Kebalian

IRASEC-NUS Press Publications on Contemporary Southeast Asia

Pierre-arnaud Chouvy and Joël Meissonnier, *Yaa Baa: Production, Traffic and Consumption of Methamphetamine in Mainland Southeast Asia* (2004)

Guy Faure and Laurent Schwab, *Japan-Vietnam: A Relation under Influences* (2008)

Rémy Madinier and André Feillard (Wong Wee, trans.), *The End of Innocence? Indonesian Islam and the Temptations of Radicalism* (2011)

Benoît de Tréglodé, *Heroes and Revolution in Vietnam* (2012)

Renaud Egreteau and Larry Jagan, *Soldiers and Diplomacy in Myanmar: Understanding the Foreign Relations of the Burmese Praetorian State* (2013)

Vatthana Pholsena and Oliver Tappe, eds., *Interactions with a Violent Past: Reading of Post-Conflict Landscapes in Cambodia, Laos and Vietnam* (2013)

Marie-Sybille de Vienne (Emilia Lanier, trans.), *Brunei: From the Age of Commerce to the 21st Century* (2015)

Renaud Egreteau and François Robinne, eds., *Metamorphosis: Studies in Social and Political Change in Myanmar* (2016)

Kebalian

The Dialogic Construction
of Balinese Identity

Michel Picard

Published by NUS Press in association with IRASEC

Revised, expanded and updated version of *Kebalian. La construction dialogique de l'identité balinaise*. Cahier d'Archipel 44, Paris, 2017.

© 2024 Michel Picard

Published by:
NUS Press
National University of Singapore
AS3-01-02, 3 Arts Link
Singapore 117569

Fax: (65) 6774-0652
E-mail: nusbooks@nus.edu.sg
Website: http://nuspress.nus.edu.sg

ISBN 978-981-325-242-4 (paper)
ePDF ISBN 978-981-325-243-1

All rights reserved. This book, or parts thereof, may not be reproduced in any form or by any means, electronic or mechanical, including photocopying, recording or any information storage and retrieval system now known or to be invented, without written permission from the Publisher.

National Library Board, Singapore Cataloguing-in-Publication Data
Name(s): Picard, Michel, 1946-
Title: Kebalian : the dialogic construction of Balinese identity / Michel Picard.
Other Title(s): IRASEC-NUS Press publications on contemporary Southeast Asia.
Description: Singapore : Published by NUS Press in association with IRASEC, [2024]
Identifier(s): ISBN 978-981-325-242-4 (paperback) | ISBN 978-981-325-243-1 (PDF)
Subject(s): LCSH: Balinese (Indonesian people)--Ethnic identity. | Balinese (Indonesian people)--Religion. | Balinese (Indonesian people)--Social life and customs. | Group identity--Indonesia--Bali Island.
Classification: DDC 305.8992238--dc23

Cover image: Acintya (from Skt., 'the inconceivable'), a traditional Balinese representation of Sang Hyang Widhi Wasa, the official name of the One and Only God of *agama Hindu* in Indonesia (Anonymous, 1932).
Wood, height: 19.5 cm, Collection of Bali Museum, inv. number 1205 (Denpasar, Bali). Photo courtesy of Doddy Obenk

Typeset by: Bertrand Bayet (IRASEC)
Printed by: Integrated Books International

For

Kunang, Mahisa and Tashi Kyi

Contents

Preface	x
A Note on Orthography	xiii
Introduction	**1**
The discourse of *Kebalian*	3
The question of Hinduism	10
The process of 'religionization'	18
Chapter 1: A 'Living Museum' of Indo-Javanese Civilization	**29**
The 'Indianization' of Bali	30
The orientalist view	45
The Dutch colonial encounter in Bali	53
Chapter 2: Making Sense of Colonial Modernity in Bali: The Debate Between *Surya Kanta* and *Bali Adnjana* (1920s)	**64**
The formation of a Balinese intelligentsia	66
The debate between *Surya Kanta* (1925–27) and *Bali Adnjana* (1924–30)	69
The foundations of *Kebalian*: *agama* and *adat*	80
Agama Hindu Bali versus *agama Bali Hindu*	88
The aftermath of the debate between *jaba* and *triwangsa*	92
Chapter 3: From 'Living Museum' to 'Last Paradise': The Discovery of Balinese Culture (1930s)	**96**
An orientalist view of Balinese culture: *Bhāwanāgara* (1930–35)	98
The Last Paradise	108
The Island of Bare Breasts	112
The Island of Artists	114
The Island of Gods and Demons	120
A Lost Paradise?	123

Chapter 4: The Balinese Religion in Question: Bali Darma Laksana (1936–42) — 129

A social and cultural monthly journal: *Djatajoe* (1936–41) — 131
The controversy about Bali and Christian missions — 138
Conversion and its outcome — 146
Balinese queries about their religious identity — 149
From Balinese to Indonesian nationalism — 157

Chapter 5: Toward Recognition of the Balinese Religion (1942–58) — 162

Ketuhanan Yang Maha Esa — 163
In search of a name — 170
Looking to India — 181
The struggle for the recognition of *agama Hindu Bali* — 190

Chapter 6: Parisada: From *Agama Hindu Bali* to *Agama Hindu* (1958–98) — 199

Parisada Dharma Hindu Bali — 200
Parisada Hindu Dharma — 207
The New Order — 217
Parisada Hindu Dharma Indonesia — 227
The 'Hindu Revival' — 232

Chapter 7: Balinese Identity Under the Challenge of Tourism — 243

Cultural Tourism (*Pariwisata Budaya*) — 244
Cultural Tourism and touristic culture — 249
Touristification and Indonesianization — 254
Tourism development and its discontents in the late New Order — 259
Crisis and *Reformasi* — 262
The revival of *adat* under the Regional Autonomy legislation — 266
The Kuta bombing and its aftermath — 273
Ajeg Bali and the politics of Balinese identity — 278
The Benoa Bay reclamation project controversy — 284

Chapter 8: Balinese Religion in the Age of *Reformasi* — 290

The reform of Parisada Hindu Dharma Indonesia — 294
The schism within Parisada Bali — 299
Back to *agama Hindu Bali* — 308
Agama Hindu under siege — 314

Bali as the world center of Hinduism?	320
Conclusion: The Predicament of *Kebalian*	**328**
Balinese and Indonesian Organizations	347
Glossary	357
Bibliography	381
Index	438

Preface

I 'discovered' Bali in 1974, during an extended journey through Asia. Back in Paris, I had the good fortune to meet Marie-Françoise Lanfant, who offered me a position on the research team she was setting up within the French National Center for Scientific Research (CNRS)—the Unité de Recherche en Sociologie du Tourisme International (URESTI). When I was recruited by the CNRS in 1981, I was appointed to this research team.

At first, I approached the island of Bali as a field where I could explore what happens to a society that offers its culture for sale on the international tourism marketplace. After spending quite some time investigating the conversion of Balinese cultural identity into a tourist attraction, I was led by the very logic of the issues I was pursuing to go further into the study of Balinese society, while expanding my research into the Indonesian multi-ethnic and multi-religious national ensemble of which Bali is a part. And with the purpose of carrying out this research, in 1991, I became a member of the Laboratoire Asie du Sud-Est et Monde Austronésien (LASEMA), which merged in 2006 with the Monde Insulindien to form the Centre Asie du Sud-Est (CASE) at the CNRS.

Like any intellectual endeavor, this book could not have come to fruition without the support of friends and colleagues, too numerous for all to be mentioned. First among them, I must make special mention of Jean-François Guermonprez, with whom I was fortunate to share a house during part of my fieldwork in Bali, as well as to spend many hours discussing Balinese issues over the years. No less important, I would like to thank Diana Darling for editing this text and rendering my Gallic style more palatable to Anglophone readers.

Among my colleagues within the French academic milieu, I should mention Andrea Acri, Cécile Barraud, Kati Basset, Claude Bazin, Marcel Bonneff, Bénédicte Brac de la Perrière, Jacques Brunet, Christine Cabasset, Henri Chambert-Loir, Catherine Clémentin-Ojha, Georges Condominas, Andrée

Feillard, Arlo Griffiths, Denys Lombard, Rémy Madinier, Pierre-Yves Manguin, Jean Michaud, Christian Pelras, François Raillon, Dana Rappoport, Jérôme Samuel, Anikó Sebestény and Jacques de Weerdt.

In Bali and among the circles of so-called 'Baliologists' and other Indonesianists, I had the welcome opportunity to meet and befriend Barbara Ashley, Freek Bakker, Rucina Ballinger, James Boon, Georges Breguet, Edward Bruner, Ian Caldwell, Bruce Carpenter, Lokesh Chandra, John De Coney, Linda Connor, Jean Couteau, Helen Creese, John Darling, Deborah Dunn, Leslie Dwyer, Cristina Formaggia, Richard Fox, Clifford Geertz, Hildred Geertz, John Hardy, Brigitta Hauser-Schäublin, Jane Hawkins, Robert Hefner, Rana Helmi, Rio Helmi, Edward Herbst, Hedi Hinzler, Michael Hitchcock, Mark Hobart, Annette Hornbacher, Leo Howe, Thomas Hunter, Marc Jurt, Garrett Kam, Johannes Kersten, Alexandra Landmann, Stephen Lansing, Barbara Lovric, Graeme MacRae, Gill Marais, Raden Moerdowo, Arlette Ottino, Urs Ramseyer, Martin Ramstedt, Larry Reed, Thomas Reuter, Raechelle Rubinstein, Abby Ruddick, Henk Schulte Nordholt, Norbert Shadeg, Narendra Dev Pandit Shastri, Cody Shwaiko, Yadav Somvir, John Stowell, David Stuart-Fox, Michael Tenzer, Adrian Vickers, Wayne Vitale, Carol Warren, Margaret Wiener, Made Wijaya and Peter Worsley.

My research in Bali has been carried out under the auspices of the Indonesian Institute of Sciences (Lembaga Ilmu Pengetahuan Indonesia, LIPI) and benefited from the patronage of Professor I Gusti Ngurah Bagus, head of the Anthropology Department at Udayana University in Denpasar. I am grateful to him for his kind support, and to all the other Balinese men and women who had to answer my numerous questions, such as Ida Bagus Gede Agastia, Ide Anak Agung Gde Agung, Anak Agung Gede Putra Agung, I Gusti Putu Rai Andayana, Anak Agung Alit Ardi, Odeck Ariawan, Anak Agung Gede Raka Arimbawa, Ida Padanda Gde Ketut Sebali Tianyar Arimbawa, Jero Arsa, Putu Alit Bagiasna, Ida Padanda Gde Ngurah Bajing, I Made Bakta, I Made Bandem, I Dewa Nyoman Batuan, I Dewa Putu Dani, Prabu Darmayasa, Cokorda Raka Dherana, I Wayan Dibia, Anak Agung Made Djelantik, I Made Djimat, Ida Bagus Gde Dosther, Putu Wirata Dwikora, AA. GN. Ari Dwipayana, Ida Bagus Made Geriya, Ida Bagus Gunadha, Ida Padanda Gde Made Gunung, I Wayan Jendra, I Wayan Juniartha, I Gusti Ketut Kaler, Cokorda Raka Kerthyasa, I Nyoman Sugi Lanus, I Ketut Madra, Anak Agung Gde Mandera, Ida Bagus Adnyana Manuaba, Ni Wayan Murni, I Gede Natih, I Ketut Natih, Ida Bagus Oka, Ibu Gedong Bagoes Oka, I Nyoman Oka, I Gede Parimartha, I Gusti Gede Ngurah Pemecutan, I Nyoman Suwandhi Pendit, I Gusti Putu Phalgunadi, I Gde Pitana, Ni Made

Pujawati, I Gusti Agung Gede Putra, I Nyoman Darma Putra, Ngakan Putu Putra, I Ketut Rinda, I Dewa Gede Windhu Sancaya, I Gusti Ketut Sangka, Degung Santikarma, I Wayan Sayoga, Putu Setia, I Made Sija, Ida Bagus Putu Suamba, Putu Suasta, I Gede Tapa Sudana, Ida Bagus Putu Sudarsana, Tjokorda Rai Sudharta, I Wayan Sudirta, I Ketut Sumarta, I Gusti Made Sumung, I Gede Sura, I Nyoman Suradnya, I Wayan Surpha, Luh Ketut Suryani, I Ngurah Suryawan, I Wayan Suta, I Wayan Mertha Sutedja, I Made Wedastera Suyasa, I Dewa Gede Ngurah Swastha, I Made Titib, Ni Made Tjanderi, Ida Bagus Gde Yudha Triguna, Anak Agung Kusuma Wardana, I Gusti Ngurah Arya Wedakarna, I Ketut Wiana, I Made Aripta Wibawa, I Nyoman Wijaya and I Wayan Windia.

I am moreover particularly indebted to I Gusti Ngurah Bagus, Norbert Shadeg, I Made Wedastera Suyasa and I Nyoman Wijaya for having generously allowed me to consult their personal archives.

I extend my thanks to the academic journal *Bijdragen tot de Taal-, Land- en Volkenkunde*, a Brill publication, for granting me permission to reproduce excerpts of the following article in Chapter 5: "Balinese Religion in Search of Recognition: From *agama Hindu Bali* to *agama Hindu* (1945–1965)", *Bijdragen tot de Taal-, Land- en Volkenkunde* 167, 4, 2011: 482–510.

Part of the contents of Chapters 2, 3 and 4 had previously been published in the journal *Archipel*:

- "La polémique entre *Surya Kanta* (1925–1927) et *Bali Adnjana* (1924–1930), ou comment être balinais à l'ère du progrès", *Archipel* 58, 1999: 3–38.
- "En quête de l'identité balinaise à la fin de l'époque coloniale", *Archipel* 75, 2008: 27–62.
- "Le christianisme à Bali: visées missionnaires, objections orientalistes et appropriation balinaise", *Archipel* 81, 2011: 11–46.

Last but not least, the publication of this book could not have been finalized without the efficient assistance of Jérôme Samuel, Peter Schoppert, Julie Willis and Maria Whelan. I would like to thank them all sincerely for their help and dedication.

A Note on Orthography

The spelling system of Malay/Indonesian in Latin script has been modified three times: in 1901, the Dutch colonial government normalized the Van Ophuijsen Spelling System; in 1947, the government of the Republic of Indonesia imposed the Soewandi Spelling System; finally, in 1972, a 'Perfected Spelling System' (*Ejaan yang Disempurnakan*) harmonized spelling differences between the languages of Indonesia and Malaysia.

The Soewandi Spelling System replaced /oe/ with /u/.

The Perfected Spelling System replaced /tj/ with /c/; /dj/ with /j/; /nj/ with /ny/; /sj/ with /sy/; /j/ with /y/; and /ch/ with /kh/.

Indonesian nouns are not morphologically marked for singular or plural.

The Balinese orthography has been adjusted to fit the official Indonesian spelling system in 1974, but it remains fluctuating. By and large, I follow the *Kamus Bali-Indonesia* (Warna et al. 1990) except for its Indonesianized spelling of the prefix vowel /e/ in terms such as *pedanda* and *kekawin*. To reflect Balinese orthography more accurately, these terms are written *padanda* and *kakawin*.

Besides, in Balinese as in Indonesian, the letter /e/ notates both phonemes /é/ and /e/.

In dealing with the historical variations in Indonesian and Balinese orthography, I have used the modern spelling throughout to facilitate reading, except for the names of persons who are best known by their original spelling.

Also to facilitate reading, I decided to romanize the Sanskrit and Kawi vocabulary and to dispense with the use of diacritics. Kawi is a linguistic register that incorporates Old and Middle Javanese, as well as various forms of Sanskrit and literary Balinese. In Balinese and in Kawi, /v/ is replaced by /w/ in terms derived from Sanskrit.

Unless otherwise indicated, all English translations from Balinese, Indonesian, Dutch and French are my own.

Map of Indonesia

Source: IRASEC

Map of Bali

Source: IRASEC

Colonial-style map of Bali

Source: PT. Repro International / PT. Matra

Introduction

> "Religion (*agama*), culture (*budaya*) and
> traditional social institutions (*adat*) are indivisible in Bali"
>
> (I Dewa Nyoman Batuan, in Ramseyer 1977: 15).

Unlike those scholars who, after a vain attempt to avoid the tourists in their midst, reluctantly included them within their field of observation,[1] I became interested in tourism before pursuing my research on Balinese society. And if I am no longer involved in tourism studies proper, it is not because I have lost interest in this topic but because the study of tourism in Bali led me to raise other questions. Thus it is that, while I went to Bali to investigate the local implications of international tourism, I ended up exploring the dialogic construction of Balinese identity.

When I began doing research in Bali in the 1970s, foreign observers, tourists and Balinese authorities alike were anxiously asking the question: 'Can Balinese culture survive the impact of tourism?' Whatever their opinion on the matter, the problem was in the very question itself. Indeed, to speak of the 'impact' of tourism is misleading, as it results in seeing the host society as a target struck by a projectile, like an inert object passively subjected to external

---

[1] Prior to the initiative of Dennison Nash to publish the personal histories of anthropologists and sociologists who were pioneers in the field of tourism studies (Nash 2007; Picard 2007), few of them had deemed it relevant to recount how they came to get involved in the study of tourism. A significant exception is the Japanese anthropologist Shinji Yamashita, who went to Sulawesi in the 1970s with a view to study the ritual system of the Toraja: "At first, he disliked the tourists, because he felt that they were an eyesore, and because they interrupted his research on 'traditional' culture in Toraja. [...] Later, however, he realized that this was a mistake. It was wrong to see Toraja culture as something 'pure', and as isolated from the rest of the contemporary world system. [...] It thus appeared to be necessary to take tourism into account in writing a 'dynamic ethnography' of Toraja society, [...] and to regard tourism as one of the primary objects of research on the Toraja" (Yamashita, Eades and Din 1997: 14; see Yamashita 2003)."

factors of change. By dissociating tourism from society, and thus depriving the local people of their agency, this approach does not permit an understanding of the process through which a society becomes a tourist product.

Contrary to this spontaneous vision of an external force striking a society from without, I contend that the process of touristification proceeds from within, by blurring the boundaries between the inside and the outside, between what is 'ours' and what is 'theirs', between what belongs to culture and what to tourism. This implies that tourism cannot be conceived of outside culture—it is inevitably bound up in an ongoing process of cultural construction. Indeed, as soon as a society offers itself for sale on the tourism market, as soon as it attempts to enhance its appeal in the eyes of foreign visitors, the consciousness that its members have of themselves is affected. In this regard, the local people are not passive objects of the tourist gaze (Urry 1990), but active subjects who construct representations of their culture to attract tourists. These representations are based on both their own frame of reference and their interpretation of the tourists' expectations. What's more, such representations are the result of rival strategies of social actors in competition to define an authorized version of their cultural identity.

Accordingly, the question should no longer be whether or not Balinese culture has been able to withstand the impact of tourism, but how tourism has taken part in the forming of the very notion of a 'Balinese culture'. This is not to be confused with whatever it is that could be described by anthropologists as the culture of the Balinese people. It is instead the dialogic fashion in which the Balinese themselves came to use the touristic image of their culture as an identity marker. In other words, as Shinji Yamashita formulates it in his review of my own work: "Culture in this context is, therefore, not the body of 'unconscious customs' with which conventional anthropology had previously been concerned but rather it is an object of conscious manipulation, invention, and consumption, within a broader social, economic, and cultural context" (Yamashita 1999: 181).

As it happened, the decision of Balinese leaders to promote a 'Cultural Tourism' (*Pariwisata Budaya*), in response to the touristic appeal of Bali's artistic and ceremonial pageantry, has made the Balinese people conscious of their culture. It was as though the interest evinced by tourists—like the amount of money they were willing to spend—had convinced the Balinese that they 'have a culture', something precious and perishable which they perceive as both a capital to be exploited and a heritage to be protected. And in this way their culture became reified and externalized in the eyes of the Balinese, turning it into an object that could be detached from themselves in order to be displayed, performed and marketed for others[2]—but also, as a result, that they could lose.

As soon as they were convinced of its value as well as its precariousness, their culture turned out to be not only a source of profit and pride, but also a cause of anxiety for the Balinese, who began wondering whether they were still authentically Balinese. Thus, called upon to conform to their image, the Balinese people are required not only to be Balinese but furthermore to live up to the demands of their idealized identity—positioned by an alien discourse not of their making, they have to become signs of themselves. For all their attempts to assert their identity, they are forever in the grip of this existential charge. Such is the challenge of tourism: enjoined to preserve and promote their culture in response to its fame as a tourist attraction, the Balinese have come to search for confirmation of their identity in the mirror held to them by the tourists (Picard 1996a).

The discourse of *Kebalian*

Faced with this challenge, the Balinese took refuge in an essentialized vision of their identity, in what they call their 'Balinese-ness' (*Kebalian*), which they metaphorically liken to a tree whose roots are their 'religion' (*agama*), the trunk their 'tradition' (*adat*), and the fruits their 'culture' (*budaya*). If the roots stay well-grounded, they claim, the trunk will grow vigorously and will bear beautiful fruits, implying that their identity would remain intact. Now, while anthropologists continue to argue over analytic definitions of 'religion', 'tradition' and 'culture', they have only recently begun to pay serious attention to local uses of these concepts.

My purpose is neither to undermine nor to support local claims about *Kebalian*, but to elucidate how the Balinese happened to construct their identity in those terms. This is the issue I decided to tackle, by shifting the focus of my study from the challenge that tourism poses to Balinese identity, to the dialogic construction of *Kebalian*. By 'dialogic', I don't specifically refer here to the works of George Herbert Mead (1934), Valentin Voloshinov (1973) or Mikhail Bakhtin (1981), nor even to Dennis Tedlock's 'dialogical anthropology' (1987),

---

[2] This reminds us of the process of objectification which Bernard Cohn attributes to the colonial encounter: "Not only have the colonial peoples begun to think of themselves in different terms, not only are they changing the content of their culture, but the way that they think about their culture has changed as well. [...] They in some sense have made it into a 'thing'; they can stand back and look at themselves, their ideas, their symbols and culture and see it as an entity. [...] What had been unconscious now to some extent becomes conscious. Aspects of the tradition can be selected, polished and reformulated for conscious ends" (Cohn 1987: 228–9).

but more generally to the iterative shaping and reshaping of *Kebalian* through the dialogues which Balinese have been led to hold both among themselves and with various significant Others in order to reflexively construct their identity. In this perspective, 'identity'—like 'religion', 'tradition', or 'culture'—is neither an analytic concept nor an empirical feature, but it is rather an ideological construct with performative effects, and as such it is a contested field, the outcome of a protracted argument, subject to public debate, an object of discourse as much as an issue of power.[3]

The very polysemy of these terms is precisely what makes them interesting, in that they are derived from categories of academic discourse which have been appropriated by the very people they purport to describe in order to reinterpret their own practices. Whereas such practices were once taken for granted, they have become objects of reflection and evaluation. In that respect, one must be cautious not to confuse the etic and emic uses of these categories—those of analysis and those of practice—but instead one should distinguish their native interpretation from their anthropological one. In particular, one should examine how these categories came to be objectified as normative frames of reference for practices to which local people take a deliberate standpoint, whether of assertion or rejection depending on the way these practices are thought to be seen by outsiders. This does not imply that this self-conscious construction of identity should simply be dismissed as inauthentic. On the contrary, as a collective representation, identity is a social fact, and it should be investigated as such. Accordingly, what interests me here is what the local actors themselves have to say about their identity, and thus I set out to investigate how the categories *agama*, *adat* and *budaya* have emerged in Balinese discourse and what their role has been in it.

Perhaps more than any other ethnic group in Indonesia, the Balinese people appear particularly prone to asserting their cultural identity and especially successful in demonstrating the worth of their culture. To a large extent, this success is due to the vigorous promotion of Balinese culture as a tourist attraction. The fact is that, by the 1980s, the initial fears of the Balinese authorities at the prospect of a tourist invasion of their island appeared to recede. Tourism was now said to contribute to the preservation of Balinese culture and even to its

---

[3] The literature on the categories 'identity', 'religion', 'tradition' and 'culture' is enormous. See, e.g., Lévi-Strauss (1977), Bourdieu (1980), Wagner (1981), Gleason (1983), Hobsbawm (1983), Handler and Linnekin (1984), Marcus and Fischer (1986), Clifford (1988), Keesing (1990), Jolly (1992), Linnekin (1992), Friedman (1993), Tonkinson (1993), Handler (1994), Kahn (1995), Vermeulen and Govers (1997), Kuper (1999), Sahlins (1999), Brubaker and Cooper (2000), Hobart (2000), Sökefeld (2001), Babadzan (2009). I deal specifically with the category 'religion' later in this Introduction.

regeneration, since it had become a source of both income and prestige for the Balinese people.[4] This flattering reputation not only prevails among the Balinese themselves but it has led to their being a model for other Indonesian ethnic groups who are eager to promote their own cultural identity on the tourist market.

In view of this remarkable situation, one might think that the construction of Balinese identity would attract scholars' attention. Yet, while several Indonesianists have studied the process of identity construction among various ethnic groups,[5] so far this question has not quite motivated the reflection of Baliologists. Besides, a certain revisionism has appeared in reaction to the culturalist vision long prevalent in Bali studies, and the few authors who have paid some attention to this topic have tended to over-emphasize the role played by colonial administrators, orientalists and anthropologists—not to mention tourism operators—in the invention of cultural 'traditions' which the Balinese claim today as their own.[6] This is a gross oversimplification, in that it does not take into account the Balinese people's agency and the strategies they have deployed in order to assert their Balinese-ness.

What we are witnessing here is the expression by the Balinese people of a vision of themselves generated by their dealings with powerful outsiders. This movement of identity affirmation began long before the influx of foreign tourists on the island in the 1970s. It goes back to the conquest of Bali and its subsequent integration into the colonial empire of the Netherlands East Indies at the turn of the 20th century, which compelled the Balinese to define themselves in terms set by non-Balinese. And it was reactivated after Indonesia's independence, when the Balinese people became citizens of the new nation-state. Such a reflexive objectification of their identity is not unique to the Balinese; it appears to be the common lot of indigenous peoples engaging in a process of self-identification

---

[4] Here is not the place to assess such claims, supported as they are by foreign observers who vaunt the resilience of traditional Balinese culture to the encroachment of tourism. Suffice it to say that, even if one has reasons to assert that Balinese culture has so far proved remarkably resilient, the point is that these claims betray a confusion between etic and emic construals of 'Balinese culture', between its anthropological understanding and its promotional image as a tourist attraction.

[5] I am referring to a series of works on Sumatra (Kahn 1993; Rodgers 1993; Kipp 1993; Perret 1995; Vignato 2000), Java (Hefner 1985; Pemberton 1994a; Florida 1995; Sears 1996; Kumar 1997), Sulawesi (Volkman 1984; Atkinson 1987; Adams 1995; Robinson 1997) and Borneo (Schiller 1997).

[6] See, e.g., Boon (1977), Schulte Nordholt (1986, 1994), Pollmann (1990), and Robinson (1995). In this regard, I must confess that my own work on 'Cultural Tourism' in Bali contributed to the demystification of Balinese cultural traditions, as can be seen in the Introduction to a collective volume on tourism in Southeast Asia: "Indeed where would Balinese culture be without tourism, given that tourism has provided the main impetus for its invention, transformation and support?" (Hitchcock, King and Parnwell 2009: 17; see also, Yamashita 2003).

when confronted with an intrusive and dominant force, most often following their incorporation into a modern state, whether it be colonial or post-colonial.[7]

Ever since the post-colonial critiques of both orientalist (Said 1978) and ethnographic (Marcus and Fisher 1986) discourses, the power to represent other cultures has been denounced as a form of epistemic imperialism, and the question has been raised as to "who has the authority to speak for a group's identity or authenticity?" (Clifford 1988: 8). However, ethnic groups are not merely the passive recipients of an external gaze, be it colonial, academic or touristic. They actively respond to foreign narratives, by telling their own version of the story.[8] Hence, the identity position of an ethnic group should not be understood as a straightforward alternative between acknowledgement or rejection of exogenous identity ascriptions. Neither should it be seen as the expression of an intrinsic principle, but rather as a localized response to a global situation. Thus we should beware of seeing locally proclaimed identities as opposed to those assigned from outside, as if we were dealing with two disconnected domains, the one characterized by inherent authenticity, the other by complete fabrication. Rather, we must pay attention to the dialogic mediations by which identity representations are constructed, as well as to the interactive processes through which their advocates negotiate their respective claims.[9]

Accordingly, I hold that the articulation of *agama*, *adat* and *budaya* by which the Balinese define their *Kebalian*—far from expressing a primordial essence and an indissoluble unity, as they would have it—is the outcome of a process of semantic borrowing and conceptual recasting which they had to make in response to the colonization, the Indonesianization and the touristification of their island. Combining Berger and Luckmann's (1966) reflections on the social construction of reality with Foucault's (1971) understanding of a discursive field, I address the formulation of Balinese identity as a transcultural discourse. Describing *Kebalian* as a discourse stresses its constructed, historical formation, while qualifying it as transcultural points to its dialogic, interactive character. As well as being reactive and reflexive, this discursive construct is performative, in

---

[7] As Marshall Sahlins remarked: "The cultural self-consciousness developing among imperialism's erstwhile victims is one of the more remarkable phenomena of world history in the later twentieth century. 'Culture'—the word itself, or some local equivalent, is on everyone's lips. Tibetans and Hawaiians, Ojibway, Kwakiutl, and Eskimo, Kazakhs and Mongols, native Australians, Balinese, Kashmiris, and New Zealand Maori: all discover they have a 'culture'" (Sahlins 1993: 3).

[8] Edward Bruner once observed that we have not known how to handle indigenous ethnographies written for a local audience, because—besides the threatening fact that they blur the distinction between anthropologists and natives—they do not fit our already established categories (Bruner 1987–88: 8).

[9] Margaret Wiener's study of the respective Balinese and Dutch representations of the colonial encounter provides a superb example of the approach advocated here (Wiener 1995).

the sense that it is both a body of cultural assumptions about reality and a set of social practices which produce that reality according to the authority of its authors. In that sense, it is as much a structure of power as it is a structure of meaning. To some extent, the discourse of *Kebalian* can be qualified as derivative (Chatterjee 1986), or counter-hegemonic (Gramsci 1971), in the sense that while its authors are indeed Balinese, their words are shaped by categories and premises that were imposed on them by dominant agencies, whether colonial, national, Islamic or touristic. Furthermore, it is conducted not in their own Balinese language but in Malay-Indonesian[10]—not to mention Dutch in colonial times, and today increasingly in English. Thus, 'authorized' by an alien discourse (Hobart 1990), compelled to use a 'stronger' language than their own (Asad 1986), indigenous intellectuals are no longer the ones to set the terms of the discourse they tell about themselves. In these conditions, there may be a cognitive dissonance between what Balinese speakers 'say' about their identity and what they actually 'know' but cannot articulate using alien categories (Sweeney 1987: 7). For all that, while we must concede that the Balinese are not in a position to determine the terms of their discourse, we must acknowledge that they have appropriated and reinterpreted them according to their own cultural values and political objectives.

When I talk here about 'the Balinese' (a problematic term), I am referring to the authors of the discourse of *Kebalian*, that is, to those Balinese authorized to speak in the name of their compatriots and who are thus in a position to claim the symbolic power to produce legitimate representations of their identity—people such as academics, journalists, officials, politicians and community organizers, entrepreneurs and professionals, students and activists, who make up the island's public opinion. These opinion leaders, most of whom lived in Singaraja during the colonial era and nowadays reside in Denpasar, comprise the modern Balinese elite. They are the ones who formulate, debate, propagate and explain contemporary issues and emergent ideas to the rest of the population. In that respect, they at once speak to, about, and from within the Balinese community (Fox 2010). It would be mistaken, however, to assume that they share the same views or concerns, not only because *Kebalian* is a contested field, but because such individuals' social positions and economic agendas, political affiliations and religious convictions, may differ greatly. Still, the fact is that the

---

[10] Mark Hobart once deplored the fact that "most scholarship on Bali depends on the remarkable ability of Balinese to convey their culture to the researchers in Indonesian" (Hobart 1989: 22). While this is indeed the case, it does not mean that one should dismiss as irrelevant the discourse of those Balinese conveying in Indonesian to fellow Balinese an authorized definition of what *Kebalian* is about.

members of this social and intellectual elite occupy an ambivalent position, since they function as mediators between two worlds: traditional and modern, rural and urban, local and global, Balinese and Indonesian. As such, they make up an 'intelligentsia' (*cendekiawan*), which should be distinguished from the 'literati' (*sastrawan*), who are custodians of a traditional knowledge that is specifically Balinese. Whereas the literati remain entrenched in the village sphere whose parochial views and values they uphold, members of the intelligentsia bestride two worlds, the ethnic group from which they originate and the larger context in which they participate.

The explicit discourse of the Balinese intelligentsia is thus superimposed on the implicit meaning of local practices, advocating an interpretation that concerns the foreign anthropologists—whether it be to request confirmation of their acknowledged expertise or, to the contrary, to contest the legitimacy of their outsider position. In these circumstances, the said anthropologists can no longer disregard this indigenous discourse, but need to take into account the ideological manipulations and political aspirations of the local actors involved in their quest for identity (Friedman 1993).

To understand how the Balinese have constructed their *Kebalian*, I set about deconstructing its genesis by tracing the dialogues they have engaged in both among themselves and with their foreign interlocutors[11]—European orientalists, Dutch colonial administrators, Javanese nationalists, Muslim clerics, Christian missionaries, Hindu gurus, as well as artists, anthropologists and tourists, not to forget Indonesian government officials, all of whom attempted to fashion Balinese society in their own vision of how it should be. Responsive to the inquisitive gaze of these diverse interlocutors, some Balinese, particularly urban intelligentsia, have questioned the legitimacy of their own practices, and they felt either proud or defensive, according to whether these outside points of view were complimentary or disparaging. Hence, they tended to adopt a reflexive stance, which led them to validate some practices while disavowing others. To the extent that Balinese practices were equated by outsiders with their religion, their tradition, or their culture, their vindication became conflated with a defense of 'the Hindu religion', 'the local tradition', or 'the Balinese culture'. By thus attributing certain practices to *agama*, *adat*, or *budaya*, understood as encompassing frames of interpretation, this internalization of outside views contributed to the objectifying of these categories (Johnsen 2007).

---

[11] My epistemological predicament is further complicated by the fact that I myself am an interlocutor of the Balinese I investigate, in the sense that some of the discourses I analyze refer to my own work, whether it be on Cultural Tourism or on the Hinduization of the Balinese religion.

In practical terms, I reconstruct here the way Balinese have construed their identity from the turn of the 20th century until the present day, while locating their views within the context of the states, colonial and post-colonial, under whose authority Bali has fallen during this period: the Netherlands East Indies (1908), the Japanese occupation (1942), the Republic of Indonesia (1945), the New Order established by Suharto (1965), and the age of *Reformasi* initiated by his demise (1998).

In the 1920s, the first generation of Balinese educated in colonial schools began to view themselves both as an ethnic group, characterized by their own customs, and as a religious community, threatened by the proselytizing of Islam and Christianity. Specifically, they construed their identity—which they glossed as *Kebalian*—as being based on both 'religion' (*agama*) and 'tradition' (*adat*). It was only in the 1930s—when tourism was developing in earnest—that 'culture' (*budaya*) was added as the third component of *Kebalian*. Once they had become Indonesian citizens, the Balinese people would be compelled to discriminate what belonged to their religion and what to their tradition, in order for their religion to be formally recognized by the state. In so doing, Balinese tradition was deprived of its former religious authority, while some of its most spectacular aspects were being distinguished for their artistic quality and ascribed to the field of culture. Later, with the government's involvement in the promotion of tourism and its exploitation of regional cultures, Balinese culture was enlisted as a resource and was required to contribute to both the development of international tourism in Indonesia and the construction of Indonesian national culture. Thus, with their tradition secularized and their culture touristified, their religion has become for the Balinese the diacritical marker of their identity, even though they had to detach it from its ethnic origin in order to comply with national regulations.

Bali is commonly depicted, by foreign observers as well as by Balinese themselves, as a Hindu island in a Muslim Archipelago. This pervasive cliché, which makes their religion that which differentiates the Balinese from other ethnic groups in Indonesia, raises two kinds of problems. The first concerns the difficulty of establishing to what extent the rites practiced by the Balinese people are actually Hindu, which amounts to determining which Indic traditions have been transmitted to Bali and how they have been appropriated there. Considering that the Balinese religion is just as difficult to delineate as Hinduism, this question has received highly conflicting answers since the first European orientalists visited the island in the 19th century. But there is another problem, which stems from the claim that, unlike their Javanese neighbors, the Balinese people have been successful in defending their Hindu heritage against the intrusion of Islam. Yet, by implying that the Balinese are still following what is assumed to be their traditional religion, one fails to take into account the deliberate movement of 'Hinduization' in which they have been engaged since the incorporation of their island into the Dutch colonial empire at the turn of the 20th century. What passes today for evidence is in fact borne out of a controversial history, which appears to have been erased from the memory of most Balinese—and of a few Baliologists. Indeed, once their religion had been acknowledged as a legitimate branch of Hinduism, the Balinese tended to behave as if it had always been agreed on as being basically Hindu. Hence the importance of retracing through which processes and within which contexts the Balinese religion came to be construed as Hinduism. Far from being a return to their Indian roots as asserted by its initiators, this result amounts in fact to a twofold invention: first, of a 'Balinese religion' (*agama Bali*) proper, and second, of the Balinese religion as 'Hinduism' (*agama Hindu*).

The question of Hinduism

The question remains as to what is meant by 'Hinduism'. As is well known, the terms Hindu and Hinduism are exonyms. The word 'Hindu'—a Perso-Arabic variant on the Sanskrit word 'Sindhu' (meaning 'river', and specifically the Indus river)—was originally a geographic and ethnic identifier, used by the Persians to designate the inhabitants of the country they named Hindustan (the land of the Hindus) (Lorenzen 1999; Sharma 2002; Von Stietencron 2005; Clémentin-Ojha 2014). For the Persians, Hindus were Indians who were not Muslims. Some of those designated as Hindus began to use that word self-referentially by the 16th century in order to distinguish themselves from the 'foreign and barbarous' peoples, the *mleccha*, who were not thought of primarily as 'Muslims' (Sanderson 2015: 156, n. 2). It was not before the 18th century that Hindus began to acknowledge that those barbarous foreigners were Muslims—thereby identifying them along religious lines (O'Connell 1973). But even when used by indigenous Indians, the term Hindu did not necessarily have a religious denotation, since in the 18th century it was still common to refer to natives who had converted to Islam or Christianity as 'Hindoo Muslims' and 'Hindoo Christians' (King 1999b: 163; Frykenberg 2005: 85).

In the course of the 18th century, European observers took the term Hindu to designate the followers of a particular Indian religion, after having long wondered whether they were dealing with a heterogeneous collection of traditions or with a coherent system of beliefs and practices (Marshall 1970; Sweetman 2003; Gelders 2009; Fisher 2018). Through a process of reification, the word 'Hindooism' was first coined in 1787 by the Evangelical missionary (and subsequent chairman of the East India Company) Charles Grant to name 'the religion of the Hindoos' (Oddie 2006: 71)—an imagined religion that had never existed as a 'religion' in the minds of Hindus themselves. Hitherto, there had been only multiple communities identified by locality, language, caste (*jati*), lineage, occupation and sectarian allegiance (*sampradaya*). Indeed, Hindus could not consider themselves to be members of a single religious community, because their idea of *dharma* focused upon distinctions between heterogeneous groups.

The concept of *dharma* is complex and cannot be reduced to one general principle. Nor is there one single translation that covers all its meanings—which span ritual, law, custom, conduct and ethics—all of which are distinct in the Western perspective. It is an all-encompassing category, both considerably broader in scope and much more specific than 'religion'. *Dharma* may be defined as that which upholds the world and supports order. It is both an account of the cosmos and a norm on which to base social life, a worldview and an ethos, which at once describes how things are and prescribes the way they ought to be. Furthermore, the rules of conduct that it determines are always context-sensitive. In the Dharmashastras,[12] the word *dharma* refers specifically to the *varnashrama dharma*, the duties and qualifications incumbent on Hindus according to their social class (*varna*) and their stage of life (*ashrama*).[13] That is to say, the differential norms of *varnashrama dharma* apply only to the *svadharma* of the male members of the 'twice-born' *varna* (*brahmana, kshatriya, vaishya*). *Dharma* is thus an exclusive and personal norm, as attested by the well-known verse from the *Bhagavad Gita*[14] that states: "It is better to perform one's own *dharma* badly than to perform another's *dharma* well" (B.G. 3.35).

---

[12] The Dharmashastras are Sanskrit treatises of the Brahmanical tradition that refer to the branch of learning (*shastra*) pertaining to the subject of *dharma*. They deal with social observance and ritual functions (*acara*), legal procedures (*vyavahara*) and expiation (*prayaschitta*). They are considered part of the *smriti* ('that which is remembered', i.e., the 'tradition') and find their source in the transcendent authority of the Vedas—the *shruti* ('that which is heard', i.e., the 'revelation').

[13] According to P.V. Kane's authoritative study of the Dharmashastras, after several transitions of meaning the most prominent significance of the word *dharma* came to be "the privileges, duties and obligations of a man, his standard of conduct as a member of the Āryan community, as a member of one of the castes, as a person in a particular stage of life" (Kane 1968: 3; see Rocher 2003 and Holdrege 2004).

[14] The *Bhagavad Gita*—the 'Song of the Lord'—is a philosophical poem in Sanskrit set in the narrative framework of a dialogue between Arjuna and Krishna, inserted into the *Mahabharata*.

The point is, *dharma* did not signify anything like a belief system one adhered to.[15] Now, as a result of the demands of British colonial administration on the one hand, and the pursuits of Christian missionaries on the other, the concept of *dharma* would be both fragmented and expanded. In his Judicial Plan of 1772, Warren Hastings, the first British governor-general of Bengal, decreed that Hindus should be governed by the laws of the Shastra, and Muslims by the law of the Quran (Rocher 1993: 220). This decision implied that native laws would apply only to 'religious' matters, that is, matters corresponding to that which in Britain fell under the purview of ecclesiastical law. This put British administrators in the position of having to discriminate the religious from the secular in all subjects relating to Hindus. By doing so, they could "manipulate the porous boundaries between religion as defined by texts and the customs they wished to ban" (Rocher 1993: 242). In consequence, law and religion, which were inextricably enmeshed in the Dharmashastras, were artificially set apart.

Then, in the early 19th century, when Baptist missionaries in Bengal translated the Bible—which they titled *Dharmapustaka* ('the Book of *dharma*')—into Sanskrit, they chose the term *dharma* as a gloss for the word religion and began to proclaim Christianity (*Khristadharma*) as the 'true *dharma*' (*satyadharma*).[16] By thus depriving Hindus of their own *dharma*, which they taught was a false religion, the missionaries channeled their reaction in two directions (Halbfass 1988: 342; see Young 1981). On the one hand, in order to meet the Christian challenge, Hindus themselves began using the word *dharma* in the sense of religion, with the result that the Hindu *dharma* became one religion among others, to be compared and opposed to the Christian *dharma* or the Muslim *dharma*, even though they be defective and fallacious. On the other hand, some Hindus rejected the exclusive character of the *varnashrama dharma* and attempted instead to universalize *dharma*, by invoking the inclusive notion of *sanatana dharma* as the 'eternal and universal religion' (Halbfass 1988: 343–6).

---

[15] In Sanskrit, the terms closest to this conception would have been rather *sampradaya* (lineages of spiritual masters who carry and transmit the religious tradition: Shaivism, Shaktism, Vaishnavism and Smarta) or else *darshana* (orthodox schools of Hindu philosophy: Nyaya, Vaisheshika, Samkhya, Yoga, Mimamsa and Vedanta).

[16] In contrast, in South India, where Jesuit missionaries had been translating the Bible since the close of the 16th century, 'religion' was commonly rendered by the terms *veda* and *mata*. Thus, Christianity was dubbed the 'true Veda' (*satyavedam*) and the Bible was titled *Vedapustaka* (Tiliander 1974; Thangaraj 1999). It is worth noting that in Ceylon it was the term *agama* that was chosen by the missionaries as the vernacular equivalent of 'religion'. Referring to Christianity in terms of *Kristiyani agama*, they named the 'religion of the Buddha' *Buddhagama*. Later on, this name gained acceptance among the Sinhala Buddhists as a term of self-reference. Eventually, in the 1880s, the compound *agamadharma* became used in the sense of a system of teaching (*dharma*) based on canonical texts (*agama*). On the colonial construction of Buddhism as a 'religion' in Ceylon, see, e.g., Southwold (1978), Carter (1993), Scott (1996) and Malalgoda (1997).

In that respect, *dharma* was considered a principle superior to and, moreover, encompassing all religions.

In 1816, the term 'Hindooism' was first adopted by a Hindu, the Bengali religious reformer Rammohun Roy, who was also the first Indian to speak of *dharma* in the sense of religion (Killingley 1993: 60–3). In due course, that new name was taken up by the Anglicized Indian elites, in their attempt to establish a religion that could compete with Christianity and Islam for equal standing. For the members of this Western-educated intelligentsia, the English language was not just a means of communicating with a foreign culture; it also served as a medium in which they articulated their self-understanding and reinterpreted their own traditions. They initiated reform movements that drew on models from both contemporary Europe and an idealized Indian past that was being actively uncovered by British orientalists (Kopf 1969). So while Hindu practices were traditionally localized, sectarian and segregated, reformers created pan-Indian associations that promoted the idea of a single inclusive religion for all Hindus, now being defined as a national religious community (Thapar 1989).

In the evolutionary worldview of 19th-century Europe, monotheism was seen as the highest form of religion. Embracing the missionaries' emphasis on sacred texts as the locus of religion, reformers endeavored to construct a 'pure' religion called Hinduism by identifying its tenets and codifying them into fixed sets of beliefs. Modeled on Judeo-Christian conceptions of the nature of religion, this process amounted to what Indian historian Romila Thapar called the 'Semitization' of Hinduism (Thapar 2000: 55). Specifically, reformers singled out Vedic and Brahmanical scriptures as canonical, while dismissing popular religious practices. They claimed that Hinduism was originally a monotheistic religion, whose true doctrines were to be found either in the Vedas,[17] the Upanishads or the *Bhagavad Gita*, but which had degenerated into polytheism and image worship during the Puranic period. In this, they aligned themselves with the orientalists, for whom true Hinduism was the pristine religion of bygone India and not that which was commonly observable in their time.

---

[17] The Vedas ('knowledge' in Sanskrit) are a body of texts considered to have been 'revealed' (*shruti*) to inspired seers (*rishi*), supposed to have been composed orally between the 15th and the 5th centuries BCE. They were assembled into 'collections' (*samhita*)—the *Rig-Veda*, the *Sama-Veda*, the *Yajur-Veda* and the *Atharva-Veda*—that consist in *mantra* and hymns to the Vedic gods. The *samhita* were completed by the Brahmanas (ritual speculations), the Aranyakas (esoteric speculations), and the Upanishads (philosophical speculations). The orientalist Henri Colebrooke was the first foreigner to study the Vedas, in 1805. Promoting the image of Vedic India as a Golden Age, he believed he detected in the Vedas a primordial monotheism predating the era of decline marked by the polytheism of the Puranas (texts related to the cult of major deities such as Vishnu, Shiva and Devi) and the idolatry of modern India. On the discovery of the Vedas and their study, see Staal (2008).

In response to missionary criticism and for fear of conversion to Christianity, reformers pressed their co-religionists to eradicate what the missionaries described as 'demonic' practices, and they set about drawing a distinction between true Hinduism and mere traditions. This distinction was commonly framed in terms of a contrast between what belonged to *dharma* and what to *acara*—the established rules of conduct that constitute *varnashrama dharma*, which are thus endorsed by the Dharmashastras but which the reformers did not consider to be an essential part of Hinduism. In fact, reformers held divergent opinions on the principles of reform Hinduism.[18] Whatever their particular agenda, all these reform movements met with resistance from Hindu traditionalists, who formed conservative organizations dedicated to the defense of the *sanatana dharma*.[19] Despite their claims that this was the 'eternal religion', *sanatana dharma* is as modern a construct as Hinduism, in that it emerged as a self-conscious reaction to both Christianity and reform movements (Halbfass 1988: 343–6).

In any case, it was not before the book *Hinduism* was published in 1877 by the renowned British Sanskritist Sir Monier Monier-Williams that the term Hinduism gained full currency in English (Monier-Williams 1877). But even then, it was not universally accepted in India itself. Thus, when the British colonial government introduced a census between 1868 and 1872, many Indians either did not understand the label Hindu or else refused it outright (Haan 2005). Then, at the time of each successive decennial census, a recurring debate would emerge among Hindu pandits, political activists and colonial administrators over a workable definition of Hinduism. But a definition was not forthcoming, for there appeared to be no single shared attribute among Hindus. For want of criteria for deciding who is and who is not Hindu, government officials resolved that Hinduism could only be defined residually, that is, Hindus were Indians who were neither Muslims, nor Christians, nor Parsis, nor Sikhs, nor Jains, nor

---

[18] One customarily distinguishes three main reform-minded responses to the Christian attack on Hinduism. Raja Rammohun Roy (1772–1833) and the Brahmo Samaj (founded in 1828) saw Christianity as one instance of universalist religion, and combined elements of Advaita Vedanta, Sufism and Christian Unitarianism to formulate a 'rational Hinduism' with strong deist tendencies (Kopf 1979; Mitter 1987). Later on, Swami Dayananda Sarasvati (1824–83) and the Arya Samaj (founded in 1875) adopted a more radical position by rejecting Christianity altogether and calling for the Aryas to 'Go back to the Vedas', considered a monotheistic religion and the ultimate source of knowledge (Jordens 1978; Llewellyn 1993). A third response was developed by Swami Vivekananda (1863–1902) and the Ramakrishna Mission (founded in 1897), who argued that Christianity was simply a lesser form of the universal spirituality found in all religions, which had reached its highest level in Advaita Vedanta (Radice 1998; Basu 2002).

[19] Overall, even though traditionalists were as diverse as the reformists, one might say that traditionalists recognized the authority of both *shruti* and *smriti*, whereas reformists rejected the latter, which they regarded as either deviant or corrupt.

Buddhists, and so on. In other words, Hindus were those who were left after others had set themselves apart.[20]

It was only after the publication in 1923 of the book *Essentials of Hindutva*[21] by Vinayak Damodar Savarkar—which popularized the neologism *Hindutva* ('Hindu-ness'), based on the idea of a Hindu nation (*rashtra*), a Hindu race (*jati*) and a Hindu civilization (*sanskriti*)—that Hinduism became a common denomination in India, and was framed within an ethno-nationalist perspective. According to Savarkar, all followers of religions of Indian origin—Hindus, Buddhists, Jains and Sikhs—were to be included in the Hindu community. After independence, the Indian constitution and subsequent legislation adopted this inclusive definition of 'Hinduism' by classifying Buddhists, Jains and Sikhs as 'Hindus', thus making a distinction between Hindus by law and Hindus by creed (Clémentin-Ojha 2019).

The point here is that defining Hinduism is not only problematic but contentious as well, because 'Hinduism', as an ideological construct, is a contested category.[22] It is fundamentally a fiction, there being no single religious practice or belief that unites all putative 'Hindus' in the premodern period. In effect, the 19th-century reform movements did not so much describe what Hinduism was, as prescribe what it should be. Hence the name 'Neo-Hinduism' commonly given to this idealized reform Hinduism (Hacker 1995), influenced as it was by European ideas and models, which in fact never concerned more than a tiny minority of those regarded as Hindu, who continued worshipping their gods, singing their songs and telling their stories.[23] Be that as it may, once detached from its social context, objectified and individualized, Neo-Hinduism could be embraced by anyone, anywhere, and thus become a universalist religion.

---

[20] This has led Frits Staal to argue that "Hinduism does not merely fail to be a religion; it is not even a meaningful unit of discourse. There is no way to abstract a meaningful unitary notion of Hinduism from the Indian phenomena, unless it is done by exclusion, following the well-worn formula: a Hindu is an Indian who is *not* a Jaina, Buddhist, Parsi, Christian, Muslim, Sikh, Animist ..." (Staal 1996: 397).

[21] Reprinted in 1928 under the title *Hindutva: Who Is a Hindu?* (Savarkar 1928).

[22] Numerous studies have been published on the construction of 'Hinduism' as a 'religion'. See, e.g., Marshall (1970), Inden (1986), King (1989), Thapar (1989), Fitzgerald (1990), Hawley (1991), Frykenberg (1993), Dalmia and Von Stietencron (1995), Staal (1996), Dalmia (1997), Von Stietencron (1997), Lorenzen (1999), King (1999a, 1999b, 2011), Brekke (2002), Sharma (2002), Sugirtharajah (2003), Sweetman (2003), Sontheimer and Kulke (2005), Balagangadharan (2005), Pennington (2005), Lipner (2006), Jha (2006), Oddie (2006), Lardinois (2007), Bloch, Keppens and Hegde (2010). Of particular relevance for the construction of the Balinese religion is the ethnographic study conducted by Mark Elmore on the discovery and maturation of Himachali religion in the Western Himalayas (Elmore 2016).

[23] This does not imply that Hindu traditions were static and that the modernization of Hinduism was exclusively the outcome of its encounter with Christianity and colonial modernity, as convincingly demonstrated by the study of the Tamil Shaiva reformer Ramalinga Swami by Richard Weiss (2019).

In this regard, there is a striking similarity between the construction of Indian Neo-Hinduism and the construction of a Balinese religion as *agama Hindu*. Besides the stress on monotheism in response to criticism leveled by Muslims and Christians alike, both these movements have been informed by Orientalism, colonialism and nationalism. In addition, they have been marked by a proselytizing drive which was originally foreign to them both.[24] Also, in their determination to assert an indigenous religious identity, Balinese elites, like their Indian predecessors, had to resort to foreign conceptual categories—by means of English for the Indians and of Malay-Indonesian for the Balinese. And one observes in Bali a similar kind of opposition between reformers and traditionalists as encountered in India.

But the similarity between India and Bali might go deeper, concerning the way of thinking common to their respective peoples. This I found expounded in Attipate Krishnaswami Ramanujan's famous essay titled 'Is there an Indian Way of Thinking?' (Ramanujan 1989). The author noticed that Indians seem to have a different relationship to outside reality, compared to that encountered in the West. This is because, he claimed, Indians' behavior abides preferably by context-sensitive rules: it tends to be particularistic, whereas the Western Judeo-Christian tradition is ideally based on a premise of context-free universality. According to Ramanujan, this pervasive emphasis on context is related to the Hindu concern with *jati*—the logic of bounded classes and species, of which human *jati* are only one instance. In such a world view, each class of man has his own laws, his own proper ethic, his own *dharma*, not to be universalized. Now, it appears to me that the Balinese notion of *soroh* is comparable to the Indian notion of *jati*, in that it refers to a group of people, animals or things sharing common features that characterize them as belonging to the same species. Each *soroh* defines a structure of relevance, a frame of reference enabling Balinese to decide what can or should be done in a given context. This is, I think, what the notion of *patut* is about, which indicates that what is considered proper in Bali is highly context-sensitive, varying according to the place, the time and the circumstance (which is neatly encapsulated in the neo-traditional slogan *desa, kala, patra*).

Following Ramanujan further, one might see the process of 'modernization' as a general movement from the context-sensitive to the context-free, a particular instance of which is in the contemporary Hinduization of the Balinese religion,

---

[24] However, Shaivite and Vaishnavite *sampradaya* did practice proselytizing to recruit their followers, in the name of the universal character of their doctrine of salvation, unlike the supporters of Brahmin orthodoxy according to whom religious membership is determined solely by birth.

with highly contextualized ritual traditions becoming universalized into a Neo-Hindu brand of *agama Hindu*. As Clifford Geertz puts it, in his characteristic virtuoso style:

> Traditional religions consist of a multitude of very concretely defined and only loosely ordered sacred entities, an untidy collection of fussy ritual acts and vivid animistic images which are able to involve themselves in an independent, segmental, and immediate manner with almost any sort of actual event. Such systems [...] meet the perennial concerns of religion [...] piecemeal. [...] Rationalized religions, on the other hand, are more abstract, more logically coherent, and more generally phrased (Geertz 1973: 172).

In any case, the fact is that, a century apart—and initially without any Indian influence other than mediated by Dutch orientalists—the Balinese people have retraced in their own fashion the movement through which Indian reformers have turned Hinduism into a 'religion'. To that end, they recast their Indo-Javanese heritage, first as an ethnic religion, then as a national one, and finally as a universalist 'Hindu' religion. Specifically, in order to have their religion recognized by the Indonesian state, Balinese reformers, in the manner of their Indian forerunners, undertook to 'purify' the ritual practices of their co-religionists by embracing current religious standards—that is, those of the Abrahamic religions—all the while presenting their reform as a return to the Indic sources of their religion.

The Balinese were not the only ones among the peoples of the Indonesian Archipelago to question their religious traditions in the wake of their incorporation into the colonial empire of the Netherlands East Indies. Indeed, the struggle of Balinese intellectuals to reform their religion is in many ways similar to other modernizing reform movements which had started around the turn of the 20th century (Howell 1978, 1982). Yet the contemporary Hinduization of the Balinese religion is a singular process, different both from the conversion of followers of a traditional religion to a universalist religion (such as Islam or Christianity), and from the reform that nominal members of a world religion (such as Javanese *abangan*)[25] had to carry out in order to make their religious practices conform to a more orthodox version of their faith. What Clifford Geertz called a process of 'internal conversion' (Geertz 1973) is a more ambiguous

---

[25] *Abangan* (lit. 'the red ones')—as opposed to *santri* or *putihan* (lit. 'the white ones')—are so-called 'nominal' Muslims, who used to compose the majority of the Javanese people. On the controversial question of Javanese religion (*agama Jawa*), or 'Javanism' (*Kejawen*), and its relation to Islam, see, e.g., Geertz (1960), Bachtiar (1973), Ellen (1983), Koentjaraningrat (1985), Woodward (1989), Stange (1990), Beatty (1999), Ricklefs (2007), Ali (2007), Hefner (2011), and Van den Boogert (2015).

phenomenon, in the sense that the Balinese had to become the Hindus that they were already supposed to be.

The process of 'religionization'

At issue is not only the alleged 'Hinduism' of the Balinese people but the category 'religion' as well, which cannot be taken for granted. To begin with, 'religion' is notoriously difficult to define. To this day, there is no scholarly consensus as to what 'religion' really is. As Maurice Bloch reminds us, "anthropologists have, after countless fruitless attempts, found it impossible to usefully and convincingly cross-culturally isolate or define a distinct phenomenon that can analytically be labelled 'religion'" (Bloch 2008: 2055). One could say that there is no such thing as 'religion' out there, "only a wide variety of human practices, beliefs, or experiences that may or may not be categorized as such, depending on one's definition" (Hanegraaff 2016: 582). In other words, the category 'religion' is an empty signifier, the meaning of which is construed and negotiated by competing sets of actors to specific ends within particular socio-political contexts.

The various existing definitions of religion may be categorized according to a distinction between 'substantivist' and 'functionalist' interpretations (Saler 2000). According to the former, religion consists of paying homage to the gods, and their anthropological formulation begins with Edward Burnett Tylor's famous minimal definition of religion as 'belief in spiritual beings' (Tylor 1871) and extends to Melford Spiro's 'culturally patterned interaction with culturally postulated superhuman beings' (Spiro 1966). For their part, functionalist definitions focus on what is of 'ultimate concern' (Tillich 1969), to either an individual or to a social group. The problem with both these approaches is that substantivist definitions are too narrow to account for situations occurring in cultures that do not conceive of an explicit distinction between religious and non-religious domains, while functionalist definitions are too broad to set any substantive boundary to religion and to thus distinguish it from other socio-cultural phenomena (Arnal 2000). Following Émile Durkheim, religion has been further characterized as concerned with the relationship between man and the 'sacred' (Borgeaud 1994), which was construed as an ontological category manifest in feelings of awe by phenomenologists like Rudolf Otto and Mircea Eliade, for whom the human being is a *homo religiosus*—thereby substituting a hierocentric definition of religion supposedly found in all cultures for the previous theocentric model.[26]

Alan Strathern has recently proposed a way out of the quandary faced when attempting to define 'religion': "there is at least one very good reason why 'religion' tends to defeat attempts at encapsulation: it strains to cover two distinct phenomena" (Strathern 2019: 3). He is not the first scholar of course to have highlighted this point. Without going all the way back to Max Weber, numerous authors have emphasized the contrast between traditional and rationalized religions, ethnic and world religions, ritualistic and salvation religions, polytheism and monotheism, and so forth. To categorize this contrast, Strathern suggests instead the labels 'immanentism' and 'transcendentalism', which he deems more encompassing. Immanentist societies attribute conscious agency to powerful entities which are immanent in the world and with whom human beings must maintain good relations in order to flourish. Strathern borrows the notion of 'metapersons' from Marshall Sahlins (2017, 2021) to designate all those forces and beings usually called spirits, gods, ancestors, ghosts, demons and the like. Rites and sacrifices are attempts to bridge the divide that separates these metapersons from the world inhabited by humans. The fundamental object of ritual activity is the harnessing of their power for human purposes. That is to say, in cultures of immanence, religion is not differentiated from society, because religion provides the framework, not only for the elaboration of social norms, but for the categories from which all reality can be conceived.

While, according to Strathern, immanentism can be considered a universal feature, found in the great majority of societies recorded in history and ethnography, transcendentalism is not. It is the consequence of a series of cultural revolutions that took place in certain areas of Eurasia during what Karl Jaspers called the 'axial age' of human history—the middle centuries of the first millenium BCE. Further, transcendentalism is always involved in a push and pull relationship with immanentism. It is characterized by an ontological breach between a transcendent and a mundane form of being that divides previously monistic worldviews between a natural and a supernatural order of existence. This transcendent dimension is construed as a longed-for escape from mundane existence, which is attained by salvation or liberation. In this perspective, religious activity is profoundly restructured, with a shift of concern from ritual

---

[26] Durkheim formulated his social definition of religion as "beliefs and practices relative to sacred things [...] which unite into one single moral community [...] all those who adhere to them" (Durkheim 1965: 62). Otto called the religious experience 'numinous', which he expounded as *mysterium tremendum et fascinans*' (Otto 1950). Eliade used the word 'hierophany' to designate the manifestations of the sacred (Eliade 1958).

obligations to adherence to ethical norms. That is to say, transcendentalism refashions the meaning of relations with metapersons according to ethical and soteriological principles. As a result, it is no longer the social group but the self which becomes the most fundamental focus of religious life.

While in immanentist societies the concept of religion has no emic relevance, being alien to their subjects' self-understanding, it takes on full significance with transcendentalism. The question remains, however, to decide whether the emic absence of the category religion amounts to denying its etic relevance. Whatever the case, it appears that this problematic term is here to stay, and even though I personally tend to favor the concept of 'heteronomy' (Gauchet 1997) for what is usually called 'religion', I must admit that it is proving difficult to do away with the word religion itself. That being granted, instead of imputing a fixed essence to the category religion it is essential to historicize it.

This is precisely what has been done for several decades now by a number of scholars who deny the prevalent assumption of the religious studies discourse: the universality of religion as a distinct domain of human societies. They propose instead to submit religious phenomena, like all other social facts, to the critical analysis of the social sciences, an approach deemed 'reductionist' by their opponents, the so-called 'religionists', who claim that religion is a *sui generis* phenomenon. These critics argue that religion is neither natural nor universal, but instead a specifically Christian, Eurocentric, modern category that has been unduly imposed upon ancient and foreign cultures.[27]

In effect, 'religion' is neither a descriptive nor an analytical term but a prescriptive and normative category, and a contentious one at that. Originating in the Roman notion of *religio*, it was appropriated by Christian theologians, who radically shifted its meaning by uprooting it from its 'pagan' framework (Sachot 2007). To the Romans, *religio* was what *traditio* is all about, a set of ancestral practices developed by a people and transmitted over generations.[28] Just as there are different peoples, so are there different traditions. As a set of practices, the

---

[27] See, e.g., Goody (1961), Smith (1962), Segal (1983), Asad (1993), Staal (1996), Gauchet (1997), McCutcheon (1997, 2004), Fitzgerald (1997, 2000, 2007), Smith (1998), King (1999a, 2011, 2013), Saler (2000), Nye (2000), McKinnon (2002), Peterson and Walhof (2002), Beyer (2003), Dubuisson (2003, 2007, 2016, 2019), Balagangadhara (2005), Masuzawa (2005), Bell (2006), Tarot (2008), Chidester (2014), Nongbri (2014), Horii (2015), Hanegraaff (2016), and Barton and Boyarin (2016). For some of these authors at least, the critique of the category religion appears to be part of the postmodern-cum-postcolonial denunciation of dominant Western worldviews and epistemologies.

[28] As is well known, Cicero's etymology related *religio* to *religere*, meaning 'to retrace' or 'to read anew'. In this sense, *religio* involved the scrupulous reiteration of the ritual traditions of one's ancestors. In the early 4th century, the Christian theologian Lactantius rejected Cicero's etymology, arguing instead that *religio* derives from *religare*, meaning 'to bind' or 'to link', thus defining *religio* as a fundamental bond between man and God.

predicates 'true' and 'false' are not applicable to tradition. By claiming to be the true *religio*, Christianity opposed its doctrines to the prevalent practices, rejected as false beliefs marred by *superstitio* (Sachot 1991). This distinction between *vera religio* and *falsa religio*, established by the Christian apologist Tertullian, marked a conceptual shift characterized by a scriptural turn, a substitution of dogma for ritual, of orthodoxy for orthopraxy, that introduced a novel kind of truth: a revealed, absolute truth (Assmann 2009; Bettini 2016; Barton and Boyarin 2016). The Christian appropriation of *religio* thus established the exclusivist monotheism of Christianity as the normative paradigm for understanding what a religion is. Religion became a matter of adherence to a particular doctrine rather than to customary ritual practices. The religious field, previously embedded in the culture of a particular society, then turned into an autonomous domain that could be taken up by other societies. The question remains as to how this Christian theological category, issued from a specific polemical context, evolved to the point of becoming the central explanatory category of religious studies.

It is important to note that for most of the history of European Christendom, the word 'religion' (*religio*) meant something very different from what it does in contemporary usage (Smith 1962; Despland 1980; Smith 1998). 'Religion' is a secular category, in the sense that its modern understanding as a 'system of beliefs and practices' is a product of secularization, that is, of the differentiation between religious and non-religious spheres of life in modern societies (Bourdieu 1971; Asad 2003; Dressler and Mandair 2011). Specifically, secularization refers not only to the formal institutional separation of Church and State, but further to an epistemic turn in which a field of beliefs and practices comes to be constituted as 'religion' as such. This religious field emerged during the Renaissance, evolved as a result of the Reformation, and was reworked in the Enlightenment, before acquiring its present significance in the course of the 19th century.

The Protestant doctrine of salvation focused attention on inner piety and personal faith. With this emphasis on private religious consciousness, institutional forms of liturgy, priesthood and church were relegated to merely external social phenomena. This shift to belief as the defining characteristic of religion resulted in a change from an institutionally based understanding of exclusive salvation within the Catholic Church to a propositionally based understanding that thereafter conceived of religion as a set of propositions to which believers gave assent (Fitzgerald 2007). Hence, the fragmentation of Christendom following the Reformation resulted not only in confessional disputes and 'Wars of Religion', but also in critical comparisons of competing forms of Christianity. Polemics and apologetics among Christians prompted the proponents of 'deism' to deal with these disputes by trying to determine the lowest common denominator of the various Christian persuasions, an approach that was eventually extended to all creeds, since 'propositional religion' allowed for the comparison of various religions by juxtaposing the content of their beliefs. The search for a universal core of religion based on reason instead of revelation produced a substantive definition of what came to be known as 'natural religion'—as distinct from the 'revealed religion' of Christianity—defined as a set of beliefs (which hinged upon the existence of one supreme being), practices (in the form of sanctioned worship), and ethics (a code of conduct based on rewards and punishments after this life), supposed to be common to all peoples (Asad 1993: 40; see Bossy 1985; Byrne 1989; Harrison 1990; Stroumsa 2010).

While this universal core of religion was being devised, the discovery of the rites and creeds of faraway peoples in the Americas, Africa, Asia and Oceania, as well as the re-discovery of antiquity, were calling into question the biblical framework for understanding the world. These combined circumstances set the stage for construing the peoples of the world as being divided into different religions, conceived as objectified doctrinal systems, each with their own distinct claims to propositional truth. Thus, from the 17th century onward, the conventional classifying of the peoples of the world in terms of Christians, Jews, Mohammedans and heathens turned into a division among four sorts of religions—Christianity, Judaism, Mohammedanism and heathenism[29]—but with only one 'right' way of worshipping God. In this perspective, Christianity—and more specifically Protestantism—provided the norm to which Judaism and Mohammedanism could be somehow related as competing 'Abrahamic religions',[30] as opposed to heathenism, long perceived as an indiscriminate lump.

As the voyages of exploration and the subsequent rise of colonialism were providing opportunities for European travelers, scholars, administrators and missionaries to acquire some first-hand knowledge of heathens' manifold customs, this latter category was progressively disaggregated into distinct religions. In the course of the 19th century, the prevalent fourfold division of

---

[29] In this process, heathenism (or, alternatively, paganism or idolatry), became a central organizing category governing much of Europe's early relationship to both the new worlds discovered by travelers and missionaries, and the ancient worlds recovered by archeologists and philologists (Ryan 1981; Augé 1982; Bernand and Gruzinski 1988; Barbu 2016).

[30] Notwithstanding the fact that each of these 'Abrahamic' religions claims to be the sole rightful heir to Abraham's covenant, there is a considerable degree of family resemblance among them, in the sense that they share references, beliefs and practices—such as a singular God, similar scriptural traditions, and a common patriarch in faith—that distinguish them quite radically from other traditions, from Hinduism in particular (Von Stietencron 1997). For a critical assessment of Abraham's religious legacy, see, e.g., Hughes (2012) and Levenson (2012).

humanity declined, to be replaced by a list of 'world religions' that could be compared with one another as particular instances of the universal genus 'religion' (Masuzawa 2005). The common assumption of Western scholarship was that these world religions shared essential similarities with Christianity—even though, weighed against what was considered to be God's last word, they were necessarily found wanting—in the terms of which they were assessed: namely, formal soteriological doctrines resting on canonical authority, enforced by a priestly hierarchy and sustained by congregational worship. From the prevailing evolutionist perspective of the times, world religions were considered advanced religions, as opposed to ethnic religions, regarded as 'primitive' or 'animist'.

In sum, the contemporary understanding of religion emerged out of both the encounter of Christendom with other religions during the great march of European discoveries and colonial expansion, and Enlightenment struggles to differentiate between rational knowledge and revealed dogmas in order to emancipate society from the smothering power of the Church—in such a way that it eventually became conceivable to separate the study of religion from its apologetics. Thus presented in a secular garb by post-Reformation and post-Enlightenment thinkers, the Christian conception of religion became a scholarly construct with the development of the so-called 'science of religion' (*Religionswissenschaft*) (Sharpe 1986). As a result, at issue is the fact that the category religion is too imbued with Christian theology, as well as with European colonialism and Western modernity, to have a transcultural or a trans-historical relevance. It is an emic category of Christian doctrine that is used as though it were an etic category in the academic study of religions. Consequently, 'religion'—as with other emic categories such as *din, mana, tao, dharma, bhakti, sampradaya, shraddha, sasana* or *agama*—ought not be taken for a conceptual tool but, rather, should itself be the object of analysis (Saler 2000). Furthermore, one should assess what is lost in the translation of these vernacular words in terms of religion.[31] That is to say, instead of essentializing religion as if it were a universal and generic category, one needs to proceed to its epistemological and genealogical deconstruction.[32]

---

[31] Conversely, one could ask what might be gained from a reversal of this translation process and the mapping of Western traditions in terms of such vernacular categories (King 2011: 50). See Sharma (1994) for an attempt at addressing religious studies in terms of *dharma* as well as of *din*, rather than through the conceptual framework of religion; as well as Turner (2014) for using *sasana* to question religion as a universal comparative frame.

[32] One of the first scholars to deconstruct the category religion was Wilfred Cantwell Smith (1962). Yet he too clung to essentialism. In retracing the genealogy of the category religion, Smith separated 'faith' from what he called 'cumulative tradition'. And in taking faith to be primary and transcendent in opposition to religious traditions,

While in the Christian context 'religion' exists as a category to its own participants, outside of this context it is a second-order category, constructed by observers from a variety of phenomena whose actors do not necessarily combine into a coherent institution and for which they usually do not possess a corresponding word (Cohn 1969). Now, it appears that the terms under which Christianity defines itself as a religion are comparable to the terms under which Judaism and Islam recognize themselves as religions. Therefore, the category religion is to some extent common to these three Abrahamic traditions, which are related by a similar belief in one exclusive God and divine revelation recorded in a holy book. In contrast, there was no corresponding indigenous terminology in Indic and other traditions prior to the modern period. In my view, if there is no equivalent term in another culture, it is not only the word which is missing, but also that particular entity 'religion' itself—understood in the sense of a set of beliefs and practices with some kind of systemic coherence and to which one could 'convert' as if it were one among several possible options. In that respect, I concur with Ludwig Wittgenstein that analyzing a concept amounts to analyzing the use of a word in a given language. Indeed, where there is no conceptual disembedding of religion from other facets of life, and thus no vernacular vocabulary to designate it, it is blatantly misleading to apply this category to the society under examination.

However, the fact that religion is "a Western folk category that contemporary Western scholars have appropriated" (Saler 2000: ix) does not imply that it is "solely the creation of the scholar's study", as Jonathan Smith would have it (1982: xi)—not only because, historically, the concept of religion was not created by scholars, but emerged over the centuries as a discursive construct proper to Christendom, but, more to the point, because members of other cultures have now appropriated the term religion—or its vernacular equivalent—to define some of their practices as differentiated from others. Hence the issue is to investigate the historical process whereby the category religion has become self-evident even to those for whom it was previously unknown (King 2011: 45).

As it happened, it was not enough for missionaries, along with orientalists and colonial administrators, to impute characteristic features of Christianity to Asian traditions to bring forth such 'religions' as Hinduism, Buddhism, Jainism, Sikhism, Taoism, Confucianism, Shintoism and so on[33]—as if local people were

---

treated as its secondary worldly expressions, he held to a typically Protestant outlook, which is not surprising coming from a Presbyterian minister.

[33] See, e.g., Oberoi (1994), Lopez (1995), Jensen (1997), Girardot (1999), Brekke (2002), Flügel (2005), Mandair (2009), Goossaert and Palmer (2011), Josephson (2012), Van der Veer (2014), and Horii (2018).

mere onlookers and had no agency of their own in the matter. While not disregarding the power imbalance in this process of negotiation, one should be aware that their native interlocutors had further to claim for themselves the privilege of possessing their own religion, construed as a soteriological system on a par with Christianity. To do this, they emphasized the doctrinal features as well as the ethical precepts in their traditions, while condemning blind superstition, mindless priestcraft and backward customs. By conforming orthopraxy to orthodoxy, reformers attempted to discriminate between 'true religion' and 'mere tradition'. As they expanded their global reach, these new religions demarcated their boundaries and consolidated their corporate identity, while trying to control the various rituals and observances that they encountered, in a process that can be called 'religionization'.[34] This replacement of disparate local traditions by a scriptural and de-territorialized form of religion was marked by rationalization (the formulation of a canonical corpus, its institutionalization, and its effective socialization) (Hefner 1993a), as well as by secularization (the desacralization of the immanent concrete in favor of an abstract and transcendent divine) (Hefner 1998). In addition, it usually brought about a politicization of religion, which was used to articulate ethnic or national identities.

Thus, if it is indeed true that 'religion' was not a vernacular category, it has become so as a consequence of the colonial encounter and broader Western political and epistemic domination across the world, which made native interlocutors of orientalists, administrators, and missionaries assert that they, too, had a proper religion. In the words of Daniel Dubuisson: "The West did not only conceive the idea of *religion*, it has constrained other cultures to speak of their own religions by inventing them for them" (Dubuisson 2003: 93).

In order to understand what is at stake with this invention, we should mark out the vernacular conception of a religious field, by assessing how the category 'religion' is construed locally and how it operates in relation to other categories. Indeed, far from being autonomous, religion is part of the semantic field it composes with related categories, such as tradition, culture, politics, law, ethics, ritual, superstition, idolatry, magic and so on. The relationship is one of mutual definition by mutual exclusion. That is to say, as a category, religion is a classificatory device, which involves the construction and maintenance of boundaries. This taxonomy is discursively constructed and rhetorically deployed by different

---

[34] I use the term 'religionization' in the sense given to it by Robert Hefner, that is, "the reconstruction of a local or regional spiritual tradition with reference to religious ideals and practices seen as standardized, textualized, and universally incumbent on believers" (Hefner 2011: 72–3). This process is very similar to the concept of 'religion-making' introduced by Arvind-Pal S. Mandair and Markus Dressler as "the way in which certain social phenomena are configured and reconfigured within the matrix of a world-religion(s) discourse" (Mandair and Dressler 2011: 3).

actors to particular ends within specific socio-political contexts. Therefore, one should address the practical work accomplished through the use of religion as a taxonomy, that is, both what it includes and what it excludes (Asad 2001).

Thus, when Balinese claim to 'have a religion', they are in effect asserting that some of their practices and beliefs are 'religious' and others are not. Hence, by investigating local productions of meaning I seek to understand the 'natives' point of view', that is, how the category religion operates for the Balinese who appropriate it and what they do with it. This amounts to saying that, in methodological terms, 'religion' is that which is regarded as such by local actors, which may or may not correspond to what counts as religion for the observer.[35] Furthermore, these actors do not necessarily concur regarding what their religion is about, as religion is a contested issue, having to do with institutionalized values and their relation to authority and its legitimation. In short, my purpose is not to determine what the religion of the Balinese actually is, but rather to elucidate what in Bali gets—or does not get—identified and legitimized as religion, by whom, in what circumstances, for what purposes, and under what configurations of power.

In contemporary Indonesia, the category religion has been appropriated by way of the Sanskrit loanword *agama*, which does not have any equivalent in the vernacular languages of Indonesia. Most Indonesianists appear to take for granted that *agama* is a direct translation of the word religion. And indeed, this is the meaning one finds in bilingual Indonesian dictionaries. However, this translation is not as straightforward as it might seem, because *agama* refers to a much narrower semantic field than does the common understanding of the word religion, for which Indonesians draw on the Dutch loanword *religi*. The fact is that the Indonesian state imposes on society its definition of what religion is. In this respect, *agama* is the peculiar combination of a Christian view of what counts as a 'world religion' with a restrictive and prescriptive Islamic understanding of what defines a 'proper religion'—namely, a prophet, a holy book, and a belief in the One and Only God.[36] Accordingly, Indonesian religious

---

[35] Regarding this point, opinions diverge widely, as between Wilfred Cantwell Smith, who declared that "no statement about a religion is valid unless it can be acknowledged by that religion's believers" (Smith 1959: 42), and Claude Lévi-Strauss, who argued that "no common analysis of religion can be given by a believer and a non-believer" (Lévi-Strauss 1972: 188). On this epistemological issue, see Segal 1983.

[36] Given that the Indonesian notion of *agama* is congruent with the Islamic understanding of 'religion', it is equated by some observers with the Arabic word *din* as used in the Quran (Hefner 1999: 212; Ramstedt 2004a: 9; Hosen 2005: 426, n. 21). However, these observers do not seem to have asked why it is the word *agama* rather than the word *din* that has come to be used in Indonesia to convey the meaning of 'religion'. In this respect, it is important to note that, before being glossed as 'religion' in the course of the 20th century as a result of the need for consistency in translation, the word *din*—which signifies 'practice, custom, law'—referred to "the corpus of obligatory

politics can be labeled 'religionization' (*agamasasi*), implying that followers of local traditions 'do not yet have a religion' (*belum beragama*), and therefore are due to be '*agama*-ized'—meaning that they could, and should, be a target of proselytizing (Cederroth 1996; Ramstedt 2019). For Indonesian authorities, to 'have a religion' is to be civilized and, therefore, it is an attribute of good citizenship. On that account, *agama* is the object of competing claims between, on one hand, proponents of indigenous cosmological frameworks and customary ritual practices, who consider these practices to be self-sufficient and deserving of the label *agama* in their own right, and, on the other, advocates of a world religion of foreign origin, who deny that such local traditions qualify as *agama*. In fact, in many cases this tension may coexist within the same actors, who are faced with the predicament of having to integrate both their own indigenous traditions and the locally prevailing world religion into the same socio-cosmic order (Aragon 2003).

In Bali, this opposition has taken the form of a protracted conflict between those Balinese who want to retain their ancestral traditions, and those who aspire to reform local practices in accordance with what they assume to be Hinduism. The first group has been mainly composed of the 'conservative' nobility, whereas the second has consisted mostly of educated commoners displaying a 'progressive' outlook. The debates between traditionalists and reformers regarding their religion have focused on two sets of questions:

> First, how is 'religion' (*agama*) connected with 'tradition' (*adat*), and how to discriminate between their respective fields?

> Second, how is *agama Bali* linked to *agama Hindu*, that is, how far does the 'Balinese religion' relate to the 'Hindu religion'?

I have dealt with these issues in parallel, by accounting for the articulation between ethnic and religious identity, on the one hand, and between Balinese religion and Hinduism, on the other. I must emphasize that I am not concerned with deciding whether the only 'real' Hinduism is to be found in India, nor whether Balinese religion is 'syncretic'. In other words, my purpose is not to assess whether the Balinese people are Hindu, neither whether they have been Hindu, nor even whether they are becoming Hindu. My objective is twofold: first, to elucidate the reasons why Balinese have come to turn *agama Hindu* into

---

prescriptions given by God, to which one must submit", according to the *Encyclopaedia of Islam* (Gardet 1965: 293; see further Karamustafa 2017 and Abbasi 2021).

the foundational marker of their ethnic identity, and second, to account for what resulted from their endeavor.

Chapter 1

A 'Living Museum' of Indo-Javanese Civilization

Time and again, Bali has been depicted as an island of Hinduism in a sea of Islam. This cliché is misleading, in that it assumes that the Balinese people have merely managed to preserve their Hindu heritage from the intrusion of Islam. Yet the fact that the island of Bali had been 'Indianized' does not necessarily mean that the Balinese religion is 'Hinduism'. Indeed, what may appear as Hindu to outside observers may not be understood as such by Balinese. That is to say, historical facts are not sufficient to establish that a people are of a particular 'religion', in the sense that a religious identity is relational—it is dialogically constructed through iterative processes of assertions and ascriptions constrained by power relations. More specifically, by presuming that the Balinese are still faithfully attached to their religious traditions, one fails to consider the movement of 'Hinduization' which has taken place on their island following its incorporation into the Netherlands East Indies in the early 20th century. This development was an outcome of the colonial encounter, which introduced to Bali the alien categories of both 'religion' and 'Hinduism'. As it happened, long before the Balinese began defining themselves as Hindu, orientalists had already Hinduized them, at a time when they had yet to learn the word Hinduism (Guermonprez 2001: 272).

After briefly outlining what is known about the so-called 'Indianization' of Bali, I will relate the circumstances under which European orientalists, Indian nationalists and Dutch colonial administrators came to view the Balinese people as Hindu, in order to then recount how the Balinese construed themselves as the Hindus that they were already supposed to be.

The 'Indianization' of Bali

To begin with, one should know that the long-standing interest in Bali shown by foreigners was initially not so much addressed to this island and its people as to the Indian and Javanese vestiges that could be discovered there: "In Western eyes there was never a Bali *per se*, but only a Bali derived" (Boon 1977: 17). The early orientalists were influenced by their Indic references: "What they saw on Bali, in their contacts with Brahmins and rulers, reminded them of [Hinduism]. True, they also saw many things that struck them as being anything but Hindu, but they saw such things through Hindu spectacles, and so had a distorted view" (Swellengrebel 1960: 25).[1] Accordingly, they regarded the island as a 'living museum' of Indo-Javanese civilization, the only surviving heir to the Hindu heritage swept away from Java by the coming of Islam. Such a preconception was compounded further by the fact that the Balinese seek the origins of their religious and social order outside their island, without differentiating clearly between that which came from India and that which came from Java. Later on, foreign observers would tend to emphasize instead the indigenous features of the Balinese religion, to the extent of viewing Hinduism as a superficial veneer tacked onto an Indonesian substratum,[2] while at the same time Balinese reformers were attempting to find in Hinduism the foundation of their religious identity. The issue has still not been settled, some authors asserting that "Bali is as much Hindu as India" (Miller 1984: 38; see Acri 2011), while others maintain that the religion of the Balinese differs "markedly from any form of Hinduism found in India" (Hooykaas 1964a: 33; see Guermonprez 2001).

In many respects, Bali appears typical of Southeast Asian Indianized societies, and its study has followed the usual evolution in two main phases, first focusing attention on transregional dynamics, then on local ones. In the colonial era, the European powers considered Indianization a forerunner of their own contemporary imperialist enterprise. For their part, Indian nationalists gathered in the Greater India Society[3] sought in their glorious past as 'benevolent

---

[1] One wonders how Bali would have been perceived if, instead of wearing 'Hindu spectacles', the early European observers had come from the Pacific Ocean; as James Boon remarked, "outside its Hinduized rites and Sanskritic texts, Bali can appear as much Polynesian as Indic" (Boon 1977: 18–19).

[2] This view was first expressed in Jacob Cornelis Van Leur's thesis, defended in 1934, according to which Indian influence in the Indonesian Archipelago was no more than "a thin and flaking glaze; underneath it the whole of the indigenous forms has continued to exist" (Van Leur 1955: 95). The same opinion was held by Christiaan Hooykaas, who contended in his study on religion in Bali that "under the more or less Hinduised layer of the last ten centuries there is the common Indonesian base" (Hooykaas 1973a: 1).

[3] The Greater India Society was founded in 1926 in Calcutta by Bengali historians and philologists, such as Ramesh Chandra Majumdar, Suniti Kumar Chatterji and Kalidas Nag, under the spiritual aegis of Rabindranath Tagore, for the purpose of promoting research into Indian culture in the regions they designated as 'Greater India'. They

colonizers' a revenge against their prestent humiliating colonized condition. They portrayed the peoples of 'India beyond the Ganges' as the passive and cultureless recipients of India's 'cultural colonization',[4] which had left its imprint in architecture, iconography, epigraphy, mythology, law, literature, theatre and rites, attesting to the Indianization of the local royal courts. Indian models had supposedly been transferred into Southeast Asia by means of a diffusionist process which paid little attention to endogenous dynamics.

This process of Indianization has been subjected to a series of theories according to the social groups supposed to have played the determining role in the diffusion of India's contribution—the *kshatriya*, *vaishya* and *brahmana* hypotheses reviewed by Frederik David Kan Bosch in his inaugural address *The Problem of the Hindu Colonization of Indonesia*, delivered at the University of Leiden in 1946 (Bosch 1961). Thus, the Bengali historian Ramesh Chandra Majumdar spoke of 'Hindu colonies in the Far East', postulating wholesale conquest and colonization by Indian settlers (Majumdar 1944). Due to the lack of evidence for this alleged colonization, orientalists such as Nicolaas Johannes Krom and George Coedès saw in Indian merchants the transmitters of Indian civilization (Krom 1926; Coedès 1968). However, doubts were soon raised as to the capacity of merchants to be the purveyors of aristocratic values, elaborate rites and erudite lore. Consequently, Jacob C. Van Leur and Frederik D.K. Bosch argued that this scriptural knowledge could only have been imparted by Brahmins and Buddhist monks summoned by local chiefs for the purpose of sacral legitimation (Van Leur 1955; Bosch 1961). In any event, all these theories attributed the effects of Indianization to an external intervention, whether imposed or solicited.[5]

After the Second World War and the formation of independent nation-states, the focus of interest shifted to the indigenous substratum common to the whole monsoon Asia—a hypothesis already advanced by Jean Przyluski, Sylvain Lévi and Paul Mus (Mus 1977)—as well as to the cultural specificities of what

---

promoted the view that culturally advanced Indians brought Indic ideas, values and religions to the uncivilized natives of foreign shores. Between 1934 and 1959 (with an interruption between 1947 and 1954) the society published the *Journal of the Greater India Society* as well as a monograph series (Kwa 2013). Several of its influential thinkers had studied in Paris with celebrated Indologists Sylvain Lévi and Jean Przyluski, and they drew on their work to support their own vision of ancient Indian cultural colonization and to counter the disparaging outlook of British orientalists. In 1936, a special memorial number was dedicated to Sylvain Lévi, praised for highlighting India's *mission civilisatrice* (Bayly 2004, 2007).

[4] Ramesh Chandra Majumdar, the most vocal promoter of the Greater India paradigm, expressed these views in explicit terms: "The Hindu colonists brought with them the whole framework of their culture and civilisation and this was transplanted in its entirety among the people who had not yet emerged from their primitive barbarism" (quoted in Manguin 2011: xi).

[5] See, e.g., Reynolds (1995), Lukas (2003), Formoso (2006), Acharya (2013), and Acri (2017b).

Horace G. Quaritch Wales called the 'local genius' (Quaritch Wales 1951). Whereas formerly Southeast Asia was treated simply as an extension of Indian civilization, increasing emphasis was being placed on the continuity of native cultural traditions, while the local peoples were being granted an active agency in their appropriation of Indic cultural features. By the same token, the very concept of Indianization was exposed to extensive criticism in that it implied a transfer of civilizing elements from an Indian 'motherland' to benighted outer reaches, all the while presupposing the existence of a homogeneous entity named 'India' before India became a historical fact (Mabbett 1977; Wheatley 1982). Critics then started speaking of interaction and convergence, implying a shared cultural complex spanning both sides of the Bay of Bengal, with the understanding that the Indianization of Southeast Asia was concurrent with, and no different from, the Indianization of South Asia itself (Heesterman 1989; Kulke 1990). This was evidenced by the spread of Sanskrit, which emerged as a language of literary, liturgical and courtly use more or less simultaneously and in very similar ways in the Indian subcontinent and Southeast Asia after the beginning of the Common Era, articulating a transregional symbolic network extending from Afghanistan to Bali which Sheldon Pollock described as the 'Sanskrit cosmopolis' (Pollock 1996, 2006).

In spite of the objections it has raised (Staal 1963), the concept of 'Sanskritization' propounded by Indian sociologist Mysore Narasimhachar Srinivas[6] is useful in highlighting the fact that what was transmitted, imitated and borrowed through the process of Indianization was the Sanskritic 'great tradition'—whether it be royal edicts, religious treatises or belletristic literature—recorded in Sanskrit texts (Gonda 1973). Once one apprehends Indianization as a transcultural movement of ideas spread by texts rather than as a movement of people, the appropriation of Indic traditions comes across as a voluntary initiative, the adoption and adaptation by local rulers of a cosmology establishing the foundations of royal authority and promoting a Brahmanical model of social order, wherein Brahmins—or, alternatively, Buddhist monks—officiate as royal chaplains and religious preceptors (De Casparis and Mabbett 1992; Bronkhorst 2011).

For Sanskrit texts to be an effective support of Indianization, however, they would have to make sense for the indigenous ruling elites. Oliver Wolters

---

[6] Srinivas defined 'Sanskritization' as a process by which a lower caste raises its status in the course of time by adopting the customs, rites, and values of the Brahmins (Srinivas 1952: 30). In this respect, the concept of 'Brahmanization' is commonly used to denote the process whereby non-Brahmanical forms of religious practices are transformed by hegemonic Brahmanical discourses (Bronkhorst 2016).

introduced the term 'localization' to account for the way Indic cultural features were appropriated locally. In this process, local people were not so much receivers as choosers, selectively embracing ideas and institutions, words and artifacts, which they reinterpreted into distinctively indigenized expressions. Thus, Sanskrit loanwords did not just rename existing categories by enhancing their status but, by wedging themselves into the structure of vernacular languages, they created new semantic fields (Reynolds 1995: 433).[7] Wolters specified further that not only did Indic materials have to be localized everywhere but they had to be re-localized before they could be appropriated in another region. He gave as an example the way Javanese 'Hindu-Buddhist' traditions were re-localized to fit into a different cultural milieu in Bali. This means that indigenous cultural systems did not remain unchanged when they had localized foreign materials: "local and foreign elements were 'universalized' and 'parochialized' respectively" (Wolters 1999: 56).

Following the increasing recognition of the predominant role played over an extended period of time by the maritime routes of trade between the Indian Ocean and the South China Sea—much of which was probably in the hands of Malay-speaking communities—current scholarship has moved beyond the diffusionist paradigm postulating a South Asian center and Southeast Asian peripheries, focusing instead on long-distance networks and processes (Hoogervorst 2013; Acri 2016). Thus, on the basis of recent archaeological findings, Pierre-Yves Manguin talks about a millennium-long phase of exchange across the Bay of Bengal that predated the beginnings of 'Indianization' proper. He concludes that "by the time Indian-inspired temples, statues and epigraphy appeared in Southeast Asia, sometime between the third and the fifth century CE, the relationship between Southeast Asian and Indian societies had already come a very long way" (Manguin 2011: xix–xx; see further Manguin 2022).

Thus it is that Indic traditions later subsumed under the respective generic labels 'Hinduism' and 'Buddhism'[8] surfaced in Southeast Asia around the 4th century CE. Data available for the 5th to 7th centuries indicate that Vaishnavism and Buddhism played prominent roles in the early phases of the Indianization process of coastal polities, both continental and insular. In the

---

[7] This is precisely what happened with the localization of the word *agama* in Indonesia.
[8] Apart from the fact that these terms are anachronistic, as they came to the fore and became reified only in the 19th century, one may wonder whether they are actually relevant to the situations they claim to describe. Thus, following De Casparis and Mabbett (1992: 288), Johannes Bronkhorst advocates speaking of Brahmanism instead of Hinduism, in order to stress the fact that Brahmanism was primarily a social order rather than a 'religion' (Bronkhorst 2011: 270). Further, particularly with regard to the situation prevailing in East Java, some authors go so far as to reject the terminological distinction between 'Hinduism' and 'Buddhism' altogether (see, e.g., Nihom 1994: 15; Jordaan and Wessing 1996: 63).

Indonesian Archipelago, Theravada Buddhism seems to have predominated before the end of the 7th century, when the inscriptions of the thalassocracy of Sriwijaya, in Sumatra, testify to the precedence of Mahayana and Vajrayana, which henceforward would remain the only forms of Buddhism attested in the Archipelago.[9] Whereas Buddhism prevailed in Sumatra and the Malay peninsula until the coming of Islam, in Central Java it coexisted with Shaivism, both cults being supported by the rulers alternately or even simultaneously, with a growing prevalence of royal support for Shaivism. In the 10th century, the center of power shifted to East Java. While Vaishnavism had considerable ascendancy during the Kadiri period (1042–1222), Shaivism was predominant, alongside Buddhism, during the Singhasari (1222–92) and Majapahit (1293–1527) periods. From the end of the 14th century, there are very few Buddhist remains and Buddhism seems to have faded away even before the fall of Majapahit and the ensuing Islamization of Java. Traces of the Indic cultural legacy progressively declined, while indigenous Javanese religious and aesthetic characteristics came gradually to the fore, suggesting that contacts with South Asia were diminishing.

Following Johan H.C. Kern, Nicolaas J. Krom and Willem H. Rassers, it has long been assumed that Shaivism and Buddhism merged into a syncretic cult of Shiva-Buddha in East Java during the Singhasari and Majapahit times, due to the pervasiveness of common significant soteriological and ritual tantric elements that contributed to the blurring of distinctions between the two persuasions.[10] As it happened, from the 13th century onwards, deceased kings were given a Buddhist as well as a Shaivite sanctuary. But the last king of Singhasari, Kertanagara, was deified after death and portrayed in the inscriptional and literary record as *Bhatara Śiwa-Buddha*, thus uniting in his own person the respective powers of Shaivism and Buddhism (Gonda 1975; Ensink 1978). Further, in the Old Javanese *Sutasoma kakawin*[11] (Santoso 1975), Mpu

---

[9] Dominant in Sri Lanka and in continental Southeast Asia, Theravada (the 'Doctrine of the Elders') is in fact a modern appellation: it was promoted in the early 20th century by Allan Bennett, a former British Theosophist converted to Buddhism, in lieu of the derogatory designation Hinayana (the 'Little Vehicle'). The term was officially endorsed in 1950 by the newly founded World Fellowship of Buddhists (Perreira 2012). Mahayana (the 'Great Vehicle') was taken up in China whence it spread to East Asia, whereas Vajrayana (the 'Diamond Vehicle') —also categorized as tantric Buddhism—is practiced mostly in Tibet and Mongolia.

[10] 'Tantrism' (a 19th-century European exonym) is a heterodox path to liberation that can be found in both Hinduism and Buddhism. It derives from the term *tantra*, which refers to systems and texts that deviate from the Vedic tradition. For a comprehensive overview of the Hindu tantric world, see Padoux (2017); on tantric Shaivism, see Sanderson (2009), and on tantric Buddhism, see Davidson (2002).

[11] Old Javanese is an Austronesian language whose lexicon contains heavy borrowings from Sanskrit. It replaced Sanskrit in Javanese inscriptions from the early 9th century and developed into what Pollock called a 'cosmopolitan vernacular', that is, vernacular language that became cosmopolitan for its regional world (Pollock 1998). Old Javanese literature comprises two major genres: prose works that include the adaptations of the Sanskrit epics, the *Ramayana* and the *Mahabharata (parwa)*, as well as related works of a didactic and religious nature (*tutur* and

Tantular, a Buddhist poet at the court of Majapahit, professed that there is no essential difference between Shiva and Buddha as their doctrines are equivalent: "Buddhahood is one with Shivahood, *bhinneka tunggal ika*, they are distinct, yet they are one" (*Sutasoma* 139.5).[12]

More recent research, however, has revised the former prevalent opinion by asserting that the fusion of Shaivite and Buddhist features in the Singhasari-Majapahit period is to be specifically attributed to Kertanagara's pursuit of both political hegemony and religious salvation (Hunter 2007; Acri 2015). The fact is that in both inscriptions (*prasasti*) and religious manuscripts of either Shaivite or Buddhist persuasion (*tutur* and *tattwa*), one finds references to distinct religious structures for their respective priesthoods. Thus, Old Javanese sources from the 11th century onward mention three religious orders (*tripaksha*): the Shaivites (also called Maheshvara), the Buddhists (also called Sogata) and the Rsis (also called Mahabrahmana).[13] On the other hand, the tale of Bubhuksha ('Glutton') and Gagang Aking ('Dry Stalk') presents the Buddhist and the Shaivite priests as siblings. The elder, the Shaivite, who represents the 'right path', is a pious ascetic practicing severe austerities, while his younger brother, the Buddhist, who is equated with the 'left path', indulges in all sorts of overconsumption and transgression. Yet, it is he who is acknowledged as the more perfect one from a tantric perspective.

In short, it appears that the Javanese remained conscious of the difference between Shaivism and Buddhism. The former probably had more affinity with the native traditions than the latter, which must have been better established with the nobility than with the common people.[14] Either way, it is hardly possible to

---

tattwa); and *kakawin*, court romances modeled on the Sanskrit metrical poetry called *kavya*. To these could be added poetry in indigenous meters (*kidung*), written in a language classified as Middle Javanese by philologists (see, e.g., Zoetmulder 1974; Creese 2001; Hall 2005).

[12] The words *Bhinneka Tunggal Ika*, conventionally translated as "Unity in Diversity", have become the motto on the coat of arms of the Republic of Indonesia.

[13] There are some uncertainties regarding the identity of the Rsis. According to Alexis Sanderson they probably are the forebears of the Balinese ritual specialists known as *resi bhujangga* (Sanderson 2003–04: 376).

[14] Few Indonesianists seem to have pondered why the term commonly used in Java today to refer to the pre-Islamic era is *jaman Buda* ('the Buddhist era'), while the pre-Islamic religion is not called, as in the scholarly literature, Hindu-Buddhist but *agama Buda*, which is usually rendered as 'Buddhist religion'. This is notably the case of the Tengger people in East Java, who followed *agama Buda* even though they were Shaivites (Hefner 1985: 39). Another case concerns the Buda communities of North Lombok, which claimed descent from the Javanese nobility fleeing the Islamization of Java (MacDougall 2005: 65). A tentative explanation of the term *jaman Buda* has been proposed by Theodoor G. Th. Pigeaud, who conjectured that Javanese Muslims felt that Buddhism was foreign and belonging to another period, whereas Shaivism was familiar to them and always remained so, particularly through the repertoire of the shadow theater (Pigeaud 1960–63, vol. iv: 480). For her part, Judith Becker advanced a highly speculative hypothesis to account for the puzzling fact that only *agama Buda* appears to be remembered in common parlance: "I assume, however, that the term *agama* in *agama Buda* formerly carried its earlier meaning—as referring to Saivite sects and scriptures—and that *agama* came to be a generic term for religion only after the

ascertain the extent to which the population at large took part in the Indic cults, owing to the fact that the sources substantiating the Indianization of Java—as well as of Bali—are mostly confined to court circles, in addition to being fragmentary. Thus, in 1971 Haryati Soebadio remarked that "we do not know yet which Indian traditions have in fact influenced Indonesia and in what form" (Soebadio 1971: 8), while Teun Goudriaan asserted in 1976 that "we are quite simply insufficiently informed about the development of Śaiva theory in India and Indonesia—and about the lines of communication between these two countries" (Goudriaan 1976: 123). However, since then important advancements have been achieved with the work of Max Nihom (1994) and Alexis Sanderson (2009) on tantric Shaivism as well as on tantric Buddhism, and more specifically with that of Andrea Acri (2006, 2013, 2017a) on the corpus of Sanskrit-Old Javanese Shaiva texts known as *tutur* and *tattwa* found in Java and Bali, who established that their main doctrinal outlook was a form of Shaiva Siddhanta, scattered with Samkhya and Pashupata elements.[15]

With regard to Bali, the discovery of Indian pottery and other artifacts indicates that as early as the 1st century BCE, the island's north coast was located on a major trade route between the Indian Ocean and the South China Sea (Ardika 2018). In addition to archaeological finds such as statuary, our chief source of knowledge regarding ancient Balinese history consists of clay miniature stupas and seals, as well as stone and copperplate inscriptions (Bernet Kempers 1990). The oldest inscriptions, which date from the end of the 9th century, show no evidence of Javanese influence. They are written in Old Bali-nese interspersed with Sanskrit terms and using a script derived from what epigrapher Arlo Griffiths named "Late Southern Brahmi" (Griffiths 2014: 54; see Goris 1954a, 1967). They indicate attempts of Balinese rulers to restructure their domain in light of Indic cosmologies and conceptions of kingship, and they

---

passing centuries. Thus, *agama Buda* originally may have referred to both Tantric faiths—Agamic Saivism and Buddhism—and came to have the more restricted, literal meaning of 'Buddhist religion' only after both were in decline" (Becker 2004: 18).

[15] The Old Javanese dictionary gives for *tutur* "memory, recollection, consciousness; innermost recesses of the spiritual part of the human being, 'the inner mind' (where the union with the absolute takes place); holy tradition, *smṛti* (as opposed to *śruti*), text containing religious doctrine, religious doctrine" (Zoetmulder 1982: 2084); as for *tattwa*, besides referring to the various categories of reality according to Samkhya doctrine, it is rendered as "doctrine concerning reality, philosophy; the writings containing this doctrine" (Zoetmulder 1982: 1963). According to Acri, whereas *tutur* are esoteric and mystically minded, *tattwa* expound Shaiva doctrines in a systematic and coherent manner and are closely related to the corpus of South Asian *Siddhantatantras*. However, although *tattwa* probably formed a separate and earlier class of scriptures, in the course of time the denominations *tutur* and *tattwa* came to overlap so as to be regarded as identical (Acri 2013: 71–2).

reflect their interest in supporting a variety of Hindu and Buddhist sects (Lansing 1983).[16]

Around the turn of the 11th century, the language of the inscriptions changed from Old Balinese to Old Javanese, after the marriage of the Balinese king Udayana to the Javanese princess Gunapriyadharmapatni. Thereafter dynastic and religious relations were strengthened with East Java, from where are assumed to have come a series of legendary cultural heroes to whom are attributed various founding acts—Rsi Agastya, Rsi Markandeya, Sang Kulputih, Mpu Bharada, Mpu Kuturan, Danghyang Nirartha and Danghyang Astapaka, to name but the most famous ones. According to a court chronicle in *kakawin* form, the *Nagarakertagama* or *Desawarnana* (Robson 1995), composed by Mpu Prapanca in 1365, Kertanagara sent a military expedition against Bali in 1284. Further, in 1343 Gajah Mada, the chief minister of Majapahit, is said to have conquered Bali. Following this conquest, a Javanese court arose in Samprangan, then in Gelgel, in the southeast of the island, which led to a marked Javanization of the Balinese society.

In the late 17th century, the court of Gelgel collapsed as a result of political turmoil and was succeeded by Klungkung, which remained the central political power, if only in name, until its final demise facing the Dutch colonial armies in 1908. Meanwhile, new kingdoms (*negara*) emerged whose rulers (*raja*), while formally recognizing the primacy of the Dewa Agung of Klungkung, would repeatedly attempt to tip the balance of power in their favor by every means available, under conditions of constant instability. Besides the armed conflicts that pitted them against each other, rivalry between the royal houses (*puri*) was reflected in a proliferation of ritual and artistic activities by means of which each ruler strove to outdo his peers as well as to ensure the tutelary support of his deified ancestors (Geertz 1980). Throughout this ceaseless competition, the Balinese rulers continued to emulate the court of Majapahit, itself modeled after the mythical kingdoms of Ayodhya and Dwarawati referred to in the *Ramayana* and the *Mahabharata* (Lansing 1979).

In Balinese historiography, Majapahit functions as an all-encompassing point of origin (*kawitan*): "'In the beginning was Majapahit'; what lies before it is a chaos of demons and villains about which the Balinese knows practically nothing" (Swellengrebel 1960: 23). Specifically, the Balinese ruling houses trace

---

[16] Roelof Goris recorded the presence in Bali of nine sectarian denominations (*paksha*): Shaiva Siddhanta, Pashupata, Bhairawa, Vaishnava, Boddha or Sogata, Brahmana, Rsi, Sora and Ganapatya. He was of the opinion that the Shaiva Siddhanta superseded all the other denominations after having absorbed some of their constituent elements, to the extent of being in certain respects closer to Samkhya teachings, with a strong tantric streak as well as with some Brahmanic Smarta components (Goris 1931a).

the origins of their political authority back to Majapahit, by claiming to be descended from the Javanese nobles (*arya*) who accompanied Gajah Mada at the time of his expedition against Bali. Moreover, when Majapahit fell to Islam, the last king of Majapahit, Brawijaya, and his entourage—the nobility, the priests and the literati—are said to have fled to Bali, thereby transferring their Indo-Javanese heritage to the court of Gelgel, initiating what would be seen in retrospect as the golden age of Balinese history.

In reality, it is difficult to assess the historicity of the traditions surrounding these events, but there is little reason to believe that there ever was a migration of the Javanese elites into Bali, as the decline of Majapahit, which was gradual, occurred before the actual expansion of Islam in Java. Unfortunately, supporting archaeological and epigraphical evidence comes to an end by the late 14th century (Bernet Kempers 1990: 33–49), while extant Balinese textual records, mostly in the form of mythical charters, origin narratives and genealogies—such as *Usana Bali, Usana Jawa, Babad Dalem, Pamancangah*, etc. (Hinzler 1976, 1986a; Wiener 1995; Creese 2000)—cannot be traced back beyond the 16th century, thus leaving an extended period of time in Balinese history about which hardly anything is known. Be that as it may, recent scholarly historiography has established that it was only from the 18th century, after the fall of Gelgel and the resulting political upheaval, that Balinese aristocratic families sought to substantiate their legitimacy in reference to Majapahit. It was as though the origin myth of Majapahit served to support the authoritative credentials of new claimants to power, while ensuring their cohesion in facing the threat posed by the expansion of Islam in Java and Makassar (Hinzler 1986a, 1986b; Schulte Nordholt 1986; Creese 2000).[17]

It is problematic to trace where the legend of the Javanese migration into Bali had its origins, if only because there is now so much cross-contamination from Balinese and Western historiographies.[18] While there are some references in Javanese sources, and a few scattered hints in Balinese ones, it is clear that the first European orientalists played a major role in its diffusion. Thus, we find it mentioned in the first two orientalist accounts of Bali, those of Thomas Stamford

---

[17] Why the island of Bali escaped Islamization might be due more to circumstances than to any Balinese cultural aversion to the new faith. Following Majapahit's demise, the kingdom of Gelgel not only consolidated its hold over the whole of Bali but extended its control into East Java as well as over the islands of Lombok and Sumbawa. Thus, in the 17th century, not only was Bali a political and military power to reckon with, but the Dutch East India Company (Vereenigde Oost-Indisch Compagnie, VOC) had become a dangerous enough foe to keep the sultanates of Mataram and Makassar at bay and prevent any attempt on their part to conquer and Islamize their Balinese neighbors.

[18] I am obliged to Helen Creese for valuable information on this subject.

Raffles (1817, vol. ii: 634, 692) and John Crawfurd (1820b, vol. ii: 257). However, a few decades later it was refuted in no uncertain terms by Herman Neubronner Van der Tuuk: "The Balinese know nothing of what is related by Sir S. Raffles, and some Dutch writers, all of whom placed too much reliance on the Javanese chronicles, namely, that those Javanese who objected to adopting the new faith fled to Bali immediately after the conquest of Majapahit by the Musalmans" (Van der Tuuk 1881: 55). Van der Tuuk's rebuttal did not prevent the French orientalist Sylvain Lévi from reiterating this legend, supplemented with an extra Indic flourish:

> About the end of the XVth century, when Java fell under the sway of Islam, the last remains of Indian civilization, princes, priests, scholars, common people, who did not consent to bow before the fierce invader, fled away to Bali, carrying with them what they could save of their spiritual treasures. While the whole of Indonesia turned gradually to the Moslem faith, Bali alone kept faithful to 'Mother India' and became a repository of ancient Indian lore (Lévi 1933: 11).

And thanks to the fame of Miguel Covarrubias's *Island of Bali*, by the 1930s the legend had acquired the status of a well-established cliché:

> It was of extreme significance for the cultural development of Bali that in the exodus of the rulers, the priests, and the intellectuals of what was the most civilized race of the Eastern islands, the cream of Javanese culture was transplanted as a unit into Bali. There the art, the religion and philosophy of the Hindu-Javanese were preserved and have flourished practically undisturbed until today. When the fury of intolerant Islamism drove the intellectuals of Java into Bali, they brought with them their classics and continued to cultivate their poetry and art, so that when Sir Stamford Raffles wanted to write the history of Java, he had to turn to Bali for what remains of the once great literature of Java (Covarrubias 1937: 28).

Needless to say, Bali's connection to a flight from Islam fitted well the colonial project to protect Balinese religion and culture from the encroachment of Islam, which was strengthening its domination over the Netherlands East Indies.

Whatever the historical reality behind the legend, the fact remains nonetheless that the Balinese did inherit the Indo-Javanese textual corpus, which they have preserved and enriched to the present day. Whereas philologists distinguish between different interrelated language registers, from Old Javanese to literary Balinese, the Balinese themselves include all of these under the generic term Kawi (from Sanskrit *kavi*, 'poet'), which translates as 'poetic language'. For them, Kawi summons up the voice of their ancestors, the words of those who founded their social order and who remain the source of authority and legitimacy. It is through the Kawi literature and its enactment in dramatic performances—particularly the shadow theater (*wayang*) and the mask theater (*topeng*)—that the Balinese people have been able to view "the mythic kingdoms of the Indian epics, the medieval empires of Java, and the feudal kingdoms of Bali" (Lansing 1977: 98) as their historical and cultural heritage (Picard 2012).

The Balinese hierarchy derived from Majapahit has been modeled on the normative ideology of the *warna* (*brahmana*, *satria*, *wesia* and *sudra*), originating from the Indian version of the *varna*, which should be understood as a classificatory grid within which the Balinese have devised their own title system, called *wangsa*.[19] Balinese status distinctions are based on the relative distance to a Javanese ancestral origin, to which the nobility—as 'people of Majapahit' (*wong Majapahit*)—is supposedly closer than commoners. By extension, however, most Balinese nowadays also claim to have Javanese ancestors, because of the social prestige inherent in Majapahit. As such, they are distinguished from what are called Bali Aga ('mountain Balinese') or Bali Mula ('original Balinese'), whose villages allegedly retained their autochthonous character by managing to some extent to keep out of Majapahit's sway (Reuter 2002).

Along with the *wangsa* system, the initiated and consecrated priesthood of the *padanda*, which is the exclusive prerogative of the *brahmana*, is assumed to have originated in Majapahit (Korn 1960). Formerly *padanda* would have served as the ruler's court chaplain (*purohita* or *bhagawanta*), source of holy water (*patirtaan*) and spiritual teacher (*guru*). Today their primary function is to prepare the holy water (*tirta*) that plays a crucial role in every Balinese major ritual. There exist two categories of *padanda*, the *padanda Siwa* (Hooykaas 1966) and the *padanda Boda* (also spelled *Buda*, *Bud(d)ha*, or *Bauddha*)

---

[19] The term *wangsa*, derived from the Sanskrit *vamsha* signifying 'descent, race, genealogy, lineage', is usually translated as 'caste, nation, people'. Whether the hierarchy of the *wangsa* constitutes a 'caste system' is a question just as recurrent and debated as whether the Balinese religion falls under the category of 'Hinduism'. While the system of four classes (*catur warna*) is occasionally mentioned in Old Javanese texts and inscriptions, the scholarly agreement is that it was a purely theoretical division of society without most of the implications of the Indian caste system. In fact, only the two superior classes correspond in theory to their Indic model, in that the *brahmana* exercise a monopoly over the consecrated priesthood and the *satria* are in charge of government. The *wesia*, who are not always clearly distinguished from the *satria*, form what could be regarded as a lesser nobility; in fact, few in Bali define themselves as *wesia*. As for the *sudra*, who constitute the bulk of the Balinese population, they are subdivided into competing title groups. Rather than 'castes', then, it is more appropriate to speak of the Balinese as having a 'title system', in terms of which status and prestige are distributed. In this instance I concur with the opinion of Hildred Geertz and Clifford Geertz: "The Hindu concept of 'caste' is inappropriate and confusing when applied to Balinese status distinctions, but the Balinese themselves, less interested in precision, nonetheless use it to explain their own system to themselves" (Geertz and Geertz 1975: 6; see Howe 1985).

(Hooykaas 1973c).[20] One should not presume that these priests are respectively 'Shaivite' and 'Buddhist', if only because the *padanda Boda* are *brahmana* and are considered 'Hindu' as much as the *padanda Siwa*. Furthermore, *padanda* of both persuasions are regarded as *siwa* (or *surya*) to their clients, who are said to either *masiwa ka Siwa* or to *masiwa ka Boda*.

Whatever their respective roles might have been in the past, today the differences between *padanda Siwa* and *padanda Boda* are not doctrinal but come down to a division between kinship groups. The matter is complicated, however, as the relation between *padanda Siwa* and *padanda Boda* refers explicitly to that which applies between the Shaivite Gagang Aking and the Buddhist Bubhuksha. Similarly, the *padanda Boda* is regarded as the younger brother of the *padanda Siwa*, and he is allowed to eat everything while the diet of the *padanda Siwa* is subject to severe restrictions. All the same, for the Balinese it makes little difference whether holy water is obtained from a *padanda Siwa* or from a *padanda Boda*. Although their paraphernalia and the divinities invoked in their *mantra* are slightly different, their rituals are essentially the same. According to the nature of the rites over which they officiate, they can be either interchangeable or complementary. Usually, each *padanda* officiates alone, but in important rituals both priests work together, albeit in a ratio of four *padanda Siwa* to one *Boda*. In that case, the *padanda Boda* is granted an inferior status and a subsidiary role with respect to the *padanda Siwa*. Thus, one notices a discrepancy in the value attached to the two types of *padanda*: in Balinese ritual the *padanda Boda* has a lower rank than is given to him in the tantric doctrine of deliverance propounded in the tale of Bubhuksha and Gagang Aking.

As the successors of court priests, one may assume that formerly the *padanda* did not participate in village rituals. While they officiate in rites of passage as well as in temple ceremonies nowadays, their office is not really part of the temple liturgy, which is conducted by priests of a lower order, the *pamangku*, who are the temples' caretakers. Balinese temples (*pura*) are different from Indian as well as Javanese temples. They are most likely a continuation of the prehistoric Indonesian sanctuaries where gods and deified ancestors came down on the megalithic stones erected for them. As a result, instead of closed buildings, Balinese temple compounds consist of walled-in courtyards with a series of altars arranged according to a linear rather than to a concentric layout.

---

[20] Balinese *padanda* are supposed to be descended from two Javanese Brahmins who are alleged to have come to Bali in the 16th century, following the collapse of the kingdom of Majapahit and the Islamization of Java: Danghyang Nirartha, who is said to be the ancestor of the *padanda Siwa*, and his nephew Danghyang Astapaka, who gave rise to the *padanda Boda*, of whom there are significantly fewer than that of the *padanda Siwa*.

Whereas in India the image of the god (*murti*), placed in the innermost sanctuary (*garbha griha*), is the focus of worship, which consists of the 'vision' (*darshana*) of the god, in Bali the deities—who are indigenous and do not belong to the Hindu pantheon[21]—do not reside permanently in the *pura*. They are believed to descend (*tedun*) from on high to the seats (*palinggih*) that are reserved for them and to temporarily inhabit their effigies (*pratima*) during the temple 'anniversary' (*odalan*), when they are feted as honored guests by the congregation (*pamaksan*) supporting (*nyungsung*) the temple (Belo 1953). During their stay in the temple, the visiting deities transform specially prepared water into holy water, which is then sprinkled by the *pamangku* over the members of the congregation. Besides these periodic ceremonies in collective temples, Balinese worship their deified forefathers in their family shrine (*sanggah*). As a rule, Balinese rituals (*karya*, *yadnya*) enact a series of transactions with immaterial entities and forces from the invisible world (*niskala*),[22] in which human beings present offerings (*mabanten*, *maturan*) and reverence (*muspa*, *mabakti*)[23] in exchange for blessings of holy water that ensure the renewal of life and the regeneration of nature. Once their offerings have been consecrated, the 'leftovers' (*lungsuran*, *surudan*) are brought back home and consumed by the worshipers.

Thus, despite the presence in Bali of numerous Sanskrit words and ritual elements of Indic origin, one would be hard-pressed to find anything exactly corresponding to what we know about India. Indeed, Bali is not India, and a fairly similar signifier does not necessarily entail an identical signified (Pain 2017: 148). Furthermore, it would be misleading to think that the Balinese religion is a straightforward continuation of that prevailing in Java at the time of Majapahit. Actually, if there can be talk of 'Indianization' as well as of 'Javanization', the

---

[21] Balinese temples are dedicated to local deities, whose identity does not really concern the officiants, least of all the worshipping community: "The vast majority of religious rituals of the vast majority of the population are concerned with very local gods—in fact, deified ancestors—and involve local temples and local groups" (Forge 1980: 224).

[22] From the Sanskrit *nishkala*, signifying 'devoid of constituent part', 'nameless and formless', a term used to refer to the Indescribable One, the Brahman (Gonda 1973: 531). Rather than conceiving an explicit polarity between the sacred and the profane, the Balinese differentiate two complementary fields of experience—the manifest world (*sakala*, "what lies within the bounds of human sensorial perception") and the unmanifest world (*niskala*, "that which lies beyond the realm of the senses") (Rubinstein 2000: 49). The formless *niskala* beings must take *sakala* form to have tangible effects in the world of humans. They are tied (*kaiket*) to particular localities as well as to specific social groups. For a perceptive analysis of the ways Balinese people manage their relationships with the *niskala* beings which interfere in their lives, see Reisnour (2018, Chap. 1).

[23] While the Balinese term *bakti* is derived from the Sanskrit *bhakti*, it should not be confused with the theistic devotional Hinduism in which devotees experience a direct relationship with the divine conceived as a personally chosen deity.

fact remains that these developments have given way since the 16th century to what might be characterized as a process of 'Balinization'—amounting in fact to a 'de-Hinduization' of Balinese religious practices (Guermonprez 2001: 289). In this respect, it must be acknowledged that the Balinese people have appropriated Indian and Javanese contributions and reinterpreted them according to their own purpose: they were not passive recipients of Indian and Javanese cultural influences but active agents of their own acculturation. As a result, it is often impossible to determine whether one is faced with Balinese features under an Indian (or Javanese) guise, or else with Indian (or Javanese) material transformed by vernacularization.[24]

The fact is that applying the word 'religion' to Balinese ritual practices is deceptive. Whatever it is supposed to be, the so-called 'Balinese religion' remains little understood, to the extent that one of the most knowledgeable specialists in this field, anthropologist Hildred Geertz, once confessed: "I do not yet know, really, what a 'temple' is, what 'deities' are, what 'rituals' are supposed to accomplish, nor what 'Balinese religion' is about" (Geertz 2004: vii; see further Geertz 2000). Earlier on, Geertz had alluded to a reason for this frustrating state of affairs: "The Balinese world is one in which the many elements are never harmoniously united, in which there is no single all-encompassing principle, no way of comprehending the whole" (Geertz 1994: 95). Geertz's statement has been endorsed by fellow anthropologists Richard Fox (2018) and Margaret Wiener, who asserted that "[it] is difficult, and misleading, to render what Balinese have to say about divinities, demons, or spirits in systematic form", not only because "establishing relationships to the invisible world interests Balinese far more than reflecting upon it" (Wiener 1995: 54), but also since to attempt to do so would amount to imposing order on a body of beliefs and practices which is rife with discrepancies and contestation, as different social groups disagree about the nature of the beings and powers who are worshipped in the temples and on the purpose of that worship.[25]

For a long time, the prevalent scholarly conception interpreted Balinese religious rituals as striving for balance, harmony and order. Barbara Lovric (1987) and Hildred Geertz (1994, 1995, 2000, 2004) have challenged this well-established view by focusing on the pervasive tantric notion of *sakti*, construed

---

[24] Following Pollock, I understand vernacularization as "the historical process of choosing to create a written literature, along with its complement, a political discourse, in local languages according to models supplied by a superordinate, usually cosmopolitan culture" (Pollock 2006: 23).
[25] It should be pointed out, however, that this contention has been vehemently denied by philologist Andrea Acri, who argues that the Javano-Balinese corpus of *tutur* and *tattwa* forms the scriptural basis of a Balinese Shaiva theology (Acri 2013: 78).

as a morally undifferentiated and ambivalent power for both creation and destruction.[26] Unlike most Western observers who, hampered by a Christian conception of 'religion', tended to understand *sakti* as 'witchcraft' and to dismiss it as peripheral to Balinese religious concerns, Hildred Geertz asserts that "an inner purpose of all Balinese rituals is the mobilization of the mystical power called *sakti*", adding that "Balinese temple rituals are, in this view, best understood as ways to use *sakti* to protect the temple congregation" (Geertz 1994: 2).[27]

In any event, it might be contended that, unlike the world religions, which have a core of abstract basic tenets meaningful to peoples of diverse cultural backgrounds, Balinese religious life is highly localized, consisting of rites that connect specific groups of people to one another, to their ancestors and to their territory.[28] Participation in these rites is a customary obligation for the Balinese, which compels membership of a village community, a kinship group, and a temple congregation. Rather than something to be believed in, Balinese 'religion' is something to be carried out. Accordingly, Balinese are far more concerned with appropriate ritual behavior (orthopraxy) than with right belief (orthodoxy).[29] What is important for them is not theology but efficacy. So much so that, prior to Dutch colonization it would have been difficult to delimit in Bali a field of activity that would be specifically 'religious'[30]—and even more so to entertain the idea that the Balinese 'religion' came under the category of Hinduism. Such evidence led the Indologist Frits Staal to conclude that, "Balinese ritual is a

---

[26] Commonly glossed as 'magically powerful and dangerous', the Balinese term *sakti* is derived from the Hindu notion of *shakti*, the all-pervading power of a deity represented by its female form. Its signification has diverged from the one it has in India, where the gods commonly require female consorts—their *shaktis*—in order to act. In the Shakta tradition, devotees worship the Goddess as the source of supreme power.

[27] This '*sakti* conjecture' has been pursued further by Michele Stephen and Andrea Acri, who have stressed the tantric Shaiva character of most Balinese rites: see Stephen (2002, 2005, 2010, 2014, 2015), Acri (2013, 2017a), and Acri and Stephen (2018).

[28] In this respect, Bali is no different from other traditional Indonesian societies, where the main purpose of ritual activity is "to maintain the proper connections between people, the natural world, and the world of the spirits/ancestors, on which equilibrium the well-being of community and cosmos depends" (McVey 1999: 5; see further Reuter 2014).

[29] Clifford Geertz expressed this in his own inimitable style: "You can believe virtually anything you want to actually, including that the whole thing is rather a bore, and even say so. But if you do not perform the ritual duties for which you are responsible you will be totally ostracized, not just from the temple congregation, but from the community as a whole" (Geertz 1973: 177).

[30] Here is what anthropologist Leo Howe has to say on this subject: "Kinship groups were equally temple congregations practising ancestor worship; subsistence production was highly ritualized, with success depending on the blessings of deities and the observance of taboos; relationships between lords and subjects paralleled those between gods and people; states were not political organizations based on a social contract between ruler and ruled, but magico-religious realms underpinned by sacred kingship; and crime was not merely a legal wrong but a polluting event, which had to be rectified by a purification ritual" (Howe 2001: 4).

classic case of ritual without religion" (Staal 1995: 31). It is also a classic case of immanentism in the sense given to this term by Alan Strathern (2019).

The orientalist view

Ever since the publication of Edward Said's *Orientalism* (1978), there has been a tendency to see the forms of knowledge produced by colonial scholars, administrators and missionaries as a one-sided imposition of power, tantamount to denying agency to colonial subjects, when in fact, from the very beginning, local actors exposed to European representations of their 'religion' became active participants in orientalist discourse. In Bali, just as in India, the orientalist view fed on the dominant standpoint of the *brahmana* priesthood, and more broadly of the ruling elite, who acted as key informants to the European visitors and shaped their perspective on the Balinese religion.

Although it is known that several European ships had reached Bali previously, the earliest detailed report on the island dates from 1597, when the first Dutch fleet to attempt the voyage to the Orient in search of spices disembarked on its shore to replenish its supply of food and water.[31] According to the ship's log, the Dutch were impressed by the prosperity of the king of Gelgel and pleased by his hospitality, which differed favorably from their reception in Java. Above all, they noticed that, unlike the Javanese who had converted to Islam, the Balinese were 'heathens'.[32] In spite of a rather pleasing first impression, however, the image of Bali that was soon to impose itself on the European imagination was one of savagery: formidable warriors, quick to abandon themselves to the frenzy of *amok*, the Balinese were seen as inveterate plunderers of shipwrecks, and their princes as opium-smoking-cum-slave-trading despots, cruel and debauched, whose widows were forced to fling themselves onto their lords' funeral pyres (Boon 1977; Vickers 2012a).

---

[31] After the Portuguese had found the way to the 'Spice Islands' in the early 16th century, the Dutch, who had declared the independence of the United Provinces of the Netherlands from Spain in 1581, set sail to the East Indies in 1595 to access spices directly from their source in the Moluccas. On the arrival of the Europeans in the Malay Archipelago, see Boxer (1973, 1990).

[32] The diary of midshipman Aernout Lintgenszoon called the Balinese heathens who 'pray to whatever they first meet in the morning'. This topos would be repeated over and over again, and we find it restated nearly verbatim a century later by François Valentijn in his *Oud en Nieuw Oost-Indiën*: "they honour as a God that which they encounter first thing in the morning" (quoted in Vickers 1994: 88), as well as in an Englishman's report on Bali: "[the Balinese] are exceeding Brutish People and the Simplest of Heathens. Their God is whatever they first cast their Eye on in the Morning" (quoted in Boon 1977: 12).

During the next two centuries, Europe heard little more of Bali, chiefly because it had neither spices nor land suitable for plantation crops. In fact, the island's main commercial activity was the slave trade, controlled by Balinese rulers and boosted by the labor requirements of the Dutch East India Company (Vereenigde Oost-Indisch Compagnie, VOC), established in 1602 and based in Batavia, on the northwest coast of Java, from 1619. Over time, the VOC progressively consolidated Dutch influence in Java and, driven by its commercial interests, extended its control over ever vaster regions of the Archipelago. Heavily in debt by the end of the 18th century, the VOC went bankrupt until the Batavian Republic finally took it over in 1800. After Napoleon had annexed Holland to his empire in 1810, Lord Minto, governor-general of India, launched a military expedition in 1811 to wrest control of Java, which remained under British administration until it was returned to the newly established United Kingdom of the Netherlands in 1816 (Hannigan 2012). During the following years, the Dutch became concerned about British rivalry in the region, and with Bali lying so close to Java, this little island took on a new strategic importance.

The first orientalists to visit Bali were agents of the British East India Company, who transferred onto the island the assumptions they had formed in India regarding 'Hinduism'. From then on Bali's reputation for primitive savagery gave way to the magnified image of an Indianized society, while the Balinese people, who had previously been regarded as heathens, became Hindus.

In 1814, John Crawfurd, a Scottish orientalist who had been appointed resident-governor of the Javanese principality of Yogyakarta, was sent on a brief reconnaissance mission to Buleleng, on the north coast of Bali. In 1820, he presented at the Asiatick Society[33] a communication entitled "On the existence of the Hindu religion in the island of Bali" (Crawfurd 1820a; see further Crawfurd 1820b: 236–58). Crawfurd—who was one of the very first orientalists to use the term 'Hinduism' to refer to the religion of the Hindus—took it for granted that the Balinese were Hindu and, moreover, he used the word *agama* in the sense of religion. He declared that while the existence of the Hindu religion in Bali was a fact which had long been known, precise information on the subject was still lacking. Crawfurd obtained his own information from Brahman priests summoned by the ruler of Buleleng. These priests told him that the Balinese people embrace either 'the religion of Siva' (*Agama Siva*) or 'the religion of

---

[33] The Asiatick Society had been established in 1784 in Calcutta by the colonial administrator and orientalist William Jones with a view to promoting studies in Indian history and culture (Kejariwal 1988).

Buddha' (*Agama Buddha*).³⁴ As in India, the Balinese are divided into four castes. And the Hindus of Bali like those of India burn the bodies of their dead. But of all the customs which attest to the Hinduism of the Balinese, none is more conspicuous than the sacrifice of the widow on the funeral pile of her lord (*masatia*).

Crawfurd further observed that while the Brahmans may be considered genuinely Hindu—even if they told him that they worshipped no idol whatsoever, not even those of the Hindu mythology—the populace were "left to their local superstitions, consisting of the worship of personifications of the elements, and of the most striking natural objects which surround them" (Crawfurd 1820b: 238).³⁵ He noted that none of the temples he visited were dedicated to the gods of the Hindu pantheon. He added that the Balinese hardly show any religious fervor, that they practice no ascetic penances and know no sectarian allegiance, and above all that they demonstrate a great deal of religious tolerance, even with regard to the Muslims who have settled on their island.

Outside their religious duties, Crawfurd said, Brahmans have authority for the administration of justice. His informants provided him with manuscripts in Kawi—"the language of learning, of religion, and of the law" (Crawfurd 1820a: 144). Most of these manuscripts bore the word *Agama* in their title—"a generic term in Sanskrit for any composition treating of those sciences which are considered by the Hindus as sacred" (Crawfurd 1820a: 147). He confessed he had looked in vain, both on Java and on Bali, for any vestige of the Indian Vedas and believed that they never had any existence on these islands.

In 1817, Sir Thomas Stamford Raffles, lieutenant-governor of British Java (1811–15), published his monumental *History of Java*, in which an appendix presented an account of Bali. Raffles spent only a few days on the island in 1815, also in Buleleng, and most of his information on the Balinese religion was provided by Crawfurd. Even more so than the latter, he regarded Bali as the last living vestige of the lost Hindu civilization of Java:

> On Java we find Hinduism only amid the ruins of temples, images, and inscriptions; on Bali, in the laws, ideas, and worship of the people. On Java this

---

[34] "When interrogated respecting their religion, the natives of Bali say that they are of the religion of Siva (*Agama Siva*), or of the religion of Buddha (*Agama Buddha*); but as almost all knowledge of their religion is confined to its ministers, whose opinions and doctrines the people supinely subscribe to, it is usual to say 'the religion of the Brahmans of Siva', and 'the religion of the Brahmans of Buddha', instead of more general appellations. It is of the Hinduism of the sect of Siva only, that I can furnish any detailed information. The Buddhists are few in number [...] The sect of Siva may indeed be denominated the national religion" (Crawfurd 1820a: 129).

[35] We see in Crawfurd the orientalist prejudice which regards the Brahmins as the custodians of Hindu orthodoxy, while popular practices are deemed to have degenerated since the Vedic era.

singular and interesting system of religion is classed among the antiquities of the island. Here it is a living source of action, and a universal rule of conduct. The present state of Bali may be considered, therefore, as a kind of commentary on the ancient condition of the natives of Java (Raffles 1817, vol. 2: ccxxxv–ccxxxvi).

Setting the path for a century of orientalist scholarship by thus portraying the island of Bali as a 'living museum' of Hindu Java, Raffles saw it as his calling to protect it against the rapid advancement of Islam in the Malay Archipelago (Aljunied 2004).

The Dutch would pursue these orientalist conjectures after they regained possession of their territories in the East Indies. In the wake of the first orientalists, missionaries, Dutch as well as British, would regard Bali as a fertile ground for evangelism. In 1829, an English missionary from the London Missionary Society based in Batavia, Walter Henry Medhurst, spent three months in Buleleng with his assistant, Reverend Jacob Tomlin. His report, originally published in a missionary journal and reprinted numerous times, although not concealing the dangers facing the settlement of missionaries on the island, advocated evangelizing the Balinese people (Medhurst 1830). This led to the assignment in 1838 in Buleleng of Reverend Ennis, who remained there only a very short time without exerting any significant influence. But while British colonial authorities were in favor of converting the natives, the Dutch government would stick to the principle of strict religious neutrality, mainly out of fear of arousing anticolonial Islamic backlash (Steenbrink 1993). Under the provision of article 123 of the 1854 Governmental Regulations (*Regeerings-reglement*) of the Netherlands Indies (revised and updated in 1925), express authorization of the governor-general was to be required for missionary work with the native population.

In 1846, as the Dutch were about to launch their first military expeditionary force against the northern Balinese kingdom of Buleleng, Wolter Robert Baron van Hoëvell, the president of the Royal Batavian Society of Arts and Sciences,[36] petitioned the governor-general to attach a scholar to the expedition to document Bali's Hindu religion and culture (Van Hoëvell 1848). In fact, van Hoëvell was more interested in reconstructing the past of Java than in documenting the

---

[36] The first learned society in Asia, the Royal Batavian Society of Arts and Sciences (Koninklijk Bataviaasch Genootschap van Kunsten en Wetenschappen) was founded in 1778 by the naturalist J.C.M. Radermacher. Its members collected manuscripts and archaeological remains, they contributed reports on the history of the Malay Archipelago and on the languages of its peoples, and from 1853 they published the academic journal *Tijdschrift voor Indische Taal- Land- en Volkenkunde* [Journal of Indian Language, Land and Ethnology].

contemporary situation of Bali.[37] He was primarily concerned with the Indian texts to be found on Bali. Crawfurd and Raffles had mentioned some titles that Wilhelm von Humboldt had established to be Sanskrit. Consequently, the Batavian Society's archivist and assistant librarian, the German Sanskritist Rudolf Friederich, a connoisseur of Indian Hinduism, was sent to Bali with the task of collecting and deciphering all the manuscripts in Sanskrit and in Kawi that he was able to find:[38] "He was consequently the perfect scholar to be sent to Bali in order to deepen the knowledge of Balinese Hinduism, to confirm it as a branch of Indian Hinduism and to study the *Kawi* literature, as *Kawi* was supposed to be a branch of the Sanskrit language" (Pain 2017: 143). His mission was to ascertain what the Balinese have borrowed from India and to trace the changes that Hindu principles have undergone in their hands. After a two-year stay in the southern kingdom of Badung, Friederich wrote a 'provisional report on the island of Bali' (Friederich 1849–50), an English translation of which would be published in 1959 in Calcutta under the title *The Civilization and Culture of Bali* (Friederich 1959). Divided into three sections—"1st, language and literature; 2nd, religion, worship and cremation; 3rd, castes and royal races" (Friederich 1959: 1)—Friederich's report is the first erudite study of Bali.[39]

Like Crawfurd before him, Friederich obtained his information from *brahmana* priests, who in his view were the repositories of the Indo-Javanese heritage and of India's sacred texts.[40] But unlike his predecessor, he asserted that the Vedas were known to the Balinese, even though there remained only fragments. And he was of the opinion that they had been known in Java as well, since the priests of Bali had their origin in Majapahit. Therefore, he concluded

---

[37] "[...] on the Island of Bali the Hindu religion subsists undisturbed and alone in the whole Archipelago. [...] Arid Islam has on Java expelled and destroyed the literary and poetical life of India, but on Bali we find the key that will enable us to penetrate the knowledge of this life as it once animated the Javanese" (Van Hoëvell 1848: 152, 159).

[38] "[...] it is necessary that all Kawi and other manuscripts which can be heard of should be collected, because these are of the utmost importance for the illustration of the social and religious condition not alone of Bali itself, but also of the still more important ancient Java" (Van Hoëvell 1848: 154).

[39] While Friederich's report may be considered the first erudite study of Bali, it was preceded by the letters of Pierre Dubois, a Walloon who was the first colonial official to live on the island. From 1828 to 1831, Dubois served as civil administrator to the Badung court. Based in the harbor of Kuta, he was in charge of recruiting soldiers for service in the Dutch colonial army during the Java War (1825–30). In 1829, he received an invitation from the Batavian Society to document his observations of Bali. The letters he wrote in French for that purpose, under the title *Légère Idée de Bali en 1830*, provide a vivid ethnographic description of Balinese society, culture, religion, and politics. Dubois' letters have been beautifully presented, edited, and translated by Helen Creese (2016).

[40] "[...] the priests bring before our eye the stage at which the Javanese stood before the introduction of Muhammedanism. They are, also, the only remaining preserves of the old literature and religion. To them must every one repair who desires the elucidation of the Kavi. They are the expounders of all laws and institutions; and of the knowledge of antiquity they have scarcely lost or forgotten anything from their faithful adherence to traditions" (Friederich 1959: 2).

that it was of the greatest importance to get possession of the remains of the Vedas in Bali, as this was the only way to understand the contemporary Balinese religion, as well as the ancient religion of the Javanese.[41] Besides the Vedas, Friederich mentioned a number of texts obtained from priests, while drawing a distinction between works of a religious or didactic nature (*tutur*) and law books; the latter generally bore the word *Agama* in their title, about which he stated: "In the Malayan and common Balinese language it [*agama*] signifies religion; in the names, *Agama, Adigama, Devāgama*, it has evidently more the old Indian meaning, and especially that of law-book" (Friederich 1959: 30, n. 21).

Friederich confirmed furthermore that Hinduism and Buddhism were present in Bali, even if most Balinese were Shaivite and Buddhism was vestigial. As for the relation between Shaivism and Buddhism, the priests stated that Buddha was Shiva's younger brother and that the two sects coexisted peacefully side by side. Unlike Crawfurd and Raffles, however, who considered that the worship of the people was mere superstition which could not be called Hinduism, Friederich was convinced that the popular religion was itself also truly Hindu, notwithstanding the low esteem in which the village temples and their rituals were held by the *brahmana* priests.[42]

Baron van Hoëvell was not only an orientalist scholar, but he was also a minister to the Batavian congregation of the Dutch Reformed Church (Indische Kerk). And it is significant that at the very time he was advocating the preservation of Bali's Indo-Javanese heritage, he published a pamphlet in which he held that Hinduism was doomed to extinction on the island, while claiming that the Balinese people were favorably disposed towards Christianity. He based his opinion on early reports that Balinese, above their numerous gods, believed in a supreme deity, which he thought would make them amenable to recognizing the Christian God (Van Hoëvell 1846). He therefore recommended sending

---

[41] Had Friederich been allowed to examine the manuscripts which the priests called *weda*, he would have found out that they in no way represented the ancient Indian Vedas, not even in a fragmentary shape, but were ritual prescriptions (*kalpasastra*), interspersed with *mantra* and hymns (*stuti* and *stawa*). In the Balinese language, the word *weda* refers to the *mantra* uttered by *padanda* during their office (*maweda*) (Goudriaan 1970). The myth of the Balinese Vedas still persisted long after scholars like J.F.G. Brumund and J.H.C. Kern had found out the real state of affairs. See the remark by Christiaan Hooykaas: "For a quarter of a century we have known that *weda* in Bali is something quite different from Vedas in India. For this knowledge we have to thank Dr. Goris, for he has explained—and this was corroborated by Sylvain Lévi—that the brahmin Siwa-priest in Bali, when stating that he was engrossed in his *surya-sewana*, *weda-parikrama* or *ma-weda*, in reality was reciting (partly Tantric) *mantra* and *stawa*" (Hooykaas 1964b: 231).

[42] "In Bali, everything relating to religion is in the hands of the priests, and on the great ignorance of the people in all that is necessary according to the sacred literature for their temporal and celestial happiness, is founded the unlimited power of the priests, who are the organs of the Deity for the blindly believing people" (Friederich 1959: 13).

missionaries to Bali while calling for the Bible to be translated into the Balinese language.[43] Once Bali had been subdued by the Dutch, its evangelization could then serve as a starting point for the conversion of Java.

In 1866, the first Dutch missionaries, Rutger van Eck and Jacob de Vroom, from the Utrecht Missionary Union (Utrechtse Zending Vereeniging), settled in Buleleng where they opened a school. Van Eck published several articles on Balinese society, its history, its language, literature and customs. But their missionary work was certainly less than a success. Only after seven years did they succeed in baptizing their servant, I Gusti Wayan Karangasem, whom they christened Nicodemus. Ostracized by his own community owing to his conversion, Nicodemus had De Vroom murdered in 1881, causing the Netherlands Indies government to ban all missionary activity on the island for the next fifty years.

In any case, from Crawfurd to Friederich, the orientalist view of Bali was clearly established: the Balinese people are the sole heirs of the great Indo-Javanese civilization of Majapahit, and Hinduism—blended with Buddhism—is the core of their society and the warrant of their cultural identity. This view is informed by several assumptions: first, that the present situation of Bali reflects that of Java prior to its Islamization; second, that the Balinese religion is located in texts of Indian provenance on which the indigenous social and judicial order has been modeled; and third, that the *brahmana* priests are the depositaries of these sacred texts and the custodians of the Balinese religion. The task set for orientalists is then to compare Balinese texts to their Indic models and to remove indigenous 'corruptions' in order to recover their 'authentic source'.[44] That is to say, the texts which the orientalists were looking for in Bali were not regarded as Balinese but as an Indian—or rather Indo-Javanese—legacy that the Balinese people had the merit of preserving for posterity. It would still be a long time before philologists finally realized that the better part of this literary and religious heritage is in fact of Balinese provenance (Rubinstein 2000; Creese 2001).

---

[43] On a proposal from Van Hoëvell, the Netherlands Bible Society (Nederlandsch Bijbelgenootschap) had intended in 1862 to send to Bali the Eurasian linguist Herman Neubronner Van der Tuuk with the mission of translating the Bible into Balinese. Due to political turmoil, Van der Tuuk had to wait until 1870 to settle on the island. And instead of getting on with the task assigned to him, he resigned from the Bible Society and became a colonial civil servant in 1873. In that capacity, he set to work on a dictionary of Balinese and Kawi. His magnum opus, the monumental *Kawi-Balineesch-Nederlandsch woordenboek* [Kawi–Balinese–Dutch Dictionary] was published only posthumously.

[44] As Andrea Acri has rightfully remarked, it might be said that the Balinese religion has usually been addressed in terms of what it lacks rather than of what it does consist of, as if it were some sort of 'defective' Hinduism in comparison with the 'pure' form of Indian Hinduism, a vision the Balinese themselves appear to have introjected, as will be seen further (Acri 2011: 161, n. 11).

A telling example of willful blindness to local reality is provided by Sylvain Lévi, who went to Bali in search of Sanskrit texts on his way back from Japan in 1928. He reported the outcome of his investigations in a book published in India, *Sanskrit Texts from Bali* (1933), in which he described his arrival on the island in a way that makes one wonder whether he might have been led astray by his 'Hindu spectacles':

> [...] the only spot where faint traces of the old Sanskrit culture can still be detected is a small and remote corner of Indonesia; but there at least, the traveller finds himself surrounded by a real Indian atmosphere. Before landing at the harbour, he can see by the sea-side a temple dedicated to Varuna; among the people waiting at the pier, he will notice Brahmans, Kṣatriyas, Vaiśyas, Śūdras; as soon as he can mix with daily life, he will hear the names of Śiva [...], of Nārāyana, of Gaṇeśa, etc. The more he comes into close contact with the Balinese, the more he will be reminded of distant India (Lévi 1933: ix).

However, if truth be told, when landing at the harbor of Buleleng, Lévi was more likely to encounter Chinese, Arabs, Javanese, Madurese, Bugis, or even Muslim Indians, than Balinese. As for being able to differentiate between Balinese according to their *varna*, it would have more to do with divination than with plain observation, even with a solid formation in Indology. Nevertheless, having seen what he was looking for, and while noticing that the *padanda* perform the same worship that is practiced all over India, Lévi pointed out that their cultural horizons are confined to Java, that they have not the faintest knowledge of India, and "that they do not understand one word of the Sanskrit texts which they write, read, and chant" (Lévi 1933: x).[45]

Shortly before Sylvain Lévi's stopover, another illustrious visitor also believed he had found India in Bali. Rabindranath Tagore spent two weeks on the island in 1927, as part of a three-and-a-half-month journey to study the remains of Indian civilization in the antiquarian relics as well as the living arts in Farther India (Das Gupta 2002).[46] Reading through his travel diary, one realizes that, like Sylvain Lévi, he saw in Bali what he was looking for: "Some puranic age seemed to have come back to life before our very eyes, some picture from the Ajanta caves come out from the realm of art into the realm of life to revel in the sunshine" (Tagore 1928: 325). Yet, as a modernist reformer, spiritual leader

---

[45] This assertion has been disputed by Christiaan Hooykaas (1959: 73; 1962: 320) as well as by Jan Schoterman (1979: 334). Furthermore, as will be seen below, not only did some Balinese educated in colonial schools know about India but moreover they intended to emulate the Indian reformers of Hinduism in order to rationalize their own religious practices.

[46] Tagore described his journey to Southeast Asia as a *tirtha yatra* (pilgrimage), using *tirtha* in a metaphorical sense, implying a transition to a liminal location between histories and cultures.

of the Brahmo Samaj, Tagore had become critical of the rituals of orthodox Hinduism. Thus, much as he enjoyed what he saw on the island, he found Balinese religious life static, as if entrapped in a bygone era, where he had searched in vain for an authentic Hindu spirituality, even among the *brahmana* priests.

Tagore was accompanied on his journey by the noted philologist from Calcutta University Suniti Kumar Chatterji, one of the founders of the Greater India Society, who presented an account of his visit to Bali before the Sixth All-India Oriental Conference, held in Patna in 1930. He declared that Bali was the main evidence of Indian civilization in the lands of Greater India as, unlike the other Indianized regions of Southeast Asia, Hindu institutions were still a living reality on the island: "Bali, where a good many old Hindu institutions are still a living thing, albeit in an altered or modified shape, is in this respect the most important tract in this Greater India" (Chatterji 1931: 139). However, due to the rupture of the links with India, the Balinese people have lost contact with their Sanskrit heritage, so that their rituals have degenerated and the *mantra* used by their priests have become corrupt and unintelligible. In consequence, Chatterji called for resuming relations between Bali and India, and he advocated the cooperation of Indian scholars to reconstruct the Balinese religious history as well as to assess how far their contemporary Hindu practices have preserved pre-Hindu rituals.[47]

This view would be disseminated in numerous articles of the *Journal of the Greater India Society*, which bear witness to a mixture of fascination and condescension towards the island of Bali. To cite only one example: "To Indians that mysterious little island, still a replica of Hindu India of early times, with its simple faith, primitive rites and native social customs and life, is of peculiar interest—as it visualizes in a living form a typical image of Ancient India—which has passed away on the continent" (Gangoly 1936: 124).

The Dutch colonial encounter in Bali

My purpose in this section is not to provide a detailed account of Dutch colonial policy in Bali, but to emphasize the crucial role played by the colonial encounter in the emergence of a reflexive Balinese identity. While the Dutch knew little of the island over which they had stretched their empire, they had certain ideas

---

[47] During his stay in Bali, Tagore had promised to send scholars to investigate the survival of Indic cultural and religious traditions on the island (Kraemer 1933b: 107; Ramstedt 2011: 533; Stowell 2011: 114).

about what it should be like, and they eagerly strove to make it conform to their preconceptions.[48] As noted above, before colonial administrators embarked on reorganizing Balinese society, it had been construed by European orientalists as 'the island of Hinduism'.[49] In the guise of a restoration of what they regarded as the Balinese 'traditional order', the colonial authorities initiated a veritable 'traditionalization' of Balinese society.

The island of Bali was one of the last regions of the Indonesian Archipelago to be subjugated by the Dutch. Its conquest was far from an isolated or incidental event: it was carried out in the course of a territorial expansion that, starting with the consolidation of the VOC's power in Java, saw the transformation of what had initially been a mere commercial enterprise into the imposition of colonial authority throughout the Archipelago (Ricklefs 2008). This required the subjugation of those regions still under native rule and the reinforcement of the colonial administration, which completed the formation of the empire of the Netherlands East Indies (Nederlands Oost Indië) around 1914. It is significant that at the time it was building up its colonial empire and expanding its boundaries, the Dutch government adopted an 'Ethical Policy' (*Ethische Politiek*), officially inaugurated in 1901, in which the Netherlands acknowledged a 'debt of honor' (*eereschuld*) toward the peoples of the Indies. At the instigation of Christiaan Snouck Hurgronje, advisor on Native Affairs, this paternalistic ideal was expected to lead to a twofold association, between the motherland and the colony on the one hand, and among the various peoples within the colony on the other. In reality, the Ethical Policy was to entail a much deeper penetration of local societies by the colonial administration, which felt both obliged and justified in acting to reform them in the cause of peace, order, welfare, and progress (Van Niel 1984).

After they regained their East Indies possessions from the British, in 1816, the Dutch undertook the establishment of diplomatic relations with Balinese rajas, whom they coerced into signing treaties acknowledging their sovereignty, which the rajas either misunderstood or ignored, thereby clearing the field for a military intervention. The pretext was provided by the Balinese custom of *tawan karang*, or the right of rajas to salvage any wreck stranded off the coast of Bali;

---

[48] My argument rests mostly on the works of Boon (1977), Schulte Nordholt (1986, 1994, 1996), Robinson (1995), Wiener (1995), and Vickers (2012a). In what follows, it should be understood that the colonial state was not a monolithic agent—'the Dutch' is no less an oversimplification than 'the Balinese'—and that its policy underwent significant changes during the period under investigation.

[49] See the remark by the colonial administrator Victor Emanuel Korn: "Every civil servant who arrives to take up duty on Bali knows that he has been transferred to the island of Hinduism" (*Ieder bestuursambtenaar, die op Bali komt dienen, weet zich verplaatst naar het eiland van het Hindoeïsme*) (Korn 1932: 57).

this triggered a 'punitive' action in 1846 after a Dutch ship was looted. It was to take no fewer than seven expeditions for the colonial armies to subjugate the entire island. The rajas of Buleleng and Jembrana were compelled to acknowledge the foreign sovereignty from 1849 onward. The Dutch foothold in the north disrupted the Balinese political balance and set off internecine conflicts among the remaining kingdoms. One after the other, the rajas of Karangasem (1896), Gianyar (1900) and Bangli (1909) chose to submit themselves to the Dutch and thus conserve a relative degree of autonomy. The remaining independent kingdoms of Badung, Tabanan and Klungkung were subdued by military force between 1906 and 1908, and were placed under direct Dutch rule (Agung 1991; Hanna 2016).

The circumstances of the final conquest of Bali merit recounting. The colonial government had been looking for an excuse to put an end to the rebellious rajas and seized the pretext of the right to shipwreck when, in 1904, a Chinese schooner foundered off the shores of Sanur in the southern kingdom of Badung. The owner claimed damages, addressing his plaint to the Dutch authorities established in Singaraja on the north coast. They in turn claimed damages from the raja of Badung, whom they considered responsible for the plunder. The raja declared the claim unfounded and rejected it. This refusal finally led to the landing of troops on Sanur beach in 1906. The soldiers rapidly ploughed their way to the *puri* of Denpasar where a strange spectacle awaited them: heading toward them was a procession led by the raja carried on a palanquin, flanked by his priests, his family and his entire court, arrayed in all their finery and heraldic weapons. As the Balinese drew closer, they broke into a run, brandishing lances and daggers (*keris*). The Dutch troops opened fire on the procession. Among the first to fall was the raja; at this, a frenzy broke out, and his followers began to kill themselves and each other. The Dutch kept firing. The massacre turned to plunder, and it is said that the Balinese threw their gold and jewels at the invaders in contempt. The same scene repeated itself that afternoon before the neighboring palace of Pamecutan, and shortly afterwards, the raja of Tabanan, allied with Badung, was captured and thrown in jail, where he committed suicide (Creese, Putra and Schulte Nordholt 2006). Two years later, another pretext resulted in the sack of the *puri* of Klungkung, seat of the Dewa Agung, Bali's most prestigious raja, who was forced to surrender (Wiener 1995). And so it was that the encounter between Bali and Europe, begun under the best auspices, came to a head in the 'fight to the end' (*puputan*) by three of the island's leading royal houses, who chose to die rather than give themselves up to a foreign master.

The Dutch government was highly embarrassed by the uproar provoked in Holland and foreign diplomatic circles by the bloody conquest of Bali. To obliterate the memory of their brutal intervention, they undertook to develop a more worthy image of their colonial policy on the island—an image based on the 'restoration' of traditional Balinese society and the preservation of its culture.[50] Hence, the colonial authorities restricted the introduction of plantation crops and commercial firms, while prohibiting widow sacrifice and eliminating slavery. On the other hand, they imposed a state monopoly on the sale of opium (*opiumregie*) and a heavy tax system. Above all, they unified the island, not only by subjecting it to a uniform administrative structure, but also territorially, by building roads and bridges. Furthermore, to address the needs of colonial administration, Dutch scholars and colonial officials began to study Balinese society and its history. One issue in particular captured their attention, that of the relation between indigenous social organization and religious institutions of Indian or Javanese origin. Thus, in the 1920s Willem Frederik Stutterheim (1929) carried out an inventory of archaeological remains, while Victor Emanuel Korn (1932) conducted research on customary law and Roelof Goris (1926) studied the Balinese religion, its texts as well as its rites. According to the now well-established orientalist view, they regarded Bali as a Hindu haven to be protected by the enlightened paternalism of colonial tutelage from the intrusion of Islam which had strengthened its grip on the greater part of the Archipelago, as well as from Christian missionaries eager to set foot on the island.[51]

Once the kingdoms of Buleleng and Jembrana had been brought under direct colonial rule, in 1882, the first colonial administrators, chief among them Frederik Albert Liefrinck,[52] focused attention on the historical separation between the nobility of Javanese descent and the commoners of indigenous origin, initiated by the orientalists. But whereas his predecessors had been mostly

---

[50] Thus writes Vicki Baum in the preface to *Love and Death in Bali*, published in 1937: "I would like to believe [...] that the self-sacrifice of so many Balinese at that time had a deep significance, since it impressed upon the Dutch the need of ruling this proud and gentle island people as considerately as they have, and so kept Bali the paradise it is today" (Baum 2011: 15).

[51] The following quotation by the colonial official Gerrit Pieter Rouffaer sums up the prevailing position of the Dutch administration rather well: "Let the Balinese live their own beautiful native life as undisturbed as possible! Their agriculture, their village-life, their own forms of worship, their religious art, their own literature—all bear witness to an autonomous native civilization of rare versatility and richness. No railroads on Bali; no western coffee plantations; and especially no sugar factories! But also no proselytizing, neither by Mohammedan (by zealous natives from other parts of the Indies), nor Protestant, nor Roman Catholic. Let the colonial administration, with the strong backing of the Netherlands government, treat the island of Bali as a rare jewel, that we must protect and whose virginity must remain intact" (quoted in Robinson 1995: 41).

[52] F.A. Liefrinck held the position of *controleur* in Buleleng several times in the years 1870–80. He became the *resident* of Bali and Lombok from 1896 to 1901, and he was sent to Bali as special advisor to the government during the military expedition against Badung and Tabanan in 1906.

interested in the priests and the princes, and in the Indo-Javanese legacy of which they were the alleged custodians, Liefrinck directed his attention to the Balinese village. This he construed as an autonomous community—a little 'village republic' (*dorpsrepubliek*)—governed by its own *adat* law, whose traditional prerogatives had been encroached upon by the interference of the royal courts (Liefrinck 1890). Thus, after the Dutch had succeeded in extending their control over the whole island, they considered themselves to be replacing the Balinese rulers and set out to "simplify the village administration and return it to its original state" and to "purge village administration of royal impositions and intrusions" (Assistant-Resident H.J.E.F. Schwartz 1909, quoted in Schulte Nordholt 1986: 32). One can indeed readily understand that the new masters would prefer to identify Bali with its villages rather than with the courts whose resistance they had so ruthlessly crushed. In this way, they could present themselves as liberators of the peasantry, freed by their benevolent intervention from the oppression of 'foreign' despots.

The Balinese rajas had built their power and manifested their authority through rituals that comprised closely interwoven political, social and religious features. The ruling houses held sway over villages (*desa*) by means of complex and competing networks of personal relationships between lords and followers. Considering these bewildering local variations an impediment to the requirements of rational administration, the colonial state imposed a uniform administrative structure throughout Balinese society. The island of Bali—to which was added its eastern neighbor Lombok—became a *residentie* administered by a *resident* established in Singaraja, on the north coast, with an *assistent-resident* posted in Denpasar, in the south. The former kingdoms, whose boundaries had been fluid and disputed, were either directly ruled by the colonial government or—for those who had willingly submitted themselves—headed by a Balinese regent (*stedehouder*) flanked by a Dutch *controleur*. They were divided into districts placed under the authority of Balinese civil servants, the *punggawa*, who had hitherto been the rajas' representatives. The Village Act of 1906 established a new type of village, the 'administrative village' (*gouvernementsdesa*), divided up according to demographic and territorial criteria, typically consisting of several 'customary villages' (*adatdesa*) grouped together under a new name (Schulte Nordholt 1991: 11–16; Hauser-Schäublin 2011: 196; see further Warren 1993).[53] Headed by a *perbekel* appointed by the

---

[53] This law became fully effective only in the 1930s. The administrative village was later renamed *desa dinas* (from the Dutch word *dienst*, referring to the obligations and services to be rendered for the colonial government), while

government, the village then became the basic administrative unit. By instigating such a dichotomy between customary matters, which they left to the Balinese, and administrative jurisdiction, which they appropriated, the Dutch thought they could rule Bali while leaving its traditional order untouched. But in doing so, they initiated an unprecedented distinction between religious tradition and secular power.

Thereafter, colonial officials would be torn between two contradictory objectives: the restructuring of the island's administration, on the one hand, and the restoration of the Balinese traditional order, on the other. And though they claimed to protect the villagers against the tyranny of the rajas, they ended up reinstating the latter's authority. The reason for this was that, despite the suspicion and low esteem in which the Dutch held the Balinese nobility, they realized that they required their collaboration to govern effectively, as well as to minimize their expenses. Thus, they fell back on the orientalist vision of the four castes and decided, in 1910, to uphold the 'caste system' (*kastenstelsel*), which they regarded as the primary foundation of a proper Hindu society (Korn 1932: 55; Robinson 1995: 33). As a result, the former hierarchical order, which had been eminently variable and mobile, was replaced with a uniform and rigid system of three closed aristocratic castes, the *triwangsa*,[54] who were marked out as a 'ruling class', differentiated from the commoners, referred to as *sudra*. The colonial authorities thus placed themselves in the position of deciding who did and who did not belong to the Balinese aristocracy. This 'caste system' was then legally enforced by courts of law set up in each of the former kingdoms.

The administration of justice in Bali had been traditionally dispensed by a council of *brahmana* priests convened by the ruler, called *kerta* (Creese 2009a). When the Dutch established their authority on the northern part of the island in 1882, they took over the Balinese legal system and adapted it to their colonial needs by setting up courts of justice which they renamed Raad van Kerta[55] (Korn

---

the customary village became known as *desa adat*, and more recently as *desa pakraman*. In the syntagm *desa adat*, we have the original combination of Sanskrit and Arabic loanwords to designate a typically Austronesian institution.

[54] The Balinese nobility is composed of the *triwangsa* (the 'three peoples': *brahmana, satria, wesia*), who are differentiated from the *wong jaba* (the 'outsiders', that is, those who are outside the sphere of the courts, as opposed to the *wong jero* the 'insiders'), the commoners, who make up over ninety percent of the Balinese population. According to their myth of origin, the *triwangsa* claim to be the descendants of the Javanese conquerors from the kingdom of Majapahit who subjugated the island of Bali in the 14th century. According to Hildred Geertz, "[t]he term '*triwangsa*' itself has very likely been adopted [...] under the colonial administration, to refer to what might have been a new social concept of 'nobility'. Before the coming of the Dutch, there was probably no need for such an all-encompassing category, since the social distinctions of titles were multiple, fluid, and highly particulate" (Geertz 2004: 256, n. 2).

[55] A Dutch-Balinese syntagm which translates as 'Customary Council'. The Sanskrit loanword *kerta* refers to various meanings such as prosperity, order, peace, and perfection (Zoetmulder 1982: 895).

1932: 42; Creese 2009b: 525). The judges were expected to base their sentences on ancient law codes written in Kawi, the *Agama*, derived from the Indian Dharmashastras, in accordance with the mistaken belief that these codes embodied Hindu law, whereas they primarily conveyed the Hinducentric ideology of the *brahmana* and actually took account of indigenous *adat* law (Lekkerkerker 1918). Then, once they had imposed their rule over the entire island, Dutch colonial officials had the main *Agama* law codes (*Adi-agama*, *Agama*, *Poerwa Agama*, and *Koetara Agama*) edited and translated by a Balinese scholar (first into Balinese, in 1909, and later into Malay, in 1918), because they deemed that the judges sitting at the courts of law were unable to adequately understand the archaic language of these Kawi texts. By thus homogenizing and fixing the *Agama* codes in printed editions, the very essence of Balinese judicial practice, based on exegetical textual traditions open to flexible and contextualized interpretation, was fatally undermined (Creese 2009b: 545). Moreover, the establishment of a *padanda*-dominated judicial system greatly increased the 'Hindu' character of Balinese society, while conferring a legal basis for the 'caste system'—now sanctioned by the coercive power of the colonial state—within which the paramount role was played by *brahmana*.[56] Further, by giving prominence to Hindu law codes, colonial officials and Balinese judges would be in a position to manipulate the boundaries between 'religion', as textually defined, and the customs they wished to eradicate—a purpose which, as will be seen below, would be taken over by Balinese religious reformers.

From then on, most of the new village and district heads were recruited from among the *triwangsa*, whose power was thus considerably increased to the detriment of commoner title groups—such as Bendesa, Pasek, Pande, Sengguhu and Dukuh—who lost their former positions of political authority and who were henceforth lumped together under the disparaging label *sudra*. Furthermore, those Balinese acknowledged as belonging to the *triwangsa* were exempted from the corvée labor (*heerendienst*) that the Dutch started imposing on the Balinese in order to undertake their public works projects. This issue sparked off some jockeying for status, with people maneuvering to be classified as *triwangsa*, while various commoner title groups launched protest movements to defend what they regarded as their ancestral rights.

In the 1920s, Dutch colonial policy underwent a conservative turn: the progressive ideal of the 'civilizing mission' upon which the Ethical venture had

---

[56] In accordance with what they assumed to be the situation prevailing in India, Dutch orientalists took it for granted that *brahmana* were at the apex of the Balinese caste hierarchy. In effect, the colonial policy strengthened the *brahmana*'s dominant position in Bali, at the expense of the *satria* in particular (see Howe 1996).

been founded was giving way to a growing concern about the safeguard of 'peace and order' (*rust en orde*), with colonial rule now firmly relying on the cultivation of cultural segregation between colonizer and colonized (Benda 1966; Van der Meer 2020, Chap. 5). This new direction received the academic endorsement of the University of Leiden, where most colonial administrators were trained and which had been the birthplace of the Ethical Policy. The promotion of native elites through Dutch education was now being accused of alienating Indonesians from their cultural roots, as well as of arousing anti-colonial unrest (Gouda 1995: 97). In place of the association advocated by the Ethici, and in opposition to a unified judicial system, the legal scholar Cornelis van Vollenhoven recommended a dual system for the colonial society, with the idea of strengthening the indigenous communities through enforcing their own '*adat* law' (*adatrecht*, that is, '*adat* with legal consequences', glossed as *hukum adat* in Malay).[57] In spite of the liberal position of most *adatrecht* specialists, the stress laid on the diversity of ethnic cultures in the Archipelago fueled a divide-and-rule policy aimed at preventing the emergence of a national Indonesian identity. In this regard, it was particularly important for the colonial authorities to increase the legally binding character of *adat* so as to counteract the prescriptive weight of Islam.

In Bali, this orientation was advocated by Resident Henri Titus Damsté who, in 1923, encouraged the administrator Victor Emanuel Korn—who had studied with Van Vollenhoven—to conduct research on Balinese *adatrecht* (Korn 1932). Even though Korn made a point of emphasizing local variations within Balinese *adat*, the very fact of laying down in one volume what were in fact flexible rules of conduct, negotiable according to the context, transformed them into fixed legal prescriptions, henceforth backed by the bureaucratic apparatus of the colonial state.

Korn was also instrumental in promoting the image of Bali as a sanctuary, a world apart, fragile and unique, which should be insulated from pernicious foreign influences and the traumatizing impact of modernity (Korn 1925). That such an idea was so willingly accepted by colonial officialdom was due not only to a genuine concern that the uniqueness of Balinese culture might be destroyed

---

[57] Van Vollenhoven is not the initiator of this Arab-Dutch syntagm, which was coined by the scholar of Islam Christiaan Snouck Hurgronje in the context of his study on Aceh (Snouck Hurgronje 1893, I: 16). Snouck Hurgronje emphasized the limitations which *adat* law imposed upon the authority of Islamic law (*syariah*). Accordingly, he advocated giving primacy to *adat* over *syariah* in matters of legal practice, while the colonial government undertook to forge bonds with traditional *adat* leaders, in order to counterbalance the dreaded influence of Islamic teachers. The ensuing codification of *adatrecht* by Cornelis van Vollenhoven and its followers turned it into a legal system competing with the *syariah*, thus exacerbating the antagonism between endogenous *adat* and exogenous Islam (Van Vollenhoven 1928; Holleman 1981; Burns 2004; Fasseur 2007; Von Benda-Beckmann and Von Benda-Beckmann 2011).

by indiscriminate contact with the outside world, but also because it suited their political agenda. Over the years, the Dutch came to regard Bali as the cornerstone of their effort to contain the spread of Islamic radicalism and various nationalist and communist movements which had arisen in Java and Sumatra. Given this vigilant outlook, it was becoming apparent to the colonial authorities that the Balinese nobility, whom they regarded as the pillar of its traditional Hindu order, was the best barrier against the threat of Islam and the seepage of subversive ideas into the island.[58]

In 1917, the island of Bali was hit by a massive earthquake which badly damaged villages, temples and palaces. This and other calamities were readily attributed by Balinese to the neglect of ritual purifications incumbent upon the rulers, who were responsible for ensuring the well-being of people and land alike. Unfortunately, these rituals had been discontinued after the colonial takeover. The ruler of Karangasem, in concert with his peers in Gianyar and Bangli, who had managed to preserve some political leverage due to their timely surrender to the Dutch, made a plea for resuming required religious observances. Appropriating the colonial distinction between 'religion' and 'politics', they pleaded to be allowed to recover their ritual duties, which was essentially a way to vindicate their role as rajas. Heeding their appeal, in 1929 the governor-general appointed designated descendants of the former ruling houses as *negara-bestuurders* ('rulers'), who were permitted to assume their hereditary titles.[59] In 1931, under the auspices of the colonial government, the Balinese rulers established a council called the Paruman Kerta Negara, presided over by the *negara-bestuurder* of Karangasem. By forming this body, the Dutch tightened their control over the Balinese social order.

Thereafter, the *negara-bestuurders* requested the Dutch government that they be fully reinstated as rajas, while suggesting that the peace and order would be ensured all the better. In 1938 the governor-general would eventually fulfil their demand by granting them the status of *zelfbestuurders* ('self-rulers'), with a measure of autonomy over the affairs of their respective territories

---

[58] As evidenced by this assertion from Assistent-Resident Berkhout in a letter to Korn in 1921: "We must, in the very first place, uphold the caste system, otherwise the religion is done for and the Muslims will take their chance" (quoted in Schulte Nordholt 1994: 104).

[59] In Buleleng, Jembrana, Gianyar and Bangli the *negara-bestuurders* bore the title *Anak Agung*; in Karangasem, *Anak Agung Agung*; in Badung and Tabanan, *Cokorda*; and in Klungkung, *Dewa Agung*. While the restoration of the rajas in Karangasem, Gianyar and Bangli did not pose too much of a problem, since they had managed to maintain a significant part of their former prerogatives, on the other hand, in the *negara* which had been conquered by force of arms, colonial administrators had to make a critical choice between competing contenders for the title of *negara-bestuurder*. These choices did not fail to arouse bitter rivalries between *puri*, the repercussions of which are still felt to this day.

(*landschapen*)—this, of course, under the strict supervision of the colonial state, which remained in place until the Japanese invasion of the Archipelago in 1942. Each *landschap* was endowed with a Consultative Council, the Paruman Negara, and to coordinate the administration of the *residentie*, a Council of Kings, the Paruman Agung, composed of the *zelfbestuurders* and their advisors, was set up in Denpasar under the chairmanship of the Dutch *resident*.

So it is that Bali's former rajas, once regarded by the Dutch as inept despots to be disposed of, became viewed as the indispensable custodians of a colonial 'traditional' order. Although they had lost their previous political power and no longer actually ruled their kingdoms, the *zelfbestuurders* were given authority over the disposal of all locally generated revenue and received regular allowances from the government. In their new position, most of them managed to build up their wealth and to strengthen their control over the people, to the point that, by the late colonial period, the Balinese felt that they were administered not only by the Dutch government but also once again by their traditional rulers. While the *zelfbestuurders* had become effectively agents of the colonial state and grown rich from it, the severe increase in land tax imposed by the government resulted in a surge of landlessness and a drastic impoverishment of tenant farmers, with a concentration of land in the hands of the ruling families.

Yet it was not enough that Bali's 'traditional order' be rescued from the onslaught of modernization and sheltered from disruptive outside influences. The Balinese people, furthermore, must be taught by their new overlords how to keep on being authentically Balinese—they had to be 'Balinized'. Such was the aim of the cultural-cum-educational policy known as *Baliseering* ('Balinization'), launched in the late 1920s by Resident Damsté, which was expected to produce a state-sponsored 'renaissance' of Balinese culture, with a view to checking the spread of Islam and nationalism from neighboring Java and strengthening the position of the pro-Dutch Balinese elite. Conceived by Hendrik te Flierhaar, a Dutch former teacher who had become a civil servant—with the support of administrators, orientalists, and artists, such as Victor Emanuel Korn, Roelof Goris, Willem Frederik Stutterheim, Walter Spies and Rudolph Bonnet—this policy took its inspiration from the educational theories of Ki Hadjar Dewantara, Rudolf Steiner and Jacques Dalcroze. It was specifically intended for native youth, who must be made conscious of the value of their cultural heritage by means of an education focusing on Balinese language—with the strict observance of its status-marking language levels—traditional literature and the arts, all the while actively discouraging any improper expressions of modernism regarding architecture, dress or behavior.[60]

To conclude, notwithstanding the Dutch government's pretension to make Bali a showcase of enlightened colonialism, its conservationist policy of 'peace and order' profoundly disturbed Balinese society. For one thing, while the imposition of a hegemonic power over the whole island put an end to overt manifestations of political rivalry among the kingdoms and princely houses, the structure of the colonial state and its system of indirect rule sowed the seeds of a confrontational situation. By reinstating the privileges of the royal courts and tightening their hold over the village population after having undermined the very foundations of their traditional authority, the Dutch exacerbated latent social tensions and generated new grounds for conflict between commoners and the nobility. In this manner, they managed to deflect toward their Balinese auxiliaries the frustrations and resentments provoked by their policy, rather than giving rise to Balinese solidarity against the colonial state. In addition, by claiming to restore Balinese society to what they assumed to be its traditional order—and particularly by enforcing their patronizing *Baliseering* policy—colonial officials would antagonize antifeudal commoner intellectuals who aspired to reap the supposed benefits of modernity.

Furthermore, by looking for the singularity of Bali in its Hindu heritage, while conceiving of Balinese identity as formed through an opposition to Islam, the Dutch established the framework within which the Balinese were going to define themselves. In other words, their colonial policy "ensured that Balinese social and political discourse came to focus heavily on matters of interpretation of tradition, religion, caste, and culture" (Robinson 1995: 32). Finally, by attempting to preserve Bali's distinctiveness from the rest of the Indies, the Dutch ended up accentuating it far more than they had ever envisioned, all the while turning it into a challenge for the Balinese.

---

[60] It is rather difficult to assess the circumstances which led to the launching of the *Baliseering* policy. The only available information is provided by Hendrik te Flierhaar himself in a belated article that tells much about the measures advocated for educating the Balinese youth but says very little about their actual implementation (Te Flierhaar 1941). The starting point appears to have been the refusal of influential members of the Balinese ruling elite, backed by orientalists working for the colonial administration, to let Catholic missionaries open a school in Bangli in 1924 (Korn 1925; *Bali Adnjana* 1925, No. 16: 4). Shortly thereafter, an educative and cultural foundation named Sila Dharma was set up in Klungkung, under the aegis of the ruling houses of Karangasem, Klungkung, and Gianyar. In 1928 the foundation opened an elite private school, the Hollandsch-Inlandsche School Siladarma, subsidized by the government, whose curriculum focused on traditional Balinese education. This Siladarma school, headed by Te Flierhaar, served as a model for the policy of *Baliseering* (see Djelantik 1997: 41–2).

Chapter 2

Making Sense of Colonial Modernity in Bali

The Debate Between *Surya Kanta* and *Bali Adnjana* (1920s)

In Bali, as in other parts of the Netherlands East Indies, the colonial encounter manifested itself not only through the imposition of military force, economic exploitation and administrative reorganization, but also through the introduction of new ideas and values that undermined the very foundations of the traditional order. In Gramscian fashion, one could say that the colonial authority was established by means of 'domination by consent', an epistemic hegemony whereby the consciousness of colonized peoples was fashioned by the discourse of the colonial power. This has led some authors to claim that "the Balinese 'tradition' so admired by foreign observers until this day was essentially an artifact of Dutch colonial policy" (Robinson 1995: 21; see also Pollmann 1990; Schulte Nordholt 1994). The problem with this colonial 'invention of tradition' (Hobsbawm 1983) is that it amounts to denying the Balinese people the status of subjects of their own history as if they had no agency of their own in the matter (Hobart 1997). As Marshall Sahlins reminds us, one should refrain from crediting the colonial masters with the exclusive power of making history, as if "the main historical activity remaining to the underlying people [was] to misconstrue the effects of such imperialism as their own cultural traditions" (Sahlins 1993: 6). Furthermore, historians and anthropologists alike have pointed out that indigenous peoples tend to assert their identity when it can no longer be taken for granted, such as following their incorporation into a colonial state.[1] Thus,

---

[1] Besides Sahlins (1993), see, e.g., Cohn (1987), Keesing (1989), Dirks (1992), and Thomas (1994).

rather than viewing the colonial encounter in terms of foreign impact, one should identify the active agency of the colonized peoples as they engaged with and accommodated colonial impositions, thereby redefining the terms of that confrontation for their own purposes.

While it is true that the Balinese "were not allowed to participate in Western discourses about themselves" (Schulte Nordholt 1994: 119), in the sense that they were not asked for their opinion, it happens that some Balinese left written accounts of the colonial times, so that we know something of how they perceived and interpreted what was happening to their world. The fact is that, notwithstanding the Dutch attempt to insulate Balinese society from disturbing foreign influences, Bali actually underwent rapid and profound changes as a result of the colonial government's increasing interference in native affairs. The introduction of a monetary economy, the imposition of taxes and forced labor, the enlistment of the former rulers into the colonial bureaucracy and the access of a minority of Balinese youth to Western-style education undermined the relationships which had prevailed between the peasantry and the traditional elites. In particular, the requirements of a modern administration were instrumental in the formation of a Balinese intelligentsia, since the colonial state needed educated natives to provision the lower echelons of the civil service and to mediate between the local population and their European overlords. These Dutch-educated Balinese strove to make sense of the changes brought about by the opening up of their island to what they viewed as the advent of 'modern times' (*zaman modern*).

Not only did the emerging Balinese intelligentsia have to face the disruption of the familiar references which ordered and gave meaning to their lives,[2] they were confronted with alien discourses telling them who they were and how they ought to conduct themselves. So much so that, while the upheaval inflicted by the colonial occupation of their island was compelling the Balinese to question the foundations of their identity, the inquisitive gaze of foreigners in their midst impelled them to explicitly account for the definition of what it meant to be Balinese in terms comprehensible to non-Balinese (Creese 2000: 34).

In this chapter, I will examine how the first generation of Balinese educated in colonial schools attempted to make sense of the predicaments of modernity, by investigating the periodicals published on the island during the 1920s—*Bali Adnjana* (1924–30) and *Surya Kanta* (1925–27).

---

[2] In 1917, a prominent *padanda* described the Dutch colonial conquest of Bali in a poem entitled 'The Destruction of the World' (*Bhuwanawinasa*) (Creese 2018). In general, Balinese writings referred to the precolonial times as 'when the world was still steady' (*dugas gumi nu enteg*).

The formation of a Balinese intelligentsia

Singaraja, the cosmopolitan harbor town of the kingdom of Buleleng on the north coast of the island, long opened to the outside world, became the seat of the colonial government in 1882. The presence of a sizeable population of Chinese, Arabs and various Indonesian groups, not to mention Europeans, resulted in a society more receptive to change and innovation than in the more conservative southern interior. This is where the Balinese intelligentsia (*kaum terpelajar*) originated, those natives educated in the schools opened by the Dutch to produce a new generation of Western-trained officials to fill the lower ranks of the colonial bureaucracy.[3] This intellectual elite, composed mostly of clerks and teachers, founded the first modern Balinese organizations. These organizations can be qualified as 'modern', in the sense that they were voluntary associations (*perkumpulan*) of like-minded people with wide-ranging purposes and highly formalized structures, complete with an elected board, statutes, written regulations, membership fees, and Dutch terminology. In this respect they differed from the various customary organizations regulating Balinese social relations, such as kinship affiliation groups (*dadia*),[4] temple congregations (*pamaksan*), neighborhood communities (*banjar*), irrigation societies (*subak*) and cooperatives formed for specific tasks (*sekaa*).

Besides opening private schools and religious foundations, these organizations started to publish periodicals, a complete novelty for Bali, though already occurring elsewhere in the Netherlands Indies at that time (Adam 1995). These publications, addressing mainly social and religious issues, were printed

---

[3] The first primary school in Bali (Tweede Klasse Inlandsche School) was opened in Singaraja in 1875. But it was only from 1908 onward that village elementary schools (Volksschool) were established in various parts of the island. At first, it was difficult to get parents to send their children to school. In the early stages, most of the pupils and their teachers were commoners, as aristocrats shied away from schools, since they were concerned that their children's status might be debased by indiscriminate social interactions. Some of the teachers were Javanese, like Sukarno's father, even though the colonial authorities were wary of importing teachers from Java, for fear of nationalist or Islamic contamination. In 1914, a school providing education based on the Dutch curriculum (Hollandsch-Inlandsche School, HIS), and as such reserved for the Balinese elite, was opened in Singaraja, followed in 1918 by a second one in Denpasar. Besides reading, writing and arithmetic, the pupils were learning Malay and Dutch. According to the census of 1920, 8 percent of the men and 0.35 percent of the women in Bali were able to read and write in Latin script (Parker 2000: 59). After having completed the HIS program, Balinese who intended to continue their secondary level education—and whose family could afford the expense—had to go either to Java (mostly to Banyuwangi, Probolinggo, Surabaya, Malang, Yogyakarta or Batavia), or to Makassar in Celebes. In 1927, some sixty Balinese were pursuing secondary level education in Java and about a dozen in Makassar (*Surya Kanta* 1927, No. 3–4: 33–4). And in 1929, there were three HIS, 29 Tweede Klasse Inlandsche Scholen and 109 Volksscholen in Bali (Putra Agung 1983: 57).

[4] This is how Hildred Geertz and Clifford Geertz defined the *dadia*: "an agnatic, preferentially endogamous, highly corporate group of people who are convinced, with whatever reason, that they are all descendants of one common ancestor" (Geertz and Geertz 1975: 5).

in Latin script and written in Malay, the lingua franca of trade and Islam in the Archipelago, which had been adopted by the Dutch as the language of education and administration, soon to become that of Indonesian nationalism (Hoffman 1979; Maier 1993).[5] The use of Malay—profusely interspersed, moreover, with Dutch terms—rather than Balinese, to address thoroughly Balinese topics intended for an exclusively Balinese readership (a very limited one for sure, a few hundred people at the most), indicates that the emerging Balinese intelligentsia were already conscious of being an integral part of a larger entity, as a result of the incorporation of their island into the colonial state.[6] In this respect, resorting to Malay enabled them to address new issues brought about by Western modernity, such as egalitarian aspirations. Thus, the same process that prompted the Balinese to question their identity was dispossessing them of their own words, by inducing them to think about themselves in a language which was not their own, but rather that used by both their fellow countrymen and their colonial masters. Such a linguistic substitution marked a reflexive distancing from the Balinese socio-cosmic order, which was decontextualized, relativized and homogenized in the process.

The history of the foundation (and disbanding) of successive or concurrent organizations in the 1920s is rather confused, as the scattered pieces of information one is able to gather from the publications of the time are not only sparse but also imprecise, and at times even contradictory. The first of these organizations, Setiti Bali ('Bali Association'), was founded in 1917 by I Gusti Bagus Tjakra Tanaya, the district head (*punggawa*) of Sukasada, to counter the Javanese Islamic association Sarekat Islam, which had recently opened a branch in Singaraja.[7] It lasted until 1920 and was succeeded the following year by a new

---

[5] These publications were thus radically different from the texts hitherto written by Balinese literati—such as *kakawin, kidung, babad* or *gaguritan*. Those literary genres addressed conventional topics, using Javanized idioms (Kawi) and a script of Indian origin (*aksara*) inscribed on palm-leaf manuscripts (*lontar*) (Picard 2012). However, it should be noted that these modern writings had been preceded by the appearance, at the turn of the 20th century, of hybrid literary forms, either resorting to traditional genres to cover modern topics or else using Malay in a traditional genre (Liem 2003; Creese 2007; Putra 2011).

[6] This is not unique to Bali, as most indigenous newspapers and periodicals published in the Netherlands Indies since the turn of the 20th century were written in Malay. And even a movement as deeply rooted in Javanese tradition as Budi Utomo ('Noble Endeavor') used, from its inception in 1908, Malay rather than Javanese (Nagazumi 1972).

[7] Sarekat Islam ('Islamic Association') was initially an association of Muslim traders founded in 1912 in Surakarta, which rapidly evolved into a nationalist political organization (Shiraishi 1990). It should also be noted that a branch of Budi Utomo was established in 1919 in Denpasar by the Javanese theosophist Sutatmo Suriokusumo. Its leaders were influential members of the Balinese elite: its president was Tjokorda Gde Raka Sukawati, the *punggawa* of Ubud and Balinese delegate to the Volksraad (the People's Council founded in Batavia in 1918); its chief administrator was I Ktut Sandi, the *punggawa* of Mengwi; and its advisors were I Gusti Bagus Djlantik, the regent (*stedehouder*) of Karangasem, and Ide Anak Agung Ngurah Agung, the regent of Gianyar.

organization called Suita Gama Tirta ('Service of the Religion of Holy Water'), founded by I Ktut Nasa, the principal of the primary school in Bubunan. Presided over by I Gusti Putu Djlantik,[8] member of the Raad van Kerta in Singaraja and a descendant of the raja of Buleleng, this organization was dedicated to the propagation of religious instruction. But it broke up within a year, apparently because of some disagreement between Ktut Nasa and Putu Djlantik. In 1923, members of a savings and credit cooperative society (*sekaa jongkok*) founded the Santi ('Peace', also spelled Santy or Shanti) association under the leadership of Putu Djlantik, Tjakra Tanaya and Ktut Nasa. Santi opened a girls' school, provided *gamelan* music lessons, furthered the study of Kawi and promoted the translation into Balinese and Malay (in Latin script) of texts from the Indo-Javanese literary and religious heritage in order to facilitate their circulation.[9] On January 1, 1924, the association started publishing its own journal, *Santi Adnjana* ('Thoughts from Santi').

All these organizations were open to the nobility (*triwangsa*) and commoners (*jaba*) alike, but tension appears to have been rife between the two groups, for the *jaba* objected to various privileges claimed by the *triwangsa*. In May 1924, a conflict arose between the leaders of each faction (and joint editors of *Santi Adnjana*), Tjakra Tanaya and Ktut Nasa, and soon afterwards the publication of the journal was taken over solely by Tjakra Tanaya, who changed its title to *Bali Adnjana* ('Thoughts from Bali'). The conflict escalated until a schism between *jaba* and *triwangsa* grew inevitable. This happened in May 1925 through a dispute over the name of the Balinese religion during a meeting of Santi's members. In October 1925, Ktut Nasa started publishing his own journal, *Surya Kanta* ('The Beautiful Sun'), and the following month he established an eponymous organization whose membership was restricted to the *jaba*. The president was Ktut Sandi, the former *punggawa* of Mengwi, who had recently been appointed *punggawa* of Singaraja,[10] the vice-president Ktut Nasa, and the secretary Nengah Metra, a young teacher at the Hollandsch-Inlandsche School (HIS) in Singaraja. Although the foundation of Surya Kanta did not spell the end of Santi, its membership dwindled as most of the *jaba* were joining Surya Kanta,

---

[8] I Gusti Putu Djlantik had surrendered allegiance to the Dutch and accompanied the colonial troops during their campaigns against Badung, Tabanan and Klungkung as a language interpreter (Schulte Nordholt 1992: 56). A colonial civil servant as well as a competent scholar, it was he who had translated the main *Agama* law codes at the request of the Dutch authorities. In recognition of his good and loyal services, Putu Djlantik was chosen to become the *negara-bestuurder* of Buleleng in 1929, even though his legitimacy within the Buleleng dynasty was far from being established.

[9] Among the texts translated and circulated by Santi, one finds the following titles: *Sarasamuscaya, Usana Bali, Usana Jawa, Ramayana, Bharatayuda, Arjuna Wiwaha, Yama Tatua*, etc.

[10] Ktut Sandi was one of the very first commoners to reach the higher levels of the colonial administration in Bali.

while the *triwangsa* lost interest in the association. In July 1926, during Santi's last meeting, its leadership formed a committee composed of members of each faction in a final attempt to resume the collaboration between *jaba* and *triwangsa*. But this move did not succeed in reversing the decline of Santi, which appeared to cease its activities by the end of that year.

The situation became even more confused after May 1926 with the foundation in Klungkung of an organization named Tjatur Wangsa Deriya Gama Hindu Bali (shortened to Tjwadega Hindu Bali, 'Association of the Four Castes for the Hindu Balinese Religion'), for the purpose of preventing 'caste conflicts' (*pertentangan kasta*)[11] on the island. Professing to reconcile the interests of all 'four castes' (*catur wangsa*)—and discreetly backed by the colonial government, anxious to defuse the rising tension—this new organization was in fact controlled by the *triwangsa* and used *Bali Adnjana* as its mouthpiece. Its president was the regent of Karangasem, I Gusti Bagus Djlantik,[12] the vice-president was Tjokorda Gde Raka Sukawati, and Tjakra Tanaya was the delegate from Buleleng. A few months later, an association of *brahmana* priests (*padanda*), named Setiti Gama Siwa Buda ('Association of the Shiva-Buddha Religion'), was founded in Karangasem under the patronage of I Gusti Bagus Djlantik (Korn 1932: 125).[13]

The debate between *Surya Kanta* (1925-27) and *Bali Adnjana* (1924-30)

Authors who have commented on these organizations and their publications have tended to stress the conflict between the *jaba* and the *triwangsa*, while construing that conflict in terms of a contest between 'modernist' and 'traditionalist' factions, which could be explained by reference to the familiar struggle between the forces of progress and those of reaction (Vickers 1996: 34).[14] True, the debate

---

[11] The word *kasta*, derived from the Portuguese *casta*, is a neologism borrowed from the Dutch, who construed Balinese hierarchy in terms of *kastenstelsel*, as if it were similar to the caste system in India, which is far from being the case as we have seen.

[12] In the same year, Gusti Bagus Djlantik authored a booklet defending the *catur wangsa* hierarchy by the law of *karma*, *Dharmasoesila*, strewn with references to Indo-Javanese religious literature (Djlantik n.d.).

[13] For the sake of completeness, I should mention the foundation in December 1924 in Karangasem, also under the aegis of Gusti Bagus Djlantik, of Satiya Samudaya Bau Danda Bali Lombok, an organization aimed at raising funds for sending Balinese children to pursue their secondary-level education in Java.

[14] The formation and development of these modern organizations in Bali, as well as the contents of their publications, have been only briefly mentioned in foreign publications: Korn (1932: 46–7, 124–5), Kraemer (1933b: 48–50), Goris (1933b: 33–6), Connor (1982: 265–7; 1996: 182–9), Bakker (1993: 39–44), Robinson (1995: 33–6), Parker (2000: 52–3), Vickers (2000: 90–4; 2012a: 212–14, 220–1), Liem (2003: 130–66). While more prolific, Balinese publications on that topic have remained rather superficial: Bagus (1969, 1972, 1975, 1996), Putra Agung

between *Surya Kanta* and *Bali Adnjana* was concerned to a large extent with 'caste' (*kasta*) privileges, which had been aggravated by colonial policy. The commoners were challenging the alliance between Dutch interests and the Balinese nobility, their aim being to overturn the archaic feudal order in the name of 'progress' (*kemajuan*). Yet, as much as a 'caste conflict' (*pertentangan kasta*), the opposition between the *jaba* and the *triwangsa* was a generation gap. Furthermore, by overemphasizing their differences, one risks losing sight of what these factions had in common. Even if they diverged in their respective ideological orientations, their leaders shared the same presuppositions on most fundamental questions—and specifically, the acknowledgement that the times were changing and, consequently, that their identity as Balinese could no longer be taken for granted and had to be redefined accordingly.

In any case, the proximity between *Surya Kanta* and *Bali Adnjana* was apparently closer than one might have assumed, since the two journals shared the same director in the person of Ktut Sempidi until his death in April 1926. Besides, their respective leaders were all members of Santi's board and kept attending its meetings until its demise. As a matter of fact—except for Tjakra Tanaya and the main leaders of Surya Kanta—very little is known about the contributors to either journal, their opinions, or their relationships. The situation is rendered yet more obscure by the inclination of the authors to sign their articles with their initials only, and even to often hide their identity behind pseudonyms—such as 'The Newsman' (*I Gatra*), 'The Commoner' (*I Jaba*), 'The Progressive' (*Suka Maju*), 'The Old-Fashioned' (*I Kolot*), 'The Worried Father' (*Nang Keweh*), or 'The Full-Blooded Balinese' (*Bali Totok*). Thus the analysis of the articles published in these periodicals poses a question of interpretation, compounded by a lack of knowledge of their precise context.

In addition, attention has been focused mainly on *Surya Kanta*, whose positions are more easily comprehensible today, as they appear seemingly 'rational' as well as more forthcoming and straightforward than those of *Bali Adnjana*, which tend to be couched in rather ambiguous and allusive terms. The general tenor of these publications is fairly different, more clear-cut in the one, more convoluted in the other, and the *jaba*'s use of Malay reminds one of the roughness of lower Balinese, while the *triwangsa*'s style evokes the literary verbosity of high Balinese. Furthermore, *Bali Adnjana* is not as accessible as *Surya Kanta*, since the available copies of the journal are scattered, forming an incomplete set, besides being poorly stenciled, which renders them difficult to

---

(1972, 2001), Kutoyo (1977–78), Padmawati (1982), Diantari (1990), Wijaya (1990, 2007, 2009), Atmadja (2001), Ari Dwipayana (2001, 2021), Putra (2011).

decipher. Finally, *Bali Adnjana* was published more frequently and for a longer period of time than *Surya Kanta*, hence its contents are more wide-ranging and its coverage of issues greater.[15]

Published under the leadership of Ktut Nasa, *Surya Kanta*[16] aimed to raise the position of the *jaba* in Balinese society and to defend their rights. Most of its founders and members were young schoolteachers and petty officials, and a number of them were former pupils of Ktut Nasa. For them, European education had been a means of social mobility. After graduating from the HIS in Singaraja, where they had learned both Malay and Dutch, those who came from better-off families pursued their studies in Java, particularly at the teachers' training college (Kweekschool) or at the school for the training of local government officers (OSVIA) in Probolinggo, where they mixed with their fellow Indonesians, according to a process well described by Benedict Anderson (1991: 120–3).[17] The command of Dutch, besides being a marker of status, was an opening for them to the Western world, with its values of rationalism and progress, its ideas of nationalism and democracy. Back in Bali, they either found employment as teachers in a HIS or in the schools which the Dutch were progressively opening in the villages, or else they filled positions in the lower echelons of the colonial bureaucracy. There, they experienced frustration from both their own and colonial society, neither of which lived up to their freshly acquired ideals.[18] Specifically, they were vexed with the attitude of the *triwangsa*, who refused to acknowledge the status to which they felt entitled due to their education, and they

---

[15] *Surya Kanta* was a 16-page monthly journal, published from October 1925 to September 1927 in Singaraja (but printed first in Surabaya, and later on in Yogyakarta). According to Goris, *Santi Adnjana* was replaced by *Bali Adnjana* around September or October 1924 (Goris 1933b: 35). The latter title appeared every ten days on six mimeographed pages till November 1930 (irregularly after June 1929). Issues of *Bali Adnjana* are available only from after January 1925, while no copies of *Santi Adnjana* seem to have survived.

[16] *Surya Kanta* (Sanskrit, 'The Sunlight') refers to a crystal, the emanation of the sun's rays. Its initiators were obviously conscious of bringing enlightenment to their Balinese brethren who remained in obscurity (*kegelapan*).

[17] The presence of young Balinese in Java would soon become a source of concern for the colonial authorities, anxious to prevent their contamination by Islamic activism as well as by nationalist ideas nurtured in Javanese schools. As early as 1919, Balinese delegates had attended the second congress of Jong Java, the youth organization of the Budi Utomo, in Yogyakarta. In 1925, the Dutch decided to close the OSVIA in Probolinggo to Balinese, who had henceforth to enroll at the OSVIA in Makassar. This provision was eventually withdrawn in December 1926, in response to Putu Djlantik's request in his role as Santi's president (*Surya Kanta* 1927, No. 3–4: 33–4).

[18] Needless to say, there is nothing specifically Balinese in this plight, which appears to be the common lot of the native intelligentsia in a colonial situation. Their predicament is deeply contradictory, as depicted by John Plamenatz, involving as it does a rejection, "in fact, two rejections, both of them ambivalent: rejection of the alien intruder and dominator who is nevertheless to be imitated and surpassed by his own standards, and rejection of ancestral ways which are seen as obstacles to progress and yet also cherished as marks of identity" (quoted in Chatterjee 1986: 2). One is also reminded of the dispute between Tjipto Mangunkusumo and Sutatmo Suriokusumo in 1918 (Shiraishi 1981), and its continuation in the famous 'polemic on culture' (*polemik kebudayaan*), in which some of the leading Indonesian intellectuals in the 1930s debated about the extent to which the emerging national culture should borrow from the West (Mihardja 1948).

resented the fact that their access to the higher echelons of the bureaucracy was hampered by the colonial government, which favored the nobility.

This frustrated group of native intellectuals strove to enlighten the Balinese people and prepare them for the advent of 'modern times' (*zaman modern*), as they proudly announced in the sentence opening the first issue of *Surya Kanta*: "Our intention in publishing this journal is to lead the Balinese people out of obscurity and backwardness towards a life of progress in this world."[19] While appearing occasionally under the guise of the predicate 'modern' (rendered by the Dutch word *modern*), modernity as such is actually not dealt with explicitly in *Surya Kanta* (nor, for that matter, in *Bali Adnjana*). The most common, indeed ubiquitous, allusions to modernity are references to the 'changing of the times' (*peredaran zaman*), which distinguishes the 'present' (*zaman sekarang*) from the 'past' (*zaman dahulu*). The present time is an age of 'movement' (*pergerakan*) (Shiraishi 1990), of 'change' (*perobahan*), of 'contest' (*perlombaan*), an 'age of ideas' (*zaman pikiran*); it is the 'age of newspapers' (*zaman surat kabar*), which are the signs of progress for a people (*tanda kemajuan bagi sesuatu bangsa*)—in short, it is the 'age of progress' (*zaman kemajuan*).[20] The contrast between the present and the past is commonly expressed by means of such pairings as 'new/ancient' (*baru/kuno*), 'young/old' (*muda/tua*), 'bright/dark' (*terang/gelap*), 'progressive/backward' (*maju/kolot*), 'already aware/still ignorant' (*sudah sadar/masih bodoh*). What is striking for today's readers is the fact that the 'times' appear to be credited with an agency of their own (*zaman punya kemauan*)—it is as if the 'will of the times' (*kemauan zaman*) requests the reforms advocated by *Surya Kanta*. These reforms are not simply the wishes of mere humans but they are in truth 'God's will' (*kodrat Tuhan*).

The reforms advocated by *Surya Kanta* are formulated in the following manner in the statutes of that organization: a) to foster reason and character (*mengutamakan budi*);[21] b) to improve the economy (*memperbaiki economie*); c)

---

[19] "*Bahwa maksud kami mengeluarkan surat kabar ini, ialah hendak memimpin bangsa Bali yang terbilang 'gelap' budinya dan jauh kebelakang tentang kemajuan hidup didunia ini*" (*Surya Kanta* 1925, No. 1: 1).

[20] Such is the title of the first article published in *Surya Kanta*, signed 'N' (for Ktut Nasa), that opens with these words: "As for 'Progress', its meaning is more and more perfect, and a people is said to 'progress' when it is more and more perfect in all aspects of its humanity, that is, all aspects that differentiate mankind from animals" (*Adapun 'Kemajuan' artinya bertambah-tambah sempurna, dan suatu bangsa dikatakan 'berkemajuan', apabila bangsa itu bertambah-tambah sempurna dalam segala sifat kemanusiaan, yaitu segala sifat yang membedakan manusia dari pada hewan*) (*Surya Kanta* 1925, No. 1: 1). Progress applies to four different fields, each designated by a Dutch term: *physiek, aesthetiek, intellectueel* and *moreel*.

[21] The term *budi* (from Sanskrit *buddhi*, meaning 'wisdom, comprehension, intelligence')—taken as emblem by the first modern organization in Java, Budi Utomo—refers to a spiritual value nurtured by education and forged by character. It was, moreover, specifically associated with both the intellectual modernity of European learning and

to improve and protect the fate of the commoners (*memperbaiki dan melindungi nasib kaum Jaba*); d) to change customs that are contrary to the progress of the times (*mengubah adat yang berlawanan dengan kemajuan jaman*) (*Surya Kanta* 1925, No. 2: 16).

The means to these ends, they said, is Western-style education (*pendidikan cara Barat*), which is deemed to be the foundation of progress (*pangkal kemajuan*). The Balinese are summoned to move forward and advance themselves (*memajukan diri*), failing which they will be left behind (*ketinggalan zaman*). In that, they should follow the lead of other peoples (*bangsa*), such as the Javanese or the Malays, who are more advanced on the way to progress than themselves. They should pursue education not only in Bali, but also in Java and even in Holland if they can. And Balinese girls should be educated as well as the boys.

Once properly educated, the Balinese will be in a better position to improve their economic situation, which has been deteriorating lately.[22] Specifically, they should strive to free their economy from the grasp of foreign capital by setting-up cooperatives. Considering the importance of economy as the foundation of all progress (*economie itu pokok segala kemajuan*), which is stressed right from the first issue of *Surya Kanta*, it is no wonder that numerous articles of that journal should relate to economic matters. Besides, Balinese have to become aware of the importance of being thrifty, particularly as concerns ruinous customary rituals, that more often than not are ostentatious demonstrations of wealth destined to increase the prestige of their initiators rather than to fulfil their religious obligations.[23] The reason for this unfortunate situation arises from the fact that Balinese do not know how to differentiate that which is *adat* from that which is agama (*tidak tahu membedakan yang mana adat dan mana agama*) (*Surya Kanta* 1925, No. 3: 1).

---

the prestige of *agama Buda* in the eyes of the Javanese elites opposed to Islamic reformism (see Ricklefs 2007: Chap. 7).

[22] While the Balinese people have been spared the foreign plantations and commercial cultures which badly affected Javanese society, the colonization of their island resulted nonetheless in their relative pauperization. The deterioration in their economic situation was not the result of the takeover of foreign capital but of the taxes and corvée labor imposed by the colonial state. With the imposition of a land-tax system in 1922, the Balinese people were subjected to the heaviest taxation in the Netherlands Indies. To pay these taxes, which had to be remitted in Dutch currency, the Balinese had to engage in export trade of agricultural and livestock products, such as copra, rice, coffee, pigs and cattle. Their increasing dependency on export goods was to lead to serious difficulties after 1931, when the value of these goods dropped dramatically as the effects of the economic depression were beginning to be felt on the island. One of the main consequences of the depression in Bali was a high incidence of landlessness (see Robinson 1995: Chap. 3).

[23] Funeral rites (*ngaben*) were particularly targeted, as they often caused the ruin of whole families (Connor 1996). In this respect, one notices that Tjakra Tanaya had published in 1924 a booklet written by Putu Djlantik in which he advocated simplified and cheaper cremations (Djlantik 1924). Needless to say, *Surya Kanta* was equally critical of the use of opium and of the habit of gambling at cockfights, widespread among Balinese.

Education is expected to enlighten the Balinese people by supplying them with both 'intelligence' (*kepandaian*) and 'reason' (*budi*). Thanks to these qualities, the Balinese will then know how to discriminate among their customs (*adat*) between those which they should conserve or rejuvenate and those which they should reform or abandon, in accordance with the 'progress of the world' (*kemajuan dunia*). For whoever keeps defending customs that are no longer suitable for the present time is guilty of hampering the progress of one's people.[24]

In Bali, the main obstacle to progress is 'caste' prejudice and the privileges which the *triwangsa* enjoy in such areas as language, etiquette, cross-caste marriage, corvée labor, and so on.[25] These privileges are legally founded on the *Agama* treatises and imposed by law courts (Raad van Kerta) dominated by *padanda*. This is no longer acceptable for the *jaba*, who demand for themselves the same station in life and society as the *triwangsa*—'solidarity and equality' (*sama rasa sama rata*).[26] Such an equality of status was simply inconceivable for most *triwangsa*, in that it implied that they would be assigned to the colonial corvée in the same way as the *jaba* and that they would have to share their part of collective labor within their *banjar*, which involves such debasement as accepting the leftover food from *jaba* offerings and taking charge of their corpses during funerary rituals.

Instead of feeling proud to inherit a title of nobility from one's father (*Ida, Cokorda, Dewa, Gusti*), modern Balinese should strive to obtain academic titles (*Professor, Meester, Doctor, Insinyur*), as in the present time it is knowledge that determines the value of a human being (*pengetahuanlah yang menentukan harga manusia*) and it is knowledge that becomes power (*pengetahuan itulah yang menjadi kekuasaan*). Indeed, by means of acquiring a proper education, the *jaba* will rise in social status and will then be paid due respect by the *triwangsa*. In

---

[24] "*Barang siapa yang masih membela adat yang tiada dikehendaki lagi oleh zaman, maka orang yang demikian adalah sebagai mengurung jiwa bangsanya didalam peti besi atau menghalangi kemajuan bangsanya*" (*Surya Kanta* 1926, No. 2: 24).

[25] In particular, the rules governing alliances between 'castes' (*Asu Pundung, Alangkahi Karang Hulu*), based on the prohibition of female hypogamy, met with vehement criticism from the *jaba*, who were forbidden to marry *triwangsa* women under penalty of banishment (*selong*). Such was the fate of Nengah Metra, first the secretary, then the president of Surya Kanta, who was exiled in Lombok for having married a *brahmana* woman (Vickers 2000: 90). In 1927, a law alleviated to some extent the punishment for cross-caste marriage (*Surya Kanta* 1927, No. 7: 82–3; No. 8–9: 98–9). But this improvement did not suffice to placate the *jaba*, who published in *Surya Kanta* a theater play (written in all likelihood by Nengah Metra) titled 'Woman's Fidelity' (*Kesetiaan Perempuan*), to denounce the suffering inflicted by such iniquity (*Surya Kanta* 1927, No. 3–4: 42–3; No. 5: 61–4; No. 6: 75–6; see Bagus 1996).

[26] This slogan was coined in 1917 by the Javanese journalist Mas Marco Kartodikromo, publisher of the newspaper *Doenia Bergerak* ('The World in Motion'), and later popularized by both Sukarno and the communists (Shiraishi 1990: 88–90).

other words, status in Balinese society should no longer be ascribed but achieved; it should stem from merit and not from birth.[27] This, claimed *Surya Kanta*, concurred with the teachings found in Balinese *lontar* as well as in the sacred books of India, which state that a true *brahmana* is not someone who is born into a *brahmana* family (*brahmana-turunan*), but someone who lives up to *brahmana* ideals (*brahmana-budi*).[28] Such a view implied that the *jaba* were claiming the right to the status of *brahmana* priesthood, a right that is still hotly disputed to this day, as we will see below (*Surya Kanta* 1925, No. 1: 5).

Faced with such virulent attacks, the *triwangsa* attempted to defend their prerogatives as best as they could in *Bali Adnjana*.[29] Yet, it would be an oversimplification to conclude that this journal was their mouthpiece. First of all, until August 1926 when its motto was removed from the mast head, *Bali Adnjana* was still officially the 'voice of Santi' (*Muat suara Santi dan keperluan untuk umum*), whose members were mostly *jaba*. And the fact is that until that time, which also corresponds to the last meeting of Santi, the opinions expressed in its pages were fairly diverse and often frankly polemical. Besides, unlike *Surya Kanta*, which was avowedly partisan, *Bali Adnjana* was always careful to present itself as neutral in the feud between *jaba* and *triwangsa*. It was dedicated to the common good of the Balinese people as a whole, that is, to the so-called 'four castes' (*catur wangsa*).[30] Yet, after the foundation of Tjwadega Hindu Bali in May 1926, *Bali Adnjana* became the unofficial organ of this new organization, and it grew more conservative over the years.

---

[27] Whereas for the *triwangsa*, the *wangsa* hierarchy was founded upon their relation to pre-colonial dynasties, the Dutch introduction of the word *kasta* to describe the Balinese social system provided the *jaba* with the opportunity to appropriate the notion of *warna* by referring it to one's function in society. They then projected that idealized norm onto a bygone era by asserting that the Javanese invaders from Majapahit had distorted the differentiation between functions (*catur warna*) into a hierarchical distinction between title groups (*catur wangsa*), which they intended to abolish.

[28] It goes without saying that such an interpretation of the nature of 'castes' and their foundation was refused by the *triwangsa*. In this instance, both factions claimed to base their position on religious manuscripts (often the same ones, in particular the *Sarasamuscaya* and the *Brahmakta Widisastra*). *Surya Kanta* would add references to the *Bhagawad-Gita*, even though it was still unknown in Bali, as it would only be translated into Malay in the 1930s by the Muslim poet Amir Hamzah (Hamzah 1933–35). A new translation, complete with commentaries and the Sanskrit original, would be published by a Balinese author in 1967 (Mantra 1967).

[29] *Bali Adnjana* (Kawi and Balinese) literally signifies 'Thoughts from Bali', or, in the words of Tjakra Tanaya: "*Bali Adnjana* signifies the primacy of the Balinese character" (*Bali Adnjana adalah berarti keutamaan Budi Bali*) (*Bali Adnjana* 1925, No. 15: 2).

[30] This is why Tjakra Tanaya refused the proposal put forward in *Bali Adnjana* in December 1925 to create a *triwangsa* association (Tjandra Kanta, Sanskrit, 'The Moonlight'), in order to counter Surya Kanta's influence, arguing that it was preferable to revivify Santi rather than exacerbate dissension among the Balinese. That proposal was supported by Surya Kanta, whose leaders were expecting that the *triwangsa* would form their own association in order for both factions to share their views on the best ways for the Balinese to move forward.

Besides, while *Surya Kanta* was produced by teamwork, in the course of time *Bali Adnjana* became for the most part the undertaking solely of Tjakra Tanaya. Unlike the leaders of Surya Kanta, who were representative of the 'younger generation' (*kaum muda*) of modernist Balinese who had received a Western-style education, Tjakra Tanaya considered himself a member of the 'older generation' (*kaum kuno*), that of the traditionalists.[31] Born into a family of *punggawa*, and a retired *punggawa* himself, he had been educated in the traditional Balinese manner through reading *lontar*. And he never missed an opportunity to assert his old-fashioned inclinations, at times using rather provocative formulations to convey his opinion: "What is new is cheap, because it is impure or fake. What is old is expensive, because it is pure or genuine."[32] For his part, Tjakra Tanaya sternly refused to use the modern term of address *Tuan* ('Mr.'), favored by educated commoners, alleging that it should be reserved for Westerners.

The position defended by Tjakra Tanaya was delineated in the issue of *Bali Adnjana* published immediately after the launching of *Surya Kanta* in October 1925, in which he replied to those who complained that *Bali Adnjana* lacked clear directions, siding at times with *triwangsa* and at times with *sudra*. Without ever mentioning *Surya Kanta*, he imparted his opinion regarding status within Balinese society, by driving home that being a *brahmana* or a *sudra* has nothing to do with character (*budi*) but everything with birth (*asal usul turunannya*). Then he declared his intentions (*tujuan*) as (1) reconciling the Balinese people (*perdamaian*), (2) strengthening the religion (*keteguhan berlakunya Agama*), (3) changing outdated customs (*perobahan adat yang sudah kurang baik pada jaman ini*), and (4) eliminating the oppression of insolent people (*menghapuskan tindasannya si angkara murka*) (*Bali Adnjana* 1925, No. 29: 2). In the ensuing issue of *Bali Adnjana*, Tjakra Tanaya inserted a short mention of *Surya Kanta*, in which he explicitly acknowledged the new publication and even extended his wishes for its success.

After this somewhat placatory—or rather sarcastic—start, the exchanges between Ktut Nasa and Tjakra Tanaya grew more aggressive, while the latter kept accusing Surya Kanta's leaders of being motivated by greed and envy in their foolish pursuit to abolish caste hierarchy. He warned them that by

---

[31] In more than one respect, the debate between *Surya Kanta* and *Bali Adnjana* reminds one of the conflict between *kaum muda* and *kaum tua* which had raged in Java, West Sumatra and Malaya during the early decades of the 20th century (Roff 1962; Abdullah 1971; Kahn 1993; Adam 1995).

[32] "*Barang baru harga murah, sebab campuran atawa palsu. Barang kuno harga mahal, sebab tulen atawa aseli*" (*Bali Adnjana* 1927, No. 30: 3).

challenging the *triwangsa*, they were dividing the Balinese people, with the risk of weakening their resilience and of sowing dissension in their ranks. Not only did the Balinese inherit the hierarchical order from their ancestors, but it is based on religious teachings found in *lontar*, which stipulate that one's current status is the fruit of one's *karma*. Accordingly, it is very dangerous to challenge the caste system (*sistem kasta*) in Bali, as this might undermine the religious foundations of Balinese society[33]—if only in that access to the status of *padanda* is the exclusive prerogative of *brahmana*. And, as if to drive his point home, in addressing his opponents Tjakra Tanaya obstinately refused to substitute the term *jaba* for that of *sudra*, which commoners objected to as being derogatory.[34]

In numerous articles, Tjakra Tanaya repeatedly launched virulent attacks against 'progress', stressing its ominous consequences. Far from improving the situation of the Balinese people, the 'lust for progress' (*hawa nafsu maju*) is bringing about poverty and misery to Bali, as it has done in Java. Unaware that they are heading for ruin, the Balinese have started selling their wealth in order to be able to buy imported goods.[35] Foreign capitalists are flattering their vanity, all too eager to sell them their manufactured products, which are gradually replacing Balinese artisanal products.[36] For the time being, agriculture in Bali is still in the hands of the Balinese, unlike the situation that prevails in Java, where it is controlled by foreign capital. But this might not be for long. Therefore, far from taking the Javanese as a model, as *Surya Kanta* urges them to, the Balinese people should be wary of foreign influences, be they Javanese or Western, which can cause only problems to their island.

---

[33] "The *Triwangsa*'s disappearance would mean the disappearance of the Hindu-Balinese Culture, Religion and Tradition, because it is the *Triwangsa* who are responsible for their preservation" (*Dengan lenyapnya Triwangsa, adalah berarti kelenyapannya Peradaban dan Agama serta Adat yang bersifat Hindu Bali, sebab kaum Triwangsalah yang harus meneguhkan hal itu*) (*Bali Adnjana* 1926, No. 17: 1).

[34] Unlike the term *sudra*, which implies an inferior status in relation to the *triwangsa*, the word *jaba* refers to an outsider position in contrast to *jero*, which denotes the position of an insider. The way it is used in *Surya Kanta*, it signifies that the commoners are outside the world of Balinese nobility and thus unrelated to the hierarchical system which they challenge (*Surya Kanta* 1926, No. 4: 61–2).

[35] On this as on other issues, Tjakra Tanaya's warnings would be taken up by foreign observers, concerned to see the Balinese people becoming victims of the introduction of a cash economy into their island. One of the first to voice his apprehension was André Roosevelt—an American adventurer from a prominent family, who spent several years in Bali in the late 1920s—who admonished the Balinese in these terms: "If you keep this up, buying from the outside, in a very short time Bali, instead of being one of the richest lands in the world, will become impoverished and you [...] will have to do like the people in Java—work for a living, nine or ten hours a day, for a mere pittance. You will become a nation of coolies" (quoted in Powell 1930: xv).

[36] Among the foreign goods which some of the wealthier and more urbanized Balinese dreamed of possessing were automobiles, symbols of status as much as of progress. The fact that Tjakra Tanaya held such questionable dreams up to ridicule did not prevent *Bali Adnjana* from advertising newly released models of automobiles for sale in Singaraja.

The blame for making Bali prey to such unwanted influences lies with those half-baked Balinese 'intellectuals' (*intellectueelen*), whom Tjakra Tanaya accuses of being 'arrogant' (*sombong*) for pretending to lead their unenlightened brethren along the path to progress. In their eagerness to pursue Western knowledge, they have forgotten their Balinese-ness (*lupa pada kebaliannya*).[37] Preferring to express themselves in Malay or even in Dutch, they are no longer able to speak correct Balinese, that is, to use the respectful language prescribed by customary etiquette (*sor-singgih*).[38]

Tjakra Tanaya's plea in favor of the Balinese language is reminiscent of the position held a decade earlier by Suwardi Suryaningrat, who objected to the idea advocated by Tjipto Mangunkusumo to replace Javanese with Dutch among the Javanese intellectual elite (Scherer 1975: 80–1). Neither Tjakra Tanaya, using Malay, nor Suryaningrat, writing in Dutch, appeared to see any contradiction in resorting to a foreign language to advocate the importance of their mother tongue in sustaining their cultural identity. This is all the more striking as, in Balinese as in Javanese, and even in Malay, the word for both 'language' and 'speech' (*basa, bahasa*, derived from Sanskrit *bhasha*), has a much broader semantic field than in English, including, as Benedict Anderson once remarked, "the notions of civility, rationality, and truth" (Anderson 1990: 28), as well as denoting good manners. Even for such conservatives as Tjakra Tanaya or Suryaningrat, language had started to lose its esoteric character and thus its power over the world.

More generally, Tjakra Tanaya feared that Balinese educated in Dutch schools would look down on their parents as being 'backward' (*kolot*) and would no longer want to engage in farming.[39] This does not mean that he denied the

---

[37] When mocking them, Tjakra Tanaya dubs them 'Balinger': "*Orang Bali yang tiada tahu akan kebaliannya disebut BALINGER*" (*Bali Adnjana* 1927, No. 2: 5).

[38] One should know that the Balinese language is divided into what is commonly construed as 'language registers', a qualifier which does not really account for the linguistic complexity encountered in Bali. The Balinese linguistic system is in all likelihood derived from the interaction between the Javanese nobility from Majapahit and the Balinese population, and to this day one still comes across the most elaborate language differentiation within the sphere of influence of the old royal courts. However, this does not mean that variations in the way of talking could be summarized in a binary opposition between refined (*basa alus*) and coarse (*basa kasar*) language, itself indexed to the status hierarchy distinguishing the *triwangsa* from the *jaba*. The system of language registers depends both on the relationship and status of those speaking—in the sense that each utterance involves a series of lexical choices which rest on the respective position of the speaker, of his or her interlocutor, as well as of the persons referred to— and on the context, more or less formal or familiar, of the utterance; so that the way Balinese people talk is not specific to the speakers themselves, but is conditional on what is deemed appropriate to the circumstance of the act of speaking.

[39] Tjakra Tanaya's denunciation of the young Balinese educated in Java would find a similar echo a decade later in the concluding remarks of Covarrubias's *Island of Bali*: "The younger generation is rapidly being cut off from a cultural environment which they have learned to regard as below them, considering their parents, formerly their

Balinese people access to modern education, but he considered that academic titles were useless for them (except for that of medical doctor). In order for Balinese children to become proficient farmers, he contended that it is enough for them to learn reading, writing and arithmetic, besides acquiring some basic notions of trade and craftsmanship. And it is more important that they study the Balinese language and script, as well as the traditional teachings (*tutur dan tatua*) contained in the *lontar*.[40]

Yet, for all this, Tjakra Tanaya claimed to be a true advocate of progress. But his idea of progress was the one that prevailed in the past, when the aim was to fill one's mind (*kemajuan cara dulu, adalah kemajuan untuk mengisi pikir*), and not according to the present, when it is only a matter of filling one's stomach (*kemajuan cara sekarang, adalah kemajuan untuk mencari isi perut*) (*Bali Adnjana* 1926, No. 28: 5). Progress is welcome, as long as it does not uproot the Balinese from their identity. Progress should not be forced upon the Balinese, the vast majority of whom are 'still ignorant' (*masih bodoh*), but must come gradually and naturally, according to the changing of the times. In short, it should be the result of an 'evolution' (*evolutie*) and not of a 'revolution' (*revolutie*).[41]

This conciliatory stance was to bring Tjakra Tanaya rather close at times to the position of his opponents concerning the necessity of balancing the values of tradition with the benefits of progress. Thus, one finds in both journals similar admonitions to the effect that the Balinese should accept and emulate what is valuable in Western education without losing sight of their own identity. Moreover, the terms used to refer to each of these worlds, the foreign and the indigenous, are remarkably consistent and present a coherent vision that contrasts

---

model of behaviour, as rude peasants who have not gone to school. [...] those young Balinese who have gone to Java to become teachers for the Western-style Government schools have returned convinced that what they learned in Java is the essence of knowledge and progress. They have become conscious of the contempt of Europeans for the native cultures and have been influenced to believe that the philosophy, arts and habits of their country are signs of peasant backwardness" (Covarrubias 1937: 394).

[40] While Andrea Acri claims that "Tuturs and Tattvas constituted, to a great extent, the very object of debate among the various factions of the Balinese intelligentsia who sought to reform their religion" (Acri 2013: 79), the fact is that in *Bali Adnjana* the words *tutur dan tatua* do not specifically designate the corpus of Sanskrit-Old Javanese Shaiva texts which he analyzed, but rather a vague repository of Balinese wisdom found in various literary texts in Kawi such as *kakawin*. What's more, *tutur* and *tattwa* are no longer peculiar to the Balinese scriptural heritage, to the extent that Tjakra Tanaya exhorts his fellow Hindu Balinese to study their *tutur* and *tattwa*, just like Muslims or Christians are studying their own *tutur* and *tattwa* (*Kalau mau keutaman Bali Hindu, pelajarilah tutur dan tatua Bali Hindu, tetapi kalau mau keutaman Islam atau Christen, pelajarilah tutur dan tatua Islam atau Christen. Sebab semua tutur dan tatua itu membawa keutamannya masing masing*) (*Bali Adnjana* 1926, No. 28: 5). The only mention of *tutur* I have been able to find in *Surya Kanta* is strongly disparaging, referring to outdated teachings found in *lontar*, that ought to be replaced by Western education (*Surya Kanta* 1926, No. 9–10: 145).

[41] Tjakra Tanaya's stance reminds one of the position held in the same period by the conservative Javanese press regarding social change, which should not be imposed but which would come gradually once society was ready for it (Van der Meer 2020: 107–9).

the material West—coarse (*kasar*), material knowledge (*ilmu lahir*), worldly knowledge (*ilmu dunia*), manifest realm (*sakala*), etc.—with the spiritual East—refined (*halus*), spiritual knowledge (*ilmu batin*), eternal knowledge (*ilmu akhirat*), non-manifest realm (*niskala*), etc.[42]

It would certainly be difficult to find a more eloquent illustration of the Balinese ambivalence towards progress and Western influences than the image which adorned the masthead of *Bali Adnjana* between September 1925 and July 1926—two Balinese men, one dressed in Western garb, the other in Balinese attire, stand facing each other, separated by a pair of scales on one side of which are piled books (*buku*) and on the other side palm leaf manuscripts (*lontar*). And one encounters that same intent to benefit from both worlds in *Surya Kanta*'s motto—'Propagator of heirloom scriptures and torchbearer of common progress' (*Penyebar kitab-kitab pusaka dan sesuluh kemajuan umum*).

The foundations of *Kebalian*: *agama* and *adat*

Beyond the much-publicized polemic between *Surya Kanta* and *Bali Adnjana*, it turns out that both factions shared a common preoccupation with their Balinese identity and were eager to preserve its foundations. As far as I could assess, it is in the debates within and between these publications that, for the first time, the Balinese viewed themselves as a singular entity—as a people: 'we, the Balinese people' (*kita bangsa Bali*).[43] Of course one could assert that a sense of pan-Bali identity already existed through reference to Klungkung, Gelgel, or, especially, Majapahit (Creese 2000), but it is doubtful that the Balinese could have apprehended their island as an integrated whole prior to its incorporation within the colonial state (Wiener 1994: 357). Until then, their identities were

---

[42] There is, of course, nothing uniquely Balinese in such a contrast, which was already formulated by 19th-century Indian reformers such as Vivekananda, who emphasized the opposition between 'Hindu spirituality' and 'Western materialism'.

[43] The Malay word *bangsa*, which, like its variant *wangsa*, refers primarily to blood nobility, conveys the idea of a people sharing the same origin and a common culture. According to the context, it can take the meaning of race or nation. It acquires a primordial quality in that it supposes that cultural features are inseparably associated with a specific people, that is, carried by a community whose unity derives from a single origin. Besides *bangsa*, the authors who wrote in these journals also commonly used such terms as *negeri* (country), *tanah* (land), and *tanah air* (fatherland) to refer to Bali. In this respect, *Surya Kanta* was indubitably more concerned with the island of Bali as a unified entity than was *Bali Adnjana*. Testimony to this is the position of Ktut Nasa during the discussion of the colonial government's project to grant a representative council to Bali as part of its policy of regional decentralization. He vigorously opposed the idea of establishing local councils (*localeraad*), favored by the *triwangsa*, as this would divide the island along the lines of the former kingdoms. He instead proposed one council for the whole of Bali (*Bali-raad*), so as to develop a 'national sentiment' (*perasaan sebangsa*) among the Balinese people (*Surya Kanta* 1927, No. 5: 54–7).

particularistic, in the sense that Balinese identified themselves as members of a village and of a descent group, or as subjects of a particular lord, rather than as 'Balinese' (Howe 2001: 8). Their collective identity, based on an awareness of shared characteristics and adherence to unifying values, took shape during the colonial period, when they attempted to define themselves as different from the foreign colonizers as well as from the other peoples in the Indies.

In their publications, *jaba* and *triwangsa* alike defined themselves as both an ethnic group, characterized by their own customs, and a religious community, threatened by the proselytizing of Islam and Christianity. Specifically, they construed their identity—which they called *Kebalian*—as being based on *agama* and on *adat* (*Kebalian kita berdasar agama dan adat*). Now, the very fact of the Balinese resorting to these terms to define their identity testifies to the conceptual shift occurring on their island after its takeover by a foreign power. Far from expressing a primordial essence, as they would have it, these categories were alien and had to be appropriated by the Balinese according to their own references and concerns.[44]

The word *agama*[45] is commonly translated as 'religion'. However, as already mentioned, *agama* covers a much more restricted semantic field than does the prevalent understanding of religion. In effect, the use of this Sanskrit loanword in Indonesia results from a distinctive fusion of a Christian view of what counts as a world religion with an Islamic understanding of what defines a true religion. Moreover, *agama* has not always signified 'religion' in the Archipelago. In order to assess how this word came to acquire such a meaning, it is necessary to examine its significance in Sanskrit.

Etymologically derived from the verb root /gam/, meaning 'to go', and the preposition /ā-/, meaning 'toward', the word *āgama* refers to that which has come down to the present, and it can be glossed as 'tradition'.[46] As such, *agama* is one

---

[44] The problem is that, as early as the 1920s, we are faced with a conception of Balinese identity which is already fully framed in terms of *agama* and *adat*. Thus, unfortunately, the investigation of these publications does not allow us to elucidate how the Balinese arrived at this conception, which presupposes not only the awareness of a distinctive identity but also the attribution of such a distinction to some specific entities and their imminent reification.

[45] One also encounters the forms *gama*, *igama* and *ugama*.

[46] This is how the Sanskritist Jan Gonda accounts for the appropriation of *āgama* in the Archipelago: "In Sanskrit *āgama*, apart from other use, designates 'a traditional precept, doctrine, body of precepts, collection of such doctrines'; in short, 'anything handed down as fixed by tradition'; it is, moreover, the name of a class of works inculcating the so-called tantric worship of Śiva and Śakti. In Old Javanese it could apply to a body of customary law or a Dharma-book, and to religious or moral traditions, and the words *sang hyang* 'the divine, holy' often preceding it emphasize its superhuman character. The term is, moreover, used to signify the religious knowledge of a brahman [...], and also that of a high Buddhist functionary. Islam, in the spread of which many compatriots of Shivaists and Buddhists who had led the way into the Archipelago took an important part, adopted the term, and so

of the sources of knowledge—the *pramana*—the criterion for valid argument, which vary according to the different 'points of view' (*darshana*) that comprise Hindu philosophy. *Agama-pramana* refers to authoritative scripture as a means of valid cognition and is usually considered equivalent to *shabda- pramana*, that is, revealed knowledge. Additionally, *agama* is the name of a genre of non-Vedic scriptures that specific Hindu orders regard as revelation, and which became prominent during the early medieval period. This genre includes the Shaiva *agama*, the Vaishnava *samhita* and the Shakta *tantra* centered on the cult of the Goddess. In some Shaiva texts, the term *agama* is used as a synonym for *tantra*. More specifically, it applies in particular to the canonical texts of the Shaiva Siddhanta order (Brunner n.d.).[47]

Surprisingly few Indonesianists appear to have wondered how this Sanskrit loanword, laden with Indic references, could have come to designate an Islamic conception of what 'religion' is about. One notable exception is Jane Atkinson, who attempts to trace the historical development of the term *agama* into what she called the 'Indonesian civil religion' (Atkinson 1987: 174–8). However, she does not specify why it was precisely the word *agama* that came to stand for religion in Indonesia. Judith Becker attributes this to the paramount importance of the Shaiva *agama* in Java and Bali (Becker 2004: 16).[48] Yet this leaves many questions unanswered, since in Shaiva Siddhanta, *agama* does not signify religion, a notion that was unknown to the Indian world before the 19th century.

Although it is difficult to establish exactly when the word *agama* came to mean religion in Indonesia, we know that it entered modern Indonesian via Old Javanese *agama*, glossed by Zoetmulder as "sacred traditional doctrine" (Zoetmulder 1982: 23). We know further that in Javanese and Balinese literary traditions, the generic title *Agama* "used to refer to a range of texts dealing with moral, religious and legal sanctions and practices" (Creese 2009a: 242, n. 2; see also Hoadley and Hooker 1981, 1986). These texts were mainly drawn from the Sanskrit *Manava Dharmashastra*, or *Manu-Smriti*—the 'Laws of Manu'—the oldest and most prominent of the Dharmashastras (Rocher 2003). According to

---

did, in the course of time, Christianity. Nowadays *agama* [...] is in Javanese, Malay etc. 'religion'" (Gonda 1973: 499–500).

[47] Shaiva Siddhanta, 'the final truth of Shiva', is the most important of all the Shaiva schools. Originally a dualist tantric sytem originating in North India, it is now established predominantly in Tamil Nadu. The primary sources of Shaiva Siddhanta are the 28 Shaivagamas, a body of Sanskrit texts that are treated as authoritative because they claim to have been revealed by Shiva to his *shakti* Parvati. They usually consist of four parts: theology (*jnana*), concentration (*yoga*), ritual (*kriya*) and observances (*carya*). On Shaiva Siddhanta and the Shaivagamas in India, see Davis (1991); on Shaiva Siddhanta in Java and Bali, see Hooykaas (1962).

[48] This is also the conclusion reached by Christiaan Hooykaas (1966), Hélène Brunner (1967: 416), and Frits Staal (1995: 45), who investigated the connections between the Shaiva *agama* and Balinese ritual.

epigraphic and textual evidence from as early as the 12th century, law codes in use in the Indic courts of Java and Bali were thus modeled on Hindu legal thought, thoroughly adapted and contextualized to suit indigenous needs.

In her study of Old Javanese legal traditions in pre-colonial Bali, Helen Creese informs us that the titles of some of the main legal texts—namely the *Agama*, *Adhigama* and *Dewāgama*—were also generic terms for particular kinds of judicial knowledge and practice that were hierarchically ordered:

> [...] *agama* refers to texts and social practices in which the teachings of Manu are invoked, that is the written texts; *adhigama* reflects the legal jurisdiction of the ruler in cases brought before the council of priests and the application of the *agama*; while *dewāgama* refers to the administration of sacred oaths as an integral part of the judicial process, but one which drew its authority not from human princes or priests but from the gods (*dewa*) themselves (Creese 2009a: 283).

Furthermore, *agama* texts overlap with didactic texts—the *sasana* ('teaching, precept, doctrine')—which also draw on Dharmashastra and Nitishastra[49] traditions, that prescribe appropriate behavior for particular social groups, especially for members of the nobility (Creese 2009a: 249).

This is also how the Bengali historian Himansu Bhusan Sarkar interpreted the word *agama* in his study of *Indian Influences on the Literature of Java and Bali*, published by the Greater India Society (Sarkar 1934). His chapter on 'The Āgama or Dharmaśāstras of Indonesia' is divided into two sections: (1) the Niti literature, which expounds moral precepts and maxims—e.g. *Sārasamuccaya*, *Kuñjarakarna*, and *Navaruci*; and (2) the legal literature, or jurisprudence—e.g. *Śivaśāsana* or *Pūrvādhigama*, *Āgama* or *Kutāramānava*, and *Ādigama*. He deemed it significant that the Sanskrit term *agama*, which refers to a *shastra* handed down by the gods, has been retained in the Javanese and Balinese law codes, which are predicated on a divinely ordained set of rules drawing their legitimacy from Shiva's supreme authority. Sarkar's interpretation is substantiated by Sylvain Lévi (1933: xi), who explains that in Bali the *Agama* comprise the Dharmashastra, the Sasana, and the Niti literature, that is, legal, philosophical and political texts corresponding to the Indian Dharmashastras and Nitishastras.

Now, while *agama* is equated with *dharma* in Old Javanese and Balinese legal texts from the 12th century onward, we know moreover that in Malay chronicles dating back to the 14th century the term *agama* is systematically

---

[49] Nitishastra refers to a class of texts on ethics and politics.

associated with Islam and used in a sense equivalent to that of *din*. Therefore, we must conclude that for centuries the word *agama* had two distinct denotations in the Archipelago, that of *dharma* as well as that of *din*, according to the context and language in which it occurred.[50] By appropriating the word *agama*, Indonesian Muslims endowed it with new meaning, namely, the exclusive worship of the One and Only God and the requirement to convert to a foreign doctrine whose teachings are contained in a holy book revealed by an inspired prophet. As a result, a sharp distinction was drawn between 'infidels' and 'true believers'. Later on, through its adoption by Christian missionaries, *agama* became associated with an ideal of social progress, while 'pagan' beliefs were scorned as antiquated superstitions and viewed as a cause for shame.

As *agama* came to mean 'religion'—in a process similar to that which occurred with the category *dharma* in India—the term was dissociated not only from 'law' but also from 'tradition', which was one of its original senses in Sanskrit. In contemporary Indonesia, this notion is rendered by the Arabic generic loanword *adat*, commonly translated as 'custom'. But this translation does not do justice to the importance of *adat* in traditional Indonesian societies, which Hans Schärer aptly conveyed regarding the Ngaju in Borneo: "[*Adat*] certainly means more than simply usage, custom, habit. [...] the notion has a double meaning. Firstly, that of divine cosmic order and harmony, and secondly, that of life and actions in agreement with this order" (Schärer 1963: 74–5). In the same fashion as *dharma*, the term *adat* is thus both a worldview and an ethos, at once describing the ideal order and prescribing the behavior required to achieve that order.

The comprehensive customary scope of *adat* was fragmented through a series of reductions (Whittier 1978; Hollan 1988; McVey 1999; Aragon 2000). First by Islamic proselytizers—Christian missionaries later followed suit—who strove to curtail the religious import of *adat* by confining its significance to the habits and customs of a people (*adat kebiasaan*).[51] By thus regarding *adat* as those customs that do not have an explicit religious legitimation, they could be

---

[50] This is not unlike what happened in 19th-century colonial India where, once the word *dharma* had acquired the sense of 'religion', one noticed on the part of religious reformers, Hindus as well as Muslims, a convergence between *dharma* and *din* as two distinct embodiments of that same category (Pernau 2011: 37).

[51] In a personal communication, Catherine Clémentin-Ojha pointed out a certain similarity in the relationship between *agama* and *adat* in Indonesia, and that between *dharma* and *acara* in India. The term *acara* refers to the customary rules of conduct governing the correct performance of social and ritual duties constitutive of the *varnashrama dharma*, as endorsed by the Dharmashastras. Unlike traditionalists, for whom the *acara* are inseparable from *dharma*, 19th-century Hindu reformers disparaged them as not falling under the scope of religion. Similarly, some Balinese authors, such as I Gede Pudja (Bakker 1993: 131) and I Wayan Surpha (Bakker 1993: 273), draw an analogy between *adat* and *acara* (see Surpi Aryadharma 2011: 55).

neutralized; no longer considered a challenge to *agama*, they were reduced to superstitions and old-fashioned ways. Subsequently, Dutch jurists of the Leiden School codified the indigenous customary rules of the various peoples on whom they had imposed their colonial empire: *adat* became '*adat* law' (*adatrecht*). By attributing to each ethnic group its own *adatrecht*, the Dutch colonial policy widened the divide between *adat* and Islam. That way, the word *adat* entered the language of Islamized populations to refer to indigenous 'customary law' as contrasted with Islamic 'religious law' (*hukum*).[52]

This dissociation between *agama* and *adat* entailed certain consequences that are worth considering. Whereas in *adat*, practices are followed because they have been handed down from generation to generation, in *agama*, practices are obeyed out of belief. And while different *agama* make exclusive claims about being the true revelation, it would be a category mistake to attribute the predicates 'true' and 'false' to *adat*. Moreover, *adat* as a specific set of practices inherited from one's ancestors is tied to a particular ethnic group that differentiates it from others, as opposed to *agama* whose intrinsic proselytizing drive explicitly aims to transcend ethnic boundaries. This detachment of a transcendent divine from the immanent practices of ancestor worship and customary village rituals amounts to an unprecedented process of secularization.

This is, briefly, how *agama*, *hukum* and *adat* have come to mutually define each other in Indonesia, the boundaries of each category being continually redefined through the process of their interaction. Whereas in the past the semantic field of the word *agama* encompassed that which Indonesians characterize respectively as *hukum* and *adat*, today 'religion' is dissociated from both 'law' and 'tradition', particularly in Islamized and Christianized societies (Abdullah 1966; Von Benda-Beckmann and Von Benda-Beckmann 1988). The emergence of the category *agama* in the sense of religion thus amounts to its differentiation from the categories *hukum* and *adat*. As such, instead of assuming the autonomy of these concepts, it is only by addressing their articulation that their respective semantic fields can be appropriately circumscribed and analyzed.

In Bali, the use of the words *agama* and *adat* in the sense of 'religion' and 'tradition' dates from the colonial period. Introduced by the Dutch, the word *adat* replaced a diverse terminology for locally variable customs (*dresta, kerta, sima,*

---

[52] For a nuanced and complex view of the articulation between *adat* and Islam, see Roy Ellen: "There is a general tendency throughout the Malayo-Islamic area to see the terms *adat* and Islam (*hukum*) as representing complementary versions of a unitary concept of the right and proper. But, where distinctions are drawn between bodies of custom distinguished terminologically by these labels, no *a priori* assumptions can be made about the content to which they refer" (Ellen 1983: 68).

awig-awig, tata krama, tata loka cara, etc.), which had "a field of meanings covering ritual obligation, social institution, legal regulation, and ancestral evocation" (Warren 1993: 4).[53] These customs governed the relationships between social groups and infused villages with a sense of communal solidarity. The appropriation of the term *adat* by the Balinese entailed a twofold consequence. First, it created a new conceptual category, that of 'tradition',[54] which initially was contrasted not with 'religion' but with 'administration' (*dinas*, from the Dutch *dienst* meaning 'service'), referring to that which came under the authority of the colonial state. Second, the incorporation of a miscellaneous assortment of context-sensitive customs into this generic term altered their meaning for the Balinese. What had until then been an interplay of significant and deliberately fostered differences between villages was becoming the locus of Balinese ethnic identity, in the sense of a customary body of inherited values, norms and institutions which governed the lives of the Balinese people.

Admittedly, we don't know when the Balinese started using the word *agama* in the sense of 'religion'. However, we know that, in contrast to Islamized or Christianized areas of Indonesia, in Bali the word *agama* has retained its original polysemy. This is attested by the official Balinese-Indonesian dictionary, which translates *agama* as (1) *agama* ('religion'), (2) *hukum* ('law'), and (3) *adat istiadat* ('customs and traditions') (Warna 1990: 7).[55] The question, then, is to investigate how the Balinese came to differentiate these semantic fields.

We don't know either when the Balinese actually chose to label their own *agama* as *Hindu*. But we do know that, long before they defined themselves as

---

[53] Here is how Carol Warren accounts for the correspondence between the word *adat* and Balinese terminology: "*Dresta*, the closest Balinese equivalent concept to *adat*, is the customary basis of local institutions handed down from community ancestors with whom ongoing relations are maintained through ritual. It refers to the accumulated experience of forebears, iterated and vitalized through community practice (*tata krama*), of which local regulations (*sima, awig-awig*) are codified expressions" (Warren 1993: 4–5). Balinese literati refer customarily to the *caturdresta*, which Jan Gonda glosses in the following manner: "[...] in administrating justice attention must be paid to the *caturdresta* [...] i.e. 'the four points to be taken into consideration' [...], to wit the *lokadresta* 'the reputation of the justiciables to whom the law is administered' [...]; the *purwadresta* 'the traditional and exemplary custom, the conventions of society which decide what is proper etc.' [...]; the *desadresta* 'the customary law of the villages' [...]; *sastradresta* 'the line of conduct and rules laid down in the *āgamas*' ([...] 'a book or treatise of divine authority, a manual of rules, a religious or scientific treatise')" (Gonda 1973: 295).

[54] Without necessarily endorsing the distinction drawn by Eric Hobsbawm (1983), I chose to render *adat* as 'tradition' rather than as 'custom' in order to stress its normative quality as well as the self-consciousness involved in its appropriation by the Balinese. In this acceptation, *adat* is not an inheritance passively handed down from one generation to the next, but a conscious model of past ways of life. It is a contested field, involving a process of interpretation, a symbolic construction of the past in the present, employed strategically by competing social groups. In this respect, the use of *adat* is not unrelated to the notion of *kastom* in Melanesia (see, e.g., Keesing and Tonkinson 1982; Borsboom and Otto 1997; Babadzan 2009).

[55] On the other hand, the Balinese religious scholar Sri Reshi Anandakusuma translated *agama* as *dharma* in his Indonesian-Balinese dictionary (Anandakusuma 1986: 234).

Hindu, the Balinese had already been Hinduized by orientalists. Thus, both Crawfurd and Friederich took it for granted that the Balinese were Hindu—and moreover, they glossed the word *agama* as religion. Yet, this begs the question whether in their time the word *agama* already meant 'religion' for the Balinese, as this would have required that they discriminate clearly among the respective senses of *agama* as 'religion', 'law', and 'tradition'. I think this is unlikely, as *agama* still retained the meaning of *dharma* in Bali throughout the colonial period.

Evidence of this comes from the fact that the *Agama* codes continued to be used for the administration of justice in the Balinese courts of law which the Dutch had renamed Raad van Kerta. Further testimony that *agama* still had the common denotation of *dharma* in Bali during the colonial era is provided by the Kirtya Liefrinck-Van der Tuuk, the library that the Dutch authorities set up in 1928 in Singaraja to preserve traditional manuscripts. In the library catalogue, established by Balinese scholars, the entry *agama* refers not to 'religion' but to legal, political, and ethical literature related to the Dharmashastras, the Nitishastras and the Sasanas. There is no entry corresponding to the category 'religion'[56] (Kadjeng 1929).

On the other hand, it is no coincidence that when the first generation of Balinese educated in colonial schools were assessing their identity—in Malay this time—they used the word *agama* in the sense of 'religion'. Indeed, they were seeking to promote their own religion on a par with Islam and Christianity in an attempt to resist Muslim and Christian proselytism. However, for the Balinese, Islam and Christianity were seen not only as a threat but also as a model of what a true religion should be. Thus we find in *Surya Kanta* numerous injunctions for the Balinese to follow the example of Muslims and Christians in defending their own religion and spreading its teachings.[57] Faced with Muslim schoolteachers and Christian missionaries, the Balinese were under pressure to formulate exactly what their religion was about. This proved to be a highly contentious issue that triggered a protracted conflict between those Balinese who wished to retain their local traditions and those who wanted to reform them in accordance with what they assumed to be Hinduism.

---

[56] There is no entry for *adat* either, nor for *hukum*.
[57] "*Marilah kita selidiki usaha orang Kristen dan Islam tentang meneguhkan dan mengembangkan agamanya masing-masing*" (*Surya Kanta* 1925, No. 3: 7). Moreover, one also finds in *Surya Kanta* an article on the efforts of the nationalist party Hindu-Mahasabha to strengthen Hinduism in India, with the aim of preventing conversions to Islam and Christianity (*Surya Kanta* 1927, No. 6: 78–80).

Agama Hindu Bali versus *agama Bali Hindu*

While *jaba* and *triwangsa* shared a common reference to *agama* and *adat* as the foundations of their *Kebalian*, they held different opinions as to how their respective fields were articulated, as well as to how Balinese religion related to Indian Hinduism. And it is this divergence, as much as the more visible 'caste conflict', which explains the famous schism within Santi. For the founding members of Santi, things were still relatively unproblematic: its statutes proposed to strengthen the Hindu religion (*meneguhkan agama Hindu*) (*Bali Adnjana* 1926, No. 30: 5). While *Bali Adnjana* determined to buttress both tradition and religion (*meneguhkan Adat dan Agama*), *Surya Kanta* wanted to reform *agama* while ridding *adat* of all the customs deemed incompatible with the 'will of the times' (*meneguhkan Agama dan merobah adat istiadat yang bertentangan dengan kemauan zaman*) (*Surya Kanta* 1926, No. 8: 99).[58] Thus, for the *triwangsa*, Balinese religion was based on tradition (*agama kita wong Bali berdasar adat*), from which it was inseparable (*adat dan agama tak boleh bercerai*) (*Bali Adnjana* 1926, No. 21: 3), whereas for the *jaba*, religion should be dissociated from a traditional order seen not only as unfair but also as a hindrance to progress. Yet, they proved unable to differentiate between what belongs to *adat* and what to *agama* ([*kita*] *tidak tahu membedakan yang mana adat dan mana agama*) (*Surya Kanta* 1925, No. 3: 1).

The inability of the Balinese to dissociate *agama* from *adat* did not stem solely from the polysemy of these terms, whose respective semantic fields overlap, but also from the fact that up until then the Balinese people did not regard religion as a bounded field that could be demarcated from the customary order. One could even say that it was not singled out as 'religion', in the sense of a set of beliefs and practices internally consistent and liable to be labelled with a specific name.[59]

Hence, *agama* could not become a boundary marker for the Balinese until they began to view Islam and Christianity as a threat, and I concur with Adrian Vickers (1987: 35) that hitherto religious differences were construed as

---

[58] As a matter of fact, on occasion, Tjakra Tanaya came surprisingly close to a similar position: "*Meneguhkan Agama yang sudah ada dan memperbaiki adat yang sudah tidak sesuai dengan keadaan jaman*" (*Bali Adnjana* 1925, No. 30: 3).

[59] Margaret Wiener substantiates this assertion in a most compelling way: "Balinese praxis and discourse blur the lines between sacred and secular, for almost everything Balinese do involves seeking the aid of auspicious forces or asking for protection against inauspicious ones. In precolonial Bali there was no clear demarcated domain of action that could be termed 'religion', since all power was understood to derive from relationships to invisible forces" (Wiener 1995: 73–4).

variations in ritual practices, as signs used to distinguish groups seen as having basic similarities. From this perspective, Islam was conceived as belonging to the same cultural sphere as Bali, and Muslims were considered their 'siblings' (*nyama Selam*) by the Balinese (Couteau 1999b, 2000; Hauser-Schäublin 2004). Indeed, even in *Surya Kanta*, so eager to impute Balinese identity to Hinduism, one finds references to Balinese who embrace Islam alongside those who follow Hinduism: "The Balinese people practice two religions, that is: there are Balinese Muslims and Balinese Hindus" (*Bangsa Bali memeluk dua agama, yaitu: bangsa Bali beragama Islam dan bangsa Bali beragama Hindu*) (*Surya Kanta* 1926, No. 1: 17).

Yet, from reading both *Surya Kanta* and *Bali Adnjana*, it appears clearly that the times had changed. The authors no longer saw fellow Muslims as *nyama Selam* but denounced the conversion of Balinese to Islam—as well as, though to a lesser extent, to Christianity. Both publications reminded their readers that the Balinese were the only people in the Archipelago to have faithfully upheld the Hindu religion of their ancestors. It was therefore their utmost responsibility to defend it against the thrust of Islamic and Christian proselytizing. *Jaba* and *triwangsa* disagreed, however, about what should be done to strengthen their religion.

According to *Surya Kanta*, the problem was that the Balinese did not really know their religion and were the unenlightened victims of 'superstitions' (*takhyul*) arising from the restrictions placed by the *padanda* on their access to sacred knowledge contained in *lontar* (*Surya Kanta* 1925, No. 3: 7).[60] As long as they contented themselves with blindly following the priests who led their ceremonies (*milu-milu tuara nawang*), without understanding the true signification of their rites,[61] the Balinese would easily fall prey to Muslim or Christian indoctrination (*Surya Kanta* 1925, No. 3: 7–8; see also *Bali Adnjana* 1925, No. 32: 2). In order to remedy this unfortunate situation, the *padanda* were

---

[60] Traditionally in Bali, knowledge was perceived as dangerous, in that it dealt with the mysterious powers (*sakti*) of the world beyond the senses (*niskala*). Hence, manuscripts treating of religious matters were shrouded in secrecy and protected by prohibitions (*aja wera*, lit. 'do not divulge'), under threat of being cursed (*kapongor, tulah*) and becoming mentally ill (*buduh*). Their access was largely restricted to those persons who had been ritually purified (*kawintenin*) and had acquired the appropriate skills to study them with an appropriate teacher, thereby becoming immune to hazardous forces from the *niskala* world. Even then, one should bear in mind Jane Belo's observation that the temple priests she interviewed either misunderstood the prayer formulae they uttered, or disclaimed any knowledge of their meaning, saying "I would not dare to understand that" (Belo 1953: 9).

[61] When asked about the signification of their rites, Balinese commonly reply '*nak suba mula keto*', which is usually rendered as 'that's the way we've always done things here'. Actually, this idiomatic expression is more significant that it might appear at first glance, as the word *mula* refers to the 'origin', a notion which in Bali encapsulates the foundational power of ancestry.

urged to become religious teachers (*guru agama*), with the mission of imparting to the Balinese people knowledge of their own religion.[62]

For *Bali Adnjana*, on the contrary, as long as the Balinese held firmly onto their *agama* and to their *adat*, which is an heirloom inherited from their ancestors (*yang menjadi pusaka dari nenek moyang leluhur kita*) (*Bali Adnjana* 1926, No. 15: 1), they were not likely to fall prey to another faith. Indeed, they had no reason to feel ashamed of their rites and beliefs, which did not suffer from comparison with those of the Muslims or Christians. Witness the long-standing interest for the Balinese religion evinced by numerous foreigners—not only Dutch orientalists and administrators but also Indian Hindus such as Rabindranath Tagore, who had visited Bali on the occasion of his journey to Java in 1927 (*Bali Adnjana* 1928, No. 2: 3). If there was indeed a problem, it resulted from the critical stance adopted by Surya Kanta's intellectuals towards their own religion, and in their ensuing intention to transform it as they thought fit.

Viewed from this perspective, the controversy that erupted between *jaba* and *triwangsa* over the name that the Balinese religion ought to adopt makes perfect sense. One should know that in the past—and even, as will be seen later, up until the 1950s—the Balinese had no generic name to designate their 'religion'. Once they adopted the word *agama* for this purpose, they referred to their religion simply as *agama Bali*. Later, the Balinese started using a variety of names for their religion. Those that I found in both *Bali Adnjana* and *Surya Kanta* are *agama Tirta*, *agama Siwa* and *agama Buda*, as well as *agama Siwa-Buda*. I also found *agama Hindu*, *agama Bali Hindu* and *agama Hindu Bali*, as well as, infrequently, *agama Trimurti*.[63] Hence the rhetorical question asked by *Surya Kanta*: "Between these different names which is the right one and how should it be practiced?" (*Diantara nama-nama yang tersebut manakah yang sebenarnya dan bagaimanakah jalannya?*) (*Surya Kanta* 1926, No. 8: 102).

---

[62] "*Hendaklah Pandita itu memberi pengajaran kepada kita dan hal agama dengan sejelas-jelasnya, sebab menurut rontal memang sudah kewajibannya Pandita itu menjadi guru agama*" (*Surya Kanta* 1926, No. 4: 12). Yet, Surya Kanta's leaders entertained no illusion about the *padanda*'s goodwill, as they had already thwarted Santi's project to open a religious school in Singaraja.

[63] *Agama Tirta* refers to the holy water prepared by the *padanda*, which is required for most religious rites. *Agama Siwa* and *agama Buda* pertain to the two categories of initiated *brahmana* priests—the *padanda Siwa* and the *padanda Boda*—while *agama Siwa-Buda* points more specifically to the tantric combination of Shaivism and Buddhism that originated in East Java in the 13th century. The name *agama Trimurti* designates the Hindu triad Brahma, Wisnu, and Siwa, respectively personifying the cosmic functions of creation, maintenance and destruction. Finally, we find *agama Bali Hindu*, *agama Hindu Bali*, and *agama Hindu*. In this respect, we should bear in mind that it is only through the work of Dutch orientalists that educated Balinese elites became acquainted with the word 'Hindu' in the 20th century.

The question was to surface in a most pressing fashion during the meeting which sealed the fate of Santi, in May 1925, when the chairman of the meeting, Nyoman Kadjeng, proposed to change the association statutes by replacing *agama Hindu* with *agama Hindu Bali*, arguing that there were numerous forms of *agama Hindu* and that it was therefore necessary to specify the Hindu religion the way it was actually practiced in Bali (*artinya agama Hindu yang ada di Bali*). It appears that his proposition met largely with approval, but it was firmly rejected by Ktut Nasa, who declared that "the Hindu religion in Bali was damaged" (*agama Hindu di Bali rusak*), and that it should be reformed accordingly (*Bali Adnjana* 1925, No. 15: 1; see also *Bali Adnjana* 1925, No. 18: 3; 1926, No. 30: 5; and 1929, No. 5: 3; as well as *Surya Kanta* 1926, No. 8: 98–9). A year later, in May 1926, Article 1 of the statutes of the newly created association Tjatur Wangsa Derya Gama Hindu Bali declared as its purpose "to strengthen the Hindu Bali religion" (*Meneguhkan Igama Hindu Bali*) (*Bali Adnjana* 1926, No. 14: 4).

Nyoman Kadjeng's proposition was substantiated by Tjakra Tanaya in the following manner: there exist two main religious trends in Bali, *agama Siwa* and *agama Budha*, with their respective priests, the *padanda Siwa* and the *padanda Budha*; their convergence over centuries resulted in *agama Siwa-Budha*, which Tjakra Tanaya personally adheres to; most Balinese resort to holy water (*tirta*) for their ceremonies, hence the name *agama Tirta* given to their religious rites; yet, there are some minority groups in Bali, such as the Pande or the Bali Aga, who dispense with the services of the *padanda* and refuse their *tirta*; thus, Tjakra Tanaya advocated the name *agama Hindu Bali* in order to accommodate the practices of these various Balinese religious communities (*Bali Adnjana* 1925, No. 29: 4–6, and No. 30: 6).

In defending *agama Hindu Bali* as the proper name, Tjakra Tanaya and the *triwangsa* were asserting that the Balinese people had appropriated and reinterpreted *agama Hindu* to such an extent that it had become indigenous to their island. In this way, they were clearly trying to preserve the established social and religious order of yore, by endorsing the religion that the Balinese actually practiced (*nama Hindu Bali yaitu yang bererti meneguhkan agama Hindu yang sudah ada dan dipeluk olih wong Bali*) (*Bali Adnjana* 1926, No. 17: 2). Whereas in advocating the name *agama Bali Hindu*, Ktut Nasa and the *jaba* were claiming that the Balinese were truly Hindu, even if their religious practices were corrupted by superstition, owing to their ignorance of the true nature of their religion.[64] Consequently, in order to become the true Hindus they were supposed to be, the Balinese had to discard all indigenous accretions that contaminated their religious practices. Hence, Tjakra Tanaya accused Surya Kanta of attempting to promote a 'pure' (*murni*) form of Hinduism, similar to that found in India.[65] This, he claimed, amounted to inventing a new religion, which was alien to the Balinese, because their religion originated not in India but in Majapahit.[66] It was therefore the duty of the Balinese to remain faithful to the religion their ancestors had brought to Bali at the peril of their lives, when they were fleeing the propagation of Islam in Java after the fall of Majapahit.[67]

The aftermath of the debate between *jaba* and *triwangsa*

The publication of *Surya Kanta* was discontinued in September 1927, but the organization still held a last meeting in February 1928. After that, it seems that its leaders had faced pressure from the colonial authorities and nothing more was heard from Surya Kanta. The fact is that Dutch administrators were wary of the *jaba* movement, which they dismissed as "a small group of Balinese youth who are filled with foreign theories, and who see salvation only in the complete dismantling of Balinese society as it now exists" (quoted in Robinson 1995: 47). Nonetheless, it appears likely that the defection of its members might be a more decisive reason for the disappearance of Surya Kanta than government pressure

---

[64] As a matter of fact, one commonly encounters both names in *Bali Adnjana*—*agama Hindu Bali* as much as *agama Bali Hindu*—the latter appearing to be the most popular during the colonial period. In any event, Frederik Bakker (1993: 40-1), Geoffrey Robinson (1995: 34, n. 52), and Lynette Parker (2000: 53) were mistaken in assuming that the commoners rejected the term *Hindu Bali* because it placed too great an emphasis on the Hindu components of Balinese religion and, therefore, also on caste hierarchy. In addition, one remarks that the *jaba*, who resorted to Hinduism in order to challenge the customary privileges of the *triwangsa*, here took a stance opposite to that of the Dutch orientalists, who saw in Balinese *adat* an egalitarian ethos standing up to the despotism of the Hinduized courts (Ramstedt 2002: 150).

[65] "*Keteguhan kita pada AGAMA akan berobah menjadi LEMAH dan RUSAK, apabila menuruti hawa nafsunya salah seorang pemimpin SURYA KANTA, yang bermaksud mengembangkan Agama Hindu yang murni, katanya sebagai Agama Hindu yang dilakukan di Hindustan*" (*Bali Adnjana* 1926, No. 20: 4). The fact is that references to India are frequent in *Surya Kanta*, which quotes Hindu canonical texts such as the *Bhagawad Gita* as willingly as Mahatma Gandhi, Rabindranath Tagore or Krishnamurti.

[66] "*Jikalau sekarang kita meneguhkan Agama cara di Hindustan, adalah berarti kita membikin Agama BARU.* [...] *dalam lontar kita tak ada terdapat perkataan atau ukara yang menerangkan asal kita dari HINDU. Tetapi apabila kita perhatikan keadaan kita berasal dari Mojopahit*" (*Bali Adnjana* 1926, No. 17: 2–3).

[67] "[...] *ingat pada leluhur saya punya keteguhan hati pada Agama dan Adatnya, sehingga terpaksa ia membuang derajatnya dan meninggalkan Negerinya pulau Djawa yang makmur lantas berpindah di pulau Bali yang sekecil ini, yaitu karena cinta pada Agama dan Adat. Bukankah perbuatan hina sekali kalau sekarang dengan omong saja saya lantas mesti suka membuang Agama dan Adat?*" (*Bali Adnjana* 1929, No. 7: 6).

against its leaders. From the early issues of the journal, there had been pressing injunctions against readers who did not pay their membership fees, a critical concern for this organization as well as for its successors.

In retrospect, it should be noted that until the end Surya Kanta remained the matter of a restricted elite and never became a mass organization, unlike Sarekat Islam for example. Its meetings never gathered more than a few dozen participants and the influence of its publication was limited, despite the opening of several local branches, in Bali as well as in Lombok, which had a sizable Balinese minority. One can therefore conclude that, at the time at least, the desire for progress promoted by the *jaba* intelligentsia did not appear to have exerted significant influence on the course of events nor on Balinese society at large.

The failure of Surya Kanta's reform project is thus not attributable solely to the *triwangsa*'s opposition nor to Tjakra Tanaya's invectives in *Bali Adnjana*. The fact remains that in the 1920s, Balinese society was still very conservative and that the majority of commoners were far from sharing Surya Kanta's reforming urge. Despite the disruptions caused by the colonial occupation, the social hierarchy that made Balinese peasants the subjects (*panjak*) of the rajas and the clients (*sisia*) of the *padanda* remained firmly rooted, legitimized as it was by *adat* and *agama* alike.

On the other hand, it seems surprising that, notwithstanding its frequent references to Java, presented as a model to emulate, there was so little mention in *Surya Kanta* of the movement of 'national awakening' (*kebangkitan nasional*) which was at the time stirring the Netherlands Indies, and, especially, neighboring Java. Certainly the fear of censorship was a valid reason for the prudence of the *jaba* intellectuals, most of them civil servants and as such banned from politics. And Surya Kanta's statutes explicitly stipulated that "this association has no political contents" (*perkumpulan ini tiada sekali-kali mengandung politiek*) (*Surya Kanta* 1925, No. 2: 16). But the fear of censorship, justified as it may be, is not sufficient to explain Surya Kanta's apparent lack of interest in the emergence of nationalism in Java. The more likely reason is that the zeal of progressive intellectuals was aimed more at denouncing the *triwangsa*'s arrogance and privileges than at fighting colonial domination. And indeed, it appears that not only the *jaba* but also the *triwangsa* had adjusted rather well to Dutch tutelage. Be that as it may, Surya Kanta's leaders demonstrated compliance to the law and order imposed by the colonial state, which they much preferred to the arbitrary power (*sekitawenang*) of the former rajas (*Surya Kanta* 1927, No. 5: 55).

Clearly, for the Balinese intellectuals in the 1920s, Indonesian nationalism was not (yet) on the agenda: for them, Indonesia was still the Indies (*Hindia*). This is evidenced by their use of the term *bangsa* which, if it already denoted the idea of a 'nation', did not refer to Indonesia as a whole but to the main ethnic groups in the Archipelago—the Javanese, the Malays, the Bugis, etc., not to mention the Balinese themselves.

Surya Kanta's politicization would occur, however, but rather belatedly. In March 1926, the association's members were authorized to conduct political activity as individuals (*Surya Kanta* 1926, No. 4: 61). And in December of the same year, the article of statutes stipulating that the association had no political contents was revoked (*Surya Kanta* 1927, No. 1–2: 6). In fact, it is in the issue immediately following this decision that we find the first explicit reference in *Surya Kanta* to the Indonesian nationalist movement: "In the Indies, people are busy thinking about the plight of the natives. Well-informed people are becoming involved in political activities. [...] Bali is only separated from Java by a narrow strait; the national feeling is the same. Bali should not lag behind in the general movement."[68] Eventually, in February 1928, during Surya Kanta's last meeting (which Tjakra Tanaya was invited to attend), it was decided that the organization would henceforth be open to *triwangsa* membership and that it should become more 'national' (*nasional*, in the sense of Indonesia as a whole this time) in its focus (*Bali Adnjana* 1928, No. 7: 1).

After the communist uprisings of November 1926 in Java and of January 1927 in Sumatra, and the ensuing crackdown, the colonial authorities became suspicious of Surya Kanta. The Dutch blamed its leaders' diatribes against the traditional social order for several incidents caused by *jaba* title groups who refused allegiance to the *triwangsa*.[69] Furthermore, they suspected them of being influenced by communist propaganda, which had reached Bali via Singaraja in 1924 (McVey 1965: 184). This suspicion was fueled by Tjakra Tanaya, who accused Surya Kanta of being a 'communist hotbed' (*S.[arang] K.[ominis]*) and warned that its leaders would end up in Boven Digoel[70] (*Bali Adnjana* 1927, No. 28: 3).

---

[68] "*Ditanah Hindia sedang ramai orang memikirkan nasib Bumiputera. Orang yang berpengertian sedang asyik menjalankan aksi dalam kalangan politik. [...] Tanah Bali hanya dipisahkan Straat Bali dari Jawa; perasaan bangsa sama. Tanah Bali harus tak ketinggalan dimedan pergerakan umum*" (*Surya Kanta* 1927, No. 1–2: 3).

[69] I am alluding here to the scandal caused during a cremation in Mengwi in November 1926 by Pande who demanded for their priests (*mpu*) the privilege of producing their own holy water (*tirta*) instead of receiving it from a *padanda* as required (*masiwa brahmana*). On the Pande's priesthood and their demands, see Guermonprez (1987).

[70] After the failure of the uprisings launched by the Indonesian Communist Party (PKI) in 1926–27, hundreds of its leaders were interned in the Boven Digoel camp in New Guinea.

As for Tjakra Tanaya, he was more than ever a faithful supporter of the government, especially since its colonial policy was becoming increasingly conservative. Thus, in June 1929, he declared that *Bali Adnjana* had lost its relevance since the Dutch had made known their intention to restore the Balinese rulers' former prerogatives and to govern Bali according to its *adat* (*Bali Adnjana* 1929, No. 15–16: 8). Two months later, he hailed the re-establishment of the Balinese rajas as *negara-bestuurders* in an editorial titled 'The Island of Bali Will Become Bali Again' (*Pulau Bali Akan Kembali Menjadi Bali*) (*Bali Adnjana* 1929, No. 19: 1–4).

Chapter 3

From 'Living Museum' to 'Last Paradise'

The Discovery of Balinese Culture (1930s)

The tension between *jaba* and *triwangsa* receded in 1928, thanks to the combined efforts of Balinese dignitaries and Dutch officials, who did their best to defuse what they rightly perceived as a threat to the established order. Indeed, they both had valid reasons to be worried by the spread of the national Indonesian awakening and political activism to Bali. In the context of the conservative turn taken by their colonial policy, combining vigilant monitoring and indirect rule inspired by the precepts of *adatrecht*, the Dutch endeavored to 'culturalize' Balinese identity in order to prevent its politicization. This is not to say that the celebrated Balinese culture is a colonial invention—contrary to what a postcolonial reading might be inclined to surmise—but rather that Dutch scholars and officials promoted the image of a Balinese traditional culture reduced mainly to its ceremonial displays and its artistic manifestations, thereby obscuring the social, political and economic disruptions caused by the colonial occupation of the island. And from the early 1930s onward, one finds growing evidence that the Balinese intelligentsia were appropriating this colonial construction in order to define themselves in terms of their 'culture'.

The Dutch colonizers were not the only interlocutors of the Balinese to be involved in this dialogic construction. Alongside orientalists and administrators engaged in conserving Bali as a 'living museum', the first tourists—preceded by artists and followed by anthropologists—were visiting this island which would be soon portrayed as the 'last paradise'.

The discovery of 'Balinese culture' is concomitant with a radical transformation in the anthropological category of culture. After the trauma of the

First World War, faith in Europe's 'civilizing mission' began to crumble and there appeared a growing disenchantment with the promises of progress, opening the door to cultural relativism. The hitherto prevalent evolutionist view, in which all the peoples in the world were expected to pass through the same development cycles, gave way to a differentialist model, that saw distinct societies as discrete cultures evolving on their own terms. Instead of a hierarchy of peoples ranked in relation to their level of evolution on the scale of civilization, one was now dealing with a mosaic of incommensurable cultures, irreducible one to another in a civilizational metanarrative.

The universalist notion of culture as *Civilisation* that had arisen during the French Enlightenment, which posited the possibility of a graded comparison between societies (Maine, Tylor, Morgan, Frazer), was thus replaced by a particularistic conception issued from the German idealist Romantic idea of *Kultur* (Herder), introduced by Franz Boas into American anthropology (Kroeber, Lowie, Sapir, Benedict, Mead, Linton, Kardiner). Instead of 'Culture', anthropologists, following Boas, began to write about 'cultures' (Kuper 1999: 60). Previously regarded as an accretion of disparate elements, in the Boasian perspective the idea of 'a culture' was developed as a bounded and integrated system of shared ideas, values and customs, expressed in symbols and embodied in religion and the arts. It came to be a source of explanation in itself, endowed with an agency of its own, in the sense that individual members of a given society were supposed to be 'patterned' by their culture, understood as 'personality writ large' (Benedict 1934). They found a sense of identity through absorbing their culture's ethos and making it their own. This psychological approach of culture, labeled 'Culture and Personality', was popularized by Margaret Mead, who studied the links between cultural patterns, personality types and modes of enculturation. It turns out that Bali played a significant role in the formulation of this theory, as witnessed by a couple of remarkable publications—*Balinese Character* (Bateson and Mead 1942) and *Traditional Balinese Culture* (Belo 1970)—that presented Balinese culture as an unbroken continuum with hardly any internal development, only recently threatened by the disruptions engendered by the colonial intrusion and the influx of foreign visitors in its wake.

This new cultural paradigm was reflected in Dutch colonial policy. While at the time of the Ethical Policy, *adat* was perceived as a source of backwardness for Indonesian societies—which the colonial administration had a mission to civilize, to modernize and to develop according to European standards—from then on government officials trained at Leiden University would focus attention on the uniqueness of indigenous cultural traditions and on the need to safeguard them, so that colonized peoples would be allowed to evolve in accordance with their own specific concerns and values:

> If nineteenth century colonial ideology had come to be informed by a view of a passive, backward, even decadent Indonesia ripe for the civilising and developmental influence of the more advanced European power that ruled it, this gave way to very different images of uniquely Indonesian (or Javanese, Balinese, Minangkabau, etc.) forms of cultural, social and economic organisation and developmental trajectories (Kahn 1995: 89).

The idea of distinctive and timeless Indonesian cultures, deeply rooted in this Dutch colonial ideology (C. van Vollenhoven, J.H. Boeke), was now being substantiated by the anthropological theory of culture, which was conducive to maintaining the status quo without making way for social change.

In line with the previous chapter, I will first investigate how the orientalist view of Balinese culture began to take shape in a publication sponsored by the colonial government—*Bhāwanāgara*. Then I will show how the opening of Bali to tourism contributed to the development of this view: at the same time that their island was becoming a tourist destination extolled for the wealth of its cultural expressions, the Balinese people were depicted by culturalist anthropologists as passive subjects of their culture, a culture conceived as an abstract and coherent essence, insulated and atemporal.

An orientalist view of Balinese culture: *Bhāwanāgara* (1930–35)

On September 14, 1928, in the presence of the *resident* of Bali and Lombok, L.J.J. Caron, the governor-general of the Netherlands Indies, A.C.D. de Graeff, inaugurated a foundation dedicated to the collection and study of Balinese manuscripts, the Kirtya Liefrinck-Van der Tuuk,[1] named after two major figures of Balinese studies. The decision had been taken at a meeting convened by

---

[1] The foundation was originally to be called Stichting Liefrinck-Van der Tuuk. At the instigation of I Gusti Putu Djlantik, wishing to confer a Balinese character, the Dutch term *stichting* was replaced by the Old Javanese word *kirtya*, derived from Sanskrit *kirti* ('glory, fame, renown'), which refers to a meritorious foundation (Gonda 1973: 633; Zoetmulder 1982: 879). I Gusti Putu Djlantik was one of the Kirtya's founders and the first Balinese to entrust his manuscript collection to it. A building with three rooms was constructed on his *puri*'s land, which became known as the Gedong Kirtya. The foundation was managed by a team of twelve curators, presided over by the *resident* of Bali and Lombok, assisted by a secretary, and composed of representatives of the eight *negara* of Bali and two delegates from Lombok. Putu Djlantik, who was the representative of Buleleng, was the vice-president. Of the nine Balinese curators, six were *padanda*. The post of librarian was held by I Nyoman Kadjeng, until his replacement in 1932 by I Wayan Bhadra.

Resident Caron in June of that year to collect Balinese manuscripts, for fear that the Balinese people might sell them to tourists and thus become cut off from their literary heritage (Hooykaas 1973b: 37). In fact, the foundation was initially dedicated not only to Balinese manuscripts but also to other cultural productions, such as sculptures, paintings and archeological remains. Most of these objects would later be transferred to the Bali Museum, opened in 1932 in Denpasar—on the grounds where the royal palace once stood—and partly funded by the Kirtya.[2]

In September 1929, shortly before his departure for Makassar where he had been appointed governor of Celebes, Resident Caron had proposed that the Kirtya should publish a cultural journal in order to become "a center of knowledge on the culture of Bali and Lombok" (*pusat pengetahuan tentang peradaban tanah Bali dan Lombok*) (*Bhāwanāgara* 1930: 4). It was up to his successor, Resident H. Beeuwkes, to bring this wish to fruition in April 1930, by granting official authorization to launch this publication, with funding from the Kirtya until it was supported by subscriptions from its readers. In September of that year a trial issue (*proefnummer*) of the new journal, called *Bhāwanāgara*,[3] was finally published, which outlined its objectives, first in Balinese, then in Malay:

> The purpose of this periodical is to increase knowledge of our culture (*peradaban*) while paying attention to new opinions as well as to changes coming from the West. Besides articles on religion, tradition and literary heritage, in this periodical one will find articles dealing with medicine, pharmacology, agriculture and other topics according to the Western point of view.[4]

Thus, while the focus was clearly on religion (*agama*), tradition (*adat*) and literary heritage (*ilmu kitab kuna*), the journal was not confined to the study of traditional manuscripts but was intent on giving the Balinese people the chance

---

[2] The idea of building the Bali Museum is attributed to W.F.J. Kroon, *assistent-resident* in Denpasar, and goes back to 1910. His original intention was to preserve specimens of traditional Balinese architectural styles, of temples (*pura*) as well as of palaces (*puri*). In 1932, a Bali Museum Association (Vereeniging Bali-Museum) was established to disseminate knowledge of Balinese architecture, arts and crafts and ethnography (Resink 1938; Budiastra 1998; Stowell 2011: 158–61).

[3] The name of the journal was glossed in the following manner in Malay: "*Bhawa* signifies the state of being true; *nagara* refers to the lands of Bali and Lombok" (Bhawa *artinya: keadaan yang sejati*; nagara *maksudnya: tanah Bali dan Lombok*) (*Bhāwanāgara* 1930: 7). The Sanskrit term *bhava* signifies 'state, condition, disposition, behavior' (Gonda 1973: 470; Zoetmulder 1982: 226).

[4] "*Tujuan surat berkala ini umumnya: menambah pengetahuan tentang peradaban kita sendiri dengan memperhatikan juga akan pendapatan baharu dan perobah-perobahan cara Barat. Kecuali karang-karangan tentang hal agama, adat, dan ilmu kitab kuna, dalam surat berkala ini akan dimuat juga karang-karangan tentang ilmu kesehatan, ilmu obat, ilmu tentang perusahan tanah dan sebagainya menurut pendapatan cara Barat*" (*Bhāwanāgara* 1930: 5). In the Balinese version the category of 'culture' is rendered by the term *sangaskara*, which is glossed as follows: "*Sangaskara* signifies *peradaban* (Malay), *cultuur* (Dutch)" (*Sangaskara mateges: peradaban (basa Melayu), Cultuur (basa Belanda)*) (*Bhāwanāgara* 1930: 1).

to benefit from the discoveries and progress introduced by the West. The editorial content of *Bhāwanāgara* was divided into headings labeled in Balinese, followed by a gloss in Malay: (1) Linguistics and literature. (2) Religion. (3) Chronicles and inscriptions. (4) Traditions. (5) Astrology. (6) Pharmacology. (7) Arts and crafts. (8) Agriculture and livestock farming. (9) Economy. (10) Education. (11) Public security. (12) Other matters ("as long as they are related to our culture").[5]

In that same inaugural issue, the editorial board insisted that, even though *Bhāwanāgara* was established under the auspices of the *resident* of Bali and Lombok in his capacity as the Kirtya's president, the new journal was not in any way an organ of the colonial government but a forum offered to Balinese who would like to contribute their opinion. In particular, it was suggested to potential contributors to pay attention to customary variations encountered in Bali from one region to the next, and even from one village to the next, so that the Balinese people might get to know each other beyond the many parochial features that distinguish them from one another. Despite such appeals to contribute to the journal, however, *Bhāwanāgara*, like its predecessors, would be written mostly by members of its editorial board.

Bhāwanāgara's editorial board was initially composed of a Dutch orientalist, Roelof Goris, and four Balinese, I Gusti Putu Djlantik, I Gusti Gde Djlantik, I Nyoman Kadjeng and I Wayan Ruma, these latter two being former members of Surya Kanta. For good measure, their main opponent, former editor of *Bali Adnjana* I Gusti Tjakra Tanaya, featured prominently in the first issues. In June 1932, Goris and Putu Djlantik were appointed as advisors, while the board was reduced to three members: I Nyoman Kadjeng, I Ktut Widjanagara and I Nyoman Mas Wirjasutha, a former leader of Surya Kanta, who was replaced in November 1933 by I Gusti Putu Djiwa. Besides the members of the editorial board and a handful of regular contributors (among whom were the first two Balinese with a law degree, I Gusti Ketut Pudja and I Gde Panetje), among occasional contributors were prominent representatives of reigning families, such as Tjokorda Gde Raka Sukawati (the *punggawa* of Ubud and member of the Volksraad in Batavia), Anak Agung Agung Anglurah Ketut Karangasem

---

[5] *"(1) Basa sastra (tentang ilmu bahasa dan ilmu kitab baru dan kuna). (2) Kasewasogatan (tentang agama). (3) Babad prasasti (tentang tambo dan ceritra-ceritra yang berhubung dengan kebangsaan). (4) Catur dresta (tentang keadaan adat istiadat). (5) Wariga (tentang ilmu menghitungkan hari baik dan jahat). (6) Kausadan (tentang ilmu obat cara kuna dan baru). (7) Gaginan (tentang perbuatan kerajinan dan ilmu seni). (8) Patanian patik-wenang (tentang ilmu bertani: bercucuk tanam, dan berternak). (9) Guna-kaya (tentang perusahan economie). (10) Sekolahan (tentang pengajaran dalam sekolah dan lain-lainnya). (11) Kertaning negara (tentang keamanan negeri). (12) Hal yang lain-lain (Karang-karangan tentang hal yang lain dari pada yang tersebut di-atas, asal saja berhubungan dengan peradaban kita)"* (*Bhāwanāgara* 1930: 7).

(*negara-bestuurder* of Karangasem), Ida Dewa Agung Oka Geg (*negara-bestuurder* of Klungkung), and Anak Agung Ngurah Agung (*negara-bestuurder* of Gianyar).

Besides *Bhāwanāgara*, specifically intended for a Balinese readership, between 1929 and 1941 the Kirtya published a series of 'Communications' (*Mededeelingen*) in Dutch at irregular intervals, as well as monographs, such as an inventory of archaeological remains by W.F. Stutterheim, the study by V.E. Korn on Tenganan Pagringsingan, and editions of Javanese and Balinese texts by C.C. Berg and Ch. Hooykaas. Furthermore, the manuscript collection was going ahead, since from less than 500 in 1930, the Kirtya's collection had grown to 2,100 *lontar* in 1941. These manuscripts had been either bought from their owners or borrowed to be copied and transliterated (Hooykaas 1979a). In the first issue of the *Mededeelingen*, I Nyoman Kadjeng, the Kirtya's librarian, classified the different manuscripts into six headings: (1) *Weda*[6]: ritual literature (*kalpasastra*), hymns of praise (*stuti* and *stawa*), and *mantra*. (2) *Agama*: codes (*sasana, palakerta, sima*), legal and political literature derived from the Indian Dharmashastras and Nitishastras. (3) *Wariga*: technical literature on astrology and calendrical divination (*wariga*), cosmology and mysticism (*tutur*), medicine (*usada*), grammar, metrics, mythology, crafts and sorcery (*kanda*). (4) *Itihasa*: epic and poetic literature (*parwa, kakawin, kidung, gaguritan*). (5) *Babad*: historical literature, chronicles, genealogies (*pamancangah*). (6) *Tantri*: popular literature (*satua*) and fables of Indian origin (Kadjeng 1929; Hooykaas 1979b: 10–12).[7]

Bhāwanāgara was published monthly for four years, from June 1931 till May 1935, with 16 pages per issue.[8] Its articles were markedly different in tone and content from those in *Bali Adnjana* and *Surya Kanta*. To begin with, the former publications were written in Malay, a language through which the Balinese intelligentsia could express the novel ideas of progress and equality,

---

[6] While the Old-Javanese word *weda* is obviously derived from the Sanskrit Veda, its semantic scope is wider. Zoetmulder's dictionary gives the following definition: "the books of holy revelation; sacred formulas and texts in general; the recitation of these" (Zoetmulder 1982: 2250).

[7] Pace Andrea Acri, while there is indeed mention of *tutur* in the Kirtya's nomenclature, *tattwa* is conspicuous for its absence.

[8] I have no information on the reason why *Bhāwanāgara* discontinued its publication, but the motive was likely financial, judging from repeated calls from the editorial board for the readers to pay their subscription fees. Moreover, even prior to its first issue, in a communication presented in April 1931 at the Royal Batavian Society of Arts and Sciences (Koninklijk Bataviaasch Genootschap van Kunsten en Wetenschappen), the Dutch orientalist Christiaan Hooykaas had criticized the decision to publish the journal, on the grounds that its cost would put a severe strain on the Kirtya's budget, provoking a sharp rebuttal from Roelof Goris (*Bhāwanāgara* 1931, No. 6: 90). Whatever the case, the decision to suspend the publication of *Bhāwanāgara* must have been taken some time in advance, since the last issue ends the fourth year of publication and bears the mention 'final' (*Penghabisan*).

unlike the Balinese language, with its lexical markers indicating the respective hierarchical position of its speakers. In contrast, when he announced the launching of *Bhāwanāgara*, Resident Beeuwkes specified that its language would be Balinese. This is understandable considering that the colonial government had an obvious interest in fostering the consciousness of a Balinese cultural identity, as opposed to an identity based on caste difference or, worse, on national Indonesian unity.[9] That being said, the *resident* conceded that the new journal could also accept contributions in Malay for the benefit of the Sasak readership in Lombok. In fact, one has only to browse *Bhāwanāgara* to realize that articles in Malay were largely as numerous as those written in Balinese.

In addition, the polemical character that marked the debate between *Surya Kanta* and *Bali Adnjana* had made room for the scholarly style that befits an academic publication, particularly concerning the articles written in Balinese.[10] As signified by its motto, *Bhāwanāgara* was expressly dedicated to 'Balinese culture' (*Surat bulanan untuk memperhatikan peradaban Bali*). Until then, 'culture' (and 'art') as a specific topic had been conspicuously absent from Balinese reflections on their identity. In fact, just as the Balinese language has no terms for 'religion' or 'tradition', it also has none for 'culture' or 'art'. In keeping with their marked preference for concrete verbal forms as opposed to abstract concepts, the Balinese have always been concerned with specific activities, inseparable from their context, which were therefore not perceived as belonging to domains coming under generic labels such as 'culture' or 'art'. Nevertheless, one begins to encounter occasional references to these topics in both *Bali Adnjana* and *Surya Kanta* shortly after the setting up of the Tjatur Wangsa Derya Gama Hindu Bali in 1926. Thus, in *Bali Adnjana*, the syntagm *peradaban Bali* tended to become a substitute for *Kebalian* to designate

---

[9] On October 28, 1928, the Indonesian Youth Congress, held in Batavia, had taken a pledge (*Sumpah Pemuda*, the 'Youth Pledge') proclaiming the ideal of one fatherland (*Tanah Air Indonesia*), one nation (*Bangsa Indonesia*), and one language (*Bahasa Indonesia*) (Foulcher 2000). As far as I could tell, there were no Balinese delegates in attendance.

[10] According to V.E. Korn, one of the best sources of information on colonial Bali, the publication of *Bhāwanāgara* had been specifically intended by the Dutch authorities to appease the dispute between *jaba* and *triwangsa*: "Like the Balinese people, the style of these polemical writings [*Surya Kanta* and *Bali Adnjana*] is fiery and insolent. The Western administration was alarmed that the frequent disparaging expressions toward the *triwangsa* could result in an undesirable decline of their prestige and it is with the monthly *Bawa Nagara* [sic], open to contributors from both sides, that it is hoped to achieve the expression of a more suitable opinion" (*Opbruisend en vrijpostig als de Baliër is, is ook de schrijftrant dezer strijdschriften [Surya Kanta en Bali Adnjana]. Het Westersch Bestuur voorzag van de vaak zeer laatdunkende uitingen ten aanzien der triwangsa een ongewenschten teruggang van het aanzien der adelshoofden en het is door het maandblad Bawa Nagara, dat openstaat voor schrijvers van beide richtingen, dat men hoopt tot meer gepaste meeningsuiting te geraken*) (Korn 1932: 47).

'Balinese culture', conceived of as being based on tradition and religion.[11] On the other hand, in *Surya Kanta*, one sometimes finds the Dutch term *cultuur*, and Ktut Nasa even dedicated a whole article to explaining the meaning of that word, which was glossed as the 'soul of a people' (*jiwa bangsa*) and understood as including *adat*, *agama* and *seni*, a Malay word signifying 'art' (*Surya Kanta* 1926, No. 9–10: 128). At the time, though, 'art' was still more commonly rendered by the Dutch term *kunst*.

Thus, if the word for 'religion' (*agama*) had been borrowed from Sanskrit and that for 'tradition' (*adat*) from Arabic, the notions of 'culture' (*cultuur*) and 'art' (*kunst*) were initially acquired from Dutch, before being appropriated through Malay.[12] *Bhāwanāgara*'s motto referred to *peradaban*, and one finds the recurrence of both the terms *cultuur* and *peradaban* in its articles. Afterwards, the Dutch word *cultuur* would be progressively replaced by *peradaban*, and then later by *kebudayaan*, from the root *budaya*—a neologism of Sanskrit origin, based on *budi*, 'mind, reason, character', and *daya*, 'energy, capacity'—which referred to the development of reason and to the character of an individual before acquiring the meaning of 'culture'. As for the word *kunst*, it would be replaced by *seni*—which meant 'fine, refined' before taking on the sense of 'art'—or by its affixed form *kesenian*.[13]

As for the topics of *agama* and *adat*, while they were indeed on *Bhāwanāgara*'s agenda, they were dealt with very differently than in *Bali Adnjana* and *Surya Kanta*. While formerly a crucial question for the Balinese in their attempt to formulate their identity in response to the challenge of changing times, and hence concerned to draw a distinction between what belongs to *agama* and what to *adat*, these topics were now a matter of orientalist erudition. Thus, rather than seeking to differentiate *agama* from *adat*, most articles dealing with these topics addressed them as if they were one and the same category—'*adat agama Bali*'. Furthermore, in *Bhāwanāgara* we find both meanings of the term

---

[11] *Peradaban* is derived from the Arabic loanword *adab*, which initially signified 'habit, custom' before taking on the meaning of 'politeness, civility', while its affixed form *peradaban* acquired the sense of 'culture' or 'civilization', as well as that of 'education'.

[12] Actually, we saw that in the Balinese version of the objectives assigned to *Bhāwanāgara*, the category of 'culture' was rendered by the Old Javanese term *sangaskara*, derived from Sanskrit *samskara*, signifying 'purification, consecration, installation, initiation, sanctifying ceremony' (Zoetmulder 1982: 1659). As far as I could determine, though, this term, which belongs to the literary style, remained little used in Bali and it seldom appeared in *Bhāwanāgara*.

[13] Denys Lombard noticed the emergence of the terms *budaya* and *seni* in the vocabulary of Indonesian writers and artists in the 1930s. He specified that *budaya* was to be found neither in Klinkert's Malay dictionary (1926) nor in Wilkinson's (1932). While *seni* did appear in both, it was only in the sense of 'fine, refined' (Lombard 1990, I: 148 and 244, n. 394).

agama, the legal as well as the religious, without any specification regarding their respective usages. A case in point is the disparity between the nomenclature of the Kirtya's manuscripts, which classified under the heading *agama* the legal and political literature, and the editorial content of *Bhāwanāgara*, in which *agama* referred to religious matters, glossed as *kasewasogatan*, from *Sewa*, Siwa's worshippers, and *Sogata*, Buddha's devotees, in reference to the two categories of *brahmana* priests in Bali, the *padanda Siwa* and the *padanda Boda*.

Even if most contributions to *Bhāwanāgara* are from Balinese authors, the editorial orientations of the journal owe much to Roelof Goris, who served as the Kirtya's scientific advisor until his replacement by Christiaan Hooykaas in 1939. The author of a doctoral dissertation from Leiden University on Indo-Javanese and Balinese theology (Goris 1926), Goris had obtained a position as a linguist at the Archaeological Service in Batavia, where he was in charge of publishing a corpus of Old Javanese inscriptions. He accompanied Rabindranath Tagore during his visit to Bali in August–September 1927, and in 1928 he was transferred to Singaraja with the mission of studying the Kawi literature on religion, law, astrology and medicine contained in the Kirtya library, and of investigating the customs and religious life of the Balinese people (Swellengrebel 1966).[14]

Goris published a number of articles in *Bhāwanāgara* (some of which he signed under his Balinese pen name, I Made Sweta, meaning 'white' in both Sanskrit and Balinese), dealing with topics such as religion, ancient history, language and literature. I mention in particular the publication (spread over several issues) of a lecture entitled 'Bali as a Field for Scientific Work' (*Bali als arbeidsveld voor wetenschappelijk werk*), which he presented on August 5, 1931, at the Koninklijk Bataviaasch Genootschap van Kunsten en Wetenschappen (Goris 1931b).

As a preamble to his lecture, Goris quoted the opinion expressed in a letter addressed in 1863 by a Ds. Brumund[15] to the Bataviaasch Genootschap: "I went for a one-month excursion to Bali. During all that time I was isolated from the civilized world. [...] I hope that I'll never have to return to this island."[16] To which

---

[14] Unlike most of his Dutch colleagues, Goris ended his career in Indonesia, whose nationality he acquired in 1949. A war prisoner in Java during Japanese occupation, he went back to Bali in 1947. He was appointed head of the Institute for Linguistic and Cultural Research (Lembaga Penyelidikan Bahasa dan Kebudayaan) in Singaraja, before becoming librarian at the faculty of literature (Fakultas Sastra) of Udayana University in Denpasar, where he taught the epigraphy and ancient history of Bali.

[15] This was the orientalist and Protestant minister Jan Frederik Gerrit Brumund, stationed in Surabaya and the author of a study on Hinduism in Java.

[16] "*Saya pernah bertamasya satu bulan lamanya di Bali. Didalam waktu itu saya terasing dari dunia beradab. [...] saya harap, agar saya jangan kembali lagi dipulau itu*" (*Bhāwanāgara* 1932, No. 12: 192).

he replied: "My opinion, as one who has been living in Bali for already three years, differs radically from that of this writer." [17] By the early 1930s, Bali had indeed become 'civilized' (*beradab*) in the eyes of the Dutch.

In this lecture, Goris took stock of the work already done in Bali, while stressing the urgency of the remaining tasks, as the Balinese cultural heritage was in danger of rapid erosion due to the disruptions affecting the island. After reviewing the scholarly achievements of Dutch and other European scholars in different fields—language (*bahasa*: H.J.E.F. Schwartz), customary law (*adatrecht*: V.E. Korn), religion (*agama*: P. Wirz),[18] arts (*seni*: J. Kunst for music and P.A.J. Moojen for architecture), chronicles and antiquities (*surat-surat riwayat dan barang kuna*: P.V. Van Stein Callenfels and W.F. Stutterheim)—he concluded that much still remained to be done (*Pendeknya masih banyak sekali yang harus dikerjakan itu*) (*Bhāwanāgara* 1932, No. 6: 90).

To the best of my knowledge, it is in this lecture that the vision of Bali as a unified field of research was outlined for the first time, and that this research was presented according to the main headings seen to make up Balinese culture: religion, customary law, history and archaeology, architecture, visual arts and crafts, performing arts and music, language and literature. It is this very same nomenclature that would be followed by Goris when the Kirtya issued a bibliography of the main publications on Bali that had come out since the seminal study of Cornelis Lekkerkerker, the archivist of the Bali-Instituut in Amsterdam[19] (Lekkerkerker 1920; Goris 1937). Furthermore, and most importantly, in Goris's research program the study of Bali was considered an objective in its own right and no longer—as it had been for the scholars preceding him—of interest for what it could teach us about the situation in Java before the coming of Islam.

But if Goris did indeed help to dissociate the study of Bali from that of Java, he certainly contributed to a rapprochement between the Balinese and India by making them aware of the Indic components of their culture, and in particular by pointing out that Hinduism (and Buddhism) had flourished in Bali long before its conquest by Majapahit.[20] Moreover, he was very likely the author of a note published by the editorial board in the trial issue of *Bhāwanāgara*, which

---

[17] "*Pendapatan saya, yang telah berdiam 3 tahun, agaknya dalam segala hal berbeda sekali dengan pengarang tersebut*" (*Bhāwanāgara* 1932, No. 12: 192).

[18] In his presentation of research already carried on, Goris bemoaned the fact that no one had yet investigated in depth issues of religion and tradition (*Tentang agama dan adat belumlah ada orang yang mempelajari sedalam-dalamnya*) (*Bhāwanāgara* 1932, No. 5: 75).

[19] The Bali-Instituut was established in 1915 as part of the Koloniaal Instituut to collect documentation on Balinese society.

[20] "*Orang harus perhatikan, bahwa telah limaratus tahun sebelum berdirinya kerajaan Majapahit agama Hindu itu (serta agama Buda) berkembang di Bali!*" (*Bhāwanāgara* 1931, No. 5: 72).

enjoined the Balinese people to learn about the canonical texts of Hinduism and to study Sanskrit. He assisted them in this instance by publishing a lengthy study of Sanskrit, complemented by a Sanskrit–Balinese lexicon, spread over several issues of the journal. In this way and in many others, Goris and his orientalist colleagues were instrumental in Hinduizing Bali, by framing the 'Balinese religion' within the context of an Indianized world beyond the shores of the island.

This interest in India was clearly shared by many Balinese contributors to *Bhāwanāgara*, as can be seen in articles on the Vedas, the Upanishads and the *Bhagawad Gita*. Regarding this topic, we have the precious testimony of the Indian philologist Suniti Kumar Chatterji, who accompanied Rabindranath Tagore during his journey to the Dutch Indies. In his account of his sojourn on Bali, he asserted the readiness of the Balinese to renew contact with India and in particular to resume the study of Sanskrit literature.[21] To make his point, he mentioned a letter from Goris, who claimed that the Balinese expressed the keenest interest for 'the real Hinduism', as practiced in India.[22] He added that they sought Hindu texts, which should be translated into Balinese or into Malay so that they could have access to Hinduism as practiced by their Indian brethren.[23]

While stating that the Balinese religion fell fully within the purview of Hinduism, Goris was nonetheless aware of the particularities that differentiate Bali from India. This is illustrated, among other things, by his insistence on dispelling the stubborn preconception that the Vedas had been passed down to Bali, where they had fallen into disuse, just like in India. This delusion, long propagated by orientalists—and soon to be promoted by the Balinese—goes back, as we saw, to the report published by Rudolf Friederich in the mid-19th century.[24]

---

[21] "The earnest desire of the Balinese priests, princes and people to be once more in cultural rapprochement with India was manifest everywhere [...] and in this the Dutch officers were frankly and freely sympathetic. There was a desire also among priests and the chiefs to revive the study of Sanskrit" (Chatterji 1931: 135).

[22] "The present Balinese have very vivid interest in the real Hinduism, and all that now to day is remaining over there (i.e. in India) from the old religion, culture and art; and there exists a real desire to exchange the modern views about Hindu culture" (Goris, in Chatterji 1931: 140).

[23] "There are some English-knowing Balinese, and they, as pioneers in a newly revived cultural rapprochement between India and Bali [...] will, in the words of Dr. Goris, 'select the most important portions of these books and translate them into Balinese (or Malay) for their brethren, so that all the interested Balinese people will share in the progress of knowledge about Hinduism as already attained by their Hindu brothers'" (Chatterji 1931: 140).

[24] See, for example, Goris's article entitled '*Artin mantra sané sering kamargiang*' ('The meaning of current *mantra*'): "What is called *wéda* here in Bali is only *sloka*; this is very different from the *wéda* practiced by the priests in India, such as the *Rgweda*. Here in Bali what is called *wéda* is none other than worship (*stotra, stuti, stawa*) as well as *mantra* taken from Hindu literature, such as the *pūrāna*" (*Sané kawastanin wéda iriki ring jagat Bali wantah seloka punika; sakéwanten séwes pisan ring wéda-wéda sané kamargiang antuk Padanda-Padanda ring tanah Hindu, sakadi Rgweda. Iriki ring Bali sané mawasta wéda, tan lian pangalem (stotra, stuti, stawa)*

Aside from issues concerning the Balinese religion and its connection with Hinduism, in his lecture at the Bataviaasch Genootschap, Goris highlighted the riches of the Balinese artistic traditions, while pointing out the need to study them and to secure their preservation. This was in particular the mission assigned to the Bali Museum in Denpasar, which was expected to conserve antiquities and works of art in order to prevent their being sold to tourists. Additionally, the museum was supposed to control the quality of artistic productions specifically destined for the tourist trade, while making sure they were not sold off at reduced prices.

The performing arts were also taken into account, and Goris suggested that Walter Spies was the most qualified person to write on these topics. But it was Goris himself who in 1933 published the first overview of theater, dance and music in Bali (Goris 1933a).[25] One would have to wait for the *Bali Congres* held by the Java-Instituut[26] in October 1937 for Goris to publish, in collaboration with Spies, a general presentation of Balinese dance and theater (Spies and Goris 1937). The following year saw the publication of *Dance and Drama in Bali*, the masterly study written by Beryl de Zoete, with the valuable assistance of Walter Spies (De Zoete and Spies 1938; see Hitchcock and Norris 1995).

It is undoubtedly the interest expressed by foreign scholars for the Balinese arts that led the Balinese people to discover the value of their artistic heritage. In May 1933, an article in *Bhāwanāgara* bemoaned the fact that Balinese who wanted to know more about their artistic traditions were forced to refer to studies written by foreign scholars in a foreign language.[27] In 1934 the first article written by a Balinese on music and dance was published in this journal. The author—who lived in Brussels and signed 'Balyson'—reproached the younger generation for its lack of interest in the classical repertoire, inexorably replaced by novelties which he deemed trivial, such as the *janger* or the *komedie stambul*.[28] But what

---

miwah mantra-mantra sané katedun saking pustaka-pustaka Hindu, sakadi pūrāna-pūrāna) (*Bhāwanāgara* 1933, No. 8–9: 143; see also Goris 1926, Appendix 1: 137–50).

[25] In this respect, it is rather surprising that one finds no mention in *Bhāwanāgara* of the great sensation created by the troupe of Balinese dancers and musicians headed by Tjokorda Gde Raka Sukawati at the Paris International Colonial Exposition from May to November 1931, where Bali was presented as the Dutch showpiece (Bloembergen 2006: Chap. 6 and Epilogue; Ladeira 2022). This is all the more puzzling in that Goris had written for the occasion two promotional brochures on Bali, one of them illustrated with photographs by Spies, in which a great deal of emphasis was placed on theater, dance and music (Goris 1930, n.d.).

[26] The Java-Instituut was set up in 1919 in Surakarta with a view to preserving and restoring 'traditional Javanese culture', understood as extending to Sunda, Madura and Bali. From 1921 to 1941, the Java-Instituut published the journal *Djawa*, which became the accredited organ of colonial Javanology.

[27] "*Bangsa kita yang hendak mempelajari seni bangsanya sendiri terpaksa memakai buku yang dikarang oleh lain bangsa asing dalam bahasa asing*" (*Bhāwanāgara* 1933, No. 12: 180).

[28] These are two related genres of Balinese performing art dating back to the early 20th century. The *janger* is a heterogeneous entertainment using the rhythmic and vocal accompaniment of the *sanghyang* trance dances (De

stood out in this article is a growing awareness of the reputation of the Balinese for being an artistically inclined people, which they can be legitimately proud of: "[...] 'because the Balinese are an artistic folk; they are born architects, sculptors, actors, dancers, musicians. [...]'. Such is the foreigners' opinion. We, the Balinese people, a people that cherishes art, we have the right to be proud of this renowned quality of ours."[29]

We have come a long way from the reaction expressed a few years earlier in an article in *Surya Kanta* entitled 'Bali as a museum of antiques' (*Bali sebagai Museum barang kuno*), which vehemently rejected the image of a 'living museum' (*museum hidup*) propagated by the orientalists, all the while denouncing the policy of cultural preservation implemented by the colonial government, accused of acting as a 'museum curator' (*museum beheerder*) (*Surya Kanta* 1927, No. 3–4: 29–30). Unlike modernist intellectuals of the 1920s, who reproached their fellow Balinese for letting themselves be seduced by the fame of their island abroad and who refused to see it become a 'tourist island' (*pulau turisten*) fossilized in its outdated customs and conservatism (*kekolotan*), in the 1930s some Balinese were beginning to embrace the process of idealization and reification of their culture initiated by the Dutch orientalists—all the more so since at the time when the Dutch were engaged in culturalizing Bali, the cultural image of the island was being both endorsed and enhanced by its tourism promotion.

The Last Paradise[30]

Before the island of Bali could become a tourist destination, it had to meet two prior conditions. First, the island of 'plunderers', 'amok-running warriors' and 'barbaric cults' had to be narratively domesticated in order to be made attractive to travelers in search of the exotic. Second, those regions of touristic interest must be made accessible to visitors. Barely six years after its military conquest, Bali fulfilled both these conditions.

Zoete and Spies 1938: 211–17; Bandem and deBoer 1995: 97–101). As for the *komedie stambul*, it comes from a genre of popular Malay theater, using themes from both Europe and the Middle East, hence its name, derived from 'Istanbul' (Cohen 2006).

[29] "[...] '*want de Balineezen zijn een kunstzinnig volk; ze zijn geboren architect, beeldhouwers, tooneelspelers, dansers, muzikanten.* [...]'. *Begitulah pendapatan orang asing. Kita bangsa Bali, suatu bangsa yang mencintai seni, berhaklah kita membesarkan hati tentang sifat kebangsaan kita sebagai tersebut diatas*" (*Bhāwanāgara* 1934, No. 11–12: 161).

[30] Title of one of the first travelogues on Bali, published by the American journalist Hickman Powell (1930).

One may trace the beginnings of tourism in the Archipelago from 1908, the year when the last Balinese raja fell under Dutch cannon fire. That year in Batavia, an Official Tourist Bureau (Vereeniging Toeristenverkeer) was opened under the aegis of the colonial government, in charge of promoting tourism in Netherlands India (Sunjayadi 2019). Initially limited to Java, its field of action extended in 1914 to Bali—hailed as the 'Gem of the Lesser Sunda Isles'—once the pacification of the island could ensure safe journeys. But tourists did not begin to visit Bali in earnest until 1924, with the opening of a weekly service of sea connections linking Singapore, Batavia, Semarang and Surabaya to Singaraja and Makassar. This initiative came from the Royal Packet Navigation Company (Koninklijke Paketvaart-Maatschappij, KPM), which had a monopoly on shipping in the Archipelago, and which had decided to carry passengers on the ships it sent to Buleleng to take on copra, coffee, cattle and pigs. And tourists would have to wait until 1928 for the KPM to open the first hotel on the island, the Bali Hotel in Denpasar, on the very site of the *puputan* of 1906 (Picard 1996a).

While these tourist facilities were being set up, the publications of the Tourist Bureau show how Bali's image as a tourist destination was developing. When the island was opened to tourism in 1914, the Bureau published an *Illustrated Tourist Guide to East Java, Bali and Lombok* (Official Tourist Bureau, 1914), striking for its sobriety and essentially practical nature. One searches in vain for information about the history of Bali or contemporary Balinese society, nor does one find the lyrical gushing about the beauty of the island and its inhabitants that later became the standard style. Instead, the island is presented as feral and primitive, and travelers are warned of the discomfort and difficulties of the expedition they are about to undertake, as well as of the inhospitable or frankly uninteresting character of certain regions. It was only with the publication in 1923 of a booklet entitled *Short Guide to Bali* (Official Tourist Bureau, 1923) that tourists were granted slightly more substantial information. A brief introduction describing Balinese society and its history, religious traditions and arts precedes the recommended itineraries. In 1927, the Tourist Bureau began publishing a monthly magazine entitled *Tourism: A Monthly Bulletin of Information Relative to Travel in the Dutch East Indies*, which devoted several issues entirely to Bali. There one finds, among other things, announcements of important religious festivals, as well as notice of cremations for which the Bureau will charter a ship if the event is likely to be especially spectacular. It was not until 1931, with the Colonial Exposition in Paris, that the Bureau decided to provide its clients with serious information on Balinese society, entrusting to Roelof Goris the editing of a booklet entitled *Observations on the Customs and Life of the Balinese* (Goris nd.), republished in a revised edition in 1939. Publications aimed at tourists multiplied during the 1930s. Among these, one notes in particular a guide to Bali edited by a Chinese from Java, written in Malay and aimed at travelers native to the Archipelago, which describes the island and its inhabitants in a manner largely inspired by the Dutch guidebooks of the time (Soe Lie Piet nd.).

From a few hundred in the mid-1920s, the yearly number of visitors to Bali reached several thousand in the late 1930s. Among these early visitors, one must give particular consideration to the small community of foreigners who sojourned on the island between the Wars. For the most part artists and scholars—along with a handful of adventurers, traders and glitterati—these foreign residents constituted an avant-garde as well as a cultural guarantee for the elite tourism of the colonial era, and in this role they mediated between Bali and the tourists. Not only did they certify and disseminate to the West the image of Bali as paradise, they also, and above all, identified Balinese society with its culture—which they saw mostly in terms of its artistic and ceremonial manifestations.

The accounts, paintings, photographs and films that they brought back from their sojourn created an enchanting image of native life, an image that the promotional services of the emerging tourist industry quickly relayed and which is in substantial ways still with us today (MacRae 1992, 1997; Shavit 2003). Thus it is that since the 1920s the island of Bali has been advertised to the point of exhaustion as a true Garden of Eden, the cradle of a traditional culture that has remained insulated from the vicissitudes of the modern world, whose exceptionally gifted inhabitants devote a remarkable amount of their time and wealth to staging colorful ceremonies for their own pleasure and that of their gods—and now, in addition, for the delight of their visitors as well.[31]

What is the source of this image that so seduced the West between the Wars? More than a simple transcription fashioned from an existing reality, it is the product of a construction; indeed, one could say that it is the result of an objective connivance among colonialism, Orientalism, cultural anthropology and tourism, in the sense that the concern for peace and order (*rust en orde*) of the Dutch administration supported the visitors' interest in the Balinese cultural

---

[31] While numerous visitors complained about the filth and expressed their irritation at the pestering of snarling dogs, few ever mentioned in their travel accounts the endemic poverty of the Balinese people, hard hit by the economic crisis of the 1930s, and even fewer noticed behind the all too apparent façade of harmony the results of a forced Pax Neerlandica. Even if Bali appeared as a paradise in the eyes of the tourists, it was no paradise for most Balinese.

traditions unearthed by the orientalists and studied by the anthropologists. The fact remains that before they became famous for the riches of their culture, the Balinese were known for the beauty of their women, and before that, for their ferocity as warriors and the cruelty of their princes. This implies that the image of the 'Other' in the hegemonic discourse was fashioned in a self-serving way: before their conquest, the Balinese had to be perceived as savages to be pacified; once the conquest was accomplished, they could become an exotic curiosity to be gazed at.

Although one could hardly call the first European travelers to Bali tourists, their accounts nonetheless already bear the mark of what would later become a touristic cliché. The label 'last paradise', which greatly contributed to the promotion of Bali in the 20th century, carries a reverberating echo of the reported enchantment of the first visitors at the end of the 16th century. Or rather, it is the story surrounding the 'discovery' of the island that retroactively establishes the first link in a long chain of images that Bali has generated during the turbulent history of its relationship with the West (Vickers 1994).

According to the chroniclers, the European sailors' encounter with Bali was love at first sight. Note, for example, the terms in which this event is described by Miguel Covarrubias:

> In 1597 a fleet of Dutch ships, headed by a former employee of the Portuguese, Cornelius Houtman, discovered Bali. He and his men fell in love with the island and made excellent friends with the king, a good-natured fat man who had two hundred wives, rode in a chariot drawn by two white buffaloes which he drove himself, and owned fifty dwarfs whose bodies had been distorted into resemblance of *keris* handles. After a long sojourn in the island, some of the Dutch returned to Holland to report the discovery of the new 'paradise'; others refused to leave Bali. The news created such a sensation in Holland that in 1601 the trader Heemskerk was sent to Bali with presents of all sorts for the king, who in turn presented him with a beautiful Balinese lady (Covarrubias 1937: 29).

The truth is that the Hollanders' first visit to Bali lasted sixteen days and that only two of them stayed on, for reasons we do not know. This no doubt excited the imagination of the chroniclers, obviously tempted to attribute the defection of the young men to the irresistible allure of the Balinese women—an allure that the first photographers of Bali did not fail to exploit.

The Island of Bare Breasts[32]

Among the earliest image-makers of Bali, two were of particular importance. The first was the Dutch graphic designer Wijnand Otto Jan Nieuwenkamp, who arrived in Bali in 1903 and returned a number of times, including once in 1906 when, invited to accompany the invasion force, he witnessed the *puputan* of the Badung court. It is to him that we owe the first albums, abundantly illustrated with drawings by the author, describing for the general public the island of Bali, the daily life of the people, and their artistic traditions (Nieuwenkamp 1910; Carpenter 1997). Above all, it was he who first called the attention of his compatriots to the beauty of the island that they had just conquered. Here is what he wrote to his wife upon his arrival on Bali in 1903: "It is very picturesque, beautiful trees, beautiful mountains, beautiful beach, beautiful temples, and friendly people. In short, it is a wonderful place, a tiny paradise" (quoted in Bakker 2018: 20).

But it was certainly Gregor Krause, a German physician appointed in 1912 by the colonial administration as a military doctor in Bangli, where he served for eighteen months, who made the decisive step in the touristic promotion of Bali with the publication in 1920 of two volumes illustrated with nearly four hundred photographs depicting the people and the land, village life, temple festivals and cremation ceremonies (Krause 1920, 1930, 1988; Krause and With 2000). In these photographs, the Balinese appear to live in sensuous harmony with nature. To a large extent, the success of his book, as its subsequent editions attest, is no doubt related to the great care with which the author emphasizes the beauty of Balinese bodies and to his enthusiasm for the photographic theme of Balinese women at their bath. It was, especially, the seduction of these photos that induced the Mexican artist Miguel Covarrubias, as well as the Austrian novelist Vicki Baum, to make the voyage to Bali. Their books, both published in 1937, remain to this day the most celebrated of all that the island has inspired—*Island of Bali* (Covarrubias 1937) and *Liebe und Tod auf Bali*, translated into English as *Love and Death in Bali* (Baum 2011).

While the breasts of Balinese women undeniably constituted a major attraction to the island during that time, the text accompanying Krause's photographs gives us better idea of the European perception of Bali when the first tourists were beginning to arrive:

---

[32] Title of a novel by Édouard de Keyser (1933).

The inhabitants of Bali are beautiful and, incredible as it may seem, inconceivably beautiful. Anyone in Bali, sitting at the roadside or elsewhere, who takes the trouble just to look at what passes before him will begin to doubt the reality of what he sees. Everything is beautiful, perfectly beautiful—the bodies, the clothes, the gait, every posture, every movement. How is this beauty possible? How is this incredible harmony with their surrounding attained? The traveller's feet never grow weary, his eyes do not cease to be charmed as long as a lucky star lets him pass far from the dwellings of the officials, the European traders and the tourist industry whose sole preoccupation is to learn how to assimilate Bali as quickly as possible to the Moloch of civilisation (Krause 1988: 8–9).

This inconceivable beauty Bali owes primarily to its women: "Balinese women are beautiful, as beautiful as one can imagine, with a physiologically simple and dignified beauty, full of Eastern nobility and natural chastity" (Krause 1988: 55).[33] But it is also the charm emanating from a rich and happy country whose inhabitants have a genius for festive celebrations: "For these happy people, life on earth seems to be an almost uninterrupted festival, an ecstasy of overflowing joy in life and of gratitude and devotion to the Gods" (Krause 1988: 89). One understands how in such heavenly conditions our author comes to exclaim: "I [...] took it amiss of God that I was not born a Balinese" (Krause 1988: 69).

To read Gregor Krause, and especially to glance through his photographs, one would think that Bali had succeeded Tahiti as the ultimate image of South Sea Island glamour. This, indeed, was the opinion put forward by Miguel Covarrubias:

The remote little island only became news to the rest of the Western world with the advent, a few years ago, of a series of documentary films of Bali with a strong emphasis on sex appeal. These films were a revelation and now everybody knows that Balinese girls have beautiful bodies and that the islanders lead a musical-comedy sort of life full of weird, picturesque rites. The title of

---

[33] This seems far from the time when Elisée Reclus could write, in his *Nouvelle géographie universelle* which appeared in 1889: "The civilization of Bali displays great decadence... The use of opium, which is widespread among all the castes, the civil wars between provinces, the expeditions of slave traders, and finally the debasement of women, reduced to being nothing more than a piece of merchandise, are the causes of the backwardness of the Balinese civilization... In the mountainous regions, goiters are extremely common; in some districts more than half the population are afflicted with them, and one hardly finds a woman who is not deformed by these excrescences..." (*La civilisation de Bali témoigne d'une grande décadence... L'usage de l'opium, qui est répandu dans toutes les castes, les guerres civiles de province à province, les expéditions de marchands d'esclaves, enfin l'avilissement de la femme réduite à n'être plus qu'un objet de trafic, ont été les causes de ce recul de la civilisation balinaise... Dans les régions montagneuses, les goîtres sont extrêmement communs; en certains districts, plus de la moitié des habitants en sont affligés, et l'on ne rencontre presque pas de femmes qui ne soient déformées par ces excroissances ...*) (quoted in Lombard 1990, Vol.1: 48–50).

one of these films, *Goona-goona*, the Balinese term for 'magic', became at the time Newyorkese for sex allure. The newly discovered 'last paradise' became the contemporary substitute for the nineteenth-century romantic conception of primitive Utopia, until then the exclusive monopoly of Tahiti and other South Sea Islands (Covarrubias 1937: 391-2).

The Island of Artists[34]

Persuasive as it appears, however, Covarrubias's argument only partly conveys Bali's seduction. In any case, Margaret Mead challenged him on this, pointing out how much the image of Bali, elaborated during the 1930s, differed from that of the South Seas that prevailed in the 1920s. According to Mead, while the South Sea image crystallized the dreams of hedonistic idleness and erotic gratification of a West soured by war and its privations, the force of Bali's attraction lay, by contrast, in the obvious contentment its people found in a life entirely occupied with religious festivals, generating a profusion of art forms unknown elsewhere. And Mead concludes:

> Many Americans in the 1920s sought for an escape as single individuals from a society which denied them self-expression. Many in the 1930s sought for a formula by which we could build our society into a form which would make possible, on a firm economic base, both simple happiness and complexity of spiritual expression. Of such a dream, Bali was a fitting symbol (Mead 1970: 340).

By the early 1920s, Bali had found a place in the Western imagination thanks to the beauty of its women, but it had yet to find someone to communicate to the world the artistic creativity of the Balinese people and the profuse diversity of their island's cultural riches. That role would be played by the German painter and musician Walter Spies, who did more than anyone else to shape the image of Bali, not just as a tropical paradise, but as a land of art and culture, of mystery and spirituality (Rhodius and Darling 1980; Stowell 2011). It was, incidentally, after seeing the photographs of Gregor Krause that the young Spies left in 1923 for the Netherlands East Indies. In 1927, he established himself in Bali, at the invitation of Tjokorda Gde Raka Sukawati, the *punggawa* of Ubud, where he

---

[34] "[...] the Balinese are the greatest artists of this age, and still more, [...] every Balinese, man or woman, is an artist" (Roosevelt, in Powell 1930: X). For some interesting comments on the clichéd and romantic view that 'all Balinese are artists', see Kam (1993: 71-3).

built himself a house in Balinese style.[35] Thereafter, his reputation as a connoisseur of things Balinese made him sought after by artists, writers, anthropologists and other celebrities traveling in Bali, and his house in Ubud became a mandatory stop for visitors eager to distinguish themselves from the other tourists.[36]

Walter Spies thus acted as the key cultural broker for other Westerners visiting Bali, and indeed most of the foreigners who sojourned on the island during the 1930s acknowledged how much they owed to his competence and unselfish good will.[37] It was his first recordings of Balinese music that attracted to this island the Latvian-born American art historian Claire Holt (1967), as well as the Canadian composer Colin McPhee (1944, 1966) and his American wife, the anthropologist Jane Belo (1949, 1953, 1960, 1970); it was Spies who inspired the novelist Vicki Baum and who guided Miguel Covarrubias in his approach to Balinese society (Williams and Chong 2005); and it is to him that André Roosevelt, Victor von Plessen and Henry de la Falaise owe the enduring allure of their films *Goona-Goona* (1929), *Insel der Dämonen* (1931) and *Legong: Dance of the Virgins* (1935). But it was not enough for Walter Spies to share his fascination with Balinese culture and record its different manifestations. He is equally credited with the renaissance of Balinese arts that flourished during the 1930s (Stutterheim 1932a; Kats 1939).

Before the colonial conquest of Bali, the modern Western conception of art and of the artist expressing his own individual creativity was unknown among the Balinese. Rather than artists, it would be more appropriate to speak of master craftsmen working in the service of temples (*pura*) and palaces (*puri*), devoting their skills to celebrate their gods and their lords. With the collapse of the patronizing role held by the rajas, on the one hand, and with the growing numbers of foreign visitors, on the other, there occurred a shift in patronage. At the same time, the heavy taxes imposed by the colonial government, combined with the impoverishment engendered by the economic depression of the 1930s, fueled a

---

[35] Spies's house, which he eventually turned into a hotel for visitors attracted by his fame, served as a model for a reinterpretation of the Balinese architectural style intended for foreign expatriates that has thrived on the island ever since.

[36] "Thanks to Walter Spies—Bali is, for me, the island of a hundred dances, of magic, of trances—without him I would have been one of a thousand tourists" (excerpt from Walter Spies's guest book, 1938).

[37] Here is what Jane Belo wrote about Walter Spies in the introduction of the collective volume *Traditional Balinese Culture*: "Perhaps more than any one person in the period preceding World War II, he contributed to the knowledge and appreciation of Balinese culture in its many manifestations, by steeping himself in the lore of the people—their arts, their religion, their customs—and by taking up with great enthusiasm, combined with complete disregard for personal credit, the particular interest of foreign scholars or investigators who came to him for help" (Belo 1970: xvii).

need for cash incomes that prompted many Balinese to meet the tourist demand by making and selling works that did not have a ceremonial function, whether they be paintings, woodcarvings or dances.

Those famous dances which have become the iconic marker of Bali's touristic image could only be recognized as an art form after being detached from their performative context, the numerous ceremonies (*yadnya*) that punctuate everyday life: temple festivals, rites of passage, sacrifices, and so on. The dances performed in the course of a ceremony are at once an act of devotion (*ngayah*) for the dancers and a communal obligation for the members of the congregation responsible for organizing it. In this sense, it is not only a spectacle to be watched, but also—and in a way difficult to dissociate—a ritual to be enacted. This difficulty of differentiating ritual from spectacle was neatly expressed by Jane Belo, who observed that the Balinese view their dances as an offering, while they stage their presentation of offerings as a performance: "In Balinese culture no very sharp line was drawn between the performance of ritual and dramatics; any dramatic performance was in itself an offering to the gods, and the presumption was that the better the performance, the better the gods would be pleased" (Belo 1960: 115).

Furthermore, for Balinese dances to become a distinct artistic genre they had to be dissociated not only from ritual but also from theater. Indeed, just as there are no words in Balinese for 'art' or 'artist', neither are there for 'music', 'dance' or 'theater'. The terms in use for dancing and acting (*ngigel* or *masolah*, in low and high Balinese respectively), as well as for dancer and actor (*pragina*, meaning someone who beautifies), encompass the choreographic and dramatic aspects of a performance, which are not conceptually distinguished by the Balinese.[38] Thus, the first references to these topics in *Bhāwanāgara* had to resort to Dutch terms, such as *musiek*, *dans* and *tooneel*. Later on, Balinese authors turned to Malay/Indonesian terminology, which qualifies dance as an art form (*seni*) among others and differentiates between 'dance' (*seni tari*) and 'drama' (*seni drama*).

The decontextualization of Balinese dance, though achieved for their own use by the Balinese themselves, required the intercession of an external gaze: that is to say, in order for the Balinese to perceive their dances as an art form, these dances had to be recognized as such by non-Balinese (Picard 1996b; Hobart 2007). Specifically, Balinese dances acquired the prestige that they have today

---

[38] See the fitting comment by the American photographer, Philip Hanson Hiss: "It is almost impossible to separate dance from drama, or either from music, and all three are inextricably bound up with religion. In spite of this, each is highly specialized" (Hiss 1941: 61).

only after becoming a tourist attraction (Picard 1990). It is significant that the arrival of the first tourists in Bali in the 1920s followed soon after the artistic revolution of *kebyar*, a new musical style whose main consequence was to allow dance to be detached from its theatrical content as well as from its ritual context in order to be turned into an art form in its own right (Tenzer 2000). Once freed of the constraints which hindered its autonomous development, Balinese dance could be made accessible to spectators unfamiliar with the linguistic codes, dramaturgic conventions and literary references of the traditional theater. Above all, dance had to become autonomous before it could be treated as a product to be exploited at will for commercial ends. After the opening of the Bali Hotel in Denpasar in 1928, the management took the innovative step of organizing regular dance performances conceived specially for its clientele. So, when the Dutch government invited a troupe of Balinese dancers and musicians to perform at the Colonial Exposition in Paris in 1931, the performances destined for a foreign public were already well established.

The first article specifically dedicated to Balinese dances as an art form in its own right opened with these words: "Is there anybody in Europe who knows anything about the Balinese dances?" (De Kleen 1921: 127). It appeared in the *Sluyters' Monthly*, the first tourist magazine of the Netherlands Indies, and was written by Tyra de Kleen, a Swedish artist who had come to Bali in 1920 to study its 'sacred dances'. Seeking to convey to her readers—the would-be travelers to the island—the singular appeal of Balinese dances, she informed them that in Bali dance is closely bound to religion, as the Balinese are "a very religious people" (De Kleen 1921: 129). But unlike the Hindus in India, theirs is not a religion of asceticism and self-torture: "It is their aim, on the contrary, to make existence as agreeable as possible, and at their temple feasts they combine two good purposes, namely to please their gods and amuse themselves. I would even say that these two things are identical with the Balinese" (De Kleen 1921: 129). Tyra de Kleen elaborated in particular on two genres of dance, the *legong*[39] and the *calonarang*.[40] What is remarkable, reading her article a century later, is the

---

[39] Indisputably the most iconic of all Balinese dances, *legong* achieved its modern form in the early 20th century. Danced as a rule by prepubescent girls, it combines elements borrowed from different traditions: from *sanghyang dedari*, an ancient ritual dance executed by two young girls in trance; from *gambuh*, the prototype of all forms of Balinese dance theater, probably originating in Java (Bandem and deBoer 1978; Picard 1998); and from *nandir*, a dance for young boys. From *sanghyang* to *legong* by way of *gambuh* and *nandir*, one sees a movement toward the creation of a 'pure' dance, detached from all ritual function and all dramatic content, and refined for the pleasure of the senses. On the origins and evolution of *legong*, one may refer to Bandem (1983), Davies (2008), and Vickers (2009).

[40] *Calonarang* is a 19th-century dramatic enactment drawn from an ancient Javanese text of tantric magic that stages the ritual encounter between the masked figures of the 'witch' Rangda and the 'dragon' Barong, which are seen as

fact that, for all its inaccuracy and naivety, it immediately laid the foundations of the conceptual grid used later on—including by the Balinese themselves—to frame the perception and interpretation of the performing arts in Bali: first, the difficulty of distinguishing entertainment from ritual, of separating what the Balinese do to 'please their gods' and what they do to 'amuse themselves'; and second, the tension between the alluring image of the 'dancing girl' and the hideous sight of the 'witch', which has marked the image of the island ever since.

Thus, one encounters this conceptual framework in the first general presentation of Balinese dance and theater by Spies and Goris in 1937. Although acknowledging the inadequacy of Western principles of classification to the Balinese situation, the authors asserted that the best division of the subject was in two groups: "ceremonies, which one can describe as *sacred* dance or theater (including some processions) and *secular* dances (or theater)".[41] This article established the taxonomy of Balinese performing arts. Accordingly, the following year, De Zoete and Spies organized their comprehensive catalogue of dance and drama in Bali along the same lines. But this neat division between sacred and secular performances proved difficult to put into practice, as they found when they attempted their minute descriptions of specific dances. This is because, as they kept warning their readers, in Bali dance is organically integrated to the religious life of the community:

> We shall have to emphasize again and again in the course of this book the fact that all dancing in Bali is religious in the sense that it is connected with the temple and organic in the life of the village, which is inseparable from temple rites; for all dance in Bali is an offering, and acceptable at a feast for whatever purpose it may be celebrated (De Zoete and Spies 1938: 46).

While investigating Balinese dramatic traditions, Walter Spies and his circle of friends helped to revive the interest of the Balinese people for certain forms of performing arts that had fallen into disuse, and they also incited the creation of new compositions. But it is in the domain of painting and sculpture that Spies

---

manifestations of Durga and Siwa. Their confrontation is not a question of good versus evil, but rather an issue of power, as these masked figures are fundamentally ambivalent powers that are at once destructive and protective, in the sense that the Balinese perceive them as being simultaneously responsible for epidemics or other catastrophes and for their prevention. The masks that represent them are subjected to certain rites of consecration after which they become the receptacle of a supernatural power (*sakti*). In order for the ritual enactment to be efficacious, it is necessary for the dancer wearing the mask of Rangda to become possessed by the power of Durga. On Rangda and Barong, see Belo (1949, 1960), Rickner (1972), Emigh (1984), Geertz (1994), Stephen (2001), and Cerita and Foley (2022).

[41] "*Ceremoniën, die men het best als* sacralen *dans of tooneel kan omschrijven (inclusief sommige processies) en* saeculaire *dansen (of tooneel)*" (Spies and Goris 1937: 205).

was most influential. Assisted by the Dutch painter Rudolf Bonnet, who had arrived in Ubud in 1929 (De Roever-Bonnet 1993), he was instrumental in renewing both the techniques and the thematic content of the fine arts.[42] Under their influence, Balinese painters and sculptors put aside the constraints of iconographic conventions to start exploring the subjects of daily life, and they set about signing their work, becoming 'artists' aware of their personal creativity. In many ways, Spies and even more so Bonnet took over the traditional role as patrons of Balinese artists, which goes some way to explaining why they were so easily accepted by them. Above all, they turned the painters and sculptors into 'professional' artists by advising them to produce works meeting the demands of a foreign public and to be sold on the budding tourist market.

If they encouraged Balinese artists to work for the tourist market, Spies and Bonnet were conscious of the risks of commercialism and mass production, and they strove to consistently control the artistic quality of the works offered to tourists (Bonnet 1936). To achieve this goal, they first resorted to the Bali Museum—of which Spies was the honorary curator—where they exhibited contemporary artworks intended for sale to visitors. Thereafter, in 1936, they established in Ubud, under the aegis of Tjokorda Gde Raka Sukawati and his younger half-brother Tjokorda Gde Agung Sukawati, and with the famous artist I Gusti Nyoman Lempad (Carpenter 2014), an association dedicated to the promotion of the Balinese fine arts. Named Pita Maha (a Sanskrit term referring to Brahma, the 'God of Creation', and symbolizing the 'great ancestors' under whose spiritual authority its members placed themselves), this association brought together some 150 Balinese artists and remained active until the Japanese invasion.[43]

Other foreign artists settled in Bali during that time, among whom one should mention the American Maurice Sterne, the Austrian Roland Strasser, the Swiss Théo Meier (Meier 1975), the Belgian Adrien Jean Le Mayeur de Merprès (Ubbens and Huizing 1995), the Dutch Willem Hofker (Carpenter and Hofker-Rueter 1993), and the Slovak Arthur Fleischmann (Jansen 2007). But, unlike Spies and Bonnet, they did not exert much influence on the evolution of Balinese arts.[44]

---

[42] Actually, Spies was much less a teacher for the Balinese artists than Bonnet. Moreover, contrary to what has often been claimed, these foreign artists were not the initiators of a movement that had already started before their arrival in Bali (Couteau 1986).

[43] In 1938, the leaders of Pita Maha designed the project of a museum for contemporary Balinese fine arts, that would eventually open in Ubud in 1956, thanks to the joint efforts of Tjokorda Gde Agung Sukawati and Rudolf Bonnet, under the name of Puri Lukisan, Museum Kesenian Bali Modern (Couteau 1999a).

[44] On the evolution of Balinese arts, see e.g. Holt (1967), Ramseyer (1977), Moerdowo (1983), Kam (1993), Spruit (1995), Vickers (2012b), and Bakker (2018).

The Island of Gods and Demons

After the artists came the anthropologists, the most prominent among them being Jane Belo, Margaret Mead and her husband Gregory Bateson, as well as Katharane Mershon.[45] Strongly influenced by Walter Spies, they found in Bali an island where culture and nature converged in subtle correspondences, the cradle of a stable and harmonious society periodically agitated by spectacular rituals.[46]

Unlike the orientalists, when Mead and Bateson approached Bali in the wake of their work in New Guinea, they chose to deliberately overlook the Indic components of Balinese culture, as Mead explained in a letter written in 1938 to her mentor Franz Boas:

> I remember asking you once whether you thought it would be possible to work in Indonesia without an extensive knowledge of Indian religions, the high ones, and you said yes. It certainly provides an entirely different approach from that of scholars who approach everything in Bali from the standpoint of a knowledge of Hinduism and Buddhism and see every Balinese form as a degradation and very often miss the essence of it altogether (Mead 1977: 213).

Inspired by the theories of their colleague Ruth Benedict (1934), Bateson and Mead sought to discover how culture shaped the Balinese personality. In their book *Balinese Character* (1942), the patterned behavior of the Balinese literally embodies their culture, which is constitutive of their distinctive character or ethos.[47] They perceived the ritual and artistic effervescence of the Balinese as a symptom to be interpreted through the grid of a culturalist psychology. In particular, Margaret Mead asked the question 'why are the Balinese artists?': "What is the difference between the society in which the arts are an integral part of everyday life, enriching it and enhancing it, and the society in which the arts are almost wholly dispensed with?" (Mead 1970: 335). She looked for an answer

---

[45] The bibliography on the work of these anthropologists in Bali is extensive. See, e.g. Bateson and Mead (1942), Mead (1972, 1977), Belo (1949, 1953, 1960, 1970), Mershon (1971), Boon (1986), Jacknis (1988), Pollmann (1990), Geertz (1994), Hitchcock and Norris (1995), Sullivan (1999), and Ness (2008).

[46] While the influence exercised by Spies on the anthropologists is undeniable, it should be noted that there were divergences of interest, sensibility and method between Belo, on the one hand, and Mead and Bateson, on the other, and above all, between these anthropologists and artists such as Spies, Covarrubias and De Zoete. This is particularly illustrated by a series of photographs in which De Zoete mocks the ethnographic methods of Mead and Bateson (Hitchcock and Norris 1995: 63). For her part, Margaret Mead was not to be outdone, as in her memoirs she went as far as identifying Beryl de Zoete with the witch Rangda (Mead 1972: 231).

[47] In a lecture Margaret Mead gave at the American Museum of Natural History shortly after her return from Bali, in 1939, she presented her study of the Balinese culture in the following terms: "Bali is an extremely rich culture, rich in symbolic forms which may be studied in relation to the types of personality which they express on the one hand, and help to create on the other" (Mead 1939: 24).

in the need for symbolic activity, a need built up by the tensions and frustrations which mark the relationship between a Balinese child and his mother.[48] For these tensions his culture is ready 'with a dozen available answers': "If his culture has developed needs and desires which can never be satisfied on the simple biological level, it has also generously provided forms which meet these needs and give satisfactions of another order also" (Mead 1970: 338).

In Mead's view, Balinese culture became a mechanism for regulating impulses, leading to a kind of institutionalized dissociative behavior, related to schizophrenia: while the Balinese normally appear quiet and well-adjusted, on certain occasions they let themselves be carried away by paroxysms of frenzy that, however spectacular and violent, remain culturally codified. Through these periodic outbursts, which take place in a state of trance, they relieve themselves of the oppressive weight of an excessively strict social control on their daily existence. Following Spies, Mead and Belo borrowed Benedict's Nietzschean distinction between Apollonian and Dionysian configurations of culture (Benedict 1934) to characterize the Balinese ethos: "Their customary poise and moderation resembles the Apollonian, while the outbreak into trance, approved and recognized in the culture, is nearer to the Dionysian" (Belo 1960: 1). They projected these alternating states on to the contrasting images of the dancer and the witch: behind the nymph-like figure of the young *legong* dancer lurked the hideous shadow of the old witch Rangda. The 'Island of the Gods' was also the 'Island of Demons',[49] a place where illness and misfortune are caused by spiritual forces and cured by those who, through trance, can control them.

Like the tourists, the anthropologists were fascinated by possession trances, and particularly by the masked figures of Rangda and Barong. Jane Belo undertook a study of the diverse manifestations of trance in Bali, which also involved Mead, Bateson, Mershon and Spies (Belo 1949, 1960). Together, they commissioned performances of Rangda and Barong, for the sake of research as well as for the entertainment of distinguished visitors. Unlike ritual enactments, which are held at night, these performances were organized in the daytime so they could be photographed and filmed, while young beautiful women provided a welcome replacement for the withered old women who were the usual performers (Mead 1972: 231).

---

[48] Mead's interpretation has been the subject of a great deal of criticism, in particular by a Balinese psychiatrist and her American colleague (Jensen and Suryani 1992; Suryani and Jensen 1993; see also Hornbacher 2021).
[49] Title of a film by Victor von Plessen, made in Bali in 1931 with the assistance of Walter Spies, as well as of a novel by Johan Fabricius (1941).

During the 1930s, relying on the fascination of visitors for trance states[50] the Balinese started designing performances exploiting the spectacular character of ancient rites of possession (Picard 1990: 56–61). At first, most visitors were taken in by the performances they saw and would not think of questioning their authenticity. Occasionally, one encounters a condescending or horrified reprobation regarding the 'barbaric rites' of the natives.[51] But once authentic Balinese events started being staged, some foreign visitors wondered whether what they saw was a 'sacred rite' or a 'tourist imitation'.[52] The problem was that the demarcation line between theatrical and trance behavior proved extremely difficult to trace, as Jane Belo was keen to remind her readers: "In Bali, not only would the entranced behave as if they were acting, but the actor would behave almost as if he were in trance" (Belo 1960: 11).

By and large, the writings of the cultural anthropologists reinforced the Dutch government in its policy of cultural protectionism by confirming the idea that Balinese society had not really been affected by colonization (Bateson and Mead 1942: 262–3). To read them, it would seem that the Balinese were too busy celebrating their culture to be bothered by the presence of a foreign administration (Pollmann 1990). Thus, in the first letter Margaret Mead sent from Bali, in April 1936, she described Balinese life under the colonial government in these terms: "It is the most extraordinary combination of a relatively untouched native life going along smoothly and quietly in its old way with a kind of extraneous, external civilization superimposed like an extra nervous system put on the outside of a body" (Mead 1977: 160–1). She and her colleagues thus provided anthropology's stamp of authority to the impressions of serene harmony reported by the visitors of that time, their analyses of the stability of Balinese society never suggesting that this may be due to its occupation by a

---

[50] "People who know nothing else about Bali know that there are dances in which men in a state of ecstasy attack themselves with their krisses, that there are other dances in which little girls who are put into a state of trance by incense smoke and singing, perform feats of acrobatics of which they would not be capable in a normal condition. Trance states are to most people much more interesting than dance states, and they have hitherto absorbed a perhaps unfair amount of attention in books and films of Bali" (De Zoete and Spies 1938: 67).

[51] Here is an example, among many others, taken from a travel book by Helen Eva Yates: "A barbaric Balinese dance is that called the Ranga. [...] I had heard too much about it to care to see it. [...] At the height of their fanatic contortions, they are said to whip out small krises, or long pins and other instruments of torture. They gouge their flesh, pull their hair, and prick their bodies until the blood runs. Then the onlookers rush up and drink the blood— but this is too terrible even to tell. I only wish that I did not have to say it is true. Though strictly forbidden by Dutch authorities, these medieval customs are carried on to-day in Bali—behind closed doors, of course" (Yates 1933: 157).

[52] To my knowledge, the most articulate expression of the perplexity evinced by some travelers of those days is an article by Stella Benson, who, upon attending a so-called 'Kris Dance', declared: "I was prepared to be impressed either by a good show or by a storm of religious frenzy, but I wanted to know which I was witnessing" (Benson 1935: 266).

colonial power. It is precisely this forced peace—imposed by the Dutch armies on an island hitherto known more for the fierce character of its natives than for their docility—that would soon be considered an inherent trait of Balinese society. In short, it appeared that from the moment matters of government were appropriated by the Dutch, the Balinese had nothing else to do but busy themselves with art and religion, elaborating their expressive culture to their hearts' content.

A Lost Paradise?

Whether as a vivacious bare-breasted village girl, a dancer in a heavy gilded headdress, or a witch in a terrifying mask, Woman is the major metaphor of Bali. But one must be aware that the power of this metaphor lies in its equivocal nature and, more precisely, in its capacity to combine the mystery of Asia with the seductiveness of the Pacific—as if Balinese harmony resulted from a rare alliance between the fertility of a traditional culture and that of a primitive natural world. Indic in its ceremonies and Polynesian in its way of life, thus did the island of Bali appear to the early European visitors, and so it remains in travelers' tales and tourist brochures many years later.

Furthermore, if Bali lends itself so easily to lyrical effusion—what the anthropologist James Boon called a 'romance' (Boon 1977)—it is not only because of its festive abundance, but perhaps even more so because the harmony it evokes appears threatened. For at the same time that the chroniclers of the 1930s presented us with an image of Bali as a theater where the artistic and ritual extravagance of the inhabitants vies for splendor with the gorgeousness of its landscape, they never failed to emphasize the archaic character of Balinese society, which they described as a medieval relic, miraculously preserved from the corrupting outrages of modernity. Thus the fascination of Bali for visitors was heightened by fear of its imminent decline, as if the image it conjured was as evanescent as 'the dream of an opium eater': "Bali is too near Java for security from the blight of European ugliness that will fall upon it; it is now like the dream of an opium eater" (Clifton 1927: 130).

The earliest expression of this fear is due probably to Victor Emanuel Korn, who, though a colonial official, was rather critical of his government's policy. In an article published in 1925, where he deplored the damage caused by the Dutch administration and pleaded against the admission of Christian missionaries on the island, he asserted that it was their religion which endowed the Balinese people with their unique character, in that it was an integral part of their daily life. For this reason, their religion was the foundation of Balinese cultural integrity and the inspiration of their artistic expressions (Korn 1925).[53] This assertion was reiterated a few years later, in a more alarmist manner, by the archaeologist Willem Frederik Stutterheim: "Should the religious life of Bali deteriorate there will be no more temples built; no more statues will be carved; no more festivities held. With the waning of the religious belief the sources nourishing the creative artistic spirit would dry up" (Stutterheim 1932a: 8–9). And even the great art-lover Walter Spies sounded the alarm by warning that: "Bali's 'modern' youth with their semi-european school-wisdom are no longer in touch with their own classic art. Danger is imminent that the art of Bali as a whole is destined to degenerate" (Spies 1936: 58).

This apprehension of looming degeneration emerges from reading travelers' accounts published between the Wars, a recurring scenario padded with preconceptions and clichés that acquired the force of truth by sheer repetition. Thus it was that so many travelers were amazed and enchanted by their discovery of the 'real' face of Bali. Made mistrustful by so many unwarranted stories about so-called enchanting islands, they came to Bali warily, with a cynical skepticism that nonetheless bore a trace of hopefulness. One account among many, written at the end of the 1930s:

> Since the day Gauguin first showed Parisians his canvasses of Tahiti, no island of original civilization has excited the spirit of artists and intellectuals sated by Europe like that 'last paradise on earth' which we have known for three centuries by seductive descriptions, the island of Bali. Idealists, breaking all ties with their past, seek refuge in this 'island of dreams'. But alarming news has reached Europe of the utter sans-gêne of the hordes of tourists and the rapid decadence of Balinese 'authenticity'. Bali is finished, they say. It has become a fair-ground of souvenirs for globe-trotters. The 'last paradise' has become a victim of its own fame. With what prudent skepticism, then, did I arm myself when I set off![54]

---

[53] It is significant that Korn's position was sternly criticized by *Surya Kanta*'s editors, who accused him of seeking to maintain Bali in its conservatism (*kekolotan*) so as to turn the island into a spectacle (*tontonan*) for the tourists (*Surya Kanta* 1927, No. 5: 49).

[54] "*Depuis le jour où Gauguin montra pour la première fois aux Parisiens ses toiles de Tahiti, nulle île de civilisation originale n'a excité l'esprit des artistes et des intellectuels rassasiés de l'Europe comme ce 'dernier paradis sur terre' que l'on connaissait depuis trois siècles déjà par des descriptions séduisantes, l'île de Bali. Des idéalistes, toute amarre avec le passé rompue, cherchaient refuge dans cette 'île de rêve'. Mais des nouvelles alarmantes ne tardèrent pas à atteindre l'Europe au sujet du sans-gêne absolu dont témoignent les hordes de touristes et de la rapide décadence de 'l'authenticité' balinaise. Bali n'est plus, disait-on. Il a dû céder la place à une foire de*

As the tourists of the 1930s disembarked in Bali, their first impression—that of the port of Buleleng with its Chinese shops and roofs of corrugated tin—was inevitably disappointing, confirming in our visitors their fear of having fallen, yet again, into a tourist trap.[55] And then, rounding a hill, leaving the main coastal town behind them, they would be seized with rapture, convinced that the tourist slogans are true after all—Bali is indeed the paradise it is vaunted to be, and surely the last:

> In the last ten years this island has been written about, filmed, photographed, and gushed over to an extent which would justify nausea. I went there half-unwillingly, for I expected a complete 'bali-hoo', picturesque and faked to a Hollywood standard; I left wholly unwillingly, convinced that I had seen the nearest approach to Utopia that I am ever to see (Gorer 1936: 42–3).

The travelers' wonder was that much more precious because of their conviction that the Balinese idyll was extremely precarious, menaced by an invasion from the West of which tourism was not the least harmful form. It was as if, since the 'discovery' of the island by an avant-garde of travelers and artists during the 1920s, the very conjuring of the name of Bali suggested the imminence of a fatal fall from a Garden of Eden in which the Balinese could not expect to indulge indefinitely. Sooner or later, this 'last paradise' was condemned to become a 'lost paradise'. So confided Margaret Mead in a letter written in June 1936: "But there is not much hope for Bali ultimately because their social system is founded on religion and that is bound to crack before the Muslims, the Christians or the modern sceptics who worship industrialism" (Mead 1977: 172).[56]

Persuaded that they were the final spectators to witness the swan-song of an exceptionally creative culture, a few visitors tried to record what they discovered before it was too late. This was the case of Covarrubias in particular, who closed the introduction of his celebrated book with the following reflection:

---

souvenirs pour globe-trotters. Le 'dernier paradis' est devenu la victime de sa renommée. De quel prudent scepticisme ne m'étais-je pas armé lorsque j'en ai pris le chemin!" (Schuh 1954: 117).

[55] Here is how Hickman Powell described his arrival in Bali in 1928: "Buleleng. Corrugated iron roofs. Chinamen in white pyjamas. Bombay traders, lost tribe of burlesque show comedians, with their shirt tails hanging out. Sweat and mosquitoes. Tin cans, through all the East the worst malfeasance of the Standard Oil Company. Dutchmen in peaked official caps, with high-buttoned choking collars" (Powell 1930: 4). Let us recall that when Sylvain Lévi disembarked at the same port of Buleleng in that same year he believed for his part that he had discovered "a real Indian atmosphere" (Lévi 1933: ix).

[56] It would take a mere three months for Mead to give up the conviction expressed in her first letter from Bali, in which she affirmed her confidence in the Balinese people's cultural resilience: "Bali seems to have learned through a couple of thousand years of foreign influences just how to use and how to ignore those influences. Accustomed to an alien aristocracy, accustomed to successive waves of Hinduism, Buddhism and so on, they let what is alien flow over their heads" (Mead 1977: 161).

> The Balinese still retain their traditions and hold to their own manner of life, but they are only too willing to adopt every new idea, good or bad, brought into their island by merchants, tourists, unsuitable education, and missionaries. The only aim of this book, therefore, is to collect in one volume all that could be obtained from personal experience by an unscientific artist, of a living culture that is doomed to disappear under the merciless onslaught of modern commercialism and standardization (Covarrubias 1937: xxv).

Faced with the urgency of this threat, observers generally took one of two positions. The first is well represented by André Roosevelt, who was backed by American Express and Thomas Cook to develop the tourist market in Bali, although this did not deter him from suggesting measures to preserve the integrity of Balinese society and its culture:

> Having leisure, my friend Spies and I started a scheme which would tend to slow down the invading forces from the West and keep the Balinese in their happy, contented ways for a few decades longer. [...] We want to make of Bali a national or international park, with special laws to maintain it as such (Roosevelt, in Powell 1930: xiv–xvi).

A few years later, Miguel Covarrubias believed that it would be in vain to try to prevent Westernization, and in particular to try to restrict tourism, which he nonetheless deplored for its corrosive effects on Balinese culture:

> It would be futile to recommend measures to prevent the relentless march of Westernization; tourists cannot be kept out. [...] To advocate the unconditional preservation of their picturesque culture in the midst of modern civilization would be the equivalent of turning Bali into a living museum, putting the entire island into a glass case for the enjoyment of hordes of tourists (Covarrubias 1937: 402–3).

The controversy was echoed in the Tourist Bureau, whose spokesmen, since the installation of their representative in Singaraja in 1924, criticized the attitude of Western artists and writers who, having helped to popularize Bali by extolling the beauty of the land and the riches of its culture, nevertheless wanted to forbid tourist access to the island. Now that the curiosity of the West was aroused, it was too late to back-paddle. It was for the Balinese to decide their future, and all the colonial administration could do was to prepare them by affirming its respect for their traditions and way of life (Van der Kop 1924: 648–9).[57]

---

[57] In this regard, the promotional literature never missed an opportunity to praise the colonial administration, which in its great wisdom had resolved to let the Balinese live their life as they wished—as witnessed by this passage from a booklet published by the Tourist Bureau: "With characteristic insight into the requirements of the situation the

The tour operators were more cynical. While they paid lip service to the enlightened paternalism of the colonial authorities, they used the argument of the imminent degradation of Bali to incite visitors to hurry and come before it was too late. A look at the tourism brochures published in the 1930s is revealing. One, entitled *Bali: The Enchanted Isle*, after assuring readers that Bali was not yet ruined by modernism and that "as yet it has not been invaded by hordes of ordinary tourists", warns them that "who knows—in another ten years, it may be spoiled by that insidious modernism". And the unsurprising conclusion follows, urging the elitist clientele to which the pamphlet is addressed, "Oh, do not wait too long to visit this extraordinary island" (Yates n.d.).

As for the colonial authorities, their attitude in regard to tourism showed a certain ambivalence. Convinced of the vulnerability of Balinese culture, the Dutch administrators tried to save it from the irreparable degradation that threatened it. Now, among the perils lying in wait for the Balinese and their culture, the most insidious was none other than the tourists themselves.[58] So that, if the decision to conserve Bali as a living museum represented the best asset for tourism promotion of the island, it required some counter-measure to preserve the Balinese cultural heritage from the harmful influences propagated by the tourists. Thus the authorities, who had already kept the Balinese from missionaries and traders, tried as well to protect them from any contact with tourists that might, in their eyes, be corrupting, in an attempt to control a quasi-monopoly on the tourism industry and to dissuade foreigners from settling in the villages.

Judging by the exemplary status that Bali soon acquired in travel literature, it seems that they were fairly successful. The French travel writer Alain Gerbault, deploring what had become of the islands of the Pacific, referred to the enviable lot of Bali: "I would have liked to make of Porapora a kind of Pacific Bali, for I have read a book about this island where the arts and indigenous customs are preserved, where tourists come but are not allowed to stay."[59]

Netherlanders have decided to rule Bali with as light a hand as possible. There was hardly any need to change the customs of the country, which lacked most of the abuses that had crept with time into the Hinduism of India. Here and there an innovation was brought about, an improvement in this direction, the removal of some abuse in that, mostly with the cooperation of the Princes and Priests of Bali, but as far as possible the Balinese have been left to themselves to live out their quiet lives in their own way" (Travellers Official Information Bureau, 1935: 3).

[58] This problem was already apparent to observers of the time, as may be seen in an article entitled 'Tourists in Bali' which opens: "The Dutch Government is trying to keep the island of Bali free of modern influences—an impossible task. Missionaries are excluded to be sure—but tourists are admitted—and tourists bring to bear the most insidious modern influence of all" (Benson 1935: 261).

[59] "*J'aurais voulu faire de Porapora une sorte de Bali du Pacifique car j'avais lu un livre sur cette île où les arts et les coutumes indigènes sont préservés, où les touristes viennent mais n'ont pas le droit de séjourner*" (Gerbault 1941: 216).

So it was that from Krause to Covarrubias, through Goris, Spies, Belo, and Mead and Bateson, 'culture' became the brand image of Bali, the chosen common ground where the views of Dutch orientalists and American anthropologists, the artists and tourists converged. Together, they originated and promoted the image of a traditional culture exceptionally prolific, still alive but ever more threatened by the growing pressure of the subversive forces of modernity. By doing so, they initiated a discourse of authenticity and corruption, of purity and pollution, reflecting a constant concern for protecting the Balinese culture against the perils it was facing. As Mark Hobart remarked, this image was deeply paradoxical: "It was a fragile culture centred on an organic unity of artistic creativity, dance and religion which needed preserving from excessive contact with the outside world, but which (with scant recognition of the irony and contradictions) people out to rush to experience in their millions (before it was too late)" (Hobart 2015: 18).

Now, while the Balinese people had clearly not been in control of the foundational identity upon which their island's tourism image was built, it would not be long before this image would establish itself not only in the tourists' imagination but also in the Balinese consciousness. In this respect, it remains to be seen to what extent this imaginary construction of their culture by foreigners has become part of their own views. This is a question that I will pursue when I address the development of international tourism in Bali from the 1970s onward.

Chapter 4

The Balinese Religion in Question

Bali Darma Laksana (1936–42)

While *Bhāwanāgara*'s orientalist perspective was manifest, and while most of its articles were of a didactic nature, some occasional contributions addressed topical issues, which reveals that the progressive aspirations borne by Surya Kanta had not disappeared from Balinese concerns.[1] As it happened, with the economic depression hitting Bali in the 1930s, the situation was alarming. No longer having the resources to pay the land taxes to the colonial government, Balinese peasants were becoming heavily indebted, which resulted in their rapid pauperization with a high incidence of landlessness (Robinson 1995: 54–9). In various articles, we encounter such terms as *jaman malaise* ('the era of malaise'), *jaman meleset* ('the era of depression'), or else *jaman keparat* ('the cursed era'). In these dire times, children deserted the classrooms, as parents could no longer pay the cost of their schooling. And yet education—for girls as well as for boys— was deemed more necessary than ever, and several authors deplored the insufficient number of schools on the island, the lack of scholarships, and the low levels of literacy among the Balinese population, still lagging behind in education compared to other peoples in the Indies.[2]

---

[1] In December 1931, an editorial reported that readers were demanding articles on modern topics: "Frequently, we hear from different quarters that, other than articles on tradition and religion, very seldom does *Bhāwanāgara* contain articles on matters somewhat more modern" (*Saban-saban kami dengar dari beberapa pihak, bahwa lain dari pada karangan tentang adat dan agama, Bhāwanāgara jarang sekali memuat karangan tentang sesuatu perkara yang agak lebih modern keadannya*). In response, it was said that the journal had yet to receive contributions on modern topics, which were called for with the following caveat: "[...] unless we consider that in this day and age such contributions might be harmful for the societies of Bali and Lombok" ([...] *kecuali kalau karangan itu atas mupakat kami untuk jaman ini masih berbahaya bagi maatschappij Bali-Lombok*) (*Bhāwanāgara* 1931, No. 7: 97).

[2] Between 1929 and 1940, the number of public primary schools in Bali rose from 140 to 324, while the number of pupils increased from 15,160 to 29,850 (Budharta et al. 1986: 75), for an overall population of 1,100,000 inhabitants

Particularly noteworthy are a series of articles written by the former vice-president of the Singaraja section of Surya Kanta, I Nyoman Mas Wirjasutha, a former *triwangsa* who had lost his title Gusti. Immediately upon becoming a member of Bhāwanāgara's editorial board, in June 1932, he published a brief programmatic article with a title taken from Multatuli[3]—*Er valt nog veel te arbeiden in ons land...* ("There is still much work to be done in our country...")— in which he called the Balinese people to work on the reforms required by the progress of the times. What's more, he took great care to underscore that Bali was part of Indonesia, a subversive view in those days and still uncommon among the Balinese.[4] The forceful, if not frankly polemical, tone of Wirjasutha's contributions, coming straight from *Surya Kanta*, appears somehow out of place in *Bhāwanāgara* and might go some way to explaining why his name disappeared from the editorial board in November 1933. Whatever the case, the discordant voices of Wirjasutha and a few others make it clear that the concerns raised in *Surya Kanta* had been stifled neither by repression nor by Balinization. They would soon re-emerge with the rise of a new Balinese organization, Bali Darma Laksana (BDL).

I will first focus on the periodical published by this organization— *Djatajoe*—with a view to investigating the debates among the Balinese

---

according to the 1930 census. Despite repeated requests from progressive Balinese elites to open more schools, the colonial government appeared reluctant to further develop education on the island, for fear that if graduates were unable to secure employment commensurate with their educational qualifications they might become discontented and swell the ranks of troublemakers. Be that as it may, numerous private schools were opened by local initiatives, including in particular the Taman Siswa schools based on the principles of traditional Javanese pedagogy, founded by Ki Hadjar Dewantara in Yogyakarta in 1924 and established in Bali in 1933 (McVey 1967; Tsuchiya 1987; Djuana 1987).

[3] Eduard Douwes Dekker, better known by his pen name Multatuli (from Latin *multa tuli*, 'I have suffered much'), was a Dutch writer famous for his critical novel *Max Havelaar*, published in 1860, which denounced the abuses of colonialism in the Dutch East Indies.

[4] "I call on all the inhabitants of Bali and Lombok, particularly the intellectuals, to contribute to the progress of Bali and Lombok, which are parts of Indonesia, by demanding as much as possible the changes and the progress of the times in good faith (Editor's note: proper, in compliance with the country's laws). Indeed, we must truly investigate the regulations that we should strengthen and those that we should change or improve. If we do not do so, surely we would lag behind and perhaps our country might be sold off as bygone and no longer attractive. [...] First we must address the problems which stand in opposition with our modern times, such as: the rights of women, of villages or wards, of marriage, the judicial system, the heritage, etc." (*Saya berseru kepada sekalian penduduk Bali dan Lombok teristimewa kepada intellectueelnya untuk turut bekerja mencapai kemajuan Bali dan Lombok, yang juga ada didalam lingkungan Indonesia, sedapat-dapatnya menuntut perobahan dan kemajuan jaman dengan jalan yang loyaal (Noot Red: patut, menurut undang-undang negeri). Bahwa sanya kita harus selidiki betul-betul aturan-aturan manakah kita patut teguhkan atau aturan-aturan manakah yang kita patut robah atau perbaiki. Jikalau kita tidak berhaluan begitu, pastilah kita akan tinggal terbelakang dan boleh jadi keadaan negeri kita boleh dijual-obral oleh sebab sudah tua dan tidak laku lagi. [...] Terlebih dulu haruslah kita mempelajari soal-soal yang agaknya sangat bertentangan dengan keadaan jaman modern ini, umpama: perkara hak-hak perempuan, hak-hak désa atau banjar, hak-hak perkawinan, rechtswezen (keadaan hukum), erfrecht (waris mewarisi), dan lain-lainnya lagi*) (*Bhāwanāgara* 1932, No. 3: 44).

intelligentsia regarding their religious identity in the aftermath of the controversy between orientalists and missionaries. Then I will assess the extent to which a nationalist spirit was rising on the island in the late colonial period. In doing so, I intend to dissociate myself from those postcolonial studies inspired by the critique of Orientalism, which leave the Balinese no other choice than to misconstrue the effects of their subjection as their own cultural traditions or to revolt against their oppression by endorsing the political agenda of Indonesian nationalism.

A social and cultural monthly journal: *Djatajoe* (1936-41)

On July 14, 1935, a few weeks after the last issue of *Bhāwanāgara* was published, the educational association Eka Laksana[5] was founded in Denpasar by I Ktut Subrata in order to "study and if possible advance the culture and arts in Bali and Lombok" (*mempelajari dan jikalau dapat memajukan cultuur dan kunst di Bali dan Lombok*) (*Djatajoe* 1937, No. 6: 153). The preamble of its statutes raised the fear that Balinese youths educated in colonial schools were becoming estranged from their own culture, with the risk of widening the gap between generations. To remedy this unfortunate situation, Eka Laksana advocated the study of traditional Balinese literature (*dengan kalimat 'mempelajari cultuur di Bali' kami maksudkan: mempelajari kebudayaan itu dari kitab-kitab dan lontar-lontar*) (*Djatajoe* 1937, No. 6: 153). In this regard, the new association was fully in line with the views of the Kirtya and of the Balinization policy.

On March 22, 1936, on the initiative of I Gusti Gde Rake, I Wayan Bhadra and I Nyoman Kadjeng,[6] an association called Balisch Studiefonds was established in Singaraja for the purpose of providing scholarships to needy Balinese pupils and students. Shortly thereafter, on July 26, 1936, Balisch Studiefonds merged with Eka Laksana in Singaraja to give rise to Bali Darma

---

[5] From Sanskrit *eka* ('one, united') and *lakshana* ('symbol, attribute, name, cause, action, behavior, way, spirit'). In Old Javanese, *laksana* is glossed as both 'mark, sign' and 'action, doing' (Zoetmulder 1982: 958).
[6] I Gusti Gde Rake belonged to a minor branch of the royal house of Mengwi, which had been defeated in 1891 in an armed conflict by a coalition led by Klungkung. After secondary education in Java, he became general collector of taxes in the residency office in Singaraja, where he petitioned in vain the colonial government for Mengwi's restoration (Schulte Nordholt 1996: 319-22). I Wayan Bhadra and I Nyoman Kadjeng were both working at the Kirtya. After his replacement as librarian by Bhadra in 1932, Kadjeng became the Buleleng representative on the board of curators.

Laksana,[7] which carried out the respective objectives of each association, namely, to provide basic education to the Balinese people while promoting the Balinese culture (*a) mengadakan studiefonds; b) berusaha mempertinggi kemajuan kebudayaan Bali*). A month later, on August 25, 1936, Bali Darma Laksana published the first issue of *Djatajoe* ('The Messenger'),[8] a 32-page 'social and cultural monthly journal' (*Surat bulanan sosial dan cultureel*).

Bali Darma Laksana is undoubtedly the most important Balinese organization of the colonial period. This is where the intellectual and political elite was formed that would lead post-independence Bali. Its founding fathers readily displayed their ambition to unify all Balinese, including those established outside their island, and they placed the association under the patronage of the eight *negara-bestuurders*, who acted as its 'protectors' (*pelindung*). It is also the association that pushed the degree of formal organization furthest, complete with an elected executive committee, written statutes, rules of procedure, annual congresses, subscription fees, financial reports, head office, regional chapters, local correspondents, and membership-registration records. Presided over by I Gusti Gde Rake, Bali Darma Laksana's executive committee consisted of a vice-president, two secretaries, one treasurer, and four assistants. After serving three terms, I Gusti Gde Rake gave up Bali Darma Laksana's chairmanship in 1939, due to his transfer to Denpasar for professional reasons. He was replaced by the vice-president, I Nyoman Kadjeng.

The membership register was regularly kept up to date and published at the time of the annual congresses of the association, held in July. From 147 members at its founding, Bali Darma Laksana's membership increased to 548 in 1937 and up to 713 in 1938, after which it decreased to 591 in 1939 and to 495 in 1940. It appears that after initial enthusiasm, the defections that occurred from 1938 onwards were due not only to a growing indifference in the association but also to financial considerations, judging by the repeated reminders issued to members to pay their subscription fee. As specified by the nominative lists published in

---

[7] The name of the association was glossed in the following manner: 'Bali *Darma* (duty) *Laksana* (the proper way)' (*Bali Darma (kewajiban) Laksana (perjalanan yang patut)*). Anak Agung Made Djelantik, a son of the *negara-bestuurder* of Karangasem, recounts in his memoirs that during his school days in Malang, in 1932, he founded with his friends a small club of Balinese students called Bali Dharma Laksana (Djelantik 1997: 70). Unlike Henk Schulte Nordholt and Adrian Vickers, who infer that the eponymous association traces its beginning from this initiative, my reading of contemporary documents suggests that it is more likely a case of homonymy (Vickers 2000: 95 and 109, n. 11; see also Putra 2011: 37).

[8] Jatayu is the name of a fabulous bird from Hindu mythology. As an ally of Rama in the *Ramayana*, he attempted to prevent Ravana from abducting Sita. Even when he was fatally injured, he managed to tell Rama where his consort had been carried away by the *raksasa*. Jatayu symbolizes at once the faithful messenger and self-sacrifice in the performance of one's duty.

Djatajoe, most of the members of Bali Darma Laksana—both *jaba* and *triwangsa*—held positions in the colonial administration as well as in the educational system. They were divided into some fifteen regional chapters, some of which were located outside Bali: namely, Mataram (Lombok), Surabaya, Malang, Yogyakarta, and Makassar. The executive committee manifested a constant concern to strengthen solidarity among members by enhancing the signs of affiliation: besides the monthly journal, Bali Darma Laksana published a calendar and produced a badge as well as a banner. Moreover, its leaders established collaborations with most of the other Balinese organizations of the time.[9] Already in decline by the late 1930s, Bali Darma Laksana was weakened further by the invasion of the Netherlands in May 1940, and it was finally dissolved after the landing of Japanese troops on Bali in February 1942. Meanwhile, *Djatajoe* had already ceased publication in August 1941.

Initially edited by I Gusti Nyoman Pandji Tisna,[10] after July 1937 *Djatajoe* was jointly edited by I Gde Panetje and I Wayan Bhadra. The editorial board welcomed contributions in three languages: Malay (more often than not now called Indonesian), Balinese and Dutch. Most of *Djatajoe*'s articles were written in Malay, despite encouragement to publish in Balinese for contributors who feared they might not be sufficiently fluent in Malay. One even encounters some occasional comments lamenting that young, educated Balinese have a better command of Dutch than of Malay. In any case, in organizational matters, the Dutch language was prevalent, generally accompanied by a Malay translation. With a view to enlightening its readership, *Djatajoe* published a Dutch–Malay glossary.

The fact is that the question of language had become a more sensitive issue for the Balinese than ever before, due in particular to the connection of Malay-Indonesian with the nationalist movement in gestation (Liem 2003; Putra 2011).

---

[9] This was in particular the case of educational associations such as Puteri Bali Sadar, founded in October 1936 in Denpasar to promote girls' education; Perkumpulan Guru-Guru Denpasar and Perkumpulan Guru-Guru Bumiputra Bali Lombok di Singaraja, which brought together teachers from both these towns; as well as the student association Persatuan Pemuda Bali Lombok, established in Surabaya in December 1938.

[10] I Gusti Nyoman Pandji Tisna was the eldest son of I Gusti Putu Djlantik, the *negara-bestuurder* of Buleleng. Brought up in a rather cosmopolitan fashion, after graduating from the HIS in Singaraja, he continued his studies in Batavia and Surabaya where he learned English, and later he studied Sanskrit with Goris. He developed more progressive views than his father and became the first Balinese author to write novels and poetry in Malay. His first novels were published in the 1930s by Balai Pustaka, the renowned colonial publishing house in Batavia, and his poems appeared in the literary journal *Poedjangga Baroe* ('The New Writers') (Sutherland 1968; Liem 2003: 167–78). After his father's death in 1944, he reluctantly replaced him and in February 1947 he was even elected chairman of the Balinese Council of Rajas (Dewan Raja-Raja), established by the Dutch after the surrender of Japan. However, in November of the same year, he resigned as chairman of the Dewan Raja-Raja and abdicated as raja of Buleleng in favor of his younger brother. Pandji Tisna's decision was probably due both to his secret conversion to Christianity in 1945 and to his growing support for Indonesian independence (Caldwell 1985).

Thus, during Bali Darma Laksana's second congress, held in July 1938 in Denpasar, I Gusti Bagus Sugriwa[11] deplored that educated Balinese, particularly those studying outside the island, neglected their own language in favor of Malay, or even Dutch. Invited to give a lecture on the Balinese religion to the congress, Sugriwa refused to do it in Malay as requested, arguing that it was not possible to speak of one's own culture in a foreign language.[12] This stance brought him a scathing retort from a certain Si Tjilik ('The Little One'), who reminded Sugriwa that if the Balinese preferred to hold their meetings in Malay rather than in Balinese, it was precisely to avoid having to comply with the deferential attitude that sanctions hierarchical distinctions.[13]

In truth, despite—or perhaps we should say due to—Bali Darma Laksana's all-embracing aspirations, differences of opinions abounded among its members. It was as if the debate between *Surya Kanta* and *Bali Adnjana*, momentarily defused by *Bhāwanāgara*, had reappeared a decade later within *Djatajoe*,[14] although admittedly somewhat tempered. This is not surprising, as in reading *Djatajoe* we come across the names of former contributors to these different publications, spanning the whole gamut of Balinese opinion leaders, from the most conservative, such as I Gusti Tjakra Tanaya and Tjokorda Gde Raka Sukawati, to the most radical, such as I Nyoman Mas Wirjasutha and I Nengah Metra,[15] not to mention several Dutch administrators. And indeed, in *Djatajoe*'s

---

[11] I Gusti Bagus Sugriwa, a prolific author born into a literate family, received a traditional Balinese education and was trained to become a schoolteacher in Bali, unlike many of his colleagues of Bali Darma Laksana who pursued secondary education in Java. Holding rather conservative views regarding culture and religion, he became a prominent nationalist during the struggle for independence and then occupied key political positions on the island (Sugriwa 1973).

[12] "*Jika membicarakan soal agama kita Bali memakai bahasa Melayu, saya rasa kurang eloknya pada congres yang berhaluan mempelajari cultuur Bali*" (*Djatajoe* 1938, No. 1: 30).

[13] "*Apabila memakai bahasa Bali, kurang leluasa, karena, mesti memakai tata, gerak tangan, metetanganan, ngelog, nyakupang tangan dan sebagainya. Jika berkata kepada orang-orang bangsawan, harus memakai bahasa ratu, singgih Pranda, anak agung, linggih I Gusti dll. Jika bahasa Melayu cukup dengan perkataan tuan sahaja dalam Vergadering-vergadering*" (*Djatajoe* 1938, No. 3–4: 127).

[14] With the exception, however, of the conflict between *jaba* and *triwangsa*, which was far from being resolved—it will re-emerge after independence and remains pending to this day—but was merely shelved in the name of Balinese unity. And while *Surya Kanta* had been accused by *Bali Adnjana* of dividing the Balinese people by attacking the caste hierarchy, one of its former leaders, I Nyoman Mas Wirjasutha, self-published in 1939, after the restoration of kingship by the colonial state, a leaflet entitled *Tjatoer Wangse di Bali* ('The Four Castes in Bali'), in which he castigated the caste system and advocated its abolition on the grounds that it stood in the way of "the national unity of the Balinese people" (*yang menjadi rem untuk mencapai persatuan nasional rakyat Bali*) (Wirjasutha n.d.: 31). Wirjasutha's leaflet was swiftly banned by the colonial authorities (Schulte Nordholt 2000).

[15] I Nengah Metra, a teacher at the HIS in Singaraja, had been one of Surya Kanta's founders. He had been exiled (*kaselong*) twice to Lombok by the colonial government, first in 1927, for having married a *brahmana*, then in 1934, for attempting to become Bali's representative to the Volksraad in Batavia, in the place of Tjokorda Gde Raka Sukawati. During his second exile, he established a chapter of Bali Darma Laksana in Mataram. An ardent

articles one encounters both *Surya Kanta*'s yearning for progress and emancipation, and a defense and illustration of Balinese culture in the manner of *Bali Adnjana* and *Bhāwanāgara*.

As an example, I cite the opinion of a member of Bali Darma Laksana regarding the contents of *Djatajoe*:

> Honorable Sir! Could not our *Djatajoe* change its attitude (which gives priority to matters that are irrelevant to our times), such as the *Ramayana*, *Baratayuda*, *Bagawan Inderaloka* and others, that it is of no interest to explain once again, since many people already know them, and other old stories, which should only serve to ornament museums. And in case a change is possible, in which direction should it go? Most of us want a new kind of information, to tread a new world. In case no change is possible, in my opinion, our *Djatajoe* could not survive as nowadays young people take no interest in these inappropriate ways.[16]

To which I Gusti Gde Rake countered that the education Balinese receive at school is 'Western' (*Westersch*), whereas *Djatajoe* aspires to provide them with an 'Eastern' (*Oostersch*) education. He concluded by warning:

> [...] our young people who don't have the opportunity to pay attention to their culture sooner or later will become strangers to their own culture. It is this cultural alienation that always provokes the divorce between the youth and their elders. Our young people have to know their culture, in order to be able to distinguish between good and bad, thereby fully appreciating what is regarded as good.[17]

This concern with culture and education on the part of Bali Darma Laksana's leadership had become all the more pressing as the economic crisis was being felt on the island, dampening somewhat the passion for progress and the confidence in the future which animated Surya Kanta. Indeed, while

---

supporter of the nationalist cause, Metra was killed in 1946 in fighting against the return of Dutch colonial soldiers (Vickers 2000).

[16] "*Meneer yth! Apakah Djatajoe kita ta' dapat akan mengubah sifatnya dari keadaanya yang sekarang (yang mementingkan lebih banyak hal hal yang ta' mencocoki dengan keadaan zaman), sebagai Ramayana, Baratayuda, Bagawan Inderaloka d.s.b. itu, yang sama sekali ta' ada gunanya diterangkan lagi, sebab toch telah banyak orang yang mengenalnya, dan ceritera kuno-kuno, yang seharusnya untuk memperhias kebagusannya meseum belaka. Dan kalau dapat diubah, dengan jalan bagaimana? Kami kebanyakan ingin penerangan secara baru, untuk menginjak dunia baru. Ande kata ta' dapat di ubah, pada hemat saya, Djatajoe kita ta' dapat akan hidup terus sebab pemuda-pemuda sekarang bukan mementingkan cara yang bukan-bukan itu*" (*Djatajoe* 1937, No. 6: 151).

[17] "[...] *pemuda-pemuda kita yang ta' mendapat kesempatan akan memperhatikan cultuurnya lambat laun menjadi asing terhadap kebudayaannya sendiri. Keasingan pada cultuur sendiri inilah, yang acap kali juga membangkitkan perceraian diantara fihak satu (dari pemuda2) sama lain (golongan yang lebih dewasa). Pemuda2 kita perlu mengenal cultuurnya, agar dapat membeda-bedakan baik buruknya, sehingga dapat menghargai mana yang terpandang baik dengan sepenuh-penuhnja*" (*Djatajoe* 1937, No. 6: 152).

acknowledging the disruptions brought to Bali by its forced opening up to the world, without, however, minimizing the importance of Western knowledge for the Balinese people, quite a few articles in *Djatajoe*—such as one in particular by Gde Panetje—urged the Balinese youths pursuing higher education in Java to learn about their culture "so as to be able to defend themselves against the assaults of another culture" (*sehingga dapat mempertahankan dirinya terhadap kepada serangan cultuur lain*) (Gde Panetje, *Djatajoe* 1937, No. 1: 10). Unfortunately, he said, young Balinese who were cut off from their cultural milieu "were not yet aware of the beauty of our culture, so that they did not yet feel a passionate love for their culture" (*belum mengarti dan merasai betapa baiknya cultuur kita, hingga belum timbul cinta yang hebat kepada kebudayaannya*) (Gde Panetje, *Djatajoe* 1937, No. 1: 11).

While Balinese youths faced the risk of forgetting their own culture, tourists were coming from all over the world to admire Bali's cultural traditions, which should make the Balinese proud of their unique culture.[18] Regrettably, as the island of Bali was becoming ever more famous, with tourists coming in ever greater numbers, the visitors were no longer the same as those of a bygone era, who were in search of the Hindu heritage nurtured in Bali after Java had surrendered to Islam. Nowadays, tourists were just looking for exoticism and entertainment, they had no real appreciation of what they saw on the island.[19] Worse, they were taking photographs of bare-breasted Balinese women, which was an offence to their sense of decency. In this day and age, Balinese women should learn to cover themselves up and no longer expose their breasts to the concupiscence of foreign visitors. To address this unacceptable situation, the Singaraja delegates to the second congress of Bali Darma Laksana, in July 1938, requested the prohibition against photographing and filming bare-breasted Balinese women.

In order to ensure that Balinese youths did not forget their own culture, they had to be 'Balinized', which was precisely the aim of the *Baliseering* colonial

---

[18] "[...] we the Balinese people—who have for centuries possessed a well-organized civilization, a culture that occupies an exceptional position, which can be said to stand out and to differ from the culture of other peoples" ([...] *kita bangsa Bali—yang sudah sejak berabad-abad mempunyai sesuatu peradaban yang teratur, sesuatu cultuur yang mengambil kedudukan teristimewa, yang dapat dikatakan berdiri dan berbeda dari pada kebudayaan bangsa lain*) (I Gusti Gde Rake, *Djatajoe* 1939, No. 10: 309).

[19] "*Mula-mula orang datang di pulau Bali kita, kebanyakan untuk mempelajari soal-soal yang berhubungan dengan agama, adat, babad enz. yang dibandingkannya dengan keadaan ditanah Hindu dan tanah Jawa sebelum didatangi oleh igama Islam.* [...] *Makin lama makin bertambahlah masyhurnya pulau kita, tourist-tourist yang mengunjunginya dari antero duniapun makin banyak bilangannya. Akan tetapi sayang sekali bahwa tamu-tamu yang sekarang ini banyak berbeda dengan mereka di waktu dahulu kala. Betul ia memujikan keadaan yang aneh yang dilihatnya, akan tetapi kebanyakan tiada bisa menghargainya, hanya dianggapnya sebagai tontonan sahaja, serta tiada diperhatikannya*" (*Djatajoe* 1938, No. 6: 185–6).

policy promoted by Hendrik te Flierhaar, the headmaster of the Siladarma school in Klungkung, regarded as a 'patron' (*darmawan*) of Bali Darma Laksana. Several articles in *Djatajoe* dealt with this topic, including in particular a two-part piece entitled *Disekitar 'Baliseering'* ('Around 'Balinization'') (*Djatajoe* 1939, No. 5: 145–9; 1940, No. 7: 214–17). It is significant that the author felt compelled from the outset to dispel some misinterpretations regarding the purpose of *Baliseering*: "So it would be completely wrong [...] to think that the aim of '*Baliseering*' is not only to maintain our culture the way it was in olden times but even to forbid us to learn about the culture of other peoples."[20] The truth, he explained, is that *Baliseering* intends to guarantee that educated Balinese do not become cut off from their cultural roots as a result of inappropriate education. In consequence, "the present education should be changed, so as to be in accordance with the situation in our society. [...] That which becomes the measure of a people is its culture, that is, an expanding feeling of nationality which is characterized by: its arts, its literature and its spiritual advancement."[21] It should be mentioned that this article provoked a rejoinder, whose author argued that it was time for the Balinese to envision themselves as being an integral part of Indonesia instead of remaining shackled by their own culture. Clearly, the *Baliseering* policy did not meet with unanimous approval among the Balinese intelligentsia. On the other hand, it was probably not as contentious as a politically correct postcolonial reading would like us to believe (Pollmann 1990: 15–17; Gouda 1995: 89–94).

In any event, while some Balinese intellectuals were beginning to heed the call of the Indonesian national awakening, reading *Djatajoe* it appears that for a significant majority the 'feeling of nationality' (*perasaan kebangsaan*) was confined to their own island, their main concern being to preserve their culture and their religion, as will be seen below.

---

[20] "*Jadi salah benar kalau orang [...] mengertikan soal bahwa dengan adanya maksud 'Baliseering' itu, kita bukan saja harus menjaga kebudayaan kita supaya tetap sebagai zaman purba (ta' ada perobahan) akan tetapi kita ta' boleh pula mempelajari atau mengetahui kebudayaan bangsa lain*" (*Djatajoe* 1939, No. 5: 146).

[21] "*[...] pengajaran yang ada sekarang harus diubah sedemikian rupa, sehingga dasar dan sifatnya sesuai dengan keadaan dalam masyarakat kita. [...] Yang menjadi ukuran derajat bangsa, ialah cultuurnya yaitu berkembangnya perasaan kebangsaan yang bersifat: kesenian, kesusastraan dan kemajuan batinnya*" (*Djatajoe* 1939, No. 5: 146–7).

The controversy about Bali and Christian missions

The questions concerning Balinese religious identity that had been hotly debated in *Surya Kanta* and *Bali Adnjana*—namely, the distinction between *agama* and *adat* on the one hand, and the articulation between *agama Bali* and *agama Hindu* on the other—after having been defused for some time by the orientalist stance of *Bhāwanāgara*, were re-emerging, more pressing than ever, in *Djatajoe*. Right from the start, queries about the nature of the Balinese religion and calls for its reform held a prominent place in the new journal. But while in the 1920s the context of religious debate had remained strictly Balinese, during the 1930s it was increasingly broadened. This debate attested to a noticeable confusion, if not a frank helplessness, due no longer solely to disagreement among the Balinese themselves but also to the fact that they were at a loss as to how to reply to accusations of 'paganism' by non-Balinese—not only Indonesian Muslims but also Christian missionaries and colonial administrators. Thus, in one of its first issues, *Djatajoe* quoted the disparaging opinion of the Balinese religion held by Victor Emanuel Korn, *assistent-resident* in South Bali and the foremost Dutch expert on Balinese *adat*:

> The words 'Bali Hindu' are inexact, as the addition of the word Hindu is supposed to show that the Balinese religion demonstrates a Hindu foundation. In truth, this is not the case. The religious foundations in Bali are 'pagan' (idolatry?) that is: ancestor worship, veneration of natural divinities such as the divinities of water, earth, sky etc. and belief in the ties between magical conditions and humanity, such as divine punishment, demonic nuisances and so on. [...] On the whole, very few Balinese know about Hinduism, and the same holds true regarding the Hindu gods.[22]

While orientalists had contrived to establish the Balinese religion squarely within the purview of Hinduism, anthropologists and other foreign observers in the 1930s tended to break away from any Indic reference in order to focus on the local Indonesian substratum, to the extent that the view expressed by Korn would soon become prevalent. It is found, for example, in Miguel Covarrubias's *Island of Bali*, where Hinduism appears as a superficial veneer tacked onto the native

---

[22] "*Perkataän 'Bali Hindu' itu, tidak benar, karena tambahan kata Hindu itu seakan akan memperlihatkan, bahwa agama Bali itu menunjukkan dasar ke Hinduan. Sesungguhnya tidak begitu. Dasar-dasar agama di Bali ialah: 'heidensch' (menyembah berhala?) yaitu: pujaan kepada nenek moyang, pujaan kepada dewa-dewanya bagian alam seperti dewanya air, tanah, langit d.l.l. dan percaya kepada pertalian antara keadaan yang gaib-gaib dengan kemanusiaan, seperti hukuman dewa-dewa, gangguan setan d.s.b. [...] Umumnya bumi putera di Bali tiada, atau sedikit benar mengetahui akan agama Hindu, demikianpun tentang déwa-déwa Hindu*" (*Djatajoe* 1936, No. 4: 92–3; see Korn 1932: 62–3).

animism: "Hinduism was simply an addition to the native religion, more as a decoy to keep the masters content, a strong but superficial veneer of decorative Hinduistic practices over the deeply rooted animism of the Balinese natives" (Covarrubias 1937: 261).

Once the Hindu foundations of the Balinese religion were thus undermined, its viability and sustainability was thrown into question, as it was threatened not only by Islam, which was tightening its grip over the greater part of the Archipelago, but also by Christianity. After the failed attempt to propagate the Christian faith among the Balinese people in the 19th century, the island of Bali had remained closed to missionaries until a Roman Catholic congregation, the Society of the Divine Word (Societas Verbi Divini, SVD), requested permission of the *resident* of Bali and Lombok in 1924 to open a Dutch-language school (HIS) for Balinese children. This request was met with vehement opposition from the Balinese political elite, efficiently relayed by Bali's representative to the Volksraad in Batavia, Tjokorda Gde Raka Sukawati, who introduced a resolution requesting the governor-general to ban Christian missionaries from entering Bali. There ensued a debate pitting representatives of Christian parties against orientalists and colonial administrators, such as Victor Emanuel Korn and Cornelis Lekkerkerker. Faced with this opposition, the SVD withdrew its request to open a school in Bali.

While the colonial government was duly concerned about the spread of Islam and subversive nationalism in Bali, not all Dutch officials were opposed to missionary activity on the island. A case in point is the former *assistent-resident* of South Bali and then *resident* of Timor, A.J.L. Couvreur, who was convinced that the Balinese religion would not withstand the pressure of Islam. To avert that threat, he proposed in 1923 that the island be Christianized by Roman Catholic missionaries. He deemed Catholicism more appropriate to the Balinese than Protestantism on account of its ritualistic propensity and its ability to adjust to local cultures. His idea was to join the Residency of Bali and Lombok to the Residency of Timor, for the purpose of creating a Christian bloc that would counter the expansion of Islam to the eastern islands. Couvreur's proposal was rejected by the *resident* of Bali and Lombok, H.T. Damsté, who argued that, to the contrary, the Balinese culture and religion should be protected through appropriate government policy. He was of the view, therefore, that all Christian missionary activity should be prohibited in Bali (Robinson 1995: 39–41). Although Damsté's position did win the day, the ban on Christianization would soon be circumvented.

The beginnings of Christianization in Bali remain poorly known and appear to have been the result of several distinct initiatives.[23] While there had been occasional inroads into Bali by Javanese and Ambonese Christian proselytizers in the late 1920s, the first documented event was the request by Reverend Robert Alexander Jaffray, head of an American evangelical Protestant organization in Makassar, the Christian and Missionary Alliance, to serve the small community of Chinese Christians in Bali. Permission was granted and in 1930 Tsang Kam Foek, later called Tsang To Hang—an evangelist of the Chinese Foreign Missionary Union founded by Jaffray to enlist Chinese missionaries in the task of opening the Dutch Indies to the gospel—settled in Denpasar, where he is said to have married a Balinese woman. Through some native women married to Chinese, Tsang came into contact with a number of Balinese families in the region of Mengwi who became attracted to Christianity and asked for baptism. In 1931, at the behest of Tsang, Jaffray came to Bali and baptized four Balinese by immersion in a river under the eyes of numerous curious onlookers; more followed suit thereafter. These incidents caused an uproar in Bali. The new converts were expelled from their village and declared socially 'dead' (*kasepekang*). The Volksraad passed a resolution, introduced by Tjokorda Gde Raka Sukawati, calling on the governor-general to keep Christian missionaries out of Bali. At the request of the *resident* of Bali and Lombok, the *assistent-resident* of South Bali, Mr. H.J. Jansen, addressed a report to the governor-general, stressing the risks of social, cultural and religious disintegration posed by Balinese conversions to Christianity. In 1933, permission for work in Bali was withdrawn for foreign missionaries, while Tsang and Jaffray were expelled from the island. They were soon replaced by two Javanese ministers from the Gereja Kristen Jawi Wetan (Christian Church of East Java)[24] who took over the care of the incipient Christian flock in Bali.

The synod of the Gereja Kristen Jawi Wetan had appointed as advisor the Protestant missionary Dr. Hendrik Kraemer, and in this capacity he paid several visits to Bali between 1930 and 1933 to monitor the religious situation on the island. In May 1932, he submitted a report to the board of the Nederlands Bijbelgenootschap (Netherlands Bible Society), following which he appealed for admittance to Bali. This report triggered off a heated controversy between

---

[23] The information presented here is based on the following sources: Kraemer (1933b: 7–11), Vandenbosch (1934: 208–9), Kersten (1940: 199–208), Swellengrebel (1948: 61–90), Steenbrink and Aritonang (2008: 731–6), and especially (Wijaya 2012).

[24] The Gereja Kristen Jawi Wetan was the first Javanese Church to become independent of the Indische Kerk (Protestant Church of the Indies), in 1931, as part of a process of indigenization of Christianity. Unlike foreign missionaries, native ministers did not need the authorization of the colonial government to work in Bali.

Kraemer[25] and orientalist members of the colonial administration—in particular, the archaeologist Frederik David Kan Bosch and the linguist Roelof Goris (Enklaar 1989). What emerges first and foremost from this controversy is the fact that its protagonists did not share the same conceptual premises and, consequently, that they could not come to an agreement. While they all debated the religion of the Balinese people, they were not really speaking about the same thing, in the sense that they did not have the same understanding of that which pertained—or did not pertain—to the category 'religion'. Counter to the 'reductionist' position of the orientalists, for whom religion came under the heading of culture, the missionary proclaimed loud and clear that religious experience was *sui generis*, and thus was not to be confused with an immanent phenomenon such as culture.

The controversy was initiated by Bosch with an article entitled 'An Inadmissible Experiment. Bali and Missions', published in September 1932 in the Dutch periodical *De Stuw* (Bosch 1932a). Kraemer replied immediately in the same periodical with the counter title 'The One and Only Admissible Experiment' (Kraemer 1932a). This first skirmish was pursued in *De Stuw* the following month (Bosch 1932b, Kraemer 1932b). Then, in February 1933, Bosch reopened the debate with an article entitled 'Bali and Missions', published in *Djawa*, the periodical of the Java-Instituut, to which Kraemer replied in the same issue with an article entitled 'Reply to 'Bali and Missions'' (Bosch 1933; Kraemer 1933a).

In his articles, Bosch is willing to admit that modern Western influences (such as colonial administration, economy, jurisdiction, education, tourism, etc.) are negatively affecting the Balinese culture. But, unlike Christian proselytizing, none of these influences is intended to be a deliberate assault on the Balinese religion. On the contrary, they are likely to raise among the Balinese an awareness of the value of their cultural heritage, which in all likelihood will bring about a religious revival. Bosch then gives an outline of the Balinese religion, which he characterizes as 'Hindu-Balinism' and claims that it is essentially part of Hinduism. In his opinion, missions are too compromised with colonial imperialism and the capitalist spirit of Calvinism to possibly be accepted by the Balinese people, to whom the monotheistic and personal conception of the God

---

[25] Hendrik Kraemer was of equal academic stature as his opponents, for whom he proved a formidable adversary. After having obtained a doctorate on a 16th-century Javanese almanac (*primbon*) with the famous Islamologist Christiaan Snouck Hurgronje at Leiden University, he worked from 1922 to 1937 in Java as a missionary of the Nederlandse Hervormde Kerk (Dutch Reformed Church), in the service of the Nederlands Bijbelgenootschap. Upon his return to the Netherlands, he was appointed professor of the history and phenomenology of religion at Leiden University.

of the Bible is absolutely foreign. Moreover, the Balinese culture is an organic whole, of which religious life forms an integral part. Therefore, the Christianization of Bali would necessarily involve the wholesale collapse of the Balinese culture. The colonial authorities should thus protect the Balinese people against the proselytizing of missionaries who would deal a fatal blow to their religion.

Kraemer then replies that while Bosch is concerned with the culture of the Balinese people, his own consideration is the salvation of their souls. The concern with cultural preservation expressed by Bosch could not be shared by the missionaries whose sole duty is to preach the Gospel in the name of Christ. While it is indeed true that the culture of Bali is an organic entity, with religion at its core, it is already irremediably subverted by Western modernity and could by no means be the support of a religious revival. And while Kraemer acknowledges that one may detect traces of Hinduization in the Balinese religion, he asserts that it cannot be claimed that what Bosch calls Hindu-Balinism is part of the world religion of Hinduism. In truth, the Balinese religion is more akin to magic, owing to the tantric mysticism in which it is steeped, than to a genuine religion. The Balinese people are not deeply religious in the true sense of the word, but they are caught up in eudemonism: they value their life in this world too much to be really preoccupied with their eternal life. And they won't be saved by a return to their Old Javanese scriptures, nor by contact of the younger generation with the spiritual mother country India, but by converting to Christianity.

Later, Kraemer would specify and develop his position in a book entitled *De Strijd over Bali en de Zending. Een studie en een appèl* ('The Controversy about Bali and Missions. A Study and an Appeal') (Kraemer 1933b; see also Kraemer 1958). This publication is an adaptation intended for a broader readership of the report to the Nederlands Bijbelgenootschap of his findings and conclusions after his visits to Bali. The book consists of four chapters: (1) a history of the missions in Bali; (2) the colonial government of Bali; (3) the religious situation on Bali; (4) the current problem of 'Bali and missions'.

After a brief account of the history of Christian missions in Bali, Kraemer exposes the current predicament of Balinese society. In spite of the colonial government's well-meaning intention to safeguard as much as possible the traditional structures of Balinese society, its foundations have been shaken to the core and will eventually collapse. The fact is that it is an agrarian society, which is only capable of solving the problems that arise in the course of its endogenous evolution, but which is ill-equipped to face up to the upheavals caused by a foreign government. Under these circumstances, the relevant issue is not the preservation of the Balinese culture—which is illusory, with all due respect to orientalists, artists, anthropologists and tourists—but the spiritual regeneration of the Balinese people.

Kraemer then describes in considerable detail—and, I have to say, quite accurately, his Christian prejudices notwithstanding—the religious life of the Balinese people, by distinguishing between Hinduism and popular religion. He needs only compare Balinese religious practices with Hinduism as observed in India to be convinced that it is thoroughly misleading to call the Balinese people Hindu. Indeed, they do not name their religion *agama Hindu* but *agama Tirta*, in reference to the holy water required for their rites. The undeniable Hindu flavor of Balinese life is of a cultural rather than a religious nature. Only the princes and the *brahmana* priests sought to model Balinese society according to norms and institutions derived from Hinduism. But even the Balinese hierarchy has little in common with the Hindu caste system, as the Balinese titles are not Indian but indigenous. The popular religion emphasizes the family, with its shrine dedicated to the ancestors (*sanggah*), and the village community of the *desa*, and it is very closely linked to the soil, the mountains, the lakes and the sea. The main duty of the village community (*krama desa*) is the maintenance and upkeep of the communal temples and the offering of sacrifices to the village deities. Hence the endless diversity of the *desa* cults, each differing from the other. In truth, under a thin Hindu veneer Balinese popular religion is a communal matter, which does not essentially differ from the religious patterns to be found among the other 'animist' peoples of the Indies.

Kraemer then denies the alleged religiosity which is said to pervade the Balinese life. In his opinion, a life ruled by tradition (*adat*) does not denote profound religiosity. And the fact is that the so-called Balinese religious life does not pertain to religion but to tradition. Like all primitive peoples, the Balinese live in a world saturated with the presence of invisible beings. What matters for them is to win the favors of the gods and to propitiate demons in order to secure a plentiful harvest, long life, health and happiness in this world (*selamat*). They are not in search of salvation but of earthly well-being. In truth, they do not worship their gods, they exploit them. Their religious life is superficial, as noted by Rabindranath Tagore, who was disappointed not to find in Bali the true Hindu spirituality which he sought. The worship of deities (*mabakti*) consists simply of gestures of reverent salutation (*sembah*), which reflect an intimacy with an ancestral deity, a family member, rather than a true communion with God. The transcendence that arouses true worship, the boundary between sacred and profane, is not sufficiently marked. The Balinese gods exist for the sake of man, and not man for the sake of God.

The Balinese religion is condemned to wither, as it is the religion of a closed and static society, which is undermined by its forced encounter with secular modernity. The fact is that no revival can be expected from within. Where his opponents see signs of revival, Kraemer detects rearguard attempts at safeguarding the customary status quo on the part of princes and especially of *brahmana* priests. The latter—the *padanda*—are still indispensable as purveyors of magical power (*sakti*), suppliers of *tirta*, and expounders of ancient scriptures. They are the conservative guardians of a tradition upon which their own social status is wholly dependent. Although by their position they ought to take the lead in a religious revival, they appear to be totally unaware that Balinese society is being shaken to the core, unlike the educated youth, who complain of the intricacy and obscurities of their religion, and who seek to understand its foundations. But the *padanda* still persist in denying access to their knowledge, which they want to keep to themselves as a precious and profitable secret. And even the young people who want to know more about their religion are motivated by an intellectual interest and not by an inner spiritual quest, which alone would be the condition of a possible religious revival.

Kraemer goes on to say that the most convincing proof that the Balinese religion is moribund is the receptivity which Christianity finds nowadays in the island, which contrasts with the rejection it faced in Van Eck's and De Vroom's time. Indeed, when Reverend Jaffray administered baptism to Balinese families, he was responding to their wish to embrace the Christian faith. This desire is a clear sign of divine providence, which legitimizes the work of missions. Under the present circumstances, the work of missions is not only legitimate but necessary and urgent. Now that there exist Christian communities in Bali, they are entitled to spiritual care, which cannot be properly given to them as long as the island remains closed to missions. In sum, the present religious situation in Bali demonstrates that the Balinese people stand in real need of an institution that is willing to undertake work of spiritual, moral and educational regeneration.

Kraemer concludes his plea by pointing out that in opening Bali to the world, the colonial government has cleared the way for all kinds of influences that are shattering Balinese society. The signs of incipient decay are only too visible behind the aesthetic seduction of ceremonies and dances. Consequently, the issue is not a false alternative between preservation of Balinese culture or its destruction as a result of missions. If the government persists in denying missionaries access to Bali, it will come into conflict with the principle of freedom of religion which underlies its colonial policy. And 'Mohammedan' propaganda should then likewise be explicitly prohibited in Bali. Finally, why should Bali be artificially closed to Christianity alone, which represents the best that Europe can bring to the Balinese people, while tourism, which reduces the Balinese religion to a mere spectacle, is being welcomed?

The riposte came this time from Roelof Goris, who published in Batavia a book entitled *'De strijd over Bali en de Zending'. De waarde van Dr. Kraemer's boek* ("'The Controversy about Bali and Missions'. The Value of Dr. Kraemer's Book") (Goris 1933b). Goris's reply to Kraemer was preceded with a preface by Tjokorda Gde Raka Sukawati, who had repeatedly expressed his opposition to the presence of Christian missionaries in Bali.

Passing through Kraemer's book, chapter after chapter, in an extremely critical manner, Goris rejects his presentation of the Balinese religion by pointing out its shortcomings, its mistakes and its Christian prejudices. He declares that in spite of all his academic credentials, Kraemer remains an uninformed and tendentious pedant, full of the assumed superiority of his own religion. Like Bosch before him, Goris asserts that the Balinese religion falls undoubtedly within the fold of Hinduism. He warns that missionary propaganda would amount to the destruction of the organic cohesion of the Balinese cultural complex of religion, society and art.[26] He concludes by stating that the Balinese who have read his book are deeply offended by Kraemer's arrogance and dishonesty. The question remains as to how many Balinese would have read Kraemer's book. In point of fact, the whole controversy appears to have gone over the head of the Balinese, with the exception of a few committed intellectuals such as Tjokorda Gde Raka Sukawati, who were only too happy to take sides with those Dutch administrators opposed to the missionaries' admittance to Bali. In any case, the controversy eventually died out.

In spite of the reservations of the colonial government, in 1936, the first Dutch Protestant ministers were finally allowed to settle in Bali, on the grounds that since there were Balinese Christians now, they were entitled to receive pastoral support. Dr. Jan Lodewijk Swellengrebel was sent to Denpasar by the Nederlands Bijbelgenootschap to translate the Bible into Balinese. He was joined by Reverends Schuurman and Gramberg, in charge of the European Christian community, but who also supervised the growing Balinese Protestant flock. Subsequently, Reverend Brill was sent to Bali by the Christian and Missionary

---

[26] Given Goris's virulence, one wonders why he did not mention in *Bhāwanāgara* the controversy between orientalists and missionaries on the question of missions in Bali. One may surmise that the official status of this periodical prevented him from broaching such a sensitive topic.

Alliance. Meanwhile, a request had been made by the Society of the Divine Word, and in 1935 Father Johannes Kersten SVD was authorized to settle as a resident priest in Denpasar.[27] His first converts were two Balinese evangelists who had been baptized by Jaffray. One of them originated from the village of Tuka, south of Mengwi. In 1936, Father Simon Buis SVD joined Kersten in Bali. The two of them moved the following year to Tuka, where the first Catholic church of Bali was built. From then on, there existed three Christian persuasions in Bali: two Protestant Churches—the Christian and Missionary Alliance and the Gereja Kristen Jawi Wetan—and one Roman Catholic. In 1937, the two Protestant Churches merged to establish the Pasikian Kristen Bali (Community of Balinese Christians), which in 1948 became the Gereja Kristen Protestan di Bali (GKPB).[28]

Conversion and its outcome

It remains to be seen under what circumstances and for what reasons some Balinese embraced Christianity in the 1930s, and to assess what resulted from their conversion. On this subject, we have the condescending opinion of Miguel Covarrubias, who contends that Tsang and Jaffray deceived Balinese impoverished by the economic crisis by making them believe that by converting to Christianity they would be relieved of all financial obligations to their village community:

> all they had to do was to pronounce the formula: '*Saja pertjaja Jesoes Kristos*— I believe in Jesus Christ'. If the man who was induced to pronounce the magic words was the head of a household, the missionaries claimed every member of the family as Christians and soon they could boast about three hundred converts (Covarrubias 1937: 396–7).

But before long, the new converts discovered that they had been misled. Not only were they not excused from their communal obligations, but they were banned from their community—they were declared socially 'dead' (*kasepekang*) and could no longer inherit from their parents.[29] Their fellow villagers no longer

---

[27] During his long career in Bali, Kersten published a grammar of the Balinese language, a Balinese–Dutch dictionary and a Balinese–Indonesian dictionary.

[28] After Indonesia's independence, denominations would become more numerous.

[29] The implications of conversion in Bali are different, depending on whether it concerns a man or a woman. The latter is able to change her religious affiliation upon marrying a man belonging to another faith, something which occurred quite frequently when Balinese women wedded Muslims. In doing so, she does not necessarily sever her relations with her own family. However, if a Balinese man converts to Christianity or to Islam, and especially if he

spoke to them (*puik*) and had to sever all ties with them, on pain of a fine. Their rice fields were no longer supplied by irrigation channels. Worst of all, they could no longer dispose of their dead, because they were not permitted to bury them in the village cemetery. Not to mention occasional violence against them. Under such duress, it is understandable that a number of these newly converted Balinese Christians chose to revert to their former religious practices.

It is possible to check Covarrubias's dismissive account with the testimonies gathered by I Nyoman Wijaya, a Hindu-Balinese historian who published a substantial history of Protestantism in Bali at the request of a Protestant Balinese foundation (Wijaya 2012). According to him, most of the first converts were men, commoners, poor and uneducated. It is hardly surprising that, in its early stages, Christianity was viewed as a religion for the poor, because the prospective converts were hoping to be exempted from the costly ceremonies that fall to the Balinese people, most particularly the cremation of the dead. There is no doubt that the material assistance supplied by Tsang and his fellow evangelists played a significant role in gaining converts. The fact is that a number of these new converts remained Christians only as long as they were receiving the coveted assistance, after which they reverted to their ancestral practices. In addition to some tangible advantages, the conversion to Christianity carried a promise of social mobility by providing access to various benefits of modernity, such as education and medicine. Indeed, Christianity has often been seen as a simple and efficient means of healing, and conversion appears in many cases to have taken place following the recovery from serious illness, after traditional health care had failed. It may also include individuals who believed themselves to be victims of 'black magic' (*pangiwa, desti*) and who had been rescued by Tsang or by one of his disciples. Christians were thought to be protected from the power of witches (*leak*), which is an appreciable boon to any Balinese.

More remarkably perhaps, it should be noted that among the early converts were a number of charismatic individuals and ritual specialists, such as literati, artists, priests (*pamangku*), healers (*balian*) and sorcerers (*anak sakti*). They viewed Christianity as a new body of esoteric 'knowledge' (*ilmu*), expected to provide access to an additional source of 'power' (*kasaktian*) as well as to the social prestige (*kawibawan*) that comes with it.[30] Some of them, who had challenged Tsang or one of his Balinese followers to a magic contest

---

does not have a brother who could fulfill his socio-religious obligations to their ancestors, the whole family of the convert is polluted (*sebel*) and the entire village to boot.

[30] This is also how Christianity had been received in Java in the 19th century (Sumartana 1991: 22–50; Ricklefs 2007: 93).

(*pangleakan*), were forced to admit defeat, following which, as is customary in Bali, they became their victor's disciple. And once they had converted, their influence and prestige persuaded their entourage to embrace the new faith as well.

These observations are corroborated by Arlette Ottino, one of the few anthropologists to have investigated the predicament of Balinese Christians (Ottino 2000a, 2000b). In the village where she conducted research, at the foot of Mount Batukaru, Christianity was brought in 1937 by Tsang's disciples. At first, it was treated as an esoteric knowledge about mystical practices, which as such posed no particular threat to the village. This would soon change, though, when the new converts were forbidden to take part in the ritual activities of their *desa adat*. They were expelled and forced to resettle away from the village. Indeed, in Bali private beliefs are of little import as long as the rules of public practices are respected.

In the Balinese conception of communal living, participation in the rituals devoted to the ancestral village deities, on whom fertility and prosperity depend, is a customary obligation that each household head must fulfill in exchange for the privilege of residing in the *desa adat*, cultivating its arable land and benefitting from its networks of mutual help (*suka duka*). However, while Balinese Christians wanted to stay in their village and cultivate their land, they no longer wanted to discharge their ritual obligations to the village deities. Not only did Tsang and Jaffray forbid them to take part in the cult of their village deities, they compelled them to burn their 'idols' and destroy their family temples (*sanggah*), which posed a threat of ancestral curse (*salahang batara*) on their household. By doing so, the converts endangered not only their own existence and that of their descendants but also the existence of the *desa adat* itself.

The most crucial problem was unquestionably the handling of the deceased. The Balinese bury their dead, awaiting their eventual cremation, at a site known as a *sema*, which is located on land belonging to the *desa adat* and is reserved to its members. And although the Hindu Balinese could not prevent Christians from destroying their family temples, they could deny them access to the village *sema*, which would be defiled (*leteh*) by Christian corpses. In some cases, and often with the involvement of the colonial authorities, the *sema* was divided, with a portion reserved for the Christians residing in the village; otherwise, a Christian cemetery was created on land belonging to a fellow convert. In other cases, the Christians had to leave their village and go into exile, either in other parts of Bali or outside the island.

Considering the challenges faced by Christians and the hostility they aroused, and with the aim of restoring social peace, the colonial government resolved to relocate them away to a new settlement. In 1938, during a meeting of Resident H.J.E. Moll with pastors and Balinese *negara-bestuurders* of regions where Christian communities had developed (Badung, Tabanan and Buleleng), it was decided to send Christian families to clear the jungle in the inhospitable wilderness at the western tip of the island, in Jembrana. It was also there that Balinese who had breached their customary obligations were being exiled (*kaselong*). Thus were founded in 1939 the Protestant village of Blimbingsari and the following year the Catholic village of Palasari, established nearby.

In cases where Balinese Christians managed to withstand ostracism and were able to stay in their village of origin, it became necessary to distinguish within communal obligations between the ritual and social spheres, between what is 'religious' and what is 'secular'. Such a distinction—which had been implemented from the outset in the new Christian villages in Jembrana—was artificial in the traditional conception of Balinese village life. In this way, the coming of Christian missionaries in the wake of the colonial encounter prompted the Balinese to proceed to an unprecedented differentiation between domains of interaction in which 'religion' (*agama*) was relevant and others where it was not. Thus, unlike Muslims, who had long been integrated within the indigenous socio-cosmic order (Couteau 1999b), the presence of Christian families in their villages challenged the Balinese to formulate what exactly their religion was about.

Balinese queries about their religious identity

While the controversy between Kraemer and his orientalist opponents does not appear to have found any echo in *Djatajoe*, the leadership of Bali Darma Laksana was clearly concerned about the conversion of Balinese people to Christianity. Thus, on May 20, 1938, I Wayan Bhadra, the co-editor of *Djatajoe*, addressed the *padanda* as follows: "Respected priests. Did you ever worry about the fact that several hundred Balinese have run to the Catholic as well as to the Protestant Church?" He went on to declare: "In my opinion, they did so because they were loath to live in a religious quandary."[31] A few months later, an anonymous contributor sounded the alarm, ever more worried, by acknowledging that the

---

[31] "*Tuan-tuan Padanda yang terhormat. Adakah Tuan pernah memikirkan pelarian beberapa ratus orang Bali ke Gereja Katholiek maupun Protestant? [...] Mereka lari, sangka saya, oleh karena mereka segan tinggal hidup dalam kegelapan Agama*" (*Djatajoe* 1938, No. 11: 323).

Balinese people were burdened by their religion, with too many costly ceremonies and obligations to bear, which explained why so many of them were receptive to the siren calls of Christianity. And he concluded his rebuke by asserting that the Christian Churches intended to subjugate the Balinese religion (*Djatajoe* 1939, No. 7: 214). Undoubtedly, the Balinese intelligentsia were alert to the warning that their religion was under threat: "our religion is like a boat without a helmsman" (*agama kita ini ibarat perahu yang tiada berjuru mudi*) (*Djatajoe* 1938, No. 9: 283).

Indicative of the Balinese frame of mind at the time is an article bearing the significant title 'Our confusion regarding religion' (*Kebingungan kita tentang agama*):

> Before the boys and girls of Bali started going to school, and before there were any newspapers on the island, the Balinese were already practicing this religion, and there was no one who criticized and blamed them; what we heard were only comments like "the tradition in this village is like this, whereas in that village it is like that", [...] Then, one did not speak of religious ceremonies, but rather of village traditions. Thus, in short, a proper religion was something unknown; what we knew about were only village traditions (*adat desa*) and the only religion we knew was Balinese religion (*agama Bali*), and it was unheard of for people to feel ashamed or angry because they had been criticized by Mr. ... So-and-So.[32]

And the author continued: "About twenty years ago, our people assented to whatever the *padanda* said and just followed whatever was going on. But now our educated youths refuse to carry out improper customs, those that are still unclear, they want to know the truth and ask for proper explanations."[33] This same author informed his co-religionists that in the eyes of foreigners:

> [...] our religion (*agama*) is based on tradition (*adat*) mixed with all sorts of extracts from Hinduism and therefore it cannot be compared to any religion found in India; thus, according to the opinion of foreigners we do not have a

---

[32] "*Sebelum putra-putra dan putri-putri Bali ada yang bersekolah, dan di Bali belumlah pernah berdiri surat-surat chabar, maka keadaan di Bali sudahlah memeluk agama ini, yang mana berjalan terus, tiadalah ada mencela dan menyalahkan, yang mana kita dengar cuma ada pembicaraan 'adat desa anu begini dan desa anu begitu', [...] Lantas ini tiada disebut upacara agama, melainkan disebut adat desa. Jadi ringkasnya agama yang sebenarnya tiada diketahui; yang diketahui perbedaannya cuma adat desa dan agama yang diketahui cuma agama Bali, dan tiada pernah kedengaran malu atau marah dicéla oleh Tuan ... anu*" (*Djatajoe* 1937, No. 5: 131).

[33] "*Kira-kira 20 tahun yang lalu, bangsa kita setuju saja apa kata Pedanda dan menurut saja apa yang sudah berjalan. Tetapi sekarang sebagian pemuda-pemuda terutama yang keluaran sekolah, sudah tiada sanggup menjalani kebiasaan yang salah ya'itu yang masih gelap, melainkan minta yang benar dan agar mendapat keterangan yang sempurna*" (*Djatajoe* 1937, No. 5: 131).

proper religion and do not worship God, but we are like fools who worship anything they happen to come across.[34]

Faced with such a disparaging opinion about their religion, some members of Bali Darma Laksana would attempt to defend it and to justify its rites, while others would endorse the criticisms leveled at it. Assessing their religion according to the norms of Islam and Christianity, the latter came to consider it not worthy of the name *agama* and that it ought to be reformed accordingly.[35] They saw the situation as critical: young Balinese studying outside their island, not knowing how to respond when asked about their religion, were converting to Islam or to Christianity for fear of being branded 'idolaters' (*penyembah berhala*) or 'animists' (*animis*) by their schoolmates. Worse still, some of them were said to have become 'free thinkers' (*vrij denker*), and even 'atheists' (*ateis*), for having been exposed to the pernicious influence of Dutch education (*Djatajoe* 1938, No. 11: 353–4).

According to other authors, however, the Balinese religion was not at issue; it did not suffer from comparison with Islam or with Christianity. They maintained not only that one religion is as good as another but furthermore that, beyond their apparent diversity, the teachings of all religions are everywhere the same.[36] Contrary to the accusations levied against them, the Balinese do not actually worship the effigies (*arca, pratima*) which they use in their rituals, as these effigies are only mediations destined to help human beings to communicate with God: "We do not worship stone, wood and so on, but we worship the One God" (*Kita tidak menyembah batu, kayu dan sebagainya, melainkan menyembah Tuhan nan Esa*) (*Djatajoe* 1937, No. 9: 246). The problem, they said, was that most Balinese did not know their religion and that, as a consequence, their rites

---

[34] "[...] *agama kita ini bersendi dari adat dan dicampuri oleh bermacam-macam sari dari agama Hindu, yang sudah tentu tiada bisa dibandingkan kepada salah satu agama di Hindu, yang mana pada pemandangan Tuan-tuan bangsa asing adalah kita tak beragama dan tiada menyembah Tuhan (Widi), melainkan kita adalah disamakan sebagai orang gila yaitu menyembah segala yang ketemu*" (*Djatajoe* 1937, No. 4: 98). This image of Balinese as heathens who 'pray to whatever they first meet in the morning' has a long history, which goes back to the first Dutch expedition to the East Indies and which would be frequently reiterated ever after (see Chapter 1, n. 32).

[35] By regarding their religion as defective according to an exogenous norm, be it Hinduism, Islam or Christianity, these Balinese reformers appear to have internalized the vision of both the orientalists and the missionaries who, as we have seen, addressed the Balinese religion from the perspective of what it lacked rather than what it comprised.

[36] Besides the fact that this opinion is widely held among the Balinese people, it attests the significant influence of Theosophy on Bali Darma Laksana's members. Indeed, several articles in *Djatajoe*, which promoted the teachings of Buddhism, were excerpted from Theosophical journals. Theosophical ideas had entered Bali through Javanese members of Budi Utomo, who had established a section in Denpasar in 1919, as well as through the Taman Siswa movement from 1933 onward. In 1937, a Javanese Theosophist, Raden Mas Kusumodihardjo, made a propaganda trip through Bali and reported that a lodge called Adnyana Nirmala had recently been founded in Gianyar by I Gusti Ketut Djelantik (Tollenaere 1996: 329; see Nugraha 2011).

displayed endless variations throughout the island. Hence, they ought to learn to understand their religion rather than merely celebrating their rites according to tradition: "[...] we should investigate the truth and the meaning of our religion so as to be able to refute the charges held against our religious ceremonies by foreigners."[37]

Alarmed that their religion was in peril, Bali Darma Laksana's leaders earnestly tried to find agreement on the true nature of their religion and to codify its rites accordingly. They were facing several problems. First of all, they had to differentiate between *adat* and *agama*, a task for which they were no better equipped than their precursors of Surya Kanta: "the fact is that we don't know which is *adat* and which is *agama*" (*ternyata bagi kami patut tiada mengetahui yang mana adat dan manakah agama*) (*Djatajoe* 1939, No. 7: 215). They had further to discriminate within their religion what came from Hinduism (and also possibly from Buddhism) from what was indigenous. But there again they were unable to reach a common view.[38] Reformers held that, for most Balinese, their religion was simply the 'Balinese religion' (*agama Bali*). They knew only how to "worship the divinities in their family shrines and in the village temples" (*menyembah dewa di sanggah atau di pura desa*) (*Djatajoe* 1937, No. 9: 246). Their religious horizons were parochial and closely related to the customs of their particular village; and they were convinced that their religion originated in Majapahit—as Tjakra Tanaya had asserted in *Bali Adnjana* in order to counter the Indian tropism of his opponents in *Surya Kanta*. Only the better educated among the Balinese people, it was said, knew that their religion originated in India and long predated Majapahit. To learn about the origins of their religion, *Djatajoe*'s contributors would resort either to Javanese-Balinese textual sources, to contemporary Indian authors, or else to the works of Dutch academics, such

---

[37] "[...] *haruslah kita menyelidiki kebenaran dan apa arti yang terpakai pada agama kita supaya bisalah kita jawab tuduhan Tuan-tuan bangsa asing tentang kehinaän upacara agama kita*" (*Djatajoe* 1937, No. 4: 98).

[38] This is evidenced by the fact that in those days the Balinese used a variety of names to designate their religion, from those which anchored it firmly in Bali to those which linked it to Hinduism, such as *agama Bali*, *agama Tirta*, *agama Siwa*, *agama Buda*, *agama Siwa-Buda*, *kasewasogatan*, *agama Trimurti*, *agama Hindu Bali*, *agama Bali Hindu*, and *agama Hindu*. The main contrast here is between *agama Bali*, which refers to a region, and *agama Hindu*, which refers to a religion (although it is well known that *Hindu* comes from *Sindhu*, which pertains to a region). However, one notices that one author objected to the name *agama Bali Hindu* on the ground that "Hindu is the name of a country not the name of a religion, and in Hindu there are all sorts of religions, therefore we are wrong to call our religion Bali Hindu" (*Hindu itu nama Negeri bukan nama agama, sedang di Hindu ada bermacam-macam agama, jadi tiada benarlah kalau kita menyebut beragama Bali Hindu*) (*Djatajoe* 1937, No. 4: 98). Whereas the debate between *Surya Kanta* and *Bali Adnjana* had opposed respectively *agama Bali Hindu* to *agama Hindu Bali*, the most frequent term encountered in *Djatajoe* is *agama Tirta*, with reference to the holy water required for religious rites. It appears that originally the name *agama Tirta* was mostly used among the Balinese in Lombok, where it served to differentiate them from the Muslim Sasak (*Djatajoe* 1937, No. 9: 244; see Diantari 1990: 109).

as H. Kern, N.J. Krom, W.F. Stutterheim, and R. Goris (*Djatajoe* 1936, No. 5: 143–6; No. 6: 164–8).

But it was not enough to elucidate the origins of the Balinese religion, as it was still necessary to account for the notable differences between religious practices in Bali and Hinduism as observed in India. To bridge this gap, some authors suggested inviting an Indian *guru* to teach the Balinese the fundamentals of Hinduism,[39] while others were of the opinion that Balinese students should be sent to India to learn about Hinduism first-hand. Moreover, the readers of *Djatajoe*—like those of *Bhāwanāgara* before them—were provided with Malay or Dutch translations of classical texts of Hinduism as well as Western studies on Indian religions. Still, reading through this journal, one realizes that in the 1930s the Balinese intelligentsia had only a vague idea about Hinduism, both past and present.[40] They had some notion of the importance of the Vedas (*Weda*), though. Thus, for want of finding in Balinese texts the foundations of the Balinese religion, one author searched for the response to his queries in Stutterheim's book, *De Hindu's* (1932b). He drew the conclusion that, even though the Vedas are sacred to Hindus, they no longer inform their religious practices. And furthermore—as Goris had already made it clear in *Bhāwanāgara*—they were unknown to both the Balinese and the Javanese (*Djatajoe* 1937, No. 8: 236–8). But this did not prevent another author from endorsing a few months later the common belief that the Vedas contained the essence of the Balinese religion, which unfortunately was inaccessible to the Balinese people owing to the prohibition (*aja wera*) of their disclosure imposed by the *padanda*: "[...] for the majority of us, Balinese people, who have not yet studied the *weda* (we have only heard that these *weda* are a most sublime and sacred knowledge, which cannot be studied by laypeople), we are still in the dark."[41]

In these disturbing circumstances, for most of *Djatajoe*'s contributors the recourse should come from the *padanda*, whom they urged to teach their religion

---

[39] Already in 1936, a Hindu Brahmin, Pr. Hemchandra Roy, had visited Bali where he delivered religious lectures (*Djatajoe* 1937, No. 7: 208–9).

[40] With the exception of Wirjasutha, who mentioned in his booklet the organization 'Aryasamy' [sic] founded by 'Dyananda' [sic] (Wirjasutha n.d.: 7), the Balinese intellectuals did not appear to be well informed about the thinking of Indian reformers of the 19th century who had turned Hinduism into a 'religion', of the same nature as Christianity and Islam. This is all the more surprising because, as mentioned above, the Balinese experience was in many respects similar to that of their Indian precursors: the stress on monotheism in response to criticism leveled by Muslims and Christians alike, and the fact of having been informed by the interlocking influences of Orientalism and colonialism.

[41] "[...] *bagi kami bangsa Bali kebanyakan yang memang belum tahu mempelajari weda-weda (cuma dengar ceritera, weda itu pengetahuan yang maha luhur dan suci, tiada boleh dipelajari oleh orang kebanyakan), jadi masih gelaplah bagi kami*" (*Djatajoe* 1937, No. 4: 98).

to the Balinese by disclosing the contents of the *lontar* on which they based their knowledge: "[...] our priests and other knowledgeable persons should settle once and for all which religion we should profess, which hodgepodge we should get rid of, which traditions we may still conserve and which ones should be discarded as bringing about our decline."[42] Yet, other authors considered that recourse to the priests was fruitless, as the *padanda*, lacking in modern education, were confined within the narrow horizon of their village and had no experience of the outside world at large:

> For the time being, we cannot wait for the priests to improve the situation of our religion so as to free it from the criticism of foreigners, since most of them are elderly, few have been to school, which is not to say that they are ignorant of the teachings of our religion, but they do not realize and do not understand the criticism and insults of foreigners toward our religion, so that they are in no hurry to address the questions that most people are asking.[43]

Besides, far from being inclined to enlighten their followers (*sisia*) about religious knowledge and ritual ceremonies, they tended to exploit their subordination.

In this respect, one author remarked justly that even though the *padanda* were reluctant to divulge the contents of their *lontar*, foreign scholars were disseminating knowledge about the Balinese religion by studying the collection of manuscripts assembled by the Kirtya:

> I urge the priests to fulfill our aspirations. Please publish in *Djatajoe* the manuscripts stored over the years. In the Gedong Kirtya there is no dearth of manuscripts dealing with religious issues. Is it permissible to disclose the contents of these manuscripts? Of course. Even if we don't want to and attempt to prohibit it, foreigners have already done it for a long time.[44]

---

[42] "[...] *harus ditimbang oleh para Pandita-Pandita dan orang-orang yang achli mana agama yang harus dipakai, campuran mana yang harus dibuang, dan adat mana yang masih boleh dipakai dan mana yang menyebabkan kemunduran harus dibuang*" (Djatajoe 1937, No. 5: 132).

[43] "*Jika kita menunggu dari Pendita-Pendita akan memperbaiki keadaan agama kita agar terlepas dari celaan-celaan orang asing, dalam waktu ini belum bisa, lantaran Pendita-Pendita kita sekarang masih kebanyakan beliau para lingsir, apa lagi beliau-beliau cuma sedikit yang berasal pernah menduduki bangku sekolah, tentang itu bukan saja anggap beliau tiada mengerti akan arti segala 'ilmu-'ilmu yang tersangkut pada agama, melainkan karena beliau tiada berasa dan tiada mengetahui tentang celaan-celaan, dan penghinaan bangsa asing kepada agama kita, dari itu kuranglah beliau bergiat akan mencari keterangan-keterangan dan menerangkan kepada orang banyak tentang seluk beluk pengetahuan kita*" (Djatajoe 1937, No. 4: 100).

[44] "*Kepada sang Sulinggih saya bermohon, sudilah menyokong angan-angan ini. Rontal-rontal yang tersimpan bertahun-tahun itu keluarkanlah dan umumkanlah dalam Djatajoe. Digedong Kirtyapun ta' kurang rontal-rontal yang memuat soal agama. Bolehkah isi rontal itu diumumkan? Tentu saja. Walaupun kita ta' mau dan melarang, tetapi bangsa asing telah lama melakukannya*" (Djatajoe 1938, No. 9: 284).

Whatever the esteem in which they held their *padanda*, it is clear that in the opinion of Bali Darma Laksana's leaders they ought to become for the Balinese what *kiai* are for Muslims and priests and pastors for Christians, whose duty is to teach and propagate their faith. And indeed, taking Islam and Christianity as a model, the Balinese were in search of their prophet (*nabi*) as well as of their holy book (*kitab suci*), which should become for them what the Quran is to Muslims and the Bible to Christians.[45] For some, the prophet of the Balinese religion was Begawan Biyasa (Vyasa), to whom is attributed the authorship of the Vedas as well as of the *Mahabharata*, the holy book of Hinduism. And since only eight out of the eighteen volumes of the *Mahabharata* were known in Bali, the missing volumes should be translated into Balinese or else into Malay. Until that moment arrives, the Balinese should study the *Sarasamuscaya* (an Old Javanese compendium of teachings derived from the *Mahabharata*) (*Djatajoe* 1938, No. 6: 180–2). For other authors, though, the prophet of the Balinese religion would rather be Wisnu, Siwa or Brahma, or even Budha.

To find a way out of such a predicament, as early as April 1937, appeals were issued in *Djatajoe* for the Balinese to come to an agreement on the common principles underlying the diversity of their rites and most particularly on the identity of the God they worship.[46] To that end, Bali Darma Laksana's leaders were asked to make a compendium of the Balinese religion, that would serve as a holy book (*kitab suci*): "How good and useful it would be if some of our religious experts were willing to draw up regulations for our religion, which would become like a holy book, the simplest possible, so that all people, from the highest to the lowest classes (the poorest), could practice it while also understanding its purpose."[47] These appeals were reiterated during Bali Darma Laksana's first congress, in July of the same year, and on November 8, 1937, I

---

[45] "The Christians had their BOOK, the Muslim traders of Bali had their BOOK and sometimes even their mosque, but the Balinese with their faulty MSS—they were aware of that—must have felt lost" (Hooykaas 1963: 373). The ascendancy of the conceptions and vocabulary peculiar to the Abrahamic religions, particularly of modernist and scripturalist Islam, over the Balinese reformers has been patent since the 1920s, and it would only increase in time: in search of a *kitab suci* (a word of Arabic origin, referring specifically to the Quran) as well as of a *nabi* (a prophet, particularly Muhammad), in *Djatajoe* as well as in the periodicals that had preceded it, the Balinese were frequently described as *umat*, their priests as *ulama*, their profession of faith as *syahadat*, and their God as *Allah*. Furthermore, the term *takhyul*, used to condemn 'superstitions' as opposed to the true religion, is the very same one that Muslims use to differentiate Islam from faulty practices and beliefs.

[46] Just as the Balinese used a variety of names to designate their religion, they had also several to identify their supreme God. In *Djatajoe*, one encounters mostly the following terms: Widi, Sang Hiyang Widi, Sanghyang Widiwasa (Tuhan), Yang Esa (Sang Hiyang Tunggal), Tuhan nan Esa, Tuhan Allah (Dewa-Dewa).

[47] "*Alangkah baiknya dan bergunanya jika diantara ahli-ahli agama kita ada yang suka membuat dan menyusun peraturan-peraturan dalam agama kita, dijadikan seperti kitab suci, yang sesederhana-sederhananya, supaya orang2 dari lapisan yang tertinggi hingga yang terbawah (termiskin) sama dapat melakukannya, dengan mencapai maksud juga*" (*Djatajoe* 1937, No. 9: 268).

Gusti Gde Rake addressed a formal request to the president of the Paruman Kerta Negara,[48] Anak Agung Agung Anglurah Ketut Karangasem, to form a commission of *padanda* and other clerisy in charge of compiling a *kitab suci*. To that end, the commission should enlist the help of the Kirtya Liefrinck–Van der Tuuk, so as to make use of its collection of religious manuscripts. The argument put forward was that once the Balinese knew what their religion was actually about, they would be in a better position to defend it against accusations of heathenism by Muslims and Christians alike, and would be less tempted to embrace another faith: "[This Holy Book...], we the Balinese need it most, in order to know and to value as much as possible the Balinese Religion and culture, so that our faith in the Balinese Religion and culture can be sustained."[49]

Thereafter, Bali Darma Laksana's executive committee reported in *Djatajoe* that in May 1938 its president had visited each of the *negara-bestuurders* and discussed with them the project's progress, all the while emphasizing that it was a difficult and time-consuming task.[50] Subsequently, the issue was regularly mentioned at the time of the association's congresses. Eventually, *Djatajoe* published a letter from the president of the Paruman Kerta Negara dated April 8, 1940, informing its readership that the attempt at composing a *kitab suci* had failed. The reason given was that in Bali, *agama* could not be divorced from *adat*, and *adat* differed from one kingdom to the next and from one village to another, just as *lontar* dealing with religious matters diverged from each other; hence the members of the commission could not agree on a religious canon valid for the whole island.[51] *Djatajoe*'s editorial board did not hide their disappointment and maintained in response that, beyond the differences due to *adat*, the point was precisely to lay the common foundations of the Balinese religion (*dasar-dasar agama kita*) (*Djatajoe* 1940, No. 9–10: 281–2).

---

[48] This is the council established in 1931 by the colonial government to coordinate the *negara-bestuurders* who had been reinstated in 1929.

[49] "*[Kitab Suci...] kitab mana untuk kita orang Bali amat perlu sekali, supaya Agama dan kebudayaan Bali dapat kita ketahui sedalam-dalamnya dan hargai setinggi-tingginya, oleh hal mana keteguhan kepercayaan pada Agama dan kebudayaan Bali, kiranya akan dapat dipertahankan*" (*Djatajoe* 1937, No. 4: 115).

[50] Meanwhile, a contributor suggested in *Djatajoe* that, before compiling a *kitab suci*, it would be preferable for the Balinese to agree on the identity of their 'prophet' (*nabi*), whether 'Siwa, Brahma or Buda' ([...] *apakah tiada lebih baik, kalau kita menentukan dahulu 'Nabi' yang kita memuliakan? Kalau telah terang yang kita memuliakan 'Siwa, Brahma atau Buda', baharulah kita menyalin kitab-kitab itu kedalam bahasa Bali yang kelak kita namai 'Kitab Suci'*) (*Djatajoe* 1938, No. 10: 316).

[51] And for good reason, as the traditional Balinese viewpoint is characterized by diversity rather than by uniformity—as reflected in the saying *desa kala patra* ('place, time, circumstances')—so that the characteristics and demands of divinities in one place or in one temple differ from those in another place or another temple.

Be that as it may, at the end of the colonial period the Balinese religion was not (yet) a religion of the Book.

From Balinese to Indonesian nationalism

The issue of the emergence of nationalism in Bali is threatened by a twofold pitfall. On the one hand, Balinese historians, and some foreign academics, are inclined to regard Bali Darma Laksana as a nationalist organization, with the risk of committing a serious anachronism (Budharta et al. 1986: 122–3; Putra 1989: 115). On the other hand, the absence of openly nationalist aims in the statutes of this organization is no reason to conclude that its leaders were unconcerned with the nationalist ideals which inspired (some of) their future fellow-countrymen. Indeed, the repression of the Indonesian nationalist movement, marked by the arrest and exile of its principal leaders, was to lead to a cultural rather than a political form of nationalism. It is in this sense that we may talk about Bali Darma Laksana's nationalism, with the caveat that we were (still) dealing for the most part with a Balinese rather than with an Indonesian nationalism.

What could be argued on the basis of Bali's historiography is that the idea of nationalism came rather late to the Balinese people. And we may assume that their mistrust of Islam was not unrelated to their hesitation to identify with the emerging Indonesian nationalist movement. It is significant in this regard that they had not participated in the Indonesian youth congresses organized in 1926 and 1928 in Batavia by various regional organizations. Indeed, these events were not even mentioned in the Balinese publications of the period. Nor was the 'national awakening' (*kebangkitan nasional*) that was stirring up the Dutch Indies at the time, and particularly the neighboring Java, referred to in *Surya Kanta*, even though its leaders habitually presented the Javanese as a model to be emulated by the Balinese. Reading *Surya Kanta* as well as *Bali Adnjana*, it is clear that for the Balinese social and intellectual elites, Indonesian nationalism was not on the agenda in the 1920s.

Nationalist ideas and aspirations were disseminated in Bali along two main channels: by means of journals and other publications, on the one hand, and on the other, as was so well illustrated by Benedict Anderson, through colonial education (Anderson 1991: 121–3). In the latter case, nationalist ideas were spread both by Javanese teachers posted in Bali and by young Balinese who had been studying in Java. Back in Bali, many of them had the opportunity to pass on their experience to the younger generation as schoolteachers. However, it cannot be assumed that the Balinese youths studying outside their island were necessarily won over to the cause of nationalism. According to Anak Agung Made Djelantik, a son of the *negara-bestuurder* of Karangasem who was studying in Malang in the 1930s, most of his fellow students "were not at all interested in politics" (Djelantik 1997: 70). What's more, he added expressly: "The sense of Indonesian citizenship, of being Indonesian, had not yet grown in us" (Djelantik 1997: 83).

To assess the emergence of Indonesian nationalism in Bali, it might be useful to look at the referents of the syntagm *bangsa kita* (our people, our nation)—as well as related terms, such as *negeri* (country), *tanah air* (fatherland), *rakyat* (people), *masyarakat* (community, society), and so on. In *Surya Kanta* and *Bali Adnjana*, when *bangsa kita* did not refer to one or the other of various Balinese *wangsa*—and specifically to the *jaba* in their confrontation with the *triwangsa*—it denoted the Balinese people, never Indonesians as a whole. This is also the case in *Djatajoe*, where *bangsa kita* still refers to the Balinese people. This being said, starting from 1938 one notices in this journal the increasing emergence of references to Indonesia.

The first occurrence I was able to spot of a mention of 'Indonesian nationality' (*kebangsaan Indonesia*) dates from February 1938. An article titled *Menuju kearah persatuan* ('Towards Unification') criticized Bali Darma Laksana's 'provincialism' (*sifat 'Provincialistisch'*), deploring that its recruitment and interests were confined to Bali: "This era is a time of union, the time of Indonesia, it is no longer a time of insularity, why are there still insular associations?"[52] The same author reiterated his criticism in April of the same year, in an article where he reproached the Balinese for their failure to care about what was happening beyond the shores of their island. He concluded his diatribe in the following terms: "[...] only authentic Nationalists are able to create a new era, namely, to glorify the nation and the fatherland. Are there already authentic Nationalists in Bali?"[53] One can see in this article an allusion to the Greater Indonesia Party (Partai Indonesia Raya);[54] indeed this party was mentioned for

---

[52] "*Zaman ini ialah persatuan, zaman Indonesier, bukan lagi zaman kepulauan, apa sebab masih ada perkumpulan bersifat kepulauan?*" (*Djatajoe* 1938, No. 7: 196).

[53] "[...] *hanya kaum Nationalis tulen yang bisa dan sanggup untuk membangunkan zaman baru, ja'ni memuliakan bangsa dan tanah air. Sudahkah di Bali ada Nationalis tulen?*" (*Djatajoe* 1938, No. 9: 276).

[54] The Partai Indonesia Raya—better known by its acronym Parindra—was founded in Surabaya in December 1935 by merging Persatuan Bangsa Indonesia (Indonesian People's Union) of Dr. Raden Sutomo with Budi Utomo (of which Sutomo had been one of the founders). Parindra focused on educating the people with the aim of building a 'Glorious Indonesia' (*Indonesia Mulia*). Characterized by cultural nationalism and an attitude of cooperation with the colonial government, Parindra remained imbued with the values of the Javanese aristocracy and never became a mass party (Abeyasekere 1972).

the first time in another article of the same issue of *Djatajoe*, where it was presented as a political organization (*perkumpulan politiek*) struggling to improve the fate of the Indonesian people (*masyarakat Indonesia*).

It was not until 1939 that stronger political views would be voiced in *Djatajoe*. Since civil servants were prohibited from joining a political party, one can assume that the permission to publish articles under a pen-name, granted in July 1938 at Bali Darma Laksana's second congress in Denpasar, had encouraged the more cautious Balinese nationalists to make their views known. A case in point is an article titled '*Politiek*', issued in April 1939 under the Sanskrit penname Kanta Gora, that complained about the Balinese lack of interest in politics while pressing them to engage in the political movement (*pergerakan politiek*):

> In the Island of Bali it is still strange to hear the word politics as this idea is still not understood and even dangerous, as if one was afraid of a tiger. Because of that, rare are those in the Island of Bali who dare to express their opinion frankly, and even more so to get involved in politics. This is also the reason why the political movement is so far behind in Bali. [...] But now a change is beginning to be felt.[55]

This same author had previously published an article in which he called Dr. R. Sutomo and Ir. Sukarno 'Fathers of Indonesia' (*Bapak Indonesia*). He had also mentioned the *Petitie Sutardjo*, the petition submitted in 1936 to the Volksraad by Sutardjo Kartohadikusumo, which called for a conference to grant autonomy to the Netherlands Indies within a Dutch-Indonesian union over a period of ten years, and which had been rejected by the Dutch Parliament in 1938.

Other related articles would be published from time to time in *Djatajoe*— including several signed 'Patriot'. However, they constitute a very small portion of the journal's editorial content. It is only from the founding in July 1938 in Singaraja of a local branch of Parindra—the sole political party to be established on the island during the colonial period—that one can speak of Indonesian nationalism in Bali. The setting up of the Parindra was due to two influential Javanese, Doctor Murdjani, posted in Negara (the capital city of Jembrana), and Sukardjo Wirjopranoto, based in Singaraja (Sukarniti 1985). Branches were founded in 1938–39 in Denpasar, Tabanan, Negara, Klungkung, and Bangli,

---

[55] "*Di Nusa Bali perkataan politiek itu terlalu aneh didengarnya sebab anggapannya belum dimengerti dan berbahaya, seolah-olah takut kepada harimau. Lantaran itu maka di Nusa Bali jarang sekali yang berani berterusterang, baikpun mempercakapkan, maupun melakukan hal kepolitiekan itu. Sebab itu pula bahwa pergerakan politiek di Bali masih amat terbelakang. [...] Tetapi sekarang baru mulailah perobahan nampak*" (Djatajoe 1939, No. 9: 295).

several of them by members of Bali Darma Laksana.[56] Parindra opened schools, formed cooperatives, and launched a youth movement. It organized a conference in Tabanan in 1939, with the participation of leaders from the central committee (including Mohamad Husni Thamrin and KPH Wurjaningrat), who unsuccessfully requested permission from the Dutch *resident* to have a representative on the Paruman Agung. Following a second conference, held in Klungkung in 1940, a resolution was addressed to the colonial government requesting that tourists be prohibited from taking photographs of bare-breasted Balinese women, and more generally that the circulation of books and postcards of bare-breasted Balinese women be censored. Although Parindra had some influence on educated Balinese youths, it remained marginal in Bali. While this party was not officially prohibited, the activities of its members were closely monitored by the government and deliberately impeded by the Balinese 'self-rulers' (*zelfbestuurders*) (Schulte Nordholt 1996: 311).

It is questionable, however, whether Parindra's ineffectiveness was primarily due to the repression to which it was subjected, as Balinese historians would have us believe. The divergence of opinions among Bali Darma Laksana's members during congresses revealed significant breaches between generations as well as between regional branches. Thus, at the second congress, held in July 1938 in Denpasar, the Singaraja branch requested that article 5 of the association's statutes—"The statute of ordinary member is reserved solely for the Balinese people" (*Yang boleh diterima menjadi anggota biasa hanyalah orang Bali saja*)—be changed to the following: "Any Indonesian residing in Bali can become an ordinary member" (*Yang boleh diterima menjadi anggota biasa segala orang Indonesia penduduk Bali*) (*Djatajoe* 1939, No. 10: 325). After being debated and put to the vote, this request was rejected by 244 votes to 143. When the time came to elect the next president, the choice fell on Ida Bagus Putera Manuaba, a prominent member of the Denpasar branch, who had initiated the proposal to compose a holy book of the Balinese religion in April 1937. But he refused the honor in the following terms: "Frankly, I disagree with B.D.L., which only accepts Balinese people as ordinary members and closes the door to

---

[56] In the context of an inventory of Balinese organizations in *Djatajoe*, I Gusti Gde Rake presented in May 1939 Parindra's objectives: "A political organization working towards the creation of a Glorious Indonesia, by means of: a) strengthening the spirit of unification of the Indonesian nationalism, b) striving to obtain the broadest possible political rights as well as a government based on democracy and nationalism, c) improving the economy and the social life of the Indonesian people" (*Perkumpulan politik yang bermaksud hendak mencapai Indonesia Raya, dengan jalan: a) memperkuatkan semangat persatuan kebangsaan Indonesia, b) berusaha politik sehingga mendapat hak-hak politik seluas-luasnya dan mendapat suatu macam pemerintahan yang berdasar kerakyatan (democratisch) dan kebangsaan, c) memajukan perekonomian dan peri-kehidupan sociaal rakyat Indonesia*) (*Djatajoe* 1939, No. 10: 303).

other Indonesians. I am a proponent of an open-door policy."[57] This same Ida Bagus Putera Manuaba would establish a Parindra branch in Denpasar a few months later.

The delegates of the Singaraja branch insisted on the same issue during the third congress, in July 1939 in Klungkung, justifying their request in the following manner:

> [...] for we consider that the sooner we reject this 'provincialist' attitude, the closer our relationship will be with Indonesians residing in Bali and Lombok. In our age, which is an age of progress, it is inappropriate to proclaim 'Bali for Bali', but we must proclaim 'Bali for Indonesia', which makes perfect sense if we are aware that Bali is part of Indonesia.[58]

In the ensuing discussion, the president reminded the delegates that Bali Darma Laksana 'doesn't meddle in politics' (*tidak berpolitiek*). And the request of the Singaraja branch was once again rejected, this time by 344 votes to 150.

In other words, on the eve of the Japanese invasion of the Netherlands Indies, most of the Balinese intelligentsia did not yet consider themselves fellow Indonesians among others. To sum up, on the basis of the articles published in *Djatajoe*, one can conclude—in accordance with Dutch colonial officials as well as American cultural anthropologists, and contrary to Geoffrey Robinson—that in the 1930s, the Balinese were indeed more interested in art, culture, and above all in religion, than in politics.[59] That being said, it should be acknowledged that for them culture, religion and politics were not exclusive categories, since for the majority of Bali Darma Laksana's members, the issue was to assert their Balinese cultural-cum-religious identity and—for the most forward-looking of them, at least—to carve out their place in the future Indonesian nation which was slowly emerging at that time.

---

[57] "*Saya berterus terang saja, saya ta' dapat sehaluan dengan B.D.L. yang hanya menerima orang Bali saja sebagai anggauta biasa dan menutup pintunya bagi bangsa Indonesia lainnya. Haluan saya Opendeur Politiek*" (*Djatajoe* 1939, No. 1: 20).

[58] "[...] *karena kami tetap berpendapatan, bahwa semangkin lekas sifat 'provincialisme' itu dilepaskan semakin rapat akan perhubungan kita dengan bangsa-bangsa Indonesia penduduk Bali dan Lombok. Pada masa ini, yaitu masa kemajuan, ta' patut kita mengatakan 'Bali buat Bali', tetapi kita harus mengatakan 'Bali buat Indonesia', yaitu suatu hal yang logisch benar, jika kita insaf, bahwa Bali ada termasuk dalam lingkungan Indonesia*" (*Djatajoe* 1939, No. 10: 325).

[59] "The image of a harmonious, exotic and apolitical Bali gained wide acceptance in the late 1920s, when Dutch colonial power in Bali was at its height and the restoration of Balinese 'tradition' had become a central feature of a conservative Dutch colonial strategy of indirect rule. By the 1930s, the bureaucratic memoranda of Dutch colonial officials had, with a tedious uniformity, begun to describe the people of Bali as more interested by nature, in art, culture and religion—dance, music, painting, carving, ceremonies, festivals, and so on—than in 'politics'" (Robinson 1995: 5–6).

Chapter 5

Toward Recognition of the Balinese Religion (1942-58)

By the end of the colonial period, the Balinese had yet to come to an agreement on the nature of their religion. However, their debates on the question of how *agama Bali* was related to *adat* on the one hand and to *agama Hindu* on the other had prepared them to confront the pressures imposed on their ethnic and religious identity after their island became part of the Republic of Indonesia. The problem was that once the categories *agama* and *adat* had been established, the Balinese still had to explicitly differentiate them, an issue both intractable and inescapable since these categories were seen at once as too similar and necessarily set apart.

Contrary to what some foreign analysts say, what happened is not simply that the former unity of *agama* and *adat* had started to disintegrate due to the colonial encounter, as these categories were alien and had to be appropriated by the Balinese for their own purposes. It is not even, as some Balinese academics would have it, that the Balinese people had taken refuge in their religion after having been unsettled by the colonial occupation of their island and threatened by the ensuing Muslim and Christian proselytism. Before they could seek refuge in their religion, Balinese social and intellectual elites had first to conceive for themselves the very idea of a 'Balinese religion', construed according to the model of Islam and Christianity. Indeed, they had formerly no notion of a system of beliefs and practices that could be demarcated from other aspects of their life to be labeled 'religion' and to which one could 'convert'—let alone that this religion was 'Hinduism'. This implied, first, that they detach the meaning of the word *agama* from that of the word *dharma*, and, second, that they specifically distinguish between its respective senses of 'religion', 'law' and 'tradition'.

In my opinion, it was the conjunction of several distinct processes of differentiation that led to the formation of the categories *agama* and *adat* in Bali: the Dutch-enforced separation between religious tradition and secular administration; the codification of Balinese *adatrecht* by colonial jurists; the necessity of discriminating between ritual and social spheres in villages with Christian converts; and the growing urge to dissociate religion from tradition on the part of reform-minded educated Balinese. Hence, by giving rise to a sharper contrast between 'our ways' (*cara kita*) and 'their ways' (*cara kaum sana*), the colonial encounter not only led the Balinese to conceive a notion of themselves as a 'people' (*bangsa*), a unitary entity, but it also contributed to a further drawing of conceptual boundaries between hitherto undifferentiated domains within Balinese society.

This conceptual separation of *agama* and *adat* had in fact started when Balinese reformers were attempting to find a name for their religion, thereby initiating an objectification of religion as a separate field of beliefs and practices. Yet, if the Dutch had de-politicized *adat* by dissociating political power from customary authority, religion remained merged with tradition in the colonial period. Once they had become Indonesian citizens, the Balinese would be compelled to distinguish explicitly between 'religion' and 'tradition': in order for their rites to accede to the status of *agama*, they had to be detached from what was considered to belong to the domain of *adat*. In fact, the Balinese succeeded in obtaining the recognition of their religion before they actually managed to differentiate *agama* from *adat*. It was only after their religion had officially been acknowledged as a proper *agama* by the Indonesian religious authorities that the Balinese undertook this process of discrimination, which is still ongoing to this day.

Ketuhanan Yang Maha Esa

During the colonial period, Indonesian Islam had remained marginalized and closely monitored by the government. Soon after the Dutch surrender, in March 1942, the Japanese occupation authorities endeavored to win over the Indonesian Muslim community in a propaganda campaign aimed at arousing anti-Western sentiment (Benda 1983). With this purpose in mind, they set up an Office of Religious Affairs (Kantor Urusan Agama), which took over from the colonial Office for Native Affairs (Kantoor voor Inlandsche Zaken) that had been established in 1899 to advise the government on Islamic policy. Then, in November 1943, they regrouped all existing Muslim organizations, both modernist and traditionalist,[1] in a Consultative Council of Indonesian Muslims (Majelis Syuro Muslimin Indonesia, or Masyumi) (Madinier 2015). By the time the capitulation of Japan could be expected, the Masyumi's leaders, comforted by a heightened sense of their importance, were convinced that Islam would be the official religion of a prospective independent Indonesia (*Indonesia Merdeka*).

On April 29, 1945, to thwart the approaching Allied Forces, the Japanese set up an Investigating Committee for the Preparation of Indonesian Independence (Badan Penyelidik Usaha-usaha Persiapan Kemerdekaan Indonesia, BPUPKI), which was quickly taken advantage of by the Indonesian nationalist leaders. Before long, the committee came up against the question of the foundation of the future Indonesian state (*dasar negara*), pitting the 'Islamic group' (*golongan Islam*) against the 'nationalist group' (*golongan kebangsaan*). The former, confident that they represented an overwhelming majority of the Indonesian people, wanted to establish an Islamic state, whereas their opponents (most of them Muslims) were concerned that such a decision would alienate the Christians and various religious minorities—not to mention the Javanese *abangan* and other nominal Muslims, who were concerned about the legal possibility of enforcing a strict adherence to Islam—and argued in favor of a state in which religious and secular affairs would be kept separate. On June 1, the most influential nationalist leader, Sukarno, originating from a Javanist background, attempted to overcome the deadlock by outlining the five basic principles—called Pancasila—that should serve as the philosophical foundations of the Indonesian state, which would neither be an Islamic nor a secular state. The fifth principle was 'Belief in God' (*Ketuhanan*).[2] According to Sukarno, Indonesian

---

[1] In 1912, the modernist Muslim organization Muhammadiyah ('Followers of Muhammad') was founded in Yogyakarta. Inspired by ideas of Islamic reform emanating from the Middle East, this organization promoted religious, educational and social works. It developed a network of urban Islamic schools (*madrasah*) which adjoined secular learning to the study of Islam. Muhammadiyah sought to purge Javanese Islam of various customs that were regarded as polytheistic deviations (*shirk*), and which thus violated the doctrine of the Oneness of Allah (*tawhid*), while aiming to enforce a stricter compliance with the formal obligations of Islam (*syariah*). At the same time, its proponents were intent on adapting Islam to the modern world through promoting rational and personal interpretation (*ijtihad*) of the Quran and the Hadith, with a view to determining those teachings which were relevant to the requirements of modern life. Faced with such a challenge to their authority, traditionalist Muslim scholars founded in 1926 in Surabaya the Nahdlatul Ulama ('Revival of the Islamic Scholars'). Strongly established in the rural areas of East Java, where it operated private Islamic boarding schools (*pesantren*), Nahdlatul Ulama defended the value of customary learning, while remaining more accommodative toward Javanese cultural traditions. On the issue of categorizing Indonesian Islam, see Ali (2007).

[2] The Indonesian word *Tuhan* literally means 'Lord', and by extension 'God'. Unlike the name Allah, it does not carry any Islamic connotation. While the most common translation of *Ketuhanan* is 'Belief in God', it would be more correct to translate it as 'Divinity' or 'Lordship' (Darmaputera 1988: 153; Intan 2006: 73). The other principles are nationalism (*Kebangsaan*), humanitarianism (*Perikemanusiaan*), democracy by consensus (*Permusyawaratan*) and social prosperity (*Kesejahteraan sosial*). On Pancasila, see Bonneff et al. (1980); and on the long-drawn-out opposition between the Islamic and the nationalist groups, see Boland (1982).

citizens would be free to profess the religion of their choice, with no religion being granted an official, or even a privileged, status, not even Islam, notwithstanding its dominant position in the country.

Sukarno's proposition was not accepted by the Islamic group, who wanted to include a clause in the constitution stating that 'the religion of Indonesia is Islam'. The confrontation was finally resolved on June 22, when representatives of each group agreed on a compromise, known as the Jakarta Charter (*Piagam Jakarta*), which was to become the preamble to the constitution. The formulation of this charter bore the mark of the Islamic group. To begin with, the order of Sukarno's five principles was reversed: 'Belief in God' was now listed the first of the founding principles, to which the other four were subordinated. Furthermore, the independence of Indonesia was to be declared 'By the Blessing of the Mercy of Allah the Almighty' (*Atas Berkat Rahmat Allah Yang Maha Kuasa*). And finally, to the first principle was extended a clause—referred thereafter as the 'seven words'—which read: '[Belief in God] with the obligation for the adherents of Islam to carry out Islamic law' ([*Ketuhanan*] *dengan kewajiban menjalankan Syariat Islam bagi pemeluk-pemeluknya*) (Boland 1982: 23–7; Elson 2009). The Jakarta Charter thus endorsed an Indonesian citizenship differentiated along religious lines, by discriminating between Muslims and non-Muslims.

In the wake of the Japanese surrender to the Allied Forces on August 15, 1945, Sukarno and Mohammad Hatta proclaimed the independence of Indonesia on August 17, and a new Committee for the Preparation of Indonesian Independence (Panitia Persiapan Kemerdekaan Indonesia, PPKI) was convened to draft a constitution. Bending to the opposition of the nationalist group, and with Christian delegates from the Eastern islands threatening to secede from the republic, Hatta demanded for the sake of national unity that the contentious 'seven words' be removed from the preamble, while proposing as a concession to the Islamic group that the expression 'Belief in God' (*Ketuhanan*) be expanded into 'Belief in the One and Only God' (*Ketuhanan Yang Maha Esa*, a formula judiciously combining Malay and Sanskrit to express a tribute to the Muslim *tawhid*).[3] Further, the provision that the president of the republic had to be a Muslim, which had been stipulated by the Islamic group, would be omitted. Then, at the request of the delegate of the Lesser Sunda Islands—the Balinese lawyer I Gusti Ketut Pudja—the Arabic name Allah was replaced by the Indonesian word *Tuhan* in the expression 'By the Blessing of the Mercy of God

---

[3] It seems that Muslim delegates agreed to Hatta's demand because they were confident that, once national elections were held, Islamic parties would prevail and be in a position to impose their own agenda.

the Almighty'. In the end, article 29 of the 1945 constitution read as follows: "(1) The State is based upon the belief in the One and Only God. (2) The State guarantees all persons the freedom to embrace their religion and to worship in accordance with their religion (*agama*) and belief (*kepercayaan*)."[4] Thus, while the freedom of worship was guaranteed by the Indonesian constitution, the freedom of conscience was not—not to mention atheism. In the words of Bernard Johan Boland, "the new Indonesia came into being neither as an Islamic State according to orthodox Islamic conceptions, nor as a secular state which would consider religion merely a private matter" (Boland 1982: 38; see further Ichwan 2012: 5–13).

The omission of the 'seven words' would become a bone of contention for decades, with repeated attempts on the part of Islamic parties to have the Jakarta Charter reinserted in the constitution. Moreover, article 29 of the 1945 constitution contained several ambiguities which were bound to engender further debate. First, it did not explicitly delineate the relationship between religion and the state, and in particular it did not specify how far the government could interfere in the religious life of Indonesian citizens. Second, it did not define what qualified as *agama*, that is, which religions fostered 'Belief in the One and Only God', and hence were included under the protection of Pancasila. While for Muslim nationalists *Ketuhanan Yang Maha Esa* implied exclusive monotheism, in accordance with the Islamic principle of God's unicity (*tawhid*), secular nationalists construed it in a more inclusive fashion as 'Godliness'. Third, the interpretation of the notion of 'belief' (*kepercayaan*) and the way it related to 'religion' (*agama*) was to be the cause of much controversy (Butt 2020). The reference to *kepercayaan* had been added under pressure from representatives of Javanese mystical movements (*aliran kebatinan*),[5] for whom it was put on an

---

[4] "(1) Negara berdasarkan atas Ketuhanan Yang Maha Esa. (2) Negara menjamin kemerdekaan tiap-tiap penduduk untuk memeluk agamanya masing-masing dan untuk beribadat menurut agamanya dan kepercayaannya itu."

[5] The emergence in the early 20th century of mystical movements in Java and their dissociation from Islam is an outcome of the breakdown of what Merle Ricklefs called the Javanese 'mystic synthesis' (Ricklefs 2006). These movements were part of a Javanist cultural revivalism, a riposte to the Muslim reformists who repudiated the mystic strand of Islam. Javanist intellectuals increasingly combined elements of their Hindu-Buddhist heritage with Sufism, Christianity and Theosophy. The overall designation for Javanese mysticism is *kebatinan*, a term derived from Sufi traditions, which conventionally contrast the *batin* ('inner, esoteric') and *lahir* ('outer, exoteric') dimensions of religious experience. *Kebatinan* (lit. 'inwardness') is thus the 'science of the inner being', in the sense that its adepts search for the experience of the divine in their inner self. While groupings of spiritual seekers around a teacher had been a familiar sight in Java for a long time, *kebatinan* groups grew in numbers during the early years of independence and became organized into formal movements that outlived their founders. In order to monitor these groups, the Ministry of Religion established in 1954 a bureau for the surveillance of the 'currents of belief' (Badan Koordinasi Pengawas Aliran Kepercayaan Masyarakat, Bakor Pakem), that became the watchdog against heterodox mystical movements (Stange 1986; Mulder 1998; Ricklefs 2007).

equal footing with *agama* by the constitution, which acknowledged the legitimacy of both, thus allowing Indonesians the choice between one or the other option. For the Islamic group, on the contrary, only *agama* originates from divine revelation, whereas *kepercayaan* are but a cultural practice that could only be a mere semantic appendage to *agama*. The handling of this dispute would be important for the position of indigenous ethnic religions (*agama suku*) as well as for the so-called 'sects' (*aliran kepercayaan*, lit. 'currents of belief')[6] in independent Indonesia.

After Sukarno was appointed president and Hatta vice-president on August 18, 1945, the Committee for the Preparation of Indonesian Independence held a meeting to discuss the structure of the new government. There was a proposal for establishing a Ministry of Religion, but it was opposed by the Christian representatives, and religious affairs were attributed to the Ministry of Education. The same proposal was again brought forward in late November by Muslim members of the Central Indonesian National Committee (Komite Nasional Indonesia Pusat, KNIP), a provisional parliament with an advisory taskforce established to replace the PPKI, headed by the recently appointed prime minister, Sutan Sjahrir. Eventually, on January 3, 1946, as a concession to Muslim demands in exchange for Islamic Group's political support of the republican government, the Ministry of Religion (Kementerian Agama Republik Indonesia, KAGRI)[7] was established in Presidential Decree No.1/SD/1946, with regional offices spread all over Indonesia. Initially set up to advance Muslim interests, the Ministry of Religion was expanded on November 20, 1946, to include separate directorates for Protestantism and Roman Catholicism, thereby acknowledging Christianity (*agama Nasrani*) as a legitimate religion of the Book (Boland 1982: 105–12).[8] Notwithstanding the broadening of its scope, however, KAGRI's main task was directed at catering to the needs of the Muslim community.

---

[6] The term *aliran kepercayaan* designates all spiritual movements and syncretic cults considered not to fall within the ambit of revealed religions. While the word *kepercayaan* literally means 'faith, creed, belief', it connotes in fact the ideas of parochialism, superstition and backwardness. In that sense, the *aliran kepercayaan* pertain to *adat* and not to *agama*, as defined by the minister of religion in 1952: "A sect [...] is a dogmatic opinion, which is closely connected to the living customs of certain ethnic groups, especially of those that are still backward. The core of their creed is everything which has become the customary way of life of their ancestors over time" (*Aliran kepercayaan* [...] *ialah suatu faham dogmatis, terjalin dengan adat istiadat hidup dari berbagai macam suku bangsa, lebih-lebih pada suku bangsa yang masih terbelakang. Pokok kepercayaannya, apa saja adat hidup nenek moyangnya sepanjang masa*) (El Hafidy 1997: 95–6). On the issue of *kepercayaan*, see Supartha (1994), Howell (2004), Hidayah (2012), Butt (2020), and Hefner (2021).
[7] In 1966, the Ministry of Religion was renamed Departemen Agama (Depag), and then again Kementerian Agama in 2010.
[8] As a legacy from the colonial period, Catholicism (*agama Katolik Roma*) and Protestantism (*agama Kristen Protestan*) are seen as two distinct religions in Indonesia, due to the way each denomination established itself in

Now that the setting up of an Indonesian Islamic state was no longer an option, the Ministry of Religion worked towards the Islamization of the Indonesian state. Yet, if the establishment of KAGRI was largely a concession to the Islamic group, it also provided the government with a legitimate tool to monitor religious communities and their practices. And while the Ministry of Religion was controlled by *santri* Muslims, who attempted to use it in order to bring Javanese *abangan* and other nominal Muslims to commit more strictly to Islam, the Ministry of Education and Culture (Kementerian Pendidikan dan Kebudayaan), strongly influenced by the ideas of Budi Utomo, the Theosophical Society, and the Taman Siswa movement, became a Javanist stronghold and a bulwark of the *kebatinan* groups.

After four years of anti-colonial struggle against the comeback of the Dutch in an attempt to reclaim their former colony, the sovereignty of Indonesia was first acknowledged on December 27, 1949 as a federal state (Republik Indonesia Serikat, RIS), and on August 17, 1950, the Republic of Indonesia was finally established as a unitary state, with a parliamentary regime and Sukarno as president (Kahin 1952). In subsequent years, radical Muslim factions kept fighting to impose an Islamic state and instigated several secessionist movements that threatened to put an end to the territorial integrity of the Indonesian Republic. These movements, which lasted until the 1960s, vindicate the enduring suspicion directed toward political Islam on the part of the Indonesian power elite, and their failure accounts for the persisting frustration of Indonesian Muslims, resentful of their lack of political leverage.

To grasp the import of 'religion' in independent Indonesia, one should investigate what has been included in—and excluded from—the normative status of *agama*. While the 1945 constitution (as well as the federal constitution of 1949 and the provisional unitary constitution of 1950, which remained in force until the return to the 1945 constitution in 1959) guaranteed Indonesian citizens (limited) freedom to profess and to practice their own religion (Ropi 2016: 134–9), the Ministry of Religion strove to restrict the legal acceptation of acknowledged religions, in conformity with the Islamic view of what qualifies as a legitimate *agama* according to the concept of *din*—that is, an understanding of religion as exclusivist, congregational, scripturalist, universalist and proselytical. Indeed, even if Islam failed to establish itself as the official religion of Indonesia, its proponents succeeded in imposing their own conception of what

---

the Archipelago—the former through the Portuguese, the latter through the Dutch—and in accordance with the historical 'pillarization' (*verzuiling*) of Dutch society, where religious differences were expressed in political parties and their affiliated associations. For a history of Christianity in Indonesia, see Aritonang and Steenbrink (2008).

a 'religion' truly is by framing and shaping all debates about the state's religious policies (Menchik 2014; Ropi 2017). Thus, from 1952 on, the Ministry of Religion made a number of attempts at establishing a legal definition of religion. According to KAGRI, in order to be officially recognized as *agama* (*agama yang diakui*), a religion must be monotheistic, have been revealed by a prophet and written down in a holy book, possess a unified body of laws and places of regular worship for its adherents, enjoy international recognition and, further, its following should not be limited to a single ethnic group.

Such a restrictive definition was tailored to fit the three revealed Abrahamic religions (*agama samawi*): Islam, Christianity and Judaism. It excluded several categories from the status of *agama*: the non-revealed religious traditions of non-Muslim and non-Christian populations like the Balinese and Chinese Indonesians; Javanese *abangan* and *aliran kebatinan* holding heterodox views; the 'animist' tribal religions (*agama suku*) of marginalized ethnic minorities; as well as syncretic 'new religions' (*agama baru*), inspired by self-proclaimed prophets. All these groups were regarded as 'people who do not yet have a religion' (*orang yang belum beragama*), a label associated with primitive backwardness and parochialism, and implying a situation that is bound to change. While adherents of ethnic religions would be targeted for Islamic or Christian proselytizing, it was understood that *abangan*, adherents of *kebatinan* groups, and followers of new religions—subsumed by the Ministry of Religion under the heading *aliran kepercayaan*—would be pressed to 'return into the fold of their original religion' (*kembali ke agama induknya*), that is, Islam.

According to the conditions laid by KAGRI, the Balinese people did not profess a proper 'religion' (*agama*) but possessed only 'beliefs' (*kepercayaan*), which not only were limited to their island, but did not even form a coherent and unified ensemble valid for the whole island. In that respect, the Balinese religion was seen as pertaining to *adat* and not to *agama*. Consequently, if the Balinese did not want to become the target of Muslim or Christian proselytizing, they had no other recourse than to reform their religion in order to make it eligible for the status of *agama*. For this to happen, the Balinese religion had to be rationalized and redefined in transcendent and monotheistic terms so as to approximate the features of a 'religion of the Book'.

Thus, before their religion could achieve the status of *agama*, the Balinese had to agree on their reply to KAGRI's conditions—they had to decide the name of their religion, of their One and Only God, of their prophet, and of their holy book. Moreover, they had to extract their religion from the boundaries of their island and from the parochialism of their ethnic identity, so as to turn it into a universalist religion. In other words, for their religion to be officially recognized, the Balinese must be willing to let themselves be dispossessed of it.

The first question to be settled was for the Balinese to agree on the name of their religion. After lengthy debate, the leaders of competing Balinese religious organizations resolved to name their religion *agama Hindu Bali* ('Balinese Hindu religion'). Once they had reached an agreement among themselves, the Balinese still had to convince the Ministry of Religion of the legitimacy of their religion. It would take them years of lobbying before *agama Hindu Bali* would finally be recognized by KAGRI.[9]

In search of a name

In 1938, the authority of the eight former Balinese rajas was restored by the Dutch colonial government, and their kingdoms (*negara*) were acknowledged as 'self-governing regions' (*zelfbestuurder landschapen*). Consultative Councils (Paruman Negara) were set up in each region, while a Great Council (Paruman Agung), composed of the *zelfbestuurders* and their advisors, was established in Denpasar to coordinate the administration of the island under the chairmanship of the *resident* of Bali and Lombok. This system remained in place until the landing of Japanese troops on the beach of Sanur in February 1942. Following the Japanese surrender and the proclamation of independence of Indonesia in August 1945, a period of political turmoil and social unrest set in, during which the incipient republican government attempted to build up its jurisdiction over the Archipelago. On August 22, 1945, the island of Bali became a 'region' (Daerah Bali) within the Province of the Lesser Sunda Islands (Propinsi Sunda Kecil, which was renamed Propinsi Nusa Tenggara in 1954), with its capital in Singaraja, and I Gusti Ketut Pudja as its first governor. On October 8, 1945, the civil administration in Bali was officially turned over to Governor Pudja and the Regional Indonesian National Committee (Komite Nasional Indonesia Daerah,

---

[9] Although there have been a number of publications by both Balinese and foreign academics about the struggle of Balinese leaders to reform their religion and have it recognized by the Ministry of Religion, none provides enough historical detail to allow the reader to fully grasp all the implications of this movement. The fact is that Balinese authors tend to consider, in anachronistic and teleological fashion, that their religion has always been 'Hindu' and that the struggle of the reformers amounted merely to having it acknowledged as such by their co-religionists and the Indonesian authorities. It is disconcerting to note that the sole foreign academic to have dedicated a full-scale study to this topic adopted precisely that same perspective (Bakker 1993). Regarding Balinese publications, one can refer to Anandakusuma (1966), Bagus (1972), Suaryana (1982), Diantari (1990), Wijaya (1990, 2007, 2009), Sudharta and Surpha (2006), Subagiasta (2009), and Ari Dwipayana (2021); and for foreign publications, see Swellengrebel (1960), Geertz (1973), Forge (1980), Rudyansjah (1986), Shadeg (1989), Bakker (1993, 1995), Howe (2001), Ramstedt (2002, 2004a), McDaniel (2010, 2013), and Landmann (2012).

KNID), under the authority of Ida Bagus Putra Manuaba, a former leader of Bali Darma Laksana and Parindra. Despite the declaration of independence and the appointment of a new governor, Bali was still controlled by the Japanese, who supported the rajas to form a political counterweight to the regional republican administration. Their attempt led to the creation in January 1946 of a Council of Rajas (Dewan Raja-Raja) and to the reconstitution of the Paruman Agung. On January 29, Gusti Ketut Pudja and the KNID surrendered their authority to the Dewan Raja-Raja and the Paruman Agung. After Dutch colonial troops (Koninklijk Nederlands Indisch Leger, KNIL) landed at Sanur beach on March 2, 1946, the Netherlands Indies Civil Administration (NICA) resumed control of the island and restored the Residency of Bali and Lombok, while acknowledging the Dewan Raja-Raja and the Paruman Agung as holding formal authority in Bali (Van der Meeberg 1946). The Dutch reinstated their *Baliseering* policy, fostering Balinese culture, tradition and religion, and undertook to strengthen the political standing of the rajas and influential Balinese aristocrats (Robinson 1995: 142-5).

The return of the Dutch exacerbated the polarization of Balinese society, leading to what political historian Geoffrey Robinson called nothing short of a local civil war (Robinson 1995: 97). While much of the population adopted a wait-and-see attitude, seemingly little concerned about the nationalist revolution in Java, most of the rajas backed their former colonizers with the hope of recovering the authority which had been bestowed on them in 1938.[10] On the other hand, groups of 'young fighters'—the *Pemuda Pejuang*—opposed the Dutch troops with fierce guerrilla resistance (Bagus 1991). The bulk of the armed resistance was wiped out on November 20, 1946, with the last stand of Lt. Col. I Gusti Ngurah Rai and his followers, in what has become known in Bali as the *Puputan Margarana*, but violent skirmishes continued until the transfer of sovereignty to the Indonesian Republic.

On December 24, 1946, as a result of the Denpasar Conference, Bali became part of the State of East Indonesia (Negara Indonesia Timur, NIT), with its capital at Makassar, established by the Dutch as a political counterweight to the Indonesian Republic based in Java, Madura and Sumatra. Tjokorda Gde Raka Sukawati was appointed president, while Anak Agung Gde Agung became prime

---

[10] An interesting eyewitness account of the troubled situation in Bali is provided by Peter Kemp, the British commander of the small party which landed on the island on February 18, 1946, to prepare the return of the Dutch. He recounts how he had to protect both Tjokorda Gde Raka Sukawati, the raja of Ubud, and Anak Agung Gde Agung, the raja of Gianyar, against attacks by Balinese nationalists, whom they called 'terrorists'. He was also in charge of organizing a conference of the Balinese rajas, held in the palace at Klungkung a few days before the landing of the Dutch troops. With the sole exception of the raja of Badung, all the other rajas pledged to cooperate in the restoration of the Netherlands Indies Government authority (Kemp 1961).

minister. On February 26, 1947, the Pembentukan Gabungan Kerajaan-kerajaan Bali ('Formation of the Unified Kingdoms of Bali') established the structure of government in Bali, which consisted of the Council of Rajas (Dewan Raja-Raja) and a People's Representative Council (Dewan Perwakilan Rakyat, which retained the name Paruman Agung). The powers entrusted to the Representative Council were extremely limited, and the government was held by the rajas, under the supervision of the Dutch *resident*. On March 14, 1949, the Residency of Bali and Lombok was abolished and the civil authority transferred to the Dewan Raja-Raja.

On September 25, 1950, shortly after the establishment of the unitary Republic of Indonesia, the Dewan Raja-Raja and the Paruman Agung, which had been seriously compromised by their collaboration with the Dutch and NIT regimes, were dissolved. They were replaced respectively by a Regional Government Council (Dewan Pemerintah Daerah, DPD), the executive authority on the island, and by a Provisional Regional People's Representative Council (Dewan Perwakilan Rakyat Daerah Sementara, DPRDS), endowed with the legislative authority. The DPD's chairman became the Regional Head (Kepala Daerah) of Bali. Chosen by the central government from the nominees by the DPRDS, the first incumbent of the post was the young nationalist leader Anak Agung Bagus Sutedja, a member of the Jembrana ruling house. The DPRDS was presided over by I Gusti Putu Merta. In replacement of the Paruman Negara, representative assemblies and executive councils were established in each of the former *negara*, headed by their respective traditional ruler. Thus, even though they were now superseded by the republican government, the former rajas managed to retain some political leverage, due to their land wealth, their client networks and their traditional authority. Most importantly, independence did not put an end to intense status competition and political divisions, and the simmering tensions would come to a head in 1965 with the bloody confrontation between supporters of the Indonesian National Party (Partai Nasional Indonesia, PNI), backed by the Indonesian military, and alleged followers of the Indonesian Communist Party (Partai Komunis Indonesia, PKI).[11]

In this context of heightened political tensions, the controversy which for years divided the Balinese intelligentsia over the proper name of their religion merits our attention in that it reveals profound divergences in the main points of debate, that is, how *agama* is related to *adat* on the one hand, and how the

---

[11] On the political situation in Bali during these years of turmoil, see Kementerian Penerangan (1953: 32–64), Last (1955), Pendit (1979), Agung (1985), Oka (1988), Bagus (1991), Sendra (2013), Robinson (1995), and Hoek (2021).

Balinese religion is linked to Hinduism on the other. This controversy attests to a resurgence of the contest between the rising elite of progressive commoners (*jaba*) and the conservative nobility (*triwangsa*)—especially the *brahmana*, eager to preserve their monopoly on the initiated priesthood—in their attempt to hold sway over the religious life of the Balinese people. Some Balinese and foreign observers have tended to imply that, despite the highly volatile situation on the island after the proclamation of Indonesia's independence, the Islamic threat was deemed serious enough for Balinese elites of different political persuasions to close ranks in defense of their religious identity (Wijaya 1990: 6-7; Bakker 1993: 225–30; Robinson 1995: 183–4). Yet, an investigation of whatever contemporary written evidence has survived provides a different picture, one that brings forth sharp disagreement among the Balinese, not only about the strategy to be pursued to have their religion officially recognized by the Ministry of Religion, but even more so in regard to the very conception of the Balinese religion.

Debate about the Balinese religion had come to a standstill during the Japanese occupation. Then, on April 22, 1945, a few months before the capitulation of Japan, a delegation of seventeen *padanda Siwa* from different parts of Bali, calling themselves the Paruman Pandita Dharma ('Dharma Priests Council'), gathered in Klungkung under the aegis of the Japanese authorities and in the presence of the Dewa Agung, Ida Dewa Agung Gede Oka Geg, together with Anak Agung Agung Anglurah Ketut Karangasem, I Gusti Ketut Pudja and I Nyoman Kadjeng, to discuss the name of the Balinese religion and to strengthen its foundations. The *padanda* resolved to name their religion *agama Siwa* and to choose as their highest deity Siwa Raditiya, that is, Siwa as the Sun God (Sanghyang Surya) (*Bali Sinbun*, April 22, 1945). It turned out that this was a maneuver to affiliate the Balinese religion with Shintoism, by way of assimilating Tirta with Sindu, and Sindu with Shinto (Diantari 1990: 110; Wijaya 2009: 338–42).

After the Japanese surrender, the *triwangsa* power elite attempted to reassert the prerogatives they had managed to safeguard during the colonial era, and especially to maintain their customary authority in religious matters. On January 31, 1947, an association of *padanda* was founded in Singaraja, the Paruman Para Pandita (PPP, 'Council of Priests'), chaired by Ida Padanda Made Kamenuh. With the backing of the Dewan Raja-Raja, the association, initially limited to Buleleng, widened its scope and, on November 6, 1948, became the Paruman Para Pandita Bali Lombok. The aim of this organization was to unify the *agama Siwa-Budha* while adapting the *adat* prevailing in Bali and Lombok to the conditions of the time (Kamenuh 1978). With a view to securing the *padanda*'s authority over Balinese religious practices, the PPP was to provide for the education of priests and religious specialists, to compose a holy book, and to establish councils of priests in the various *negara*. On November 16–19, 1949, the Paruman Para Pandita held its first congress in Singaraja, in the presence of most of the rajas and with the official support of the president of the NIT. The main point on the agenda was the name of the Balinese religion, which took no less than two days of debate to assess the respective merits of *Tirtha, Siwa, Siwa-Budha, Hindu Bali,* and *Hindu*,[12] before a majority of *padanda* and rajas finally settled for *agama Tirtha*, all the while asserting that only *padanda Siwa* and *Budha* could ordain candidates to the priesthood.[13] Other issues dealt with during the congress concerned the standardization of religious ceremonies throughout the island and their simplification (PPP 1949). The PPP organized a second congress on October 26–28, 1952, after which it appears to have ceased any activity.

While the *padanda* were buttressing their religious hegemony, young Balinese studying in Java, Sulawesi and Bali were sending delegates to a conference (*Konperensi Pelajar Seberang*) that took place on July 14–17, 1950 in Denpasar. On August 17, 1950, a Coordinating Committee of High School Students (Badan Koordinator Usaha Pelajar, BKUP) was set up in Malang (Java), under the leadership of I Made Wedastera Suyasa—a Balinese student who had formed the movement of the Hindu-Balinese Youth (Angkatan Muda Hindu-Bali, AMHB) in June 1950 in Jakarta and who was soon to become a leader of the Indonesian National Party (PNI) (Lane 1972). The BKUP addressed a series of demands to both the Balinese authorities and the Paruman Para Pandita: that they come to an agreement regarding the name of the Balinese religion; that ceremonies be simplified in order to reduce their cost and be standardized throughout the whole island; that the *padanda* instruct their flock on the meaning of their ceremonies and publish educational books on religious matters; that a school be opened for the formation of priests, without any distinction whatsoever as to title or caste; and that customary laws which are no longer appropriate to the progress of the times be abolished. Among the latter issues, we note the revocation of the rules governing matrimonial alliances between *jaba* and

---

[12] During the discussions, *agama Tirtha* was endorsed by the delegates of Gianyar, Bangli, Karangasem and Lombok; *agama Siwa* by Klungkung and Buleleng; *agama Siwa-Budha* by Tabanan; while Padanda Gede Ngendjung opted for *agama Hindu Bali* and a delegate from Klungkung advocated *agama Hindu* (PPP 1949: 8).

[13] The question of priesthood in Bali is complex, the more so as it is contentious, owing to its link to the hierarchy of the title groups. On this issue, I refer the reader to Chapter 6.

triwangsa[14] as well as the recognition of equal rights for women (BKUP 1950; Suaryana 1982: 34–7).

When Minister of Religion K.H. Wahid Hasyim officially formulated the structure of the Ministry of Religion on September 19, 1950, it became painfully clear that the Balinese religion would not be taken into account. In response, I Gusti Bagus Sugriwa, who was in charge of religious and cultural affairs at the recently established Dewan Pemerintah Daerah, formally requested KAGRI to recognize the Balinese religion on a par with Islam and Christianity. Then, a delegation from KAGRI, led by the former minister of religion, K.H. Masjkur, paid a visit to Bali on December 26, 1950, to inquire about the religious situation on the island. Masjkur asked the name of the religion professed by the Balinese,[15] that of its God, of its prophet and of its holy book, the purpose of its ceremonies and the theological tenets of its creed. Sugriwa replied that the proper name of the Balinese religion was *agama Hindu Bali*. He explained that "Hindu in Bali refers to Siwa Buddha, that is, Hinduism of the Siwa sect and Buddhism of the Mahayana sect, merged with the Balinese religion (syncretism), which explains why there are priests of Siwa, priests of Buddha, as well as numerous priests of the Balinese religion."[16] He denied that the Balinese were polytheists as, in conformity with Pancasila, they worship the One and Only God (Sanghyang Tunggal). He explained that in their family shrine (*sanggah*), the Balinese pay homage (*berbakti*) to the purified souls of their ancestors, but they do not worship (*bukan menyembah*) them. In return, Sugriwa demanded that KAGRI take over the religious obligations which were formerly the responsibility of the rajas and, especially, that it maintain the Pura Panataran Agung at Besakih[17] and finance its rituals; support the *padanda* as well as the *pamangku*; fund the translation into Indonesian of Old Javanese religious manuscripts; and establish representations for the Balinese religion within KAGRI, not only in Jakarta, but also at the provincial and regional levels. In the end—and despite some conciliatory

---

[14] These rules (*Asu Pundung, Alangkahi Karang Hulu*) would eventually be revoked by the DPRDS in July 1951, along with those punishing commoners for giving birth to male-female twins (*manak salah*), and banishment (*selong*) in retribution for the breach of customary law. Among the other resolutions issued at the same time was the prohibition on photographing bare-breasted Balinese women.

[15] "*Yang saya ketahui nama agama saudara-saudara ada bermacam-macam, yaitu: Agama Bali, Agama Tirtha, Agama Hindu, Agama Hindu Bali, Agama Çiwa Buddha. Manakah yang sebenarnya?*" (Sugriwa 1973: 7).

[16] "*Pengertian Hindu di sini adalah Çiwa Buddha, Hindu sekte Çiwa dan Buddha sekte Mahayana, berpadu (syncritisme) dengan Agama Bali, sebab itu ada dalam kenyataan pendeta Çiwa, pendeta Buddha dan pendeta-pendeta Bali yang sangat banyak*" (Sugriwa 1973: 8).

[17] The Pura Panataran Agung ('Great State Temple') is the main sanctuary at Besakih, a large complex of temples located on the slopes of Gunung Agung, the highest volcano in Bali. It is considered the 'mother temple' (*pura induk*) of Bali and has always been associated with the political powers of the day (Stuart-Fox 2002).

promises—only a modest contribution to translation costs was granted by the Ministry of Religion (Anandakusuma 1966: 84–5; Sugriwa 1973: 6–8).

Following the visit to Bali by the delegation from the Ministry of Religion, a Provincial Office of KAGRI (Kantor Urusan Agama Propinsi Sunda Kecil, KUAP)—that is, in charge of the Province of the Lesser Sunda Islands—was set up in Singaraja, while a Regional Office of KAGRI (Kantor Urusan Agama Daerah Bali, KUAD)—that is, concerned only with the island of Bali—was opened in Denpasar. However, much to the consternation of the Balinese, both these offices dealt exclusively with *agama Islam*. The Balinese religion was consequently left in a vacuum, now that its former patrons (*Guru Wisesa*), the rajas of yore, had been replaced by the republican government. Several religious organizations would soon emerge to face this dire situation.

On December 31, 1950, I Gusti Anandakusuma and Ida Bagus Tugur founded the Majelis Hinduisme ('Council of Hinduism') in Klungkung. Their purpose was to adapt *agama Hindu* in Bali to the conditions of the time, to purify the *adat* of the customs that had become obsolete, and to remove any trace of 'animism' (*animisme*) from Balinese religious practices (*Anggaran Dasar Majelis Hinduisme*, 1950). The Majelis Hinduisme succeeded the Trimurti organization, which had been set up by the same individuals on October 16, 1939 (*Djatajoe* 1940, No. 9–10: 292–4). As indicated by the title of that organization, the name they advocated then for the Balinese religion was *agama Trimurti*.

On February 6, 1951, the Panti Agama Hindu-Bali (PAHB, 'Institution of the Hindu-Balinese religion') was established in Singaraja, under the leadership of Ida Padanda Gede Ngendjung and I Wayan Bhadra, with the aim of unifying *agama Hindu-Bali* by deepening the knowledge of its philosophy (*memperdalam pengetahuan tentang filsafat agama Hindu-Bali*), of simplifying its ceremonies (*mempersahaja upacara2 agama Hindu-Bali*), and of getting rid of outdated customs (*mengubah adat-istiadat yang ta' sesuai lagi dengan keadaan zaman*) (*Anggaran Dasar Panti Agama Hindu Bali*, 1951; see also Ngendjung 1951). In order to propagate their ideas, the PAHB's leaders launched a short-lived periodical titled *Surat Tri-Ulan*. Although this organization was presided over by a *padanda*,[18] most of its members were commoners (among them were Ketut Kandia, Nyoman Kadjeng, Putu Shanty, as well as Gusti Bagus Sugriwa). They adopted a 'progressive' (*progressief*) stance, aimed particularly at the *padanda*

---

[18] Even though he was a *padanda*, after his death in March 1955, Ida Bagus Gede Ngendjung was said to have been a communist since the 1930s (*Damai* 1955, No. 3: 18). And some members of the PAHB were associated with Lekra (Lembaga Kebudayaan Rakyat), the cultural organization affiliated with the Indonesian Communist Party (PKI), set up in 1950 (Foulcher 1986; Putra 2003).

assembled in the Paruman Para Pandita, whom they accused of being diehard 'conservatives' (*conservatief*) (Shanty 1951).[19] They denounced the prohibitions (*aja wera*) placed by *padanda* on access to religious knowledge contained in their manuscripts. Above all, they challenged the traditional vision of the 'castes' (*kasta*) as a hierarchy of title groups based on birth, and advocated a concept founded on merit and competence. For them, status should no longer be ascribed but achieved, a position that had already been championed by Surya Kanta, of which some of them had been members (Shanty 1952a). Yet, by promoting the name *agama Hindu-Bali*—which was the name advocated by the *triwangsa* in *Bali Adnjana*, against the *jaba* who defended the name *agama Bali Hindu*—they were clearly not intending to radically transform the religion of Bali in order to make it conform to Indian Hinduism: "The Panti Agama Hindu-Bali will not bring about radical change, but will endeavor to guide its followers toward one direction, that is, God—without losing the original foundations. You do not have to worry that with such change the foundations of our Culture in Bali will be lost."[20]

A few weeks later, an association devoted to the study of Balinese religious texts, Wiwada Sastra Sabha ('Society for Discussing Literature'), was founded in Denpasar, on the initiative of Ida Bagus Raka Keniten and I Gusti Bagus Sugriwa, with the aim of substantiating that Balinese religion had scriptures that met the standard for its national recognition (Anandakusuma 1966: 78).

Thus, soon after the incorporation of Bali into the Indonesian state, there were four main religious organizations on the island, representing a wide spectrum of opinions held by various Balinese elites on the nature of their

---

[19] Here is how Putu Shanty formulated the opposition between the two organizations and the names they respectively advocated for the Balinese religion: "In Bali, there are two views regarding religion. One group which consists of conservative people holding on to bygone opinions call the religion in Bali: Tirtha, whereas the new generation who have a wider point of view and a full awareness have already protested that the religion in Bali be called: Hindu-Bali" (*Di Bali ada dua buah paham nama dikalangan agama! Satu grup yang terdiri dari manusia konserpatif yang berpegang kepada dalil2 lama menamakan agama di Bali: Tirtha, sedang angkatan baru yang mempunyai pandangan lebih luas dan penuh kesadaran sudah memperotes agar agama di Bali ini dinamai: Hindu-Bali*) (Shanty 1952a: 7).

[20] "*Panti Agama Hindu-Bali tidak akan membawa perobahan yang radikal, melainkan Panti berusaha akan menyadarkan penganut penganutnya kearah satu, yaitu Widhi—dengan tidak menghilangkan dasar2 semula. Engkau tidak usah chawatir bahwa dengan perobahan yang tiba2 ini dasar2 Kebudayaan kita di Bali akan lenyap*" (Shanty 1951). In an intriguing reversal of the positions held respectively by *jaba* and *triwangsa* in the 1920s, at the time of the PAHB's first meeting, on March 11, 1951, intended to debate on the proper name of the Balinese religion, Wayan Bhadra objected to the name *agama Bali Hindu* on the ground that it referred to a bygone era, when the Balinese people were not well acquainted yet with Hinduism and were still very much influenced by their former animism. In his eyes, far from defining the Balinese people as truly Hindu, as Surya Kanta had argued, the name *Bali Hindu* was better replaced with the name *Hindu Bali* in order to signify that they had duly come to embrace Hinduism (PAHB 1951).

religion, the orientation its reform should take and its links to Hinduism. The first one, the Paruman Para Pandita, was the most conservative, staunchly adhering to Balinese particularism and anxious to defend the authority of the *padanda* and their monopoly on religious knowledge. The Wiwada Sastra Sabha represented the literary tradition, attached to Balinese cultural identity, from which religion was seen as inseparable. As for the Panti Agama Hindu-Bali, its leaders were taking over the progressive struggle, stemming from Surya Kanta and pursued to some extent by Bali Darma Laksana, of those Balinese intellectuals who wanted to modernize and reform their religion in the direction of Hinduism, without cutting it off from its indigenous roots. Finally, as its name indicated, the Majelis Hinduisme was aiming to universalize the Balinese religion in conformity with contemporary Indian Hinduism.

On June 10, 1951, representatives of these four organizations decided to send a written motion to the minister of religion, the Balinese members of the Indonesian parliament, and the governor of the Province of the Lesser Sunda Islands, putting forward the following requests: that the Balinese religion be represented in KAGRI's central, provincial and regional offices; that a committee for the writing of a textbook of *agama Hindu Bali*, to be used in the schools, be funded by the government; that the *padanda* and *pamangku* be supported on KAGRI's budget; and that a subsidy be attributed for the maintenance of the main Balinese temples as well as of the religious ceremonies taking place therein. On August 23, 1951, the minister declined all these requests and insisted instead once again on knowing the proper name of the Balinese religion—*Siwa-Budha, Tirtha, Hindu Bali* or *Hinduisme*? (Anandakusuma 1966: 85–8).

In Singaraja, a committee was set up to try to comply with KAGRI's demand, consisting of Padanda Made Kamenuh from the PPP, Wayan Bhadra and Nyoman Kadjeng from the PAHB, and Roelof Goris, who had been back in Bali since 1947 (Shadeg 1989: 3). Eventually, in order to reach an agreement on the Balinese religion, KAGRI's Provincial Office (KUAP) convened a meeting on May 25, 1952, at Tampaksiring with representatives of the four main religious organizations. At the conclusion of this meeting, the Balinese religion was officially given the name *agama Hindu Bali* (*Suara Indonesia*, May 26, 1952). The choice of *agama Hindu Bali* instead of simply *agama Hindu* was based on the agreement among the delegates that while the Balinese religion had been deeply marked by Indian Hinduism it was still significantly different enough to deserve a specific name of its own. Besides, it appears in retrospect that it was only after Balinese had started to convert to Islam as well as to Christianity that the name *agama Hindu Bali* became customary, in order to distinguish *Hindu Bali* from *Islam Bali* or *Kristen Bali*.

It is noteworthy that the representative of the Paruman Para Pandita opposed the name *agama Hindu Bali* and maintained his preference for *agama Tirtha*. In the months following this meeting, Padanda Made Kamenuh lectured extensively around Bali as well as to Balinese students in Java in defense of the name *agama Tirtha*. It was only on July 2, 1953, at the time of a lecture he delivered in Jakarta to the Indonesian Association of Balinese Students (Persatuan Siswa Indonesia Bali, PERSIB)—headed by his opponent I Nyoman Suwandhi Pendit (Pendit 1952)—that Padanda Made Kamenuh finally agreed to the name *agama Hindu Bali*. On that occasion, he specified that the One and Only God of *agama Hindu Bali* was Sanghyang Widhi (*yang berarti Tuhan yg maha esa* [*tunggal*]), that its holy book (*kitab suci*) was the *lontar Sarasamuscaya*, a compendium of the teachings of the *Asta Dasa Parwa* (*Mahabarata*), and that its prophet (*nabi*) was Begawan Biasa—the mythical compiler of the Vedas and the *Mahabharata* (*Bhakti* 1953, No. 23: 20–1). However, it was not enough that representatives of Balinese religious organizations agree on the name *agama Hindu Bali* for that name to be henceforth unanimously acknowledged by the Balinese people, as was demonstrated by the persistent embarrassment of Balinese students outside their island whenever they were asked about the name of their religion (Shanty 1954; Kandia 1954).

While the Balinese had long debated the name of their religion, they appear to have agreed rather easily on the name of their God—Ida Sang Hyang Wid(h)i (Wasa), the Balinese rendering of the Indonesian *Ketuhanan Yang Maha Esa*. The fact is that I could not find any evidence of debate on this issue, even though the Balinese had numerous names to refer to their supreme deity.[21] One might have expected that religious reformers choose rather Sanghyang Tunggal to convey the idea of the oneness of God, as it was the name put forward by Gusti Bagus Sugriwa when the KAGRI's delegation had come to Bali on December 26, 1950. In any case, prior to becoming the generic name of the One and Only God of *agama Hindu Bali*, Sang Hyang Widi was known only among the literati and was not the object of religious worship. It was a sort of abstract and all-

---

[21] One could mention, with no claim to be exhaustive, the following names: Tuhan, Allah, Batara Siwa, Iswara, Acintya, Sang Hyang Tunggal, Sang Hyang Sunya, Sang Hyang Widi, Sang Hyang Guru, Sang Hyang Embang, Sang Hyang Wenang, Sang Hyang Kawi, Sang Hyang Tuduh, Sang Hyang Suksma, Sang Hyang Jagat, Sang Hyang Wisesa, etc. On the other hand, in Javanese religious literature of the 19th century, the name Hyang Widdhi refers exclusively to Allah (Zuhri 2022: 383).

encompassing *deus otiosus*, "a kind of Fatum presiding over the universe" (Lévi 1933: xiv). This name was popularized in the 1920s by the movement of religious reform as an equivalent of the Malay word *Tuhan*. It is in fact an ancient representation of the cosmic order, already known in Java, combining the Old Javanese terms *sang* (a particle used before a noun designating a person of high rank) and *hyang* (god, deity) with the Sanskrit terms *vidhi* (rule, law; prescribed rites; destiny) and *vasha* (power, force, dominion), so that Sang Hyang Widhi Wasa could be rendered as 'God Almighty', the equivalent of *Tuhan Yang Maha Kuasa*. According to Jan Gonda: "[…] in modern Bali *Vidhi* (*Viddhi*)—the Indian designation of 'rule, destiny' which is also applied to some individual gods— denotes that principle which, representing the unity of the universe, is beyond all plurality and acts as the guardian of the cosmic and moral order" (Gonda 1975: 23). The polysemy of this name allowed it to express the conception of God the Creator peculiar to the Abrahamic religions as well as the idea of *dharma*, which implies a prevalence of the cosmic order over the gods and of gods over men (Ramstedt 2004a: 11). Furthermore, the name Sang Hyang Widi carried no reference to Shaivism and was therefore acceptable to the *padanda Boda* (Forge 1980: 229). From then on, the manifold deities of the Balinese would be said to be different manifestations of Sang Hyang Widi. Needless to say, this novel conception differed considerably from the traditional Balinese understanding of the divine, both hierarchized and multiple.

At the conclusion of the meeting of May 25, 1952, the holy books of the Balinese were defined as: a) *Shruti* (the sacred knowledge of the Vedas revealed to the primordial seers);[22] b) *Smreti* (the orally transmitted religious literature, not included in the Revelation); and, c) *Yadnya* (the Balinese manuscripts providing instructions on the correct execution of the rites). Furthermore, a Balinese profession of faith (*Sahadat*, an Islamic term) was chosen: '*Om tat sat, ekam ewa dwityam*'[23] ('We believe in the One and Only God, almighty and eternal') (*Suara Indonesia*, May 26, 1952). Shortly afterwards, a Hindu-Bali

---

[22] Numerous Balinese reformers whom I interviewed openly admitted that the Vedas were unknown until recently in Bali and that the Balinese people have very little idea of what they are about. They generally concurred that the reference to the Vedas was due to the KAGRI's pressure for the Balinese religion to cite a *kitab suci* in support of its official recognition as a bona fide *agama*, all the while conceding that the Vedas are a very different kind of holy book from the Quran or the Bible. See Acri (2011: 164, n. 41): "It should be noted that the Vedas are hardly in conformity with a Holy Book providing a coherent basis for doctrine, being written in a language which was not understood even in India from the classical period onwards."

[23] This is derived from the well-known *mahavakya*, from the *Chandogya Upanishad* (6, 2, 1), '*Ekam eva advityam Brahman*' ('God is one, there is no two'). This profession of faith was certainly not unrelated to the Islamic *syahadat*, declaring belief in the oneness of God and the acceptance of Muhammad as His prophet, which the Balinese people were requested to comply with.

division (*bagian*) was established within the KUAP, under the leadership of Wayan Bhadra, in order to deal with day-to-day matters. But this did not imply that *agama Hindu Bali* was recognized by KAGRI in Jakarta, or even by the KUAP in Singaraja.

Looking to India

Meanwhile, on February 2, 1951, the Balinese daily *Suara Indonesia* ('The Voice of Indonesia', 1948–66) had published a 'Letter from India' entitled 'The Problem of Religion in Bali' (*Soal Agama di Bali*) (Mantra 1951). It was sent by a Balinese student at Visva-Bharati, the famous Hindu university founded by Rabindranath Tagore at Shantiniketan, in Bengal. This student, the first Balinese to obtain a scholarship through the Indian Council for Cultural Relations in 1950,[24] was a *brahmana* by the name of Ida Bagus Mantra. He was preparing a PhD thesis, which he would present in 1955 on *Hindu Literature and Religion in Indonesia* (Mantra 1955).

Deploring the ritualistic propensity of the Balinese people, Mantra described their religion as being still 'primitive' (*masih bersifat primitief*). He was of the opinion that the present religion in Bali should be called *Bali Hindu*, as it was actually a haphazard mixture of Balinese and Hindu elements which is not the true Hinduism. He attributed this unfortunate state of affairs to the fact that Indian religious influences had reached the Indonesian Archipelago and combined with archaic Balinese customs at a time when Hinduism itself was still 'primitive' (*masih bersifat primitief juga*). Later, the arrival of Europeans would result in the severing of the links with India, while Hinduism was nurturing its spiritual riches. For example, the Vedas that are known in Bali are not the real ones, and in truth they are only good enough to be put into a museum (*sudah sepatutnya ditempatkan di Musium*). What is now important in India are the Upanishads, which represent the highest philosophical level in Hinduism, and which are unknown in Bali—to the extent that for the ensuing centuries the Balinese were barred access to the source of their religion, with the result that they had become spiritually impoverished. Accordingly, Mantra appealed to the Balinese to regenerate their religion by renewing contact with their spiritual

---

[24] The Indian Council for Cultural Relations was established in 1950 by the minister of education with the purpose of promoting the cultural diplomacy of independent India, especially by providing fellowships to foreign students wishing to enroll in an Indian university. An Indonesian bureau was opened in Jakarta in 1955, the Jawaharlal Nehru Indian Cultural Centre, as a result of an agreement between the two countries.

mother country India, so as to make it a true Hinduism (*agama Hindu*). For that purpose, he suggested sending Balinese scholars to India, with the mission of studying the sacred texts of Hindu literature and translating them into Indonesian in order to fulfill the spiritual needs of their co-religionists.

This open letter made a great impression upon Balinese reformers at the time and convinced many of them to look to India for a solution to their religious predicament.[25] Its influence was especially patent on the Panti Agama Hindu-Bali, as witnessed by the lecture given by Wayan Bhadra at its first meeting, on March 11, 1951, in which he took up many of the arguments put forth by Mantra, specifically by objecting to the name *Bali Hindu* as denoting a phase when the Balinese religion was still 'animistic' (PAHB 1951: 3).

A few months later, in 1952, a senior high school student in Singaraja, Ida Bagus Oka Punyatmadja, another *brahmana*, addressed 'A Letter from Bali' to Professor Raghu Vira, an eminent Indian scholar and prominent politician, founder of the International Academy of Indian Culture,[26] who had come to the Kirtya library to research the cultural history of Bali. Punyatmadja was a pupil of Wayan Bhadra and had met Raghu Vira on the occasion of his guest lectures on the cultural and religious links between India and Bali. The Indian scholar had suggested that one of Bhadra's promising students should come to his country to study the origins of the Balinese culture. Punyatmadja wrote in his letter: "I thought it was the chance of my life to learn our culture in your country, where our glorious doctrine and the essence of our (Bali) high culture was born in former time" (Vira 1978: 73–4). Throughout his lengthy and rather verbose letter, Punyatmadja expressed his love and admiration for the religious legacy of India, making recurrent references to Hindu scriptures and Shaivite theology, sprinkled with Sanskrit words, a language he was studying—as he mentioned—with Dr. Goris. All the while, he bemoaned the fact that his co-religionists were ignorant of the teachings of the Hindu scriptures:

> I feel unhappy because of the weak point of the faith of Hindu Bali devotees who do not practise their dharma, who only perpetrate the ritual of our religion and some men who will abandon their ancient high culture. Perhaps this weak

---

[25] Actually, Mantra's letter was not the first occurrence of a Balinese author resorting to Indian Hinduism in order to authorize his religion. Without going all the way back to Tjakra Tanaya accusing his Surya Kanta opponents of searching for their references in India rather than in Majapahit, one should mention a 'Textbook of the Samkhya Philosophy' (*Adji Sangkya*) composed in 1947 in Balinese by Ida Ktut Djelantik, who "must be acknowledged as the first exponent of the Balinese religious elite of the modern period to have made use of an Indian Hindu source" (Acri 2013: 89; see further Bakker 1993: 302).

[26] The International Academy of Indian Culture (Saraswati Vihar) was established in Lahore in 1932; it shifted to Nagpur in 1946 and finally to New Delhi in 1956, where it is still run by Raghu Vira's son, Dr. Lokesh Chandra.

point is caused by the fact that there are not enough educators to educate the Hindu Bali devotees, to ameliorate them, according to the teachings of our scriptures, and to educate Bali's youth [...] to love their culture. This fact is the reason why my intention is very strong to learn our culture in your country, where I will receive enlightenment about our culture and especially I can follow the faithful Hindu devotees in practising their dharma which they had received from their wise ancestors. And afterwards if I return to my island, I can bring the glorious souvenir from your country (glorious teachings and education) to perfect the faith of Hindu Bali devotees and the love of Bali's youth for their culture (Vira 1978: 79–80).

Thanks to the intercession of I Gusti Bagus Oka, vice-governor of the Province of the Lesser Sunda Islands, Punyatmadja would be granted a government scholarship to study in India in 1953, at Banaras Hindu University and at the International Academy of Indian Culture. In 1954, he was joined by Tjokorda Rai Sudharta, a *satria* from the Ubud ruling house, who had also been recommended by Raghu Vira. During their stay in India, Mantra, Punyatmadja, and Sudharta drew up plans to establish a council of Hinduism, with a view to unifying and institutionalizing the Balinese religion.[27] Back in Indonesia, each of them would pursue a high profile political-cum-religious career.[28]

At the time when Balinese students in India were pleading for their co-religionists to renew the age-old links of their island with Hinduism, an Indian man established in Bali was acknowledging the Balinese people as fellow Hindus. Shortly after Mantra's letter appeared in *Suara Indonesia*, a booklet was published under the title *Dasa Sila Agama Bali* ('The Ten Principles of the Balinese Religion'), that made Balinese religion looking suspiciously like a local version of Arya Samaj Neo-Hinduism (Shastri 1951). Its author, who signed himself Prof. Narendra Dev. Pandit Shastri, had paid a visit to Bali in 1949, where he eventually took up residence, married a Balinese girl, became an Indonesian citizen, and started trading in textiles. Citing the names of some of the foremost religious leaders of the time (Padanda Made Kamenuh, Padanda

---

[27] Interview, Tjokorda Rai Sudharta, Puri Amertasari, Ubud, June 1, 2006.
[28] After being one of the main founders of Parisada Dharma Hindu Bali, Ida Bagus Mantra became its first secretary-general (1959–64); he would go on to become president of the University of Bali (1964–68) and then director general of culture in Jakarta (1968–78), before being appointed governor of Bali (1978–88) and ending his career as Indonesian ambassador to India (1989–92). Ida Bagus Oka Punyatmadja would become vice-president of Parisada Hindu Dharma (1968–91), a member of the parliament in Jakarta (1977–92), vice-president of the World Hindu Federation (1988–92), in close contact with the Vishva Hindu Parishad, and he would be ordained a *padanda* in 1998. Tjokorda Rai Sudharta would be appointed in 1963 director of the Bali Office of Religion (Kantor Agama Daerah Tingkat I Bali), before becoming secretary-general of Parisada Hindu Dharma (1964–68) and a member of the national parliament (1977–87).

Gede Ngendjung, Wayan Bhadra, Gusti Bagus Sugriwa, as well as Roelof Goris, among others), he claimed that in its fundamentals the Balinese religion (*Agama Bali*) was no different from Hinduism as found in India. First, the Balinese manuscripts used by the *padanda* were in accordance with Indian textual tenets, and second, the Balinese ritual practices were similar to the ones followed by their Indian co-religionists, with two minor exceptions, the modalities of cremation (*ngaben*) and the consumption of beef. Above all, Shastri stated that the Balinese were monotheists, as they venerate the One and Only God, Sang Hiang Widhi, with Brahma, Vishnu, and Shiva as His manifestations (*penjelmaan*, lit. 'incarnation'). The effigies (*arca*) used by the Balinese in their rituals were only mediations destined to help human beings to communicate with God. Shastri went on to assert unhesitatingly that the four Vedas (which were still unknown in Bali)[29] were the most important sacred books (*kitab suci*) of the *Agama Bali*, along with the *Sarasamuchaya*, the *Ramayana* and the *Suta-Soma*. He claimed further that *moksha* was the ultimate purpose of every Balinese.[30] He also mentioned the *Pancha Yajna* (*Deva Yajna, Pitri Yajna, Manushya Yajna, Bhuta Yajna, Rishi Yajna*).[31] Additionally, he contended that the Indian caste system (*Chaturwangsa*) was in force in Bali (including the misconception of the *Vaishya* as traders). Finally, Shastri ended his booklet by stressing the importance of performing the *Tri Sandhya*, a compilation of Sanskrit *mantra*, the first of which is the famous *Gayatri* drawn from the *Weda Parikrama*, a manual used by the *padanda Siwa* for their daily worship.[32]

---

[29] During my interview with Narendra Dev. Pandit Shastri (Denpasar, January 3, 1994), he freely admitted that the Balinese people did not yet know the Vedas in the 1950s.

[30] "*Moksha adalah tujuan terachir dari seluruh Ummat Agama Bali*" (Shastri 1951: 8). While the concept of *moksha*, the liberation of individual souls (*atma*) from the cycle of death and rebirth (*samsara*) through union with the Brahman, was indeed known to the Balinese literati, it certainly was not the 'ultimate purpose of every Balinese', who aspire rather to reunite with their ancestors before reincarnating (*numitis*) in their own family line (Hornbacher 2014).

[31] The Sanskrit term *yajna* means 'sacrifice, offering'. These are derived from the 'five great sacrifices' (*panchamahayajna*) that a Vedic householder has to perform daily: *devayajna* (oblation to the fire), *pitryajna* (offering of food and water), *bhutayajna* (offering of a rice ball or flowers), *narayajna* (offering of food to brahmins), and *brahmayajna* (recitation of Vedic *mantra*). There are occasional mentions of these *yajna* in Javanese textual traditions as well as in *Djatajoe* (1937, No. 9: 268), but their precise doctrinal standardization is a modern innovation as we shall see further on (Hooykaas 1975).

[32] At that time, the recitation of Sanskrit *mantra* such as the *Gayatri* was restricted to *padanda*. Balinese religious practices relied on prayers in Balinese language while presenting offerings during ceremonies. There are mentions of the *trisandhya* in Old Javanese and Balinese literature, as denoting the practice of three daily acts of worship during the 'junctures' (*sandhya*) of the day: at dawn, at noon, and at dusk. I also found a very brief reference in *Djatajoe* (1938, No. 7: 222). But it is only in the 1950s, after the publication of another of Shastri's booklets, entitled *Tri Sandhya* (195?), that the *Puja Tri Sandhya* ('Celebration of the Three Daily Prayers') was to become the official Hindu prayer—the Hindu equivalent of the Muslim *salat*—taught in Balinese schools and, later, broadcast on radio

It is difficult to assess the precise influence exerted by Narendra Dev. Pandit Shastri on the contemporary Hinduization of the Balinese religion (Kapoor 1958: 33–42; Somvir 2004: 258–9; Lanus 2014: 251–7). But it was certainly decisive, if one considers that he was the first Indian Hindu to propagate a reformed version of Balinese theology and ritual, rationalized along the lines of Neo-Hinduism.[33] Yet, regardless of what his double title of 'Prof.' and 'Pandit' could lead one to assume, Shastri himself denied being a scholar, and affirmed to me that his knowledge of religious matters was rather limited. Contrary to what has been reported by several authors (Bakker 1993: 57, 227; Ramstedt 2004a: 11, 2008: 1240), he contended that he had never been sent to Bali by the Arya Samaj with the aim of Hinduizing the Balinese people.[34] He claimed that he had come to Bali by chance and that, to his surprise, he had discovered that the Balinese were fellow Hindus like himself, even though they had forgotten most of what Hinduism was about, due to the ignorance of religious matters in which they were kept by their priests. Thus he decided to bring the Balinese people back into the fold of Hinduism, for fear that if they persisted along their natural inclination, which is animism, they would become an easy prey for proselytizing, not so much Muslim as Christian, or worse, communism. To this end, he had approached the Ramakrishna Mission and the Arya Samaj in Singapore, but they could not provide any help.

It seems that Shastri was reluctant to admit his affiliation to the Arya Samaj because his intent to Hinduize the Balinese religion had met with criticism and opposition from various quarters—from *padanda* especially, who were staunchly conservative, and also from Ida Bagus Mantra, who deliberately marginalized

---

and television, like the Islamic call to prayer (*azan*) and the *Angelus*, sounded three times a day in Catholic areas around Indonesia. On the history of the *Tri Sandhya* in Bali, see Lanus (2014) and Reisnour (2018, Chap. 3).

[33] An article by Nyoman Suwandhi Pendit, a Balinese student in Jakarta who would later pursue his studies at the Visva-Bharati University, testifies to Shastri's influence. Quoting liberally from his brochure, he enjoined his co-religionists to forsake the instructions of the *padanda* and the contents of the *lontar* in exchange for the teachings of the true experts, namely, Hindu theologians from India. And he urged the Balinese authorities to engage in relations with India, "where one can further study seriously what we call the Hindu religion, complete with its philosophy" (*dimana orang dapat mempelajarinya lebih jauh dengan sungguh2 apa yang kita namakan agama Hindu, dengan falsafahnya sekaligus*) (Pendit 1952: 7). Interview, I Nyoman Suwandhi Pendit, Jakarta, April 6, 2000.

[34] Interview, Narendra Dev. Pandit Shastri, Denpasar, January 3, 1994. Yadav Somvir—an Indian lecturer of Sanskrit and Indian culture at Udayana University in Denpasar, and himself an avowed member of the Arya Samaj—confirmed to me that Pandit Shastri was indeed affiliated to the Arya Samaj and had been sent to Bali by the Birla Foundation, dedicated to the propagation of Hinduism in the world (interview, Denpasar, June 26, 2004). This assertion was corroborated by the director of the International Academy of Indian Culture, Lokesh Chandra, who informed me that Shastri had been a student of his father, Raghu Vira (interview, New Delhi, December 20, 2005). This was probably when Raghu Vira was the head of the Sanskrit department in Sanatana Dharma College in Lahore, as Shastri was originally from that city (Lanus 2014: 26).

him—which explains that his contribution to the recognition of the Balinese religion had never received the acknowledgement he thought it deserved.[35] Be that as it may, his writings clearly reflect the influence of the Arya Samaj, focusing as they do on the Vedas and the Upanishads at the expense of the Puranas and Itihasa literature—not to mention his intention of propagating the *Gayatri mantra* to Balinese laypeople, despite the resolute opposition of the *padanda*. Furthermore, in his treatise *Intisari Hindu Dharma* ('The Essence of Hinduism'), Shastri laid out the theological framework of what would become in 1964, at Mantra's instigation, the official canon of the Balinese religion as *Hindu Dharma*, the so-called 'Five Articles of Faith' (*Panca Çraddha*) (Shastri 1955a: 8–11).[36] Besides publishing eight booklets on Hinduism—most of them in collaboration with the Balinese teacher I Gusti Made Tamba, who worked as his sponsor and translator—Shastri was instrumental in the development of religious education in Bali, being involved in both the Perguruan Rakyat Saraswati and the Yayasan Dwijendra.[37] And, through his relations in Indian official milieux, he managed to obtain scholarships to send Ida Bagus Mantra, Tjokorda Rai Sudharta and other promising young Balinese to study in India.

While Narendra Dev. Pandit Shastri was engaged in Hinduizing Balinese religious practices, Roelof Goris was putting his orientalist erudition at the service of Balinese reformers by substantiating their Hindu credentials. In 1933, Goris had opposed the presence of Christian missions on the grounds that in Bali religion and social order form an indivisible whole, to the extent that by deliberately assaulting the religion of the Balinese, missionary work would inevitably bring about the demise of their entire culture. He claimed that the Balinese religion—which he called 'Hindu Balinism'—should be considered a genuine part of Hinduism, and he was of the opinion that it could find its regeneration through renewed contact with India (Goris 1933b).

---

[35] Shastri did eventually receive some posthumous recognition, with a few articles appearing in the *Bali Post* at the time of his death in June 2001. One of them was signed by Nyoman Pendit, who credited him with the official recognition of the Balinese religion by the government and dubbed him "the pioneer of the modern Hindu struggle in Bali" (*pelopor perjuangan Hindu modern di Bali*) (Pendit 2001).

[36] The *Panca Çraddha* is comprised of the belief in Sang Hyang Widhi, in *atman*, in *karmaphala*, in *samsara*, and in *moksa*. See Chap. 6.

[37] The Perguruan Rakyat Saraswati was opened in Denpasar by I Gusti Made Tamba in 1946, with a curriculum inspired by the Taman Siswa and the educational ideas of Rabindranath Tagore (Putra 1997). The Yayasan Dwijendra was established in 1953 in Denpasar by I Wayan Reta and Ida Bagus Wayan Gede. Named after Danghyang Dwijendra (a.k.a. Danghyang Nirartha), the Javanese Brahmin credited with having brought the Hindu religion from Majapahit to Bali in the 16th century, the Yayasan Dwijendra opened a religious high school, the Sekolah Menengah Hindu Bali Dwijendra (*Suara Indonesia*, July 17, 1953).

In July 1953, Goris came again to the Balinese rescue by publishing in the Balinese magazine *Bhakti*[38] an article entitled 'Is Hindu Bali Worship a Religion or a Sect?' (*Apakah: Ibadat Hindu Bali itu agama atau aliran?*) (Goris 1953). After defining the meaning of the word *agama* in Sanskrit as "whatever we have received from our ancestors" (*apa2 yang telah kami terima dari leluhur kami*), he proceeded to delineate what characterizes a true *agama*, construed as the Indonesian translation of the word 'religion'. Dismissing the Islamic requirement of a holy book (*kitab suci*) and a prophet (*nabi*), he contended that the 'great religions' consist of a dogma (*syahadat*), a code of ethics (*kesusilaan*), a liturgy (*ibadat*) and regular places of worship for the faithful. Likewise, the Balinese religion possesses its own scriptures (*lontar*), which comprise a dogma (*tutur*), a code of ethics (*çasana*) and a liturgy (*kalpaçastra*), and it also has its own places of worship (*pura* and *sanggah*). Therefore, there was no doubt that *agama Hindu Bali* was a true religion (*Maka dari itu ibadat Hindu Bali dengan hak penuh bolehlah dinamakan agama (religion)*) (Goris 1953: 13). Goris's demonstration would not be lost on the Balinese reformers, who would soon emphasize the dogmatic contents and the ethical principles of *agama Hindu Bali*, in order to disparage the ritualistic inclination of their co-religionists.

So, the point seems pretty clear for Goris. It is thus perplexing, to say the least, to compare the position he publicly defended to the opinion he expressed in handwritten letters and notes not intended for publication. I happened across some of these, written in English, in the Widya Wahana library, set up by the American Catholic priest Norbert Shadeg SVD in Tuka.[39] In his letters to Father Shadeg, Goris emphasized that, even though he was "a staunch Roman Catholic",[40] he was proud to help the Balinese in their formulation of an acceptable 'credo' in the sense of monotheism and Pancasila. In a note dating back to the time when Goris participated with Padanda Made Kamenuh, Wayan Bhadra and Nyoman Kadjeng in the debates triggered by KAGRI's refusal to recognize the Balinese religion, shortly before the Tampaksiring meeting in May

---

[38] *Bhakti* ('Devotion') was published three times a month in Singaraja from September 1952 to September 1954, under the heading *Madjalah Untuk Umum—Non Party* ('Magazine for the Public—Non Party'). It included a supplement entitled *Ruangan Kebudajaan: Seni, Sastra dan Filsafat* ('Cultural Space: Art, Literature and Philosophy'). Wayan Bhadra and Nyoman Kadjeng were the editors of the cultural supplement, while Putu Shanty and Nyoman Pendit were among the regular staff. Thus, although *Bhakti* was not politically affiliated, most of its main contributors were members of the Panti Agama Hindu-Bali and thus belonged to the progressive Balinese intelligentsia (Putra 2000: 137–9; see further Wijaya, Putra and Vickers 2021).

[39] Father Norbert Shadeg came to Indonesia shortly after his ordination, working in Makassar and Flores before accepting an assignment in Bali in July 1950. Interview, Norbert Shadeg, Tuka, May 18, 1999.

[40] One should know that while Goris had been a virulent opponent to Christian missionaries in the 1930s, he was converted to Catholicism by Johannes Kersten and Simon Buis in 1940.

1952, he claimed that all that the most prominent Balinese intellectuals knew about Hinduism came from him. While disclosing his low esteem for Padanda Made Kamenuh (he "had much more words than ideas"), he recounted that, back in the 1930s, he had warned the *padanda* that their religion would soon disappear if they did not reform it, but to no avail. Since Indonesia's independence, the pressure of Islam and Christianity has become more insistent, he said, and some of the conscious Hindu-Bali people, particularly his own pupils (such as Wayan Bhadra and Nyoman Kadjeng), are aware of the danger. But it was now too late to rescue the Balinese religion. All the more so since the Balinese remained incapable of agreeing on a consistent conception of their religion, of its name and of its creed: "Never will the best of the best of Balinese people be able to make any credo." He was of the opinion that the only possible name for the Balinese religion was *agama Hindu-Bali*. As for the name chosen by the Balinese to designate the One and Only God of their religion (Sanghyang Widhi), in the monotheistic perspective imposed by the Ministry of Religion, he contended that it amounted to the Christian conception of God, which he had explained to his Balinese friends back in the 1930s.[41] And Goris concluded his note in summarizing his impressions of the Balinese reformers: "We Hindu-Bali are fearing [...] that our religion will not be accepted by Islam! And thence the stress on mono-theism" (Goris 1952).

Goris would reaffirm the poor esteem in which he held most Balinese intellectuals, and the misconceptions they professed of their own religion, on the occasion of a lecture delivered on October 19, 1953, by I Gusti Bagus Sugriwa in front of Balinese students in Denpasar (Sugriwa 1954). After reminding his audience that, at the time of his youth, the Balinese people didn't have to worry about finding a name for their religion, which they simply called *agama Bali*, Sugriwa told them that when he was asked to give a lecture on the Balinese religion during Bali Darma Laksana's second congress, in July 1938, he had proposed the name *agama Çiwa-Buddha* or else *agama Hindu Bali*. Then, he explained that in Bali as in Java, the teachings of Shaivism and Buddhism had

---

[41] The fact is that by 1937, missionaries had adopted the name Sang Hyang Widhi in order to translate the Christian conception of God into the Balinese language, which might have contributed to popularizing this particular representation of the supreme deity (Wiryatnaya 1995: 151–8). However, contrary to what has been claimed by several Christian authors (e.g., Eck 1982: 158), we saw earlier that it was not the Christian Balinese who first came up with that name, which would later be endorsed by the Hindu Balinese. And Norbert Shadeg, who had been Goris's close confident since his assignment in Bali in 1950, doubtless grants him too much credit when he alleges that it was he who suggested Ida Sanghyang Widi as a fitting Balinese equivalent of the Indonesian *Tuhan Yang Maha Esa*, rather than Batara Siwa or Sanghyang Batara (Shadeg 1989: 5). Even if one could concede some Christian influence, the new Balinese conception of the supreme deity owed most to the influence of reformist Islam imported from the Near East in the early part of the 20th century.

merged to constitute what is now being called *agama Hindu Bali*. Among the various points touched in his lecture, he was adamant in refuting the prevalent opinion that the Balinese people are polytheists, based on the fact that they give different titles to God, in accordance with His various attributes.[42]

In the comments he wrote on this lecture, Goris did not hide his contempt for Sugriwa, claiming that "serious Hindu Bali people [...] do not even more [*sic*] read him. They despise him strongly." Besides pointing out his erroneous assertions, he contested Sugriwa's declaration that the religion of the present Balinese was directly derived from Hinduism—which is precisely what he himself had declared a few months earlier in his *Bhakti* article. He wrote:

> The present Balinese religion is a mixture of 80 to 90% primitive religion and 10 to 20% changed Hinduism (Çiwaism + Buddhism). About 60 to 80% of the Balinese still are polytheists. Believing in many 'spirits' (ghosts), good ones and evil ones. [...] The real religion of about 90 to 95% of the Balinese population is a pre-historic, 'animistic' or 'dynamistic', conception of the world.

The main bulk of Balinese beliefs and ceremonies have to do with ancestor worship. Of all their ceremonies, the only one of Hindu origin is cremation; all the others, the rites of passage, the temple ceremonies, are Old Balinese, with the sole exception of the *tirtha* made by the *padanda*, which is in fact an external addition to the ceremonies. Most Balinese have acquired their vague notions of Hinduism from Old Javanese literature, through the theatrical repertoire, the *wayang* in particular. It is only with the modern education introduced by the Dutch since the 1930s that Balinese have been able to acquire some information about Hinduism. And Goris concluded his commentary by asserting that all the philosophical ideas manipulated by Balinese intellectuals were only superficial and ill-digested notions, because, unlike Indians, the Balinese were incapable of abstract and speculative thinking: "[Sugriwa] (and with him nearly all the Balinese literate) are always 'concretizing' abstract ideas: their 'phase of thinking' is quite 'allegorical', substituting 'statues' (material images) for 'ideas'"[43] (Goris 1954b).

---

[42] "*Memang gelaran2 yang diuntukkan kepada Tuhan Esa itu sangat banyak menurut sifat2 Tuhan dalam melakukan kekuasaannya didunia Maya ini*" (Sugriwa 1954: 41).

[43] It is interesting to observe that what Goris criticizes the Balinese for is precisely what Crawfurd, in the evolutionist perspective of his time, reproached the Javanese for in his *History of the Indian Archipelago* (1820b, vol. 2: 230–2).

The struggle for the recognition of *agama Hindu Bali*

On July 4, 1952, a few weeks after the main Balinese religious organizations had finally reached agreement on the name of their religion, the minister of religion stipulated by decree the following conditions (*syarat*) for a religious tradition to be officially recognized as a proper *agama* (*Peraturan Menteri Agama No.9/1952*): it must be monotheistic, have a prophet (*nabi*), a holy book (*kitab suci*), unified teachings, and international recognition (*Merdeka*, July 4, 1952; Van der Kroef 1953: 123). Reiterating the distinction between *agama* and *kepercayaan*, this ministerial decree relegated *agama Hindu Bali*, along with other 'religious sects and movements' (*aliran/gerakan agama*) not acknowledged as genuine religions, to Division H of KAGRI, thus making it a potential target for Islamic proselytism (*dakwah*) or Christian missions. These official stipulations provoked widespread public outrage in Bali. Faced with such a setback, Balinese leaders held diverging views about how best to respond to what they perceived as a Muslim provocation. While a majority of them were resolute in pushing for KAGRI to recognize their religion, some—among them Gusti Bagus Sugriwa—were of the opinion that the Balinese had no need to seek such recognition.

The first reaction came from a Balinese member of the Provisional People's Representative Council (Dewan Perwakilan Rakyat Sementara, DPRS), the national parliament in Jakarta, Ida Bagus Putera Manuaba, the former chairman of the Komite Nasional Indonesia for the Province of the Lesser Sunda Islands and a prominent PNI politician. Putting a question to the government, he challenged the legal bases of KAGRI's conditions, which violated the religious freedom proclaimed by the constitution, while reminding his Muslim opponents that *agama Hindu Bali* was not a new religion but went back to Sriwijaya and Majapahit, and thus had been present in Indonesia centuries before Islam took its hold over the Archipelago (*Mimbar Indonesia*, July 10, 1952).

In response to Manuaba's protest, Muhammad Dimyati,[44] a Muslim member of the DPRS, published in the Indonesian weekly *Siasat* ('Inquiry') an article denouncing 'the danger of anarchism in religious matters' (*Bahaya anarsisme dilapangan keagamaan*). Having stressed that religious freedom should be restricted (*berbatas*) lest it bring about anarchism, he made clear that, for him, the Balinese religion was not a proper *agama* but pertained to *adat*, like the 'pagan' (*jahiliah*) religions of the Karo Batak in Sumatra or the Badui and

---

[44] In early 1952, Muhammad Dimyati had requested the minister of religion to specify the criteria to be met for a religion to be officially recognized as *agama* by the state (Subagya 1976: 116).

the Tengger in Java. It consisted basically of remnants of traditional 'beliefs' (*kepercayaan*), which might at most be acknowledged as such, under the condition that they remain circumscribed to their region of origin and that their propagation is prohibited (Dimyati 1952a). To which Putu Shanty retorted in the same periodical by asserting that all religions were true and respectable, as in the end they were all equivalent. Indeed, they all were given equal rights by the Indonesian constitution, and Islam had no license to take advantage of the sheer number of its followers in order to impose its views on other religions (Shanty 1952b). This brought him a rejoinder from Dimyati, taking the form of rhetorical questions: What was, in fact, the religion which the Balinese would like to have recognized by KAGRI? Was it the religion actually practiced in Bali (paganism), or the one practiced in India (Hinduism)? In case of a theological controversy in Bali, which authority was in a position to resolve the matter? Would the Balinese look for an answer in the Vedas, as Muslims refer to the Quran whenever a point of dogma is debated among the *ulama*? And our author concluded his reply by asking whether the Indonesians wanted to progress by rejecting the remnants of archaic beliefs and customs to the benefit of the sole monotheism, or whether they wanted to regress to the time when their ancestors were still worshipping statues in Borobudur and Prambanan.[45]

At the very time when this polemic was being voiced, in September 1952, Wedastera Suyasa published in *Bhakti* an article entitled 'The Balinese Hindu Religion Threatened' (*Agama Hindu Bali Terancam*) (Suyasa 1952). In the name of Pancasila and the constitution, he denounced the conditions put forward by KAGRI and appealed to the government to protect all religions, whether their adherents be a majority or a minority in the country, as well as to keep religion away from political matters. He enjoined the Balinese to close ranks under the banner of *agama Hindu Bali* instead of wearing themselves out seeking in vain its recognition by KAGRI. A similar stance was taken by several authors in the same periodical (Dirgahayu 1952). A case in point is an article by a member of the Panti Agama Hindu-Bali bearing the explicit title: 'Religion is a Matter of Faith, Not a Question of Recognition' (*Agama adalah soal kepercayaan, bukan soal pengakuan*) (Sutrisna 1954). According to the author, the proclamation of the freedom of religion in the constitution sufficed to guarantee the ongoing existence of the Balinese religion in Indonesia, which was therefore not in need of any official recognition by KAGRI. Denouncing the influence of Muslim and Christian theological conceptions over the definition of their religion by Balinese

---

[45] "*Adakah kita mau maju dan cerdas, ataukah kita ingin mundur kezaman 1000 tahun yang lalu, ketika nénék-moyang kita masih memuja patung2 dicandi Borobudur dan Prambanan?*" (Dimyati 1952b: 16).

reformers, he claimed that *agama Hindu Bali* had no need of a prophet or of a holy book, which were distinctive features of Islam and Christianity, unknown to religions such as Hinduism and Buddhism.

Meanwhile, on October 10, 1952, KAGRI's secretary-general gave a lecture in Denpasar, in which he reiterated that *agama Hindu Bali* did not fulfill the conditions allowing its official recognition (Sugriwa 1973: 8). On November 14, 1952, taking into account KAGRI's repeated refusals to open a division for *agama Hindu Bali*, the DPD addressed a request to the DPRDS pleading for the establishment of an Autonomous Office of Religion for the Region of Bali (Jawatan Agama Otonoom Daerah Bali) (*Suara Indonesia*, November 28, 1952). This was eventually granted by a vote of the DPRDS on March 24, 1953, after further unsuccessful negotiation on February 14, in Singaraja, among KAGRI's secretary-general, the governor of the province, the DPD, and the president of the DPRDS (*Pengumuman Resmi DPD Bali*, 1953; *Suara Indonesia*, March 24, 1953). The decision was not approved unanimously in Bali, as some religious leaders thought that, instead of establishing their own Autonomous Office of Religion, the regional authorities should keep struggling to obtain KAGRI's official recognition of the Balinese religion (*Bhakti* 1953, No. 7: 4–5). In any case, the Dinas Agama Otonoom Daerah Bali, which was in charge exclusively of the followers of *agama Hindu Bali*, was eventually established in Singaraja on November 1, 1954, under the leadership of I Putu Serangan, and with branches in all former kingdoms.[46] It was not recognized by the minister of religion. In retaliation, the DPD severed all institutional links with both KAGRI's provincial (KUAP) and regional (KUAD) offices, which caused a severe disruption of their operations.

While the Balinese authorities were busy setting up their own religious agency, the debate on the foundations of the Indonesian state had resurfaced in the wake of a speech delivered on January 27, 1953, by President Sukarno at Amuntai, in Kalimantan, in which he commented on a banner reading 'Indonesia a National State or an Islamic State?' (*Indonesia Negara Nasional atau Negara Islamkah?*). In his address, Sukarno criticized the attempt by some Muslim parties to establish a state based on Islam and warned that it would be the end of the national unity of Indonesia, as regions whose populations were not Islamic—

---

[46] One of the tasks of the Dinas Agama Otonoom Daerah Bali was to administer religious education in Balinese schools, in conformity with the July 16, 1951, joint regulation by the minister of education, instruction and culture and by the minister of religion stipulating that religious education should be provided in all public schools (Kaler 1957). In actual fact, education in *agama Hindu Bali* was plagued from the start by the lack of qualified teachers as well as by a want of general agreement on its basic tenets, not to mention an avowed lack of interest on the part of most Balinese to learn about their own religion in school (Kandia 1957: 6).

such as Bali and the Christian Eastern islands—would secede. This speech triggered a vehement stir in the Indonesian political arena, with Muslim circles demanding that Sukarno withdraw his statement, while the nationalist parties defended him. And of course, it was approvingly endorsed in Bali, with a series of articles appearing in *Bhakti* and in the new monthly magazine *Damai*[47] (Shanty 1953; Sugriwa 1953a, 1953b). The Balinese were clearly worried that, as a result of the coming general elections, the Islamic parties might take advantage of their majority status to impose an Islamic state.

On May 26–27, 1953, an important conference (*Pesamuan Agung*) was held in Denpasar on the initiative of the DPD. For the first time, members of the regional government, officials from the KUAP, *padanda*, and delegates of the main religious organizations gathered to discuss *agama Hindu Bali* and its predicament. The debates revolved mostly around the reforms which should be applied to rituals (*yadnya*)—particularly death rituals (*ngaben*) and so-called inter-castes (*antar kasta*) marriages—as well as to the ordination (*padiksan*) of *padanda* (*Suara Indonesia*, June 1, 1953; Sugriwa 1953c: 733–4; Kandia 1954: 2). While nothing much came out of these debates, the Panti Agama Hindu-Bali kept on actively promoting religious reforms. They were on the agenda of its first congress, on July 22–23, 1953, and in October, its chairman, Padanda Gede Ngendjung, enlisted the help of representatives of the other religious organizations to set up a committee to compile a textbook of *agama Hindu Bali* under the leadership of Wayan Bhadra (Panitia Penyusun Kitab Pelajaran Agama Hindu Bali) (Bhadra 1953b).

The textbook did not materialize but, in September 1953, Wayan Bhadra, in his capacity as head of the Hindu-Bali division at the KUAP, published a booklet with the somewhat pretentious title 'Treatise on the Hindu Balinese Religion' (*Treaty tentang Agama Hindu Bali*) (Bhadra 1953a). This was in fact a formal request addressed to KAGRI, pleading for the official recognition of *agama Hindu Bali*. In response to a declaration by the minister of religion that the Balinese religion was but one of some three hundred religions demanding to be officially recognized, and referring to the article published by Goris in July in *Bhakti*, Bhadra asserted that *agama Hindu Bali*—which he labeled *Hindu Balinisme* or else *Hinduisme Bali*—was not a sect (*aliran*) but a true religion

---

[47] *Damai* ('Peace') was issued by the Yayasan Kebaktian Pejuang Bali, a foundation established on the DPD's initiative on January 14, 1951, in Denpasar to provide assistance for the Balinese veterans of the war of independence. It was published by I Gusti Bagus Sugriwa from March 1953 to June 1956, under the heading *Madjalah Umum Untuk Rakjat* ('General Magazine for the People').

(*agama*), as its doctrinal foundations were no different from Indian Hinduism.[48] The manifest differences between Balinese religious practices and Hinduism as actually performed in India were only the result of the historical adaptation of Hinduism to Javanese and Balinese cultural specificities.[49] Quoting extensively from the works of famous Indologists and Indian religious reformers, Bhadra stressed that Hinduism (like Buddhism) did not abide by theological conceptions peculiar to the Abrahamic religions, and in this respect it was thus pointless on the part of KAGRI to demand from the Balinese the name of their prophet and of their holy book.[50]

Despite Bhadra's vigorous plea, and notwithstanding the presence of a Hindu-Bali division at the KUAP, the painful fact remained that *agama Hindu Bali* had still no official status even at the provincial level. It was not until June 30, 1955, at the outcome of a conference held by the Ministry of Religion at Tretes, in East Java, that it would be officially represented within the KUAP in Singaraja, when *agama Hindu-Bali* was promoted to Division G and endowed with three sections (*seksi*): Religious Affairs (*Urusan Agama*), Religious Information (*Penerangan Agama*) and Religious Education (*Pendidikan Agama*) (Kandia 1957: 6–8). But this concession to the Balinese religion did not imply that *agama Hindu Bali* would be represented at KAGRI in Jakarta, where it was still classified among the *aliran/gerakan agama*.

The first general elections—on September 29, 1955, for parliament (Dewan Perwakilan Rakyat, DPR) and on December 15 for the constituent assembly (Majelis Permusyawaratan Rakyat, MPR), whose task was to draft the definitive constitution for the Republic of Indonesia—were a serious disappointment for the Islamic parties, which obtained only 43.5 percent of the votes and could not even come together in cooperation. This setback marked the failure of the political struggle of Islam in Indonesia and resulted in a deadlock in the MPR, pitting the advocates of an Islamic state (*Negara Islam*) against the proponents of a Pancasila state (*Negara Pancasila*).[51]

---

[48] "*Hindu Balinisme itu bukanlah aliran tetapi Agama, yang dalil2 dan ajaran filsafatnya sama dengan aspek agama dari Hinduism di India*" (Bhadra 1953a: 1).

[49] "*Agama Hindu-Bali sebagai kami dapatkan sekarang adalah suatu akibat hasil perkembangan2 dari pertemuan2 kebudayaan Hindu (aspek agamanya, filsafat dan seninya) dengan kepercayaan (religie) Bali asli dst. pendek kata dengan Kebudayaan Bali*" (Bhadra 1953a: 3).

[50] Wayan Bhadra would reiterate his views on the changing patterns of the Balinese religion in a special issue on Indonesia of *The Atlantic Monthly Supplement*, in which he declared that "in the field of religion we are developing towards a purer, more spiritual Hinduism as certain old beliefs, remnants of pre-Hinduism animism, rapidly fall into the category of superstition" (Bhadra 1956: 71).

[51] The political deadlock would eventually be broken on July 5, 1959, by President Sukarno, who established his 'Guided Democracy' (*Demokrasi Terpimpin*) by disbanding the MPR and decreeing a return to the constitution of 1945, which provided for a strong executive presidency. This authoritarian political system, which rejected both

Needless to say, the Balinese were actively involved in the struggle for a *Negara Pancasila* (Sugriwa 1955; Suyasa 1956). This was particularly the case of the younger generation of Balinese students, who appeared impatient with their elders' temporizing. Thus, the youth movement Gerakan Kumara Bhavana (GKB), which had been founded by Wedastera Suyasa at the time of the fourth conference of the Student Coordinating Committee (Badan Koordinator Usaha Pelajar, BKUP) on May 25, 1955, in Denpasar, set up a Contact Committee (Badan Kontak Gerakan Kumara Bhavana, BKGKB) under the leadership of I Putu Wirja on November 12, 1956. This body was to initiate contacts with Balinese members of the MPR in order to urge them to pursue the struggle for the recognition of *agama Hindu Bali* (GKB 1957).

On April 27, 1957, Wedastera Suyasa, in his capacity as chairman of the Gerakan Kumara Bhavana, addressed a request to President Sukarno and his prime minister, demanding that a representative of *agama Hindu Bali* be allowed to sit in the National Council (Dewan Nasional),[52] like delegates of Islam, Protestantism and Catholicism (Suyasa 1957a). The request was granted, and Gusti Bagus Sugriwa was appointed representative of *agama Hindu Bali* in the Dewan Nasional. Then, on July 28–31, 1957, the Gerakan Kumara Bhavana organized in Denpasar the fifth conference of the Hindu-Balinese Youth (Angkatan Muda Hindu-Bali, AMHB). There were two main topics addressed during this conference: Wedastera Suyasa dealt with 'the religion and its struggle' (*Agama dan perjuangannya*), while Ida Bagus Gde Dosther treated of education, culture, and tourism. Concerning religious matters, the resolutions passed by the conference demanded: that a Hindu-Bali division be established within KAGRI; that a representative organization of *agama Hindu Bali*, comprising all the officials and experts concerned with religious matters, be instituted to replace the existing organizations, with the mission in particular of standardizing religious education; that the Dinas Agama Otonoom Daerah Bali instruct the Balinese in simplifying their rites and inform them of their meaning; and that the constitution be based on Pancasila, with specific provisions guaranteeing religious freedom and the protection of all religions by the state (Suyasa 1957b, 1957c; Kandia 1957).

After this conference, the struggle for the recognition of the Balinese religion entered its final stage—from then on, it would become much more

---

political Islam and democratic pluralism, provoked a growing tension among the military, the Islamic parties and the Communist Party (Feith 1962).

[52] The Dewan Nasional was set up by Sukarno in May 1957 to deliberate issues on general policy matters and issue recommendations to parliament.

coordinated and determined. What triggered the decisive push was KAGRI's demand in early 1958 for the Balinese authorities to disband the Dinas Agama Otonoom Daerah Bali, all the while continuing to refuse to establish a division for *agama Hindu Bali*. On June 14, 1958, a movement requesting the establishment of a Hindu-Bali division within KAGRI (*Gerakan Aksi-Bersama Menuntut 'Bagian Hindu-Bali' Dalam Kementerian Agama Republik Indonesia*), coordinated by I Gusti Ketut Kaler from the Dinas Agama Otonoom, was launched on Wedastera Suyasa's initiative.[53] Invoking the glorious memory of Sriwijaya and Majapahit, and asserting that Hinduism was the foundation of Indonesian civilization, Suyasa called on all religious organizations and concerned individuals to put pressure on KAGRI by petitioning the minister of religion, the prime minister, the president of the republic and the main political authorities at the central, provincial and regional levels. Besides reiterating the demand to establish a Hindu-Bali division within KAGRI without further ado, the petition stated that not only should the Dinas Agama Otonoom Daerah Bali not be closed, but that, rather, KAGRI should be shut down, or at the very least, thoroughly restructured so as to ensure equal treatment for all the religions of Indonesia, in conformity with Pancasila (Suyasa 1958). A few days later, a delegation led by Gusti Ketut Kaler was sent to Jakarta to convey the Balinese petition.

On June 26, 1958, representatives of eight religious organizations met in Denpasar to debate the situation of *agama Hindu Bali* (*Pertemuan Kerja Sama Organisasi Agama Hindu Bali Tentang Kedudukan Agama Hindu Bali Dalam Organisasi Kementerian Agama Republik Indonesia*): I Gusti Anandakusuma (Satya Hindu Dharma Indonesia, Denpasar),[54] Ida Bagus Wayan Gede (Yayasan Dwijendra, Denpasar), Ida I Dewa Agung Gede Oka Geg (Partai Nasional Hindu

---

[53] Interview, I Made Wedastera Suyasa, Puri Mahendradatta, Denpasar, December 13, 1994.

[54] The Satya Hindu Dharma Indonesia was founded on January 1, 1956, in Denpasar, under the leadership of Ida Pedanda Gde Wayan Sidemen and I Gusti Anandakusuma, with the aim of promoting Hinduism in Indonesia (*Memajukan Agama Hindu yang ada di Indonesia*) (*Anggaran Dasar Satya Hindu Dharma Indonesia*, 1956). Considering that *agama Hindu* was not confined to Bali, and being aware that the Javanese Hindus would not accept the name *Hindu Bali*, its promoters argued for replacing it with the name *Hindu Dharma*, thus defending an Indianized vision of the Balinese religion (Anandakusuma 1985: 3). Anandakusuma is also credited with popularizing the *swastika* as symbol of *agama Hindu*, as well as the greeting '*Swastyastu*' as an equivalent of the Indian '*namaste*'—and mirroring the Muslim '*salam alaikum*'. The following year, he was instrumental in the foundation of the Balinese branch of the Divine Life Society (Perhimpunan Hidup Ketuhanan), which propagated the teachings of Swami Shivananda, whose disciple, Swami Vishnudevananda, visited Bali in September 1957, where he delivered lectures and was officially received by the Balinese government. On Gusti Anandakusuma, see Bakker (1993: 53–100).

Bali, Klungkung),[55] Ida Bagus Tugur (Majelis Hinduisme Bali, Klungkung), Ida Pedanda Made Kamenuh (Paruman Para Pandita, Singaraja), I Ketut Kandia (Panti Agama Hindu-Bali, Singaraja), Ida Bagus Gde Dosther (Angkatan Muda Hindu-Bali, Denpasar), and Ida Bagus Gede Manuaba (Eka Adnjana, Sempidi). They formally adopted a resolution demanding that *agama Hindu Bali* be recognized on an equal footing with the other religions represented in KAGRI, while insisting that the Balinese authorities maintain the existence of the Dinas Agama Otonoom Daerah Bali until this demand was granted. The resolution was addressed to the same political authorities as on June 14 (Pertemuan Kerdja Sama, 1958).

On June 29, 1958, this resolution was presented personally to President Sukarno at his Balinese residence at Tampaksiring by a delegation of representatives from five organizations: Ida Pedanda Made Kamenuh (Paruman Para Pandita), I Gusti Anandakusuma (Satya Hindu Dharma Indonesia), Ida Bagus Wayan Gede (Yayasan Dwijendra), Ida Bagus Gde Dosther (Angkatan Muda Hindu-Bali), and I Ketut Kandia (Panti Agama Hindu-Bali). They were accompanied by the DPRD's chairman, I Gusti Putu Merta. The delegates reasserted that *agama Hindu Bali* was a proper religion, as its philosophical foundations were taken from Hinduism while its ceremonies were those of the Balinese traditional institutions.[56] And it met the requirements laid down in KAGRI'S decree (*Peraturan Menteri Agama No.9/1952*), with a profession of faith (*çraddha*), a holy book (*kitab suci*), prophets (the *maharsi* who received the revelation of the Vedas), houses of worship (*tempat2 untuk melakukan peribadatan*), a priesthood (*pemangku2 Agama*), and ethical and theological teachings (*ajaran2 tatasusila, tattwa2 dan Kitab2 Agama yang lain*). In short, *agama Hindu Bali* complied with *Ketuhanan Yang Maha Esa*, and as such it was not polytheistic but monotheistic, while it paid homage to the souls of the ancestors (*disertai dengan penghormatan terhadap arwah nenek-moyang*) (Kandia 1958; Anandakusuma 1966: 101–6; Dosther 2007: 101–2). Sukarno appeared to have been receptive to the Balinese plea,[57] and he instructed the minister of religion to come to Bali.

---

[55] The Partai Nasional Hindu Bali was founded in February 1954 by Ida I Dewa Agung Gede Oka Geg, the raja of Klungkung, in order to promote the interests of the Balinese Hindus in the national elections—in which it fared very poorly.

[56] "*Peribadatan Hindu Bali tidak dapat diragu-ragukan lagi bahwa ia adalah AGAMA, dengan dasar filsafat Agama Hindu dan upakara dan upacara menurut adat lembaga Bali*" (Kandia 1958: 2).

[57] On June 17, 1958, in Jakarta, President Sukarno delivered the opening speech at the Third Congress of Indonesian Mysticism (*Kongres Kebatinan Indonesia yang ke III*)—attended by Gusti Anandakusuma, representing the Satya Hindu Dharma Indonesia—in which he praised the spiritual loftiness of the *Bhagawad Gita*, a comforting message which did not fall on deaf ears in Bali (Anandakusuma 1966: 92).

The support of Sukarno—whose mother was a Balinese *brahmana*—proved to be decisive: on September 5, 1958, a Hindu Bali Division (Bagian Hindu Bali) was established within KAGRI (*Surat Keputusan Menteri Agama tanggal 5 September 1958 No.2, Tentang Bagian Hindu Bali pada Kementerian Agama Republik Indonesia*). Shortly afterwards, the Balinese government appointed three representatives to KAGRI's Hindu Bali Division: I Gusti Gede Raka (a former government minister and chairman of Bali Darma Laksana), I Nyoman Kadjeng (an official from the provincial government, member of the Panti Agama Hindu-Bali), and I Gusti Ngurah Oka Diputhera (a Buddhist student in Yogyakarta, member of the Angkatan Muda Hindu-Bali). On January 1, 1959, the Division of Hindu Balinese Affairs (Bagian Urusan Hindu Bali) was finally set up within KAGRI in Jakarta.

In the meantime, on August 14, 1958, Bali had become a full-fledged province of the Republic of Indonesia, with Anak Agung Bagus Sutedja as governor. And two years later, the provincial capital was moved from Singaraja to Denpasar.

Chapter 6

Parisada

From *Agama Hindu Bali* to *Agama Hindu* (1958-98)

The establishment of a Division of Hindu Balinese Affairs (Bagian Urusan Hindu Bali) within KAGRI in Jakarta was achieved by means of a twofold accomplishment—that is, not only the acknowledgement of Balinese religious traditions as a local instance of the modern idea of a world religion called 'Hinduism', but also the construal of Hinduism as a monotheism, in compliance with theological tenets peculiar to Abrahamic religions. However, this first important step did not signal the end of the Balinese struggle for the recognition of their religion.

To begin with, the fact that the division was named Hindu Balinese 'Affairs' (*Urusan*) rather than Hindu Balinese 'Religion' (*Agama*) indicates that the status of the Balinese religion as a true *agama* was still being evaded by the Ministry of Religion. Furthermore, it still remained to decide who should be in charge of *agama Hindu Bali* since the former rajas, who had previously been the patrons of the religious ceremonies on the island, had been replaced in 1957 by officials (*bupati*) appointed by the republican government, resulting in a breakdown in the management of religion in Bali.

To debate these issues, on October 7, 1958, the governor of Bali, Anak Agung Bagus Sutedja, set up a planning committee for the preparation of a Hindu-Bali Congress (Panitia Perancang Hindu-Bali Sabha), whose task was to establish an *agama Hindu-Bali* council (Dewan Agama Hindu-Bali), with the purpose of assisting the Division of Hindu Balinese Affairs within KAGRI and of coordinating all the religious activities of the Hindu-Balinese community throughout Indonesia. Chaired by Ida Bagus Mantra—who combined dual credentials, being a *brahmana* and holding a doctorate from a prestigious Indian university—this committee was composed of representatives of the Dinas

Agama Otonoom (I Gusti Ngurah Gede and I Putu Serangan), of the Dewan Nasional (I Gusti Bagus Sugriwa), and of the main Balinese religious organizations: Angkatan Muda Hindu-Bali (I Made Wedastera Suyasa), Paruman Para Pandita (Ida Padanda Made Kamenuh), Panti Agama Hindu-Bali (I Ketut Kandia), as well as I Nyoman Kadjeng and I Gusti Ngurah Oka Diputhera. On October 12, the planning committee met in Bedugul, under the auspices of the Dinas Agama Otonoom, and there again on December 6, with a delegation of Hindu Balinese from Lombok, and decided to convene a Hindu-Bali Congress in January 1959 (Panitia Perantjang 1958).

Parisada Dharma Hindu Bali

The Hindu-Bali Sabha was finally held on February 21–23, 1959, chaired by Ida Bagus Mantra at the new faculty of literature in Denpasar,[1] with representatives of the Balinese government, of the Dinas Agama Otonoom and of all the religious organizations on the island. This congress resulted in the foundation of a council of the Hindu Balinese religion—Parisada Dharma Hindu Bali (PDHB, Hindu Bali Dharma Council)—that was to replace both the existing religious organizations and the former rajas. According to its charter (*Piagam Parisada*), Parisada was charged with coordinating all religious activities of the Hindu-Balinese community (*umat Hindu Bali*), by "regulating, promoting and developing the Hindu Balinese religion" (*mengatur, memupuk dan memperkembangkan agama Hindu Bali*) (PHD 1970: 11; see Bakker 1993: 225–91). In its first few years of existence, Parisada would be accommodated at the Fakultas Sastra Universitas Udayana in Denpasar.

The Sanskrit title of the council bore the hallmark of Ida Bagus Mantra, who decided on the name of the new organization.[2] The term *parisada* was borrowed from the *Manava Dharmashastra*, the canonical foundation of Hindu society.[3] And one notices that instead of the word *agama*, rejected on account of

---

[1] The faculty of literature in Denpasar had been a stake in the conflict between the Indonesian National Party (PNI) and the Indonesian Communist Party (PKI). While the PKI wanted to set up a faculty of economics, the PNI was in favor of a faculty of literature for the purpose of promoting the Balinese language and its literary heritage. The decision to establish the faculty of literature was an outcome of the first congress of the Balinese language, held in October 1957 in Denpasar. Opened in September 1958, it was initially only a branch of the Airlangga University in Surabaya, before being officially inaugurated on September 29, 1962, as the Fakultas Sastra Universitas Udayana (Wijaya 2009: 374).
[2] Interview, Tjokorda Rai Sudharta, Puri Amertasari, Ubud, May 11, 2007.
[3] While the term *parishad* is indeed ancient, it was brought up to date by Neo-Hindu reformers in 19th-century India to designate the new pan-Hindu religious organizations and differentiate them from traditional movements such as the *sampradaya*, religious orders based on a spiritual lineage from masters to disciples (*parampara*). This is the

its Islamic connotation, it was the word *dharma*, used in India by Hindu reformers and their orthodox opponents alike to convey the normative and universalist notion of 'religion', which was chosen, by former Balinese students recently graduated from Indian universities.

Parisada was acknowledged by KAGRI as the highest jurisdiction (*majelis tertinggi*) of *agama Hindu Bali*, on the model of similar councils set up to coordinate the other officially recognized religions. It was intended to operate as a conduit between the Hindu-Balinese community and the Ministry of Religion. As it happened, in just a few years Parisada managed to impose its hegemony by superseding the various religious organizations that had taken part in its foundation, which were mostly marginalized, if not eliminated altogether. This hegemonic position was bound to provoke conflicts, notably with I Gusti Anandakusuma, who expected Parisada to cooperate with the Satya Hindu Dharma in its project of religious reform, and who was eventually evicted from its leadership (Anandakusuma 1985).

Parisada originally consisted of two assemblies—an Assembly of Priests (*Pesamuhan Para Sulinggih*) composed of eleven members (with a majority of *padanda*) and an Assembly of Laymen (*Pesamuhan Para Walaka*) of twenty-two members—assisted by an Executive Board (*Pengurus Harian*) of three members, the chairmen of each assembly, and the secretary-general (*Sekjen*), Ida Bagus Mantra (PHD 1968). While its chairman (*Ketua Umum*) was a *padanda*, Parisada was in fact controlled by a ruling elite composed of *triwangsa—brahmana* for the most part—with officials and academics in positions of leadership. It is significant that the *padanda*, who wield supreme authority in religious matters on Bali, were generally at the rearguard of religious reform, when they were not frankly hostile to it. In fact, even though *padanda* occupied a prominent position within Parisada's governing bodies, the centralization of religious decision-making deprived them of their former autonomy and of their prestige as the gatekeepers of religious knowledge. And they were readily criticized by reformers inasmuch as they confined themselves to making holy water (*tirta*) and completing rituals (*muput karya*) instead of becoming spiritual leaders, following the example of Christian priests and Muslim *ulama*.[4]

---

same term that was chosen by the Vishva Hindu Parishad (World Hindu Council), an international missionary organization with strong Hindu nationalist allegiances, founded in 1964 with the aim of defending, promoting, and propagating Hinduism in the world (Hellman 1993).

[4] In many respects, this criticism of the *padanda* by Balinese reformers concurred with that of the Brahmins by Indian reformers, which was itself similar to the criticism of Catholic priests by Protestant missionaries.

Nonetheless, their support proved to be crucial to ensuring that Parisada's decisions would be accepted by the Balinese population at large.

Notwithstanding the ambitions of its initiators, Parisada has been seriously affected from the outset with both a chronic lack of financial resources and conspicuous organizational weakness. Its financing comes from the government—both from the Ministry of Religion and from the provincial budget—as well as from a kind of religious contribution (*dana punia*), similar to the Muslim *zakat*, which it endeavors with some difficulty to collect from the Hindu-Balinese community. As regards its organizational structure, the Assembly of Priests appears mostly concerned with ritual issues, while the Assembly of Laymen is composed of academics and officials, civilian and military, who have little time and energy to dedicate to Parisada. The real power is held by the Executive Board, which make the decisions, even though these have to be endorsed by the Assembly of Priests. Furthermore, it must be pointed out that there is usually little consensus among Parisada's leadership concerning the nature and extent of the religious reforms to be pursued.

Parisada's strategy was to promote internal homogeneity in the practice of Balinese religion in order to present a united front as a Hindu minority in a predominantly Muslim nation. By means of seminars (*seminar*), assemblies (*pesamuhan*) and congresses (*mahasabha*), Parisada undertook to regulate rituals, formalize the priesthood, standardize temples, compile a theological canon (*Panca Çraddha*), publish a Hindu catechism (*Upadesa*) as well as a monthly bulletin (*Kala Wrtta Hindu Dharma*, which in 1967 became *Warta Hindu Dharma*, 'News of Hinduism'), devise a Hindu prayer (*Tri Sandhya*) as an equivalent of daily Islamic prayers, translate Hindu sacred scriptures into Indonesian, and provide religious education to the population.[5] This undertaking amounted to a 'scripturalization' of Balinese religion, in the sense that rites were now meant to comply with texts, and orthopraxy had to be substantiated by orthodoxy. In short, Parisada was displacing the traditional hegemony of rajas and *padanda* (*Guru Loka*)—based on the contentious partnership of *puri* and *gria*—and replacing it with a collaboration between a modern elite and the government. In some respects, it might be argued that the new council intended

---

[5] It is important to point out that the very idea of a formal religious education was new in Bali, in that the democratization of religious knowledge conflicted with the conviction that such knowledge should remain secret and be protected by prohibitions (*aja wera*), thus breaking the traditional monopoly of *padanda* and other literati (Nala 2004; Landmann 2012). The Balinese were now required to understand the meaning of their rites in order to be able to defend their religion against the criticism of Muslims and Christians alike. This has generated a cognitive dissonance between the way people construe what they actually do and the interpretation that is propounded by Parisada.

to play the role with the government that was formerly held by their court *padanda* with the rajas. But unlike kings and priests, who merely interceded on behalf of their subjects and clients, Parisada was now instructing the Balinese on what to believe and how to practice their religion accordingly[6]—a religion supposedly coming from India rather than from Majapahit. Stressing the theological as well as the ethical import of religion, the reformers attempted to restrain Balinese ritualistic leanings, while construing their Indo-Javanese heritage in accordance with their idea of what Hinduism—or rather, Neo-Hinduism—was about. In truth, Parisada's references were derived not only from Indian Neo-Hinduism, but equally from the prevalent religion in Indonesia, Islam.

The first decisions taken by Parisada consisted of publishing a handbook for religious instruction in schools (*Dharma Prawrtti Çastra*) (PDHB 1960), setting the date of the Saka new year[7] (*Nyepi*) valid for the whole island, and deciding which religious dates would become public holy days in Bali (*Nyepi, Pagerwesi, Galungan, Kuningan, Saraswati*).

From 17 to 23 November 1961, a General Assembly of Parisada (*Dharma Açrama Para Sulinggih dan Para Walaka Hindu Bali*) was held at Campuan, Ubud, which issued the Campuan Charter (*Piagam Campuan*), containing two sections: *Dharma Agama* and *Dharma Negara* (PHD 1970: 14–19; Supartha, Nadha and Sudibya 1995). *Dharma Negara* was intended to define the relationships between the Hindu-Balinese community and the Ministry of Religion. Among other things, the assembly demanded that *Dharma Hindu Bali* be taught in schools and universities, just like the other officially recognized religions. Specifically, Parisada urged KAGRI to normalize once and for all the institutional situation of *agama Hindu Bali*. In response, in 1962, the minister of religion opened negotiations with the Balinese government, Parisada, the Kantor Urusan Agama Propinsi, the Kantor Urusan Agama Daerah and the Dinas Agama Otonoom Daerah Bali. By decree of the minister of religion (*Keputusan Menteri Agama RI No.100 Tahun 1962*), the Dinas Agama Otonoom, the KUAP and the

---

[6] According to Margaret Wiener: "It is in assuming the power to interpret texts—to establish doctrine—and to standardize its interpretations in the form of ritual procedures to be followed throughout the island of Bali as a whole, that *Parisada*'s hegemony differs so radically from the earlier one" (Wiener n.d.: 15). This hegemony of religious exegesis resulted in marginalizing traditional interpreters such as literati, priests and mediums: indeed, deities were no longer expected to express their wishes through the utterances of mediums in trance, but their instructions were now transmitted by a bureaucratic jurisdiction on the authority of scriptural references (Hornbacher 2011).

[7] Alongside the Gregorian calendar, the Balinese make use of two ritual calendars, the Saka year of twelve lunar months, of Indian origin, and the *pawukon*, of Javanese origin, which combines a series of permutational cycles of variable lengths over a period of 210 days. To understand how these calendars articulate linear and cyclical time, and how they punctuate religious festivals in Bali, see Darta, Couteau and Breguet (2013).

KUAD were finally closed on July 10, 1963, to be replaced by a Bali Office of Religion (Kantor Agama Daerah Tingkat I Bali), headed by Tjokorda Rai Sudharta, with a section for Islam and Christianity in Singaraja, and a Hindu-Bali section in Denpasar (Anandakusuma 1966: 116–17). That same year, by decree of the minister of religion (*Keputusan Menteri Agama RI No.47 Tahun 1963*), the Division of Hindu Balinese Affairs (Bagian Urusan Hindu Bali) within KAGRI became the Bureau of the Hindu Balinese Religious Affairs (Biro Urusan Agama Hindu Bali), thereby finally acknowledging the Balinese religion as a legitimate *agama*.

Dharma Agama dealt with theology (*tattwa*), ethics (*susila*) and ritual (*upacara*), presented as the three inseparable pillars of any religion worthy of the label *agama*. It included a number of foundational pronouncements:
- the list of works composing the canon of *agama Hindu Bali* (*Çastra Dharma Hindu Bali*), with a distinction between *Weda Sruti*, comprised of *mantra*, the *Bhagawad Gita* and *tattwa*, such as the *Sang Hyang Kamahayanikan*, and *Dharma Sastra Smerti*, such as the *Sarasamuçcaya*;
- the standardization of the liturgical and astrological Hindu Balinese calendar (*pangalantaka*);
- the normalization of initiation procedures to the priesthood (*padiksan*);
- the definition of states of ritual pollution (*sasebelan*);
- the procedures to be followed for funeral rites (*atiwa-tiwa*);[8]
- the institutionalization of meditation during the 'Night of Siwa' (*Siwaratri*), hitherto a concern primarily of priests and literati;
- the classification of temples (*pura*), comprising two main categories: temples of a territorial nature, supposedly intended to the cult of Ida Sanghyang Widhi Wasa (*pura kahyangan*: kingdoms, villages, powerful places, etc.), and those of a genealogical nature (*pura kawitan*: from kinship temples to ancestral shrines);

---

[8] In order to reduce the expenses involved in funeral rites, Parisada recommended the organization of collective cremations. Whereas previously many Balinese could not afford to cremate their dead for decades, and many were never cremated, the development of collective cremations, by drastically reducing their cost, allowed most people to have access to proper death rites.

- lastly, the decision to build in all village temples (*kahyangan tiga*)[9] a *padmasana* dedicated to the One and Only God, Ida Sanghyang Widhi Wasa, in order to assert the monotheism of *agama Hindu Bali*.[10]

It was further decided to erect in the center of Denpasar, next to the Bali Museum, on the site of the *Puputan Badung*, a temple unlike any other, the Pura Agung Jagatnatha ('World Great Temple'). Its construction was started in 1962, with funding from the provincial government, Parisada and KAGRI, but it was not consecrated until 1968. In contrast to traditional Balinese temples, which usually comprise two or three courtyards (*jaba sisi, jaba tengah, jeroan*) with their many shrines (*palinggih*) dedicated to local deities, the new *pura* had only one courtyard with an immense central shrine (*padmasana*) dedicated to Siwa as Sanghyang Widhi, thereby emphasizing the monotheism and universalism of *agama Hindu Bali*. While rites performed in a Balinese *pura* normally concern only the congregation supporting it (*pamaksan*), as members of a territorial or functional community, or else a kinship group (*dadia*), the ceremonies conducted in the new temple are intended for the Hindu-Balinese community in its entirety, on the model of services held in mosques and churches. What's more, instead of calendrical festivals (*odalan*), its ceremonies are celebrated on the full moon and the dark of the moon, as well as on major religious holidays, and the officiating *padanda* delivers a sermon after having prepared the holy water. The Pura Agung Jagatnatha served as a template for the new temples that Parisada constructed outside Bali as it expanded its influence throughout Indonesia. Besides, until Parisada was able to buy land in north Denpasar, in the 1970s, its secretariat was located at the Pura Agung Jagatnatha.

Another important initiative taken at Campuan was the opening in Denpasar of a higher institute of religious education (*Açrama Pangadyayan*) for the training of officials and teachers of *agama Hindu Bali*. Inaugurated on October 3, 1963, the Institut Hindu Dharma (IHD) had four faculties: Religious Science

---

[9] Each Balinese village is said to comprise three sanctuaries (*kahyangan tiga*), that define it as a *desa adat*: the 'origin temple' (*pura puseh*, lit. the 'navel temple'), theoretically built at the time of the first settlement of the area, where the deified founding ancestors of the village are worshipped; the 'village temple' (*pura desa*) or 'great meeting hall temple' (*pura bale agung*), intended for meetings of the village council and associated with fertility rites; and the 'death temple' (*pura dalem*, lit. the 'temple of the mighty one'), place of ritual contact with the not yet purified deceased, located near the cemetery and cremation ground. In fact, numerous villages have only two main temples, a *pura puseh* combined with a *pura bale agung* at the upper end of the village, and a *pura dalem* at the lower end of the village. This is why Hildred Geertz suggested rendering the term *kahyangan tiga* as 'the three holy beings', in order to convey the idea that these three deities reign together over a *desa adat* (Geertz 2004: 47).

[10] The *padmasana* ('lotus seat') is traditionally the shrine of Siwa Raditya, that is, Siwa as the Sun God (Surya). Balinese textual traditions trace the origins of the *padmasana* to the coming in the 16th century of the Javanese Brahmin Danghyang Nirartha, the ancestor of the *padanda Siwa*, to whom numerous founding acts are attributed. But until recently most village temples had no *padmasana*, and no shrine was ever dedicated to Sanghyang Widi.

(*Ilmu Agama*), Religious Education (*Pendidikan Agama*), Religious Law (*Hukum Agama*), Religious Literature and Philosophy (*Sastra & Filsafat Agama*). It would be elevated to the rank of a university in 1993, under the name Universitas Hindu Indonesia (UNHI).

While the name *agama Hindu Bali* implied a clear recognition of its distinctive ethnic origin, it would subsequently be replaced by the more inclusive name *agama Hindu*. As far as I could ascertain, the move from *agama Hindu Bali* to *agama Hindu* has not been documented, unfortunately, and today opinions diverge as to how and why it came about. Some of my Balinese informants assumed that KAGRI had put pressure upon Parisada to universalize.[11] The fact is that the Provisional People's Consultative Assembly (Majelis Permusyarawatan Rakyat Sementara, MPRS)[12] had specified in 1960 that only acknowledged 'universal religions' (*agama universal*) would deserve government legitimation (*Ketetapan MPRS No.2, 1960*). According to others, however, it was not KAGRI that compelled the Balinese to replace *agama Hindu Bali* with *agama Hindu* but the Balinese reformers themselves who pressed KAGRI to recognize *agama Hindu* as a universal religion in no way circumscribed to Bali.

Be that as it may, in the early 1960s, the growing presence of Balinese in search of a living or education outside their island enabled Parisada to extend its influence to other regions in the Archipelago by opening branches in various provinces. Cut off from their temple networks and their deified ancestors, these Balinese migrants needed a delocalized and scriptural religion that they could carry with them. Indeed, books and doctrines being portable, they can be used by emigrants separated from their communities. Furthermore, besides the Balinese people, there were other Indonesian ethnic groups—such as the *abangan* and the Tengger in Java, for example—still practicing their traditional religion and whose rites bore the mark of Hindu-Buddhist influence.

In these circumstances, a debate emerged among Balinese religious leaders as to the proper name for their religion. Ida Bagus Mantra, endorsed mostly by Balinese who had studied in India and by those living in Jakarta—such as Tjokorda Rai Sudharta, Ida Bagus Oka Punyatmadja and Ida Bagus Gde Dosther, as well as I Gusti Anandakusuma—advocated giving up the exclusive ethnic flavor of the label *Hindu Bali* in favor of the more inclusive *Hindu Dharma*, in conformity with true Hinduism. Mantra's intention was to bring together the

---

[11] Interview, Putu Setia, Pedungan, May 15, 2007.
[12] The Majelis Permusyarawatan Rakyat Sementara was instituted by Sukarno's presidential decree as the highest legislative authority of the Republic of Indonesia after he had established his 'Guided Democracy' in July 1959.

whole Hindu-Indonesian community within Parisada and to strengthen the position of *agama Hindu* vis-à-vis Islam and Christianity in KAGRI, by vesting it with a universal scope.[13]

This move was opposed by prominent Balinese religious leaders—issuing mostly from the Panti Agama Hindu-Bali—led by I Gusti Bagus Sugriwa. For him, *agama Hindu Bali* was the result of a historical combination of *agama Hindu* and *agama Bali*, hence differing from Hinduism as practiced in India. However, *agama Hindu Bali* was not confined to the Balinese, as it was in fact the true ancestral religion of the Indonesians, complemented with Shaivism and Buddhism. According to Sugriwa, in the syntagm *agama Hindu Bali*, 'Bali' did not refer to an island, nor to an ethnic group, but it signified 'offering' (*banten*). In this respect, *agama Hindu Bali* was the religion of all those who make use of offerings to worship Sang Hyang Widhi and His manifestations (Sugriwa 1968).

Parisada Hindu Dharma

Mantra's standpoint eventually prevailed and his opponents were marginalized in the process. At his instigation, during the First Congress of Parisada Dharma Hindu Bali (*Mahasabha I*), held on October 7–10, 1964, in Denpasar, taking into account the fact that the council was not confined to Bali and was not limited solely to the Balinese people, its name was changed to Parisada Hindu Dharma (PHD, Hindu Dharma Council), thus forsaking any reference to its Balinese origins and widening its scope.[14] From then on, the designation *Hindu Dharma* would be frequently used instead of *agama Hindu*, both names becoming practically interchangeable. In fact, as early as 1956, I Gusti Anandakusuma had already proposed changing *Hindu Bali* to *Hindu Dharma*. On the other hand, some of Parisada's leaders objected to the name *Hindu Dharma* and advocated replacing it with *Sanatana Dharma*, the 'eternal and universal religion', a label endorsed by both Hindu reformers and traditionalists in India as a manifestation of self-assertion against Christianity. In any event, notwithstanding its change of name, Parisada would remain focused on Bali for a long time to come.

---

[13] Interview, Tjokorda Rai Sudharta, Puri Amertasari, Ubud, May 11, 2007.
[14] "*Berhubung Parisada tidak hanya di Bali dan tidak hanya terdiri dari suku Bali maka dengan tidak merubah makna dan tujuannya nama Parisada Dharma Hindu Bali ditingkatkan dan diluaskan menjadi Parisada Hindu Dharma*" (Dana 2005: 17).

Among the decisions adopted by the congress were regulations regarding the *desa adat*, the *banjar* and the *subak*.[15] In particular, Parisada asked the government to recognize the *desa adat* as a legal body (*badan hukum*) defined by the presence of a *kahyangan tiga*. Following the congress, Tjokorda Rai Sudharta was appointed secretary-general of Parisada in replacement of Ida Bagus Mantra, who had become president of Udayana University.

It was also during this congress that, for the purpose of defining *agama Hindu*, Ida Bagus Mantra drew up a theological canon composed of 'Five Articles of Faith' (*Panca Çraddha*), modeled on the Abrahamic religions, which—unlike Hinduism—are based on dogma (and most likely in reference to the Five Pillars of Islam, not to mention Pancasila): belief in the One and Only God (Sang Hyang Widhi, sometimes equated with the Nirguna Brahman of the Upanishads, with Parama Siwa or else with Narayana); belief in the eternity of the human soul (*atman*); belief in the ineluctable retribution of all actions (*karmaphala*); belief in reincarnation (*samsara*); and belief in the eventual liberation from the cycles of death and reincarnation (*moksa*) (Punyatmadja 1970).

While such a dogmatic formulation was indeed new, we saw that the groundwork had been prepared by Narendra Dev. Pandit Shastri, and it happened to be rather similar to the principles of the Arya Samaj as propounded by Dayananda Sarasvati. But one should understand that the *Panca Çraddha* partake of theological tenets which bear little resemblance to traditional Balinese cosmology and its related ritual practices in house and village temples. Each of these articles of faith would deserve an individual development, as the Sanskrit terminology employed by Mantra—hitherto familiar only to literati—differs from indigenous conceptions. I shall confine myself to commenting on some of the conceptual shifts implied by the obligation for the Balinese to subscribe to the compulsory monotheism imposed by the Indonesian state in order for their

---

[15] The *desa adat* ('customary village') is not really a socio-political organization nor, strictly speaking, a territorial unit, although of course it occupies territorial space in which the land belongs ultimately to the gods. It is, rather, a ritual domain, composed of the married couples of each house yard located on its territory, collectively responsible for the management of the temples associated with the *desa* (*kahyangan tiga*) and for the ceremonies that are celebrated therein. *Desa* membership (*krama desa*) is in this way defined by vertical relationships to a temple network rather than by horizontal relationships among the members of a community. The *banjar* (neighborhood association) is a residential entity largely autonomous from the *desa* which organizes community life, and whose responsibilities are at once ritual, social and administrative. They are mainly concerned with social control and public order on the one hand, and on the other, with communal co-operation in public works and ceremonial undertakings, the most important of which is the burial and eventual cremation of the dead. In this respect, *banjar* membership (*krama banjar*) is defined by horizontal relationships between all married residents in the neighborhood. As for the *subak* (irrigation society), it is a cooperative responsible for irrigation works and distribution of water among the rice fields. On the complexity of Balinese organizational forms, see, e.g., Geertz (1959), Guermonprez (1990), Warren (1993) and Ottino (2000a).

religion to receive official recognition. This does not mean that the reformed version of the Balinese religion has actually replaced the traditional ritual practices, but there is no question that Parisada is endeavoring to transform them, if only by imparting to them a new interpretation. And thanks to its increasing organizational efficiency, Parisada's instructions—endorsed by the state apparatus, in particular by the education system, and conveyed by the media—are progressively penetrating Balinese society at village level. Accordingly, generations of Balinese children are being taught that they are Hindu and they are coming to believe that *agama Hindu* has always been their religious tradition, that which distinguishes the Balinese people as a non-Muslim and non-Christian minority within the multi-religious Indonesian nation.

As previously mentioned, ritual action in Bali is construed as a concrete transaction with entities and forces of the invisible (*niskala*) world, intended to propitiate them in order to ensure their benevolence. In this understanding, it makes perfect sense that more elaborate rituals, with numerous offerings and a large number of officiating priests, would secure a greater degree of protection and well-being (*rahayu*). Yet, by teaching that religion is a matter of faith, the reform initiated by Parisada undermines the exchange logic of Balinese rituals. The onus is now on the spiritual disposition of the faithful to the detriment of ritual profligacy, denounced as useless and wasteful.[16] Henceforth Hindu Balinese are no longer expected to establish multiple transactions with immanent entities from the *niskala* world, but a personal relationship of devotion and faith with a transcendent God—Sang Hyang Widi.

The manifold entities with whom the Balinese establish exchange relations in their rituals are not clearly identified, and their usual rendering in terms of 'gods', 'ancestors' and 'demons' accounts very poorly for the reality on the ground. The imposition of Sang Hyang Widi as the monotheist God of *agama Hindu* entailed a twofold differentiation, between 'gods' and 'ancestors' on the one hand, as well as between the 'divine' and the 'demonic' on the other.

To begin with, the deities worshipped in Balinese temples—commonly referred to as *dewa* or *batara*[17]—are localized, in the sense that they are attached

---

[16] Hence the debate regarding animal sacrifices, a compulsory component of specific Balinese rites, which are criticized by reformers who advocate replacing the shedding of blood with symbolic substitutes, arguing that internal devotion in good faith is more effective than offering meat without good intentions. But villagers resist substituting the offering of intentions for the offering of live animals, since the spilling of blood upon the earth is necessary to bring forth fertility and the continuity of life.

[17] The distinction between *dewa* and *batara* is far from clear. Here is what Covarrubias had to say about it: "When a Balinese speaks of his gods, collectively called *dewas*, he does not mean the great divinities of Hinduism, but refers to an endless variety of protective spirits—*sanghyang, pitara, kawitan*, all of whom are in some way connected with the idea of ancestry. The rather vague term *dewa* includes not only the immediate ancestors

to a particular *pura*. Similarly, the Balinese are 'tied' (*kaiket*) to the particular deities of that temple. Thus, for example, they would talk about *Batara Puseh* to refer to the deity of their village origin temple, which differs from the one of another village. As a rule, Balinese belong to a network of temples, the main ones being their village and kinship temples. They worship the deities and ancestors of a particular temple during their visit at the time of the temple anniversary ritual (*odalan*); they do not worship a universal God who is always everywhere. But now, according to Parisada, the throngs of gods that attend a temple festival are said to be temporary manifestations of the One and Only God, an interpretation which goes against the grain of Balinese temple relationships. Besides, it used to be customary for a single person, generally a woman, to represent a whole house yard in temple ceremonies, to be blessed with holy water and to bring home the family's offerings after they had been consumed by the gods (*lungsuran, surudan*). This is no longer acceptable, as every Hindu devotee ought to worship for themselves, since each person is supposed to have a personal relationship to Sang Hyang Widi.

Balinese worship their ancestors in family and kinship temples (*sanggah/pamerajan, pura dadia, pura kawitan*) and they do not appear to clearly demarcate ancestors from gods. Instead, they seem to have the idea of a hierarchical continuum extending from less to more purified ancestors, who eventually become united with divinities as the outcome of a series of post-crematory rites (*nyekah, mukur, maligia*). Thus, the worship of one's own ancestral divinities by a family or a kin group emphasizes a distinction between descent groups, each with their own respective divinities, an exclusivist attitude which threatens the ideal of a Hindu community unified in the worship of Sang Hyang Widi. This novel ideal demands that a progressive gradation from ancestors to gods be replaced by an absolute dichotomy between human ancestors and a transcendent God.

---

worshipped in the family temple, or the nameless forefathers, founders of his community, to whom the village temples are dedicated, but also certain Hindu characters of his liking whom he has adopted into the Balinese race and has come to regard also as his ancestors. [...] The deities of the Hindu pantheon are mostly those worshipped in India, the high 'Lords'—*bhatara*—but in Bali they acquire a decidedly Balinese personality. Centuries of religious penetration did not convince the Balinese that the *bhataras* were their gods; they were too aloof, too aristocratic, to be concerned with human insignificance, and the people continue to appeal to their infinitely more accessible local *dewas* to give them happiness and prosperity" (Covarrubias 1937: 288–9). More recently, in the context of a village monography, anthropologist Danker Schaareman provided the following specifications: "In principle, all deities are 'déwa'; 'batara' is a honorific, only used for the more important gods. [...] 'Déwa' may also denote deified ancestors, for whom the term 'batara' is never used. [...] Both terms, 'déwa' and 'batara', however, are often arbitrarily and inconsistently used, regardless of the factual meaning of the words" (Schaareman 1986: 53).

Furthermore, *niskala* entities are inherently ambivalent, potentially protective as well as destructive, benevolent as well as malevolent (*rwa bhineda*), since in Bali the divine and the demonic are construed as transformations of each other. In short, Balinese deities can cause death and disease as well as provide life and well-being.[18] By contrast, from now on rituals are no longer supposed to be about offerings to positive and negative forces, propitiating the ones and placating the others, potentially transforming the latter into the former, but about celebrating the greatness of Sang Hyang Widi. Last but not least, since Sang Hyang Widi has long been appropriated by Balinese Christians, who like to affix stickers claiming 'Sang Hyang Widi Loves You' (in English) on the rear window of their cars, it is conceivable that in the long run their views might color those of Hindu Balinese.

Now, once the theological tenets of *agama Hindu* had been fully delineated, Ida Bagus Mantra set about composing a Hindu catechism—the *Upadesa Tentang Ajaran-Ajaran Agama Hindu* ('Instructions in the Doctrine of Hindu Religion')[19]—intended to be used as religious instruction in primary and secondary schools.[20] Following Parisada's First Congress, he assembled a team of contributors that included Tjokorda Rai Sudharta, Ida Bagus Oka Punyatmadja, Ida Bagus Gde Dosther and Parisada's chairman, Ida Padanda Gde Wayan Sidemen. The *Upadesa*, issued in 1967, is the first publication to expose in a systematic fashion a coherent doctrine of what *agama Hindu* is about, and it has been repeatedly republished since then (Sudharta and Punia Atmadja 1967). This doctrine is presented in the form of a dialogue between the *guru* Resi Dharmakirti ('Dharma's Glory') and his disciple (*sisia*) Sang Suyasa ('He Who Is

---

[18] This has been particularly well expressed by anthropologist Barbara Lovric in her dissertation: "Any confrontation between deities and demons cannot represent a conflict between good and evil because these moral categories simply do not apply [...]. Deities and demons are not directly concerned with each other or with human moral or ethical conduct. They merely demand deference. Moreover, Balinese are not concerned with the morality or virtue of deities and demons but with their power and the ambiguous nature of that power. It is not a case of lofty, exalted, high-minded deities aligned against apolaustic, iniquitous demons. Neither align to oppose, oppugn or objurgate the other. Both belong to the realm of the divine" (Lovric 1987: 63–4). See further Hobart (1985), Stephen (2002), Geertz (2004), and Acri and Stephen (2018).

[19] The Sanskrit term *upadesha* has the meaning of 'teachings, instructions', in the sense of the spiritual guidance provided by a *guru* to his disciple.

[20] The very idea of catechism is Protestant in origin, as Protestants had to reflect on what was truly the Christian religious doctrine, as opposed to its alleged corruption by the Roman Catholic Church. While the composition of a catechism was alien to Indic traditions, it is significant that two of the first leaders of the Theosophical Society, hailing from a Protestant background, had designed a catechism: Henry Steel Olcott's *A Buddhist Catechism* (1881) and Annie Besant's *Sanātana Dharma Catechism* (1902). Closer to home, Narendra Dev. Pandit Shastri had published in 1955 his own version of a Balinese catechism under the title *Dharmopadeça* ('The Teachings of Dharma'), but at the time he was dealing with the teachings of the *agama Çiwa-Buddha* (Shastri 1955b). I Gusti Ngurah Bagus in his contribution to Parisada's General Assembly held at Campuan in 1961 already suggested publishing a catechism of *agama Hindu Bali* (Bagus n.d.: 2–3; see Wijaya 2007: 307).

Renowned'), a rhetorical device which brings to mind the characteristic composition of the Upanishads. Following the publication of the *Upadesa*, all accounts of *agama Hindu* would take up its three-point framework (*kerangka dasar*)—*Tattwa* (theology), *Susila* (ethics) and *Upacara* (ritual)[21]—whose premises had already been outlined by Goris in 1953 and reiterated during Parisada's General Assembly at Campuan in 1961.

After a prologue introducing the protagonists, Resi Dharmakirti explains to his disciple that *agama Hindu*[22] (*Hindu Dharma*) is the religion of the people who follow the teachings of the *Weda* sacred scriptures, which have been revealed by Sang Hyang Widhi. He then presents the five absolute beliefs (*kepercayaan mutlak*) professed by *agama Hindu*, the *Panca Çraddha*, whose articles are developed in the ensuing chapters: "*Percaya adanya Sang Hyang Widhi, Atma, Hukum Karma Phala, Samsara, Moksa*" (Sudharta and Punia Atmadja 1967: 6).

The theology expounded in the *Upadesa* tends to combine the monism (*advaita*) of Vedanta with the dualism (*dvaita*) of Samkhya—which are not explicitly mentioned—without detracting from the monotheism imposed by the Ministry of Religion.[23] To reconcile the multiplicity of temples and deities with the conception of the One and Only God, the divinities addressed by the Balinese in their rituals (*Dewa* and *Bhattara*) are said to be 'radiations' (*sinar*) of Sang Hyang Widhi. According to a similar logic, their 'effigies' (*pratima*) are no longer conceived as vessels for the temporary residence of a local deity, but are now presented as 'symbols' (*simbol*) of the universal divine presence, on which the faithful are expected to focus their concentration during temple ceremonies. Besides its multiple emanations, Sang Hyang Widhi manifests Himself in his three functions (*Tri Sakti*): Brahma as Creator (*utpatti*), Wisnu as Preserver (*sthiti*) and Siwa as Destroyer (*pralina*). These three functions are supposed to

---

[21] We remark that both the catechism and the textbooks published by Annie Besant were divided into the same three parts—theology ('Basic Hindu Religious Ideas'), rites ('General Hindu Religious Customs and Rites'), and ethics ('Ethical Teachings')—like British Protestant catechisms at that time.

[22] In their presentation of *agama Hindu*, the authors advanced a fanciful etymology of the word *agama*, in that they construed the letter /a-/ as being privative, from which they inferred that *agama* signifies 'that which does not change, which is eternal' (*langgeng*). Unfortunately, this etymology is faulty, as in Sanskrit the prefix /ā-/ of *āgama* is long and means 'toward', the verb /gam/ means 'to go', and /ā-gam/ 'to arrive', while the suffix /-a/ indicates a nominal derivation. Thus, *āgama* signifies 'arrival', with reference to that which has been inherited from the past, in the sense of 'tradition'. I am indebted to Arlo Griffiths for this elucidation. This faulty etymology is not unique to Parisada, as it is also the one propounded by Islamic leaders in Indonesia. An early example is found in a comprehensive exegesis of the word *agama* by I Gusti Bagus Sugriwa (Soegeriwa 1938: 70).

[23] On the other hand, there is no reference whatsoever to tantric Shaivism, however prevalent it is in Balinese religious traditions.

be represented in the three village sanctuaries (*Kahyangan Tiga*): the *Pura Desa* is dedicated to Brahma, the *Pura Puseh* to Wisnu and the *Pura Dalem* to Siwa.[24]

After the lengthy exposition of the theological tenets (*Tattwa*) of *agama Hindu*, the catechism begins to lose its didactic coherence and the following sections appear as something of a catch-all. The chapter on ethics (*Susila*) is summed up by the aphorism *Tat Twam Asi* ('Thou Art That'), derived from the *Chandogya Upanishad* and unknown in Balinese textual traditions.[25] As for rituals (*Upacara*), they are intended to achieve, by means of sacrifices (*yajna*), a relationship between human beings and Sang Hyang Widhi. These sacrifices are motivated by the three 'debts' (*tri rna*)[26] that every Hindu has to discharge: to the *Dewa*, the *Pitra* and the *Resi*. This results in five sacrifices (*panca yajna*):[27] for gods (*Dewa-yajna*),[28] ancestors (*Pitra-yajna*), human beings (*Manusa-yajna*), priests (*Resi-yajna*), and 'demons' (*Bhuta-yajna*).[29] But rather than an explanation of the meaning and purpose of each of these sacrifices, the reader is

---

[24] This interpretation is most likely recent, notwithstanding that it is commonly attributed to Mpu Kuturan, the legendary Javanese priest said to have come to Bali in the 11th century, who is credited with the institution of the three sanctuaries that define a *desa adat*. Evidence of this comes from the fact that there is no mention of *kahyangan tiga* in Balinese inscriptions of the 11th to 14th centuries (Stuart-Fox 2002: 23, n. 4). Margaret Wiener convincingly rebutted this modern interpretation: "For one thing, many Balinese villages never had three village temples [...]. Second, it is not Siwa but his consort who is associated with the Pura Dalem, so the parallels are not as neat as they seem (especially as Wisnu's consort is associated with water temples rather than village temples, while Brahma's has nothing to do with temples). Third, it obscures the role of locality and history in the practice of Balinese religion. That one does not worship in any village temple anywhere in Bali [...] is the strongest indication that for Balinese the deities of village temples are not (yet) the same everywhere" (Wiener 1995: 381, n. 8; see Geertz 2004: 250, n. 36). What's more, there appears to be some confusion as regards the *pura puseh* and the *pura desa*, which are occasionally associated with Brahma and Wisnu respectively, indicating that Balinese have a hard time making sense of this official interpretation.

[25] Richard Fox (2010) has provided a witty treatment of this modern borrowing.

[26] This reference was borrowed from the *Manava Dharmashastra* by Ida Bagus Mantra, who introduced it in the *Dharma Prawrtti Çastra*, published in 1960.

[27] Like a number of recent formalizations, this categorization of Balinese rituals had been propounded by Narendra Dev. Pandit Shastri who, in his booklet *Dasa Sila Agama Bali*, had put forward a presentation close to the Vedic *pancamahayajna*, the five 'great sacrifices' that a householder should perform daily: to gods, to ancestors, to human beings, to all living creatures, and to the Vedas (Shastri 1951). The *panca yajna* were then expounded in 1954 by I Gusti Anandakusuma, who appears to have been the first Balinese reformer to endorse this formulation (Anandakusuma 1954). However, Christiaan Hooykaas (1975) pointed out that the *pañcayajña* were already mentioned in Old Javanese texts.

[28] One notices that the rites supposed to worship Sang Hyang Widhi are called *Dewa-yajna* and not *Widhi-yajna*, which indicates that the recipients of this worship are the *dewa* and not Sang Hyang Widhi, who was not the recipient of any ritual before becoming the One and Only God of *agama Hindu* in Bali. Furthermore, it is significant that the *Upadesa* does not mention the transformation of ancestors into *dewa* by means of post-crematory rites, perhaps for fear that the Hindu Balinese might be accused of practicing primitive ancestor worship (Bakker 1993: 271–2).

[29] Although usually translated into English as 'sacrifices for the demons', the *Buta Yadnya* are rituals to urge potentially malevolent forces to return to their benevolent form, in line with the tenets of tantric Shaivism (Stephen 2002; Acri and Stephen 2018; Fox 2018, Chap. 4).

provided with a detailed description of their ritual procedure, which is rather surprising given the anti-ritualist stance taken by Parisada. In the final chapter, Resi Dharmakirti expounds the *trisandhya*, the prayer to Sang Hyang Widhi that every Hindu should perform during the 'junctures' (*sandhya*) of the day: at dawn, at noon and at dusk.[30]

With the consecutive publication of both the *Panca Çraddha* and the *Upadesa*, *agama Hindu* officially became a universalist religion. Yet, while the authority claimed by the *Upadesa* is clearly buttressed by references to Indian sacred scriptures and concepts, one gets the feeling that most of these references are just tacked on rather than articulated in a coherent fashion, as the Balinese authors attempt to adjust the specific characteristic features of their own island to the normative framework provided by Neo-Hinduism. Indeed, the taxonomic organization of its topics appears more Indian than Balinese,[31] and this alien makeup plainly fails to account for actual local practices. Hence an inescapable amount of confusion that grows messier as Resi Dharmakirti's narrative proceeds, not to mention some flagrant distortions that Balinese religious leaders will be forever busy striving to repair.

The universalization of the Balinese religion as *agama Hindu* was ratified on January 27, 1965, by Sukarno's Presidential Decree No.1 of 1965 on the Prevention of the Misuse and/or the Defamation of Religion (*Penetapan Presiden No.1/1965 Tentang Pencegahan Penyalahgunaan dan/atau Penodaan Agama*), that made it illegal to slander, falsely interpret or promote teachings deviating from the core tenets of any of the state-sanctioned religions (Crouch 2012; Hefner 2018). For the first time, the decree named the six religions officially recognized as legitimate *agama* and deserving as such to be protected and to receive government assistance: *Islam, Kristen, Katolik, Hindu, Budha,* and *Kong Hu Cu* (*Confusius*).[32] This did not imply that other religions were outlawed in Indonesia (the decree cited Judaism, Zoroastrianism, Shintoism and Taoism), so long as they did not contradict the decree or other laws. But ethnic religions

---

[30] Again, like so many other Hindu innovations, the *trisandhya* had already been formulated by Narendra Dev. Pandit Shastri (195?).

[31] It is noteworthy that the authors tend to systematically substitute the vernacular Balinese terminology with a Sanskrit one, scrupulously transcribed with the proper diacritics.

[32] Even more so than the Balinese, the followers of Buddhism and Confucianism had to face institutional and theological hurdles to have their religion recognized as monotheism. Buddhist organizations managed to accommodate Chinese traditions, Theravada tenets and Javanese Vajrayana, and agreed to recognize Adi Buddha, a concept from the Old Javanese tantric Buddhist text *Sanghyang Kamahayanikan*, as the One and Only God of Indonesian Buddhism. Confucianism was articulated as *agama Khonghucu* by the Indonesian Chinese along with Buddhism. Regarding the recognition of Buddhism and Confucianism as proper *agama*, see Brown (1987, 2004), Abalahin (2005), Heriyanto (2005), Steenbrink (2013), Chambert-Loir (2015), and Ramstedt (2018).

(*agama suku*), as well as the so-called 'sects' (*aliran kepercayaan*) and Javanese mystical movements (*aliran kebatinan*) were not acknowledged as *agama*, and so were not entitled to protection by the state.

Sukarno's decree responded to the concerns of both the Ministry of Religion and the Islamic organizations. By setting out a restricted list of the religions formally recognized by the state, it laid down the legal foundation for the policing of religious heterodoxy and the prosecution of indigenous cults deemed to be deviating (*sesat*) from the state-sanctioned *agama*. In order to counter the *aliran kebatinan*, the Islamic organizations had long urged the government to establish a legal definition of religion, and KAGRI had made several attempts to do so. In response, a number of *aliran kebatinan* had formed in December 1955 the Congressional Body for Indonesian Mysticism (Badan Kongres Kebatinan Indonesia, BKKI), which kept petitioning the government to grant *kebatinan* equal status with *agama*, by claiming that theirs was the 'original religion' of Indonesia (*agama asli Indonesia*)—a clear anti-Islamic declaration. The BKKI's militancy was compounded by the political instability of the times. After Sukarno introduced his 'Guided Democracy' in 1959, he attempted to establish a coalition, the Nasakom (an acronym for 'Nationalism-Religion-Communism'), bringing together his supporters from the PNI, the conservative Muslim Nahdlatul Ulama, and the increasingly assertive PKI. A shaky combination from the start, by 1964 the three partners in Nasakom had fallen into infighting. Given the growing activism of both the *aliran kebatinan* and the Communist Party, it appears that Sukarno had decided to appease the Muslim wing of his ailing coalition.

The political infighting, which had been escalating for years, came to a head with the abortive coup of September 30, 1965, in which six army generals were kidnapped and killed. The crushing of the coup, attributed to the PKI by the right-wing army, unleashed a massive slaughter of alleged 'communists' (Robinson 2018; Roosa 2020). The repression also targeted adherents of *aliran kepercayaan* and members of Javanese *kebatinan* groups, and more generally those continuing to practice indigenous religions, who were seen as subversive elements. While the massacres affected mainly Java, they were particularly ferocious in Bali, where some estimates put the number at a hundred thousand casualties (Cribb, Soe Hok Gie et al. 1990). And yet, far from adversely affecting the image of Edenic harmony bequeathed by the colonial era, these massacres were readily attributed to Balinese cultural exoticism, like some sort of cathartic interlude, a murderous madness related to *amok* and akin to a new *puputan*. Eager to clear up what he saw as a misconception, the political historian Geoffrey Robinson argued that this veritable civil war was the outcome of rising tensions on the island since the late 1950s, as well as the polarization of Balinese society along dividing lines where class conflicts and status competition were buttressed by party rivalries and ideological divergences (Robinson 1995). In the context of seriously deteriorating economic conditions, following a series of natural disasters and pest plagues, and a devastating volcanic eruption of Mount Agung in 1963, the aggressive implementation of the Basic Agrarian Law promulgated by Sukarno in 1960 and the occupation of land belonging to palaces and temples orchestrated by the PKI were construed by their opponents as an attack on *agama Hindu* and traditional social hierarchy, as a sacrilege bringing about a cosmic imbalance in need of thorough cleansing. This interpretation discounts the role of the army and of the PNI, whose leaders had clearly decided to do away with the PKI once and for all, and who managed to achieve their ends.[33] In December 1965, the governor of Bali, Anak Agung Bagus Sutedja, accused of pro-communist leanings, was replaced by the Balinese PNI leader, I Gusti Putu Merta, who himself would be replaced in November 1967 by a Javanese military figure, Colonel Soekarmen.

While Bali had until then been among Indonesia's most politically active provinces, the trauma provoked by these appalling events brought about a forced depoliticization along with an increased focus on culture and religion, which were to become valuable commodities with the forthcoming development of tourism (Lewis and Lewis 2009). The image of a peaceful and apolitical Balinese society, inherited from colonial times, was propagated, culminating in the neo-Sanskritic motto of *Tri Hita Karana* ('The Three Sources of Well-being')— namely, the harmonious relationships of human beings with God (*parhyangan*), with people (*pawongan*) and with nature (*palemahan*). This motto was formulated on November 11, 1966, by Captain I Wayan Mertha Sutedja at a conference organized by the Board for the Struggle of the Hindu-Balinese community (Badan Perjuangan Umat Hindu Bali) in Denpasar, with the aim of strengthening the position of the Hindu-Balinese community within the new political configuration in Indonesia, by forging a veneer of theological unity over the diverse local cosmological and associated ritual traditions on the island. Popularized by I Gusti Ketut Kaler, *Tri Hita Karana* has been presented ever

---

[33] The problem with Robinson's analysis is that it completely eschews any reference to Balinese culture and emic perceptions of the events (Vickers 1998). Counter to Robinson, anthropologist Leslie Dwyer and Balinese activist Degung Santikarma contend that in Bali agency cannot be reduced to worldly politics and that in order to make sense of the violence of 1965–66 one has to engage with the *niskala* dimension of the Balinese reality. They stress in this respect the Balinese fear of *leak*, humans who are capable of changing their shape into a terrifying demon, to whom communists were readily likened (Dwyer and Santikarma 2003).

since as a 'traditional Balinese philosophy' based on the *Weda* (Wirawan 2011; Ramstedt 2014: 65).[34]

Thus it is that through their struggle to obtain recognition of their religion, the Balinese have come to turn *agama Hindu* into the diacritic marker of their ethnic identity. But it is precisely from the moment they identified themselves most explicitly as a Hindu island in a sea of Islam that one can date the foundations of a disjunction between Balinese religious and ethnic identities. This is because their identification of ethnicity and religion would soon be foiled by a twofold process of Indonesianization-cum-Indianization: on the one hand, once expressly detached from any ethnic reference, *agama Hindu* was no longer the sole property of the Balinese people, who had to open it up to other Indonesian ethnic groups; while on the other hand, the growing influence of Indian Neo-Hinduism on *agama Hindu* would render the link between religion and ethnicity ever more problematic for the Balinese.

The New Order

In the aftermath of the coup of September 30, 1965, and the ensuing elimination of the PKI and other suspected leftist elements, President Sukarno was progressively sidelined to be replaced by General Suharto, who officially became president on March 27, 1968. The 'New Order' (*Orde Baru*) which he established with a firm fist set itself the goal of redressing Indonesia's dire economic situation by calling on the aid of foreign capital and experts. Simultaneously, Suharto reinforced the authority of the state and put an end to popular mobilization and the political agitation that had marked the Sukarno years, henceforth outlawed as an impediment to the country's march toward 'modernization' (*modernisasi*) and 'development' (*pembangunan*).[35]

The new regime undertook to rely on religion to strengthen its control over the population as well as to confront the specter of 'atheistic communism'.

---

[34] While this formulation is indeed recent, the conception of the *Tri Hita Karana* is related to a number of traditional Balinese tripartitions, more particularly the concern with the three levels of the cosmos (*tri loka*): the heavens, the middle world and the underworld, now equated with the environment. Besides, it is not specific to Bali, in that it refers to a set of ideas and values which bound together the living community, its ancestral founders and the natural environment which sustains the community through time.

[35] The Indonesian terminology has three distinct words to convey the notion of 'development'—*pembangunan*, *pengembangan* and *pembinaan*—all of which imply an intentionality, a concerted effort to form, cultivate, and promote a quality that is not taken for granted but that needs to be developed in a particular direction. The objective being pursued is the mobilization of society in the service of the state. Regarding the ideology of 'development' in New Order Indonesia, see Heryanto (1988).

Pancasila, with its proclamation of *Ketuhanan Yang Maha Esa*, acquired further prominence as a state ideology. The Ministry of Religion was given increased importance and in 1966 became the Department of Religion (Departemen Agama, Depag). Placed under direct supervision of President Suharto, who oversaw the formulation and implementation of its policies, it was transformed from the bulwark of conservative political Islam into a fully-fledged instrument of state power. That same year, by presidential decree (*Keputusan Presiden RI No.170 Tahun 1966*), the Bureau of Hindu Balinese Religious Affairs (Biro Urusan Agama Hindu Bali) was put in charge of Buddhist Affairs and became the Directorate General for the Guidance of the Hindu Balinese and Buddhist Communities (Direktorat Jenderal Bimbingan Masyarakat Hindu Bali dan Buddha).[36] In 1969, Sukarno's Presidential Decree No.1 of 1965 on the Prevention of the Misuse and/or the Defamation of Religion was given full legal standing by being elevated to the status of national law (*UU No.5, 1969*).[37] This had the result of turning state-sanctioned religions into bounded and mutually exclusive categories, while keeping all religious communities under tight surveillance and putting increasing pressure on heterodox views to conform. By requiring all citizens to embrace one of the state's recognized religions, the law triggered a wave of mass conversions from adherents of ethnic traditions.

Muslim parties, which had been instrumental in fighting communism and bringing Suharto into power, thought that their time had come and pressed to have the Jakarta Charter inscribed in the constitution. But they were quickly disabused, as Suharto appeared to share Sukarno's suspicion of political Islam and undertook to control and restrict any potential opposition from Muslim activists.[38] By and large, the administration of Islam under the New Order aimed at accommodating the religious aspirations of the Muslim community while preventing the Islamic parties from meddling in public affairs. By depoliticizing Islam, this policy was to result in Islamizing Indonesian society (Ricklefs 2012).

A policy of 'building up religion' (*pembinaan agama*) was implemented, coordinated jointly by the departments of religion and of the interior. As of 1966,

---

[36] One notices that the Department of Religion had still not registered the universalization of the Balinese religion and its associated change of name, notwithstanding its official inscription in Sukarno's 1965 presidential decree.

[37] After having endured a series of restrictions since the inception of the New Order, Confucianism, regarded as an ethnic Chinese religion and hence associated with communism, would no longer be recognized as a proper *agama* as of 1979 (Abalahin 2005: 128–9). In 2006, after the fall of the New Order regime, Confucianism was officially reinstated as a recognized religion.

[38] In January 1973, to allow better control, the government forced the various Islamic parties to merge into the United Development Party (Partai Persatuan Pembangunan, PPP) while the non-Islamic parties were combined into the Indonesian Democratic Party (Partai Demokrasi Indonesia, PDI). By monitoring their leadership, the government ensured that these parties never developed effective opposition.

religious education was made compulsory, from primary school to university, each pupil being instructed in the religion declared by his/her parents (Kelabora 1976). With the coming of age of new generations of Indonesians duly educated in religious matters, this measure would drastically change the balance of power in favor of Islam. Insofar as most Indonesians consider themselves Muslims, to a greater or a lesser degree, their children would henceforth receive a Muslim education, which would eventually boost mainstream normative Islam while spurring the decline of its syncretic variants and numerous ethnic religions. In this way, Indonesian Muslims increasingly came to understand their religion as a coherent system of beliefs and practices, rather than merely a conventional way of life.

Yet, at the time, the obligation for Indonesians to be affiliated with one of the officially recognized religions did not benefit Islam as, in their quest for religious respectability and protection, numerous nominal Muslims, particularly Javanese *abangan* and members of *aliran kebatinan*, chose to repudiate Islam outright, opting instead for Protestantism or Catholicism, as well as, to a lesser extent, for Hinduism or Buddhism. Moreover, in the late 1960s, the *aliran kebatinan* received the backing of an influential faction of the political and military elite, deeply rooted in a Javanist cultural background. In 1970, the former Badan Kongres Kebatinan Indonesia (BKKI) was revived under the aegis of the government party Golkar (Golongan Karya, 'Functional Groups')[39] as the Badan Kongres Kepercayaan Kejiwaan Kerohanian Kebatinan Indonesia (BK5I), which soon after became the Coordinating Secretariat of Beliefs (Sekretariat Kerjasama Kepercayaan, SKK), formally incorporated into Golkar. From then on, the label *kebatinan* tended to be replaced by *kepercayaan*, in reference to article 29 of the 1945 constitution, while the SKK kept demanding that the constitutional position of *kepercayaan* be acknowledged on a par with that of *agama*. That demand appeared to be granted in 1973, when the new Broad Outlines of State Policy (*Garis-garis Besar Haluan Negara, GBHN*) formulated by the People's Consultative Assembly (Majelis Permusyarawatan Rakyat, MPR) declared *kepercayaan* and *agama* as separate but equally legitimate expressions of the 'Belief in the One and Only God'.[40]

---

[39] Originally established in October 1964 by the National Armed Forces as a counterweight to the PKI's influence, Golkar was turned into an electoral machine to support the New Order of President Suharto.
[40] Under the heading '*Agama dan Kepercayaan terhadap Tuhan Yang Maha Esa*', the text of the GBHN stated: "*Atas dasar Kepercayaan Bangsa Indonesia terhadap Tuhan Yang Maha Esa maka perikehidupan beragama dan perikehidupan berkepercayaan terhadap Tuhan Yang Maha Esa didasarkan atas kebebasan menghayati dan mengamalkan Ketuhanan Yang Maha Esa sesuai dengan Falsafah Pancasila*" (Subagya 1976: 125).

Even though the MPR fell short of recognizing *kepercayaan* as 'religion', Islamic groups, dreading that this might be imminent, put intense pressure on the government to make sure that it would never happen. Yielding to their demands, at the time of its next session, in 1978, the MPR officially stated that "Belief in the One and Only God is not a religion" (*Kepercayaan terhadap Tuhan Yang Maha Esa tidak merupakan agama*). From then on, *kepercayaan* would no longer come under the jurisdiction of the Department of Religion, but would be placed in the Department of Education and Culture (Departemen Pendidikan dan Kebudayaan), where shortly afterwards a new directorate was established within the Directorate General of Culture (Direktorat Jenderal Kebudayaan)—the Directorate for the Supervision of the Followers of Belief in the One and Only God (Direktorat Pembinaan Penghayat Kepercayaan terhadap Tuhan Yang Maha Esa).[41] The following year, the Sekretariat Kerjasama Kepercayaan changed its name to align itself with the new directorate and became the Association of the Followers of Belief in the One and Only God (Himpunan Penghayat Kepercayaan terhadap Tuhan Yang Maha Esa, HPK). Thus, failing to be recognized as 'religion', *kepercayaan* was finally acknowledged as 'culture', this way providing the *aliran kepercayaan* with some institutional shelter (Stange 1986: 90–1). At the same time, Indonesian citizens were required to officially register their religious affiliation, which would be stated on their identity cards (*Kartu Tanda Penduduk, KTP*). As a consequence, adherents of *kepercayaan* were expected to affiliate themselves with one of the state-sanctioned *agama*, otherwise they ran the risk of being discriminated against by the administrative authorities.

On the other hand, the official recognition of *agama Hindu* by Sukarno's decree had turned it into a de facto proselytizing religion, in the sense that any Indonesian citizen could choose to become '*Hindu*'. Thus, in the wake of the anti-communist massacres of 1965–66, groups of Javanese *abangan* and followers of *aliran kebatinan* converted to *agama Hindu* for fear of being branded 'atheists', an accusation synonymous with 'communists' in Indonesia (Howell 1977; Lyon 1977; Reuter 2001; Hefner 2004). During the following years, they were joined by several ethnic minorities which in turn took refuge in the Hindu fold hoping to be allowed to conserve their ancestral rites, *agama*

---

[41] Andrew Abalahin remarked that: "The sharp distinction that certain authorities seek to draw between *agama* and *kepercayaan* extends even to the terms covering their adherents: an *agama* has *penganut* ('those who submit [to it]') or *pemeluk* ('those who embrace [it]'), while a *kepercayaan* has *penghayat* ('those who comprehend or who practice [it]'). The further distinction reinforces the notion that an *agama* is transcendent, coming from some higher source outside the individual, outside humanity, while a *kepercayaan* is subjective, arising from within the individual, within the humanity" (Abalahin 2005: 121, n. 7).

Hindu being reputedly more accommodating in this respect than Islam or Christianity (Ramstedt 2018: 268–9).[42]

The affiliation of non-Balinese populations to *agama Hindu* raised delicate issues, for the new converts as much as for the Balinese themselves, as the Hinduization of the Balinese religion had now to adjust to the particular conditions of ethnic groups wondering what it meant to become '*Hindu*'. While they expected to be allowed to conserve at least part of their *adat*, they still needed to differentiate it from that which properly belonged to *agama Hindu*, a task for which they were even more poorly equipped than the Balinese had been before them. Furthermore, whereas the movement of religious rationalization and Hinduization in Bali had been spearheaded by an urbanized social and intellectual elite, its propagation outside the island concerned mostly rural populations, poor and undereducated. And while these new Hindu minorities were regularly the target of discrimination, harassment, and humiliation from Muslim and Christian quarters, the Balinese were impaired by their serious lack of educators and proselytizers to spread and promote the teachings of *agama Hindu*, which they were themselves currently elaborating.

It should be noted that the issue at hand here was less one of 'conversion' to a new faith than of institutional affiliation to a state-sanctioned religion, regarded primarily as a protection (*pelindung*). And indeed, once the political situation had cooled down somewhat, particularly in Java, a number of new 'Hindus' gave up *agama Hindu*, which they found as alien to their religious traditions as Islam. For if the affinities which the new converts had perceived with traditional Balinese rituals had initially facilitated their affiliation to *agama Hindu*, they would later on realize that the religious norms promoted by Parisada were completely foreign to them.

Meanwhile, the New Order regime was strengthening its hegemony over society and expanding its control over Indonesians' religious life. In 1975, to provide Islamic support and legitimacy for its policies, the government established the Indonesian Council of Islamic Scholars (Majelis Ulama Indonesia, MUI), with the function of issuing religious legal opinions (*fatwa*) and religious advice for the Indonesian Muslim community. Then, in 1978, the minister of religion issued a decree (*Keputusan Menteri Agama No.70 Tahun*

---

[42] I am referring here to various ethnic groups who succeeded in having their traditional religion recognized as a branch of *agama Hindu*: the Tengger in Java (*agama Buda*), between 1962 and 1977 (Hefner 1985); the Sa'dan-Toraja (*Aluk To Dolo*), the Mamasa-Toraja (*Ada'Mappurondo*) and the Bugis To Wani To Lotang, in Sulawesi, in 1969 (Ramstedt 2004b); the Karo Batak in Sumatra (*Pemena*), in 1977 (Vignato 2000); as well as the Ngaju and the Luangan in Kalimantan (*Kaharingan*), in 1980 (Weinstock 1987; Schiller 1997; Baier 2007).

1978 Tentang Pedoman Penyiaran Agama) prohibiting any proselytizing among populations already professing, however nominally, a state-sanctioned religion, aimed in particular at preventing the evangelization of nominal Muslim Javanese (Kim 1998). Simultaneously, the Depag was launching Islamic preaching campaigns (*dakwah*), with the aim of winning back Javanese who had converted to Christianity, as well as to Hinduism or Buddhism, after the trauma of 1965-66. Indeed, from then on, the Islamization of Java, and of Indonesia as a whole, would start off anew, together with the world revival of Islam (Hefner 2011).

In these circumstances, and notwithstanding the fact that *agama Hindu* was now an officially recognized religion, the Hindu community felt rather insecure. Thus, after having been close to the PNI and even more so to the army, Parisada's leaders were quick to endorse the New Order with the aim of protecting the Hindu community against the hostility of Muslims, who still tended to consider non-Muslims would-be 'communists'. In the course of a seminar held from June 30 to July 5, 1968, at Tampaksiring by the Angkatan Muda Hindu Indonesia (AMHI),[43] its chairman, Wedastera Suyasa—a former member of the PNI's leadership and a supporter of Sukarno—pledged his support to President Suharto and requested the affiliation of the AMHI to Golkar (AMHI 1968: 86). Parisada immediately followed suit and on July 23, 1968, three Hindu organizations officially joined Golkar: Parisada Hindu Dharma, the Angkatan Muda Hindu Indonesia and the Prajaniti Hindu Indonesia, an organization set up on June 19, 1965, under Parisada's auspices to defend the interests of the Hindu community. Thereafter, most of Parisada's leaders would be prominent members of Golkar holding important political or military positions. With its affiliation to Golkar, Parisada lost its independence and became an integral part of the New Order apparatus, a move which would increase its Indonesianization and generate serious criticism in its ranks. By the same token, its bureaucratization increased with emphasis on religious regulations and ritual procedures.

As a member of Golkar, Parisada Hindu Dharma was now required to endorse the five-year governmental development plans (*Repelita*) launched by the New Order. This was demonstrated by the theme chosen for its Second Congress (*Mahasabha ke II*), held on December 2–5, 1968, in Denpasar in the presence of President Suharto: 'The Hindu Community in the Five-Year Development Plan' (*Umat Hindu Dalam Repelita*).[44] Some thirty regional

---

[43] The Angkatan Muda Hindu-Bali had become the Angkatan Muda Hindu Indonesia on November 20, 1966, and had moved its headquarters to Jakarta in November 1967.

[44] Since tourism had become a national priority for the First Five-Year Development Plan (*Repelita 1969–1973*), the congress stated that Parisada had to promote tourism in Bali, all the while preserving religion (*agama*), tradition

delegations took part in the congress, a testimony to the expansion of Parisada, which was already established in five provinces and some forty districts (*kabupaten*). The Assembly of Priests was renamed *Paruman Sulinggih* while the Assembly of Laymen became the *Paruman Walaka*. Following the congress, two Javanese made it into the *Paruman Walaka* and a representative branch (*perwakilan*) of Parisada was set up in Jakarta.

As pointed out above, until then the heading *Hindu Bali* still prevailed in the Depag. Consequently, the congress pressed (*mendesak*) the president of the republic to instruct (*memerintahkan*) the minister of religion to replace as quickly as possible the name *Hindu Bali* with the name *Hindu* in all its offices (PHD Kabupaten Badung 1970: 16). As a result, in 1969, by presidential decree (*Keputusan Presiden RI No.39 Tahun 1969*), the Directorate General for the Guidance of the Hindu Balinese and Buddhist Communities (Direktorat Jenderal Bimbingan Masyarakat Hindu Bali dan Buddha) became the Directorate General for the Guidance of the Hindu and Buddhist Communities (Direktorat Jenderal Bimbingan Masyarakat Hindu dan Buddha).

In addition to various standardization measures concerning rites and ceremonies, the congress fixed the curriculum for the training of priests and the procedures required for their ordination, which could henceforth be sanctioned only with Parisada's due authorization. Two categories of priests were distinguished:

- the *pandita* (or *sulinggih*), a title reserved for those who undergo an initiation (*padiksan*), complete with spiritual death (*amati raga*) and rebirth with a new name, who are thus 'twice-born' (*dwijati*); their function is to guide the congregation (*memimpin umat*) and to supervise the rites (*loka pala sraya*);
- the *pinandita*, who undergo only a purification (*pawintenan*) that does not involve a spiritual death, and who are thus only 'once-born' (*ekajati*); their function is to assist the *pandita*.

The *pinandita* category, open to anybody, is comprised mostly of priests attached to the service of a particular temple (*pamangku*), specific classes of puppeteers (*mangku dalang*), mediums (*dasaran*) and healers (*balian*), as well as other kinds of priests, such as the *wasi* in Java. On the other hand, the *padiksan* initiation had always been exclusive to *brahmana* priests—the *padanda*. Already contested by Surya Kanta, as we have seen, this privilege was challenged by

---

(*adat*) and culture (*budaya*) from the putative harmful damage brought about by tourists—a regular dilemma for the Balinese authorities as will be seen later on.

various commoner descent groups (*warga*), whose leaders attempted to abolish the *brahmana*'s monopoly and impose the use of their own priests—*bhujangga, resi, bhagawan, empu* and *dukuh*—alongside the *padanda*. Under pressure from these *warga*, Parisada decreed at this congress that all Hindus (*umat Hindu dari segala warga*) could undergo the initiation rite and that all duly initiated priests would hence have the same status, and in consequence that they would be equally qualified to officiate at the same ceremonies (*Keputusan No.5/Kep/PHDP/1968*).

Furthermore, the congress insisted on the necessity of differentiating between what belongs to *agama* and what to *adat*, with the aim of preserving *adat* that conforms to the teachings of *agama* while discarding *adat* that stands in the way (*menghambat*) of *agama*. The distinction between their respective domains stated that *agama* is eternal and universal whereas *adat* is variable according to the place, the time, and the circumstance (*desa, kala, patra*). In addition, the congress requested that the rules (*awig-awig*) governing the *desa adat*, the *banjar* and the *subak* be written down in order to ensure their standardization.

It appears that in these years when the New Order was buttressing its institutional authority, the Hindu community still felt itself in a shaky position despite the protection provided by the government's Golkar, while Parisada was being criticized for not properly building up the Hindu religion. This is clearly evidenced by numerous contributions to an important conference of Indonesian Hindu intellectuals and academics (*Musyawarah Cendikiawan/Sarjana Hindu-Dharma (Indonesia) Seluruh Indonesia*), held in Denpasar on June 1–4, 1972, under the auspices of Wedastera Suyasa, the very diligent chairman of the Angkatan Muda Hindu Indonesia, who was being ostracized by Parisada's leadership.[45] Some participants suggested strengthening Parisada's organizational structure by adding an assembly of Hindu intellectuals and academics, as well as an assembly of Hindu youth, alongside the *Paruman Sulinggih* and the *Paruman Walaka*. Others demanded that all the organizations that had taken part in the foundation of Parisada be invited to its general assemblies and congresses (Sukarsa 1972).

One of the most vocal critics was I Gusti Anandakusuma, who denounced Parisada for being Bali-centered instead of promoting a universal *Hindu Dharma*, its change of name notwithstanding. As the Balinese were not instructed in the proper conduct of their religion, he said, they still went about enacting their customary rituals without really understanding what they were

---

[45] Interview, I Made Wedastera Suyasa, Puri Mahendradatta, Denpasar, December 13, 1994.

doing or why. Anandakusuma attributed this unfortunate state of affairs, at least in part, to the fact that Parisada was engaged in supporting cultural tourism (*pariwisata budaya*) in Bali, which focused on spectacular ceremonial pageants and turned religious practices into a tourist attraction. The result was that Bali was being sold to foreign commercial interests for the sake of tourism, while the Balinese people were facing the threat of land seizure and invasive immigrant labor (Anandakusuma 1972).

On another note, some participants observed that *agama Hindu* was spreading in earnest outside Bali, most particularly in Java. They urged Parisada to consolidate this promising lead, while regretting the patent dearth of Hindu proselytizers (*dharma dutta*) and religious teachers (*guru agama*). Conversely, they deplored the fact that some Hindu Balinese were forsaking their religion and converting to Islam or Christianity. To reinforce the position of *agama Hindu* vis-à-vis its competitors, one contributor recommended forging an alliance between Hindus (*Hindu Dharma*), Buddhists (*Budha Dharma*) and Confucianists (*Tri Dharma*), based on the fact that their traditions share common features that differentiate them from Abrahamic religions, such as ancestor worship in particular (Budja 1971).

It is questionable whether these various exhortations and criticisms had much effect on Parisada, which held its Third Congress (*Mahasabha ke III*) on December 27–29, 1973, in Denpasar. In fact, Parisada was becoming more bureaucratized, as illustrated by the appointment of a police officer, I Wayan Surpha, with no religious credentials, as secretary-general. Most of the decisions and recommendations issued by the congress were merely reiterations of previous ones, such as the need to clearly differentiate *agama* from *adat*. In particular, Parisada planned to design a standard curriculum for the teaching of *Hindu Dharma* from elementary school to university, as well as another for the formal religious education of *pandita* and *pinandita*; and it resolved to train teachers and proselytizers to propagate *agama Hindu* outside Bali. Clearly worried about the risk of desecration of temples and ceremonies by disrespectful tourists, Parisada declared its intention to monitor the tourism policy in Bali. Among the requests addressed to the national government, the congress asked anew that the main island-wide Balinese religious celebrations—*Nyepi*, *Siwaratri*, *Pagerwesi*, *Galungan*, *Kuningan*, *Saraswati*—become national Hindu holidays, so as to publicly acknowledge equal treatment among Hinduism, Islam and Christianity. In the end, only *Nyepi* would be declared a national holiday, and this not until 1983.

Parisada's Fourth Congress (*Mahasabha ke IV*) was held only on September 24–27, 1980 in Denpasar, after the huge celebration at Besakih of the centennial rite *Eka Dasa Rudra* that marked the turn of the Saka year 1900, on March 28, 1979, in the presence of the president of the republic, the minister of religion and the governor of Bali (1978–88), Ida Bagus Mantra, recently appointed in replacement of Colonel Soekarmen—and under the gaze of tourists, journalists and television crews from all around the world (Stuart-Fox 1982).[46] The rapid development of tourism compelled Parisada to restrict access to Balinese temples while admonishing that religious ceremonies should not become tourist attractions. Already in 1974, Parisada had issued a decree regulating access to temples (*Surat Keputusan No.42/Kep/PHDP/74 tgl 7 Pebruari 1974 Tentang Tatacara Keluar Masuk Pura*), which was ratified shortly thereafter by a governor's decree (*Surat Keputusan Gubernur Kepala Daerah Tingkat Satu Bali No.26/Kesra.II/c/339/74*). More generally, the issue was to decide what tourists were permitted to do and what ought to be prohibited, such as holding religious ceremonies specifically for them. This matter had already been addressed during a seminar held in 1971, which had unsuccessfully attempted, as we will see in the following chapter, to differentiate the sacred (*sakral*) from the profane (*provan*) regarding dance performances.

Another point of note is the procedure regulating conversion to *agama Hindu*, regularly discussed since the 1968 congress and officially adopted during a seminar organized by Parisada in February 1981. Once non-Balinese ethnic groups were being nominally affiliated to *agama Hindu*, there was a need for a rite to substantiate their conversion; notably, in order to celebrate a Hindu wedding whenever one of the spouses came from another religion. Named *Sudhi Wadani*, this rite was manifestly borrowed from the procedure (*Shuddhi*) invented by the Arya Samaj for reconverting to Hinduism those Indians who had converted to Islam or Christianity (Titib 1991; Jordens 1991; Clémentin-Ojha 1994).[47]

---

[46] This rite consists of propitiatory offerings to the eleven Rudra, representing destructive aspects of Siwa. At this occasion holy water was, for the first time, brought in from India. Although centennial in principle, the *Eka Dasa Rudra* had previously been celebrated in March 1963 for the purpose of warding off several disasters that were affecting the island (Bagus 1974). The ceremony had been disrupted by the eruption of Mount Agung, which devastated numerous surrounding villages but narrowly spared the temple complex of Besakih (Mathews 1965).

[47] The Sanskrit term *shuddhi* refers to the state of purity necessary for the performance of *dharma*; by extension, it signifies the rite of purification by which pollution is removed. The formalization of the *Sudhi Wadani* rite did not address all the problems presented by the opening of *agama Hindu* to non-Balinese. The question remained of deciding in which 'caste' to place the new 'Hindus', a question that Wayan Bhadra had raised in the time of *agama Hindu Bali*. He deemed that caste was a social and not a religious aspect of Hinduism, and he concluded that the new converts were casteless, since only those who were born Hindus belonged to a caste (Bhadra 1953b). This implied that only a Balinese could be a *brahmana* and thus that the status of *padanda* remained an exclusive

Subsequently, the need arose for a mass organization (*ormas*) of Hindu youth, Hindu students in particular, to counter the pressure of Islamic organizations, increasingly militant on campuses. For this purpose, on the initiative of Balinese students at Gadjah Mada University in Yogyakarta, the Association of Indonesian Hindu Youth (Perhimpunan Pemuda Hindu Indonesia, better known by the acronym Peradah) was set up on March 11, 1984, as a replacement for the Angkatan Muda Hindu Indonesia which had ceased being active in the 1970s. A break-up occurred the following year, when one of its founders, I Wayan Sudirta, denouncing the conservatism of Peradah and its submission to Golkar, set up in Jakarta a competing organization, the Indonesian Hindu Youth (Pemuda Hindu Indonesia, PHI).[48] But the PHI was not approved by Parisada, which acknowledged Peradah as the one and only Hindu youth organization in Indonesia, and it appeared to have remained ineffective (Wijaya 2009: 393–5).

Parisada Hindu Dharma Indonesia

After establishing branches in every province of the country, Parisada Hindu Dharma became Parisada Hindu Dharma Indonesia (PHDI, Hindu Dharma Council of Indonesia) at the close of its Fifth Congress (*Mahasabha ke V*), held on February 24–27, 1986, in Denpasar. As a consequence, a regional branch was set up in Bali on November 15, Parisada Hindu Dharma Indonesia Propinsi Bali (PHDI Bali) (Pemecutan 2007). Parisada's statutes (*anggaran dasar*) were redesigned for the occasion, with a new organization chart. Three departments were created: Religion (*Keagamaan*), Sociocultural (*Sosial Budaya*),[49] and Economy, Finance and Foundations (*Ekonomi, Dana dan Yayasan*). Besides addressing various issues, the congress submitted several requests to the Indonesian government, inter alia, that a Hindu religious jurisdiction (Lembaga Peradilan Agama Hindu) be established, that the Institut Hindu Dharma be nationalized (*dinegerikan*), and that financial assistance be provided to fund Hindu religious schools in regions with a substantial Hindu population. On the other hand, one notices that Parisada's program was closely aligned with the

---

Balinese prerogative. As a matter of fact, the highest position in *agama Hindu* accessible, at least in theory, to non-Balinese is that of *resi*, though even this is controversial since traditionally only *triwangsa* could become *resi* (Bakker 1997: 39).

[48] Interview, I Wayan Sudirta, Denpasar, May 7, 2007.

[49] A Javanese Hindu was appointed as the head of the Sociocultural Department.

government's instructions, in particular by expressly endorsing the *Pedoman Penghayatan dan Pengamalan Pancasila* (*P-4*).[50]

As a nationwide organization, the PHDI was expected to care for a growing Hindu community outside Bali as well as to promote the Indonesianization of *agama Hindu*. This new orientation paved the way for the rise of commoners, as well as of non-Balinese, within Parisada's direction. Following this congress, Parisada intensified its proselytizing initiatives, by increasing the rationalization-cum-standardization of procedures, rites, and places of worship. In 1988, it published the conclusions of a series of seminars intended to normalize *agama Hindu* (PHDI 1988a). This document contained forty-eight detailed rubrics, ranging from the observance of religious ceremonies to the dances that are to be performed with each of the main rituals, and including the classification of temples, rules governing the ordination of priests, and the implications of tourism for religious life in Bali. It is surprising that all these prescribed norms were specifically Balinese, as if we were still in the time of *agama Hindu Bali*. The fact is that most of the scriptural references were taken from Balinese manuscripts rather than from Indian texts.

In the same year, in compliance with the *P-4*, a Parisada General Assembly (*Pesamuhan Agung*) designed a guidebook that systematized the various methods of religious guidance (*pembinaan agama*), to complement formal religious instruction that ought to be pursued from kindergarten to university (PHDI 1988b). Reading it, one realizes how much the normalization of *agama Hindu*, its Sanskrit terminology notwithstanding, mirrors Islamic norms and usages:[51]

- *Dharma Wacana*: religious sermons (in the manner of Muslim *khotbah*);
- *Dharma Gita*: religious singing, particularly excerpts from the Vedas (in the manner of chanting from the Quran);
- *Dharma Tula*: debates on religious topics;
- *Dharma Yatra*: pilgrimages to sacred sites;

---

[50] During its 1978 session, the MPR had approved a decree entitled 'Guide to the Comprehension and Implementation of Pancasila' (*Pedoman Penghayatan dan Pengamalan Pancasila, P-4*), which worked toward propagating the New Order interpretation of Pancasila through ideological education courses. In a move aimed at bringing political Islam to heel, Suharto proposed in 1982 a legislation requiring that all political parties and social organizations, including religious communities, adopt Pancasila as their single ideological guiding principle—their 'sole foundation' (*asas tunggal Pancasila*). This legislation was formally passed in 1985.

[51] Such a guidebook may be viewed as a counter practice, whereby Parisada's leaders are emulating Islamic practices in order to counter them and emphasize their Hindu identity in a context where Indonesian public culture is becoming increasingly Islamic. However, in doing so they let Islam define what *agama Hindu* should be.

- *Dharma Sadhana*: personal realization of the teachings of *dharma* by means of one or the other of the four ways of *Yoga* (*Catur Marga Yoga*)—*Bhakti*, *Karma*, *Jnana* and *Raja Marga*;
- *Dharma Santi*: mutual pardon at the time of the Saka new year (*Nyepi*) (in the manner of the Muslim *Maaf Lahir dan Batin* during the Lebaran, the celebration that breaks the Ramadan fast).

The Indonesianization of what was originally the institutional organ of the Balinese religion was confirmed during Parisada's Sixth Congress (*Mahasabha ke VI*), held on September 9–14, 1991, in Jakarta—not in Bali, as it had always been. Among the resolutions passed by the congress, one notices the opening of a publishing house (PT Upada Sastra) to bring out edifying literature for the Hindu community; the transcription and translation of the Vedas in Indonesian; and the standardization of collective prayers in the temples (*Kramaning Sembah*), as well as the obligation for all Hindus to recite the *Puja Tri Sandhya*[52] three times daily, designed as the counterpart to the Islamic *salat*. Another issue worth noting is the demand addressed to the government that the Indonesian Hindu community be authorized to make use of ancient Hindu remains, such as shrines and temples (*candi*), as a place to celebrate Hindu rituals. Finally, there was the reiterated appeal to get rid, once and for all, of the label 'customary ceremony' (*upacara adat*), still used far too often instead of 'religious ceremony' (*upacara agama*), proof that the distinction between *adat* and *agama* was not yet clearly established within the Hindu community.

But for the most part, the debates focused on the question of Parisada's relocation to the capital city, advocated by the majority of provincial delegates in order to put *agama Hindu* on an equal footing with the other official religions and to better promote the interests of the Indonesian Hindu community at the national level by freeing it from the restrictive bonds that still tied it to Bali. The Balinese delegates managed to block this decision, but they could not prevent the transfer of the Executive Board's seat from Denpasar to Jakarta.

From that congress onward, Parisada set about extending its reach over the national territory by erecting a number of important temples outside Bali with a view to integrating Hindus throughout Indonesia.[53] One should mention in particular the momentous consecration on July 3, 1992, of a new Hindu sanctuary, the Pura Mandara Giri Semeru Agung, on the slopes of Mount Semeru

---

[52] As late as 1975, Christiaan Hooykaas had remarked that he had never seen anyone in Bali, whether priest or layperson, perform the *Tri Sandhya* (Hooykaas 1975: 253).
[53] These include the Pura Gunung Salak in West Java, as well as the Pura Agung Blambangan, the Pura Loka Moksa Jayabaya and the Pura Pucak Raung in East Java.

in East Java, regarded as a replica of the mythical Mount Mahameru in India, to which Mount Agung is also linked. This new temple was granted the status of a *pura kahyangan jagat* ('world sanctuary') by Parisada, implying that it was intended for the Indonesian Hindu community in its entirety, a status which until then had remained the prerogative of the Pura Panataran Agung at Besakih (Bakker 1997: 32). Thereafter, on Parisada's initiative, other *pura kahyangan jagat* were constructed in various parts of the Archipelago inhabited by significant Hindu minorities. This erection of *pura kahyangan jagat* was coupled with that of *pura agung jagatnatha*—similar to the one consecrated in 1968 in Denpasar—in the district capitals of Bali and in some provincial capitals outside the island.

The extension of Hindu sanctuaries beyond the confines of the island of Bali was replicated during the same period by a multiplication of rituals in different regions, intended to unify the whole of the Indonesian Hindu community. Thus, the national celebration of *Nyepi*, the Saka new year, was henceforth regularly held at the ancient Hindu temple of Prambanan in Central Java with government officials in attendance. On Bali itself, as a further completion of the *Eka Dasa Rudra* of 1979, two large-scale purification rituals were celebrated in the temple complex of Besakih, the *Tri Bhuwana* in March 1993 and the *Eka Bhuwana* in March 1996, whose purpose was to restore harmony and prosperity to the world (Agastia 1996). It appears that after the sensation caused by the *Eka Dasa Rudra* and the prestige it conferred to the Hindu community, Parisada recognized the interest of performing impressive ceremonies attended by high-ranking members of the national government. While Indonesian Hindus clearly needed official government backing so as to position themselves favorably with regard to Muslims and Christians, one could speculate that in supporting and attending the performance of national Hindu rituals, the New Order regime was seeking to raise its prestige by presenting itself as heir to Majapahit and the ancient Javanese kings.[54] The corollary, of course, was that the Indonesian Hindu community was expected to support the national government.

With the diffusion of *agama Hindu* throughout Indonesia and the refocusing of Parisada on Jakarta, a significant number of Balinese began to fear a loss of control over the religion whose recognition they had fought so hard to obtain. And indeed, most estimates consider that Hindus have become more

---

[54] It might seem paradoxical, however, that while advocating a simplification of rituals, Parisada has actually been fueling a ritual inflation by celebrating the largest rituals ever in the history of Bali.

numerous outside Bali.[55] But what appeared to the Balinese as the dispossession of their own religion was perceived by other Indonesian Hindus as Balinese colonization—as 'Balinization' (*Balinisasi*). Non-Balinese Hindus tend to reject what they regard as the imposition of specific Balinese norms on their own ritual practices, whether it be the setting of temples and the performance of ceremonies therein or else the conditions for gaining access to the priesthood, not to mention the particular attire Hindu worshippers are supposed to wear. Whereas for most Balinese these norms properly belong to *agama Hindu*, non-Balinese see them as pertaining to *adat Bali*. Hence the rising of a twofold tension, affecting the Balinese themselves, between the Balinization of the religious practices of various ethnic groups affiliated with *agama Hindu* on the one hand, and the Indonesianization of the Balinese religion aimed at detaching it from its ethnic origin on the other.

While the Hindu community was gaining in prominence on the national stage, Suharto's regime was facing the growing criticism of a rising middle class and a budding pro-democracy movement. At the same time, his power was challenged by sections of the military leadership, dominated by Christian and secularist factions, who had hitherto provided his main base of support, and he started to court the Islamic community while trying to burnish his own Muslim credentials. Suharto's 'Islamic turn' was indicated by a substantial legal accommodation of Islamic norms and institutions, as well as by the establishment on December 7, 1990, of the Association of Indonesian Muslim Intellectuals (Ikatan Cendekiawan Muslim Indonesia, ICMI), under the leadership of one of his closest advisors and eventual successor, Bacharuddin J. Habibie (Hefner 1993b). This highly influential association comprised an unlikely assortment of government bureaucrats, Muslim scholars and Islamic activists, all these factions having clearly diverging agendas. While observers debated whether ICMI was a vehicle for the Islamization of Indonesian society or a political instrument used by President Suharto for his own purposes, the prominence of the new association and the access of its members to leading government positions attested to an increasing prominence of Islam in Indonesian politics (Liddle

---

[55] It is difficult to know with any precision the number of adherents to *agama Hindu* in Indonesia, in that the religious composition of the population is a politically contentious matter. According to the 1990 census, there were then some six million Hindus in Indonesia. This number appeared to have been reduced to four million in the 2010 census, a figure disputed by the Directorate of Hinduism at the Ministry of Religion, which put the number at roughly ten million, while Parisada claimed that they were in fact eighteen million. According to the 2010 census, Hindus composed 1.69 percent of the Indonesian population and 83.5 percent of the population of Bali. In the opinion of many Balinese religious leaders, the proportion of Hindus is deliberately underestimated at the national level, whereas it is overestimated for Bali so as to prevent the Balinese people from knowing the true weight of the Muslim population on their island.

1996). With this Islamization of Indonesia's public sphere, the prevailing coexistence of the religious communities was seriously upset.

The 'Hindu Revival'

The Islamic resurgence in Indonesia aroused the concern of the Balinese over their religious identity and triggered in mimetic fashion a 'Hindu Revival' (*Kebangkitan Hindu*) (Setia 1993). This so-called revival was carried forth by a new generation of Hindu reformers and activists, and it manifested itself in a spate of textual editions and translations of Hindu scriptures, as well as in the emergence of new religious organizations, both in Bali and in Jakarta. And whereas their predecessors had fought to secure a position for their religion that was equal to that of Islam and Christianity, these young intellectuals did not shy away from asserting the superiority of Hinduism over other religions, including Islam and Christianity (Setia 1992).[56]

Thus, on September 29, 1991, shortly after Parisada's Sixth Congress—and just a few months after the creation of the Ikatan Cendekiawan Muslim Indonesia—a group of Balinese, commoners for the most part, founded in Jakarta the Forum of Indonesian Hindu Intellectuals (Forum Cendekiawan Hindu Indonesia, FCHI).[57] In 1993, they published the monthly magazine *Aditya* ('The Sun', which became *Raditya* in 1995), in order to diffuse their ideas in the Indonesian Hindu community. They applied themselves to fighting various prejudices highly detrimental to *agama Hindu*: that the Hindus are idolatrous (*menyembah berhala*), that they are divided into 'castes' (*kasta*),[58] that Hinduism is a 'religion of the soil' (*agama bumi*), a mere cultural production and not a

---

[56] For his part, the director general of Hinduism and Buddhism at the Department of Religion, I Gusti Agung Gede Putra, was trying to win Muslim public opinion by declaring in 1992 that 70 percent of the teachings of Hinduism were in conformity with those of Islam. As for the remaining 30 percent, they were due to cultural particularities more than to real theological differences (Kasiri and Nubaiti 1992: 103).

[57] The founding members of the FCHI included Putu Setia, Nyoman Suwandhi Pendit, Jero Mangku Ketut Subandi, I Wayan Sudirta, I Gusti Ngurah Bagus, Ibu Gedong Bagoes Oka and Ida Padanda Gde Ketut Sebali Tianyar Arimbawa as advisor (*penasehat*). Interview, Putu Setia, Pedungan, May 15, 2007.

[58] As previously noted, the issue of 'caste' has been recurrent among Balinese intellectuals. Since the polemic launched by the *jaba* against the privileges of the *triwangsa* in *Surya Kanta*, the politically-cum-religiously correct version in Bali claims that caste is a European colonial invention, which does not exist in true Hinduism. It is said to be a misconception of the idea of functional occupation (*warna*), turned into a status hierarchy based on birth (*wangsa*) after the conquest of Bali by Majapahit, due to political maneuvering of the rajas, further compounded by the Dutch colonial administration. According to this interpretation, highly influenced by a conception of merit acquired by Balinese in colonial schools as well as by the position of Indian reformers, such as Dayananda Sarasvati, a *triwangsa* title would no longer be the marker of belonging to a specific *wangsa* but only a residual element of one's personal name (Wiana and Santeri 1993; Wiana 2006; Kerepun 2007).

revealed religion (*agama wahyu*) in the same way as Islam or Christianity, and especially that it is the religion solely of the Balinese people in Indonesia.

While *agama Hindu* was facing increasing pressure from various quarters, with the Balinese people fearful of losing its institutional control, the physiognomy of Bali was being rapidly transformed, as the island was ever more narrowly enclosed by the overlapping networks of the national state apparatus and the international tourism industry. The prosperity brought by tourism was accelerating urbanization and giving rise to a Balinese middle class, whose opinion was starting to be heard on the national stage. As a religious minority, the Balinese people were particularly sensitive to the defamation of their religion by Islamic groups and more generally to anything they perceived as 'religious harassment' (*pelecehan agama*), not to mention the misuse of temples and ceremonies for tourism purposes.

In November 1993, news of a major luxury seaside resort, the Jakarta-driven Bali Nirwana Resort (BNR), scheduled for construction near Tanah Lot, one of Bali's holiest temples and most iconic tourist spots, caused an uproar on the island, which was soon shaken by an unprecedented wave of protest. Outraged by the prospect of a tourist resort rising next to this revered temple, a broad coalition of public intellectuals, academics, students and NGO activists from all over Bali and throughout the country claimed that the Tanah Lot temple would be desecrated by the resort and accused the government of trampling their faith for the sake of tourism. They urged Parisada to take up the defense of their religion. After temporizing for some time, Parisada finally enacted in January 1994 a *bhisama*,[59] the equivalent of an Islamic *fatwa*, decreeing that a 'sacred area' (*kawasan suci*) of two kilometers must be maintained between the temple and any development unrelated to religious purposes. Had it been actually applied, the decree would have wiped the BNR project off the map. But, as is so often the case in Indonesia, it was more a face-saving maneuver than a measure likely to be implemented. After what amounted to little more than window dressing, work was resumed on the resort, while the military were cracking down on protests and suppressing student demonstrations (Warren 1998a; Suasta and Connor 1999).

The failure of popular protests marked a turning point in the Balinese perception of their position within the Indonesian nation-state. More specifically,

---

[59] *Keputusan PHDI Pusat No.11/Kep/I/PHDIP/1994 tentang Bhisama Kesucian Pura*. The publication of this decree was postponed due to the reluctance of Parisada's secretary-general to sign it. It so happened that in those days that position was held by a police colonel, Ida Bagus Suyasa Negara, who had received pressure from the police hierarchy to dissuade him from signing the *bhisama*. Interview, I Dewa Gede Ngurah Swastha, Denpasar, July 21, 2011.

the sense of frustration bred by Parisada's powerlessness led to the creation on January 2, 1995, in Bali of a new organization, the Forum of Indonesians Concerned for Hinduism (Forum Pemerhati Hindu Dharma Indonesia, FPHDI).[60] This new forum aimed both to defend the Indonesian Hindu community against attacks of radical Muslims and to reform Parisada in a more democratic and universalist fashion. Among other issues, it opened a public debate on the possibility of turning Bali into an official Hindu territory (Ramstedt 2018: 275). Even though Parisada's chairman was one of its main advisors, the forum was accused of seeking to compete with it, an accusation rejected by its leaders who claimed that they only aspired to help Parisada to better carry out its missions.[61]

It was readily apparent, however, that these new Hindu organizations were highly critical of Parisada, whom they accused of being more a pressure group of conservative members of the Balinese nobility than a genuine religious body, as well as of promoting a traditionalist conception of *agama Hindu*, still very much affected by its native Balinese parochialism. They reproached Parisada for being more preoccupied with the issue of how ceremonies should be properly conducted than with instructing their co-religionists in the spiritual and doctrinal aspects of Hinduism. Yet, with the advance of formal education and the rise of a middle class, the demand to intellectually understand the tenets of their religion was growing among Indonesian Hindus. Furthermore, critics denounced Parisada's leaders for having submitted to the New Order and for remaining passive in the face of the widespread vilification of *agama Hindu*, to the point of ridiculing them by dubbing them *paraseda*—a play on words meaning 'dead men' in Balinese (Bagus 2004: 88). The fact is that while Parisada had been initially inspired by Indian Neo-Hinduism, its bureaucratization combined with its affiliation to Golkar, as well as the predominance of the *triwangsa*—of the *brahmana* most particularly—had led it to adopt a stance which became ever more conservative and Bali-centered over the years, as witnessed by the reluctance of its leadership to move to Jakarta. Accordingly, conflicts could only

---

[60] The founding members of the FPHDI were prominent Balinese opinion leaders, such as I Dewa Gede Ngurah Swastha (chairman), I Nyoman Gelebet, Ida Anak Agung Gde Agung, Anak Agung Made Djelantik, Ibu Gedong Bagoes Oka, Agus Indra Udayana, Ida Bagus Oka Punyatmadja, I Gusti Ngurah Bagus, Jero Mangku Gede Ketut Subandi, Ida Bagus Gde Dosther, Luh Ketut Suryani, I Wayan Sudirta, I Ketut Ngastawa and eleven *padanda* as advisors. Interview, I Dewa Gede Ngurah Swastha, Denpasar, July 21, 2011.

[61] Other Hindu organizations were founded around the same period, in particular the Union of Indonesian Hindu University Students (Kesatuan Mahasiswa Hindu Dharma Indonesia, KMHDI), in September 1993 in Bali; and the Association of Indonesian Hindu Youth (Ikatan Pemuda Hindu Indonesia, IPHI), in January 1995 in Jakarta, which took over from its predecessor, the Pemuda Hindu Indonesia (PHI). There was also the reactivation in November 1995 of the Prajaniti Hindu Indonesia, which had fallen into disuse since the 1980s, and the foundation in 1996 of the Forum for Religious Awakening (Forum Penyadaran Dharma) by I Gusti Ngurah Bagus. Most of these organizations fell apart at the end of the 1990s, following the change of political regime.

worsen between a traditionalist faction, established in rural communities and the nobility, focused on Bali, and a progressive faction based on the urbanized middle classes and the intelligentsia, open to Indonesia and increasingly looking towards India.

In March 1996, the Forum Pemerhati Hindu Dharma Indonesia organized a seminar to debate the problems facing Parisada and to prepare its Seventh Congress (FPHDI 1996). In September of the same year, the Forum Cendekiawan Hindu Indonesia devoted a special issue of its magazine *Raditya* to the forthcoming congress, in which it set out its reform proposals, which were similar to those of the FPHDI (*Raditya*, No. 6, September 1996: 4–67). Both these forums demanded that the various Hindu organizations—forums, NGOs (*lembaga swadaya masyarakat*) and foundations (*yayasan*)—which until then had been authorized to attend Parisada's congresses as observers (*peninjau*), be invited as fully fledged participants (*peserta*). They also proposed that Parisada's leaders be elected by the participants by secret ballot instead of being chosen by an ad hoc committee, so as to prevent rampant pressure and manipulation. And they insisted that these leaders be completely independent of the state apparatus, both civil and military. They suggested further that Parisada's chairman be a layman and no longer a priest, in order to avoid the risk that a *padanda* be embroiled in organizational or political litigations and instead could devote himself entirely to strictly religious issues. Lastly, they requested that Parisada's leadership be widely open to non-Balinese, so as to put an end to the ethnic parochialism of the bygone *agama Hindu Bali*. Proof, if any were required, that these proposals did not meet expectations: the following issue of *Raditya*, which reported on the congress, was entitled 'Parisada's Crisis' (*Kemelut Parisada*) (*Raditya*, No. 7, November 1996: 4–34).

Indeed, the latent tensions between Parisada's old guard and the reformers promoting its regeneration crystallized during the Seventh Congress (*Mahasabha ke VII*), held on September 18–20, 1996, in Surakarta. The reform-minded organizations—FCHI, FPHDI, KMHDI and IPHI—were represented, and their delegates called for the reorganization and the reorientation of Parisada. While they managed to score a few points, such as having the different Hindu organizations being invited as participants in their own right, they came away deeply frustrated, having failed to dissociate Parisada from Golkar and to widely open its leadership. Besides, the friction worsened steadily between the Balinese delegates and those from other ethnic groups.[62] By and large, the debates focused on institutional issues. Despite the opposition of the majority of Balinese delegates, the congress modified Parisada's statutes and decided to relocate its headquarters from Bali to Jakarta, leaving only a regional branch on the island. From then on, the Regional Parisada (Parisada Daerah) were placed under the authority of the Central Parisada (Parisada Pusat) and had to abide by its decisions. And whereas previously the function assigned to Parisada was not clearly specified, it would henceforth be in charge of issuing *bhisama* as well as spreading the teachings of *agama Hindu* in Indonesia.

Furthermore, with the aim of diversifying Parisada's leadership—and of preventing the *padanda*'s ascendency—the reformers succeeded in imposing the enlargement of the Assembly of Priests (now renamed *Sabha Pandita*)[63] to 33 members and of the Assembly of Laymen (*Sabha Walaka*) to 44 members. However, the committee in charge of selecting the leadership eventually appointed, exactly as before, 11 *pandita* (a majority of them *padanda*, but with the admission of two Javanese priests) and 22 *walaka*, sparking considerable irritation among reformers, some of whom came to demand the holding of an 'Extraordinary Congress' (*Mahasabha Luar Biasa*). Shortly afterwards, on September 23, 30 prominent Balinese, members of the FCHI and of the FPHDI for the most part, issued an open letter in the form of a declaration and an appeal (*Surat Pernyataan dan Himbauan*), in which they requested the election of all the members of the *Sabha Pandita* and the *Sabha Walaka*. In response, following a meeting held at the Universitas Hindu Indonesia in Denpasar, the newly appointed Parisada leadership declared on October 22, that the supplementary members—in this case, priests from commoner descent groups—would be nominated as 'assistants' (*pengabih*) to the *padanda*. This incensed the signatories, who issued once again on October 24 an inflamed declaration of their position (*Pernyataan Sikap*). While the reformers' exasperation was brewing, the crisis would not erupt openly until the next Parisada congress, and this under completely different political conditions.

The forums and other reform-minded organizations were not the only milieux where one encountered such reproaches of Parisada. They were being voiced also by two socio-religious movements which pursued distinct aims but

---

[62] In the wake of the congress, the *Hindu Kaharingan* delegates from Kalimantan threatened to withdraw from Parisada in protest against the overwhelming control of the conservative Balinese faction over its direction (*Raditya*, No. 46, May 2001: 91).

[63] Following the repeated request of reformers, it was agreed during the congress that all priests should now be called *pandita*. Still, the honorific title *sulinggih* continued to be the preferred designation for *padanda*.

whose actors stemmed from similar backgrounds—the *warga* and the *sampradaya*. Whereas the first movement revealed the Balinese people's concern with grounding their identity in their indigenous ancestry, the second attested to their eagerness to rise above the boundaries of their own island in order to adhere to a transnational Neo-Hinduism.

The *warga* movement resumed the struggle of the *jaba* against the privileges of the *triwangsa* that was initiated in the 1920s by Surya Kanta (Kerepun 2007). After Indonesia's independence, the main commoner descent groups, which had been deprived of their former status by the colonial administration, set up formal organizations, commonly called *warga* (from Sanskrit *varga*, 'class, order, clan'):

> These *warga* organizations are characterized by their ownership of a common ancestral temple or temples, an internally agreed origin myth and founding ancestor, an accepted body of rules of conduct (*warga sesana*), and the claim to possess supernaturally powerful religious regalia, in particular for the performance of death rites. Moreover, each *warga* organization generally has a written genealogy/history or *babad* (Pitana 1999: 182–3).[64]

The *warga* aim to bring together all the members of a kinship group (*soroh*) who consider themselves descendants of a common ancestor, whether real or mythical, whom they venerate in a 'temple of origin' (*pura kawitan*). Their leaders, drawn from the educated elites, attempted to convert their newly acquired social position and economic prosperity into traditional status. They struggled to have their rights acknowledged against the prerogatives of the *triwangsa*, who had managed since the inception of the New Order to recover their political and economic prominence, which had been somewhat undermined by the upheavals of the previous decades. More specifically, the *warga* sought to abolish the *brahmana*'s monopoly on the initiated priesthood by imposing the use of their own priests (*resi bhujangga* or *sengguhu*, *empu*, and *dukuh*) alongside the *padanda*. To achieve this, the *warga*'s leaders, refusing to be classified as *sudra*, resorted to genealogies asserting that their status was in fact higher than that of the *triwangsa*, in the sense that their ancestors held positions

---

[64] There are currently over thirty registered *warga* in Bali, the most important ones being the Pasek (Maha Gotra Pasek Sanak Sapta Rsi, set up in 1952) (Pitana 1997), the Bhujangga Waisnawa (Keluarga Besar Bhujangga Waisnawa, founded in 1953), and the Pande (Maha Samaya Warga Pande, established in 1975) (Guermonprez 1987). It is highly significant that the main Balinese publications on the issue of 'caste' have been authored by Pasek (Ketut Wiana, Gde Pitana), a Bhujangga Waisnawa (Raka Santeri), and a Pande (Made Kembar Kerepun). Besides, it is well known that the FCHI defends mostly the rights and interests of the Pasek, from which the majority of its members are drawn.

of power prior to the conquest of Bali by Majapahit, and hence before the *triwangsa*'s rise to prominence. Thus, whereas the *jaba* claim to be fighting for the democratization and the modernization of Balinese religious practices, it turns out that they are striving to raise their own status more than they are working for an equality between *soroh*. What is at issue with the *warga* movement is a status competition between *jaba* and *triwangsa* rather than a contestation of the hierarchical principle as such.

Under pressure from the *warga*, Parisada had decreed in 1968, during its Second Congress, that all Hindus were entitled to undergo the ordination rite to the initiated priesthood and, furthermore, that all duly initiated priests had the same status and were thus equally qualified to officiate at all ceremonies, regardless of which *soroh* they belonged to. This decree, however, did not settle the matter as, despite Parisada's official position, some of its leaders continued to defend the exclusive privileges of the *brahmana*—in accordance with the customary practice whereby no important religious ceremony would be considered 'complete' (*muput karya*) in Bali without the rituals of a *padanda*.

The issue was raised anew in 1993, when the leaders of the three main *warga*—Pasek, Bhujangga Waisnawa and Pande—requested that their priests be authorized to officiate at the *Tri Bhuwana* ceremony at Besakih. The organizing committee, dominated by *brahmana*, rejected their demand, arguing that according to the authoritative literature (*Raja Purana Pura Besakih*), only three priests—the so-called *tri sadhaka*,[65] comprising a *padanda Siwa*, a *padanda Boda* and a *resi bhujangga*—were permitted to officiate in Besakih main temple complex. The dispute was referred to the governor of Bali, Ida Bagus Oka (1988-98), himself a *brahmana*, who stated that the *Tri Bhuwana* ceremony would continue according to custom but promised that in the future the priests from different *warga* (*sarwa sadhaka*) would be included in the ceremonies held at Besakih. This promise, however, was broken at the *Eka Bhuwana* ceremony in 1996, and it was not until the change of political regime, during the *Panca Wali Krama*[66] ceremony in 1999, under the jurisdiction of a new governor, I Dewa Made Beratha (1998–2008), that the *warga* finally obtained satisfaction— not without having to confront numerous delaying tactics from their opponents,

---

[65] Like many other traditions, this term is attributed to Mpu Kuturan, who is credited with having merged the nine sects (*paksa*) present in 11th-century Bali into three—Siwa, Budha and Waisnawa. However, the priests from these three *paksa* are not equivalent in status, as the *resi bhujangga*'s office is restricted to engaging with the nether world and he is relegated to a subordinate position in relation to the *padanda Siwa* and *Boda* (Hooykaas 1964b: 241–4).

[66] Like the *Eka Dasa Rudra*, the *Panca Wali Krama* falls in the category of the *Buta Yadnya*. This ceremony is supposed to be celebrated with each decade of the Saka era, which is far from having been the case in the past (Stuart-Fox 2002: 327).

most particularly from Ida Bagus Gede Agastia, one of Ida Bagus Mantra's most vocal followers (Pitana 2001; Setia 2001).[67]

While Balinese reformers supported the demand of the *warga* that their priests be allowed to officiate on a par with the *padanda*, they were no longer satisfied with a nationally recognized religion. They aspired to universalize their religious identity by breaking the ties between *agama Hindu* and *adat Bali* and fully embracing Indian Neo-Hinduism as a world religion. Contacts of Indonesian Hindus with India had been limited to the occasional visits of Indian scholars to Bali and a handful of Balinese students enrolling in Indian universities.[68] This began to change in the early 1990s when, in response to the Islamic resurgence in their country, marked by the rise of conservative and transnational currents, Indonesian Hindus from the urbanized middle classes began to see themselves as part of a worldwide religious community and to look to India for guidance and support. This renewed Indian tropism coincided with the progress of Hindu nationalism, fueled by the surge of political Islamism in India, which struck a responsive chord in the Indonesian Hindu community similarly exposed to the pressure of Islam (Somvir 2004; Ramstedt 2008).

The turn toward India manifested itself in the promotion of Neo-Hindu concepts and practices such as vegetarianism and the sanctity of the cow, the growing use of Sanskrit *mantra* and the related tendency to substitute Sanskrit for Balinese or Kawi in religious ceremonies, or else the performance of the revived Vedic fire ritual *Agni Hotra* (Nilon Batan and Mudita 2001), which had been initiated by the Arya Samaj. Another instance of Arya Samaj influence was the introduction of the motto 'Back to Veda'[69] (in English), in the fashion of Dayananda Sarasvati. Most Balinese quoting this rallying cry, however, did not appear to be aware of its origin and seemed to have very little notion of what the Vedas really are.[70] One notices also the routine use of Sanskrit salutations—such

---

[67] Interviews, I Made Titib, Denpasar, May 9, 2007; Ida Bagus Gede Agastia, Denpasar, July 21, 2008.

[68] Among the latter, one should mention I Gusti Putu Phalgunadi, who had received a scholarship to carry out research at the International Academy of Indian Culture in 1978. A revised version of his PhD dissertation was published in 1991 under the title *Evolution of Hindu Culture in Bali* (Phalgunadi 1991). Interview, I Gusti Putu Phalgunadi, Puri Gerenceng, Denpasar, July 26, 2012.

[69] The motto 'Back to Veda' was based on the presupposition that the Vedas had been transmitted to Bali, where they had fallen into disuse, as in India. As already mentioned, this illusion, long held by orientalists, went back to the report published by the German Sanskritist Rudolph Friederich, who had been sent by the Batavian Society of Arts and Sciences with the first military expedition against Bali in 1846 to collect manuscripts and other artefacts (Friederich 1849–50). On another point, it is notable that the slogan 'Back to Veda' replicates that of conservative Islamic Indonesians, whose common rallying call has been the catchphrase 'Back to the Quran and Sunnah'.

[70] Unlike Dayananda Sarasvati, for whom the Vedas were restricted solely to the *samhita*, which he interpreted as a doctrinal canon, the Balinese have a very extensive notion of the Vedas, that comprises not only Vedic literature proper but includes the *Mahabharata* as well.

as '*Om Swastyastu*', in imitation of the Arabic '*salam alaikum*' of the Muslims—the vogue of fonts simulating the *Nagari* script and the proliferation of Indian iconography of Hindu divinities, the success of Indian television series based on the *Ramayana* and the *Mahabharata* and the tendency to name *upanayana* what is in fact a *pawintenan*.[71] Most of all, the turn towards India was manifested in pilgrimages (*tirta yatra*) organized by Balinese travel agencies to Hindu holy sites of India where Indonesian Hindus were urged to look for their religious sources in the manner of Muslims going on the *hajj* to Mecca (Titib 1997; Hornbacher 2017).

The rapprochement with India was marked not only by pilgrimages of Indonesian Hindus to Indian holy sites, but also by the progressive establishment in Indonesia of Neo-Hindu devotional (*bhakti*) movements (*sampradaya*), such as Sri Sathya Sai Baba,[72] Hare Krishna (International Society for Krishna Consciousness, ISKCON),[73] Ananda Marga, Brahma Kumaris, Transcendental Meditation, Divine Life Society, Art of Living, Anand Ashram Foundation, etc., not to mention various groups inspired by Gandhi's teachings[74] (Jendra 2007). Besides opening international schools in Jakarta and Denpasar, these movements set up ashrams (*pasraman*), most particularly in Bali, where their adepts could practice their devotion. With their universalist scope, their democratic appeal and their social message, the *sampradaya* represented a challenge to the New Order definition of acceptable religion and to its determination to monitor the officially recognized representative bodies of the particular religions. It is thus not surprising that the spread of these proselytizing movements in Indonesia met with opposition from the Department of Religion as well as from Parisada, even though some leaders of *sampradaya* held official positions in both institutions.

---

[71] *Upanayana* is an Indic initiation ceremony whereby a boy from one of the first three *varna* is conferred the Brahmanic sacred thread that marks the beginning of his apprenticeship of the Vedas with a *guru*, whereas *pawintenan* is a Balinese personal purification rite that is prerequisite for any significant spiritual undertaking.

[72] Established in Jakarta in the early 1970s, the Sai Baba Mission began to open centers throughout Indonesia in the 1980s. It now operates around one hundred centers in the country, with over thirty in Bali. After having been accused of being 'deviant' (*sesat*) by the Directorate of Hinduism at the Department of Religion, the movement was eventually taken under the umbrella of Parisada in 1994 as a spiritual study group based on the Vedas (Howe 2001, Chap. 8).

[73] In 1973, Bhaktivedanta Swami, the founder of ISKCON, visited Jakarta and met with leaders of Parisada. But his movement was found too sectarian and in 1984 it was banned by the attorney-general's office at the behest of the Department of Religion due to the alleged incompatibility of its teachings with official *Hindu Dharma*. However, during Parisada's congress of 1996, Hare Krishna was officially declared *Hindu*, as a result of which it managed to establish itself in Indonesia, where it operates around twenty centers, including five in Bali. But it remains highly controversial and its activities are effectively curtailed, with repeated moves aiming at having it banned in Indonesia (Howe 2001, Chap. 9).

[74] The Gandhi Ashram was set up in 1976 by Ibu Gedong Bagoes Oka at Candi Dasa, on the south-east coast of Bali (Bakker 1993: 195–224).

Indeed, none of these movements were conferred official status as 'religion' (*agama*) by the Department of Religion, but were classified as 'sects' (*aliran kepercayaan*). What's more, their Hindu credentials were questioned by Parisada. Specifically, its leaders feared the rise of conflicts between competing sects, which could only undermine a Hindu community already weakened by its minority position in the country and thinly spread over a number of different ethnic groups.

The *sampradaya* attracted mostly educated middle-class Balinese employed in urban-based modern occupations, who found it difficult to fulfill their ritual obligations in their village of origin. As traditional agrarian Balinese society was progressively giving way to a market and service economy, communal rituals linked with the agricultural cycle were becoming obsolete in the eyes of these Balinese, whose time and money were in short supply, and who identified readily with the simplified rites and the internalized practices advocated by the *sampradaya*. In search of a new religious identity, they saw themselves as being on a spiritual journey in quest of enlightenment. Discontented with both their traditional religion and the official *agama Hindu*, devotees focused on their emotional experience, which was unlike anything expressed by Balinese towards their gods. They claimed that membership of a *sampradaya* enabled Hindus to deepen the teachings of their religion by fostering 'spirituality' (*kerohanian*). By and large, they were critical of social hierarchy and ritualism, rejecting the use of animal sacrifice, and they were keen on practicing meditation and yoga. Conversely, they were accused by conservative Balinese of undermining their ritual traditions.

The situation in Bali has become even more confused with the proliferation of new indigenous religious movements, also regarded as *aliran kepercayaan*. Parisada is highly suspicious of these movements, which are even more disturbing than the Indian *sampradaya* as they are beyond its control. Whereas their leaders claim that their teachings conform with *agama Hindu*, the practices of their adherents are often very remote from its principles, insofar as they are typically interested in accessing and mastering 'mystical power' (*sakti*), accumulation of which was at the heart of traditional Balinese rituals but which Parisada wishes to eradicate and replace with the development of 'spirituality' (*kerohanian*), like the *sampradaya* (Howe 2001: 156–62).

Thus we see that this much-vaunted 'Hindu Revival' has in fact resulted in a fragmentation of the religious obedience of Hindu Balinese into three distinct affiliations—*Hindu-Bali, Hindu-Indonesia*, and *Hindu-India*—that will prove difficult to reconcile, as expressed in these headlines of the monthly Balinese magazine *Sarad*:[75] "How to accommodate the dispute among the three Hindu major streams in Indonesia: Bali, India, and Indonesia?" (*Bagaimana mengakomodasi pertarungan tiga arus besar Hindu di Indonesia: Bali, India, dan Indonesia?*) (*Sarad*, No. 21, September 2001: 48). From then on, neither the traditional religion, attached to the correct execution of rites, nor the official *agama Hindu* promoted by Parisada, concerned as it is with ethics and theology, were able to meet the aspirations of a growing portion of urbanized middle-class Balinese, who are in quest of religious devotion and personal conviction. This active minority is no longer content with a religion recognized nationally but is intent on universalizing its religious identity by completely severing *agama Hindu* from *adat Bali* and by taking up Indian Neo-Hinduism as a world religion.

This being said, there is general agreement that ritual activities in Bali have not decreased in cost or scope during the past decades, as the increasing prosperity due to the development of tourism prompted its beneficiaries to display conspicuous ritual consumption. However, even if Balinese ritualism is actually flourishing, it should be understood that it is consciously mobilized and staged as a response to a wider context. Indeed, with *agama Hindu* construed as a world religion, it is not surprising that Balinese would seek refuge in the intimacy of their *adat*, seen as the core of their *Kebalian*. Thus, a two-way process is taking place: concurrently with the normative universalization of *agama Hindu*, there is a revival of *adat Bali*, with its associated ritual practices. In other words, together with creating boundaries between *agama* and *adat*, there has been a contrary movement towards the blurring of boundaries between Balinese religious and ethnic identity.

To sum up, these various dynamics are the outcome of a twofold split that divides the Balinese people along two different lines, even though they tend to overlap:
- on the one hand, a status competition between *triwangsa*, mainly *brahmana*, and *jaba*, particularly commoner *warga*;
- on the other hand, an opposition between those Balinese who want to retain their ritual traditions and those who aspire to universalize *agama Hindu* after the model of Indian Neo-Hinduism, foremost among them the members of *sampradaya*.

This twofold split would eventually precipitate an open crisis within Parisada after the downfall of President Suharto in 1998.

---

[75] *Sarad*, launched in 2000, is the name of a spectacular offering which depicts all kinds of elements of the Balinese universe.

Chapter 7

Balinese Identity
Under the Challenge of Tourism

While Bali has been renowned as a tourist destination since the 1920s, international tourism to the island, as to Indonesia generally, after having come to an end with the Japanese occupation, remained very limited up to the end of the 1960s: the rudimentary state of its infrastructure and the ruinous condition of the economy, as well as endemic political agitation and the xenophobic attitude of the government, not to mention the mayhem of 1965–66, all tended to discourage visitors (Coast 1951, 1954; Last 1955; Vickers 2011). It was only after the inception of the New Order regime and the opening of an international airport on the island in 1969 that tourists began to arrive in significant numbers. Within the framework of the First National Five-Year Plan, launched that year, the Indonesian government decided to open up the country to international tourism, primarily in order to tackle a pressing national balance of payments deficit. Even if the arguments advanced in favor of the development of international tourism in Indonesia addressed mainly economic objectives, one should not underestimate the political purpose of the operation. Indeed, President Suharto needed to dispel the memory of the bloodbath that had brought him to power if he wanted to affirm the legitimacy of his New Order. In this regard, there is a striking parallel between the situation of the Indonesian government and that of the colonial government some sixty years earlier: in both cases, the promotion of tourism proved itself an opportune means of quelling the trauma of the regime's ascent to power.

Banking on the image of Bali as a tourist paradise inherited from the colonial period, the government decided to make this island the showcase of Indonesia. A French consulting firm, the SCETO, was commissioned to draw up a Master Plan for the Development of Tourism in Bali, financed by the United Nations Development Program with the World Bank as its executive agency. The

SCETO report, published in 1971 and revised in 1974 by the World Bank, proposed to confine the bulk of tourism to a luxury beach enclave at Nusa Dua, on the southern Bukit Peninsula close to the airport, while providing for a network of excursion routes linking the new resort with major attractions on the island (SCETO 1971; IBRD/IDA 1974). With the official endorsement of the Master Plan by presidential decree in 1972, tourism became a top economic priority for the province of Bali, second only to agriculture.

Thus, while at the time of the Dutch occupation the opening of Bali to tourism was initiated and controlled by the colonial authorities and foreign firms, since the independence of Indonesia the revival of international tourism has been the initiative of the central government and advised by foreign experts. The Balinese themselves were scarcely more consulted once their island had become a province of Indonesia than when it was still a possession of the Netherlands East Indies. The decision to make Bali the showcase of tourism in Indonesia was imposed upon them, just as in earlier times it had been imposed upon them that their island be conserved as a 'living museum'.

Cultural Tourism (*Pariwisata Budaya*)

Faced with a fait accompli, the Balinese authorities[1] criticized the Master Plan as a plan for the development of tourism in Bali and not a plan for the development of Bali through tourism. Turning the perspective around, they coined the slogan: 'Tourism for Bali, not Bali for Tourism' (*Pariwisata untuk Bali, bukan Bali untuk pariwisata*). By the same token, they decided to take advantage of the touristic fame of their island abroad—and of the economic importance of international tourism for the state coffers—to assert their cultural identity and to enhance their leverage over Jakarta.

In response to the Master Plan, the Balinese authorities proclaimed their own concept of the kind of tourism they deemed appropriate for their island—namely 'Cultural Tourism' (*Pariwisata Budaya*). This concept was formulated in October 1971, a few months after the publication of the Master Plan, when the

---

[1] I should point out that those I call the 'Balinese authorities' are not limited to the personnel of the Indonesian state in the province, but include opinion leaders and prescribers, that is, those Balinese who are authorized to speak in the name of their island and who are thus in a position to monopolize legitimate discourse on Bali. As such, they occupy an ambivalent position by speaking on behalf of Bali to Jakarta and simultaneously by conveying the instructions of the capital to the province. By shifting from one discursive position to another, they are in a position to affirm their Balinese identity while at the same time furthering the integration of Bali within the Indonesian nation-state.

governor of Bali convened a 'Seminar on Cultural Tourism in Bali' (*Seminar Pariwisata Budaya Daerah Bali*), under the joint aegis of the provincial agencies for tourism, religion, culture and education (Projek 1971b). The proceedings of this seminar reveal that the Balinese authorities had an ambivalent attitude toward tourism, which they perceived as a 'challenge' (*tantangan*), at once fraught with danger and filled with the promise of prosperity: 'How to develop tourism without damaging Balinese culture?' (*Bagaimana mengembangkan pariwisata tanpa merusak kebudayaan Bali?*). On the one hand, the artistic and ceremonial traditions that had made Bali famous worldwide provided its main tourist attraction, thus turning Balinese culture into the most valuable 'resource' (*sumber*) for the island's economic development. But on the other hand, the invasion of Bali by foreigners was seen as a threat of 'cultural pollution' (*polusi kebudayaan*). To prevent such a fatal outcome, the doctrine of 'Cultural Tourism' was meant to capitalize on Balinese cultural identity to attract tourists while using tourism revenues to preserve and promote Balinese culture.[2] By thus regarding Balinese culture as being both essential to and threatened by tourism, the Balinese authorities could claim to speak in the name of Bali, construed as a homogeneous and inclusive entity faced with an exogenous menace.[3]

As it happened, the Balinese appeared to be genuinely proud of the renown of their culture abroad and were eager to show their cultural traditions at their best to the tourists. Thus, contrary to the foreign consultants, who attempted to shield Balinese culture from the frontal assault of tourism, the Balinese authorities were led to link the fate of their culture to that of tourism in the sense that, not content with offering their visitors contrived attractions staged only for their benefit, they invited tourists to partake of authentic 'cultural performances' (*pertunjukan budaya*). These performances were the festivities and ceremonies of all sorts, such as temple festivals, rites of passage, processions and cremations, that provide the occasion for those exotic pageants for which their island is renowned.

But Cultural Tourism was not only a way of responding to the expectations of tourists in their quest for genuine cultural performances. It was also, and above

---

[2] During the closing ceremony of the seminar, the governor announced that its conclusions would be the subject of regulations, in order to permit the provincial government to monitor the development of tourism on the island. In 1974, he issued a Provincial Regulation on Cultural Tourism (*Peraturan Daerah Tingkat I Bali No.3 Tahun 1974 tentang Pariwisata Budaya*), which was revised in 1991, then again in 2012, and most recently in 2020. Like many others, though, these regulations were "statements of intention without teeth" (Noronha 1979: 200), in that they could not be enforced.

[3] As Adrian Vickers once remarked, no Balinese worthy of the name could refuse to adhere to the ideal of 'Balinese culture': "Nobody on Bali would seriously think to challenge the idea of Balinese culture. Even those people who oppose tourism and see themselves as defenders of tradition are supporters of the idea" (Vickers 2012a: 267).

all, meant to be a means of protecting Balinese cultural integrity. Hence the necessity of deciding the extent to which Balinese culture may be put to the service of tourism, by issuing directives allowing local people to know what they were authorized to sell to tourists and what should not be commoditized. Without being able to distinguish between that which they do for themselves and that which they do to please their visitors, the Balinese people incurred the risk of no longer being able to tell the difference between their own values and those of the tourists. And if this were the case, Balinese culture would become a 'touristic culture' (*budaya pariwisata*)—defined as a state of axiological confusion between what belongs to tourism and what to culture.

This concern for discrimination was never so pressing as when faced with a threat of 'profanation' (*provanasi*). In this respect, the subject most bitterly debated, which caused the greatest confusion and raised the thorniest problems, was the performance of ritual dances for tourists. Indeed, as we have seen, these celebrated dances that have done so much for Bali's fame are not only a spectacle to be enjoyed by both Balinese and their visitors, but they are first and foremost a ritual to be enacted (De Zoete and Spies 1938; Bandem and deBoer 1995; Dibia and Ballinger 2004). As long as their dances were being performed in their traditional context, the Balinese had no need to ask themselves where the ritual ended and the spectacle began.[4] The arrival of tourists confronted them with the unprecedented situation of having to interpret their culture before a foreign audience, compelling them to mark a boundary between what belongs to 'religion' (*agama*) and what to 'art' (*seni*). These two dimensions were to prove difficult to differentiate for the Balinese, as testified by their inability to dissociate 'sacred' from 'profane' dances.

I refer here to the 'Seminar on Sacred and Profane Arts in the Field of Dance' (*Seminar Seni Sakral dan Provan Bidang Tari*) that was convened in March 1971 with the aim of working out criteria to distinguish between the dances which might be commercialized for the tourist market and those which should not (Projek 1971a).[5] The task proved to be a delicate one, to judge from the confusion of the participants, a select group of Balinese officials, priests and academics solicited to write a paper on the subject. Their predicament was hardly

---

[4] As Edward Bruner rightly noted, such a distinction does not make sense for the Balinese: "If a Balinese troupe performs a dance drama in a temple, we call it religion; if in a concert hall in London, we call it art; if in a beach hotel, we call it tourism. But the distinction between religion, art and tourism are western categories, not Balinese realities" (Bruner 1995: 238).

[5] The commoditization of ritual dances had already been an issue in *Djatajoe* where it was pointed out that performances of *rejang*, *sanghyang dedari* and *baris pendet* should not be enacted independently of the context of a religious ceremony (*Djatajoe* 1940, No. 1: 25–8; 1941, No. 6: 120–2).

surprising, given that neither the Balinese nor Indonesian language have at their disposal the terminology that would permit their speakers to articulate the conceptual opposition between the sacred and the profane. As a result, the organizers had to resort to neologisms borrowed from Latin by way of Dutch for the very wording of the problem to be addressed. This semantic borrowing resulted in uneasy attempts on the part of the participants to forge a distinction that was alien to them. Instead of framing the problem they had to resolve as a matter of discriminating between two domains which had hitherto been undifferentiated, several contributors ended up speaking of 'sacred and profane dances' (*tari sakral dan provan*) as one and the same category, thus conferring upon the very same dances the attributes of both 'sacred' and 'profane' (Picard 1990).

Such is the challenge that tourism has flung at the Balinese. Not only were they called upon to slice into the living flesh of their culture, to draw a dividing boundary (*batas*) where they knew only a continuum, but on top of that they were compelled to think in a borrowed terminology that plainly made no sense to them. In their perplexity, they saw no other recourse than to look for rescue in the language of their former colonizers. And so they were reduced to searching within a foreign mode of thought for the concepts that were supposed to help them protect the most inalienable of their cultural values from the threat wrought by the presence of foreign tourists on their territory.

The inability of the Balinese authorities to separate the sacred from the profane, as they had intended, led the participants of the seminar to set up a nomenclature distinguishing three categories of dances, accompanied, moreover, by a gloss in English, which its authors somehow thought would make things clearer: (1) *Seni tari wali* ('sacred, religious dances'), indissociable from the carrying out of a ceremony (*pelaksana upacara*); (2) *Seni tari bebali* ('ceremonial dances'), accompanying a ceremony (*pengiring upacara*); (3) *Seni tari balih-balihan* ('secular dances'), performed as pure entertainment (*hiburan*), with no relation to a ceremony. Then, in 1973, a decree by the governor of Bali officially ratified the conclusions of the seminar by prohibiting the commercial exploitation of 'sacred dances'. This decree forbade organizing performances of *tari wali* for tourists, although visitors were still permitted to watch these dances when they were performed in the ceremonial context in which their execution was required. But this did not yet solve the problem. Not only were the provincial authorities unable to enforce the new regulation, the character of dances classified as *bebali* remained ambiguous: while not explicitly forbidding their commercialization, in principle it reserved their presentation to the context of religious ceremonies. The indecisiveness of the authorities, resulting in blurred boundaries, expressed the unresolved tension between two divergent views of dance among the Balinese. For some, it is a living tradition which runs the risk of becoming debased by being offered for tourist consumption. For others, however, the Balinese cultural heritage should be not merely "protected" (*dipertahankan*), but also "excavated" (*digali*), "cultivated" (*dibina*) and "developed" (*dikembangkan*) (Listibiya 1973: 5–6), with the aim of stimulating tourism and at the same time reinforcing Balinese cultural identity.

The patent failure to clearly distinguish 'sacred dances' from 'profane dances' led the head of the Bali Office of the Department of Religion (Kantor Wilayah Departemen Agama Propinsi Bali), I Gusti Agung Gede Putra, to shift the debate on to more familiar grounds, that of the categories *agama* and *adat*. This in fact only displaced the problem, since while now the words to address the issue were available, their semantic fields largely overlapped. While recognizing the difficulty of precisely differentiating what belongs to tradition from what belongs to religion, Putra tried to extricate himself from the difficulty by separating from *adat* all that should, according to him, belong to the sphere of *agama*. This latter part of *adat* he qualified as "religious tradition" (*adat keagamaan*) in order to distinguish it from what he considered as pertaining to "customary practices" (*adat kebiasaan*).[6] By doing this, he embarked on a semantic re-casting, where *agama*, now augmented by *adat keagamaan*, was differentiated from *adat*, a category that became residual because what remained was only that which relates to *adat kebiasaan* (Putra 1971).[7] In this way, a Balinese conception of the 'sacred' was created by dividing up the semantic field previously covered by the category *adat* and removing those practices considered non-religious. These would then be grouped with mundane activities to compose the sphere of the 'profane'.

Now, why was it so important to the Balinese authorities to separate the 'sacred' from the 'profane'? Since they perceived tourism as the unleashing of a

---

[6] We notice that it is precisely this same strategy which was chosen by the Tobaku people of Central Sulawesi converted to Christianity: "Christian converts divided their adat into two segments: religious *adat* (*agama adat*) and traditional customs (*adat kebiasaan*)" (Aragon 2000: 160; see also Whittier 1978).

[7] A characteristic example of a similar stratagem was provided by Parisada's response to the prohibition of cockfights (*tajen*) by the Indonesian government in 1981, in the framework of a national campaign to put an end to gambling. Refusing to renounce *tajen* altogether, the Balinese were constrained to discriminate between that which must be conserved as a sacrifice to chthonic forces (*tabuh rah*)—in this respect constituting a ritual requirement—and that which should be proscribed as a simple pretext for gambling (*judi*). To this end, they formulated the problem in terms of a distinction between what belongs to *agama* and what to *adat*, defined as an opposition between 'what is conceptual' (*yang bersifat konseptional*) and 'what is traditional' (*yang bercorak tradisional*) (Picard 1983).

tidal wave battering their coasts, the Balinese tried to build protective dikes against this foreign assault, to keep their most 'sacred' values from being 'profaned' by the tourists. The firm base to which they clung in confronting this assailant was their religion, conceived as the 'foundation' (*sendi*), the 'origin' (*induk*), the 'essence' (*intisari*) of their cultural identity. And having circumscribed the hard kernel of what constitutes their 'religion' (*agama*)—which henceforth defined the sphere of the 'sacred'—that which did not pertain to the religion but to the sphere of 'tradition' (*adat*) became available for 'profane' use.

The result of this conceptual re-casting is that the meaning of *adat* as the expression of a world order that is at once cosmic and social has become secularized, relativized, and, by being deprived of its religious foundations, is rendered negotiable. This secularization of *adat*, besides raising inextricable epistemological problems, has been causing widespread incomprehension and resentment among the Balinese. Be that as it may, once *adat* has been secularized, its practices can be either discarded like a worn out old 'skin' (*kulit*)—if they happen to displease the authorities or the tourists—or they might be converted into tourist attractions, thus regaining in aesthetic quality what they had lost in religious prerogatives, and thereby becoming 'art' (*seni*).[8]

Cultural Tourism and touristic culture

The Balinese concern about the tourist invasion of their island was shared by foreign observers, who wondered whether the Balinese culture would survive the impact of tourism. Their answers were strongly opinionated and differed sharply. While some accused tourism of corrupting Balinese culture by selling it off like a piece of common merchandise, others insisted that, to the contrary, the Balinese were perfectly capable of protecting their cultural heritage from whatever assaults it might undergo in the course of thoughtless touristic exploitation.

According to a rumor that was becoming ever more insistent, Bali was ruined—that is, almost... in any case, it was no longer what it used to be. The authentic traditions that had made this island famous the world over had been altered to suit the tourists, the celebrated artistic creativity of the Balinese was a

---

[8] Marked as it is by the touristification of Balinese culture, this evolution of the meaning of *adat* is not particular to Bali, as shown by the studies of Susan Rodgers (1979) and Rita Kipp (1993) on the Batak of Sumatra, and by those of Toby Volkman (1984) and Greg Acciaioli (1985) on the Toraja of Sulawesi. There is an interesting selection of articles on the relations between *adat* and *agama* in various Indonesian societies in Kipp and Rodgers (1987).

thing of the past, and the religious ceremonies had been turned into commercial shows. In short, the Balinese had let themselves be corrupted by the lure of profit, and everything on the island was up for sale. Money had got the upper hand over culture, irreversibly. And although the hordes of tourists had not yet completely submerged the Island of the Gods, it would not be long before they do so. Thus, one could read in a popular guidebook:

> How much more tourism can the island take? How much more traffic? How many more craft shops? How many more Kutas? How many more jets? The answer is that it never stops, the roads are widened, the hotels multiply, the direct flights increase. Commercialism has crept into every aspect of Balinese life. [...] It is now clear that the unbelievably complex social and religious fabric of the Balinese is at last breaking down under the tourist onslaught (Dalton 1990: 35–6).

Other observers, believing themselves to be better informed, were pleased to reply that this alarmist talk was hardly new. As we have seen, the island of Bali had scarcely been discovered by an avant-garde of travelers and artists in the 1920s before travel accounts began to warn of the imminence of its inevitable ruin. Thus it was that to each new generation of visitors, Bali seemed to be on the brink of ruin, holding out only by a reprieve from the gods. And so it was that by being so continuously repeated, this cry of alarm not only lost its edge, but it appeared to confer a certain immunity to Balinese culture. Because fear of its imminent destruction continued into the present day, and the fall was thus continuously postponed, this fear gave way to the conviction that the Balinese have adjusted to the tourist invasion of their island as they had adjusted to other circumstances of their past, that they have been able to make use of the attraction that their cultural traditions hold for foreign visitors without sacrificing their cherished values on the altar of commerce. The following quotation is a clear example of this conviction:

> Has the tidal wave of tourism sweeping over the East Indies washed away the idyllic culture that enchanted earlier visitors? With its hamburger joints, discotheques and Kentucky Fried Chicken outlets, has Bali succumbed to the gritty homogenization of the modern world? The short—and definitive— answer is: By no means! Beset by invaders for millenniums, the Balinese are responding to the latest incursion, as they have to past incursions, by becoming even more like themselves. The fabric of Balinese society is too strong and too flexible to be rent by easy money (Elegant 1987: 9).

Such is the ongoing speculation over the fate of Bali: an argument between fears of cultural destruction and confidence in the self-renewing vitality of Balinese culture in the face of potentially destructive forces.

Be that as it may, the fears aroused by the opening of Bali to international tourism in the 1970s appeared to recede in the course of the 1980s. Accused previously of being a vehicle of 'cultural pollution' (*polusi kebudayaan*), tourism was now extolled as a factor of 'cultural renaissance' (*renaissance budaya*). According to the Balinese authorities, the money brought in by tourists had stimulated the interest of the Balinese for their cultural traditions, while the admiration of foreigners for their culture had reinforced their self-esteem and their sense of identity. By becoming the patron of Balinese culture, tourism was contributing to its preservation and even to its revival, to the extent that it had turned their culture into a source of both profit and pride for the Balinese people (McKean 1989; see further McKean 1973).

This argument became the official word in Bali when it was upheld by Ida Bagus Mantra, the new governor of the province appointed in 1978 by President Suharto and replacing the Javanese colonel imposed on the Balinese eleven years earlier to bring the island back under control after the bloodshed that marked the advent of the New Order regime. For the Balinese, anxious about the expanding Javanese influence on their island, the appointment of a Balinese governor was perceived as a sign of legitimization of Balinese identity on the part of the central government. The hitherto perceptible anxiety gave way to relief, and the defensive attitude of the Balinese authorities became more confident.

Thus, to judge by the declarations of the Balinese authorities, one could surmise that Cultural Tourism—after going through an initial period of adjustment when the onslaught of foreigners on the island raised legitimate fears—had successfully accomplished its mission. However, from the threat of a 'cultural pollution' to the claim of a 'cultural renaissance', what was signified by 'Balinese culture' had undergone a revealing shift. When tourism was accused of corrupting Balinese culture, what was at stake was the desacralization of temples and the profanation of religious ceremonies, the monetization of social relations and the weakening of communal ties, as well as the relaxing of moral standards and the rise of mercantile attitudes. From then on, the issue was about what could be presented and marketed to the tourists. From being a lived experience, culture was now being designed as a product. It was with this in mind that the Balinese authorities promoted the idealized image of '*BALI*' (*Bersih, Aman, Lestari, Indah*—which can be rendered as 'Clean, Peaceful, Everlasting, Beautiful').

In the face of such evidence, it was tempting to conclude that the Balinese authorities had capitulated and sacrificed their concern for the preservation of culture to the demands of tourism promotion. In effect, rather than a commitment to preserving Balinese culture, the discourse of Cultural Tourism reflected the reaction of Balinese elites aware that their social position was being threatened by the intrusion of external capital invested in the tourism industry. In this respect, the debate on culture and tourism concealed a contest between the Balinese bourgeoisie and its Indonesian rivals competing for the spoils of tourism. For Jakarta-based investors and their local brokers, Balinese culture was to be exploited for the benefit of national development, whereas for the budding Balinese bourgeoisie, cultural commoditization ought to be kept in check so as to control the development of the island according to its own interests and capacities. It is clear that the Balinese were no match for their competitors. And the more the situation ran out of control, the more the reference to Cultural Tourism became incantatory and the more 'Balinese culture' took on added importance as an identity marker. All the while, the agrarian base on which Balinese culture is grounded was fast shrinking, as farmland was converted for tourism purposes (Couteau 2002: 236; 2003: 51–3).

However, the change of opinion in regard to tourism was not only a reflection of the Balinese failure to control its development and appropriate its revenues; it was also the outcome of a logic set in motion from the time of the very inception of Cultural Tourism. The problem addressed by this concept was to reconcile the respective interests of culture and tourism, initially perceived as conflicting. The solution provided by the discourse of Cultural Tourism would be to defuse this fundamental opposition by means of exchanging the respective attributes of tourism and culture: tourism in Bali was becoming 'cultural' as the Balinese culture was becoming 'touristic'. This was expressed by a disjunction in the Balinese view of their culture, according to whether or not it was conceived in relation to tourism.

In the discourse of Cultural Tourism, 'Balinese culture' (*kebudayaan Bali*) was presented as the distinctive marker (*ciri khas*) of Balinese identity. In this sense, their culture constituted for the Balinese a 'heritage' (*warisan*), which they should protect accordingly. With the coming of tourists, Balinese culture was no longer the exclusive property of the Balinese alone. As the main attraction of their island, it epitomized Bali's brand image (*citra*) as a tourist destination. Indeed, thanks to the appreciation that their culture inspired in the tourists, it had become a form of 'capital' (*modal*) for the Balinese, which they could exploit for a profit.

By thus viewing their culture as capital, the Balinese blurred the initial opposition between tourism and culture, between economic and cultural values. But one should understand that the Balinese view of their culture as a heritage was in fact the sign that it had already been converted into capital. Indeed, it was only once it had been enlisted as a tourist asset, available for profitable financial transactions, that the Balinese began regarding their culture as an heirloom to be carefully preserved and nurtured. Rather than being given from time immemorial, the Balinese cultural heritage is, in a sense, a product of the tourist encounter. On this account, we must conclude that what the Balinese authorities were celebrating as a 'cultural renaissance' was but the logical outcome of what they formerly denounced as a 'touristic culture'. By becoming Bali's brand image, that which distinguishes its tourist product on a highly competitive international market, 'culture' has become, indissociably, an identity marker for the Balinese, that by which they define and recognize themselves.[9] It seems to me that one could speak of a 'touristic culture' once the Balinese came to confuse these two uses of their culture, when that by which the tourists identify them becomes that by which they identify themselves, to the extent that the Balinese end up taking the brand image of their tourist product for the marker of their cultural identity.

The best evidence of this is the debate that stirred up Balinese public opinion in the late 1980s, following the publication in the main daily newspaper on the island—the *Bali Post*—of an article entitled 'The Balinese are Increasingly Losing their Balinese-ness' (*Orang Bali Semakin Kehilangan Kebaliannya*) (Sujana 1988). The author, I Nyoman Naya Sujana, a Balinese sociologist from Airlangga University of Surabaya, accused his fellow countrymen of being intoxicated with the prestige of their touristic reputation abroad and unaware that the authenticity of their cultural identity was gravely compromised. A survey among the newspaper's readers was taken on this occasion, showing that while 40 percent of the persons interviewed attributed to the influence of tourists an erosion of 'Balinese-ness', there were 60 percent who thought that, to the contrary, the increasing number of tourist arrivals in Bali was the best proof of the enduring cultural authenticity of the Balinese.

---

[9] This analysis was pursued further by Mark Hobart: "Bali's 'culture' is the product of such brilliant advertising that Balinese, let alone others, often imagine it as historical actuality rather than as successful branding" (Hobart 2015: 13).

Touristification and Indonesianization

The implications of tourism in Bali are compounded by the policy of the Indonesian state, which uses Balinese culture as a resource to contribute both to the development of international tourism in Indonesia and to the construction of an Indonesian national culture. Rather than a cultural renaissance, what is taking place is a joint process of touristification and Indonesianization of the Balinese culture.

When Suharto came to power, his New Order regime undertook to forge a national culture on the basis of Indonesian regional cultural traditions. Once the unity of the nation could be taken for granted, it looked as if the initial stress on centralization could be relaxed somewhat and emphasis placed on the country's diversity, in accordance with the slogan issued by the Directorate General of Tourism advertising Indonesia as 'a destination of endless diversity'. By the 1980s, ethnicity had become the fashion in Jakarta, to the extent that the media were talking of an 'ethnic revival' (Magenda 1988). The truth is that rather than denying the appeal of ethnicity as a focus of allegiance and identity by suppressing its manifestations, the New Order has resorted to a strategy of disempowerment and incorporation. In short, ethnic identities have not only been domesticated by the state, but they have been enlisted in the process of nation-building. The point was to celebrate cultural diversity while preventing the centrifugal force of ethnic identities.[10]

It should be emphasized, however, that only the major Indonesian ethnic groups, those showing a high degree of 'civilization' (*peradaban*), were deemed worthy of being taken into consideration. Ethnic minorities, seen as being imprisoned in their own narrow customary horizon of *adat*, were not really perceived as different specific cultures, but rather were lumped together in the residual category of 'isolated tribes' (*suku terasing*) (Colchester 1986). That is to say, in the definition of the Indonesian culture, a few superior cultures—first and foremost the Javanese and Balinese cultures—were distinguished from inferior cultures, excluded as such from contributing to the forging of the national culture.

Now, while the expression of ethnic identity appeared to have found some official sanction in New Order Indonesia, it was only as long as it remained at the level of cultural display—and even then, the kinds of cultural variations

---

[10] On Indonesian cultural policy and the construction of a national culture, see e.g. Soebadio (1985), Alexander (1989), Liddle (1989), Foulcher (1990), Zurbuchen (1990), Hooker (1993), Kipp (1993), Rodgers (1993), Pemberton (1994a), Schefold (1998), Acciaioli (2001), and Jones (2013).

which could be displayed were strictly defined by the state. Thus, the visual and decorative aspects of Indonesian ethnic cultures—such as dance and music, costumes, handicrafts, and architecture—have benefited from an unprecedented degree of official promotion: this is what Indonesians call the 'cultural arts' (*seni budaya*)[11] and which Greg Acciaioli has termed 'culture as art'.[12] What we have here is a folkloristic vision of ethnic cultures, targeting two audiences: first and foremost, Indonesians themselves, expected to endorse a contrived version of what is presented as their national 'cultural heritage' (*warisan budaya*); and, second, foreign visitors, enticed into the country to admire Indonesia's celebrated 'tourist objects' (*obyek wisata*).

Needless to say, this showcase vision did not acknowledge that which forms the core of a culture—such as language, kinship system, social organization, ritual practices, legal rules, economic activities and so on—and contributes to sustaining the sense of identity of the participants in that culture. On the contrary, the dismantling of traditional social relationships, the plundering of the environment, and the depreciation of local knowledge that ensued from the policy of 'national development' (*pembangunan nasional*) contributed to the deculturation of religion and the erosion of the ritual function of the arts (Dove 1988). In this respect, the New Order state proceeded just as the colonial administration before it had done in order to prevent ethnic differences from taking on political force: that is, by culturalizing the expression of ethnic identity as far as possible (Geertz 1990: 79).

But even this is only one side of the story, as we are not really dealing with Indonesia's ethnic cultures, even as they appear as a strictly controlled and sanitized version of themselves, but rather with what is called by Indonesian officials 'regional cultures' (*kebudayaan daerah*). Some semantic clarification is in order here. The Indonesian term that is commonly translated as 'culture' (*kebudayaan*) is at once normative and evolutionist, in the sense that it refers to the process through which the diverse ethnic groups of the Archipelago are expected to acquire the qualities judged necessary to instate order and civilization consonant with the ideals of the aspiring Indonesian nation. One should not therefore expect to find in this word the idea of a cultural specificity characteristic of each ethnic group, nor that of cultural relativism (Pelras 1977:

---

[11] The Indonesian syntagm *seni budaya* conveys a meaning of culture restricted to the sole aspects that could be represented and generate an aesthetic appreciation. With such a narrow conception of culture as art, we have come a long way from the holistic conception that prevailed in *Bhāwanāgara*, where culture included *agama*, *adat* and *seni*.

[12] "Regional diversity is valued, honoured, even apotheosized, but only as long as it remains at the level of display, not belief, performance, not enactment" (Acciaioli 1985: 161).

64–6). In this sense, *kebudayaan* and *agama* are both hallmarks of civilization, which Indonesian ethnic groups are enjoined to attain in order to be awarded a full-fledged citizenship. As for the term *daerah*, which translates as 'region', it carries an ambiguity as to the nature (ethnic or administrative) and geographic scope (local or regional) of the cultural entity under consideration.

Now, through the pervasive use of the set syntagm *kebudayaan daerah*, what we have actually been witnessing, in conjunction with the policy of national integration, was a dual process of homogenization within each province and of differentiation between provinces. The Indonesian state was aiming to induce in each of its provinces a distinctive provincial identity, grounded in a notion of culture stripped down to *seni budaya*, at the expense of the diverse ethnic cultures enclosed within their boundaries. Such provincial identities were promoted by the regional governments to be proposed to the nation for consumption and to the local populations they allegedly represent for authentication. They were exhibited in the cultural programs broadcast on television as well as in the regional museums that were being opened in the provincial capitals (Taylor 1994; Rath 1997). But the most conspicuous illustration of the official image of the country's cultural diversity is to be seen at President Suharto's pet project, the 'Beautiful Indonesia-in-Miniature Park' (Taman Mini Indonesia Indah), a grandiose theme-park opened in 1975 in Jakarta. There, each province of Indonesia is represented by a 'traditional house' (*rumah adat*), in which are exhibited 'traditional costumes' (*pakaian adat*), as well as performances of 'traditional dances' (*tarian adat*) (Pemberton 1994b; Acciaioli 1996; Errington 1997; Hitchcock 1998).

And so it is that with the creation of a provincial *adat*, the sphere of 'tradition' has become an administrative category. The focus of identity has been displaced from the ethnic group to the province: there has been a substitution of ethnic cultural identities with a provincial cultural identity. That being said, just as not all ethnic groups of a province were called upon to contribute to the related regional culture, not all the constituent elements of a regional culture were called upon to contribute to the national culture—only those judged worthy to be selected as the 'cultural peaks' (*puncak-puncak kebudayaan*) of each regional culture, a conception of the relationships between national and regional cultures expounded initially by Ki Hadjar Dewantara (1950). Thus the issue is one of a double-barreled process of selection: on the one hand, only certain ethnic groups are considered representative of the Indonesian nation, and as such their culture is destined to become a regional culture; on the other hand, only certain elements of that culture are considered significative of the related regional culture, and as such they are called upon to become part of the Indonesian national culture.

To sum up, just as 'culture' (read 'cultural arts') was being used as a means to defuse potential political problems, the risks inherent in ethnic mobilization were defused by means of a focus on the 'region' (read 'province'), that is, by shifting the locus of identification from a primordial to an administrative entity. In addition to the rather conspicuous folklorization of culture, there was a more discreet, yet no less crucial, provincialization of ethnicity. In this perspective, the promotion of provincial cultural identities by the New Order can be interpreted as a safe way for the state to bridge a gap between ethnic identities—regarded as being either irrelevant or else detrimental to the process of nation-building—and the still remote national identity.

While this cultural policy has been implemented to a certain extent within most provinces, Bali happens to be a privileged position in this respect: as the tourist showcase of Indonesia, its cultural arts stand not so much for the island itself as for the nation as a whole and as such they are expected to enhance the prestige of Indonesian culture abroad.[13] For this to be possible, however, Balinese culture had first to be divested of its anthropological singularity, in order to become commensurable—that is, both comparable and different—with other regional cultures of Indonesia and with the foreign tourist destinations with which it competes. The touristification of Bali and its Indonesianization combine their implications to place Balinese culture in a series where it has become nothing more than one item among others.

As part of this cultural policy, in accordance with the instructions of the Department of Education and Culture, several institutions were established in Denpasar by the provincial government, to teach, preserve and promote Balinese artistic traditions—specifically the performing arts: the Conservatory of Music (KOKAR-SMKI),[14] the Indonesian Dance Academy (ASTI-STSI-ISI),[15] the Arts

---

[13] Here 'Cultural Tourism' merges into 'Cultural Diplomacy' (*Diplomasi Kebudayaan*), a concept advanced by the minister of foreign affairs in 1983 to promote Indonesia's cultural image abroad. Given its prestigious touristic reputation, the province of Bali was particularly solicited to contribute. Accordingly, the Balinese troupes of dancers and musicians sent abroad on tour—now called 'artistic missions' (*misi kesenian*)—were charged with both promoting Indonesian culture and developing international tourism in Indonesia.

[14] The Conservatory of Music (Konservatori Karawitan, KOKAR) was founded in 1960 through the initiative of a few Balinese artists. In 1979, it became the Indonesian High School of Music (Sekolah Menengah Karawitan Indonesia, SMKI), to be placed under the jurisdiction of the Department of Education and Culture.

[15] The Indonesian Dance Academy (Akademi Seni Tari Indonesia, ASTI) was set up in 1967 and was integrated into the Department of Education and Culture in 1969. Its status was upgraded in 1988, when it became the Indonesian College of the Arts (Sekolah Tinggi Seni Indonesia, STSI), and in 2003 it merged with the Study Program of Art and Design (PSSRD) of Udayana University to establish the Indonesian Institute of the Arts (Institut Seni Indonesia, ISI).

Council (Listibiya),[16] and the Art Center (Werdhi Budaya).[17] To some extent, these institutions have taken over the patronage formerly exerted by the courts. They now dominate the creation of styles and the establishment of norms for their execution, the training of dancers and musicians, and the organizing and financing of performances. There is a crucial difference, however: while the courts were always careful to maintain their own distinctive style, the Indonesian government, through its regional apparatus, has been deliberately centralizing, normalizing and de-contextualizing the Balinese performing arts, with the result that artistic performances are being cut off from the source of their meaning and deprived of their evocative power, while local audiences tend to become passive viewers (Ramstedt 1992; Lindsay 1995; Yampolsky 1995; Hough 2000; Umeda 2005).[18]

The most significant example of this Indonesianization is certainly the Bali Arts Festival (Pesta Kesenian Bali, PKB), one of the first initiatives taken by Governor Mantra (Noszlopy 2002). Launched in 1979 at the Art Center—another creation of the same Mantra, when he was director general of culture—this month-long annual event is held by the provincial authorities as the best proof of Bali's cultural renaissance (Pangdjaja 1991). Even though it was initially presented as a perfect exponent of Cultural Tourism, the Arts Festival was never convincingly promoted on the tourist market and it soon became a thoroughly Balinese affair. Extensively publicized by the regional as well as by the national media, this event has evolved into the most prominent showcase for the public display of Balinese arts. In 1986, it was rendered compulsory by a provincial regulation and the following year it was ceremoniously inaugurated by no less than President Suharto himself. This national endorsement was interpreted as a signal for other provinces to start organizing their own arts festivals, modeled on the Balinese example.

At the Bali Arts Festival, the highlights of the Balinese 'cultural arts' are singled out from their original context to be combined into a performance for the consumption of the urbanized Balinese who provide the bulk of its audience.

---

[16] The Arts Council, officially called the Advisory and Promotional Council for the Regional Culture of the Province of Bali (Majelis Pertimbangan dan Pembinaan Kebudayaan Daerah Propinsi Bali, Listibiya), was established in 1966 through the initiative of a group of officials, artists, academics and professionals with the task of preserving and promoting Balinese artistic and cultural traditions. Chaired by a military officer, I Gusti Ngurah Pindha, it was further intended to purge artistic and cultural activities on the island of communist influences.

[17] The Art Center (Werdhi Budaya), inaugurated in 1976 by the minister of education and culture, was created to showcase Balinese artistic traditions.

[18] It is noteworthy that tourism operators need precisely that which is provided by the Department of Education and Culture—with whom they share a common vision of culture as art—that is, shortened, expurgated, and de-contextualized artistic performances.

Indeed, only those Balinese who are already cut off from their rural roots can recognize themselves in such an idealized image, projecting the authorized Balinese cultural identity on the national stage. But, to the extent that art forms conceived in Denpasar are then brought back to the villages by former students of the Indonesian artistic institutions—besides being broadcast by the cultural programs of Indonesian television—in the end they are recognized as being Balinese by the island's rural population itself (Picard 1996b).

Tourism development and its discontents in the late New Order

Tourism in Bali did not quite develop in the way that foreign and Indonesian experts had expected. After a promising start, it fell well below targets. It was only in the late 1980s that the development of tourism shifted to high gear, with a sharp upsurge in visitor arrivals, followed by an even more rapid rise in hotel investment and other tourism related facilities.[19] Although there are various reasons for this boom, the main one appears to be that after the slump in oil revenues in 1986, the Indonesian government undertook to actively develop international tourism. Leading international hotel chains established themselves on Bali, enticed by the deregulation of the banking system and solicited by Asian investors, most of them backed by Jakarta-based conglomerates. Thus, whereas during Ida Bagus Mantra's governorship, the growth of tourism had remained under control, his successor, Ida Bagus Oka (1988–98), opened the door for an unbridled influx of outside investment.[20] In 1988, alleging the pressure of demand, he scheduled 15 areas for development as 'tourism areas' (*kawasan wisata*), which became 21 in 1993, covering a quarter of the total surface of the

---

[19] Between 1970 and 1980, the number of foreign visitors to Bali multiplied from fewer than 30,000 to over 300,000 a year, reaching about 1 million in 1990 and up to around 2 million in 1997, when the growth of arrivals started to slow down owing to the Asian financial crisis and the ensuing Indonesian political breakdown. During the same period, hotel capacity increased from less than 500 rooms in 1970 to about 4,000 in 1980, jumping to 20,000 in 1990 and up to over 30,000 rooms in 1997. As a matter of fact, we do not know how many tourists visit Bali each year, either foreign or domestic. The only precise figures given by the Bali Tourism Office concern foreign visitors entering Indonesia through Bali on direct international flights, registered by the provincial immigration services. These figures do not take into account Indonesians or foreigners arriving on domestic flights, or arrivals at Gilimanuk on the ferry coming from Java, not to mention tourists from cruise ships mooring at Benoa or Padang. Domestic tourist arrivals have been on the rise since the 1990s, to the point of outnumbering foreign visitors.

[20] Ida Bagus Oka became a favorite target of criticism for selling off the island to outsiders: he was privately nicknamed 'Ida Bagus OK' for endorsing any development project backed by Jakarta, and particularly those involving members of Suharto's family and his cronies, in which he was accused of getting a commission. After the change of regime, he was convicted on corruption charges in 2001 and served a short time in prison before being acquitted.

island. This initiative provoked intense competition among the tourism areas, eager to attract a bigger share of tourism investment. It also led to a demand for cheap labor for building projects, which brought large numbers of migrant workers to Bali from other parts of Indonesia, mostly Muslims from the neighboring islands of Java, Madura and Lombok. These workers tend to accept lower wages than the Balinese and, unlike the latter, they don't have the inconvenient habit of taking leave unexpectedly to participate in endless ceremonies in their village.

There is no question that tourism has boosted the economic growth of Bali, to the point of displacing agriculture as the leading sector. At the close of the New Order, with the activities it has generated, such as handicrafts, garment manufacture and other cottage industries, tourism was estimated to contribute over half of the Regional Gross Domestic Product of the province, while absorbing half of the work force if one includes its indirect spin-off effects. Meanwhile, the average per capita income on the island had moved from below the national average to one of the highest-ranking provinces. However, the growing encroachment of foreign interests, as well as the uneven distribution of economic benefits within the local population and throughout the island, was becoming a matter of serious concern. The southern area, where the main resorts and most of the facilities are located, receives the lion's share of the tourism revenues. This has led to a continuous influx of internal migrants from other parts of the island and, consequently, to social tension and competition over jobs in the already overpopulated south. Furthermore, tourism has tended to accentuate social inequalities, with a widening gap between those Balinese with direct access to tourist dollars and those without.

Its disparity notwithstanding, the wealth brought about by the tourism industry has fueled the rise of a Balinese middle class, while furthering the spread of urbanization. In particular, local compradors, who served as brokers for outside investors, were able to turn themselves into a capitalist class within the tourism industry. Even though Balinese capitalists, power holders and opinion leaders had profited substantially from the early years of tourism development, they realized that they were reaping an ever smaller share of its economic benefits. As members of an ethnic and religious minority, the Balinese elites had become critically aware of the plundering of their island's natural and cultural resources in the name of 'development' and 'national interest' (Suasta and Connor 1999). They were faced with a conundrum: while concerned that they were no longer in control of tourism nor of their own culture, they were painfully aware that its commoditization formed the very backbone of their economic prosperity.

Throughout the 1990s, growing feelings of discontent were voiced against the capital-intensive tourism development initiated from Jakarta and operated by foreign investors. A number of controversial tourism 'mega-projects' (*megaproyek*) made the headlines of the *Bali Post* and triggered protests from the Balinese public—the Garuda Wisnu Kencana monument on the Bukit peninsula, the Bali Nirwana Resort at Tanah Lot, the Bali Turtle Island Development on Serangan island, the Bali Pecatu Graha Resort on the Bukit peninsula, and the beach reclamation at Padanggalak,[21] to name but the most infamous ones (Supartha 1998). Since political opposition to the government was out of the question during the authoritarian New Order, these projects were generally objected to on account of the damage they inflicted upon the island's environment (Warren 1998b). But at the same time, the Balinese were becoming highly sensitive to any move they construed as 'aggressions' (*pelecehan*) against their religion, particularly as a result of the tourist exploitation of religious sites and of the ceremonies taking place there. Complaining that Bali had become Jakarta's colony (Aditjondro 1995), influential opinion leaders accused foreign investors and their Indonesian counterparts of having made a clean sweep of prime real estate at the expense of the Balinese, who were finding themselves progressively marginalized on their own island as a result of massive land speculation and forced expropriation. They denounced the directives from Jakarta, which all too often overrode provincial regulations, as well as the collusion between corrupt officials and powerful private investors.

The fact is that as a result of inadequate development planning and lack of control, compounded by incompetent bureaucracy and rampant corruption, the environment of Bali has been heavily strained, to the point that the island is now rife with air and water pollution, beach erosion and reef destruction, freshwater and electricity shortage, saturation of solid waste disposal, rivers clogged up with plastic bags and other detritus, not to mention traffic congestion, urban sprawl, overpopulation, crime and social tensions. Worse in the eyes of the Balinese is

---

[21] In October 1997, the *Bali Post* reported on a land reclamation project for the building of a large tourist resort at Padanggalak beach, an important religious site for the village of Kesiman where ritual cleansings and post-cremation purifications are held. The news sparked a protest spearheaded by Anak Agung Kusuma Wardana, a leader of Puri Kesiman and a member of the regional parliament in Denpasar, who demanded that Ida Bagus Oka resign his governorship for having approved the project. As Ida Bagus Oka originated from Kesiman, the village council threatened him with expulsion (*kasepekang*), a sanction equivalent to social death with dire ritual consequences. The governor caved in and the beach was promptly returned to its original state. Thus, for the first time, local resistance based on *adat* sanction was able to defeat a coalition of external investors and regional government.

the transformation of land into a marketable commodity and its massive conversion, which has caused family as well as communal feuds and uprooted the local population, alienated from land ownership. This shift in the function of rice fields has important implications for the production of food and the livelihood of farmers, and it poses serious threats to the perpetuation of traditional Balinese culture, which grew out of a communal-agrarian society (MacRae 2003; Suartika 2010; Bendesa and Aksari 2015; Fagertun 2017; Wardana 2019).

Crisis and *Reformasi*

In 1997, a major financial and economic crisis hit Indonesia, which ended in the resignation of President Suharto on May 21, 1998, under pressure from students, the pro-democracy movement, segments of the military and some Muslim leaders. His successor, interim-President Bacharuddin J. Habibie, managed the transition to democracy by launching decisive reform measures, which ushered in the era known as '*Reformasi*': freedom of speech and of information, freedom to establish political parties and associations, free national elections and far-reaching administrative decentralization. Following the 1999 elections, Abdurrahman Wahid—a liberal Muslim religious and political figure, long-time chairman of the Nahdlatul Ulama—was elected president by the People's Consultative Assembly (MPR). His bold and somewhat ill-considered initiatives antagonized both Muslim conservatives and the military—all the while disappointing his reformist supporters—and he was forced to resign under political pressure in 2001. He was replaced by his vice-president, Megawati Sukarnoputri (daughter of Sukarno), deemed more conservative and easier to control by entrenched interests. She was defeated in the 2004 elections by Susilo Bambang Yudhoyono, a retired general, who became the first directly elected president of Indonesia. After the renewal of his mandate in 2009, he was succeeded by Joko Widodo in 2014, who in turn was re-elected in 2019.

The flowering of the movement for a democratic Indonesia that had brought Suharto down quickly lost momentum, with most of the old establishment remaining in place and consolidating its power via formally democratic elections, while pervasive patronage and corruption expanded through all levels of government. Meanwhile, the façade of social harmony laboriously crafted by the New Order regime was torn down, as lasting resentments and conflicts that had been simmering under a lid of political repression and cultural censorship began to surface, together with a strong reassertion of local identities. Dissension regarding issues of ethnicity, religion and social class, that hitherto had been contained, surged to the fore, against the backdrop of a lasting economic and social crisis. Thanks to tourism, Bali was less affected by the economic crisis than other regions of Indonesia, as connections with international business networks had rendered the island's economy less dependent on state subsidies (Vickers 2003: 25). In fact, the devaluation of the Indonesian rupiah boosted Bali's tourism and export-based economy (Connor and Vickers 2003; Hitchcock and Putra 2007, Chap. 8).

Moreover, Bali appeared to remain remarkably free of the political, ethnic, and religious strife that engulfed the Archipelago (Ardika and Putra 2004). The main reason for this state of affairs was not the fact that the Balinese people are Hindu and peace-loving, as they are prone to claim, but rather the widespread concern for sheltering the island's all-important tourism industry, on behalf not only of Jakarta and foreign-based conglomerates but also of Balinese politicians and business stakeholders.[22] The relative good fortune of Bali, at a time when the rest of Indonesia was in dire straits, increased the influx of migrant workers in search of jobs. At the same time, large numbers of refugees from the anti-Chinese riots that marked the fall of Suharto in Jakarta and other main cities of Java sought refuge in Bali. The Balinese did not appear to resent the arrival of these Chinese Indonesian settlers, whose ancestors have been well integrated for centuries; but the increasingly conspicuous presence of Muslim laborers and petty traders was giving rise to expressions of animosity on the island. Although there are no reliable figures as to the scope of these migrations to Bali, it is clear that it was rapidly becoming a multi-ethnic and multi-religious island.

The fact is that the development of tourism has considerably modified the social stratification in Bali, with the emergence of non-indigenous populations at both ends of the social scale: on the one hand, a wealthy Indonesian business class and its foreign associates, who control the tourism industry and appropriate most of its profits, and on the other, a growing mass of workers employed on building sites and in the informal sector.[23] Thus, "many Balinese have a growing sense that they are losing control of their own economy simultaneously from the top down and the bottom up" (MacRae 2010: 17). However, even though

---

[22] Thus, during the campaign preceding the general election in 1999, one could see roadside signs bearing slogans such as 'Bali is safe: the tourists come' (*Bali aman: Turis datang*).

[23] In addition, one should mention the significant cosmopolitan community of expatriates carrying on the romantic idyll with Bali initiated by Westerners in the 1930s, whether as managers in the tourism industry or as traders in clothing, jewelry, and other crafts, or else enjoying a comfortable retirement in the sun. They have been joined by a number of affluent Indonesians, who have built luxurious villas in the south of the island.

Balinese society has become a class society, the tensions between social classes are not expressed as such but in terms at once ethnic and religious. This is because the intrusion of outsiders triggered an intensified sense of identity among both populations—indigenous Hindus versus Muslim outsiders—sowing the seeds of ethnic and religious discrimination on the island (Couteau 2002: 235; see further Burhanuddin 2008; Hauser-Schäublin and Harnish 2014).

Indeed, disturbing signs of a growing rejection of newcomers—referred to as *pendatang* or, in euphemistic Balinese, as *tamiu dauh tukad* ('guests from west of the river')—have been on the rise since the late 1990s, as Balinese felt that their tolerance towards other ethnic and religious communities had been taken advantage of. They resented the fact that while enterprising immigrants from neighboring islands had started to make a living in Bali, numerous poor Balinese families had been constrained to resettle in other islands under the transmigration program of the Indonesian government. These new immigrants were perceived as a source of unfair economic competition and a burden on the environment and the infrastructures of the densely populated and urbanized area of southern Bali where they mostly settled.

As expressed in a critical self-portrait by representatives of the younger generation of Balinese public intellectuals, the growing heterogeneity of the population on the island and the fragmentation of the Balinese society in terms of ethnic belonging and religious affiliation has prompted, among many Balinese, "a feeling of insecurity which manifests itself in the growing readiness to use their own culture defensively against the ethnical and religiously others" (Ramseyer 2001: 11). To name only one example of this defensive attitude, all across Bali notice boards have been posted at the entrance to villages which read '*Pemulung Dilarang Masuk*' ('Scavengers Forbidden to Enter'), warnings which are meant to deter non-Balinese Indonesians from intruding. Balinese public opinion is prone to blame these outsiders for the alarming proliferation of thefts, murders, rapes, prostitution, rackets and the trade of hard drugs that have become widespread on the island.

To curb the coming of these unwelcome migrants, the municipality of Denpasar decided in January 2000 to impose a system of residence permits on *pendatang*. A few months later, a poll was conducted by the *Bali Post*, which found that over 90 percent of the respondents agreed that such a system should apply to the island as a whole (*Bali Post*, August 12, 2000). Meanwhile, it was reported in Balinese and foreign media that vigilante groups regularly conducted raids in Denpasar and elsewhere in which house-to-house checks resulted in non-Balinese Indonesians being harassed and sometimes expelled from the island—

when they were not simply put to death on accusation of crime (Santikarma 2001). The fact is that, as in other regions of Indonesia, the ineffectiveness of the weakened state in maintaining public order has led to the establishment in Bali of militia (*pacalang*), ostensibly aimed at protecting village communities from 'external' threats.[24] This kind of neo-traditional village militia was first employed to provide protection to Megawati Sukarnoputri's party, the Indonesian Democratic Party of Struggle (Partai Demokrasi Indonesia-Perjuangan, PDI-P),[25] the main political force in Bali since the demise of the New Order, when it held its first congress on the island in October 1998. It was not long, though, before *pacalang* became identified less with party politics and more with the control of *pendatang*, as all over Bali villages have established their own *pacalang* militias.

However, in these years of turmoil, social disturbances did not come only from outsiders but arose from within Balinese society itself. Witness the increasingly frequent incidence of communal clashes within and between villages fueled by conflicting claims over land or status, commonly euphemized as *kasus adat* ('customary law disputes') in the Balinese media—not to mention conflicts between supporters of competing political parties (Warren 2000; Atmadja 2010, Chap. 8). But even when these conflicts involved Balinese, local politicians and public intellectuals tended to attribute them to the work of outside provocateurs. In short, it appeared as if the Balinese were afflicted by a growing sense of anomie, further compounded by the forceful politicization of Indonesian Islam unleashed by the demise of the New Order regime, which fueled a series of confrontations between Hindu Balinese and Muslim hardliners. This challenge gave rise to a proliferation of new Hindu organizations in the island, accompanied by a profusion of publications on Balinese identity, which revealed the anxiety of a society threatened in its structures as well as in its self-image. Among these publications, one notices a flurry of magazines and newspapers with a distinct traditionalist flavor, which began to mushroom with the inception of *Reformasi*. Some were written in Balinese (*Kulkul, Buratwangi, Canang Sari*), a relative novelty on the island, where the vernacular was seen as fast disappearing under the onslaught of Indonesian and English.[26] But even those

---

[24] On the *pacalang*, see, e.g., Darling (2003), ICG (2003), MacDougall (2003), Santikarma (2003a), and Widia (2010). The *pacalang* should not be confused with gangs and other 'security organizations' euphemistically dubbed *organisasi masyarakat* ('community organizations'), such as Laskar Bali, Bali Baladika, Pemuda Bali Bersatu, or Forum Peduli Denpasar, which provide public support in exchange for political protection, and whose territory is outside the bounds of customary authority (Vandenberg and Zuryani 2021).

[25] After Megawati was forced out from the leadership of the Indonesian Democratic Party (PDI) by Suharto in 1996, she founded the PDI-P following the lifting of the limitations on national political parties.

[26] To counter this potential threat, in 2004, the governor made the teaching of the Balinese language mandatory in all secondary schools and not solely in primary schools as was previously the case.

published in Indonesian, such as *Bali Aga, Sarad* or *Taksu* targeted a local readership with topics that were strictly Balinese.

The Islamic pressure reached a climax in October 1998, following a provocative remark made during the campaign for the 1999 elections in the Muslim newspaper *Republika* by A.M. Saefuddin, a minister in Habibie's cabinet and a presidential candidate from the Islamic United Development Party (Partai Persatuan Pembangunan, PPP). He declared that Megawati, the favorite candidate of Balinese voters, could not be elected president because she worshipped Hindu gods. This was an allusion to the fact that, although Muslim, Megawati—whose paternal grandmother was Balinese—was seen praying in Hindu temples whenever she visited Bali. This gross insult against their religious identity raised an immediate uproar among the Balinese and triggered mass protests on the island. A committee of Hindu Balinese activists was formed, who threatened to fight for the independence of Bali (*Bali Merdeka*) until Saefuddin resigned. Eventually, the atmosphere cooled down, even though Saefuddin stayed in his post, but the idea of an independent Hindu Bali in a predominantly Muslim nation had taken hold of the Balinese people's imagination—all the more so as the economic prosperity ensured by tourism made it appear a feasible option. Subsequently, in October 1999, when it transpired that Muslim politicians had prevented the election of Megawati as president by the MPR, despite the fact that her party had come out ahead in the elections, her supporters rioted and caused havoc in Bali. Since then, while the idea of Bali's independence has lost its relevance, the ethno-nationalist project of 'Bali for the Balinese' has been making headway (Vickers 2002: 94; Couteau 2002: 243–4, 2003: 55–6).

The revival of *adat* under the Regional Autonomy legislation

Accordingly, the Balinese had pinned high hopes on the laws on Regional Autonomy (*Undang-Undang No.22/1999 & No.25/1999 Tentang Otonomi Daerah*)—promulgated in May 1999, implemented in January 2001, and revised in October 2004—which led to the devolution of power and fiscal responsibility from central to regional authorities. As elsewhere in Indonesia, the introduction of regional autonomy legislation led in Bali to a revival of *adat* and a revitalization of the customary village communities (Davidson and Henley 2007), as Balinese sought protection in the intimacy of the village and its *adat* against the pressures of competing national interests, penetration of external capital, influx of economic migrants from other islands and the spread of deleterious foreign cultural influences.[27]

The new laws abolished the 1974 law on Regional Government (*Undang-Undang No.5/1974 Tentang Pokok-Pokok Pemerintahan di Daerah*) and the 1979 law on Village Government (*Undang-Undang No.5/1979 Tentang Pemerintahan Desa*), which had disenfranchised the customary institutions of governance by imposing uniform administrative structures at regional and village level across Indonesia (Warren 1990). Until then, Balinese villages had been characterized by a dichotomy between customary and administrative authority, a state of affairs that went back to colonial times when, in order to govern the island efficiently, the Dutch had introduced uniform administration throughout Balinese society. A new type of village was created, the 'administrative village' (*desa dinas*), which ran parallel to the 'customary village' (*desa adat*). After the troubled period following the revolution and the early years of independence, the New Order continued the state penetration of village government in Bali from where the Dutch had left off. There was a difference, however: with the 1979 reform of village administration, village leaders became civil servants responsible to the central government rather than to the local population. As a result, the Indonesian government went much further than its colonial predecessor in the penetration of society by the state, by undermining the authority of the customary village and subordinating *adat* to the requirements of national development (Surpha 1986; Warren 1993, Chap. 9).

This marginalization of *adat* shows the suspicion in which it is held by the Indonesian state. While *adat* had proved a useful ideological weapon in the nationalist struggle in that it symbolized the common and distinctive cultural heritage of Indonesians, after independence the very diversity of *adat* bore the risk of sowing dissension between the various ethnic groups. In independent Indonesia, therefore, *adat* received an honored place due to its ideological usefulness, but since then its scope and legal import have been steadily eroded by the state (Burns 1989: 4). The successive shifts in the terminology used in Bali are highly significant in this respect. Before the colonial occupation, the Balinese village was simply termed *desa*, without further qualification. Then, for

---

[27] On March 17, 1999, Balinese representatives participated in the First Congress of Indigenous Peoples of the Archipelago in Jakarta, during which was founded the Alliance of Indigenous Peoples of the Archipelago (Aliansi Masyarakat Adat Nusantara, AMAN), whose aim was to obtain official recognition of all Indonesian customary communities (*masyarakat adat*) as 'indigenous peoples' (Acciaioli 2007). Specifically, AMAN's political platform focused on the devolution of decision-making power to indigenous institutions at village level and on the recognition of *hukum adat*. In 2001, AMAN opened a regional branch office in Bali.

the purpose of distinguishing it from the 'administrative village' (*desa dinas*) set up by the Dutch, it became the 'customary village' (*desa adat*). Finally, with the 1979 law on Village Government, the 'village' (*desa*) had become an Indonesian administrative unit, with the attributions of the *desa adat* defined in a residual manner as whatever did not come under the jurisdiction of the *desa*.

Shortly before the Indonesian state curbed the prerogatives of *adat*, the Balinese provincial government had established itself as the custodian of tradition, as much to ward off central government control over Balinese customary autonomy as to enhance its own authority over local institutions. In 1979, Governor Mantra set up the Council for the Guidance of Customary Institutions (Majelis Pembina Lembaga Adat, MPLA), with the aim of normalizing the role of customary institutions in the province. The MPLA formalized the status of 'customary law' (*hukum adat*) and promoted written codification of village regulations (*awig-awig desa*) (Dherana 1982; MPLA 1990). Then in 1986 the governor enacted a provincial regulation that imparted legal status to the *desa adat*, henceforth defined as a customary law community (*Peraturan Daerah No.6/1986 Tentang Kedudukan, Fungsi dan Peranan Desa Adat Sebagai Kesatuan Masyarakat Hukum Adat Dalam Propinsi Daerah Tingkat I Bali*). While aimed at strengthening the legal standing of *adat* in the judicial system, these initiatives severed *adat* from local knowledge and practice in order to submit it to the provincial administrative authority.

Yet, even more critical than the visible effects of impinging national law and provincial bureaucracy was the changing frame of reference within which Balinese discourse on *adat* had been taking place. Increasing focus on written codification and administrative sources of authority for its claims to legitimacy reveal a shifting balance of power between *adat* and *dinas*, between the village and the state. Hence, while the strength of customary institutions in Bali had enabled them to sustain the implementation of national development policy, conversely it was administrative functions that were used to justify the legitimacy of *adat*, and to the administration that appeals were made to redress the decline in authority of the *desa adat* (Schulte Nordholt 1991; Warren 1993, Chap. 11).

In other words, to establish the legitimacy of their *adat*, Balinese had not only to standardize it and circumscribe its sphere of authority, but they had also to put it at the service of the state. While the colonial state aimed at preserving *adat* with a view to maintaining the traditional allegiance of village communities, the Indonesian state has incorporated *adat* into its policy of national integration, economic development and public order. In the process, the locus of Balinese tradition has become the province, in effect creating a provincial *adat*.

The regional autonomy laws opened the way for a revision of the relationship between *adat* and *dinas* by giving the Balinese an opportunity to restore the customary prerogatives of their *desa adat*, which had been unduly appropriated by the state. On March 21, 2001, the governor of Bali, I Dewa Made Beratha, issued a Provincial Regulation on the Customary Village (*Peraturan Daerah Provinsi Bali No.3/2001 Tentang Desa Pakraman*), which replaced the 1986 regulation and was ratified in 2003. This provincial regulation (*perda*) restored full authority to the customary village to "run its internal affairs" (*berhak mengurus rumah tanggannya sendiri*), owing to the recognition that it constitutes an autonomous "community of customary law" (*kesatuan masyarakat hukum adat*).[28] Yet, contrary to what had been advocated in some Balinese quarters and discussed at length in the *Bali Post*, with a view to returning to the situation prevailing before the intrusion of the colonial administration, the *Perda Desa Pakraman* did not go as far as abolishing the *desa dinas* altogether. As a matter of fact, it did not address the controversial articulation between customary and administrative villages, and it did not even mention the *desa dinas*.

In order to give the newly restored customary village a more specific Balinese flavor, its name was changed from *desa adat* to *desa pakraman*.[29] The new *perda* defined the *desa pakraman* as a "Hindu religious community" (*masyarakat umat Hindu*), marked by a communal way of life based on the *Tri Hita Karana* and characterized by the presence on its territory of the three village sanctuaries (*kahyangan tiga*). Participation in communal rituals at these sanctuaries was made mandatory for the enjoyment of full citizenship rights in the *desa pakraman*. Village authority was conferred on its decision-making assembly (*krama desa*), which was placed under the supervision of the Grand Council of Customary Villages (Majelis Utama Desa Pakraman, MUDP), an overarching body which has the upper hand on all matters related to *adat* in the 1,535 *desa pakraman* in Bali, in cooperation with the governor. Furthermore,

---

[28] However, the plain fact that in Indonesia customary law is subordinated to national law drastically undermines the presumed autonomy of the *desa pakraman*. On legal and institutional pluralism in Bali, see Wardana (2019).

[29] Unlike the word *adat*, which has both a colonial and an Islamic connotation, the term *pakraman* claims its authority from Old Balinese inscriptions and is said to be derived from the Sanskrit root *krama*, meaning 'custom, rule sanctioned by tradition' (Zoetmulder 1982: 891). However, according to David Stuart-Fox, it is more probably "related to Austronesian *karaman* (from *rama*, 'father, elder'), which in pre-Majapahit inscriptions refers to the village community" (Stuart-Fox 2002: 21, n. 1). In any case, this new name suggests that, despite their actual diversity, villages in Bali were seen as self-contained uniform entities, bringing to mind Liefrinck's conception of the autonomous 'village republic' (*dorpsrepubliek*).

since then the *desa pakraman*—and no longer the *desa dinas*—has become the main recipient of provincial- and district-level government funding.[30]

Essentially, the *desa pakraman* was conceived as "the last line of defense of Balinese culture" (*benteng terakhir pertahanan kebudayaan Bali*), in the sense that it was meant to control and curb in-migration on its territory. This task was specifically assigned to the *pacalang*, acknowledged as a traditional security force (*satgas keamanan tradisional*), which was given authority to ensure law and order in the *desa pakraman*. According to the regulation, migrants—dubbed *krama tamiu* (guest citizens) or *krama dura* (foreign citizens)—are members of the *desa pakraman* with respect to social and territorial, but not religious, matters. Only natives of a *desa pakraman*—the *krama wed* (native citizens)—are "entitled to partake in the village participatory trilogy of *'palemahan'* (land), *'pawongan'* (people) and *'parhyangan'* (pantheon), the unity of which makes up the village (*desa*)" (Couteau 2003: 48; see *Sarad*, No. 34, January 2003: 22–41; No. 36, March 2003: 24–39). The result is thus a demarcation between the residents originating from the *desa pakraman*, members ex-officio of its institutions, and the newcomers, barred from worshipping the gods considered to be the legitimate owners of the village.

This provision has been criticized on various counts. To begin with, it is ambiguous, in that it does not distinguish explicitly between the rights and obligations of Hindu Balinese coming from another *desa pakraman*, and those of migrants from abroad. Specifically, Balinese who want to keep migrants away from the villages contended that they were only expected to fulfill social and territorial duties, whereas Hindu Balinese had to comply as well with ritual service obligations (*ayahan*), which are much more burdensome. On the other hand, those observers more sensitive to considerations of human rights and democracy denounced the discrimination against non-Hindu Balinese residents, who were stigmatized as outsiders as they were denied full participation in the village community (Rawski and MacDougall 2004). In any case, this controversy about membership of the *desa pakraman* testifies to the difficulties the Balinese face with the increasing heterogeneity of their society.

In short, the *Perda Desa Pakraman* reflected the concerns of an urbanized elite, who deemed that Balinese culture should be protected against external threats and saw the customary village and its *adat* as the backbone of their ethnic identity. However, the new regulation created an inequity among Indonesian citizens living in Bali by endowing the Hindu Balinese with special rights at the

---

[30] On the *Perda Desa Pakraman* and its implications, see, e.g., Surpha (2002), Warren (2007), Reuter (2008), Ramstedt (2009, 2012, 2013, 2014), and Hauser-Schäublin (2011, 2013).

expense of disenfranchised residents—Muslim and Christian Balinese as well as Chinese Indonesians who had been living in mixed villages for generations, labor migrants from other islands, and even Balinese members of Neo-Hindu *sampradaya*, in that they are generally averse to customary Balinese rituals. Furthermore, the authority conferred on the *desa pakraman* blurred the former separation of *adat* and *dinas* as well as the distinction between *adat* and *agama*, by defining the village along Hindu Balinese religious principles. While reformist Balinese leaders had been striving for decades to universalize their religion by segregating it from their indigenous traditions, the *Perda Desa Pakraman* reintegrated *agama Hindu* into *adat Bali* by compelling Hindu Balinese to comply with local *adat* regulations. Finally, while the consolidation of *adat* institutional authority might strengthen the provincial stand against competing national and foreign interests on issues such as in-migration, development projects, and land alienation, on the other hand, giving too much autonomy to customary villages could exacerbate local conflicts and undermine provincial policy (Warren 2007: 177).

Be that as it may, for the Balinese provincial government, regional autonomy was intended not only to restore the customary village and curb the coming of migrants, it was also expected to allow for controlling tourism development and appropriating a larger share of its profits. Indeed, as we have seen, even before the era of *Reformasi*, influential opinion leaders had denounced the takeover of the tourism industry by Jakarta and foreign-based conglomerates, and warned that the unrestrained inflow of investment was unsustainable in the long term. They claimed the right of the Balinese to further their own views on a tourism policy appropriate for their island and beneficial to its population. The solutions advocated revolved around the need for adequate planning and managing of tourism development, which implied both political will and legal authority for the provincial government to develop tourism in the interest of the Balinese people. Moreover, most incomes and taxes earned from the tourism industry should accrue to Bali instead of being siphoned off to Jakarta.

However, while the Balinese provincial government expected to take advantage of regional autonomy to control the development of tourism on the island and to secure a larger share of its revenue, it turned out that the new laws devolved most of the authority not to the province but to the district (*kabupaten*) and municipality (*kota*) levels. For fear that a genuine transfer of authority to the provinces might entice some of them to break away from Jakarta, they were granted only a vague mediating role between the districts. And the situation was all the more confused regarding tourism, as it was not even mentioned among the domains falling under the authority of either the regions or the center. Accordingly, as soon as the disposition of the laws became known, Balinese authorities campaigned for Bali to be granted 'special autonomy' (*otonomi khusus*) status as a province, in order to confer greater authority to the provincial, instead of district-level, government. The arguments they put forward to back their demand were twofold: some referred to tourism, others to Bali's religious specificity.

On the one hand, it was advanced that Bali is a small island with limited natural resources. As such, it is a geographical unit and it should be dealt with in a holistic manner—the so-called 'one island one management' approach (Wardana 2019). Yet, as a province, it is divided into eight districts and one municipality. Only the southern districts of Badung and Gianyar, and the municipality of Denpasar, received an adequate regional income from tourism, while the other districts were poor. With autonomy being devolved to the districts, the widely unequal distribution of profits from tourism was inciting each district to compete in issuing permits for resort development in order to boost their regional revenue, without taking into account the necessary coordination of the island's resource management and tourism development. Moreover, for the same purpose, each district might impose various taxes and fees on hotels, restaurants, and tourists. This would only increase regional imbalances, heighten interregional conflicts and result in ruining the environment as well as creating social and cultural tensions.

Consequently, the implementation of regional autonomy raised fears of disintegration. Provincial authorities were concerned that district heads (*bupati*) might turn into 'little kings' (*raja-raja kecil*), thus going back to the situation when Bali was fragmented between quarrelsome kingdoms, before the Dutch colonial forces put an end to their internecine wars by subjugating the whole island. Their concern echoed Geoffrey Robinson's study, which attributed the recurrent political conflicts among Balinese, and the absence of strong regionalist or ethnic-based movements on the island, to the historical weakness of regional powers encompassing the whole of Bali (Robinson 1995).

More interesting for my purpose is the fact that Balinese opinion leaders were calling for a special autonomy status to be granted to the province in the name of Bali's specificity, namely, its 'Balinese-ness' (*Kebalian*). Thus, one could read in the *Bali Post* statements such as these: "Bali is a unity of religion, tradition and culture. [...] When Bali is truly an autonomous region, it will automatically possess full right to govern its own area. Including in manifesting its Balinese-ness."[31] This, they maintained, did not mean that Bali intended to separate itself from the rest of Indonesia. They were not fighting for independence (*Bali Merdeka*). But, they added, if Aceh had been able to obtain special autonomy on account of Islam, Bali should get it as well because it is the island of Hinduism. As critically summarized by the Balinese activist Degung Santikarma:

> "Bali" is imagined to be an entity with clear boundaries which exists in a certain space (the island of Bali), is inherently linked to a certain language (Balinese), a certain way of life (*adat* Bali or Balinese custom), and a certain religion (Balinese Hinduism). All Balinese are, by extension, thought to share this culture and to be willing participants in the project of caring for it (Santikarma 2001: 31).

In November 2004, following the revision of the laws on Regional Autonomy, the Balinese provincial parliament (Dewan Perwakilan Rakyat Daerah, DPRD Bali) submitted a draft law to the national parliament in Jakarta (Dewan Perwakilan Rakyat, DPR) seeking special autonomy status for the province of Bali. Yet, despite intense lobbying by Balinese parliamentary representatives in Jakarta, the request for special autonomy for Bali was not granted, as it was blocked by the Indonesian government and underhandedly sabotaged by district officials keen to extend their prerogatives at the expense of the provincial government.

The Kuta bombing and its aftermath

On Saturday night October 12, 2002, a series of bomb blasts shook Bali, putting an end to the peace and prosperity the island had so jealously guarded over the years. A first bomb exploded inside Paddy's Cafe, followed a few seconds later by the explosion of a vehicle parked in front of the nearby Sari Club, two busy night spots in Kuta Beach, the most popular resort area on the island. This terrorist attack killed over two hundred people and injured many more—primarily tourists, Australians for the most part, but Indonesians as well—not to mention extensive material damage.

Traumatized by the horror of the carnage, the Balinese reacted at first with an outburst of anger toward their aggressors. Then, very quickly, came a time of

---

[31] "*Bali adalah satu kesatuan agama, adat dan budaya.* [...] *Bila Bali memang sudah menjadi daerah khusus, dengan sendirinya Bali mempunyai hak penuh mengatur daerahnya sendiri. Termasuk dalam menonjolkan Kebaliannya*" (*Bali Post*, September 14, 1999).

'introspection' (*mulat sarira*), of intense soul-searching. The bombing was seen as a warning that something must be out of balance in Bali, that all was not well on the island of the gods. Indeed, many regarded the strike as a punishment from the gods, a divine retribution for the sins of Kuta, where drugs and prostitution were allowed to flourish shamelessly. Too busy chasing the tourist dollars, the Balinese had disregarded their moral values and neglected their religious duties. Thus, in the words of one distinguished Balinese psychiatrist and medium, Luh Ketut Suryani: "The destruction happened because the Balinese people have already forgotten their Balinese-ness" (*Kehancuran terjadi karena orang Bali telah melupakan Kebalian mereka*) (*Sarad*, No. 32, November 2002: 24). As a matter of fact, this sort of reaction was not that different from the contempt expressed by the perpetrators of the bombing toward the immoral behavior of foreign tourists in Bali.

By and large, the Balinese responded to the bombing with an intensified religious fervor. Starting on the very next day, a series of rituals and prayers were convened in various locations, either by private organizations or by the provincial government. These culminated on November 15 with an elaborate and highly publicized purification ceremony (*Pamarisuddha Karipubhaya*), intended to cleanse the site of the bloodbath from all trace of pollution (*leteh*) and to restore cosmic order by liberating the souls of the dead victims from their earthly bonds. As a result, the Balinese succeeded in appropriating the traumatic event by accommodating it within their own frame of reference. In their eyes, by dealing appropriately with the situation in its intangible *niskala* aspects, it followed that it would become settled in the tangible *sakala* dimension[32] (Couteau 2003: 45). Indeed, for the Balinese, ritual is not only a material reflection of the invisible world but the real work (*karya*) of which the material world is the result.

Yet, if celebrating these cleansing rituals had comforted the Balinese and placated their gods, it hardly resolved the problems generated by the bombing, namely the collapse of an economy based on tourism and the severe social crisis which ensued. In the days following the attack on Kuta, thousands of tourists scrambled to get a flight out of Bali; during the subsequent months, the island's tourism industry almost ground to a halt. Furthermore, the attack had not only ruined Bali's economy, it had also convinced the Balinese that they were under siege and had to defend themselves against hostile outsiders. The precariousness

---

[32] Thus, it seems that many Balinese attributed to the purification ceremony the success of the chief of police, I Made Mangku Pastika (with the assistance of foreign forensic experts), in finding and arresting the perpetrators of the bombing. Building on his success, Pastika became governor of Bali in the first elections for this post in 2008, to which he was re-elected in 2013. He was succeeded in 2018 by I Wayan Koster.

of their economic situation, combined with a heightened feeling of insecurity, sharpened their sense of identity. In that way, the Kuta bombing marked a watershed in the Balinese perception of themselves as a vulnerable ethnic and religious minority within the Indonesian nation-state.

Given such a state of mind, it should not come as a surprise that one of the first Balinese reactions to the bombing had been to shut Bali off from the rest of Indonesia and specifically to close the island to outsiders. Thus, an influential Hindu Balinese intellectual, Putu Setia, the leader of the Forum of Indonesian Hindu Intellectuals (Forum Cendekiawan Hindu Indonesia, FCHI), wrote in the Indonesian news magazine *Tempo* a few days after the bombing: "The most important thing for the Balinese people now is to isolate the island of Bali [...] from the tumult and abuse of Indonesian politics" (*Yang paling penting dilakukan orang Bali sekarang ini adalah mengisolasi Pulau Bali [...] dari hingar-bingar dan carut-marut politik Indonesia*) (Setia 2002: 7).

In these circumstances, one might have expected a backlash by Hindu Balinese against Muslim communities when it transpired that the bombing had been committed in the name of Islam. Especially so as rumors circulated on the island that fanatical Muslims were attempting to extend religious and ethnic violence to Bali with the purpose of eventually securing an Islamic state. The fact that there was no communal retribution, barring a few exceptions, is due to several factors. First of all, even though there were some Balinese among the Indonesian victims, none of them were natives of Kuta. This was no doubt due to the fact that the shops and businesses around the bomb site did not belong to the local population, and that most of their employees were outsiders. Indeed, the bombing took place away from the settlement areas and moreover the nearby shrines (*palinggih*) remained relatively unscathed. Therefore, the Kuta community did not perceive the attack as directed against them but specifically against foreign tourists. Besides, not only were there numerous Muslims among the victims, but one of the first rescue volunteers to arrive on the site was an aid group headed by the leader of Kuta's Muslim community, Haji Agus Bambang Priyanto. Furthermore, leaders of the regional and national Muslim organizations were unanimous in readily condemning the bombing (Couteau 2003: 43).

But the most significant factor was certainly the calls for restraint from the local and provincial authorities and the cautious attitude of the Balinese media, intent on avoiding inter-religious and inter-ethnic conflicts. Early morning the very day after the bombing, a group of prominent public intellectuals, religious leaders from various denominations, security officers and government officials, who had gathered in the governor's office, made a solemn appeal to the population, urging them to remain calm and to preserve unity and solidarity on the island. In the weeks following the bombing, the provincial government and various local organizations managed to provide the people with inter-religious vigils and ritual outlets, through which they could channel their emotions and strengthen the cohesion between different communities. Moreover, the police's seriousness and effectiveness in investigating the bombing and arresting its perpetrators played a crucial role in defusing the tension-filled situation. Finally, and importantly, the Balinese—particularly tourism stakeholders—were very much aware that any inter-communal strife would further aggravate their economic problems and might destroy the island's prospects of getting tourists back. This was especially so at a time when Bali was being scrutinized by international media (Anggraeni 2003). Yet, behind an appearance of composure, discriminative measures were taken against non-Balinese immigrants through the authority of the *desa pakraman* and the empowerment of their *pacalang*. In addition, restrictions were enforced on migration from Java, allowing only those with valid identity cards and guaranteed jobs to enter Bali. But it turned out that after a few months this policy of population control was no longer rigorously enforced, as it appeared to be impossible to prevent internal migration to Bali.

In the meantime, various measures were being taken to assist the Balinese and restore the island's economy. A few days after the bombing, Indonesia's minister of culture and tourism, I Gede Ardika, a native Balinese, held a press conference in Bali outlining a tourism recovery plan. Thereafter, a Bali Tourism Recovery Committee was set up in Jakarta by key figures from government and business circles, who coined the slogan 'Bali for the World'. They came to Bali with lots of money and little understanding of the real issues facing the Balinese people. With the help of celebrities from the media and show business, they invited top Indonesian and international entertainers to the island to celebrate the New Year holidays in the presence of President Megawati and several members of her cabinet. This initiative was cold-shouldered by Balinese opinion leaders, who accused the committee of wasting precious money in orchestrating mega-concerts instead of using it more effectively to address Bali's urgent problems. In particular, they objected to the slogan 'Bali for the World', which they construed as selling out Bali for the sake of tourism, and advocated instead 'The World for Bali' (Wedakarna 2002; Putra 2004a: 217–20).

This was not the only disagreement between the Balinese and other parties. The idea of a memorial at the site of the bombing had been voiced soon after the attack. While the Australian government pushed for organizing a commemoration ceremony, the Indonesian authorities and the Badung district, which presides over Kuta, were eager to promote a sense of restored harmony that would boost Bali's recovery as a tourism destination. They wanted to erect a monument in time for the first commemoration ceremony of the bombing in October 2003 when world attention would again be turned toward Bali. This idea was hotly debated in Balinese media, as many Balinese opinion leaders believed that the memorializing of a catastrophe would only perpetuate its adverse spiritual and social impact (Lewis, Lewis and Putra 2013).

Precisely one year after the bombing, in October 2003, a joint report was issued by the World Bank, the United Nations Development Programme and the United States Agency for International Development (UNDP/World Bank 2003). Upon releasing the report, the country director for the World Bank stated that there had been no comprehensive policy response to Bali's economic crisis, because of poor coordination, planning and budgetary mechanisms among the various government agencies. The report found that Bali was facing a harsher, longer economic crisis than initially expected. Average incomes across Bali were down 40 percent while 30 percent of workers were affected by job losses, and children were increasingly dropping out of school. Among those losing their jobs, many had returned to their home villages. There, they had to rely on their relatives or try to eke out a living as farmers. But toiling in the muddy rice fields was by no means easy, especially after one had become accustomed to the financial rewards and prestige attached to a job in tourism. Moreover, plots of cultivable land were generally too small to accommodate any additional labor force.

Most importantly, the report deplored the fact that the economic crisis had not led to a fundamental reassessment by Balinese policy-makers about the island's development priorities. The aim of the recovery plan implemented by the government was to bring the tourists back as fast and as many as possible, both foreign and domestic.[33] Former questions about the sustainability of tourism

---

[33] After a sharp slump in foreign arrivals, tourism began to recover in earnest in 2004, until Bali was hit for the second time by an Islamist terrorist attack on October 1, 2005. Unlike what had happened previously, there was no mass exodus of tourists. Nonetheless, arrivals went down markedly in 2006, to rise sharply anew from 2007 onward, with an average annual growth of visitors arrivals of about 15 percent. But the composition of the market had changed significantly, with mostly Asian and domestic tourists, as government agencies had developed a new strategy that sought to stimulate domestic tourism and diversify the source of international visitors. Thus, in 2019, before tourism was hit by the Covid-19 pandemic, Bali welcomed around 17 million visitors, a number comprised of about 6.3 million foreign tourists and some 10.7 million domestic travelers. To deal with this massive influx of visitors, the Ngurah Rai International Airport was expanded in 2014 in order to be able to accommodate 25 million passengers per year. All this for a 6,500 km2 island, with a population of about 4.5 million inhabitants, including several tens of thousands foreign residents. With hotel facilities standing at close to 150,000 rooms, to which one should add thousands of condominiums, luxury estates and villas owned by Indonesians and foreigners alike, the

growth were only given lip service. The report's final recommendation was for Bali to diversify its economy in order to make it more resilient, which implied seeking a more sustainable model of tourism instead of chasing ever more tourist dollars. Accordingly, it stressed that a concerted effort must be made to wean Bali off its overdependence on tourism by developing opportunities in handicrafts and agriculture.

By the time international agencies were assessing the current economic and social situation in Bali, a group of concerned Balinese opinion leaders and policy makers were formulating their own views on the direction they wanted their island to take.

Ajeg Bali and the politics of Balinese identity

On August 1, 2003, a seminar entitled '*Strategi Menuju Keajegan Bali*' ('Strategy towards a strong and resilient Bali')[34] was organized in an international hotel by the *Bali Post*. The papers presented at this seminar were then published in a special edition of the *Bali Post* to celebrate its 55th anniversary on August 16. They were reprinted in book format in January 2004 (Satria Naradha 2004), along with a collection of essays by prominent public intellectuals (Putra 2004b). In his editorial, the chief editor (and owner) of the *Bali Post*, Anak Bagus Gede Satria Naradha,[35] explained that the purpose of the *Ajeg Bali* strategy was to "defend Balinese identity" (*menjaga identitas Bali*) and to "preserve Balinese culture" (*melestarikan kebudayaan Bali*). The problem, he said, is that the Balinese have forgotten their Balinese-ness (*Kebalian*), "which is based on religion, tradition and culture" (*berdasarkan agama, adat dan budaya*). They have to strengthen themselves if they want to avoid being overcome by the cultural hegemony of globalization, with its trail of consumerism, commercialism and commodification. The critical situation of

---

tourist carrying capacity of Bali has long been considerably exceeded—it had been estimated by the SCETO report to be around 24,000 rooms.

[34] *Ajeg* is a Balinese word, which translates in Indonesian as *tegak* (upright, erect) or *kukuh* (strong, firm) (Warna 1990: 9). The term has a further connotation of stability, tenacity and resilience (Bawa 2004: 251).

[35] Anak Bagus Gede Satria Naradha is the son of Ketut Nadha, who founded *Suara Indonesia* in 1948, which after undergoing several name changes became the *Bali Post* in 1972. He progressively took over the paper in the 1990s and gave it a more assertive orientation. Since then, and particularly since the onset of *Reformasi*, the *Bali Post* has become the main channel for the Balinese ethnic revival. Over the years, Satria Naradha has built the powerful Bali Post Media Group, which includes a TV station (Bali TV), several radio stations, and a number of newspapers and magazines. These combined media have a major influence on the dissemination of information and the formation of public opinion in Bali (MacRae and Putra 2007: 174–5).

Bali is due not only to the bombing but also to the fact that the Balinese people have lost control of their island, which is overloaded with construction, exploited by foreign investors, colonized by Jakarta, invaded by migrant workers and threatened by Islam. Now, "Bali is on the verge of destruction" (*Bali di ambang kehancuran*), and "the Balinese feel like foreigners on their own land" (*orang Bali merasa terasing di tanahnya sendiri*). In short, "Bali must be rescued" (*Bali harus diselamatkan*). In this critical situation, *Ajeg Bali* aims to "preserve the Balinese culture so that Bali does not lose its Balinese-ness" (*melestarikan kebudayaan Bali agar Bali tidak kehilangan identitas Kebaliannya*) (Satria Naradha 2004: 2–5).

The slogan *Ajeg Bali* was initially coined by the governor of Bali, I Dewa Made Beratha on May 26, 2002, at the opening of the Bali TV Station, whose mission was "to bring forth a strong and resilient Bali" (*mewujudkan Ajeg Bali*). And one of the regular programs of Bali TV has been a cultural talk show called *Ajeg Bali*. But it was only after the Kuta bombing that *Ajeg Bali* became a pervasive catchword, which one encountered not only in *Bali Post* articles and Bali TV talk shows, but also in seminars and public events, as well as in electoral meetings.[36] Clearly, the *Ajeg Bali* discourse was used to secure the power of local elites, who positioned themselves as saviors of Balinese identity against real and perceived threats at the island's shores by establishing an 'us versus them' politics.

Satria Naradha had a definite political agenda in launching his *Ajeg Bali* campaign. He was concerned not only with the predicament of post-bomb Bali but also with the political fragmentation of the island, which had been exacerbated by the laws on regional autonomy. In order to strengthen and unify Bali, and to attract political support from the rest of Indonesia, Satria Naradha invited high-ranking officials and dignitaries (not only the governor, *bupati*, and the mayor of Denpasar, but also the Indonesian president and cabinet ministers, the Sultan of Yogyakarta, etc.) to sign stone inscriptions (*prasasti*) endorsing his *Ajeg Bali* campaign. This was a practice inspired by former royal patronage, by which rulers made solemn proclamations, and which had been taken over by the New Order regime to commemorate official events. These inscriptions are now set on the façade of the head office of the Bali Post Media Group, an imposing

---

[36] Thus, one could read on banners erected during the campaign for the 2004 presidential election: 'Bring forth a strong and resilient Bali / Choose a President with Balinese blood / Megawati Soekarnoputri' (*Wujudkan Ajeg Bali / Pilih Presiden Berdarah Bali / Megawati Soekarnoputri*). To drive the point home, the words *berdarah Bali* (to have Balinese blood) were outlined in bright red.

building called the Gedung Pers Bali K. Nadha, located in the suburbs of Denpasar.

However, apart from the vaguely phrased intentions to strengthen Balinese culture from within and protect it against threats from outside (MacRae 2010: 18), the fact remains that very few practical solutions were suggested by the participants of the *Ajeg Bali* seminar in August 2003. Admittedly, besides having become a compulsory reference in Balinese public discourses, as well as the topic of further seminars—including one entitled 'Ajeg Bali, between Slogan and Implementation' (*Ajeg Bali, antara Slogan dan Implementasi*)—the so-called *Ajeg Bali* strategy resulted in several initiatives. In addition to *Ajeg Bali* competitions among schoolchildren and prizes awarded to *Ajeg Bali* teachers, the main practical measure was the launching by Satria Naradha in May 2005 of a cooperative (Koperasi Krama Bali, KKB), to strengthen the economic standing of the Balinese people vis-à-vis their competitors by granting soft loans to needy local small traders and entrepreneurs. Thanks to these grants, it was hoped that Balinese would no longer be tempted to sell their land to foreign investors.[37] Another initiative taken by Satria Naradha was the establishment in August 2005 of the Lembaga Kajian Strategis Ajeg Bali (Institute of Strategic Studies to Make a Strong and Resilient Bali), to solicit contributions from Balinese intellectuals eager to work toward the recovery of Bali. The new institute was inaugurated on October 8, 2005, a few days after the second Islamist terrorist attack, during a seminar titled 'Challenges and Opportunities of Ajeg Bali in the Global Era' (*Tantangan dan Peluang Ajeg Bali dalam Era Global*).

At first sight, *Ajeg Bali* would appear to be a mere follow-up of the discourses of *Kebalian* and *Pariwisata Budaya*. In Bali, traditional values have periodically been drawn upon at critical moments, and the new slogan seems to carry the same message as before in a new guise. Indeed, in Balinese *ajeg* denotes the idea of persistence, just like the word *lestari* in Indonesian, which brings *Ajeg Bali* very close to the catchphrase *pelestarian budaya* (cultural preservation), in vogue during the New Order. Yet, in the meantime the situation had changed rather drastically, and *Ajeg Bali* differed on at least two counts from previous articulations of Balinese identity. On the one hand, since the Kuta bombing the Balinese were clearly on the defensive and their plea had a stronger sense of urgency—even of desperation—than ever before. Accordingly, the discourse of *Ajeg Bali* captured a much harder-edged notion of Balinese-ness, one that was

---

[37] As the saying goes, in *Ajeg Bali* parlance: 'The Balinese sell their land to buy *bakso*, whereas the newcomers sell *bakso* to buy land' (*Krama Bali jual tanah untuk beli bakso, warga pendatang jual bakso untuk beli tanah*). *Bakso* is a popular Indonesian dish of meatball soup peddled by itinerant street vendors.

under siege on a number of fronts and in need of guarding itself against the perils assailing the island from all sides—globalization, tourism, Jakarta, immigrants, Islam, terrorism and so on. The bombing had hurt the Balinese not only in their economic mainstay but even more so in their honor, if not in their virility.[38] It shook their nerves and raised their sense of *jengah*, which is a particular Balinese feeling of shame mixed with anger. Hence the character at once protective and assertive of their new posture, much more exclusive than the statement of their identity in terms of *Kebalian*. Whereas the discourse of *Kebalian* was descriptive, *Ajeg Bali* was meant to be performative.

On the other hand, *Ajeg Bali* was much more divisive than previous articulations of Balinese identity. Even though the policy of Cultural Tourism did not really meet the expectations of its initiators, the ideological discourse which supported it is still being eagerly embraced by most Balinese. And even when tourism development in Bali was contested in the 1990s, it was precisely in the name of Cultural Tourism. Now, contrary to Satria Naradha's purpose, the *Ajeg Bali* campaign, which appealed to the Balinese people to close ranks in the face of external threats, gave rise to both skepticism and criticism from various quarters on the island (Allen and Palermo 2005).

To begin with, in the eyes of a number of Balinese (and foreign) observers, *Ajeg Bali* was really no more than an empty shell, a rhetorical device, to which public figures were simply expected to pay lip service.[39] Moreover, the formula was vague enough to mean different things to different people, and to be manipulated by powerful actors for their own ends. For some, it was an assertion of ethnic and cultural identity, a way to remind the Balinese to be faithful to their *Kebalian*; for others, it was a nostalgic retreat to a perceived authentic and unadulterated Balinese past; for still others, it was a filter through which to select from external influences those that fit Balinese cultural values; for yet others again, it was an aspiration for Bali to become peaceful and prosperous with the return of the tourists. In any event, two main positions can be distinguished in the Balinese reaction that gave rise to the *Ajeg Bali* slogan—a primordialist

---

[38] It is significant that whereas the discourse of Cultural Tourism portrayed Bali in the guise of a pretty girl whose virtue was threatened by visitors vying for her favors, in the *Ajeg Bali* campaign the island was depicted in terms much more masculine and aggressive (Santikarma 2003c).

[39] In Indonesia, social problems tend to be treated as moral problems. Hence an inclination for a normative approach, expressed through the recurrent use of injunctions, such as *harus*, *mesti* ('must'), *perlu* ('necessary'), *harap*, *moga-moga*, *mudah-mudahan* ('let's hope'), *jangan* ('don't'), and so forth. Hence also a taste for incantatory maxims and mottoes, which seem to acquire a life of their own, as if the situation would be under control once it has been labelled. In this respect, both *Pariwisata Budaya* and *Ajeg Bali* function as discourses without authors, as some sort of *mantra* giving the assurance that the material reality will coincide with what one says about it. This goes a long way to explaining that, from one slogan to the next, it is difficult to escape a certain sense of déjà-vu.

posture fostering an exclusive ethnic and religious identification that reflected a sense of disenfranchisement, and an instrumentalist tool to withstand the economic competition of newcomers by fighting for increased empowerment of the Balinese community (Putra 2004a: 227; Ari Dwipayana 2005: 10; Schulte Nordholt 2007: 60).

As for the critics, they came from two opposing sides, which is clear evidence of the ambivalence of *Ajeg Bali*.[40] Progressive public intellectuals reproached its promoters for freezing Balinese society by preserving outdated customs and values that buttressed abusive privileges of traditional elites whose power had been jeopardized by *Reformasi*. Quite a few of them saw in *Ajeg Bali* a return to the Dutch cultural policy of *Baliseering*, which they denounced as an attempt to turn Bali into a living museum for the sole enjoyment of tourists (Suryawan 2009, Chap. 4). They recalled that the *Baliseering* policy, which had the backing of the conservative nobility assembled behind *Bali Adnjana*, was rejected by the modernist commoner movement Surya Kanta, whose leaders wanted the Balinese people to adapt to the changing times. Further, they charged that, in fostering social stability and normative consensus, the *Ajeg Bali* campaign resulted in putting down any dissent and criticism, by accusing its opponents of disturbing the romantic image of Bali promoted by the tourism industry.

According to these critics, the problem at hand was not one of preservation—as if Bali was already *ajeg* and had to be kept that way—but of transformation, in order for the Balinese to become better equipped to confront the challenge of globalization. Instead of complaining about migrant workers and foreign investors taking over the tourism industry and appropriating its revenue, the Balinese people should acquire the professional proficiency that would allow them to compete for job and business opportunities with their challengers. Otherwise, they would be pushed aside by outsiders and would indeed become foreigners in their own island.

Furthermore, these same critics objected to the reified and simplistic vision of Bali as a homogeneous and harmonious society threatened from outside, which was not only illusory but dangerous. They denounced a xenophobic ideology that fostered primordial ethnic and religious identification by erecting boundaries between Balinese and non-Balinese and by sparking Hindu

---

[40] An issue of the magazine *Sarad* was devoted to a debate on *Ajeg Bali*, bringing together Ketut Sumarta, Made Kembar Kerepun, Gusti Ngurah Bagus, Nyoman Wijaya, and AA. GN. Ari Dwipayana (*Sarad*, No. 43, November 2003: 20–41). See also Santikarma (2003b, 2003c), Suryawan (2004), Wijaya (2004), Ari Dwipayana (2005) and Atmadja (2010).

fundamentalism as a response to Islamic pressure. This protectionist stance was delusive, they said, for Bali's plight did not come from beyond its shores but arose from within Balinese society itself. Witness the incidence of social strife on the island, which had risen sharply after the collapse of the New Order. Thus, in December 2003, the Balinese magazine *Sarad* dedicated its main feature to debating intra-Balinese conflicts. Its investigators registered no less than 88 violent mass conflicts since 1997, most of them having to do with customary law disputes, referred to as *kasus adat*, others between political parties or youth gangs (*Sarad*, No. 44, December 2003: 20–37).

Whereas progressive intellectuals associated *Ajeg Bali* with the rise of Hindu fundamentalism, Hindu religious leaders accused its promoters of fostering Balinese cultural and ethnic identity to the detriment of the Hindu religion. Thus, the Hindu magazine *Raditya* framed its December 2004 headlines on the question: '*Ajeg Bali* or *Ajeg Hindu?*' (*Raditya*, No. 89, December 2004: 7–15).[41] According to its chief editor, Putu Setia, if the purpose of *Ajeg Bali* was to preserve and promote Balinese culture, then it concerned Muslim and Christian Balinese as much as it did Hindu Balinese. If this were the case, Bali was doomed to meet with the same fate as Java after the fall of Majapahit under the pressure of Islam, when the Javanese discarded their religion while holding on to their culture. Conversely, if the aim was to curb the coming of Muslim migrants and to limit the construction of mosques on the island, *Ajeg Hindu* should be promoted instead. Indeed, "as long as the Hindu religion is still *ajeg* in Bali, the Balinese culture will be *ajeg* as well" (*sepanjang agama Hindu masih ajeg di Bali maka kebudayaan Bali akan tetap ajeg*), as "Balinese culture has its source in the Hindu religion" (*kebudayaan Bali bersumber dari agama Hindu*) (*Raditya*, No. 89, December 2004: 7). In short, for Hindu fundamentalists, it was religion and not culture or tradition which was the ultimate guarantor of Balinese identity.

All in all, *Ajeg Bali* proves to be a discursive articulation meant to suture the disjunctures and antagonisms that fracture contemporary Balinese society (Fox 2010). However, the contradictory criticism around *Ajeg Bali* attests to the disintegration of the discursive construction of *Kebalian*, torn between *adat* and *agama*, between ethnic belonging and religious affiliation. While progressive public intellectuals attempt to make their society adapt to the challenges of a globalized world, and Hindu fundamentalists are busy devising a universal religion true to their idealized vision of Vedic India, most Balinese are inclined

---

[41] There were contributions from Putu Setia, Ketut Wiana and Made Titib. See also Titib (2005).

to find refuge in the parochial ideal of their customary village community. Since what defines them as a non-Muslim and non-Christian minority in a multi-religious nation is no longer their exclusive property, while their religious identity has become controversial, it is understandable that, faced with an aggression from outside, the Balinese are withdrawing into what is most exclusively theirs, that is, not *agama Hindu* but *adat Bali*.

The Benoa Bay reclamation project controversy

Over time, *Ajeg Bali*'s appeal eventually faded away and a new rallying cry has taken its place: '*Bali Tolak Reklamasi Teluk Benoa*' ('Bali Rejects Benoa Bay Reclamation'), this time in response not to an Islamist attack but to an aggression of another nature, a gigantic tourism development project in the heart of the south of the island (Cabasset, Couteau and Picard 2017; Bräuchler 2018, 2020; Wardana 2019, Chap. 6).

In July 2013, the Balinese learned from the press that four major investors were competing for a massive reclamation project in Benoa Bay that would see the development of luxury tourist facilities, including a Disneyland-style theme park, apartments, hotels, villas, entertainment centers, a golf course and even a Formula One racing circuit. Then, during a plenary meeting between the governor and the Balinese provincial parliament (DPRD Bali), a legislator suddenly interrupted the meeting to ask about the project. The governor, Made Mangku Pastika, denied any knowledge of it, despite all the evidence to the contrary. At the same time, he argued that land reclamation would be preferable to building tourism facilities on productive and fertile land.

Shortly after this official denial, the *Bali Post* informed its readership that six months earlier, on December 26, 2012, out of the public eye, the governor had in fact issued a permit authorizing the company PT Tirta Wahana Bali Internasional (TWBI)—based in Jakarta and headed by an influential businessman, Tomy Winata, owner of the powerful conglomerate Artha Graha—to utilize, develop and manage 838 hectares in Benoa Bay (over half of its surface area), with a 30-year concession and the possibility of an additional 20-year extension.[42] This authorization was allegedly based on a feasibility study from Udayana University's Community Research Center and a recommendation letter issued by DPRD Bali, which stated that the development of Benoa Bay would

---

[42] *SK 2138/02-C/HK/2012 tentang Izin dan Hak Pemanfaatan, Pengembangan dan Pengelolaan Wilayah Perairan Teluk Benoa.*

not cause any environmental damage. However, when questioned by journalists, the Udayana researchers insisted that their feasibility study was not completed, and could therefore not be used as grounds for the Bali provincial administration to issue a development permit.

Very soon, a number of Balinese tourism stakeholders, academics, and environmentalists expressed concern about the reclamation project. They reminded the provincial administration that, due to the oversupply of tourist facilities in southern Bali, a moratorium on hotel development had been imposed in 2011 by Governor Pastika himself, even though the *bupati* of Badung and Gianyar, as well as the mayor of Denpasar, had openly ignored it. Any massive tourism development in what was already the most densely populated area on the island would increase the number of immigrants, worsen the shortage of water and electricity, and exacerbate traffic congestion and endemic pollution. Moreover, the reclamation project would increase coastal erosion and flooding, and cause irremediable damage to the marine ecosystem and to the mangroves bordering Benoa Bay. Critics recalled the ecological disaster caused by the reclamation of nearby Serangan Island, whose unfinished development had been imposed by two of Suharto's sons in 1994. Since then, nearby reefs were swamped in sediment, seaweed farms destroyed and wave patterns changed. And finally they pointed out that Benoa Bay had been designated a 'conservation area' (*kawasan konservasi*) by a 2011 presidential regulation,[43] so the governor's decree was illegal.

In August 2013, opponents of the project regrouped into the Balinese People's Forum Against Benoa Bay Reclamation (Forum Rakyat Bali Tolak Reklamasi Teluk Benoa, better known as ForBALI), a Denpasar-based coalition of opinion leaders, NGO activists, youth groups, journalists, academics, students, artists, musicians and village representatives, under the leadership of I Wayan Gendo Suardana, an outspoken lawyer and former head of the Balinese branch of the Indonesian Environmental Society (Wahana Lingkungan Hidup Indonesia, WALHI), the oldest and largest environmental organization in Indonesia, affiliated with Friends of the Earth International.[44] They staged protests against the planned reclamation and demanded that the governor revoke his permit. Bowing to the extent and the determination of the growing public opposition, Pastika caved in and revoked the reclamation permit on August 16. But in the

---

[43] *Peraturan Presiden (Perpres) RI No.45 Tahun 2011 tentang Rencana Tata Ruang Kawasan Perkotaan Denpasar, Badung, Gianyar, dan Tabanan.*

[44] The proponents of the reclamation project, far fewer than its opponents, have joined together to establish the Forum Bali Harmoni.

process, he gave the green light to TWBI to carry out a forecast study of the Benoa Bay reclamation.[45]

In September 2013, the president of Udayana University declared that the Community Research Center found the reclamation of Benoa Bay plan to be unviable technically, environmentally, socially, culturally, and economically (*Hasil Final FS Unud. Reklamasi Tak Layak*, Bali Post, September 3, 2013). Nonetheless, at the seeming behest of Tomy Winata, President Susilo Bambang Yudhoyono issued on May 30, 2014, shortly before the end of his term of office, a presidential regulation (*Peraturan Presiden No.51/2014*) revoking his own previous regulation that had declared Benoa Bay a conservation area and reclassifying its status into a 'cultivation area' (*kawasan budidaya*), henceforth liable to reclamation. Yudhoyono's outgoing administration then issued the official state permits for the project just before President-elect Joko Widodo was due to be sworn in.

Emboldened by this propitious turnaround, Tomy Winata promoted his project with renewed vigor. Referring no longer to *reklamasi* but to *revitalisasi*, he claimed that he would revitalize Benoa Bay's ecosystem which was already in a state of advanced degradation. In its new guise, called Nusa Benoa, his $3 billion reclamation project, now reduced to 700 hectares, includes the creation of twelve artificial islets connected by bridges and the establishment of luxury resorts, condominiums, villas, malls, a yacht marina, a water theme park, a botanical garden and other residential facilities. The planned development is structured around the Bali Mandara Toll Road connecting Sanur, the airport, Nusa Dua and Benoa harbor, which was inaugurated in 2013 and appears in retrospect as the first step of TWBI's reclamation project.

President Yudhoyono's new decree triggered a wave of protests, which are so far the largest social mobilization critical of tourism development in Bali. While Governor Pastika appeared to temporize, ForBALI's lawyers prepared a judicial review request before the Supreme Court in an attempt to block TWBI's project on legal grounds, but this came to nought. Failing on this front, ForBALI began organizing mass demonstrations, marches, debates and concerts involving ever-growing numbers of participants. At numerous crossroads all over southern Bali, huge artistically decorated billboards sprang up with the constantly recurring slogan '*Bali Tolak Reklamasi Berkedok Revitalisasi Teluk Benoa / Batalkan Perpres 51/2014*' ('Bali Rejects Reclamation Masquerading as Revitalization of Benoa Bay / Revoke Presidential Decree 51/2014'). After the

---

[45] *SK 1727/01-B/HK/2013 tentang Izin Studi Kelayakan Rencana Pemanfaatan, Pengembangan dan Pengelolaan Wilayah Perairan Teluk Benoa.*

election of the new president, Joko Widodo, in October 2014, ForBALI pressed him to abrogate his predecessor's decree and return Benoa Bay to its original status as a conservation area. Meanwhile, the issue had become so politically sensitive that a debate on Benoa Bay reclamation scheduled at the prominent Ubud Writers and Readers Festival in October 2015 was cancelled by the police and Wayan Gendo Suardana was banned from speaking.

It is interesting to compare the opposition to Benoa Bay reclamation to the first Balinese resistance against a large tourism resort in 1993, the Bali Nirwana Resort near the seaside temple of Tanah Lot. The protests were driven by academics, students, and Hindu activists, supported by the *Bali Post*, and their argument mainly revolved around the religious significance of the site. Despite having succeeded in forcing Parisada to enact a *bhisama* decreeing that a 'sacred area' must be maintained between the temple and the resort, this first opposition movement eventually failed, repressed by the police and suppressed by the government, but it marked a turning point in the Balinese attitude toward tourism development on their island.

Twenty years later, the protest was predominantly directed against environmental destruction and socio-economic damages, but it soon evolved into growing exasperation, and even despair, among a broad and sustained portion of Balinese public opinion, confronted with capitalist exploitation and massive expropriation. So angry and distressed were some of the opponents that they threatened to 'fight to the death' (*puputan*), after the fashion of their glorious ancestors, if the project went ahead. They viewed their fight as a resistance to a new form of colonization driven by investors from Jakarta with the support of the government.

Above all, by combining offline and online activism, the Benoa Bay protest benefited from a much wider exposure than its predecessor ever did, in Bali as well as abroad. Through their savvy use of the web and social media, such as Twitter, Facebook, Instagram and YouTube, relayed by advocates of social and environmental causes the world over, the ForBALI activists were able to reach a large audience by soliciting support outside Bali: an online petition was circulated on Change.org, a documentary film titled *Bali versus Mass Development* was broadcast on YouTube, and the whole affair was widely reported in both national and foreign media.

Despite this widespread support, however, the focus on the environment eventually failed as a sustainable argument, as both sides claimed that they wanted to protect and restore Benoa Bay. In order to gain stronger grassroots legitimacy, ForBALI needed to mobilize the Balinese population at large along the lines of *adat* and *agama*. In January 2016, 39 customary villages around Benoa Bay united in the Pasubayan Desa Pakraman Tolak Reklamasi Teluk Benoa, an umbrella organization for coordinating anti-reclamation activities and to win over new villages. What really made the *desa pakraman* move was a specifically religious argument, the identification of Benoa Bay as a 'sacred area' (*kawasan suci*) that was threatened by the reclamation plan. To compile knowledge about sacred sites in Benoa Bay, ForBALI set up a student investigation team that conducted research in the villages around the bay. They identified 70 sacred sites which they set out on a map, including visible (*sakala*) and invisible (*niskala*) temples and spots used for specific rituals. The map of sacred sites became an important legitimation tool for the resistance movement, and it was presented to Parisada in early April 2016 (Lanus 2016).

Up to that time, Parisada had remained in cautious expectancy, despite the demands of reclamation opponents that it take an official stand on what they regarded as an aggression against Balinese religious identity. The problem was that its leaders were divided over what decision to take in respect of the development project. Moreover, there were insinuations that Parisada had benefited from generous hand-outs from TWBI, which might explain its hesitancy about taking sides.[46] Finally, building on the 1994 *Bhisama Kesucian Pura*, Parisada issued a decree on Benoa Bay on April 9, 2016. However, internal power struggles—between the Assembly of Priests (*Sabha Pandita*) and the Assembly of Laymen (*Sabha Walaka*), but also within the priesthood—prompted the PHDI to issue two Benoa Bay related decrees on that same day (Bräuchler 2018: 380; see also Bräuchler 2020). One clearly defined Benoa Bay as a sacred area in its title (*Keputusan Pesamuhan Sabha Pandita PHDI No.1/Kep/SP PARISADA/IV/2016 Tentang Kawasan Suci Teluk Benoa*); the title of the other omitted the word 'sacred' (*Keputusan Pesamuhan Sabha Pandita PHDI No.03/Sabha Pandita Parisada/IV/2016 Tentang Rekomendasi Kawasan Strategis Pariwisata Nasional Besakih dan Kawasan Teluk Benoa*). The latter included a contested paragraph that opened doors for reclamation, stating that Benoa Bay "can be utilized and processed for the welfare of the people as long as it does not tarnish and undermine its sanctity values" (*dapat dimanfaatkan dan diolah untuk kesejahteraan rakyat sepanjang tidak menodai serta merusak nilai-*

---

[46] This was the case in particular for one of the most vocal advocates of the project, I Ketut Wiana, a member of the PHDI's Executive Board, accused of being Tomy Winata's 'spiritual advisor' (*penasihat spiritual*). Parisada was not the only authority suspected of taking bribes, as the Bali Corruption Watch organization formally requested in May 2016 the Indonesian Committee for the Eradication of Corruption (Komite Pemberantasan Korupsi, KPK) to investigate allegations charging the governor with accepting a bribe to approve TWBI's project.

nilai kesuciannya). It so happened that the president of the PHDI, Ida Padanda Gde Ketut Sebali Tianyar Arimbawa, a dedicated opponent of Benoa Bay reclamation, could not attend the meeting on April 9 as he was being treated in hospital. And while the head of the *Sabha Walaka*, Putu Wirata Dwikora, was clearly committed to supporting the resistance movement, the *Sabha Pandita* refused to take a firm stand on the reclamation issue.[47]

Subsequently, on August 25, 2018, TWBI lost the location permit of the land reclamation project because the company failed to get the project's feasibility study approved by the Ministry of Marine Affairs and Fisheries before the permit's expiration date. The newly elected governor and deputy-governor, I Wayan Koster and Tjokorda Oka Artha Ardhana Sukawati, seized that opportunity to publicly declare that the controversial reclamation project would not be allowed to proceed under their administration. However, what the resistance movement thought was victory quickly turned into a disappointment when the Ministry of Marine Affairs and Fisheries issued a new permit for TWBI on November 28, 2018. Shortly thereafter, on December 21, Governor Koster sent a letter to President Joko Widodo requesting he abrogate the 2014 presidential resolution and restore Benoa Bay's status as a maritime conservation area. While this letter remained unanswered, it so happened that, in October 2019, the Ministry of Marine Affairs and Fisheries issued a decree which designated Benoa Bay as a conservation area.

In any event, with the Covid-19 pandemic striking Bali with full force, the future of Benoa Bay—indeed of Bali as a tourism destination—remains pending.

---

[47] Interview, Ida Padanda Gde Ketut Sebali Tianyar Arimbawa, *Dharma Adhyaksa* PHDI Pusat and Putu Wirata Dwikora, *Ketua Sabha Walaka* PHDI Pusat, Dewan Perwakilan Daerah, Denpasar, May 16, 2016. See '*Dualisme Keputusan PHDI*', *Majalah Bali Post*, No. 138, May 16–22, 2016: 8–11; *Media Hindu*, No. 146, April 2016: 17–26; *Raditya*, No. 226, May 2016: 20–1.

Chapter 8

Balinese Religion in the Age of *Reformasi*

Indonesia's impressive political democratization after the downfall of President Suharto in May 1998 has hardly been conducive to religious pluralism. Instead, it has led to increasing conflict over just what constitutes a proper and legal form of religion (Hefner 2021). Although constitutional and regulatory reforms were introduced that appeared to strengthen rights to religious freedom, the gradual enforcement of conservative Islamic orthodoxy actually led to a pattern of worsening religious intolerance, making religious minorities more anxious about their status (Lindsey and Butt 2016). What happened is that, whereas religion had been kept under strict surveillance by the authoritarian New Order regime, democracy allowed the rise of public religious expression, which resulted in increasing Islamization of Indonesian polity and society.

Initial signs of religious liberalization were promising, as on September 13, 1998, the Indonesian People's Consultative Assembly (MPR) adopted a new Human Rights Charter which provided for the freedom of citizens to practice their religion without specifying any particular religion (*Ketetapan Majelis Permusyawaratan Rakyat Republik Indonesia No.17/1998, Tentang Hak Asasi Manusia*). Yet, to this day, much of the politics and laws regulating religion inherited from the pre-*Reformasi* era are still in existence, obstructing a fuller realization of freedom of religion in Indonesia.

While only six religions are officially recognized,[1] the law also states that other religions and beliefs—falling within 'Beliefs in the One and Only God' (*Kepercayaan terhadap Tuhan Yang Maha Esa*)—are not forbidden. In some respects, the boundaries of limited religious pluralism in Indonesia might even appear to have been stretched in the *Reformasi* period, with a widening choice

---

[1] In January 2000, President Abdurrahman Wahid issued a formal presidential decision abrogating Suharto's presidential instruction that banned public celebration of Chinese religious and customary practices. Confucianism (*agama Khonghucu*) was officially reinstated as a legitimate religion in January 2006.

not only within normative religions but between 'religion' (*agama*) and 'belief' (*kepercayaan*) as well (Howell 2004, 2005). Thus, on December 29, 2006, the Indonesian parliament (Dewan Perwakilan Rakyat, DPR) passed the Population Administration Law (*Undang-Undang No.23/2006, Tentang Administrasi Kependudukan*) that authorized citizens whose religion or belief was not yet acknowledged as *agama* to leave blank the religious affiliation space on their national identity card (*Kartu Tanda Penduduk, KTP*). In practice, however, citizens without a bona fide religious affiliation would still see their civil rights discriminated against in matters of marriage, birth and funeral. It is precisely because of such discrimination that in November 2016 the Population Administration Law was challenged in the Constitutional Court (Mahkamah Konstitusi)[2] by representatives of several *aliran kepercayaan* and indigenous religions, who demanded to be allowed to fill in the name of their own religion/belief on their *KTP*. On November 7, 2017, the court decided that, alongside the recognized religions, the government should create a separate category for belief-followers (*Penghayat Kepercayaan*) on identity cards, without however specifying the particular belief adhered to. While the court's decision has been heralded as a constitutional recognition of 'beliefs' in Indonesia, in fact this recognition is still confined to 'Beliefs in the One and Only God', which implies monotheism (Butt 2020: 471). Indeed, when the Ministry of Interior issued regulations about new types of *KTP* in June 2018, these cards had a space with the mention '*Kepercayaan terhadap Tuhan Yang Maha Esa*' instead of '*Penghayat Kepercayaan*', as the court had required (Butt 2020: 472). That is to say that the religious issue remains unsettled in Indonesia, as no consensus has been achieved so far on freedom of religion, while the government is clearly reluctant to let go of state control over religion (Aragon 2021).

Additionally, the liberalization of the political system after four decades of tight control gave rise to a mushrooming of parties of all colors and convictions. With the requirement to adopt Pancasila as the sole foundation of political parties no longer enforced, leaving them free to choose their ideological orientation, new Islamist[3] parties and organizations sprang up that asked for a formal endorsement

---

[2] The Mahkamah Konstitusi was established in 2003 as part of democratic efforts to strengthen the separation of state powers in Indonesia.

[3] Regarding the distinction between 'Islamist' and 'Islamic', I align myself with the following position of Edward W. Walker: "By 'Islamism', I mean the normative political ideology that has as its core program the establishment of Islam as a state religion and the implementation of Islamic law (*shari'a*). [...] The adjective that I will use for Islamism is 'Islamist', while for Islam in general it is 'Islamic'" (Walker 2003: 22, n. 1; see further Mozaffari 2007). In other words, 'Islamism' is the product of the twin process of the religionization of politics and the politicization of religion.

of Islam by the state while seeking to impose the implementation of its tenets in private and public life. Yet, this forceful reassertion of political Islam has not translated into increased support for Islamist parties in the national elections, held every five years since 1999 (with direct presidential and gubernatorial elections held since 2004). Nonetheless, nominally 'secular' political parties have steadily Islamized their own image over the years to appeal to an electorate that is growing more self-consciously Muslim than in the past.

Most dramatically, the resurfacing of political Islam in Indonesia manifested itself during the early transition period with the emergence of a radical fringe of Muslim fundamentalists expressing themselves through street politics, engaging in *jihad* against Christians, as well as perpetrating terrorist acts (Van Bruinessen 2002; Feillard and Madinier 2011). While outbreaks of communal violence and terrorism abated eventually, radical Islamist groups and civil militias continue to harass and persecute religious minorities. Faced with the growing assertiveness of these vocal and visible few, the mainstream Muslim community appears to be paralyzed, while Islamist hardliners attempt to impose their own interpretation of the meaning of Islam, with a view to establishing their political legitimacy to regulate the social life of their co-religionists.

In 2000, seizing the opportunity of the debate over constitutional reform, two Islamist political parties in the newly elected parliament demanded reinsertion of the Jakarta Charter into the constitution in order to have official recognition of Islamic law with the Indonesian legal system. Their proposal was extensively discussed in the 2001 and 2002 MPR sessions, but it was rejected due to the opposition not only of the secularist and Christian parties but also of the two largest Muslim organizations, Nahdlatul Ulama and Muhammadiyah. Later, the debates shifted from the project of Islam becoming the foundation of the state to the obligation of the government to implement *syariah* (Hosen 2005; Hasan 2008). Whereas in the past the aim of the militant Islamist groups was to establish an Islamic state, by either legal or violent means, now their strategy appears to be to take over the state by establishing an Islamic society.

Thus, while failing to amend the constitution in order to impose *syariah* law nationwide, Islamist activists and political parties—with the backing of some secular nationalist parties eager to flaunt their Islamic credentials—took advantage of the enhanced authority of regional parliaments under the new regional autonomy legislation to get elements of *syariah* adopted into regional bylaws (*peraturan daerah syariah Islam*); this, despite the fact that religious matters fall specifically within the competence of the central government. Over the years, dozens of districts across the country promulgated *syariah*-inspired regulations setting out dress codes and norms of good behavior for women, banning the retail sale of alcohol, and requiring religious observances for Muslim schoolchildren and public servants (Hefner 2012; Buehler 2016). Civil rights activists, religious minorities, and some members of parliament have expressed growing concern over what they perceive as a rampant maneuver to force *syariah* law in Indonesia. They assert that such *syariah*-based regulations violate the constitution and have called on the government to exercise its constitutional jurisdiction to revoke these bylaws, but to no avail.

Muslim conservatives and Islamist militias have also made use of Sukarno's 1965 presidential decree on religious defamation—elevated to the status of national law in 1969 and commonly known as the 'Blasphemy Law'—to launch campaigns against so-called 'deviant sects' (*aliran sesat*). Arguing that the government has the obligation to prohibit interpretations that depart from the core teachings of the state-sanctioned religions, they demanded that sects propagating 'heretical' teachings about Islam be banned. And the fact is that the government is closely monitoring those groups associated with forms of Islam viewed as outside the mainstream, whose members are regularly harassed and charged with heresy, blasphemy, and insulting Islam (Olle 2006). Exclusivist trends in Muslim debates have been reinforced by the growing influence and conservative moralism of the Indonesian Council of Islamic Scholars (Majelis Ulama Indonesia, MUI) (Hefner 2019). In July 2005, MUI issued a highly controversial *fatwa* forbidding 'Religious Pluralism, Liberalism, and Secularism' (*Fatwa No.7/2005 Tentang Pluralisme, Liberalisme, Dan Sekularisme Agama*) as contrary to Islamic teachings (Ichwan 2013). To counter this conservative turn, a coalition of liberal non-government organizations lodged an application in October 2009 for judicial review of the Blasphemy Law with the Constitutional Court, on the grounds that it contravenes the freedom of religion guaranteed by the 1945 constitution and exposes religious minorities to persecution. The court's April 2010 judgement held that the Blasphemy Law did not contradict the constitutional right to freedom of religion and concluded that the state had legal authority to prohibit any interpretation that differed from mainstream religious teachings—thus confirming the right of the state to enforce Islamic orthodoxy as defined by MUI (Crouch 2012; see further Mursalin 2019, Chap. 7).[4]

Another step in the direction of strictly policing Indonesian social life to comply with conservative Islamic standards was the enactment of the

---

[4] It turns out that the PHDI, like institutional representatives of Indonesian Buddhism and Confucianism, but not of Protestantism and Catholicism, opposed the revision of the Blasphemy Law.

Pornography Law. In 2006, legislators from Islamist parties submitted to the parliament the draft of an Antipornography and Pornographic Action Bill (*Rancangan Undang Undang Antipornografi dan Pornoaksi*) (Allen 2007). This legislation criminalized not only publications and performances with sexually explicit content, but also the display of nudity or any behavior deemed indecent according to the codes of Muslim puritanism. The draft bill sparked heated debate and led to large demonstrations both for and against. Due to the public outcry, Indonesian lawmakers revised the draft to take into account cultural traditions and local sensitivities, and changed the bill's name to the Pornography Bill (*Undang-undang No.44/2008 Tentang Pornografi*). Eventually, despite vehement protests, the parliament passed the disputed Pornography Law in October 2008. The passage of the law was quickly slammed by human rights organizations, claiming that it threatens national unity, discriminates against minority groups and women, and harms religious pluralism in the country (Pausacker 2008).

Nowhere was the resistance to the Pornography Bill stronger than in Bali, where the governor vowed to oppose the new law, a stance that triggered a vehement polemic between Hindu Balinese and Islamist activists. Initially the bill had been viewed by the Balinese as an offense to their cultural identity and a threat to their tourism industry, but Islamist militancy convinced them that what was at risk was their own religious freedom (*Media Hindu*, No. 57, November 2008: 8–17). However, far from closing ranks to resist Islamist pressure, the Balinese Hindu community became more divided than ever on the issue of *agama Hindu*.

The reform of Parisada Hindu Dharma Indonesia

As seen in the previous chapter, by actually subsuming *agama Hindu* within *adat Bali*, the provincial regulation on *Desa Pakraman*, issued on March 21, 2001, led to a blurring of the distinction between *adat* and *agama*. The revival of Balinese *adat* accentuated tensions between Parisada's old guard and reformers promoting its regeneration, pitting a conservative faction grounded in village communities and courtly circles against a reform-minded faction driven by the urbanized middle class and the intelligentsia, who denounced Balinese customary ritual practices as parochial and outdated. Positions hardened on both sides, in that both ethnic and religious primordialism on the one hand, and democratic and reform-minded aspirations on the other, both formerly repressed, were henceforth given free rein. Furthermore, the demands of commoner descent groups (*warga*) were becoming more pressing, while institutional obstacles to the spread of Neo-Hindu devotional movements (*sampradaya*) had been removed.

This strife, which had been building up since Parisada's Seventh Congress in 1996, would come to a head during the Eighth Congress (*Mahasabha ke VIII*), held on September 20–24, 2001, at the Radisson Hotel in Sanur, Bali. Emboldened by the new wind of freedom, critical Hindu reformers had pinned high hopes on the upcoming congress and were calling for a true '*Parisada Reformasi*', free from the political manipulations that had prevailed under the New Order. And thanks to the newly granted press freedom, the media coverage of the congress and its repercussions were more important than ever.

Immediately upon President Suharto's resignation in May 1998, *Raditya* magazine had published an issue titled 'Hinduism and Reform' (*Hindu dan Reformasi*) (*Raditya*, No. 16, May 1998: 4–16). It appears that in the eyes of the reformers, Parisada had lost its legitimacy as a result of its compromises with the fallen regime. They objected to the leaders chosen by the Seventh Congress and requested their collective resignation. They reproached them for remaining passive during the political crisis that marked the end of the New Order, instead of taking a public stance in favor of *Reformasi*. They also criticized the lack of transparency in Parisada's financial management and accused its administrators of embezzlement (*Korupsi Kolusi Nepotisme*, *KKN*). Furthermore, they demanded the convening of an 'Extraordinary Congress' (*Mahasabha Luar Biasa*) to debate Parisada's future in the new political circumstances. Additionally, some activists advocated the creation of a Hindu political party (Partai Nasionalis Hindu Indonesia), to defend the interests of the Hindu community in the parliament in Jakarta and counter the newly established Islamist political parties.

The conservatives were not idle in the face of the wind of reform that was beginning to blow. Thus, in May 2000, a coterie of *padanda* from Karangasem publicized a solemn declaration (*kretesemaya*) stipulating that its signatories refused to officiate alongside priests belonging to other kinship groups (*soroh*). They also forbade their clients (*sisia*) to receive holy water (*nunas tirta*) from any other priests but themselves. This show of force was interpreted by reformers as a sign that the *padanda* were beginning to worry that their flock might escape their control (*Raditya*, No. 39, October 2000: 4–17).

One can no doubt see a reformers' riposte in the General Assembly of the Indonesian Hindu Community (*Pesamuan Agung Umat Hindu Indonesia*) convened by the Forum for Religious Awakening (Forum Penyadaran Dharma) under the leadership of I Gusti Ngurah Bagus in June 2000 at the Grand Bali Beach Hotel in Sanur. The assembly decided to found a Center for Hindu Studies (Pusat Kajian Hindu) to assist the Indonesian Hindu community in dealing with the urgent issues that it was facing.[5] According to some of its initiators, this center aimed to rival Parisada, while others asserted that it intended to compete with Universitas Hindu Indonesia, deemed too conservative. In any case, the Pusat Kajian Hindu never really became operational and virtually ceased its activities after the untimely death of Gusti Ngurah Bagus in October 2003.

In preparation for the Eighth Congress, the central Parisada (PHDI Pusat) organized four regional seminars in 2001 to debate the emergence of a 'new paradigm' (*Seminar Paradigma Baru Parisada*)—in Denpasar, Medan (Sumatra), Jakarta, and Palu (Sulawesi). To ensure a more democratic outcome in accord with the current spirit of reform, participants in the Denpasar seminar, held on May 20, proposed that from then on Parisada's leaders should be elected directly by the congress and no longer appointed by ad hoc committees. This was in order to avoid manipulation and pressure, as well as to put an end to the continuing domination by the *brahmana*. The new leaders should be able to fulfill their mission full time and they may not join political parties. Furthermore, Parisada's chairman would no longer be a priest but a layman, to ensure that the *padanda* could fully devote themselves to religious issues and that they did not run the risk of becoming involved in mundane controversies[6] (*Raditya*, No. 47, June 2001: 37–40). While reserving the place of honor for the priests, the reformers made no secret of their low esteem for the *padanda*, whom they reproached for confining themselves to their ritual practices and for being ignorant of ethical and theological issues—a criticism that had been raised in similar terms in *Djatajoe* magazine back in the 1930s. Under the leadership of a layman, Parisada should no longer limit its role to issuing 'instructions' (*bhisama*), but it should take an active part in leading the Indonesian Hindu community and in defending it against any offence or attack from hostile quarters. Moreover, the various Hindu organizations, NGOs (*lembaga swadaya masyarakat*) and foundations (*yayasan*), as well as the *warga* and the *sampradaya*, should now be given full recognition as an integral part of Parisada. Finally, Parisada should no longer be dominated by Balinese but be fully representative of the Indonesian Hindu community in its diversity (*kebhinekaan*),

---

[5] Interview, I Gusti Ngurah Bagus, Denpasar, April 15, 2001.
[6] The actual risk was all the more present in view of the allegations of misappropriation that were becoming increasingly pressing against Parisada's leadership, whom the reformers threatened to bring to justice. Therefore, they were eager to ensure that a *padanda* could not be implicated in an embezzlement case.

and *agama Hindu* ought to become a missionary religion in order to counter Muslim and Christian proselytism, following the example of the Vishva Hindu Parishad in India (*Raditya*, No. 48, July 2001: 6–29; *Sarad*, No. 20, August 2001: 26–40).

On July 21, 2001, Parisada Bali convened a symposium at Universitas Hindu Indonesia in response to the seminar organized in Denpasar by Parisada Pusat, which its leaders had refused to attend in protest against the presence of representatives of NGOs, foundations, *warga* and *sampradaya*. During this symposium, an official of the Bali Office of the Department of Religion (Kanwil Depag Propinsi Bali), I Gusti Gede Goda, embarked upon a critical offensive against the *sampradaya*, which he accused of being 'deviant sects' (*aliran sesat*), whose dissenting practices aroused controversies within the Hindu community and damaged its cohesion. This earned him an indignant rebuke from I Ketut Wiana, a prominent member of Parisada's Executive Board, who argued that the *sampradaya* were not to be confused with *aliran kepercayaan* but were in truth 'spiritual groups' (*kelompok spiritual*), originating in India and grounded in the Vedas. According to him, the actual *aliran sesat* were the traditionalist Balinese who refuse to conform to the Vedic tenets. The fault lay with the age-old collusion between princes and priests—between *puri* and *gria*—who conspired to perpetuate their hegemony by keeping the Balinese populace ignorant of its true religion[7] (*Raditya*, No. 50, September 2001: 6–33).

In view of this rising tension, it came as no surprise that Parisada's Eighth Congress was chaotic. One of the main issues under debate was the status of the *sampradaya*. Despite the opposition of most delegates of Parisada Bali—and especially of the *padanda*—the steering committee had formally invited representatives of the *sampradaya* as full-fledged participants (*peserta*) and not as mere observers (*peninjau*) as had been the case until then. With their support and that of the majority of the regional delegations, and regardless of the objections of Parisada Bali, the congress decided that Parisada would henceforth be headed by the chairman of the Executive Board—a layman—and no longer by the chairman of the Assembly of Priests—a *padanda*. This was a milestone in the reform process, since it had been the *brahmana*'s exclusive rights over the function of *padanda* which until then had allowed Balinese to maintain their domination over Parisada, and hence, over the fate of *agama Hindu*.[8]

---

[7] Interview, I Ketut Wiana, Denpasar, May 9, 2007.
[8] Another significant change was the fact that the democratization of election procedures to Parisada's leadership allowed it to loosen the shackles of far-reaching interference from the Directorate General for the Guidance of the

Parisada's statutes were modified accordingly, with an Assembly of Priests (*Sabha Pandita*) composed of 33 members (with only 11 *padanda*) occupying the highest position, an Assembly of Laymen (*Sabha Walaka*) of 55 members, and an Executive Board (*Pengurus Harian*) of 15 members. The mission assigned to the *Sabha Pandita* was to issue *bhisama* and to resolve divergences of opinion on the interpretation of theological and doctrinal matters. Its chairman—the reformer Ida Padanda Gde Ketut Sebali Tianyar Arimbawa (who did not appear to be well regarded by his peers due to his radical views)—was henceforth designated by the lofty title *Dharma Adhyaksa* ('Superintendent of Religion').[9] He was assisted by a vice-chairman (a Pasek *empu*) and a secretary (the head of the Hare Krishna *sampradaya* in Bali). The *Sabha Walaka* was charged with submitting proposals to the *Sabha Pandita* and with contributing to its deliberations. Its chairman (*Ketua*) was a *jaba*, a retired senior army officer, I Putu Sukreta Suranta, and its members were mostly Balinese intellectuals and government officials. As for the Executive Board, it was entrusted with implementing the *bhisama* issued by the *Sabha Pandita* and the resolutions adopted during congresses, as well as carrying out administrative tasks. While its chairman (*Ketua Umum*) was a Balinese, a *jaba* lawyer, I Nyoman Suwandha, the key position of secretary-general (*Sekretaris Umum*) was held by a Javanese, and the influential jurisdiction of religious issues (*Bidang Keagamaan*) was entrusted to the Pasek I Made Titib. Among the numerous resolutions adopted by this congress, it is noteworthy that Parisada was now called to 'protect' (*mengayomi*) the *sampradaya*, which for their part were required to consult with Parisada and to comply with its decisions (*Sarad*, No. 21, September 2001: 48–56; *Raditya*, No. 51, October 2001: 4–29; Dana 2005: 106–22; Sudharta and Surpha 2006: 132–52).

It is thus hardly surprising that Parisada Bali objected to the decisions adopted by the Eighth Congress, most of all to the nomination of a layman to Parisada's chairmanship, not to mention the conspicuous presence in its leadership of non-Balinese as well as of prominent members of NGOs, foundations, commoner *warga* and—especially—*sampradaya*. In fact, Parisada Bali's objection was arguably not so much due to the choice of a layman instead of a *padanda* as the formal head of Parisada, as to the Balinese conservative

---

Hindu and Buddhist Communities (Ditjen Bimas Hindu dan Buddha) at the Department of Religion, which had formerly controlled their nomination.

[9] This title is found in the *Nagarakertagama*, where it refers to high religious dignitaries at the court of Majapahit charged with the guardianship of religious institutions. There was one *Dharma Adhyaksa* for the Shaivites and another one for the Buddhists (Zoetmulder 1974: 355).

elite's refusal to admit priests of commoner *warga* on an equal footing with *padanda*, in effect displacing them as the rightful gatekeepers of religious knowledge. Behind the pretext of the choice of its chairman, disagreement within Parisada was in truth due to the recurrent conflict between *wangsa*, at a time marked by a general decline of aristocratic power. In any event, after heated debate and as a mark of protest (*ngambul*), some fifteen *padanda* ostentatiously left the conference hall of the congress. The following day, the press reports mentioned an exchange of insults and even of blows between participants from opposing factions.

The schism within Parisada Bali

In order to formalize its position, Parisada Bali embarked on the preparation of its own congress, the fourth one since its foundation in 1986. The chairman of Parisada Pusat's Executive Board, Nyoman Suwandha, ordered that this regional congress conform to the newly adopted national statutes. When it was found not to be the case, Parisada's leaders attempted to prevent its taking place, while on November 21 a delegation of reformers petitioned the governor to suspend the holding of the congress. Despite these maneuvers, however, and after the failure of an ultimate confrontation between representatives of the two parties at the governor's office, Parisada Bali held its Fourth Congress (*Lokasabha IV*) on November 23, 2001, at Campuan, in Ubud, under the chairmanship of Tjokorda Rai Sudharta and with the joint patronage of Governor Dewa Made Beratha and Puri Ubud—a long-standing stronghold of Golkar—but in the absence of delegates from Parisada Pusat (PHDI Propinsi Bali 2001; *Raditya*, No. 54, January 2002: 4–21; *Sarad*, No. 22, January 2002: 8–9).

The venue for the congress was the Pura Gunung Lebah, a historic temple associated with Rsi Markandeya, the legendary priest from East Java who is credited with establishing Hinduism in Bali in the 8th century. This location had not been chosen randomly, as it was there that forty years earlier, to the day, Parisada's foundation text, the Campuan Charter (*Piagam Campuan*), had been signed. Accusing the national leadership of undermining Balinese cultural values by unduly Indianizing *agama Hindu*, the conveners stressed from the outset their identity as a 'Hindu-Balinese community' (*komunitas umat Hindu Bali*), distinct from other Hindu communities in Indonesia.[10] They re-elected the very popular and highly charismatic Ida Padanda Gede Made Gunung (who had not been

---

[10] Interview, I Gusti Putu Rai Andayana, *Ketua Pengurus Harian* Parisada Campuan, Denpasar, May 15, 2007.

invited to Parisada's Eighth Congress) as chairman of Parisada Bali, all the while pressing for the nomination of a *padanda* at Parisada Pusat's chairmanship. Most importantly, they firmly rejected the resolutions passed by the *Mahasabha VIII* on the grounds that they did not conform to Parisada's statutes nor to the Campuan Charter.

The Campuan Congress was conspicuously dominated by *padanda*, and its steering committee—headed by I Gusti Gede Goda, from the Kanwil Depag Propinsi Bali—consisted of a majority of *triwangsa*.[11] It is clear that the latter, and most particularly the *brahmana*, were striving to re-establish their hegemony, adversely affected by the demands of commoner *warga* and the dissenting practices of the *sampradaya*. Referring explicitly to Sai Baba and Hare Krishna, they expressly refused the admission of the *sampradaya* into Parisada on the grounds that, far from being an integral part of the Hindu-Balinese community, these were but cliques of devotees of a religious leader adhering to different religions, whose legal status had ever been dubious in Indonesia.

The following day, Parisada Pusat convened an emergency meeting in Jakarta, and on December 7 the chairman of its Executive Board, Nyoman Suwandha, formally stated that he would not acknowledge the Campuan Congress,[12] given that it was not in compliance with the statutes ratified by Parisada's Eighth Congress. In retaliation, the newly elected chairman of Parisada Bali, Ida Padanda Gede Made Gunung, declared that he would break off all relationships with Parisada Pusat and would no longer recognize the decisions made at the Eighth Congress, since they did not conform to the original statutes of Parisada as specified by the Seventh Congress.[13] The schism within Parisada Bali was operative, and it put Hindu institutions, both Balinese and Indonesian, in an embarrassing position. The director general for the Guidance of the Hindu and Buddhist Communities (Dirjen Bimas Hindu dan Buddha) called for dialogue and conciliation, all the while suspected by the reformers of underhandedly supporting the Balinese dissidents. The district branches

---

[11] The steering committee of the Campuan Congress comprised 95 members, of whom 58 were *triwangsa*. A special commission was set up, with 23 *padanda* of the 25 *pandita* and 12 *triwangsa* of the 14 *walaka* (PHDI Propinsi Bali 2001: 68–72).

[12] "*Tidak mengesahkan dan tidak mengakui pelaksanaan Lokasabha IV Parisada Propinsi Bali*" (PDHB 2007: 66).

[13] "*Parisada Hindu Dharma Indonesia Propinsi Bali menolak hasil Mahasabha VIII Parisada Hindu Dharma Indonesia, karena pelaksanaan Mahasabha VIII melanggar Anggaran Dasar dan Anggaran Rumah Tangga Parisada, sebagai ketetapan Mahasabha VII Parisada Hindu Dharma Indonesia yang seharusnya dijadikan pegangan dan acuan*" (Pemecutan 2007: 399; interview, Ida Padanda Gede Made Gunung, Gria Purnawati, Blahbatuh, June 23, 2004).

(Parisada Kabupaten) of Parisada Bali were manifestly divided,[14] while most of Parisada from other provinces (Parisada Daerah) were adopting a cautious wait-and-see approach. At the same time, several of Parisada's historical founders—including Tjokorda Rai Sudharta, Ida Bagus Gde Dosther and Ida Padanda Oka Punyatmadja—publicly resigned from Parisada Pusat. Furthermore, the split affected other Hindu organizations, some of which—such as the Forum of Indonesians Concerned about Hinduism (Forum Pemerhati Hindu Dharma Indonesia, FPHDI)—had to cease their activities failing agreement between their members.[15]

Under the aegis of Parisada Pusat, Balinese reformers and activists, led by the Pasek lawyers Wayan Sudirta and Putu Wirata Dwikora, convened—also with the backing of the governor, and despite the opposition of four Parisada Kabupaten (Denpasar, Badung, Gianyar and Klungkung)[16]—a competing regional congress on March 29, 2002, at Besakih.[17] This is another site with a highly symbolic value, as it is the location of the main sanctuary on the island, the Pura Panataran Agung, effectively representing the community of Indonesian Hindus in its entirety. After Parisada Besakih had duly ratified the decisions of the Eighth Congress, it was acknowledged on May 27 by Parisada Pusat as the one and only official Parisada Bali, with I Made Artha—the head of the Maha Gotra Pasek Sanak Sapta Resi, the most influential of the *warga* movements—as chairman of the Executive Board (Dwikora 2002; *Sarad*, No. 25, April 2002: 10–11; *Raditya*, No. 58, May 2002: 4–21).

Meanwhile, Parisada Campuan had been lobbying—without success—to convene an 'Extraordinary Congress' (*Mahasabha Luar Biasa*) with the aim of revoking the Eighth Congress. Stressing the distinctive character of *agama Hindu* in Bali, Padanda Gunung announced that he would change the name Parisada Hindu Dharma Indonesia Bali to Parisada Hindu Dharma Bali Indonesia, with the declared purpose of "preserving the purity of the Hindu religion as it has been inherited in Bali" (*Kita benar-benar ingin menjaga keutuhan agama Hindu yang diwarisi di Bali*) (*Bali Post*, March 13, 2002). This change of name did not in fact materialize, and from then onwards there were

---

[14] Two Parisada Kabupaten out of nine, those of Buleleng and Tabanan, had refused to attend the Campuan Congress.
[15] Interview, I Dewa Gede Ngurah Swastha, *Ketua* FPHDI, Denpasar, July 21, 2011.
[16] It is certainly not just a coincidence that these districts were precisely those headed at that time by *triwangsa*.
[17] In the hope of creating a diversion, Parisada Campuan organized that very same day a solemn purification ceremony (*Wana Kerthih*) at the Pura Luhur Batukaru, a very important temple located on the slopes of Mount Batukaru. This ceremony was funded on the budget of the provincial government.

two competing Parisada Bali, respectively known as Parisada Besakih and Parisada Campuan.

A few months later, on October 26–29, 2002, Parisada Pusat held its annual General Assembly (*Pesamuhan Agung*) in Mataram (Lombok), which issued two important *bhisama* that had been decided during the Eighth Congress, one on the priesthood, the other on the interpretation of the *warna*. The *bhisama* on the priesthood (*Bhisama Sabha Pandita PHDI Pusat Tentang Sadhaka*) in fact merely reiterated the decision of Parisada's Second Congress, according to which all *pandita* have the right to conduct *yadnya*. This was necessary to resolve the conflict of interpretation that had arisen during the celebration of the *Tri Bhuwana*, the *Eka Bhuwana*, and the *Panca Wali Krama* ceremonies at Besakih in the 1990s. The conflict was between the *brahmana* and the commoner *warga*. The *brahmana* held that only priests belonging to the three original *paksa* (*tri sadhaka*)—the *padanda Siwa*, the *padanda Boda*, and the *resi bhujangga*—were authorized to officiate; while for the *warga*, all *pandita* (*sarwa sadhaka*) had the right to officiate at these important ceremonies. The commoner *warga* finally won the case, which was officially reaffirmed by the *bhisama* that declared that once they have undergone an initiation (*padiksan*) all *pandita*, irrespective of their *wangsa* title and their *soroh*, become *brahmana* by law.[18] This meant that a *pandita* is actually released from his/her original *wangsa* and consequently that *pandita* should not be discriminated on the basis of their *soroh* (Dana 2005: 146-8).

The *bhisama* on *warna* (*Bhisama Sabha Pandita PHDI Pusat Tentang Pengamalan Catur Warna*) declared that the division of society into four classes (*catur warna*) is a divine provision set forth in the Vedas, that assigns the division of tasks according to the 'qualities' (*guna*) and the 'deeds' (*karma*) of different people. Unfortunately, it said, this wise institution was distorted during the historical development of Hinduism, degenerating into the system of *jati* in India and into that of *wangsa* in Bali, based on birth and no longer on merit. What needs to be done, therefore, is to return to the original meaning of the *catur warna*, as stated in the Vedas.[19] Otherwise, the persistence of distinctions between *wangsa* and between *soroh* in Bali might arouse conflicts that would divide the Hindu community. Indeed, Balinese ancestral descent groups cannot be easily subsumed within a monotheistic framework because they emphasize

---

[18] This explains that in order to differentiate the religious function of *brahmana* from the *wangsa* title acquired by birth into a *brahmana* family, the reformers prefer the term '*soroh Ida Bagus*' to speak of the latter.

[19] This echoes the position of Dayananda Sarasvati and the Arya Samaj, according to whom—contrary to the orientalists' opinion—in the Vedas the *varna* were functional and thus non-hereditary distinctions.

difference and exclusivity, including hierarchical prohibitions on worshipping at other descent groups' temples. Therefore, as claimed by Parisada, such distinctions should be relevant only in the context of funeral ceremonies (*Pitra Yadnya*), to honor the ancestors of a particular *soroh*. They should neither govern social relationships nor be used as a criterion for *adat* purposes (Dana 2005: 149-56).

These *bhisama*, theoretically based on canonical Hindu scriptures, are supposed to have legally binding force for the Indonesian Hindu community. However, while they were approved by the reformers, they were greeted with some skepticism, considering that those which had preceded them—such as the *Bhisama Kesucian Pura* enacted in 1994 to protect religious structures after the scandal caused by the Bali Nirwana Resort in Tanah Lot—remained in most cases a dead letter.

During the following years, each Parisada Bali would claim to be the legitimate representative of the Hindu-Balinese community, while attempting to enlist the support of both the provincial authorities and the Balinese people at large for their respective positions. In the Balinese media, they were commonly characterized in terms of 'progressive' (*progresif*) versus 'conservative' (*konservatif*). The latter were described by their opponents as a 'traditionalist and feudal clique' (*persekongkolan tradisionalis dan feodalis*) that sought to 'Balinize' (*Balinisasi*) the religious practices of the Indonesian Hindu community. In response, they accused the reformers of seeking to unduly 'Indianize' (*Indianisasi*) *agama Hindu*, undermine *adat Bali* and subvert the authority of the *desa pakraman*. In particular, the conservatives reproached the *sampradaya* for attempting to impose the systematic practice of the Vedic rite *Agni Hotra* in place of the variegated Balinese customary rituals, and especially for seeking to suppress blood sacrifices (*pacaruan*) that form an integral part of the *Buta Yadnya*.

As expected, the contrast between the composition of their respective leadership was revealing. Parisada Besakih was headed by the leaders of the main commoner *warga*, while Parisada Campuan was controlled by *triwangsa* and more specifically by *padanda*.[20] And while Parisada Besakih had the backing of the intelligentsia and the urbanized middle class, as well as Balinese established

---

[20] The Assembly of Priests (*Paruman Pandita*) of Parisada Besakih comprised 22 members, of whom there were only two *padanda*, and it was moreover chaired not by a *padanda* but by a priest from a commoner *warga*. Besides, there were only three *triwangsa* among the 36 members of its Assembly of Laymen (*Paruman Walaka*) (Dwikora 2002: 41–3). Conversely, the *Paruman Pandita* of Parisada Campuan comprised 11 priests, of whom six were *padanda*; and 16 out of 22 members composing its *Paruman Walaka* were *triwangsa* (PHDI Propinsi Bali 2001: 37–8).

outside their island, Parisada Campuan was unquestionably more in phase with the village population of Bali. As for the governor and for the head of the Bali Office of the Department of Religion (Kakanwil Depag Propinsi Bali), while they maintained a façade of official neutrality, they were repeatedly charged by Parisada Besakih of being partial to Parisada Campuan (*Raditya*, No. 77, December 2003: 10–12). In fact, after the inception of Parisada Besakih, the governor severed all connections with both factions and suspended all financial contribution to Parisada,[21] whose leaders accused government authorities of unduly appropriating religious attributions that fall within their prerogatives (Sudharta and Surpha 2006: 153–5). This, by the way, would only be a return to the traditional pattern of yore, when the rajas were in charge of the ceremonies that were held in the temples located in their kingdom.

Every now and then calls were addressed to the feuding factions, aiming to bring them to the negotiation table, but the impending reconciliation never occurred as each side kept accusing the other of having initiated the schism. Thus it is that *Sarad* magazine organized a debate on the theme '*India vs Bali*', with Tjokorda Rai Sudharta confronting representatives of *sampradaya* (*Sarad*, No. 27, June 2002: 29–43). After duly paying lip service to the pluralism and the tolerance intrinsic to Hinduism, the participants attempted to reconcile the ritualistic leaning of the conservatives with the spiritual aspirations of the followers of *sampradaya*, all the while stressing that reforms should be done cautiously and gradually, in such a way that they can be selectively filtered out by the 'local genius' (*kearifan lokal*) proper to the Balinese culture. Some of them even ventured to claim that, although the Vedas never reached Bali, in fact Hinduism remained there more faithful to its Vedic origins than in India, where it was subjected to numerous reforms throughout the course of its history due to its confrontation with Islam and Christianity. Therefore, the Balinese did not need to 'return' to the Vedas since their religious practices already conformed to Vedic teachings that were collected in the Upanisad, the Purana, the Itihasa, the Dharmasastra, etc. Overall, what was particularly striking in this debate were Sudharta's remonstrances to those Balinese who cut themselves off from their cultural roots to join an Indian *sampradaya*, and his diatribes against the sheer arrogance of those who presume to reject their ancestors' religious practices. This amounted to stating that Bali is different from India and intends to remain so (*Hindu di Bali beda dengan India*).

---

[21] That being said, it must be pointed out that Parisada Campuan was accommodated in a building belonging to the provincial government.

Not to be undone, the reformers displayed their alleged commitment to reconciliation by publishing an issue of *Raditya* magazine titled 'Rituals of Indian or of Balinese persuasion?' (*Ritual keIndia-Indiaan atau keBali-Balian?*) (*Raditya*, No. 67, February 2003: 6–17). They in turn intoned the refrain of the diversity and tolerance intrinsic to Hinduism, which has been able to adjust to the cultural specificities of the various societies in which it was established. Rituals, which pertain to culture, may vary in form, as long as their essence (*inti*) remains faithful to the Vedas. Ultimately, it is up to believers to decide which rituals are right for them, provided that they do not attempt to impose them on other ethnic groups.

Notwithstanding these attempts at reconciliation, the fact remains that the reformers were afflicted by the persistent schism within Parisada Bali, which weakened the Hindu community and made it a laughingstock to the other Indonesian religious communities. In particular, they feared that such weakening might be used to advantage by Christian and Muslim proselytizers in order to convert Hindus. And they deplored Parisada Pusat's inability to impose its authority, citing the example of the monthly *Warta Hindu Dharma*, which had remained in the hands of Parisada Campuan after the Eighth Congress, to the extent that Parisada Pusat had to publish a competing monthly in Jakarta—*Media Hindu* (*Raditya*, No. 77, December 2003: 10–12).[22]

Seeing no end to the dispute, some prominent reformers declared that Parisada—which had lost much of its former luster in the eyes of Balinese opinion leaders—should be disbanded altogether, in order to make a new start on sounder foundations. They emphasized that what separated the parties was more personal antagonism, coupled with social conflict, than any theological disagreement on the nature of *agama Hindu* in Bali.[23] Be that as it may, it does not appear that the religious situation in Bali was in the least affected by the competition between the two Parisada Bali, which remained a matter of concern for only an elite few. This testifies to the rather limited hold exercised by Parisada

---

[22] Nothing ever being really clear in Bali, it turned out that *Media Hindu* rapidly took equivocal positions on the schism within Parisada Bali, at times coming close to supporting Parisada Campuan by shifting responsibility for the split to Parisada Besakih (*Media Hindu*, No. 38, April 2007: 32–3; when I interviewed the chief editor of *Media Hindu*, Ngakan Putu Putra, in Sanur on June 27, 2018, he plainly avoided the issue). This partiality was denounced by one of the leaders of Parisada Besakih, Putu Wirata Dwikora, who likened the debates between *Raditya* and *Media Hindu* to the contention between *Surya Kanta* and *Bali Adnjana* (interview, Putu Wirata Dwikora, *Paruman Walaka* PHDI Bali, Denpasar, May 7, 2007; see *Sarad*, No. 79, November 2006: 12–13).

[23] According to some of my informants, the split between Parisada Bali factions went back to the conflict between the Hindu youth organizations Peradah, affiliated with Golkar, and Pemuda Hindu Indonesia, set up by Wayan Sudirta to denounce Golkar's conservatism (interview, I Wayan Surpha, former secretary-general PHDI Pusat, and I Dewa Gede Windhu Sancaya, *Paruman Walaka* Parisada Campuan, Denpasar, July 2, 2011).

on the daily life of the Balinese people, who are more concerned with their village affairs than with regional or national institutions that purport to speak and to act on their behalf.

Meanwhile, in January 2006, the minister of religion finally complied with a repeated request of Parisada by deciding the partition of the Directorate General for the Guidance of the Hindu and Buddhist Communities (Direktorat Jenderal Bimbingan Masyarakat Hindu dan Buddha) in order to separate the Hindu and Buddhist authorities. The president of Universitas Hindu Indonesia, Ida Bagus Gde Yudha Triguna, was appointed to head the new Directorate General for the Guidance of the Hindu Community (Direktorat Jenderal Bimbingan Masyarakat Hindu) in June 2006. Although he did not take a public stance regarding the confrontation between the two factions of Parisada Bali, it was clear—at least in the eyes of his opponents—that Ida Bagus Triguna had the *brahmana*'s interests at heart and that he was partial to Parisada Campuan.[24]

As the next national congress was drawing near, calls for reconciliation were becoming more pressing. The general expectation was that the Ninth Congress would provide a welcome opportunity to settle the Balinese controversy once and for all. With a view to facilitating the rapprochement, the steering committee, infiltrated by supporters of Parisada Campuan, invited its chairman, Ida Padanda Gede Made Gunung, to the congress, and even promoted him to the status of 'advisor' (*penasehat*), despite the opposition of Parisada Besakih, while openly challenging the validity of the decisions taken by the Eighth Congress. Several preparatory meetings were held in Denpasar, some organized by Universitas Hindu Indonesia (a stronghold of Parisada Campuan), others by the Institut Hindu Dharma Negeri (a bastion of Parisada Besakih),[25] without reaching any agreement.

For the reformers, it was a matter of deep concern that the conservatives intended to return to the Campuan Charter, which would take the Hindu community back to the time when *agama Hindu Bali* was not yet universalized

---

[24] Whereas his position required him to exercise restraint in his official declarations (*tak boleh berpihak*), Ida Bagus Gde Yudha Triguna did not conceal his partisan preferences during our various interviews, in particular on July 21, 2013, at his home in Denpasar.

[25] The history of the Institut Hindu Dharma Negeri goes back to the Sekolah Menengah Hindu Bali Dwijendra, opened in 1953 by the Yayasan Dwijendra in Denpasar, which became Pendidikan Guru Agama Hindu in 1959, was renamed Akademi Pendidikan Guru Agama Hindu in 1993, then Sekolah Tinggi Agama Hindu Negeri in 1999, and was eventually upgraded to Institut Hindu Dharma Negeri (IHDN) in 2004 (Nala 2004). While the Universitas Hindu Indonesia (UNHI), a private university originating in 1993 from the Institut Hindu Dharma opened by Parisada in 1963, is a bastion of conservative *brahmana*, the IHDN, which is under the Department of Religion, is known for its progressive and universalist positions. On February 2, 2020, the IHDN became the first Hindu state university in Indonesia and was renamed Universitas Hindu Negeri I Gusti Bagus Sugriwa Denpasar (UHN). This is ironic given the traditionalist position of I Gusti Bagus Sugriwa in religious matters.

under the aegis of *agama Hindu*. Such a regression entailed the risk of splitting the Indonesian Hindu community by inducing other regional Parisada to establish their own religion, such as *agama Hindu Jawa*, *agama Hindu Tengger*, *agama Hindu Kaharingan*,[26] and so on. Besides, several leaders of Parisada Campuan were openly accused of embezzlement, and their opponents saw their determination to appoint a *padanda* to Parisada's chairmanship as a subterfuge to protect themselves against a likely incrimination, with the assumption that no one would dare to bring a *padanda* to justice, owing to the prestige inherent in their high status.

Parisada's Ninth Congress (*Mahasabha ke IX*) was held on October 14–18, 2006, at Taman Mini Indonesia Indah in Jakarta and re-elected Ida Padanda Sebali Tianyar Arimbawa as *Dharma Adhyaksa*, though not without some reservations on the part of a number of participants, who feared that his intransigence might prevent the eventual reconciliation between the feuding Balinese factions (PHDI 2006a, 2006b). Despite pressure from supporters of Parisada Campuan, the split of Parisada Bali was not put on the agenda by the convenors of the congress, who considered the matter already settled since Parisada Besakih had been recognized as the one official Parisada Bali. Furthermore, while Ida Padanda Gede Made Gunung had indeed been invited to the congress, it was as an observer (*peninjau*) and not as a participant (*peserta*), so that he was not granted the right to vote. As a consequence, in a fit of pique, he withdrew from the plenary session. He told me later that his supporters, banking on his undeniable popularity, had hoped to win over the delegates to elect him as the new chairman of Parisada Pusat.[27] He seemed to have been very upset by his failure, and some of his opponents—such as Ida Padanda Sebali Tianyar Arimbawa—attributed to his disappointment the decision of Parisada Campuan to radicalize its position.[28]

---

[26] The risk was very real because, since the loosening of religious control under the presidency of Abdurrahman Wahid, the leaders of the *Hindu Kaharingan* community were lobbying the Department of Religion to recognize *agama Kaharingan* as an autonomous religion, distinct from *agama Hindu* (*Raditya*, No. 50, September 2001: 4-5).
[27] As an observer, while he did not have the right to vote, he was nevertheless eligible for election. But he accused Padanda Sebali and Wayan Sudirta of having tampered with Parisada's rules of procedure in order to prevent his eligibility (interview, Ida Padanda Gede Made Gunung, Gria Purnawati, Blahbatuh, May 10, 2007).
[28] Interview, Ida Padanda Gede Ketut Sebali Tianyar Arimbawa, PHDI Bali, Denpasar, May 9, 2007. See further *Taksu*, No. 163, September–October 2006: 6–32; *Raditya*, No. 110, September 2006: 16–25; No. 111, October 2006: 39–53; No. 112, November 2006: 7–15; *Media Hindu*, No. 31, September 2006: 14–27; No. 33, November 2006: 17–27; *Sarad*, No. 79, November 2006: 9–13; No. 80, December 2006: 18–33.

Back to *agama Hindu Bali*

On January 28, 2007, Parisada Campuan held its Fifth Congress (*Lokasabha V*), notwithstanding the attempts by Parisada Pusat to prevent its taking place (PDHB 2007).[29] Ever mindful of potent symbols, its leaders had chosen for its venue the Pura Samuan Tiga, in Bedulu. This is where, in the 11th century, the legendary East Javanese priest Mpu Kuturan is said to have merged the nine religious sects (*paksa*) operating on the island into three—Siwa, Budha and Waisnawa—and to have laid down the canonical tenets of the Hindu Balinese religion. According to Parisada Campuan's leadership, the proliferation of *sampradaya* was bringing Bali back to the critical situation that prevailed at the time of Mpu Kuturan, and it was therefore necessary to renew his original act. Hence the congress's decision to promulgate the Samuan Tiga Charter (*Piagam Samuan Tiga*), which determined to return to the 'true self' (*jati diri*) of the Balinese religion—that is, to *agama Hindu Bali*—implying to see its origins in Majapahit rather than India. By the same token, the delegates decided to revert to the name originally chosen by their founding fathers and renamed themselves Parisada Dharma Hindu Bali (PDHB)[30]—thus formally ending the dualism within Parisada Bali while further increasing the Balinese schism (Pemecutan 2007).[31]

It was up to Ida Bagus Gde Dosther, as one of Parisada's historical founders, to open the congress by recalling the noble deed of the great ancestors who bestowed upon Bali the custody of *agama Hindu* after the fall of Majapahit and the ensuing Islamization of Java.[32] This was the heritage that the Balinese people had treasured in their manuscripts and rituals through the ages. And Dosther pointed out that if Parisada had now expanded throughout Indonesia, it was born in Bali, and for that reason Bali had remained the center (*pusat*) from

---

[29] The congress had been prepared by a meeting of the *Paruman Sulinggih* held on December 3, 2006, where the priests solemnly declared that the *sampradaya* had no place in Parisada (*Sampradaya nenten patut sarengang ring Parisada*) (PDHB 2007: 8). Even though, as head of the steering committee, Padanda Gunung retained ultimate control over the resolutions and decisions adopted during this congress, his mandate as chairman was not renewed—at his own request, he claimed, as he wanted to be able to devote himself fully to his religious teaching in the ashram he had opened in 2004, the Pasraman Yogadiparamaguhya (interview, Ida Padanda Gede Made Gunung, Gria Purnawati, Blahbatuh, May 10, 2007; see *Media Hindu*, No. 38, April 2007: 22–5). Instead of retaining the chairmanship, he became the head of a team of eight 'advisors' (*penasehat*), all *triwangsa*.

[30] While the leadership of Parisada Campuan was partly renewed during the congress, the PDHB's organizational structure remained the same: its *Paruman Pandita* likewise comprised 11 priests, of whom six were *padanda*, and 16 of its 22-strong *Paruman Walaka* were *triwangsa* (PDHB 2007: 89–90).

[31] The fact that several leaders of Parisada Pusat had threatened to sue Parisada Campuan for misappropriating the name Parisada Hindu Dharma Indonesia Bali (officially reserved for Parisada Besakih) had something to do with Parisada Campuan's decision to change its name to Parisada Dharma Hindu Bali (interview, Putu Setia, *Wakil Ketua Sabha Walaka* PHDI Pusat, Pedungan, May 15, 2007).

[32] Interview, Ida Bagus Gde Dosther, Denpasar, July 16, 2008.

which *agama Hindu* spread out and blossomed (PDHB 2007: 20–3). While Dosther's speech was delivered in Indonesian, a significant proportion of the congress report was in Balinese and the terms *sulinggih* and *wiku* were used throughout to refer to the initiated priesthood instead of the more neutral term *pandita*.

In his address to the congress, the chairman of the Executive Board, Ida Bagus Putu Sudarsana, explained that the return to *agama Hindu Bali* did not concern solely the Balinese people since it was in fact the true ancestral religion of Indonesian Hindus (*cikal bakal Hindu Nusantara*) and, in consequence, it ought to become the model of *agama Hindu* in Indonesia. That is to say, the issue was not, as one might suppose, to promote *agama Hindu Bali* in Bali, *agama Hindu Jawa* in Java, and so on, but to establish the foundations of the Hindu religion such as it was effectively practiced in Bali, since it was fundamentally the same in Java and everywhere else in the Archipelago. According to the interpretation put forward by Sudarsana, in the syntagm *agama Hindu Bali*, 'Bali' did not refer to the island known by that name nor to the ethnic group which inhabits it, but it signified 'offering' (*banten*). In that sense, *agama Hindu Bali* was the religion of Hindus who make use of offerings to worship Sang Hyang Widhi and His manifestations.[33] Besides, taking into account the fact that the practices of *agama Hindu* are differentiated according to the ethnic and cultural specificities of the areas where it is established, the PDHB called for setting up a series of regional Parisada, such as Parisada Dharma Hindu Jawa, Parisada Dharma Hindu Tengger, Parisada Dharma Hindu Kaharingan, Parisada Dharma Hindu Toraja, and so on, each one of them to be placed under the national coordination of a Parisada Dharma Hindu Indonesia (PDHB 2007: 1-4).[34]

In the light of this, the emergence of the PDHB could be construed as an extension of regional autonomy to the religious domain, even though religion

---

[33] This interpretation was taken directly from the exegesis put forth in the 1960s by I Gusti Bagus Sugriwa to defend the name *agama Hindu Bali* against the proponents of the name *agama Hindu*. In his view, *agama Hindu Bali* was the result of a historical combination between *agama Hindu* and *agama Bali*, and in consequence it differed from Hinduism as practiced in India (see Chap. 6). Moreover, the report of the Samuan Tiga Congress contained excerpts from Sugriwa's booklet *Sedjarah dan Falsafah Agama Hindu Bali* (Sugriwa 1968; PDHB 2007: 69–82).

[34] It so happened that several Hindu councils of ethnic persuasion were established around the same time in Indonesia, such as the Chinese Majelis Hindu Tionghoa, the Indian Sabha Dharma Nusantara, and the Javanese Majapahid. These initiatives were received favorably by the Dirjen Bimas Hindu, Ida Bagus Gde Yudha Triguna, who suggested that Parisada take the form of a federation so as to better account for the ethnic and cultural variations of Hinduism in Indonesia (*Raditya*, No. 135, October 2008: 28–9). That being said, *agama Hindu Bali* was not officially recognized by the Ditjen Bimas Hindu, and in fact the PDHB made no attempt whatsoever to obtain its recognition (interview, Ida Bagus Gunadha, former secretary-general Parisada, former president UNHI, Denpasar, March 19, 2013; interview, Ida Bagus Gde Yudha Triguna, Denpasar, July 21, 2013).

was not included among the fields attributed to the regions. Besides, the regionalization of *agama Hindu* in Indonesia did not stop at the provincial level but went down to the level of the district, as illustrated by the decision of the PHDI Kota Denpasar during its congress held on February 14, 2008, to rename itself PDHB Kota Denpasar (*Sarad*, No. 95, March 2008: 8–9). And, as claimed by the leaders of Parisada Dharma Hindu Bali, other Parisada *kabupaten* were to follow in the footsteps of the PDHB Kota Denpasar.[35]

In order to understand what is at stake with this return to *agama Hindu Bali*, one has to refer to the six-point declaration of the Samuan Tiga Charter (PDHB 2007: 53). According to this document, *agama Hindu Bali* is based on the *Sruti* (the knowledge revealed in the Vedas), the *Smerti* (the texts of the Vedic tradition), the *Darsana* (the orthodox doctrinal 'viewpoints' of Hinduism) and the *Tantra* (the texts revealed by Siwa), the essence of which has been contained and transmitted in traditional manuscripts (*lontar*), where it was filtered, interpreted and appropriated by Balinese 'local genius' (*kearifan lokal*). The foundation of its 'faith' (*Sradha*) is Shaivite and more specifically monistic (*Siwa Tattwa dengan paham Monisme*), which contravened the obligation incumbent upon Indonesian citizens to adhere to a religion complying with the strict monotheism of Islam—a point that, curiously, does not appear to have provoked any controversy.[36] Equally contentious is the declaration that, besides the officially recognized appellation Sang Hyang Widhi, God was referred to as *Bhatara Siwa*, *Dewa Dewi*, and *Hyang Laluhur* ('Deified Ancestors')—which nearly amounted to an acknowledgement of polytheism and ancestor worship, a fact which had been until then carefully obliterated in Parisada doctrinal literature. The other points of the Samuan Tiga Charter referred to the sociocultural context specific to Balinese ritual practices (*Panca Yadnya*), with their shrines (*sanggah/pamerajan*), their temples (*pura*), and their offerings (*banten*).[37]

---

[35] Interview, Ida Bagus Putu Sudarsana, *Ketua Pengurus Harian* PDHB, Sesetan, July 16, 2008; interview, Ida Bagus Gede Agastia, *Sabha Walaka* PDHB, Denpasar, July 21, 2008. In fact, this did not happen, as only Parisada Kota Denpasar adopted the new name (interview, I Gusti Ngurah Oka Pemecutan, *Ketua III Pengurus Harian* PDHB, Denpasar, July 18, 2011).

[36] Interview, I Gede Sura, *Sabha Walaka* PDHB, Denpasar, June 16, 2009.

[37] It is significant of the swing back to a distinctive Balinese religious identity that I Dewa Gede Ngurah Swastha, the initiator and former chairman of the Forum Pemerhati Hindu Dharma Indonesia, who had been at the forefront of religious reform in the 1990s, published in 2016 a book in which he fully endorsed the return to *agama Hindu Bali* (*nama Hindu Bali perlu dipergunakan kembali oleh para pemuluknya*) (Sukahet 2016: 3). Since 2014, he has presided over the *soroh* that gathers the descendants of Sri Kresna Kepakisan, the first sovereign of Bali after the conquest of the island by Majapahit in the 14th century, with the lofty title Ida Pangelingsir Agung Putra Sukahet. Among other issues, he rejected the slogan 'Back to Veda', by claiming that *agama Hindu Bali* was already based on the *Kitab Suci Weda*, which meant that the Balinese did not have to 'return' to the Vedas. He emphasized the

In many respects, the return to *agama Hindu Bali* is consonant with the reaffirmation of Balinese identity expressed in the *Ajeg Bali* movement and the reinstatement of the customary village (*desa pakraman*). With a view to firmly establishing Parisada Campuan in the villages, the congress organizers had indeed taken care to invite representatives of the Grand Council of Customary Villages (Majelis Utama Desa Pakraman). And among the recommendations from the congress, one notices that the 'vision and mission' (*visi dan misi*) of the PDHB was to ensure that the *agama Hindu* that has been bequeathed to Bali be '*ajeg*' (*Ajegnya agama Hindu yang diwariskan di Bali*) (PDHB 2007: 38).

Curiously enough, while the split of Parisada Campuan had been extensively debated in the Balinese media, the return to *agama Hindu Bali* and to the name Parisada Dharma Hindu Bali elicited only brief comments, as if it did not really matter that much. This is not to say that the event did not excite the ire of reformers, however. To mention just one example, *Raditya* magazine issued a special report on the Samuan Tiga Congress under the title '*Hindu versus Hindu Bali*' (*Raditya*, No. 116, March 2007: 7–25). In his editorial, Putu Setia gave free rein to his sarcastic verve by making a detailed rebuttal of the Samuan Tiga Charter. He had little difficulty pointing out that the contents of the *lontar* did not constitute a coherent and comprehensive theological canon, mostly dealing with minute instructions for specific rituals, to say nothing of the fact that they differ widely from one another—as the leaders of Bali Darma Laksana had been forced to admit to their great chagrin back in 1940. In these conditions, it would make more sense to go back to the Indian Vedas themselves than to accord much credit to the motley assortment of their local interpretations, all the more so since for the Balinese people, *lontar* are heirlooms (*pusaka*) to be venerated more than to be read. Above all, they could not constitute a sacred book (*kitab suci*) as they are not the product of a divine revelation (*wahyu*), but only reflect the personal opinion of their authors or their sponsors. And in any case, today Hindu youth are more inclined to seek answers to their religious aspirations on the Internet than in *lontar*. Indeed, they tend to think critically and thus they no longer blindly obey injunctions without understanding their reason.

With regard to the proclaimed Shaivism of *agama Hindu Bali*, Putu Setia emphasized that even if Siwa Siddhanta was historically predominant in Bali, the

---

essential character of the variegated rituals and the profusion of offerings, wrongly criticized for their profligacy by the reformers. Most importantly, he explained that the *Pitra Yadnya* were intended to transform the dead into ancestors (*pitara*) and the ancestors into deities (*Dewa Pitara*, or else *Batara Kawitan*), who eventually merged with Ida Sang Hyang Widhi (*amor ring Acintya*). He concluded his book by stressing that Parisada is a priestly institution and that, consequently, it ought to be chaired by a priest (*sulinggih*) and not by a layman (*walaka*).

Balinese people acknowledged the Hindu *Trimurti* and venerated Brahma and Wisnu alongside Siwa.[38] And he highlighted the central significance of the *Bhagawad Gita*, which is of Vaishnavite persuasion. But it is undoubtedly the importance attached by the PDHB to offerings and other Balinese cultural specificities that most aroused his biting irony, as he rhetorically asked how Balinese Hindus are expected to practice their religion when they happen to live outside their island. Furthermore, he criticized those Balinese who at great cost import coconut palms from Java and fruits from Australia to make their offerings, instead of simply using what is available in their surrounding environment. In so doing, they become impoverished for the greater benefit of outsiders (*pendatang*). And he concluded by stating that for his part he embraced *agama Hindu universil*, instead of regressing to *agama Hindu Bali*—which, in his eyes, is only a 'sect' (*aliran kepercayaan*) and not a true 'religion' (*agama*).

Despite such objections from reformers, the Fifth Congress (*Lokasabha V*) of the official Parisada Bali, held on April 29, 2007, on the campus of the Institut Hindu Dharma Negeri in Denpasar, went almost unnoticed (*Raditya*, No. 119, June 2007: 30–1). As far as I could assess, the return to *agama Hindu Bali* was not included on the agenda of the congress. Yet, for Parisada Bali, this was a most unfortunate regression, a typical manifestation of the deplorable 'feudal' leanings evinced by the old guard of the Balinese nobility compromised with Golkar, particularly in evidence among the *brahmana* eager to preserve the *padanda*'s monopoly on the initiated priesthood. Construing the discord between the PHDI and the PDHB as a conflict between reason and tradition, the reformers viewed their own struggle against those remnants of the past as a resurgence of the 'caste conflict' (*pertentangan kasta*) of the 1920s, pitting the progressive *jaba* of *Surya Kanta* against the conservative *triwangsa* represented by *Bali Adnjana*.[39]

It is true that the similarities between the position of the PDHB and that exposed in *Bali Adnjana* are striking—starting with the very name given to the Balinese religion. Thus, one finds in the statements of the PDHB's leaders the same reference to the 'religion of our ancestors' (*agama leluhur*) and to the legacy of Majapahit—rather than of India—which was already emphasized by Tjakra Tanaya. Furthermore, for some of its advocates at least, the return to

---

[38] It should be pointed out that Siwa Siddhanta is not seen in a very good light by the Balinese reformers, in that it is connected to Danghyang Nirartha and to the *padanda*'s hegemony which he imposed on the Balinese religion. As previously noted, Neo-Hinduism, which they prefer, objects to any sectarian exclusivism and favors instead a universalist religion.

[39] Interview, Putu Wirata Dwikora, *Paruman Walaka* PHDI Bali, Denpasar, May 7, 2007.

agama Hindu Bali appears clearly like a yearning for the religious-cum-social order of yore, when *agama* was deemed to be inseparable from *adat*. And one could find some similarities between the accusation of sowing dissension within the 'four castes' (*catur wangsa*) made by Tjakra Tanaya against Surya Kanta, and the criticism leveled at the *sampradaya*, whom the PDHB charged with weakening the Hindu-Balinese community by dividing it between competing sects. Yet, for all that, there is much more to the creation of the PDHB than a withdrawal into Balinese parochialism coupled with a religious cover-up of mundane ambitions on the part of a clique of diehard reactionaries, as their opponents contended.

The schism within Parisada Bali is the outcome of multiple divisions that cannot be reduced to a mere theological dispute. It is first of all predicated on perennial tensions between *jaba* and *triwangsa*, and most particularly on the commoner *warga*'s intention to abolish the *brahmana*'s monopoly on the initiated priesthood. It also results from the attempt of conservative Balinese elites to regain control of their religion in order to put an end to both its Indonesianization and its Indianization, by winning back the direction of Parisada which they lost following the establishment of its headquarters in Jakarta in 1996. The crux of the matter is the displacement of Parisada Pusat outside Bali, with the increasing domination of non-Balinese and commoner *warga* over its leadership to the detriment of *padanda*, and the ascendancy of *sampradaya* aiming to get rid of age-old religious traditions with the intent of forcing their own rites upon the Balinese people.

In this respect, the comeback of *agama Hindu Bali* might be understood as a return to a meaning of *agama* untainted by its Islamic and Christian interpretations, when *agama* had not yet been separated from *adat*. One could say that Parisada Dharma Hindu Bali reclaimed the power to identify as *agama* that which pertained to *adat* for Parisada Hindu Dharma Indonesia, just as the latter had earlier claimed the power to designate as *agama* that which the Indonesian Ministry of Religion had classified as *adat*. In short, the promoters of *agama Hindu Bali* are deliberately reversing the process of universalization of the Balinese religion by relocalizing it.[40] In so doing, they are displaying a

---

[40] This was precisely the position advocated by Gusti Bagus Sugriwa, as recalled by some of his former students during a seminar organized in March 2008 at the Universitas Hindu Indonesia, who stressed the fact that he had not only Hinduized the Balinese traditions but that he had also localized the teachings of Hinduism (*Sugriwa* [...] *bukan sekadar melakukan peng-hindu-an atas tradisi Bali, tetapi juga melakukan pelokalan terhadap ajaran-ajaran Hindu*) (*Sarad*, No. 96, April 2008: 8).

heightened sense of Balinese empowerment—something which could not have been possible during the New Order.

Agama Hindu under siege

Over the years, the conflict between the two Balinese religious factions appears to have faded somewhat, although the reasons for its initial outbreak have yet to be properly addressed. It must be acknowledged in this respect that the PDHB seems to have quickly reduced its initial ambitions; in fact, it has not held a congress since its foundation, and a number of observers consider that it has fallen into abeyance. This does not mean, however, that the endorsement of *agama Hindu Bali* is no longer prevalent in Bali, far from it. Moreover, the nonacceptance of *sampradaya* is still widespread among Balinese villagers and has remained a bone of contention to this day.

Meanwhile, some *sampradaya* joined forces on September 19, 2008, to set up, under Parisada's auspices, the United Council of Balinese Ashrams (Dewan Persatuan Pasraman Bali, DPPB), which initially gathered about a dozen 'spiritual groups' (*kelompok spiritual*) claiming to be more or less based on the Vedas. Their stated objective was to strengthen the institutional representation of *sampradaya* so as to obtain government protection, and to this end they specifically requested to be attached to the Department of Religion and not to the Department of Culture, unlike the *aliran kepercayaan* (*Raditya*, No. 159, October 2010: 31).[41] In effect, there has been a mushrooming of ashrams in Bali in recent years, concurrently with the promotion of meditation and yoga—and of 'spirituality' (*spiritualitas*) more generally (*Media Hindu*, No. 122, April 2014: 8–25).

For all that, the hope of reconciling the warring Balinese factions had not disappeared, as reflected in the commemoration in March 2009 of the fiftieth anniversary of Parisada's foundation, under the joint aegis of the two archenemies, Padanda Sebali and Padanda Gunung, who had agreed to collaborate for the first time since 2001.[42] The event was highlighted by the organization of seminars on the 'Indonesian Hindu Revival' (*Kebangkitan Hindu*

---

[41] Interview, I Made Aripta Wibawa, chairman of the Dewan Persatuan Pasraman Bali, Batubulan, July 12, 2011.
[42] They could be seen smiling and shaking hands under the approving gaze of Ida Bagus Gde Dosther on the cover of the *Sarad* issue devoted to this commemoration, calling together for a 'complete reshuffle of Parisada' (*Rombak Total Parisada*) (*Sarad*, No. 109, May 2009: 12–18). However, as reported in *Media Hindu*, both Padanda Sebali and Padanda Gunung insisted that any expectation of reconciliation between the PHDI and the PDHB in the near future was a vain hope (*Media Hindu*, No. 63, May 2009: 36).

Indonesia)—in Jakarta, Palangkaraya (Kalimantan), Surabaya, Palu (Sulawesi) and Denpasar. Their proceedings were published in two collective volumes, prefaced together by both *padanda* (Mantik 2009; Budiarna 2009).

All the parties involved in Parisada since its foundation were invited to participate in these seminars, and in fact their proceedings demonstrated the prevalence of the positions advocated by the PDHB. Thus the chapter relating the history of Parisada's first fifty years blamed the schism within Parisada Bali squarely on the aggressiveness of the *sampradaya* and the commoner *warga*, which were accused of attempting to hijack its leadership in order to further their own interests (Jelantik 2009). Overall, rather than celebrating an 'Indonesian Hindu Revival', numerous contributors were critical of Parisada, judging that it had lost the initial impetus of its founding fathers, had worn itself out and had now exhausted its working capacity. This had led to a growing disaffection of the Hindu community with Parisada, which was all the more worrying in view of the fact that there had been recently an alarming increase in conversions of Balinese Hindus to Islam and Christianity.

Indeed, according to the decennial censuses the proportion of Hindu Balinese has been declining sharply over the past decades. While in 1990, 93.1 percent of the population of Bali declared themselves Hindu and 5.2 percent Muslim, in 2000, the figures were respectively 87.4 and 10.3 percent (67 and 25 percent in Denpasar), and in 2010, 83.5 and 13.6 percent (65 and 27 per cent in Denpasar)—with some 2 percent Christians of various denominations,[43] as well as a handful of Buddhists and Confucians. By comparison, as assessed by the first Dutch census in 1920, the breakdown was then estimated to be 97.84 percent Bali Hindu, 1.38 percent Bali Islam, and 0.78 percent Indonesians from elsewhere (Swellengrebel 1960: 6).

Whatever the validity of such figures, there is a general consensus among Hindu Balinese that they are on the wane in their own island, and will soon even become a minority in Denpasar. Some Balinese opinion leaders go so far as to accuse the Department of Religion of deliberately weakening the position of *agama Hindu* in Bali, for the reason that its subsidies to the provinces are allocated according to the national breakdown of adherents to each of the officially recognized religions. Thus, about two-thirds of the budget of the Bali Office of the Department of Religion (Kanwil Depag Propinsi Bali) is granted to Muslims, while Hindus, Protestants, Catholics, Buddhists and Confucians have

---

[43] The majority of Balinese Christians belong to the Gereja Kristen Protestan di Bali. A significant proportion of the Roman Catholic community (Gereja Katolik) in Bali consists of immigrants from other islands, particularly Flores.

to share the remainder (*Raditya*, No. 110, September 2006: 7). Similarly, critics denounce the Department of Religion for appointing more Muslim than Hindu civil servants to its Bali Office. They emphasize the fact that there are more Muslim schools than Hindu schools in Bali, and that 80 percent of the religious teachers on the island are Muslim and only 10 percent Hindu, a proportion equivalent to that of Christian teachers (*Sarad*, No. 85, May 2007: 32–3). Furthermore, they take issue with the fact that other religious communities are allowed to establish places of worship in Bali, whereas Hindus are hindered from doing the same outside the island (*Raditya*, No. 76, November 2003: 42–8). Indeed, since the 1990s there has been a sharp increase in funding by the Department of Religion for the construction of mosques and other Muslim places of worship on Bali, where they have multiplied.

After the terrorist attacks of 2002 and 2005, followed by the passing of the Pornography Law of 2008, the Balinese people have felt themselves threatened (*terancam*), looking like easy prey to Islamist aggression against their religious identity. In 2011, an article in *Media Hindu* magazine expressed concern about the growing popularity among Indonesian Muslims of pilgrimages to graves said to be the resting places of seven Muslim saints—the *Wali Pitu*—dispersed throughout Bali. This practice went back to 1992, when a Javanese Muslim claimed that a divine voice had told him that there were seven *wali* buried on Bali and that he should go and find their graves. These were then construed as 'sacred sites' (*keramat*), from which Bali was due to be Islamized, in the same way that Java is said to have been Islamized by legendary nine saints—the *Wali Songo*. The author of the article warned his readers that according to Muslim zealots, the history of Islam in Java, when Hinduism had to yield to Islam after the fall of Majapahit, was going to repeat itself in Bali (*Media Hindu*, No. 88, June 2011: 72–3; see also Quinn 2012; Slama 2014; and Zuhri 2022). In this respect, one should note that most Indonesian Muslim organizations support a policy of conversion of the Balinese people, and one observes further a disturbing progression of radical Islamist movements on the island.

Along with the growing Islamization of Indonesia, the Balinese people have recently faced repeated Islamic interference in their own affairs. To give just one example, in 2014, the government promulgated the Law on Halal Product Certification (*Undang-undang No.33/2014 Tentang Jaminan Produk Halal*), which asserted that all products which enter, are distributed and are traded in Indonesia must be *halal*-certified (permissible according to Islamic law). Thereafter, numerous food stalls appeared on the island bearing signs such as *Warung Muslim*, *Warung Islam* or *Warung Halal*. Some Balinese reacted by putting up the sign *Warung 100% Haram* (prohibited according to Islamic law) on their food stalls. Then a prominent but controversial Balinese Hindu activist, I Gusti Ngurah Arya Wedakarna—the son of Made Wedastera Suyasa, the founder of Angkatan Muda Hindu-Bali—who had recently been elected to the Regional Representative Council (Dewan Perwakilan Daerah, DPD) in Jakarta, launched the *Sukla Satyagraha* movement. He wanted to certify Balinese food stalls with the label *sukla* ('ritually pure', in Balinese), in order to persuade the Balinese people to patronize the *Warung Sukla* instead of the *Warung Halal*. His initiative gave rise to heated public debate, with Balinese religious figures claiming that *sukla* food should be offered only to deities (*dewa-dewi*) or ancestors (*laluhur*), rather than being sold to human consumers. Only after having been consumed by their proper recipients can *sukla* food then be eaten by devotees as 'leftovers' (*lungsuran*). The polemic eventually petered out.

Another Islamic slight to Balinese identity took the form of plans for establishing *syariah* tourism in Bali, which were fiercely resisted by the same Gusti Ngurah Arya Wedakarna, who insisted that tourism in Bali should be developed only on the base of its Hindu culture. The plans were eventually dropped in March 2016, but they re-emerged in February 2019, when Sandiaga Uno, the running mate of presidential candidate Prabowo Subianto, declared that Bali should become a *halal* tourism destination (*Pariwisata Halal*). This declaration generated an uproar on the island, whose officials, from the governor to the head of tourism, abruptly refused to develop *halal* tourism, arguing that Bali was already known the world over as a destination of Cultural Tourism (*Pariwisata Budaya*). They conceded that *Pariwisata Halal* might be promoted in Muslim regions, such as Lombok, Sumatra Barat or Aceh, but certainly not in Bali, which is the Hindu island of Indonesia. As Prabowo was defeated, the issue lapsed into oblivion, even though Sandiaga Uno was appointed minister of tourism and creative economy by President Joko Widodo.

Yet, despite increasing Islamic pressure, the Balinese appear to aim their denunciations more readily at the proselytism of Christian Churches than at Islamic *dakwah* (*Sarad*, No. 122, June 2010: 44–5; *Media Hindu*, No. 99, May 2012: 10–24). It may well be that it is less risky for Hindus to lash out at another minority religion than at Islam, with its powerful institutional channels in Bali. In any case, debate on the evangelization of the Balinese people has increased in recent times. The contention is particularly acute regarding the enculturation of the Christian message, namely, the appropriation of symbols and references which Balinese Hindus consider to be legitimately theirs. While Christian missionaries initially demanded that new converts destroy their family shrines and cut off any link with Balinese customary activities, from the 1970s onward Balinese Christians have sought a religious practice more in tune with their ethnic culture. They opted for using Balinese music and dance and for wearing traditional Balinese garb in church contexts, and they started building their churches in Balinese architectural style.[44] Such a 'Balinization' of Christianity aroused the hostility of Hindu Balinese, who criticize it precisely for blurring the boundaries between Christians and Hindus in order to facilitate conversions. Indeed, what Balinese Christians regard as being part of culture (*budaya*), and in this respect as belonging to all Balinese, is deemed by Balinese Hindus to pertain to religion (*agama*), and to be therefore their exclusive property (Surpi Aryadharma 2011; Wijaya 2012).

In particular, Balinese Hindus have still not accepted the appropriation of the name Sang Hyang Widi by Balinese Christians. To mention just a few related protests, Hindu Balinese remonstrated against the use of Sang Hyang Widi to name God the Father and of Sang Hyang Yesus to refer to his Son, on the occasion of a *sendratari* performance titled 'Jesus the Redeemer' (*Yesus Sang Penebus*), broadcast on Balinese television by the Tri Tunggal Maha Kudus Catholic Church in Tuka on Christmas Day 1999. More recently, protesters denounced several Christian institutions for claiming the right to make use of Sanskrit terminology which Hindu Balinese intend to retain for themselves. Thus, on the Catholic side, the Yayasan Swastiastu was forced to change its name to Yayasan Insan Mandiri, while the Sekolah Swastiastu was renamed Sekolah Santo Yoseph. Protestants, too, have not been spared, as the Yayasan Widya Pura was renamed Yayasan Harapan, and the Sekolah Widya Pura became Sekolah Harapan (Dhana 2014; Wiebe 2014).

In order to prevent what they called the 'evil of conversion' (*kejahatan konversi*), as well as to bring back the victims of conversion to the fold of *agama Hindu*, a group of Balinese Hindu activists, priests and academics founded on June 1, 2018 in Denpasar, under the patronage of Parisada, the Forum for the Advocacy of Hinduism (Forum Advokasi Hindu Dharma, FAHD).[45] They were intent on protecting the rights of Hindus and defending them against all possible 'discrimination' (*diskriminasi*), 'abuse' (*pelecehan*), and 'attacks' (*serangan*) perpetrated by followers of other religions. They demanded that the heads of all government bodies in Bali be bona fide Hindus. And they announced their aim

---

[44] Hindu Balinese appear to be particularly incensed at the sight of Christian churches (*gereja*) looking like Hindu temples (*pura*). There was recently in *Media Hindu* a special report on this topic, entitled 'Could temples be transformed into churches?' (*Dapatkah Pura Dijadikan Gereja?*) (*Media Hindu*, No. 174, August 2018: 8–12).

[45] Interview, I Wayan Sayoga, founder and chairman of the Forum Advokasi Hindu Dharma, Denpasar, June 28, 2018.

to build up solidarity and unity among Hindus worshipers throughout Indonesia, very much along the lines of majoritarian Muslims. However, they do not appear to have been particularly active, as their main achievement so far has been the organization on May 25, 2019, of a symposium on 'The Impact of the Change in the Demographic Structure of Bali on the Way of Life of the Balinese People that is Based on the Hindu Dharma Noble Values' (*Dampak Perubahan Struktur Penduduk Bali terhadap Tatanan Kehidupan Masyarakat Bali yang dilandasi Nilai-Nilai Luhur Hindu Dharma*). The recommendations from this symposium demanded that the provincial government keep pushing for special autonomy (*otonomi khusus*) status for Bali, rejected *Pariwisata Halal* and *Warung Halal*, stated that the proportion of immigrants should not exceed 20 percent of the whole population of the island, and above all urged the provincial authorities to take the necessary steps to prevent religious conversion of Hindu Balinese. The Balinese should become committed Hindus and defend their Hindu identity against any defamation from followers of other religions. For this to happen, instead of setting supporters of *Hindu Bali* against advocates of *Hindu India*, all Hindus should acknowledge that, in essence, *agama Hindu* thrives on diversity (Sayoga 2019).

Along similar lines, on the initiative of the Balinese branch of the Prajaniti Hindu Indonesia (whose chairman is none other than Wayan Sayoga, the head of the Forum Advokasi Hindu Dharma), an international conference was held on December 22, 2018, in Denpasar on the theme 'Hindu Temples as Centers of Excellence' (*Pura Hindu sebagai Pusat Keunggulan*). In the first session, titled 'Hindu Under Siege' (*Hindu Dalam Kepungan*), the speakers denounced both Muslim and Christian proselytizing, while deploring the fact that Balinese have no qualms about converting to either Islam or Christianity. They were of the opinion that Hindu temples should not come to life only on the date of their 'anniversary' (*odalan*) but should become veritable religious centers, following the example of mosques and churches (*Media Hindu*, No. 181, March 2019: 8-17).

By and large, Balinese religious advocates criticize Parisada for not protecting the Hindu community against Muslim and Christian proselytizing, and they urge its leaders—as well as the governor—to exercise increased vigilance with regard to religious conversions. However, they willingly acknowledge that such conversions are due not only to the zeal of missionary religions, but even more so to the shortcomings of Balinese religious practices. At issue is the excessive complexity (*keruwetan*) of traditional rituals and their exorbitant cost—further compounded by the ritual inflation fueled by the revenue from tourism—to the extent that their religion has become a financial burden (*beban*) for the Balinese people. This, they say, is because people just go about blindly practicing their rites (*gugon tuwon*), without trying to understand their meaning (*mula keto*), an accusation already made in similar terms in *Surya Kanta* and *Djatajoe*. In order to prevent further conversions, Parisada should thus simplify rituals (*upacara*), while providing a religious education that stresses ethics (*susila*) and theology (*tattwa*), in order to strengthen the faith (*iman*) of Balinese Hindus. By learning what Hinduism truly is, they will become proud of their own religion and they will then be able to defend it against the proselytism of Abrahamic religions.

Be that as it may, it does not yet appear that such admonitions have had any significant effect on Balinese religious practices.

Bali as the world center of Hinduism?

It is thus in critical circumstances that Parisada held its Tenth Congress (*Mahasabha ke X*) on October 23–26, 2011, in Sanur, following which Ida Padanda Sebali Tianyar Arimbawa was once again re-elected as *Dharma Adhyaksa*. This provided an opportunity for Parisada, two years after the commemoration of its fiftieth anniversary, to project itself for the next fifty years by devising a *Grand Design Hindu Dharma Indonesia 2011–2061*—as ambitious in its declared objectives as it was modest in its effective reach. More interesting for my purpose were two initiatives proceeding from the congress, which aimed to unify Hindus, not only in Bali but also in Indonesia, and even worldwide.

One can see a response to the spread of Islamic 'sacred sites' (*keramat*) throughout Bali in the project to strengthen Hinduism in Indonesia by setting a network of nine temples located in relation to the points of the compass and the center—the *Padma Bhuwana Nusantara* (lit. 'Lotus World Archipelago'). This is based on a principle already in existence in Bali (and also in India), where a complex of nine temples protects the island against harmful influences from the invisible world (*niskala*). It is derived from the scheme of cosmological classification known in Java and Bali as *nawa sanga*, a tantric mandala that associates a series of items with the points of the compass: gods, weapons, colors, syllables, numbers, days, etc. (Acri and Stephen 2018: 172–8). Extended to the entire Indonesian Archipelago, the *Padma Bhuwana Nusantara* is presented as the "bastion of the resistance of Hinduism" (*benteng ketahanan Hinduisme*) (PHDI 2011: 112). Within this framework, Bali occupies the southern position, with the Pura Luhur Uluwatu, on the coast of the Bukit Peninsula, where Danghyang Nirartha is said to have achieved *moksa* (liberation from the cycle of death and rebirth). This project, attributed to Padanda Sebali, has been criticized by other *padanda*, who pointed out that in the *nawa sanga* the Pura Luhur Uluwatu is located in the southwest and not in the south, which happens to be an inauspicious direction in the Balinese (and Indic) cosmology. Overall, critics pointed out that Bali should remain the center of Hinduism in Indonesia, whereas in the *Padma Bhuwana Nusantara* the center is occupied by the Pura Pitamaha in Palangkaraya (Kalimantan). Furthermore, it is well known that as soon as the project was announced, leaders of various regional Parisada began fighting to obtain a *Pura Padma Bhuwana Nusantara* in their own area (*Raditya*, No. 175, February 2012: 7–21).

In any event, Parisada's ambitions extend beyond the boundaries of Indonesia: as of late its leaders aspire to promote Bali as center of Hinduism for the world. In fact, it appears that after the Balinese had successfully managed to persuade the Indonesian Ministry of Religion to recognize *agama Hindu* as a legitimate monotheistic religion—even though in the opinion of hardline Islamist organizations the Balinese people are still downright idolaters—they sought to convince Indian Hindus that their own religion was a genuine local offshoot of Hinduism. As already noted, starting in the 1990s, Balinese religious leaders endeavored by various means to demonstrate a firm connection to Indian Hinduism, from embracing Neo-Hindu devotional movements (*sampradaya*) to organizing pilgrimages (*tirta yatra*) to Hindu holy sites of India. In 2002, the governor of Bali, I Dewa Made Beratha, approached the Indian prime minister, Atal Bihari Vajpayee, leader of the Hindu nationalist Bharatiya Janata Party, with a view to developing Indian investments in Bali and to promoting the island as a choice destination for Indian tourists. Some time later, the *bupati* of Bangli went to India with Yadav Somvir at the request of the governor with the aim of considering the possibility of building a Balinese temple in Rishikesh, on the banks of the Ganges, to reciprocate the opening of the Indian Cultural Centre in Bali.[46] Although a great number of Indian tourists visited Bali in the following years, a Balinese temple has yet to be built in India. Besides, judging by the disappointment of Balinese pilgrims when they are denied access to certain Hindu temples in India, it is painfully clear that Indian Hindus do not yet acknowledge them as fellow co-religionists (Hornbacher 2017: 168).

---

[46] The Indian Cultural Centre was opened by the Indian Council for Cultural Relations in 2004 in Denpasar. Headed by Yadav Somvir, it was intended to promote academic exchanges and allocate scholarships to Indonesian students, besides teaching yoga, Sanskrit, and Indian dance and music.

Institutional relations have been more fruitful, however. Thus, Parisada managed to affiliate itself with the World Hindu Federation (WHF, a.k.a. Vishwa Hindu Mahasangh), an umbrella organization established in 1981 in Nepal under the patronage of King Birendra to coordinate the activities of Hindu-based movements the world over.[47] One of the founding fathers of Parisada, Ida Bagus Oka Punyatmadja, was vice-president of the WHF from 1988 to 1992, the year it held its third international conference in Bali under his chairmanship. For the occasion, the WHF even published a book by Punyatmadja (1992). The growing interaction of Balinese with global Hinduism advanced further in November 2004, when Bali hosted the First World Hindu Youth Summit with the backing of the Vishva Hindu Parishad, bringing together Hindu youth leaders from thirteen countries to debate the theme 'Shaping the Next Generation of Leaders of the Hindu Resurgence'. One outcome of the meeting was the establishment of the World Hindu Youth Organization, placed under the chairmanship of Gusti Ngurah Arya Wedakarna.[48]

The World Hindu Federation was seriously compromised by the abolition of the Nepalese monarchy in 2008, and its leaders have been trying to revive their organization ever since. The following year, during the commemoration of the fiftieth anniversary of Parisada's foundation, the question of the future of the WHF was raised by Padanda Sebali and AS. Kobalen (an Indonesian of Indian origin, founder of the Sabha Dharma Nusantara) (Kobalen 2009). After Parisada's Tenth Congress, Padanda Sebali traveled to Bangalore, in India, to meet with the vice-president of the WHF, Maharaj Jayapataka Swami, who was also the leader of the International Society for Krishna Consciousness (ISKCON). They decided to launch a new organization with a view to uniting Hindus throughout the world, which would be an equivalent of what the Organization of Islamic Cooperation is to Muslims (*Raditya*, No. 178, May 2012: 7–15). To this end, a World Hindu Summit was convened in Bali, under the auspices of Governor I Made Mangku Pastika and President Susilo Bambang Yudhoyono, which gathered from 9 to 12 June 2012 some two hundred delegates from fifteen countries on the theme 'Build Harmony to the World, from The Island of the Gods, Bali, Indonesia' (*Raditya*, No. 180, July 2012: 18–21). They issued the Bali Charter (*Piagam Bali*), which resolved to set up in Denpasar a World Hindu Centre (Pusat Hindu Dunia), in charge of implementing a World Hindu Parisad (Parisada Hindu Dunia), "an organization to unify Hindus,

---

[47] While the World Hindu Federation has no formal link with the Indian militant organization Vishva Hindu Parishad, both nonetheless share a common fundamentalist approach of Hinduism (Bouillier 1997).

[48] Interview, I Gusti Ngurah Arya Wedakarna, Istana Mancawarna, Tampaksiring, April 27, 2014.

coordinate activities and propagate Hindu Dharma globally" (*The Bali Charter*, June 9, 2012).

The World Hindu Summit was coordinated by four authorities: Parisada; the United Council of Balinese Ashrams (Dewan Persatuan Pasraman Bali); the Forum of Balinese University Presidents (Forum Rektor Bali); and the provincial government. A working committee was set up to implement the resolutions of the Bali Charter, assisted by a 45-member board of advisors chaired by Padanda Sebali and manned mostly by Balinese, with a handful of Indians representing various institutions, ashrams, and *sampradaya*, such as the Vishva Hindu Parishad, the Arya Samaj, the International Society for Krishna Consciousness, Sri Sathya Sai Baba, Brahma Kumaris, the Sri Aurobindo Centre, the Art of Living, etc. As for the Balinese members, they were clearly supporters of universal Neo-Hinduism, with the notable exception of Padanda Gunung, curiously placed at the forefront of the list of the board of advisors. This list also included Ida Bagus Yudha Triguna, in his capacity as director general for the guidance of the Hindu community (Dirjen Bimas Hindu) at the Ministry of Religion, the governor and the deputy-governor of Bali, and the chairman of the provincial parliament.

A second World Hindu Summit was convened in Bali from 13 to 17 June 2013, with an impressive opening ceremony held in the presence of the minister of religion, Suryadharma Ali, at the Pura Samuan Tiga, chosen once again with reference to the founding gesture credited to Mpu Kuturan. But while in the 11th century the purpose was to bring together Hindu sects within the limited context of Bali, a millennium later the objective was to unify Hindus across the whole world. This second World Hindu Summit officialized the foundation of both the World Hindu Centre (WHC) and the World Hindu Parisad (WHP), with the Parisada's *Dharma Adhyaksa*, Ida Padanda Sebali Tianyar Arimbawa,[49] as chairman, and the president of Udayana University, Professor I Made Bakta, as secretary-general. All Hindu organizations and *sampradaya* are welcome to become members of the World Hindu Parisad, with no restrictions whatsoever. The decision was taken to organize annual meetings in Bali, oddly named 'World Hindu Wisdom Meet', to discuss problems and challenges facing Hindus around the world and to provide the required solutions to address them (*Raditya*, No. 192, July 2013: 16–20).

The theme chosen for the first World Hindu Wisdom Meet, held in Denpasar on April 16–18, 2014, was 'Hinduism Based Education', which

---

[49] After Ida Padanda Sebali Tianyar Arimbawa passed away in February 2017, the WHP's chairmanship was entrusted to the governor of Bali, I Made Mangku Pastika.

allowed the various participants to talk ad libitum about their respective favorite topics. Thus, while Indian speakers stressed the continuing relevance of the principles of Vedic education (*gurukula*) and mentioned the numerous cutting-edge scientific discoveries contained in the Vedas—which, they claimed, were recognized as the source of all knowledge in the world—the Balinese for their part emphasized the Vedic wisdom that inspires the *Tri Hita Karana*. Unlike their Indian colleagues, however, more often than not outspoken and full of self-importance, Balinese speakers appeared frequently faltering and ill at ease. They were obviously disadvantaged by their generally poor command of English, and quite a few of them chose to present their speech in Indonesian, even though they were well aware that most foreign delegates would not understand them. But both Balinese and foreigners seemed to feel the need to defend and justify Hinduism, complaining that it was unfairly underestimated even though it is the oldest religion in the world and clearly superior to all the other religions, as it is the 'eternal religion' (*sanatana dharma*).[50] And they agreed on the need for further meetings on the same theme, by convening on June 9–11, 2015, a second World Hindu Wisdom Meet, this time entitled 'Hindu Dharma Based Education',[51] that did not add much to the previous one.

Besides the publication of the proceedings of these meetings, the World Hindu Centre launched a wide-ranging publishing program in both Indonesian and English. As examples of this, I mention a collective volume entitled *Konsep dan Praktik Agama Hindu di Bali* (Tim Peneliti WHP/WHC 2015), the Indonesian translation of H.D. Swami Prakashanand Saraswati's *The True History and the Religion of India: A Concise Encyclopedia of Authentic Hinduism* (Saraswati 2014), and even an English-language journal grandly named *BĀLIJYOTIḤ—International Journal of Theology, Philosophy, and Eastern Culture*. Its chief editor is the head of the World Hindu Centre, I Ketut Donder, and half of the 36-member board of editors is made up of foreigners, mostly Indian academics. Unfortunately, some of the contributions authored by Balinese are in such broken English as to be barely readable.

According to its leaders,[52] the launching of the World Hindu Parisad aimed to overcome past divisions, both in Bali and in the rest of Indonesia, which

---

[50] In 2016, the WHP's website published a long article in English entitled '*Sanatana Dharma* as a major world civilization', launching a well-argued, if somewhat veiled, critique of both the materialistic West and dogmatic religions such as Islam and Christianity.

[51] The change of title was due to the proposal of an Indian speaker at the World Hindu Wisdom Meet of 2014, who insisted on substituting 'Hindu Dharma' for 'Hinduism', a term rejected as being of foreign origin.

[52] Interviews with I Made Bakta, secretary-general of the World Hindu Parisad, Denpasar, July 9, 2013; Prabhu Darmayasa, chairman of the Organizing Committee of the 2014 World Hindu Wisdom Meet, April 29, 2014; Ida

weakened the Hindu community. Above all, it was intended to provide the Balinese with much-needed international backing against the growing pressure of Islam, by securing institutional ties with powerful global Hindu networks. It was expected further to instill in the Balinese people the high values of the Vedas so that they would not easily be converted to other religions. When I asked how it was that the tiny island of Bali had been chosen to host the world organization of Hinduism, my interlocutors alleged that it resulted from a Balinese initiative and that, as a Hindu minority in Indonesia, the people of Bali constituted a kind of microcosm of Hinduism and its predicament. Besides, Indian Hindus were divided between competing sects and organizations, and thus were unable to agree among themselves. This is the reason why their representatives decided that the World Hindu Parisad would be located in Bali.

It was initially planned to establish the World Hindu Centre on land belonging to the provincial government. Until that day, which is not foreseen in the near future, the World Hindu Parisad is accommodated in the Provincial Office for Culture (Dinas Kebudayaan Provinsi Bali) in Denpasar. Its funding is shouldered by the provincial budget, until hypothetical subventions from the relevant Hindu stakeholders can take over. In the meantime, its Balinese initiators are forced to admit that their human and financial resources are extremely limited. One may have an idea of their difficulties when one consults the WHP's website, which is seldom updated.[53]

It is painfully clear that since the World Hindu Summit of 2012 the initial enthusiasm has rapidly waned, judging by the sharp decline in the number of foreign delegates to the successive World Hindu Wisdom Meet over the years.[54] While the audience had always been mainly Balinese, it tended to become sparse as soon as the opening ceremony, invariably lavish and solemn, was over—not to mention that many Balinese could be seen chatting, playing with their smartphones or even sleeping during the sessions. The organizers of these meetings regularly bemoaned the fact that many invited foreign participants were not able to come to Bali, while asking the Balinese in the audience to beat the

---

Padanda Sebali Tianyar Arimbawa, chairman of the World Hindu Parisad, May 16, 2016; Ngakan Putu Putra, member of the Organizing Committee of the 2018 World Hindu Wisdom Meet and chief editor of *Media Hindu*, June 27, 2018.

[53] At the time of writing, the website of the World Hindu Parisad is no longer active. On the other hand, the website of the World Hindu Federation, now based in Delhi, does not even mention the World Hindu Parisad. What's more, I could not find any mention of the WHP in the proceedings of the Parisada's Eleventh Congress (*Mahasabha ke XI*), held in Surabaya on October 21–24, 2016 (PHDI 2016).

[54] The following yearly meetings chose different themes: 'Hindu Dharma Contributions to the World Civilization and Science' (2016); 'Para and Apara Vidya as the Basic Hindu Body of Knowledge' (2017); and 'Hindu for Better Life' (2018).

drum to fill up the venue of the meeting. Needless to say, these appeals did not have the desired effect. The World Hindu Wisdom Meet of 2018—the last one to be convened thus far—even had a somehow downbeat tone, as reflected by the opening speech of Made Mangku Pastika, as chairman of the World Hindu Parisad, who stressed the unfortunate fact that Hindu Balinese were on the wane in their own island.

What's more, a number of Balinese religious leaders are openly dismissive of the whole enterprise and do not hold out much hope for its chances of success. Indeed, it is rather doubtful whether the Balinese stakeholders are up to the task, as the discrepancy between the WHP's lofty objectives and its available means is glaring. Not only are the Balinese riddled by division and beset by poor management skills, but some of the project's initiators have admitted that they were encountering strong resistance from various quarters—Balinese as well as Indonesian and Indian. Even the Indian advisors to the working committee did not hide their impatience with the timidity of their Balinese colleagues, whom they deemed unable to take up their responsibility and to truly benefit from the support offered by Indian Hinduism. It would seem that the foreign signatories to the Bali Charter harbor no illusions about the Balinese capacity to bring about their project and that they are inclined to leave them to their own devices. As for the Balinese people at large, it must be acknowledged that, for the most part, they appear unconcerned with the World Hindu Parisad, when they are not simply unaware of its existence. Furthermore, numerous critics have pointed out that Parisada is not even able to properly manage *agama Hindu* in Balinese villages, how then could it hope to successfully champion Hinduism worldwide.[55]

This unfortunate state of affairs was recently illustrated by a controversy surrounding the Hare Krishna movement (ISKCON) which flared up in Balinese social media in June 2020, in the midst of the Covid-19 pandemic crisis. It seems that the protracted rejection of this particular *sampradaya*, seen as the most radical, had reached a boiling point, with numerous Balinese openly accusing its followers of disrupting and jeopardizing customary village rituals. To quell the growing controversy, the chairman of PHDI Bali, I Gusti Ngurah Sudiana, convened a meeting on June 30, 2020, whereupon he deferred the matter to PHDI Pusat and to the Ditjen Bimas Hindu, asking for official instructions. On July 22, several Hindu organizations approached Parisada Bali, demanding that it put an end to the activities of Hare Krishna in the island, since its teachings deviate from the Hindu traditions bequeathed by their ancestors and cause unrest in the Hindu-

---

[55] "*Umat Hindu di Bali masih amburadul, Parisada tak kedengaran di desa pakraman, lha, ini kok ngurusi Parisada Dunia, ya?*" (*Raditya*, No. 178, May 2012: 6).

Balinese community. Pointing out that ISKCON had been banned by the attorney general in 1984, they queried the decision of Parisada's Eighth Congress to 'protect' (*mengayomi*) the Hare Krishna *sampradaya*. On August 3, Hindu organizations grouped together in the Forum Komunikasi Taksu Bali organized a mass demonstration in Denpasar to demand the ban of Hare Krishna as contrary to *agama Hindu Bali*. Two days later, the head of the newly established Council of Customary Villages (Majelis Desa Adat Provinsi Bali, MDA),[56] Ida Pangelingsir Agung Putra Sukahet, instructed all *desa adat* in Bali to prevent members of *sampradaya*, and specifically of Hare Krishna, from carrying out their ritual practices in village temples and other public facilities operated by customary village authorities. By the same token, Putra Sukahet asked Parisada Pusat to officially reject Hare Krishna as a recognized Hindu religion in Indonesia and to withdraw its publications from public circulation as heretical and contradicting mainstream Hindu Bali religious teachings. Frustrated by the lack of response from Parisada Pusat, Parisada Bali and the Majelis Desa Adat issued on December 16, 2020, a joint decree—henceforth known as the *Bali Deklarasi*—formally restricting all activities of non-traditional *sampradaya* in Bali.[57] Endorsed by Bali's incumbent governor, I Wayan Koster, concerned about protecting Balinese culture and religion, this decree forbids all followers of *sampradaya*, on pain of legal sanctions, to interfere with the teachings and practices of *agama Hindu* in Bali, and specifically to proselytize the *umat Hindu Bali*. Eventually, on July 30, 2021, responding to Balinese pressure, Parisada Pusat officially withdrew its protection to ISKCON.[58] However, it is doubtful that this decision would suffice to settle the issues raised by the presence of *sampradaya* in Bali.

In brief, while the all-embracing World Hindu Parisad has clearly lost its luster, *agama Hindu Bali* appears strongly entrenched, with the PHDI Bali now aligning itself with the insular stance formerly championed by the PDHB.

---

[56] After the enactment of the National Law No. 6/2014 on Villages, the Majelis Desa Adat Provinsi Bali was set up on May 28, 2019, by a new Provincial Regulation on the Customary Village (*Peraturan Daerah Provinsi Bali No.4/2019 Tentang Desa Adat di Bali*), which replaced the *Peraturan Daerah Provinsi Bali No.3/2001 Tentang Desa Pakraman*.

[57] *Surat Keputusan Bersama (SKB) Parisadha Hindu Dharma Indonesia Provinsi Bali (PHDI) dan Majelis Desa Adat (MDA) Provinsi Bali Nomor: 106 PHDI-Bali/XII/2020 & Nomor: 07/SK/MDA-Prov.Bali/XII/2020 Tentang Pembatasan Kegiatan Pengembangan Ajaran Sampradaya Non-Dresta Bali di Bali.*

[58] *Surat Keputusan Nomor: 374/PHDI Pusat/VII/2021 tentang Pencabutan Surat Pengayoman Hare Krishna (ISKCON).*

Conclusion

The Predicament of *Kebalian*

The island of Bali is commonly depicted as a Hindu sanctuary in a Muslim Archipelago. Such a pervasive cliché is misleading, in that it assumes that the Balinese people, unlike their Javanese neighbors, have been successful in defending their Hindu heritage against the encroachment of Islam. By thus presuming that they still faithfully adhere to their religious traditions, one fails to consider the twofold process of 'religionization' and 'Hinduization' in which the Balinese engaged following the incorporation of their island into the Netherlands East Indies in the early 20th century. Far from being a return to their Indian sources as claimed by its initiators, this process amounts to the construction of Balinese 'religion' as 'Hinduism' (*agama Hindu*). Indeed, the Balinese had formerly no notion of a system of beliefs and practices that could be demarcated from other aspects of their life to be labeled 'religion'—let alone that this religion was 'Hinduism'. This required constructing the separate existence of religion as an encompassing frame of reference for the interpretation of practices which were then formulated as enactments of Hinduism. Such an undertaking was an outcome of the colonial encounter, which introduced to Bali the alien categories of both religion and Hinduism.

While the Balinese society has indeed been 'Indianized', in the sense that it is pervaded by Indic references, the fact is that the Balinese people used to attribute the origin of their social order and their religious traditions not to India but to the conquest of their island by the Javanese kingdom of Majapahit in the 14th century. It is on this origin myth that the Balinese nobility—the *triwangsa* (*brahmana*, *satria*, *wesia*)—bases the legitimacy of its status, by claiming to be descended from the Javanese lords who allegedly settled in Bali after the conquest. And it is also from Majapahit that the initiated priesthood of the *padanda* originated, which remained the exclusive prerogative of the *brahmana*. According to Balinese historiography, when Majapahit fell to Islam at the end of the 15th century, the nobility, the priests and the literati who refused to convert to the new religion are said to have found refuge in Bali, where they have carefully preserved their Javanese heritage.

Whatever the case, it would be wrong to infer that contemporary Balinese religious life is a straightforward continuation of that prevailing in Java at the time of Majapahit. On the contrary, it must be emphasized that the Balinese people have appropriated Indian and Javanese contributions and reinterpreted them in accordance with their own purposes: they were not passive recipients of external influences but active agents of their own acculturation. This means that despite the presence in Bali of numerous Sanskrit words and ritual elements of Indic origin, Balinese religion is fundamentally indigenous and localized, as it consists of rites relating specific groups of people to one another, to their ancestors, and to their territory.

Grateful to the Balinese for having preserved Hindu texts and rituals from the depredations of Islam, the early European orientalists construed Bali as a 'living museum' of Indo-Javanese civilization, the only surviving heir to the Hindu heritage swept away from Java by the coming of Islam. Hence, long before the Balinese began defining themselves as Hindu, orientalists had already Hinduized them, at a time when they had yet to learn the word Hinduism. In line with this orientalist view, Dutch colonial administrators held Hinduism to be the core of Balinese society and the warrant of its cultural integrity. Accordingly, it had to be protected through the enlightened paternalism of colonial tutelage from both the intrusion of Islam, which had strengthened its grip on the greater part of the Archipelago, and Christian missionaries, eager to set foot on the island. This conservative colonial policy was to have long-lasting implications. For one thing, by looking for the singularity of Bali in its Hindu heritage, while conceiving of Balinese identity as formed through an opposition to Islam, the Dutch established the framework within which the Balinese would define themselves. Furthermore, by attempting to preserve Bali's particularism from the rest of the Indies, they ended up accentuating it, while turning it into a challenge for the Balinese.

Notwithstanding the Dutch attempt to insulate Balinese society from disturbing foreign influences, Bali actually underwent rapid and profound changes as a result of the colonial encounter. To begin with, the colonial state imposed a uniform administrative structure throughout Balinese society by establishing a new type of village, the 'administrative village' (*desa dinas*), typically consisting of several 'customary villages' (*desa adat*). By instigating this dichotomy between customary matters, which they left to the Balinese, and administrative jurisdiction, which they took over, the Dutch initiated an unprecedented distinction between religious tradition and secular power. Next, the requirements of a modern administration were instrumental in the formation of a Balinese intelligentsia, since the colonial state needed educated natives to mediate between the local population and their European overlords. These Dutch-educated Balinese strove to make sense of the changes brought about by the opening up of their island to what they viewed as the advent of 'modern times' (*zaman modern*). Not only did they suffer the disruption of the familiar references which ordered and gave meaning to their lives, they were confronted with alien discourses telling them who they were and how they ought to conduct themselves. The upshot was that the turmoil of the colonial occupation drove the Balinese to question the foundations of their identity, while the inquisitive gaze of foreigners in their midst forced them to define what it meant to be Balinese in terms comprehensible to non-Balinese.

As it happened, since the 19th century the Balinese have increasingly been subjected to the views of outsiders—European orientalists, colonial administrators, Javanese nationalists, Muslim schoolteachers, Christian missionaries, Indian gurus, as well as artists, anthropologists and tourists, not to forget Indonesian government officials. Thus, Balinese identity has been constructed dialogically, through repeated assertions and ascriptions controlled by powerful outsiders, and in this way the Balinese appropriated the conceptual framework of influential foreigners with whom they had to engage.

In the 1920s, the first generation of Balinese educated in colonial schools founded modern organizations and started publishing periodicals, a complete novelty for Bali. These publications, devoted chiefly to social and religious issues, were written not in Balinese but in Malay, the language of Islam as well as of colonial modernity. Thus, the same process that led the Balinese to question their identity was dispossessing them of their own words, by making them think about themselves in a language that was not their own but that used by both their fellow countrymen and their colonial rulers. This linguistic substitution marked a reflexive distancing from the Balinese frame of reference, which was decontextualized, relativized and homogenized in the process.

In these publications, the Balinese began viewing themselves, for the first time, as a singular entity—as a 'people' (*bangsa Bali*). Until then, their identities were particularistic, in the sense that Balinese identified themselves as members of a village, a kinship group or a temple network, rather than as 'Balinese'. Now, as a people, the Balinese were defining themselves as an ethnic group, characterized by their own customs, and as a religious community, threatened by the proselytizing of Islam and Christianity. Specifically, they construed their identity—which they called their 'Balinese-ness' (*Kebalian*)—as being based on *agama* ('religion') and *adat* ('tradition'). The very fact of the Balinese resorting to these foreign terms to define their identity testifies to the conceptual shift occurring on their island after its takeover by a foreign power. Far from expressing a primordial essence, as they would have it, these categories were alien and had to be appropriated by the Balinese according to their own references and concerns.

Agama has not always meant 'religion' in Indonesia. In Shaiva tantric texts, *agama* signifies 'authoritative scripture', and it applies to anything handed down as fixed by tradition. Although it is difficult to establish when exactly the Sanskrit loanword *agama* came to mean religion in Indonesia, we know that in Javanese and Balinese textual traditions from the 12th century onward, it applied to law codes related to the Indian treatises on *dharma*, in which legal and religious features are not distinguished. We also know that in Malay chronicles dating back to the 14th century, *agama* is associated with Islam and used in a sense equivalent to that of *din*. Therefore, one has to conclude that for centuries the word *agama* had two distinct denotations in the Archipelago, that of *dharma* and that of *din*, according to the context and language in which it occurred. By appropriating this word, Indonesian Muslims endowed it with new meaning, namely, the exclusive worship of a transcendent God along with the requirement of conversion to a foreign doctrine whose teachings are contained in a holy book revealed by an inspired prophet. Later, through its adoption by Christian missionaries, *agama* became associated with an ideal of social progress, while 'pagan' beliefs were scorned as bygone superstitions and viewed as a cause for shame.

By taking on the meaning of 'religion', *agama* was not only being dissociated from 'law' but also from 'tradition', rendered in Indonesia by the Arabic loanword *adat*, which refers to both a worldview and an ethos, at once describing the ideal order and prescribing the behavior required to achieve that order. This comprehensive scope of *adat* was fragmented by Islamic proselytizers—and later by Christian missionaries—who confined its purview to customs that did not have an explicit religious legitimation. In particular, the word *adat* entered the language of Islamized populations to refer to indigenous 'customary law' as opposed to Islamic 'religious law' (*hukum*).

Introduced to Bali by the Dutch, the word *adat* replaced diverse terms for locally variable customs that governed the relationships between social groups and sanctioned the sense of communal solidarity in the villages. The decontextualization of a miscellaneous assortment of local customs and their incorporation into this generic term altered their meaning for the Balinese: what had until then been an interplay of significant and deliberately fostered differences between villages became the locus of Balinese ethnic identity, in the sense of a customary body of inherited values, norms, and institutions governing the lives of the Balinese people. As such, in Bali *adat* was not distinguished from *agama*. Indeed, *adat* pertains to the religious worldview of the Balinese, since it refers both to an immutable cosmic order and to the social order instituted accordingly by their deified ancestors.

While the word *agama* still conserved the meaning of *dharma* in Bali during the colonial period, it is no coincidence that when the Balinese were assessing their identity in the 1920s they used this word in the sense of 'religion', as they were seeking to promote their own religion to an equal standing with Islam and Christianity in order to resist their proselytism. For the Balinese, however, Islam and Christianity were seen not only as a threat, but also as a model of what a true religion should be. Confronted with Muslim schoolteachers and Christian missionaries, they were challenged to formulate what exactly their religion was about. This proved to be a highly contentious issue, which triggered a protracted conflict between those Balinese intending to retain their ritual traditions and those who wanted to reform them in accordance with what they assumed to be Hinduism. This conflict set the rising elite of educated commoners (*jaba*) against the conservative nobility (*triwangsa*) in their attempts to hold sway over the religious life of the Balinese people.

Although both commoners and nobility shared a common reference to *agama* and *adat* as the foundations of their *Kebalian*, they held different opinions as to how their respective fields were connected, and how Balinese religion related to Hinduism. Whereas the *triwangsa* were determined to strengthen both tradition and religion, the *jaba* wanted to reform *agama* while ridding *adat* of those customs they deemed obsolete. Thus, for the nobility, Balinese religion was based on the traditional social order, within which *agama* was inseparable from *adat*, while for the commoners, religion should be dissociated from a traditional order seen not only as unfair but also as an obstacle to progress. Yet, they proved unable to differentiate between what belonged to *agama* and what to *adat*.

This should come as no surprise given that, in contrast to Islamized or Christianized areas of Indonesia, in the Balinese language *agama* refers at once to 'religion' (*agama*), 'law' (*hukum*) and 'customs' (*adat-istiadat*). Yet, the difficulty of the Balinese in dissociating *agama* from *adat* does not stem solely from the polysemy of these terms, whose respective semantic fields largely overlap, but also from the fact that up until then the Balinese did not regard religion as a specific and circumscribed domain to be distinguished from other aspects of their social life. Hence, *agama* could not become a boundary marker for the Balinese people until they began to view Islam and Christianity as a threat.

In the 1930s, 'culture' (*budaya*)—together with 'art' (*seni*)—would be added to 'religion' and 'tradition' as a constituent part of *Kebalian*. The advent of the category of culture is due primarily to the persistence of the orientalist vision of Bali as a 'living museum' of Indo-Javanese civilization, further enhanced by the decision of the colonial government to culturalize Balinese identity in order to prevent the contamination of Bali by the nationalist and communist agitation that was rife in Java. At the time when the Dutch were engaged in culturalizing Bali, the cultural image of the island was being endorsed and magnified by its promotion as a tourist destination. Along with tourists, the artists and anthropologists who sojourned in Bali between the World Wars were influential in popularizing the spectacular extravagance of Balinese ceremonial pageants. The accounts, paintings, photographs and films that they brought back created an enchanting image of native life, an image that the emerging tourism industry quickly exploited. Not only did they certify and disseminate to the West the image of Bali as the 'last paradise', they also identified Balinese society with its culture—a culture essentially reduced to its ritual and artistic expressions. It would not be long before this idealized image would establish itself not only in the tourists' imagination but also in the Balinese consciousness.

This, briefly, is how the Balinese came to formulate their identity in terms of *agama*, *adat* and *budaya*, all alien conceptual categories that they had to appropriate and reinterpret for their own use. The emergence of the categories *agama* and *adat* results from a twofold process of differentiation: on the one hand, the Dutch-enforced separation between religious tradition and secular administration, and on the other, the growing urge to dissociate religion from tradition on the part of reform-minded educated Balinese. Afterwards, thanks to the contributions of orientalists and anthropologists, of artists and tourists, the Balinese adjoined the category *budaya* as a component of *Kebalian*. Now, with their tradition secularized and their culture touristified, their religion was becoming for the Balinese the diacritical marker of their identity.

After Indonesia's proclamation of independence, in 1945, the question of the foundation of the new state came rapidly to a head, pitting the 'Islamic group' (*golongan Islam*) against the 'nationalist group' (*golongan kebangsaan*). The former, confident that they represented an overwhelming majority of the Indonesian people, wanted to establish an Islamic state, whereas their opponents, concerned that such a decision would alienate Christians and other religious minorities, argued in favor of a state in which religious and secular affairs would be kept separate. This confrontation resulted in a compromise: the Indonesian state placed 'Belief in the One and Only God' (*Ketuhanan Yang Maha Esa*) first among its founding principles (Pancasila), without making Islam an official or even privileged religion. As a concession to the Islamic group, however, a Ministry of Religion was set up in 1946. Initially designed to promote Muslim interests, it was soon expanded to include separate sections for Protestantism and Roman Catholicism, thereby acknowledging Christianity as a legitimate religion.

Whereas the 1945 constitution guaranteed Indonesian citizens the freedom to profess and practice their own religion, the Ministry of Religion endeavored to restrict the legal scope of acknowledged religions in conformity with the Islamic view of what qualifies as a legitimate *agama*—that is, an understanding of religion as exclusivist, congregational, scripturalist, universalist and proselytical. Thus, even though Islam failed to establish itself as the official religion of Indonesia, its proponents succeeded in imposing their own conception of the relations between religion and the state, by framing and shaping all debate about religion. In 1952, the Ministry of Religion stipulated the following conditions for a religion to be officially recognized as *agama*: it must be monotheistic, have been revealed by a prophet and written down in a holy book, possess a codified system of law for its adherents, enjoy international recognition and, further, its following should not be limited to a single ethnic group.

According to these conditions, the Balinese did not have a proper 'religion' (*agama*) but only 'beliefs' (*kepercayaan*), which not only were limited to their island, but did not even form a coherent and unified ensemble valid for the whole island. In this sense, Balinese ritual practices were considered to belong to the domain of *adat* and not to *agama*. As a result, like other ethnic minorities who still practiced their traditional religion, the Balinese were classified as 'people who do not yet have a religion' (*orang yang belum beragama*), a label associated with primitive backwardness and parochialism. Consequently, if the Balinese did not want to become the target of Muslim or Christian proselytizing, their only recourse was to rationalize their religion and redefine it in transcendent and monotheistic terms, in order to make it eligible for the status of *agama*.

The first question to be settled was for the Balinese to agree on the name of their religion. After lengthy debate, they resolved in 1952 to call the Balinese religion *agama Hindu Bali*. In the past, the Balinese had no generic name to designate that which would later become known as their religion. Once they had adopted the word *agama* for this purpose, they referred to their religion simply as *agama Bali*. It is only after some Balinese had converted to Islam or to

Christianity that the name *Hindu Bali* became customary, in order to distinguish *Hindu Bali* from *Islam Bali* and *Kristen Bali*. But before it was officially adopted as the name of the Balinese religion, *Hindu Bali* was just one name among many.

However, even though the Balinese had finally reached an agreement among themselves, they still had to convince the Ministry of Religion of the legitimacy of *agama Hindu Bali*. Consequently, during the following years, they kept pressing for the recognition of their religion. While some religious leaders looked for the seeds of regeneration in their own indigenous traditions, young Balinese who were studying in India urged their co-religionists to return to the fold of Hinduism, which they presented as the source of their rites. Stressing the theological and ethical import of religion, they attempted to restrain the Balinese ritualistic leanings, while construing their Hindu heritage in accordance with the tenets of Islam and Christianity.

In 1958, after years of lobbying, a Hindu Bali division was finally established within the Ministry of Religion, a few weeks after Bali had become a full-fledged province of the Republic of Indonesia. The next step was to decide who should be in charge of *agama Hindu Bali*, now that the former kings, who had previously been the patrons of the main rituals on the island, had been replaced by the republican government. For that purpose, a council was set up in 1959 to coordinate the religious activities of the Hindu-Balinese community—Parisada Dharma Hindu Bali. Parisada's strategy was to promote internal homogeneity in the practice of Balinese religion in order to present a united front as a Hindu minority in a predominantly Muslim nation. With the backing and subsidies of the provincial government, Parisada undertook to regulate rituals, formalize the priesthood, standardize temples, compile a theological canon (*Panca Çraddha*), publish a Hindu catechism (*Upadesa*), devise a Hindu prayer (*Tri Sandhya*) as an equivalent of daily Islamic prayers, translate Hindu sacred scriptures into Indonesian and provide religious education to the population. This undertaking amounted to a 'scripturalization' of Balinese religion, in the sense that rites were now meant to comply with texts, and orthopraxy had to be substantiated by orthodoxy. Unlike the kings and priests of yore, who merely interceded on behalf of their subjects and clients, Parisada was now instructing the Balinese on what to believe and how to practice their religion accordingly—a religion said to come from India rather than from Majapahit.

This Hinduization of indigenous ritual practices rested on a democratization of religious knowledge that constituted a drastic break with traditional ideas of secret knowledge, as the Balinese had to understand their religion in order to be able to defend it from the questioning of followers of other religions. Thus, for the first time, Balinese individuals other than priests and literati were enjoined to find in their religion a logically coherent set of theological tenets and moral values. Furthermore, the newly instituted monotheism implied that, instead of collective transactions with immanent entities and forces from the invisible world (*niskala*), Balinese Hindus were expected to establish a personal relationship of faith and devotion with their One and Only God—Sang Hyang Widi. This in turn entailed a twofold differentiation, between 'gods' and 'ancestors', as well as between the 'divine' and the 'demonic'. While there were formerly no clear lines of demarcation between ancestors and gods, but instead hierarchical ideas of less and more purified ancestors who eventually became merged with divinities, now there had to be an absolute dichotomy between human ancestors and a transcendent God. Besides, whereas *niskala* entities were inherently ambivalent, potentially benevolent as well as malevolent, Sang Hyang Widi had become an entirely positive figure.

During the 1960s, the growing presence of Balinese communities outside their own island enabled Parisada to extend its influence across the Archipelago. Cut off from their temple networks and their deified ancestors, these Balinese migrants needed a delocalized and scriptural religion which they could carry with them. In these circumstances, Parisada leaders who had studied in India advocated giving up the exclusive label *Hindu Bali* in favor of the inclusive *Hindu Dharma*, in order to strengthen the position of their religion vis-à-vis Islam and Christianity. As a result, during its first congress, in 1964, Parisada Dharma Hindu Bali changed its name to Parisada Hindu Dharma, thus forsaking any reference to its Balinese origins. And when, the following year, President Sukarno specified the religions that would qualify for official recognition, it was *agama Hindu* and no longer *agama Hindu Bali* that was retained.

Thus it is that through their struggle to obtain recognition of their religion, the Balinese came to define their ethnic identity in terms of *agama Hindu*. But it is precisely from the moment they began to identify themselves as a Hindu island in a sea of Islam that one can date the premises of a disjunction between the Balinese religious and ethnic identities. This is because their identification of ethnicity and religion would soon be foiled by a dual process of Indonesianization-cum-Indianization: on the one hand, the affiliation of other Indonesian ethnic groups with *agama Hindu* dissociated it from the Balinese, while on the other hand, the growing influence of Indian Neo-Hinduism on *agama Hindu* rendered the link between religion and ethnicity ever more problematic for the Balinese.

Once detached from any ethnic reference, *agama Hindu* was no longer the sole property of the Balinese people, who had to open it up to other ethnic groups. In the wake of the anti-communist massacres of 1965–66, which established the New Order of President Suharto, its official recognition prompted Javanese nominal Muslims to become affiliated with *agama Hindu* for fear of being branded 'atheist', an accusation synonymous with 'communist' in Indonesia. In the following years, several ethnic minorities took refuge in the *Hindu* fold hoping to be allowed to conserve their ancestral rites, *agama Hindu* being reputedly more accommodating in this respect than Islam or Christianity. The diffusion of *agama Hindu* outside Bali continued to such an extent that Balinese began to fear a loss of control over the religion whose recognition they had fought so hard to obtain. But what appeared to some Balinese as the dispossession of their own religion was perceived by other Indonesian Hindus as Balinese colonization. Hence the rising of a tension between the Balinization of the religious practices of various ethnic groups affiliated with *agama Hindu* on the one hand, and the Indonesianization of the Balinese religion aimed at detaching it from its ethnic origins on the other.

In due time, this tension would eventually affect Parisada itself. After having established branches in every province of the country, at the time of its fifth congress, in 1986, Parisada Hindu Dharma became Parisada Hindu Dharma Indonesia. As a consequence, non-Balinese as well as Balinese commoners were promoted to Parisada's leadership, hitherto dominated by *triwangsa*. Then, in 1996, at the time of its seventh congress, overriding the opposition of Balinese delegates, Parisada headquarters were relocated from Bali to Jakarta, leaving only a regional branch on the island.

In the 1990s, the Islamic resurgence in Indonesia aroused the concern of the Balinese over their religious identity and triggered in mimetic fashion a 'Hindu Revival' (*Kebangkitan Hindu*). This movement resulted in the founding of new religious organizations which were critical of Parisada, whom they accused of being more a pressure group of conservative members of the Balinese nobility than a genuine religious body, and of promoting a traditionalist conception of *agama Hindu*, still very much affected by its native Balinese parochialism. This criticism was expressed particularly by two socio-religious movements which pursued distinct aims but whose actors originated from similar milieux—the *warga* and the *sampradaya*.

The *warga* movement resumed the commoners' struggle against the privileges of the nobility initiated in the 1920s. After Indonesia's independence, the main *jaba* title groups set up formal organizations uniting all members of a kinship group who considered themselves the descendants of a common ancestor. Their aim was to have their rights acknowledged against the prerogatives of the *triwangsa*, and specifically to abrogate the *brahmana*'s monopoly on the initiated priesthood by imposing the use of their own priests alongside the *padanda*. Under pressure from the *warga*, Parisada had decreed during its second congress, in 1968, that all Hindus were entitled to undergo the ordination rite to the initiated priesthood and, furthermore, that all duly initiated priests had the same status and were thus equally qualified to officiate at all ceremonies. This decree, however, did not settle the matter as, in spite of Parisada's official position, some of its leaders continued to defend the exclusive privileges of the *brahmana*.

While supporting the *warga*'s demand that their priests be allowed to officiate on a par with *padanda*, Balinese reformers were no longer satisfied with a nationally recognized religion. They began a renewed turn towards India, marked by the promotion of Indian concepts and practices, such as vegetarianism or the performance of the revived Vedic ritual *Agni Hotra*. They introduced the motto 'Back to Veda', according to the erroneous assumption that the Vedas had been transmitted to Bali, where they had fallen into oblivion, as in India. Pilgrimages were organized to the Hindu holy sites of India (*tirta yatra*), where Indonesian Hindus were urged to seek the sources of their religion, in the manner of Muslims going on the *hajj* to Mecca. Above all, this rapprochement with India was marked by the rise in Indonesia of Neo-Hindu devotional movements (*sampradaya*), such as Sai Baba and Hare Krishna, the most popular among them. The propagation of these movements in Indonesia met with some opposition from the Ministry of Religion as well as from Parisada, who feared conflicts between rival sects that might undermine the Hindu community, already weakened by its minority position and divided by the diversity of its ethnic origins.

It thus turns out that this much-vaunted 'Hindu Revival' has in fact resulted in a fragmentation of the religious allegiance of Hindu Balinese into three distinct persuasions—*Hindu-Bali, Hindu-Indonesia* and *Hindu-India*—that would prove difficult to reconcile. From then on, neither the traditional religion, attached to the correct execution of rites, nor the official *agama Hindu* promoted by Parisada, concerned with ethics and theology, were able to meet the aspirations of a growing portion of urbanized middle-class Balinese, who are in quest of religious devotion and personal conviction. This active minority is intent on universalizing its religious identity by completely severing *agama Hindu* from *adat Bali* and by fully embracing Indian Neo-Hinduism as a world religion.

To sum up, these various dynamics are the outcome of a double-edged split that divides the Balinese people along two different lines, even though they tend to overlap:
- on the one hand, a status competition between *triwangsa*, mainly *brahmana*, and *jaba*, particularly commoner *warga*;
- on the other hand, an opposition between those Balinese who want to hold on to their local traditions and those who aspire to universalize *agama Hindu* after the model of Indian Neo-Hinduism, foremost among them the members of *sampradaya*.

The resignation of President Suharto in 1998 resulted in a major political restructuring while unleashing centrifugal forces in the regions. It opened up an era of reforms (*Reformasi*), marked by a process of decentralization and a spate of cultural, ethnic, and religious identity politics, against a background of severe economic and social crisis. Thanks to tourism, Bali was less affected by this crisis than other regions of Indonesia, and its relative prosperity prompted a massive influx of labor migrants—Muslims for the most part—in search of a better livelihood. The growing heterogeneity of the population on the island created stirrings of resentment among Balinese Hindus, accompanied by outbreaks of rejection of newcomers.

The promulgation of laws on regional autonomy in 1999 led in Bali to a revitalization of the customary village communities, whose traditional prerogatives had been unduly appropriated by the state during the New Order regime. The purpose of the provincial regulation on the customary village (*Perda Desa Pakraman*), issued in 2001, was to restore full authority to Balinese villages to run their internal affairs. In order to give the newly reinstated customary village a more specific Indic flavor, its name was changed from *desa adat* to *desa pakraman*. Unlike the word *adat*, which has both a colonial and an Islamic connotation, the term *pakraman* is said to be derived from Sanskrit and claims its authority from Old Balinese inscriptions.

One of the most contentious points of the *Perda Desa Pakraman* concerned the role attributed to the villages in controlling immigration. By defining the *desa pakraman* as a Hindu religious community, the regulation discriminated between Hindu Balinese, ex-officio legitimate members of village institutions, and non-Hindu residents, who were stigmatized as outsiders as they were denied full participation in the village community. Furthermore, while Balinese reformers had been striving for decades to universalize their religion by segregating it from their indigenous traditions, the *Perda Desa Pakraman* subsumed *agama Hindu* under *adat Bali* by compelling Hindu Balinese to comply with local customary regulations. Consequently, there has been an upsurge in Balinese ritualism, which the reformers had tried in vain to reduce.

This resurgence of Balinese *adat* accentuated tensions between Parisada's old guard and reformers promoting its regeneration, pitting a conservative faction grounded in village communities and courtly circles against a reform-minded faction driven by the urbanized middle class and the progressive intelligentsia, who denounced Balinese customary ritual practices as parochial and outdated. This strife came to a head during Parisada's eighth congress, in 2001. The Balinese branch of Parisada objected to several decisions adopted by the congress, namely the nomination of a layman to Parisada's chairmanship, which had hitherto been monopolized by *padanda*, not to mention the conspicuous presence in its direction of non-Balinese as well as prominent members of commoner *warga* and *sampradaya*. A few weeks later, the Balinese Parisada convened its own congress at Campuan. Accusing the central leadership of undermining Balinese identity by unduly Indianizing *agama Hindu*, the Campuan congress demanded the nomination of a *padanda* as chairman while refusing the admission of *sampradaya* into Parisada.

Soon afterward, the central Parisada refused to recognize Parisada Campuan and convened a competing regional congress at Besakih. After Parisada Besakih had duly ratified the decisions of the eighth national congress, it was acknowledged as the official Balinese branch of Parisada. During the following years, each of the two Balinese Parisada claimed to be the legitimate representative of the Balinese Hindu community. While Parisada Besakih had the support of the middle-class urban intelligentsia and those Balinese living outside the island, Parisada Campuan appeared to be more in line with the village population.

In 2007, Parisada Campuan convened its own congress, which decided to return to the 'true self' (*jati diri*) of the Balinese religion—that is, to *agama Hindu Bali*—implying to see its origins in Majapahit rather than India. By the same token, the congress resolved to revert to the name originally chosen by their founding fathers, Parisada Dharma Hindu Bali. This return to *agama Hindu Bali* reveals itself to be much more than a withdrawal into Balinese parochialism on the part of a group of die-hard reactionaries, as contended by their opponents. The schism within the Balinese Parisada illustrates a divide centered on two interrelated issues: the desire of preserving *brahmana*'s priestly authority on the one hand, and the challenge to Balinese leadership over *agama Hindu* in Indonesia on the other. Conservative Balinese elites were attempting to regain control of their religion in order to put an end to both its Indonesianization and its Indianization, by winning back the direction of Parisada that they lost since the establishment of its headquarters in Jakarta in 1996. The crux of the matter is indeed the displacement of Parisada outside Bali, with the increasing domination of non-Balinese and commoner *warga* over its leadership to the detriment of *triwangsa*, and the ascendancy of *sampradaya* aiming to get rid of age-old religious traditions with the intent of forcing their own rites upon the Balinese people.

Over the years, the conflict between the two Balinese factions appears to have faded somewhat, although the reasons for its outbreak have yet to be properly addressed. In any event, the comeback of *agama Hindu Bali* might be understood as a return to a meaning of *agama* untainted by its Islamic and Christian interpretations, when *agama* had not yet been separated from *adat*. One could say that Parisada Dharma Hindu Bali reclaimed the power to identify as *agama* that which Parisada Hindu Dharma Indonesia considered *adat*, just as the latter had earlier claimed the power to designate as *agama* that which the Ministry of Religion had classified as *adat*. In short, the promoters of *agama Hindu Bali* are deliberately reversing the process of universalization of the Balinese religion by relocalizing it. In so doing, they are displaying a heightened sense of Balinese empowerment—something which would not have been possible during the New Order.

Conservative Balinese elites were not the only ones to assert themselves in the era of *Reformasi*, since the rise of public religious expression allowed by the demise of the New Order resulted in increasing Islamization of Indonesian society. New Islamist parties and organizations sprang up that demanded a formal endorsement of Islam by the state while seeking to impose the implementation of its tenets in private and public life. Most dramatically, the resurfacing of political Islam manifested itself in outbreaks of communal violence and acts of terror perpetrated against religious minorities. The island of Bali was the target of a major Islamist terrorist attack in 2002—followed by a second one in 2005—which convinced the Balinese that they were under siege.

Besides some rather ineffective attempts at closing the island to outsiders, the feeling of insecurity caused by the terrorist attack brought about a renewed formulation of *Kebalian*. During the ensuing months, a party of journalists, academics and politicians launched the slogan *Ajeg Bali* ('Bali Erect'), which was to become an obligatory reference in Balinese public discourses for years to come. According to its promoters, the critical situation of Bali was due not only to the terrorist attack, but also to the fact that the Balinese people had lost control of their island, which was exploited by foreign investors, invaded by immigrant workers, and threatened by Islam and Christianity.

Far from inducing the Balinese people to close ranks in the face of external threats, however, the *Ajeg Bali* campaign gave rise to criticism from various quarters on the island. Progressive intellectuals reproached it for freezing Balinese society by preserving outdated customs and values in order to buttress abusive privileges of conservative elites whose power had been jeopardized by the *Reformasi*. They denounced a xenophobic ideology, which fostered primordial ethnic and religious identification by erecting boundaries between Balinese and non-Balinese, and by sparking Hindu fundamentalism as a response to Islamic pressure.

While progressive intellectuals associated *Ajeg Bali* with the rise of Hindu fundamentalism, Hindu religious leaders accused its promoters of fostering Balinese cultural and ethnic identity to the detriment of the Hindu religion. According to them, if the purpose of *Ajeg Bali* was to preserve Balinese culture, then it concerned Muslim and Christian Balinese as much as it did Hindu Balinese. If this were the case, Bali was doomed to meet with the same fate as Java after the coming of Islam, when the Javanese discarded their religion while holding on to their culture. Conversely, if the aim was to defend Balinese religion against the intrusion of Islam and Christianity, *Ajeg Hindu* should be promoted instead. As long as the Hindu religion is alive in Bali, they claimed, Balinese culture would be resilient as well since it has its source in Hinduism.

The slogan *Ajeg Bali* is now mostly a thing of the past. Yet the problems it was meant to address have not disappeared, as the encroachment of Islam and Christianity on Bali is more pressing than ever. The fact is that *agama Hindu* is threatened not only by the settling of Muslim immigrants in Bali and aggressions of Islamist hardliners, but also by the dramatic increase in conversions of Balinese to Islam and Christianity, to the point that Hindu Balinese are beginning to fear that they might eventually become a minority in their own island. Hence, in order to prevent conversion, as well as to bring back the victims of conversion to the fold of *agama Hindu*, Balinese religious leaders and Hindu activists have taken renewed measures to defend the Hindu community against Islamic and Christian proselytizing—all the while denouncing Parisada's failure to do so.

Aware of these criticisms, Parisada leaders were to take a particularly ambitious initiative to strengthen the position of *agama Hindu* in Indonesia. After the Balinese had successfully managed to convince the Ministry of Religion to acknowledge *agama Hindu* as a proper monotheistic religion, they sought to convince Indian Hindus that Bali was truly a local branch of Hinduism. Thus,

Parisada succeeded in affiliating itself with the World Hindu Federation, an umbrella organization established in 1981 in Nepal under the patronage of King Birendra to coordinate the activities of Hindu-based movements the world over.

The World Hindu Federation was seriously compromised by the abolition of the Nepalese monarchy in 2008, and its leaders have been trying to revive their organization ever since. Following Parisada's tenth congress in 2011, its chairman seized the opportunity to meet with the World Hindu Federation's leadership in India, and they decided to launch a new organization with a view to uniting Hindus throughout the world, which would be an equivalent of what the Organization of Islamic Cooperation is to Muslims. To this end, a World Hindu Summit was convened in 2012 in Bali, which gathered dozens of delegates from wide-ranging Hindu organizations, with Bali's governor and Indonesia's president in attendance. They issued the Bali Charter, which resolved to set up in Denpasar a World Hindu Centre, in charge of implementing a World Hindu Parisad, an organization to unify Hindus, coordinate their activities, and propagate Hindu Dharma globally. A second World Hindu Summit was convened in 2013, which officialized the foundation of both the World Hindu Centre and the World Hindu Parisad, with the head of Parisada as chairman. On that occasion, it was decided to organize annual meetings in Bali, oddly named 'World Hindu Wisdom Meet', to discuss problems and challenges facing Hindus around the world and to provide the required solutions to address them.

According to its leaders, the launching of the World Hindu Parisad aimed to overcome divisions within the Hindu community, both in Bali and in the rest of Indonesia. Above all, it was intended to provide the Balinese with much-needed international backing against the growing pressure of Islam, by securing institutional ties with powerful global Hindu networks. However, one may wonder what can come of their efforts, as the discrepancy between the World Hindu Parisad's lofty objectives and its available means is glaring. Not only are the Balinese riddled by division and beset by poor management skills, but some of the island's religious leaders are openly dismissive of the whole enterprise and do not hold out much hope for its chances of success. Besides, several of the project's initiators openly admitted that they were encountering strong resistance from various quarters—Balinese as well as Indonesian and Indian. As for the Balinese people at large, it must be acknowledged that, for the most part, they appear unconcerned with the World Hindu Parisad, when they are not simply unaware of its existence. Furthermore, numerous critics have pointed out that Parisada is not even able to properly manage *agama Hindu* in Balinese villages, how then could it hope to successfully champion Hinduism worldwide.

Be that as it may, while the initial ambitions of the World Hindu Parisad have rapidly waned, the divide has widened further between those Balinese concerned with preserving the specificity of their indigenous traditions and those who aspire to reform local practices by bringing *agama Hindu* into line with Neo-Hinduism. This divide attests to the disintegration of the discursive construction of *Kebalian*, torn between two alternative referents—*adat* and *agama*—which resulted in a contentious fragmentation of Balinese religious identity. With ever growing disagreement over whether *adat* should be religionized or *agama* traditionalized, what constitutes 'religion' in Bali is no longer a unified field of practices and beliefs, but it has become a contested arena in which political, ethnic, and religious struggle is played out. While Hindu fundamentalists are busy inventing a world religion true to their idealized vision of Vedic India, conservative elites are seeking to reinstate their Majapahit credentials, whereas common folk are inclined to take shelter in the parochial haven of their customary village community. Indeed, since what defines the Balinese as a Hindu minority in Indonesia is no longer their exclusive property, while their religious identity has become controversial, it is understandable that faced with what they perceive as a multifarious menace from outside, the Balinese would tend to retreat into the intimacy of their *adat*.

Thus, a two-way process has been taking place: concurrent with the universalization of *agama Hindu*, there has been a contrary movement of re-localization, with a return to *agama Hindu Bali* together with a revival of *adat Bali* and its associated ritual practices. Such is the predicament of *Kebalian*: while in order to obtain recognition of their religion by the Indonesian state it had been necessary for the Balinese to dissociate their religious affiliation from their ethnic belonging by setting up boundaries between *agama* and *adat*, after the loosening of normative constraints permitted by *Reformasi*, one observed a blurring of boundaries between *adat* and *agama*, with attempts at reunifying the Balinese religious and ethnic identities.

In retrospect, it appears that the contemporary Hinduization of the Balinese religion is the result of a misapprehension. Although their embrace of *agama Hindu* has allowed the Balinese to counter to some extent Islamic and Christian proselytizing, it was effected at the expense of a denial. Far from restoring their Indian heritage as they claimed, by means of internal rationalization and alignment with transnational Neo-Hinduism, the Balinese reformers have in fact dissociated themselves from their religious roots—including those derived from tantric Shaivism. By thus renouncing their ancestral practices, although of Indic origin, in order to embrace a Neo-Hindu orthodoxy that was perfectly alien to them, they assumed that they could withstand the Abrahamic religions on their own ground. In doing so, they ended up appropriating the Islamic criteria of what a true religion should be, and this long before the Indonesian Ministry of Religion imposed its requirements for the official recognition of their religion. The semantic evolution of the word *agama* provides a revealing account of this substitution, since while it formerly referred to texts belonging to Shaiva tantric traditions, it has come to designate a particular Abrahamic religious conception.

One should therefore distinguish between two distinct processes of religionization—the enforcement of certain religious politics by Indonesian state institutions on the one hand, and the determination of Balinese social and intellectual elites to appropriate the category 'religion' as a means of empowerment vis-à-vis authoritative discourses and practices on the other. While there were negative incentives for the Balinese to affiliate with Hinduism as a world religion, such as the threats posed by Islamic and Christian pressures, there were also positive motivations, since the claim of belonging to a world religion could bring access to both government recognition and influential global networks. Yet, there are potentially adverse consequences as well, since the compulsion to define their identity in religious terms obliged the Balinese to determine what counts as religious and what is dismissed as superstition, or in other words, what is acknowledged as a legitimate exercise of religion and what is not. As we have seen, this dual process of religionization has provoked a tension between Balinese eager to defend their own indigenous cosmological frameworks and customary ritual practices, who consider these practices to be self-sufficient and deserving of the label *agama* in their own right, and advocates of Neo-Hinduism as a world religion, who deny such local traditions the qualification of *agama*.

Like other ethnic groups around the world, the Balinese people are struggling to shield themselves from the challenges of globalization by clinging to what they claim as their roots. So much so that they are inclined to seek refuge in a primordial definition of their identity at a time when the boundary between the inside and the outside of Bali is proving increasingly difficult to draw and to enforce, if only because of the growing heterogeneity of the people who have made this island their home—not only fellow Indonesians of various ethnic origins and religious denominations, but also thousands of foreign expatriates, and of course the millions of visiting tourists.

As a result, Bali is today in a paradoxical situation. On the one hand, tourism has opened up the island and increased its dependence on the outside world. But on the other hand, their religious particularism, their ethnocentric inclination, and the perils they feel threatened by have led the Balinese to retreat into their insular identity and to develop a siege mentality which hardly prepares them to solve the problems they face.

Balinese and Indonesian Organizations

Akademi Seni Tari Indonesia (ASTI): Indonesian Dance Academy, founded in 1967 in Denpasar; it became the Indonesian College of the Arts (Sekolah Tinggi Seni Indonesia, STSI) in 1988, and in 2003 it merged with the Study Program of Art and Design of Udayana University to become the Indonesian Institute of the Arts (Institut Seni Indonesia, ISI).

Aliansi Masyarakat Adat Nusantara (AMAN): Alliance of Indigenous Peoples of the Archipelago, founded on March 17, 1999, in Jakarta with the aim of obtaining official recognition of all Indonesian customary communities as 'indigenous peoples'.

Angkatan Muda Hindu-Bali (AMHB): Movement of the Hindu-Balinese Youth, established in June 1950 in Jakarta; it became the Movement of Hindu Youth of Indonesia (Angkatan Muda Hindu Indonesia, AMHI) on November 20, 1966.

Badan Kongres Kebatinan Indonesia (BKKI): Congressional Body for Indonesian Mysticism, set up in 1955 with the aim of obtaining for 'mysticism' (*kebatinan*) a status equal to that of 'religion' (*agama*); in 1970, its was revived as Badan Kongres Kepercayaan Kejiwaan Kerohanian Kebatinan Indonesia (BK5I), which soon after became the Coordinating Secretariat of Beliefs (Sekretariat Kerjasama Kepercayaan, SKK).

Badan Koordinasi Pengawas Aliran Kepercayaan Masyarakat (Bakor Pakem): bureau for the surveillance of the 'currents of belief' (*aliran kepercayaan*), established in 1954 by the Ministry of Religion.

Badan Koordinator Usaha Pelajar (BKUP): Coordinating Committee of High School Students, set up on August 17, 1950, in Malang.

Badan Penyelidik Usaha-usaha Persiapan Kemerdekaan Indonesia (BPUPKI): Investigating Committee for the Preparation of Indonesian Independence, established by the Japanese occupation authorities on April 29, 1945.

Bagian Urusan Hindu Bali: Division of Hindu Balinese Affairs, established within the Ministry of Religion on January 1, 1959.

Balai Pustaka: 'Bureau of Literature', the main colonial publishing house, founded in 1917 in Batavia as the Kantoor voor de Volkslectuur.

Bali Darma Laksana (BDL): socio-cultural Balinese organization founded on July 26, 1936, in Singaraja, which published the monthly journal *Djatajoe* from 1936 to 1941.

Bali-Instituut: institute established in 1915 in Amsterdam as part of the Koloniaal Instituut to collect documentation on Balinese society.

Bali Museum: museum opened in 1932 in Denpasar with the aim of preserving examples of traditional Balinese architectural styles and other cultural artifacts; that same year, a Bali Museum Association (Vereeniging Bali-Museum) was established to disseminate knowledge of Balinese architecture, arts and crafts, and ethnography.

Balisch Studiefonds: association founded on March 22, 1936, in Singaraja for the purpose of providing scholarships to needy Balinese pupils and students.

Biro Urusan Agama Hindu Bali: Bureau of the Hindu Balinese Religious Affairs, which replaced the Bagian Urusan Hindu Bali in 1963 within the Ministry of Religion.

Budi Utomo: 'High Endeavor', the first native political society in the Dutch East Indies, founded on May 20, 1908, in Batavia.

Departemen Pendidikan dan Kebudayaan: Department of Education and Culture.

Dewan Nasional: National Council, set up by President Sukarno in May 1957 to deliberate issues on general policy matters and issue recommendations to parliament.

Dewan Pemerintah Daerah (DPD): Regional Government Council; the executive authority on the island of Bali, established on September 25, 1950.

Dewan Persatuan Pasraman Bali (DPPB): United Council of Balinese Ashrams, set up on September 19, 2008, to obtain government protection for ashrams in Bali.

Dewan Perwakilan Daerah (DPD): Regional Representative Council, established in 2004; together with the Dewan Perwakilan Rakyat (DPR), it makes up the Majelis Permusyarawatan Rakyat (MPR).

Dewan Perwakilan Rakyat (DPR): People's Representative Council, established after the general elections of 1955.

Dewan Perwakilan Rakyat Daerah Sementara (DPRDS): Provisional Regional People's Representative Council; the legislative authority on the island of Bali, established on September 25, 1950; it became the Regional People's Representative Council (Dewan Perwakilan Rakyat Daerah, DPRD) after the general elections of 1955.

Dewan Raja-Raja: Council of Balinese Rajas, established in January 1946 as a counterweight to the regional republican administration.

Dinas Agama Otonoom Daerah Bali: Autonomous Office of Religion for the Region of Bali, established in Singaraja on November 1, 1954, to take charge of the followers of *agama Hindu Bali*.

Direktorat Jenderal Bimbingan Masyarakat Hindu: Directorate General for the Guidance of the Hindu Community, established in 2006 to institutionally separate Hinduism from Buddhism within the Department of Religion.

Direktorat Jenderal Bimbingan Masyarakat Hindu Bali dan Buddha: Directorate General for the Guidance of the Hindu Balinese and Buddhist Communities, established within the Department of Religion in 1966.

Direktorat Jenderal Bimbingan Masyarakat Hindu dan Buddha: Directorate General for the Guidance of the Hindu and Buddhist Communities, established within the Department of Religion in 1969.

Direktorat Jenderal Kebudayaan: Directorate General of Culture.

Direktorat Pembinaan Penghayat Kepercayaan Terhadap Tuhan Yang Maha Esa: Directorate for the Supervision of the Followers of Belief in the One and Only God, established in 1978 within the Department of Education and Culture to monitor the 'currents of belief' (*aliran kepercayaan*).

Eka Laksana: educational association founded on July 14, 1935, in Denpasar.

Forum Advokasi Hindu Dharma (FAHD): Forum for the Advocacy of Hinduism, founded on June 1, 2018, in Denpasar to protect the rights of Hindus.

Forum Bali Harmoni: forum set up in 2013 by supporters of the Benoa Bay reclamation project.

Forum Cendekiawan Hindu Indonesia (FCHI): Forum of Indonesian Hindu Intellectuals, founded on September 19, 1991, in Jakarta.

Forum Komunikasi Taksu Bali: a grouping of Balinese Hindu associations opposed to Hare Krishna as contrary to *agama Hindu Bali*.

Forum Pemerhati Hindu Dharma Indonesia (FPHDI): Forum of Indonesians Concerned for Hinduism, founded on January 2, 1995, in Denpasar to defend the Indonesian Hindu Community against attacks of radical Muslims and to reform Parisada in a more democratic and universalist fashion.

Forum Penyadaran Dharma: Forum for Religious Awakening, founded in 1996 in Denpasar.

Forum Rakyat Bali Tolak Reklamasi Teluk Benoa (ForBALI): Balinese People's Forum Against Benoa Bay Reclamation, a Denpasar-based coalition of opponents of the Benoa Bay reclamation project, set up in August 2013.

Gandhi Ashram: ashram founded in 1976 at Candi Dasa, to propagate Gandhi's teachings.

Gerakan Kumara Bhavana (GKB): Hindu youth movement founded on May 25, 1955, in Denpasar.

Gereja Kristen Jawi Wetan: Christian Church of East Java, established in 1931.

Gereja Kristen Protestan di Bali (GKPB): Christian Protestant Church in Bali; the name adopted by the Balinese Protestant Church in 1948, formerly known as the Pasikian Kristen Bali.

Golongan Karya (Golkar): 'Functional Groups'; originally established in October 1964 by the National Armed Forces as a counterweight to the PKI's influence, Golkar was turned into a political party to support the New Order of President Suharto.

Himpunan Penghayat Kepercayaan terhadap Tuhan Yang Maha Esa (HPK): Association of the Followers of Belief in the One and Only God, established in 1979.

Hollandsch-Inlandsche School (HIS): Dutch Native Schools providing education based on the Dutch curriculum, first established in 1914 in Bali as part of the Ethical Policy.

Ikatan Cendekiawan Muslim Indonesia (ICMI): Association of Indonesian Muslim Intellectuals, established on December 7, 1990, in Malang.

Ikatan Pemuda Hindu Indonesia (IPHI): Association of Indonesian Hindu Youth, set up in January 1995 in Jakarta.

Indian Cultural Centre: cultural center opened in 2004 in Denpasar to promote academic exchanges and allocate scholarships to Indonesian students, besides teaching yoga, Sanskrit, and Indian dance and music.

Institut Hindu Dharma (IHD): Hindu Dharma Institute; higher institute of religious education for the training of officials and teachers of *agama Hindu Bali*, founded by Parisada Dharma Hindu Bali on October 3, 1963, in Denpasar; it became a university under the name Universitas Hindu Indonesia (UNHI) in 1993.

Institut Hindu Dharma Negeri (IHDN): National Hindu Dharma Institute, established in 2004 in Denpasar under the Department of Religion; it became a state university under the name Universitas Hindu Negeri I Gusti Bagus Sugriwa Denpasar (UHN) on February 2, 2020.

Java-Instituut: Institute of Javanese Studies, set up in 1919 in Surakarta with a view to preserving and restoring traditional Javanese culture.

Kantoor voor Inlandsche Zaken: Office for Native Affairs, established in 1899 to advise the government on Islamic policy in the Netherlands East Indies.

Kantor Agama Daerah Tingkat I Bali: Bali Office of Religion, established on July 10, 1963, as a regional office of the Ministry of Religion; its name was changed to Kantor Wilayah Departemen Agama Propinsi Bali in 1966, and then to Kantor Wilayah Kementrian Agama Provinsi Bali in 2010.

Kantor Urusan Agama Daerah Bali (KUAD): Regional Office of the Ministry of Religion, opened in 1951 in Denpasar.

Kantor Urusan Agama Propinsi Sunda Kecil (KUAP): Provincial Office of the Ministry of Religion, opened in 1951 in Singaraja.

Keluarga Besar Bhujangga Waisnawa: association of the Bhujangga Waisnawa *warga*, set up in 1953.

Kementerian Agama Republik Indonesia (KAGRI): Indonesian Ministry of Religion, established on January 3, 1946, in Jakarta; it was renamed Departemen Agama (Depag) in 1966, then again Kementerian Agama in 2010.

Kesatuan Mahasiswa Hindu Dharma Indonesia (KMHDI): Union of Indonesian Hindu University Students, founded in September 1993 in Bali.

Kirtya Liefrinck-Van der Tuuk: foundation dedicated to the collection and study of Balinese manuscripts, established by the Dutch colonial government on September 14, 1928, in Singaraja, more commonly known as the Gedong Kirtya.

Komisi Pemberantasan Korupsi (KPK): Indonesian Committee for the Eradication of Corruption, set up in 2002 in Jakarta.

Komite Nasional Indonesia Daerah (KNID): Regional Indonesian National Committee, established in Bali as a provisional parliament on October 8, 1945.

Komite Nasional Indonesia Pusat (KNIP): Central Indonesian National Committee, established by President Sukarno on August 29, 1945, in replacement of the Preparatory Committee for Indonesian Independence (Panitia Persiapan Kemerdekaan Indonesia, PPKI); it gave way to the Provisional People's Representative Council (Dewan Perwakilan Rakyat Sementara, DPRS) when Indonesia became a unitary state in 1950.

Koninklijk Bataviaasch Genootschap van Kunsten en Wetenschappen: Royal Batavian Society of Arts and Sciences, founded in 1778 to collect manuscripts and archaeological remains.

Koninklijk Nederlands Indisch Leger (KNIL): Royal Netherlands Indies Army.

Koninklijke Paketvaart-Maatschappij (KPM): Royal Packet Navigation Company, the main inter-island shipping company in the Archipelago during the colonial era.

Konservatori Karawitan (KOKAR): Conservatory of Music, founded in 1960 in Denpasar; in 1979, it became the Indonesian High School of Music (Sekolah Menengah Karawitan Indonesia, SMKI), to be placed under the jurisdiction of the Department of Education and Culture.

Koperasi Krama Bali (KKB): cooperative set up in May 2005 in Denpasar to strengthen the economic standing of the Balinese people vis-à-vis their competitors by granting soft loans to local small traders and entrepreneurs.

Lembaga Ilmu Pengetahuan Indonesia (LIPI): Indonesian Institute of Sciences, Jakarta.

Lembaga Kajian Strategis Ajeg Bali: Institute of Strategic Studies to Make a Strong and Resilient Bali, established in August 2005 in Denpasar to solicit contributions from Balinese intellectuals eager to work toward the recovery of Bali.

Lembaga Kebudayaan Rakyat (Lekra): Institute for the People's Culture; a cultural organization affiliated with the Indonesian Communist Party (PKI), set up in 1950.

Lembaga Penyelidikan Bahasa dan Kebudayaan: Institute for Linguistic and Cultural Research, established in 1947 in Singaraja.

Maha Gotra Pasek Sanak Sapta Rsi: association of the Pasek *warga*, set up in 1952.

Maha Semaya Warga Pande: association of the Pande *warga*, set up in 1975.

Mahkamah Konstitusi: Constitutional Court, established in 2003 as part of democratic efforts to strengthen the separation of state powers in Indonesia.

Majelis Desa Adat Provinsi Bali (MDA): Council of Customary Villages of the Province of Bali, set up in 2019 to replace the Majelis Utama Desa Pakraman Bali (MUDP).

Majelis Hinduisme: Council of Hinduism, founded on December 31, 1950, in Klungkung to promote *agama Hindu* in Bali.

Majelis Pembina Lembaga Adat (MPLA): Council for the Guidance of Customary Institutions, set up in 1979 by the governor of Bali to formalize the status of customary law and promote written codification of village regulations.

Majelis Permusyarawatan Rakyat Sementara (MPRS): Provisional People's Consultative Assembly, instituted by Sukarno's presidential decree as the highest legislative authority of the Republic of Indonesia after he had established his 'Guided Democracy' on July 5, 1959; following the legislative elections of 1971, it became the Majelis Permusyarawatan Rakyat (MPR).

Majelis Pertimbangan dan Pembinaan Kebudayaan Daerah Propinsi Bali (Listibiya): Consultative and Promotional Council for the Regional Culture of the Province of Bali, established in 1966 in Denpasar to preserve, monitor and promote Balinese artistic and cultural traditions.

Majelis Syuro Muslimin Indonesia (Masyumi): Consultative Council of Indonesian Muslims, set up in November 1943 in Jakarta by the Japanese occupation authorities to control Islamic organizations in Indonesia.

Majelis Ulama Indonesia (MUI): Indonesian Council of Islamic Scholars, established in 1975 by the government with the function of issuing religious legal opinions and religious advice.

Majelis Utama Desa Pakraman Bali (MUDP): Grand Council of Customary Villages, established on March 21, 2001, by the Provincial Regulation on the Customary Village.

Muhammadiyah: 'Followers of Muhammad'; reformist Islamic organization founded in 1912 in Yogyakarta with a view to purifying Indonesian Islam of local syncretic practices.

Nahdlatul Ulama: 'Revival of the Islamic Scholars'; traditionalist Islamic organization founded in 1926 in Surabaya that defends the value of customary learning while remaining accommodative toward Javanese cultural traditions.

Negara Indonesia Timur (NIT): State of East Indonesia, established on December 24, 1946, by the Dutch colonial government as a political counterweight to the Indonesian Republic.

Netherlands Indies Civil Administration (NICA): organization established in 1944 to restore Dutch colonial rule after the capitulation of the Japanese occupation forces in the Netherlands East Indies.

Panitia Penyusun Kitab Pelajaran Agama Hindu Bali: committee set up in October 1953 by the Panti Agama Hindu-Bali to compile a textbook of *agama Hindu Bali*.

Panitia Persiapan Kemerdekaan Indonesia (PPKI): Preparatory Committee for Indonesian Independence, established on August 7, 1945, to prepare for the transfer of authority from the Japanese and to draft the first Indonesian constitution.

Panti Agama Hindu-Bali (PAHB): Institution of the Hindu-Balinese Religion; religious organization founded on February 6, 1951, in Singaraja.

Parisada Besakih: name given to the legal faction of the Balinese Parisada after the congress convened on March 29, 2002, at Besakih.

Parisada Campuan: name given to the splinter faction of the Balinese Parisada after the congress convened on November 23, 2001, at Campuan, Ubud.

Parisada Dharma Hindu Bali (PDHB): Hindu Bali Dharma Council; the initial name of Parisada at the time of its founding on February 23, 1959; this name was taken over by the Parisada Campuan at the end of its congress on January 28, 2007, at the Pura Samuan Tiga, Bedulu.

Parisada Hindu Dharma (PHD): Hindu Dharma Council; the name adopted by the Parisada Dharma Hindu Bali at the end of its first congress on October 10, 1964, in Denpasar.

Parisada Hindu Dharma Indonesia (PHDI): Hindu Dharma Council of Indonesia; the name adopted by the Parisada Hindu Dharma at the end of its fifth congress on February 27, 1986, in Denpasar.

Parisada Hindu Dharma Indonesia Propinsi Bali (PHDI Bali): name of the Balinese branch of the Parisada, set up on November 15, 1986, in Denpasar.

Parisada Hindu Dunia: World Hindu Parisad, founded on June 17, 2013, in Denpasar to unify Hindus, coordinate their activities, and propagate Hindu Dharma globally.

Partai Demokrasi Indonesia (PDI): Indonesian Democratic Party, set up in January 1973 by the New Order government to merge the non-Islamic political parties.

Partai Demokrasi Indonesia-Perjuangan (PDI-P): Indonesian Democratic Party of Struggle, founded by Megawati Sukarnoputri after she was forced out from the leadership of the Indonesian Democratic Party (PDI) by President Suharto in 1996.

Partai Indonesia Raya (Parindra): Greater Indonesia Party, founded in December 1935 in Surabaya by merging Persatuan Bangsa Indonesia with Budi Utomo.

Partai Komunis Indonesia (PKI): Indonesian Communist Party, founded in 1924.

Partai Nasional Hindu Bali: Hindu-Balinese National Party, founded in February 1954 by the raja of Klungkung to promote the interests of the Balinese Hindus in the national elections of 1955.

Partai Nasional Indonesia (PNI): Indonesian National Party, founded in 1927.

Partai Persatuan Pembangunan (PPP): United Development Party, set up in January 1973 by the New Order government to merge Islam-based political parties.

Paruman Agung: Council of Balinese rulers, composed of the 'self-rulers' (*zelfbestuurders*) and their advisors, established in 1938 in Denpasar by the Dutch colonial government to coordinate the administration of Bali.

Paruman Kerta Negara: Consultative Council, established in 1931 by the Dutch colonial government to coordinate the Balinese 'rulers' (*negara-bestuurders*) who had been reinstated in 1929.

Paruman Negara: Consultative Council, established in 1938 by the Dutch colonial government in each of the Balinese kingdoms (*negara*).

Paruman Pandita Dharma: Council of Dharma Priests; association of *padanda* set up on April 22, 1945, in Klungkung under the aegis of the Japanese occupation authorities.

Paruman Para Pandita (PPP): Council of Priests; association of *padanda* set up on January 31, 1947, in Singaraja.

Pasikian Kristen Bali: Community of Balinese Christians, established in 1937 by the merging of the Christian and Missionary Alliance and the Gereja Kristen Jawi Wetan.

Pasubayan Desa Pakraman Tolak Reklamasi Teluk Benoa: organization set up in January 2016 regrouping the customary villages opposed to the reclamation of the Benoa Bay.

Pemuda Hindu Indonesia (PHI): Indonesian Hindu Youth; a splinter organization of Peradah, set up in 1985 in Jakarta.

Perguruan Rakyat Saraswati: Hindu religious school opened in 1946 in Denpasar.

Perhimpunan Hidup Ketuhanan: Balinese branch of the Divine Life Society, founded in 1957 to propagate the teachings of Swami Shivananda.

Perhimpunan Pemuda Hindu Indonesia (Peradah): Association of Indonesian Hindu Youth, set up on March 11, 1984, in Yogyakarta, affiliated with Parisada.

Persatuan Siswa Indonesia Bali (PERSIB): Indonesian Association of Balinese Students, founded in 1952 in Jakarta.

Pesta Kesenian Bali (PKB): Bali Arts Festival; annual event organized since 1979 at Werdhi Budaya Art Center in Denpasar.

Pita Maha: association dedicated to the promotion of the Balinese fine arts, set up in 1936 in Ubud.

Prajaniti Hindu Indonesia: political organization set up on June 19, 1965, under Parisada's auspices to defend the interests of the Hindu community.

Puri Lukisan, Museum Kesenian Bali Modern: museum for contemporary Balinese fine arts, opened in 1956 in Ubud.

Pusat Hindu Dunia: World Hindu Centre, founded on June 17, 2013, in Denpasar, in charge of implementing the World Hindu Parisad.

Raad van Kerta: Customary Council; courts of justice set up by the Dutch colonial government in each of the former Balinese kingdoms.

Republik Indonesia Serikat (RIS): United States of Indonesia; a federal state to which the Netherlands transferred sovereignty of the Dutch East Indies on December 27, 1949, following the Dutch-Indonesian Round Table Conference in The Hague; it was replaced by the unitary Republic of Indonesia on August 17, 1950.

Santi: 'Peace'; socio-religious organization founded in 1923 in Singaraja.

Sarekat Islam (SI): Islamic Association; association of Muslim traders founded in 1912 in Surakarta, which rapidly evolved into a nationalist political organization.

Satiya Samudaya Bau Danda Bali Lombok: organization founded in December 1924 in Karangasem to raise funds for sending Balinese children to pursue their education in Java.

Satya Hindu Dharma Indonesia: Indonesian Association for the Hindu Religion, founded on January 1, 1956, in Denpasar with the aim of promoting Hinduism in Indonesia.

Sekolah Menengah Hindu Bali Dwijendra: Hindu Bali Dwijendra High School, opened in 1953 in Denpasar by the Yayasan Dwijendra.

Setiti Bali: Bali Association; organization founded in 1917 in Singaraja to counter the Javanese Islamic association Sarekat Islam.

Setiti Gama Siwa Buda: Association of the Shiva-Buddha Religion; association of *padanda* founded in 1926 in Karangasem.

Sila Dharma: 'Foundation of Dharma'; educational and cultural foundation set up in 1926 in Klungkung, under the aegis of the ruling houses of Karangasem, Klungkung, and Gianyar.

Suita Gama Tirta: Service of the Religion of Holy Water; organization founded in 1921 in Singaraja to promote religious instruction.

Surya Kanta: 'The Beautiful Sun'; organization founded in November 1925 in Singaraja to defend the position of the commoners (*jaba*) against the privileges of the nobility (*triwangsa*); it published an eponymous monthly journal from 1925 to 1927.

Taman Mini Indonesia Indah: 'Beautiful Indonesia-in-Miniature Park', opened in 1975 in Jakarta.

Taman Siswa: 'Garden of Students'; educational institution based on the principles of traditional Javanese pedagogy, founded in 1924 in Yogyakarta.

Tjatur Wangsa Deriya Gama Hindu Bali (Tjwadega Hindu Bali): Association of the Four Castes for the Hindu Balinese Religion; conservative religious organization founded in May 1926 in Klungkung.

Universitas Hindu Indonesia (UNHI): Hindu private university that took over from the Institut Hindu Dharma in 1993 in Denpasar.

Universitas Hindu Negeri I Gusti Bagus Sugriwa Denpasar (UHN): Hindu state university that took over from the Institut Hindu Dharma Negeri on February 2, 2020, in Denpasar.

Universitas Udayana (UNUD): public university established on September 29, 1962, in Denpasar.

Vereenigde Oost-Indisch Compagnie (VOC): Dutch East India Company, established in 1602 and based in Batavia from 1619; ceased operations on December 31, 1799.

Vereeniging Toeristenverkeer: Official Tourist Bureau, opened in 1908 in Batavia under the aegis of the Dutch colonial government, in charge of promoting tourism in the Netherlands Indies.

Volksraad: People's Council; advisory council established in 1918 in Batavia by the Dutch colonial government.

Wahana Lingkungan Hidup Indonesia (WALHI): Indonesian Environmental Society; the oldest and largest environmental organization in Indonesia, set up in 1980 in Jakarta.

Werdhi Budaya: Art Center, inaugurated in 1976 in Denpasar by the minister of education and culture to showcase Balinese artistic traditions.

Wiwada Sastra Sabha: Society for Discussing Literature; association devoted to the study of Balinese religious texts, founded in 1951 in Denpasar.

Yayasan Dwijendra: Dwijendra Foundation; educational foundation established in 1953 in Denpasar to develop the teaching of *agama Hindu Bali*.

Yayasan Kebaktian Pejuang Bali: foundation established on January 14, 1951, in Denpasar to provide assistance for Balinese veterans of the war of independence.

Glossary

A: Arabic
B: Balinese
D: Dutch
J: Javanese
OJ: Old Javanese
S: Sanskrit
The unmarked terms are Malay/Indonesian

abangan (J): 'the red ones'; Javanese term for 'nominal' or 'syncretic' Muslims, as opposed to *santri* or *putihan* ('the white ones').

acara (S, OJ): conduct, good behavior; the established rules of conduct governing the correct performance of social and ritual duties constitutive of the *varnashrama dharma*, as endorsed by the Dharmashastras.

adat (A): tradition, custom, and by extension customary law.
    adat istiadat: customs and traditions.
    adat keagamaan: religious tradition.
    adat kebiasaan: habits, customs.
    adatrecht (D): '*adat* with legal consequences'; customary law.

advaita (S): 'non-dual', a term used to describe the unitary philosophies and religious movements in India.

āgama (S, OJ): 'That which has come down'; authoritative scripture; sacred traditional doctrine; name of a genre of non-Vedic scriptures regarded as revelation by Shaivite orders such as Shaiva Siddhanta.

Agama (S): generic term referring to Javanese and Balinese texts drawn from the Dharmashastras dealing with moral, religious and legal sanctions and practices.

agama (*gama*, *igama*, *ugama*) (S): religion, in the restricted sense of those religions claiming to be monotheistic and universalist, and as such officially recognized as legitimate by the Indonesian state.
    agama Bali: Balinese religion.

agama Bali Hindu: Hindu Balinese religion; the name of Balinese religion promoted by the periodical *Surya Kanta* in the 1920s.

agama bumi: 'religion of the soil', a mere cultural production as opposed to revealed religion (*agama wahyu*).

agama Hindu: Hindu religion, Hinduism.

agama Hindu Bali: Balinese Hindu religion; the name of Balinese religion defended by the periodical *Bali Adnjana* in the 1920s; the official name of the Balinese religion between May 1952 and October 1964.

agama Jawa: Javanese religion.

agama Katolik Roma: Roman Catholicism.

agama Kristen Protestan: Protestantism.

agama leluhur: ancestral religion.

agama Nasrani: Christianity.

agama samawi: the three revealed Abrahamic religions: Islam, Christianity and Judaism.

agamasasi: 'religionization', the act of making religious.

agama Siwa and *agama Buda*: names given to Balinese religion in reference to the two categories of initiated *brahmana* priests, the *padanda Siwa* and the *padanda Boda*.

agama Siwa-Buda: name given to Balinese religion in reference to the tantric combination of Shaivism and Buddhism that originated in East Java in the 13th century.

agama suku: indigenous ethnic religion.

agama Tirta: name given to Balinese religion in reference to the holy water which is required for most religious rites.

agama Trimurti: name given to Balinese religion in reference to the Hindu triad Brahma, Wisnu and Siwa.

agama wahyu: revealed religion.

Agni Hotra (S): 'Fire offering'; Vedic fire ritual that had fallen into disuse until its restoration by the Arya Samaj.

aja wera (OJ, B): 'do not divulge'; prohibition protecting manuscripts devoted to religious matters, considered dangerous for the uninitiated.

Ajeg Bali (B): 'Bali Erect'; slogan launched by the main Balinese media group at the time of the 2002 Islamist terrorist attack.

Ajeg Hindu (B): slogan promoted instead of *Ajeg Bali* by the Hindu magazine *Raditya*.

aksara (S): letter, syllable; script of Indic origin traditionally used to write Javanese and Balinese.

Alangkahi Karang Hulu (B): prohibition on hypergamous alliances between a *sudra* or *wesia* man and a *wesia* or *satria* woman, respectively; abrogated in July 1951.

aliran: 'current, stream'; a social grouping or religious sect.

aliran kebatinan: Javanese mystical movement.

aliran kepercayaan: 'current of belief'; a spiritual movement or syncretic cult considered not to fall within the ambit of acknowledged religions (*agama*).

aliran sesat: 'deviant sect'; pejorative term applied to religious movements considered heretical.

amok: a Malay culture-bound syndrome referring to an act of furious and murderous madness.

Aranyaka (S): 'Forest texts'; esoteric speculations about the Vedic rituals.

arca (S, B): effigy serving as vehicle for a deity.

arya (S, B): title for Javanese nobles who are said to have come to Bali from Majapahit.

ashrama (S): the system of four stages in the life of a Hindu according to the Dharmashastras: Brahmacharya (student), Grihastha (householder), Vanaprastha (forest dweller) and Sannyasa (renunciate).

Asu Pundung (B): prohibition on hypergamous alliances between a *sudra*, *wesia* or *satria* man and a *brahmana* woman; abrogated in July 1951.

atiwa-tiwa (B): cremation.

atma (S), *atman*: inner self, soul.

awig-awig (B): customary regulations (of *desa*, *banjar*, *subak*, *sekaa*).

ayahan, *ngayah* (B): ritual service obligations (to *desa*, *banjar*, *pura*, *puri*).

azan (A): call by the muezzin for ritual prayers.

babad (J, B): literary genre consisting of chronicles and genealogies of title groups.

BALI (*Bersih, Aman, Lestari, Indah*): promotional slogan: 'Clean, Peaceful, Everlasting, Beautiful'.

Bali Aga (B): 'mountain Balinese'; autochthonous inhabitants and villages, as opposed to the *wong Majapahit*, the Balinese who claim to have Javanese ancestors.

Bali Congres (D): congress of Balinese studies held in October 1937 by the Java-Instituut.

Bali Deklarasi: joint directive issued on December 16, 2020, by Parisada Bali and the Majelis Desa Adat restricting all activities of non-traditional *sampradaya* in Bali.

Bali Merdeka: 'Independent Bali'; a slogan that emerged in 1999, in response to what the Balinese perceived as Islamic provocations.

Bali Mula (B): 'original Balinese'; autochthonous inhabitants and villages, as opposed to the *wong Majapahit*, the Balinese who claim to have Javanese ancestors.

balian (B): healer, spirit medium, witch-doctor.

Baliseering (D): 'Balinization'; policy launched in the late 1920s by the colonial administration to produce a 'renaissance' of Balinese culture, with a view to checking the spread of Islam and nationalism from neighboring Java and strengthening the position of the pro-Dutch Balinese elite.

bangsa (S): people, nation, race.
> *kebangsaan*: nationality, nationalism.

banjar (B): neighborhood community within a *desa*, which organizes communal life and whose responsibilities are at once ritual, social and administrative.

banten (OJ, B): offering, sacrifice.

baris pendet (B): ritual male dance in which the performers carry vessels filled with flower petals.

Barong (OJ, B): generic term for a range of large masks, mostly in animal form, animated by *niskala* beings; a guardian effigy, venerated by local communities; the 'dragon' confronted with the 'witch' Rangda in the *Calonarang* drama.

batara (S, B): deity; title for Hindu gods.

batin (A): inner, esoteric, as opposed to *lahir*.
> *kebatinan*: inwardness, spirituality, mysticism.

bendesa (B): traditional title for village official; head of *desa adat*.
> *Bendesa*: commoner descent group (*warga*) whose ancestors held positions of power prior to the conquest of Bali by Majapahit.

berhala (S): idol.
> *penyembah berhala*: idolater.

Bhagavad Gita (S): the 'Song of the Lord', a philosophical poem in Sanskrit set in the narrative framework of a dialogue between Arjuna and Krishna, inserted into the *Mahabharata*.

bhagawan (S), *begawan* (B): holy person; priestly title for *wangsa satria*.

bhagawanta (S, B): court priest; religious advisor and ritual expert to a raja.

bhakti (S), *bakti* (B): homage, devotion, worship.

bhasha (S), *basa* (B), *bahasa*: speech, language.

Bhinneka Tunggal Ika (OJ): 'Unity in Diversity'; motto on the coat of arms of the Republic of Indonesia, derived from the *Sutasoma kakawin* composed by Mpu Tantular, a Buddhist poet at the court of Majapahit.

bhisama (S): religious stipulation of Parisada having moral force for Indonesian Hindus, the equivalent of an Islamic *fatwa*.

Bhujangga Waisnawa (B): a prominent commoner descent group (*warga*).

Brahmana (S): ritual speculations that are part of the Vedas.

brahmana (S, B): highest of the four *wangsa* in the Hindu-Balinese title system, who have the exclusive prerogative of the initiated priesthood, the *padanda*.

budaya, kebudayaan (S): culture, civilization.
> *budaya pariwisata*: 'touristic culture', defined by the Balinese authorities as a state of confusion between the values of culture and those of tourism.

kebudayaan daerah: 'regional culture'; the acknowledged cultural manifestations deemed representative of a province and expected as such to contribute to the building of the national Indonesian culture.

budi (S): sense, mind, reason, intellect, character.
    budidaya: cultivation, effort.

buduh (B): mad, senseless.

bupati (S): government head of a district (*kabupaten*).

buta (S): living being; element; demon, ogre.
    buta kala (B): spirits of the underworld; earthly forces responsible for all sorts of calamities.
    Buta Yadnya (B): 'sacrifices for the demons'; rituals to urge potentially malevolent forces to return to their benevolent form.

Calonarang (OJ, B): dramatic enactment drawn from an Old Javanese text of tantric magic that stages the ritual encounter between the masked figures of the 'witch' Rangda and the 'dragon' Barong.

caru, pacaruan (S, B): blood sacrifices to the *buta*.

catur wangsa (S, B): the so-called 'four castes'; the four social groups ranking the Balinese hierarchy by birth: *brahmana*, *satria*, *wesia* and *sudra*.

catur warna (S, B): the division of society into four classes based on a differentiation between functions, according to Balinese reformers: *brahmana*, *satria*, *wesia* and *sudra*.

cendekiawan (S): intellectual.

ciri khas (S): distinctive feature, identity marker.

citra (S): brand image.

dadia (B): agnatic, preferentially endogamous kinship group.

dakwah (A): Islamic proselytism.

dana punia (S, B): funds, alms; religious contribution of Hindu followers, similar to the Muslim *zakat*.

Danghyang Astapaka: Javanese Brahmin who is alleged to have come to Bali in the 16th century, considered the ancestor of the *padanda Boda*.

Danghyang Nirartha: Javanese Brahmin who is alleged to have come to Bali in the 16th century, considered the ancestor of the *padanda Siwa*.

darshana (S), *darsana* (B): point of view, vision; term referring to the six orthodox schools of Hindu philosophy.

dasaran (B): trance medium.

Demokrasi Terpimpin: 'Guided Democracy'; authoritarian political system established by Sukarno in 1959 to replace the former parliamentary democracy.

desa (S, B): village.
> *desa adat*: customary village.
> *desa dinas*: administrative village.
> *desa kala patra*: 'place, time, circumstances'; principle justifying the diversity of customs in Bali.
> *desa pakraman*: name given to Balinese customary villages in 2001.

desti (OJ, B): black magic, bewitchment.

dewa (S, B): deity.
> *Dewa Agung* (B): title of the raja of Klungkung.
> *Dewa Yadnya* (B): rituals addressed to gods.

dharma (S, B): cosmic order, law, duty; in the Dharmashastras, *dharma* refers specifically to the *varnashrama dharma*, the duties and qualifications incumbent on Hindus according to their social class (*varna*) and their stage of life (*ashrama*).
> *Dharma Adhyaksa*: 'Superintendent of Religion'; title of the chairman of Parisada's Assembly of Priests since its eighth congress in 2001.
> *dharma dutta*: Hindu proselytizers.
> *Dharma Gita*: religious singing, particularly excerpts from the Vedas.
> *Dharma Sadhana*: personal realization of the teachings of *dharma* by means of one of the four ways of *Yoga* (*Catur Marga Yoga*)—*Bhakti*, *Karma*, *Jnana* and *Raja Marga*.
> *Dharma Santi*: mutual pardon at the time of the Saka new year (*Nyepi*).
> *Dharmashastra*: Sanskrit treatises of the Brahmanical tradition that refer to the branch of learning (*shastra*) pertaining to the subject of *dharma*; the *Manava Dharmashastra* (Laws of Manu) is considered the first and most authoritative text on *dharma*.
> *Dharma Tula*: debates on religious topics.
> *Dharma Wacana*: religious sermons.
> *Dharma Yatra*: pilgrimages to sacred sites.

diksa, *padiksan* (S, B): ordination of a *padanda*; initiation to the status of *pandita/sulinggih* according to Parisada.

din (A): practice, custom, law, religion.

dinas (D): service, agency, office.

Diplomasi Kebudayaan: 'Cultural Diplomacy', launched by the minister of foreign affairs in 1983 to promote Indonesia's cultural image abroad.

dorpsrepubliek (D): 'village republic'; term used by Dutch colonial administrators to refer to the old Balinese villages, construed as autonomous communities.

dresta (S, B): the customary basis of local institutions handed down from community ancestors with whom ongoing relations are maintained through ritual.

dukuh (OJ, B): hermit; priest of a commoner descent group.

dvaita (S): 'dualist', a term used to refer to the notion that God is completely separate and different from the human soul.

dwijati (S, B): 'twice-born'; refers to priests who undergo an initiation (*padiksan*), complete with spiritual death and rebirth with a new name, designated as *pandita* by Parisada.

eereschuld (D): 'debt of honor' that the promoters of the Ethical Policy acknowledged toward the peoples of the Dutch East Indies at the turn of the 20th century.

Eka Bhuwana (S, B): large purification ritual celebrated in the temple complex of Besakih in March 1996.

Eka Dasa Rudra (S, B): huge purification ritual celebrated in the temple complex of Besakih in March 1979 that marked the turn of the Saka year 1900; this rite consists of propitiatory offerings to the eleven Rudra, representing destructive aspects of Siwa.

ekajati (S, B): 'once-born'; refers to priests who undergo a purification (*pawintenan*) that does not involve a spiritual death, designated as *pinandita* by Parisada.

(e)mpu (OJ, B): title of the priests of some commoner descent groups (*warga*), such as Pasek and Pande.

Ethische Politiek (D): the official policy of the colonial government of the Dutch East Indies between 1901 and 1942.

fatwa (A): legal opinion of a Muslim jurist.

gaguritan (B): poems written in Javanese-Balinese indigenous meters.

Galungan (OJ, B): main Balinese holiday held every 210 days according to the *pawukon* calendar.

gambuh (OJ, B): genre of Balinese court theater featuring stories of the Javanese hero Panji.

gamelan (OJ, B): a set of mostly percussion musical instruments making up an orchestra.

garbha griha (S): the innermost sanctuary of a Hindu temple.

Garis-garis Besar Haluan Negara, GBHN: the Broad Outlines of State Policy formulated by the People's Consultative Assembly (Majelis Permusyarawatan Rakyat, MPR).

Gayatri (S): a highly revered *mantra* from the *Rig-Veda*; the first section of the *Puja Tri Sandhya*.

golongan Islam: 'Islamic group'; members of the Investigating Committee for the Preparation of Indonesian Independence (Badan Penyelidik Usaha-usaha Persiapan Kemerdekaan Indonesia, BPUPKI) who wanted to establish an Islamic state in independent Indonesia.

golongan kebangsaan: 'nationalist group'; members of the Investigating Committee for the Preparation of Indonesian Independence (Badan Penyelidik Usaha-usaha

Persiapan Kemerdekaan Indonesia, BPUPKI) who wanted to establish a religiously neutral state in independent Indonesia.

gria (S, B): residence of a *brahmana* family.

guna (S): quality; force, energy, magic.

guru (S): spiritual teacher, master.
> *gurukula*: Vedic education system.
> *Guru Loka*: traditional joint authority of rajas and *padanda*.
> *Guru Wisesa*: traditional government authority.

hajj (A): Muslim pilgrimage to Mecca.

halal (A): permissible according to Islamic law.

haram (A): prohibited according to Islamic law.

heerendienst (D): corvée labor imposed by the Dutch colonial administration.

Hindia (D): the (Dutch East) Indies.

Hindutva (S): 'Hindu-ness'; Hindu nationalist ideology articulated by Vinayak Damodar Savarkar in 1923.

hukum (A): law; religious law as opposed to customary law (*adat*).
> *hukum adat*: customary law; Indonesian rendering of the Dutch word *adatrecht*.

hyang (OJ): deified being.
> *hyang laluhur* (OJ, B): deified ancestors.
> *kahyangan tiga* (B): 'the three deified beings'; the temple complex defining a Balinese village as a *desa adat*: the 'origin temple' (*pura puseh*), the 'village temple' (*pura desa*) and the 'death temple' (*pura dalem*).

ibadat (A): service to God, worship, religious observance, liturgy.

ijtihad (A): rational and personal interpretation of the Quran and the Hadith.

ilmu (A): science, knowledge, esoteric knowledge.

itihasa (S, B): 'traditional accounts of past events'; in the Kirtya nomenclature it pertains to epic and poetic literature (*parwa, kakawin, kidung, gaguritan*).

jaba (B): outside, outsider; term designating commoners (*wong jaba*), those who are outside the sphere of the courts, as opposed to members of the nobility (*wong jero*), the insiders.
> *jaba sisi*: outermost courtyard of a Balinese temple (*pura*).
> *jaba tengah*: central courtyard of a Balinese temple (*pura*).

jahiliah (A): 'Age of Ignorance'; paganism.

jaman Buda (A): 'the Buddhist era', referring to the pre-Islamic era in Java.

janger (B): modern heterogeneous dance-drama using the rhythmic and vocal accompaniment of the *sanghyang* trance dances.

jati (S, OJ): birth, caste, group, kind; social status based on lineage; a group of people, animals, or things sharing similar features that characterize them as belonging to the same species.

jengah (B): a particular feeling of shame mixed with anger.

jero (B): inside, insider; term designating the nobility (*wong jero*), those who are inside the sphere of the courts, as opposed to the commoners (*wong jaba*), the outsiders.
> *jeroan*: innermost courtyard of a Balinese temple (*pura*).

jihad (A): holy war to defend Islam against infidels.

kabupaten: administrative district below the level of province.

Kaharingan: name given to the religious practices of the peoples of southern Borneo in the 1940s, eventually acknowledged as a branch of *agama Hindu* in 1980.

kaiket (B): tied.

kakawin (OJ, B): Old Javanese epic court poetry modelled on Sanskrit metrical principles.

kalpasastra (S, B): ritual prescriptions; part of *Weda* in the Kirtya nomenclature.

kapongor (B): to be cursed by arousing the ire of the gods or the ancestors.

karma (S): action, deed, work, fate; one of the ways of *Yoga*.
> *karmaphala*: the ineluctable retribution of all actions.

Kartu Tanda Penduduk, KTP: Resident's Identity Card.

karya (S, B): work, particularly ritual work.

kasepekang (B): expulsion from one's village due to a serious offense, a sanction equivalent to social death with dire ritual consequences.

kasewasogatan (B): 'religion'; from *Sewa*, Siwa's worshippers, and *Sogata*, Buddha's devotees, in reference to the two categories of *brahmana* priests in Bali, the *padanda Siwa* and the *padanda Boda*.

kasta (D): caste; a neologism, derived from the Portuguese 'casta', borrowed from the Dutch, who construed Balinese hierarchy as being similar to the caste system in India.

kastenstelsel (D): caste system.

kasus adat: 'customary law disputes'; euphemism for *adat*-related conflicts.

kaum (A): race, tribe, group.
> *kaum kuno, kaum tua*: the older generation; the traditionalist Muslim movement.
> *kaum muda*: the younger generation; the modernist Muslim movement.
> *kaum terpelajar*: intelligentsia.

kavi (S): poet.

kavya (S): Sanskrit epic court poetry.

kawasan: area, region, territory.

kawasan budidaya: cultivation area.
kawasan konservasi: conservation area.
kawasan suci: sacred area.
kawasan wisata: tourism area.

Kawi (S, OJ, B): poet, poetic language; linguistic register that incorporates Old and Middle Javanese, as well as various forms of Sanskrit and literary Balinese.

kawitan (B): origin, foundation, ancestry; ancestral origin of a descent group.

kearifan lokal (A): local genius.

Kebalian (B): 'Balinese-ness'; the Balinese religious, ethnic and cultural identity.

Kebangkitan Hindu: 'Hindu Revival'; movement born in the early 1990s in response to the Islamic resurgence in Indonesia.

kebyar (B): popular modern Balinese musical style and dance genre.

Kejawen (J): 'Javanism'; Javanese customs and beliefs.

kelompok spiritual: spiritual group; euphemism for Neo-Hindu devotional movements (*sampradaya*).

kepercayaan (S): faith, creed, belief; refers to cultural practices not recognized as proper 'religion' (*agama*) in Indonesia.

keramat (A): holiness, sanctity, sacred site.

keris (OJ): ceremonial dagger.

kerohanian (A): spirituality.

kerta (S, B): prosperity, order, peace, perfection; council of *brahmana* priests convened by the ruler for administering justice.

Ketuhanan Yang Maha Esa: 'Belief in the One and Only God'; the first principle of Pancasila, combining Malay and Sanskrit to express a tribute to the Muslim *tawhid*.

kiai (J): title given to Islamic religious scholars (*ulama*).

kidung (OJ, B): poetry in indigenous meters written in Middle Javanese.

kirtya (S, OJ): meritorious foundation.

kitab suci (A, S): holy book.

komedie stambul: a genre of Malay theater, using themes from both Europe and the Middle East, popular in Bali in the 1920s.

krama (S, B): custom, rule sanctioned by tradition; corporate membership.
    krama banjar: full membership of a *banjar*.
    krama desa: full membership of a desa *adat/pakraman*.
    krama dura: 'foreign citizens'; members of the *desa pakraman* with respect to social and territorial, but not religious, matters.
    krama tamiu: 'guest citizens'; members of the *desa pakraman* with respect to social and territorial, but not religious, matters.

krama wed: 'native citizens'; full members of the *desa pakraman*.

Kramaning Sembah: collective prayers in Balinese temple.

lahir (A): outer, exoteric, as opposed to *batin*.

laluhur (J, B): what is above, superior, and by extension ancestors, ancestral spirits.

landschap (D): region.

leak (B): witch; sorcerers who have acquired the ability to transform themselves and propagate illness.

pangleakan: the fact of becoming a *leak* with the intention to harm others.

legong (B): court dance performed by prepubescent girls.

lembaga swadaya masyarakat: non-governmental organization.

leteh (OJ, B): state of ritual pollution.

lontar: palm-leaf manuscript.

lungsuran (OJ, B): what an inferior asks for and receives from a superior; leftovers of food offerings whose essence has already been absorbed by the deity and which can therefore be consumed by the worshipers (*surudan*).

madrasah (A): Islamic school combining general education with Islamic studies.

Mahabharata (S): Indian epic poem narrating the heroic adventures of the descendants of Bharata, and the conflict between the Pandava and their cousins, the Kaurava, for the conquest of the land of the Arya.

Majapahit: East Javanese kingdom (1292–1527) that conquered Bali in the 14th century, from which Balinese nobility claims descent.

maligia (B): highest level of post-cremation ritual to purify and deify deceased ancestors.

mantra (S): holy formula using Sanskrit words and powerful syllables.

Manusa Yadnya (S, B): rituals addressed to human beings; rites of passage.

masolah (OJ, B): high Balinese term for dancing and acting.

masyarakat (A): society, community.

masyarakat adat: Indonesian customary communities as indigenous people.

misi kesenian: 'artistic mission'; name given to troupes of musicians and dancers sent on tour abroad to promote Indonesian culture and develop tourism to Indonesia.

mleccha (S): term referring to foreign and barbarous peoples in ancient India, as contradistinguished from Arya.

modal: capital.

moksha (S) *moksa* (B): the liberation of individual souls (*atma*) from the cycle of death and rebirth (*samsara*) through union with the Brahman.

Mpu Kuturan: legendary Javanese priest who is credited with having merged the nine sects (*paksa*) present in 11th century Bali into three (Siwa, Budha and Waisnawa), as well as with the institution of the three sanctuaries (*kahyangan tiga*) that define a *desa adat*.

mukur (B): post-cremation ritual to purify deceased ancestors.

mulat sarira (B, S): introspection.

muput karya (OJ, B, S): 'to complete the ritual', to ensure its completeness and therefore its success.

murti (S): form, embodiment; the image of a deity, placed in the innermost sanctuary of a Hindu temple.

museum hidup: 'living museum'; in reference to the orientalist view of Bali as a living museum of Indo-Javanese civilization.

nabi (A): religious prophet, specifically in reference to Muhammad.

nandir (B): a dance performed by young boys, a forerunner of *legong*.

Nasakom: acronym for '*Nationalisme-Agama-Komunisme*'; a coalition established by President Sukarno in 1959 to bring together the PNI, the Nahdlatul Ulama and the PKI.

nawa sanga (S, OJ, B): a cosmological tantric mandala that associates a series of items with the points of the compass, important in Balinese classification and mysticism.

negara (S, OJ): state, country, nation; the name given by the Dutch to former Balinese kingdoms.

    negara-bestuurder (D): ruler; title conferred to the Balinese rajas by the Dutch colonial administration in 1929.

negeri (S, OJ): country.

ngaben (B): (to hold) cremation rituals.

ngayah (B): to perform volunteer ritual labor or service.

ngigel (B): low Balinese term for dancing and acting.

nishkala (S), *niskala* (B): 'devoid of constituent part', 'nameless and formless'; designates in Bali that which is not perceived by the senses, the 'unmanifest world', as opposed to *sakala*, that which is perceptible to the senses, the 'manifest world'.

Nitishastra (S): a class of texts on ethics and politics teaching appropriate social, moral and political behavior.

numitis (OJ, B): to be reincarnated.

Nusantara (S): the Indonesian Archipelago.

nyama (B): sibling, parent.

nyekah (B): post-cremation ritual to purify deceased ancestors.

Nyepi (B): the 'Day of Silence' that marks the date of the Saka new year.

nyungsung (B): to support à temple.

obyek wisata: 'tourist object'; any officially designated tourist attraction.

odalan (B): Balinese temple anniversary ceremony according to the *pawukon* or Saka calendars.

Om Swastyastu (S): Indonesian Hindu greeting, equivalent of the Indian *namaste* and the Arabic *salam alaikum*.

orang yang belum beragama: 'people who do not yet have a religion', implying that they should and will embrace a state-sanctioned religion (*agama*).

Orde Baru: 'New Order'; the regime established by Suharto after the aborted 1965 coup d'état.

organisasi masyarakat: 'community organization'; euphemism for gangs and 'security organizations' which provide public support in exchange for political protection.

otonomi khusus: 'special autonomy', a status demanded for the province of Bali within the framework of the regional autonomy legislation promulgated in 1999.

pacalang (B): neo-traditional militia which was given authority to ensure law and order in the Balinese customary villages by the 2001 provincial regulation on the *desa pakraman*.

padanda (S, B): initiated and consecrated Balinese *brahmana* priesthood, of which there are two categories, the *padanda Siwa* and the *padanda Boda* (also spelled *Buda*, *Buddha*, or *Bauddha*).

Padma Bhuwana Nusantara (S): 'Lotus, World, Archipelago'; a configuration of nine Hindu temples located at the cardinal points of the Indonesian Archipelago, established at Parisada's tenth congress in 2011.

padmasana (S, B): 'lotus seat'; shrine of Siwa Raditya in Balinese temples, supposedly established by Danghyang Nirartha and formalized by Parisada in 1961 to signify the monotheism of *agama Hindu Bali*.

paksha (S), *paksa* (B): sectarian denomination.

    pamaksan: congregation collectively supporting a Balinese temple.

    tripaksha: the three religious orders present at the court of Majapahit, the Shaivites, the Buddhists and the Resis.

palinggih (OJ, B): 'seat'; shrine for a deity in Balinese *pura* and *sanggah*.

pamancangah (B): genealogy.

pamangku (OJ, B): Balinese priest attached to the service of a particular temple.

Pamarisuddha Karipubhaya (S, B): a major purification ceremony held on November 15, 2002, to cleanse the site of the Islamist bombing of October 12 from all trace of pollution and to restore cosmic order by liberating the souls of the dead victims from their earthly bonds.

pamerajan (B): household temple of nobility dedicated to the veneration of family ancestors, called *sanggah* in the case of a commoner household.

Panca Çraddha (S, B): the 'Five Articles of Faith' of *agama Hindu*, promulgated at Parisada's first congress in 1964: belief in Sang Hyang Widhi, in *atman*, in *karmaphala*, in *samsara* and in *moksa*.

Pancasila (S): the 'Five Principles' on which the Indonesian state is officially based, formulated by Sukarno in 1945: Belief in the One and Only God (*Ketuhanan Yang Maha Esa*), nationalism (*Kebangsaan*), humanitarianism (*Perikemanusiaan*), democracy by consensus (*Permusyawaratan*) and social welfare (*Kesejahteraan sosial*).

Panca Wali Krama (S, B): purification ritual celebrated with each decade of the Saka era at the Pura Panataran Agung at Besakih.

Pande (OJ, B): metal smith; a prominent commoner descent group (*warga*).

pandita (S, B): title of priests who undergo an initiation (*padiksan*), whose function, according to Parisada, is to guide the congregation and to supervise the rites.

panengen (OJ, B): white magic (lit. 'of the right').

pangalantaka (B): Balinese liturgical and astrological calendar.

pangiwa (OJ, B): black magic (lit. 'of the left').

panjak (B): subject, servant, slave.

parampara (S): spiritual lineage from masters to disciples, responsible for transmitting the religious teachings of a *guru*.

parishad, parisada (S): assembly, council.

Pariwisata Budaya: 'Cultural Tourism'; the official tourist doctrine adopted by the Balinese authorities in 1971.

parwa (S, OJ, B): prose works in Old Javanese adapted from the *Mahabharata*.

Pasek (B): a prominent commoner descent group (*warga*).

Pashupata (S): devotional and ascetic movement, considered to be the oldest Shaiva order.

pasraman (S, B): ashram.

patut (OJ, B): proper, appropriate.

pawintenan (B): initiation into the spiritual realm.

pawukon (J, B): calendar of Javanese origin combining a series of permutational cycles of variable lengths over a period of 210 days, which schedules most religious rituals in Bali.

Pedoman Penghayatan dan Pengamalan Pancasila (*P-4*): 'The Guide to the Comprehension and Implementation of Pancasila'; a parliamentary resolution passed in 1978 which propagated the New Order interpretation of Pancasila through mandatory ideological education courses.

pelecehan agama: religious harassment.

pelestarian budaya: cultural preservation.

pembangunan: development.

pembinaan agama: religion building.

Pemuda Pejuang: the 'young fighters' who fought against the return of the Dutch after Indonesia's declaration of independence in 1945.

pendatang: 'newcomer'; euphemism for Indonesian Muslim immigrants to Bali.

penjelmaan (S): incarnation, manifestation.

peradaban (A): culture, civilization, education, proper behavior.

peraturan daerah: provincial regulation.

perbekel (OJ, B): administrative village head.

pergerakan: movement; the incipient political movement toward independence of Indonesia.

pertentangan kasta: caste conflict.

pertunjukan budaya: cultural performance.

pesamuhan (B): assembly.

Petitie Sutardjo: petition submitted in 1936 to the Volksraad by Sutardjo Kartohadikusumo, which called for a conference to grant autonomy to the Netherlands Indies within a Dutch-Indonesian union over a period of ten years.

piagam (J): charter.

> *Piagam Bali*: the 'Bali Charter', issued in 2012, which resolved to set up in Denpasar a World Hindu Centre, in charge of implementing a World Hindu Parisad.
>
> *Piagam Campuan*: the 'Campuan Charter', issued at Parisada's general assembly held at Campuan in 1961.
>
> *Piagam Jakarta*: the 'Jakarta Charter'; a compromise between the 'Islamic group' and the 'nationalist group' in 1945, which was to become the preamble to the Indonesian constitution and whose withdrawal has remained a source of controversy between the two factions.
>
> *Piagam Parisada*: the 'Parisada Charter', issued at the founding of Parisada in 1959.
>
> *Piagam Samuan Tiga*: the 'Samuan Tiga Charter', issued at Parisada Campuan congress held at Pura Samuan Tiga in 2007, which decided to return to *agama Hindu Bali*.

pinandita (S, B): title of priests who undergo only a purification (*pawintenan*), rather than the *padiksan* initiation, and whose function, according to Parisada, is to assist the *pandita*.

pitara (S, B): ancestors; spirits of the dead.

Pitra Yadnya (S, B): funerary rites; ancestors worship.

polemik kebudayaan: the 'polemic on culture', between 1935 and 1939 when Indonesian intellectuals were divided over the question of how much the developing national culture should borrow from the West.

polusi kebudayaan: cultural pollution.

pragina (OJ, B): performer, dancer.

pralina (S, B): dissolution of the universe.

pramana (S): 'valid means of knowledge', which varies according to the different 'points of view' (*darshana*) that comprise Hindu philosophy.

prasasti (S): inscription on stone, copper, etc.; commemorative plaque.

pratima (S, B): image; a small effigy into which a deity descends at a temple ceremony.

prayaschitta (S), *prayascitta* (B): expiation, atonement, penance.

puik (B): attitude of mutual avoidance between feuding people.

puncak-puncak kebudayaan: 'cultural peaks'; in reference to those elements of regional cultures that are deemed worthy of contributing to Indonesian national culture.

punggawa (S, B): formerly a regional lord vassal of a raja; a district head under the colonial administration.

puputan (B): fight to the end; act of resistance to colonial rule, as in *Puputan Badung* (1906), *Puputan Klungkung* (1908) and *Puputan Margarana* (1946).

pura (S, B): temple.

> *pura agung jagatnatha*: 'world great temple'; temples erected in the district capitals of Bali and in some provincial capitals outside the island, on the model of the temple inaugurated by Parisada in 1968 in Denpasar.
>
> *pura bale agung*: 'great meeting hall temple', intended for meetings of the village council and associated with fertility rites.
>
> *pura dadia*: kinship temple.
>
> *pura dalem*: 'temple of the mighty one', place of ritual contact with the not yet purified deceased, located near the cemetery and cremation ground.
>
> *pura desa*: 'village temple', intended for meetings of the village council and associated with fertility rites.
>
> *pura kahyangan*: temples of a territorial nature, supposedly intended to the cult of Ida Sanghyang Widhi Wasa according to Parisada's nomenclature.
>
> *pura kahyangan jagat*: 'world sanctuary'; temples intended for the Indonesian Hindu community in its entirety, erected by Parisada in various parts of the Archipelago inhabited by significant Hindu minorities.
>
> *pura kawitan*: temples of a genealogical nature, from kinship temples to ancestral shrines, according to Parisada's nomenclature.
>
> Pura Mandara Giri Semeru Agung: temple erected by Parisada in 1992 on the slopes of Mount Semeru in East Java.

Pura Panataran Agung: 'Great State Temple'; the main sanctuary at Besakih, on the slopes of Mount Agung, considered the 'mother temple' of Bali.

pura puseh: 'navel temple'; the 'origin temple', where the deified founding ancestors of the village are worshipped.

Purana (S): texts related to the cult of major deities such as Vishnu, Shiva and Devi.

puri (S, B): royal palace, noble house, residence of a *satria* family.

purohita (S, B): court priest; religious advisor and ritual expert to a raja.

pusaka (S): heirloom, inheritance.

rahayu (OJ, B): well-being and safety.

raksasa (S): monster, giant, ogre, demon.

rakyat (A): people, nation.

Ramayana (S): Indian epic poem narrating the adventures of Prince Rama and his wife Sita.

Rangda (S, OJ, B): 'The Widow'; mask representing the terrifying transformation of deities or sorcerers, venerated by local communities as a tutelary deity; character of the 'witch' confronted with the 'dragon' Barong in the performances of *Calonarang*.

Reformasi: 'Reformation', in reference to the period of democratic reform initiated in the aftermath of President Suharto's resignation in 1998.

rejang (B): female temple dance.

religi (D): religion.

Repelita (*Rencana Pembangunan Lima Tahun*): five-year governmental development plans launched by the New Order in 1969.

rishi (S), *resi*, *rsi* (B): seer, holy man, religious ascetic and mystic, priest.

resi bhujangga: title for the priests of the Bhujangga Waisnawa descent group (*warga*), equivalent to *sengguhu*.

Resi Yadnya: rituals for the priesthood.

Rsi Markandeya: legendary cultural hero said to have come from East Java in ancient times to establish Hinduism in Bali and to have founded the Pura Panataran Agung at Besakih.

rust en orde (D): peace and order.

rwa bhineda (OJ, B): unity of opposites; principle of complementarity of positive and negative forces.

sabha (S, OJ): assembly, council, society, congress.

lokasabha: regional congress of *Parisada*.

mahasabha: national congress of *Parisada*.

sadhaka (S, B): person performing religious practices.

sarwa sadhaka: name given by the commoner descent groups (*warga*) to the demand that their priests be allowed to officiate at the ceremonies in the Pura Panataran Agung of Besakih, as opposed to the tradition of *tri sadhaka* defended by the *brahmana*.

tri sadhaka: the three priests traditionally entitled to officiate at the ceremonies in the Pura Panataran Agung of Besakih, namely, a *padanda Siwa*, a *padanda Boda* and a *resi bhujangga*.

Saka (S, B): lunar calendar of Indian origin, which begins in the year 78 CE.

sakala (S, B): material, concrete; designates in Bali that which is perceptible to the senses, the 'manifest world', as opposed to *niskala*, that which is not perceived by the senses, the 'unmanifest world'.

salahang batara (B): threat of ancestral curse.

salat (A): the ritual prayer prescribed by Islam to be recited five times a day at stipulated times and in a stipulated way using Arabic phrases.

sama rasa sama rata: 'solidarity and equality'; slogan coined in 1917 by the Javanese journalist Mas Marco Kartodikromo and later popularized by both Sukarno and the communists.

samhita (S): collections of *mantra* and hymns from the four Vedas: the *Rig-Veda*, the *Sama-Veda*, the *Yajur-Veda* and the *Atharva-Veda*.

Samkhya (S): one of the six orthodox systems of Hindu philosophy (*darshana*), based on an ontological dualism between male spirit (*purusha*) and female matter (*prakriti*).

sampradaya (S, B): religious order based on a spiritual lineage from masters to disciples (*parampara*).

samsara (S, B): the cycle of life, death and rebirth.

samskara (S), *sangaskara* (OJ): purification, consecration, initiation; literary term used to render the category of 'culture' in *Bhāwanāgara*.

sanatana dharma (S): 'eternal *dharma*'; name given in the 19th century by traditionalists to Hinduism, considered an eternally and universally valid religion, in reaction to both Christianity and reform movements.

sanggah (B): household temple of commoners dedicated to the veneration of family ancestors, called *pamerajan* in the case of a nobility household.

sang hyang (OJ, B): deity; a genre of performances involving spirit possession.

sanghyang dedari: an ancient ritual dance executed by two pre-pubescent girls possessed by the spirits of celestial nymphs.

Sang Hyang Wid(h)i (Wasa): the official title given by the Balinese to the supreme God of *agama Hindu (Bali)*, in conformity with the official monotheism of the Indonesian Ministry of Religion.

santri (J): student of an Islamic boarding school; used to refer to religiously observant Muslims.

pesantren: private Islamic boarding school, typically for study of the Islamic sciences including jurisprudence.

Sarasamuscaya: Old Javanese compendium of teachings derived from the *Mahabharata*.

sasana (S, B): teaching, precept, doctrine, in Hinduism and Buddhism.

satria (S, B): class of kings and lords, former holders of temporal power, second in the hierarchy of *wangsa*.

satua (B): story, narrative, popular literature.

satya (S), *satia* (B): loyalty, faithfulness.
    satyadharma: Christianity as the 'true *dharma*'.
    satyavedam: Christianity as the 'true Veda'.
    masatia: to commit an act of loyalty, referring to the immolation of a widow on the funeral pyre of her lord.

sebel, sasebelan (B): state of ritual pollution.

sekaa (B): voluntary association, formed for specific purposes.

selamat (A): safe, secure.

selong (B): banishment, exile.
    kaselong: to be sent into exile.

sema (OJ, B): cemetery and cremation ground.

sembah (OJ): worship, veneration, reverential salutation.

sendratari: '*seni, drama, tari*'; modern pantomimic dance-drama.

sengguhu (B): title for the priests of the Bhujangga Waisnawa descent group (*warga*), equivalent to *resi bhujangga*.

seni, kesenian: art.
    seni budaya: 'cultural arts'; a conception of culture restricted to aspects that can be represented and generate an aesthetic appreciation.

Shaiva Siddhanta (S): 'The final truth of Shiva'; the most important of all the Shaiva schools, whose doctrine has deeply marked the religious life in Java as in Bali.

shakti (S): active power of a deity represented by its female form.
    sakti, kasaktian (B): mystical and magical power.

shastra (S), *sastra* (OJ): precept, rule, knowledge, scripture, literature; term used in reference to Sanskrit treatises dealing with all branches of knowledge and laws.
    sastrawan: man of letters, literati.

shirk (A): the sin of idolatry or polytheism in Islam.

shraddha (S), *sradha* (B): faith, belief.

shruti (S): 'that which is heard', i.e., the 'revelation'; sacred knowledge of the Vedas, which was heard by ancient seers and orally transmitted from generation to generation.

shuddhi (S): state of purity necessary for the performance of *dharma*; rite of purification by which pollution is removed; procedure invented by the Arya Samaj for reconverting to Hinduism those Indians who had converted to Islam or Christianity.
    Sudhi Wadani: rite of conversion to *agama Hindu* formalized by Parisada in 1980.

sima (S, B): local customary regulation.

sisia (S, B): disciple, student, client, of a priest or spiritual master.

siwa (or *surya*) (S, B): honorific term for a *padanda*.
    masiwa brahmana: to receive holy water from a *padanda*.

Siwaratri (S, B): the 'Night of Siwa', a time for fasting and meditating.

Smarta (S): orthodox Hindu tradition conforming to the prescriptions of the *smriti*.

smriti (S): 'that which is remembered', i.e., the 'tradition'; a body of Hindu texts usually attributed to an author, traditionally written down but constantly revised, in contrast to *shruti* considered authorless, that were transmitted orally through the generations and fixed.

sor-singgih (OJ, B): low and high; the respectful Balinese language prescribed by customary etiquette.

soroh (OJ, B): a group of persons or things of the same kind; members of a kinship group who consider themselves, by virtue of a presumed genealogical relationship, the descendants of a common ancestor and are therefore regarded as similar.

stawa (S, B): hymns of praise.

stedehouder (D): Balinese regent during the Dutch colonial occupation.

sthiti (S, B): preservation of the universe.

stuti (S, B): hymns of praise.

subak (B): cooperative of wet-rice farmers, responsible for irrigation works and distribution of water among the rice fields.

sudra (S, B): commoner; the lowest in the hierarchy of *wangsa*, to which the great majority of the Balinese belong, as opposed to the minority *triwangsa*.

suka duka (S, B): a system of mutual help between members of a neighborhood or kinship group, especially during the rites of life and death.

sukla (S, B): ritually pure; new or never used.

suku: group, family, genus.
    suku bangsa: ethnic group.
    suku terasing: ethnic minorities construed as 'isolated tribes'.

sulinggih (OJ, B): honorific title for *padanda*; the equivalent of *pandita* in Parisada's nomenclature.

Sumpah Pemuda: the 'Youth Pledge', first taken at the Indonesian Youth Congress held in Batavia on October 28, 1928.

surudan (OJ, B): leftovers of food offerings whose essence has already been absorbed by the deity and which can therefore be consumed by the worshipers (*lungsuran*).

surya-sewana (S, B): devotional rite performed daily by *padanda Siwa*.

susila (S, B), *kesusilaan*: ethics; one of the three pillars of the *Dharma Agama* according to Parisada.

svadharma (S): the duties and qualifications incumbent on Hindus according to their social class (*varna*) and their stage of life (*ashrama*).

syahadat (A), *sahadat*: creed, dogma; the Muslim confession of faith.

syariah (A): Islamic law.

tabuh rah (B): blood sacrifice to chthonic forces.

tajen (OJ, B): cockfight.

takhyul (A): superstition.

taksu (B): inspiration of a divine or magical origin; shrine in household temple dedicated to forces mediating between divine and human worlds.

tanah air: fatherland.

tantra (S, B): esoteric traditions of Hinduism and Buddhism, constituting a post-Vedic revelation reserved for initiates, that developed in India from the middle of the first millennium CE onwards; in a specific sense, texts from the Shakta tradition, which worship the Goddess as the source of supreme power (*shakti*).

tantri (S, B): popular literature (*satua*) and fables of Indian origin in the Kirtya nomenclature.

tari: dance.
> *tari balih-balihan* (B): 'secular dances', performed as pure entertainment, with no relation to a ceremony.
> *tari bebali* (B): 'ceremonial dances', accompanying a ceremony.
> *tari wali* (B): 'sacred, religious dances', indissociable from the carrying out of a ceremony.

tata krama (S, OJ): code of conduct, etiquette, good manners; local customary practices.

tattwa (S, B): doctrine, philosophy, theology; one of the three pillars of the *Dharma Agama* according to Parisada.

Tat Twam Asi (S): 'Thou Art That', famous aphorism from the *Chandogya Upanishad*

tawan karang (OJ, B): the right of rajas to salvage any wreck stranded off the coast of Bali.

tawhid (A): the Islamic principle of God's oneness.

tirtha (S), *tirta* (B): holy water.

tirta yatra: pilgrimage.

patirtaan: padanda as a source of holy water.

topeng (OJ, B): mask; masked theater based on historical chronicles of the Balinese ruling families.

Tri Bhuwana (S, B): large purification ritual celebrated in the temple complex of Besakih in March 1993.

Tri Hita Karana (S, B): 'The Three Sources of Well-being', namely, the harmonious relationships of human beings with God (*parhyangan*), with people (*pawongan*) and with nature (*palemahan*).

tri loka (S, B): the three levels of the cosmos, the heavens, the middle world and the underworld.

Trimurti (S, B): 'three forms'; the Hindu triad Brahma, Vishnu and Shiva, respectively personifying the cosmic functions of creation, preservation and destruction.

tri rna (S, B): the three 'debts' that every Hindu must discharge, to the *Dewa*, the *Pitra* and the *Resi*.

Tri Sakti (S, B): 'three powers'; alternative designation of the *Trimurti*.

trisandhya (S), *Puja Tri Sandhya* (B): the prayer to Sang Hyang Widhi that every Hindu should perform during the 'junctures' (*sandhya*) of the day: at dawn, at noon and at dusk; it became the official daily prayer of *agama Hindu* after Parisada's Sixth Congress in 1991.

triwangsa (S, B): the three descent groups of *brahmana*, *satria* and *wesia*, composing the Balinese nobility, as opposed to the commoners, called *sudra* and more generally *jaba*.

tulah (OJ, B): to be cursed by arousing the ire of the gods or the ancestors.

tutur (OJ, B): esoteric texts dealing with mystical, cosmological and ritual speculations.

ulama (A): Islamic religious scholars.

umat (A): religious community, specifically Islamic.

upacara (S, OJ): ritual, ceremony; one of the three pillars of the *Dharma Agama* according to Parisada.

upadesa (S, B): 'teachings, instructions', in the sense of the spiritual guidance provided by a *guru* to his disciple; Hindu catechism, formulated by Parisada in 1967.

upanayana (S): initiation ceremony whereby a boy from one of the first three *varna* is conferred the Brahmanic sacred thread that marks the beginning of his apprenticeship of the Vedas with a *guru*.

Upanishad (S): philosophical speculations supplementing the Vedas and illuminating them with commentaries.

usada (OJ, B): remedy, medicine, medical science.

utpatti (S, B): creation of the universe.

vamsha (S): descent, race, genealogy, lineage.

varga (S): class, order, clan.

varna (S): Brahmanic ideology of hierarchizing society into four classes: *brahmana*, *kshatriya*, *vaishya* and *shudra*.
> *varnashrama dharma* (S): duties and qualifications incumbent on Hindus according to their social class (*varna*) and their stage of life (*ashrama*).

Veda (S): 'knowledge'; a body of texts considered to have been 'revealed' (*shruti*) to inspired seers, supposed to have been composed orally between the 15th and the fifth centuries BCE, composed of four 'collections' (*samhita*): the *Rig-Veda*, the *Sama-Veda*, the *Yajur-Veda* and the *Atharva-Veda*.

Vedanta (S): 'End of the Veda'; term referring to the Upanishads as well as to a major philosophical tradition (*darshana*) divided into several schools, the main ones being non-dualism (*advaita*), qualified non-dualism (*vishishtadvaita*) and dualism (*dvaita*).

vyavahara (S): legal procedure.

wahyu (A): divine revelation.

walaka (S, B): lay people; specifically, a *brahmana* who is not a *padanda*.

Wali Pitu (A, J): the seven Muslim saints whose graves are supposed to become the starting point for the Islamization of Bali.

Wali Songo (A, J): the legendary nine saints to whom the Islamization of Java is attributed.

wangsa (S, B): caste, nation, people; Balinese hierarchical system of titles ordered according to the Indian terminology of *varna* and based on the proximity to an ancestral Javanese origin.

warga (S, B): Balinese formal organization aspiring to unify all members of a kinship group (*soroh*) who consider themselves, by virtue of a presumed genealogical relationship, the descendants of a common ancestor.

wariga (OJ, B): technical literature on astrology and calendrical divination.

warisan budaya: cultural heritage.

warna (S, B): normative ideology modeled on the Indic version of the *varna* providing a classificatory grid within which the Balinese have devised their own title system, called *wangsa*.

wayang (OJ, B): shadow; generic term, designating both shadow puppet theater (*wayang kulit*) and dramatic genres performed by actors (*wayang wong*), among other forms.

weda (S, B): sacred formulas; Balinese liturgical manuscripts composed of ritual prescriptions (*kalpasastra*), *mantra* and hymns (*stuti* and *stawa*), used by *padanda* during their daily worship (*maweda*).
> *Weda Parikrama*: manual used by *padanda Siwa* for their daily worship.

wesia (S, B): warriors and administrators of lesser nobility, not always clearly distinguished from the *satria*, third in the hierarchy of *wangsa*.

wibawa, kawibawan (S, B): authority, power, charisma, prestige.

wiku (OJ): sage, ascetic, priest.

wong Majapahit (OJ, B): the 'people of Majapahit', as opposed to the Bali Aga or Bali Mula; members of the Balinese nobility who claim to be descendants of the Javanese conquerors from the kingdom of Majapahit who subjugated the island of Bali in the 14th century.

yajna (S), *yadnya* (B): sacrifice, devotion, worship, offering; generic term designating the religious rituals of *agama Hindu*.

 panchamahayajna (S): the five 'great sacrifices' that a Hindu householder should perform daily: to gods, to ancestors, to human beings, to all living creatures and to the Vedas.

 panca yadnya (B): the five categories of rites of *agama Hindu*, formalized at Parisada's first congress in 1964: for gods (*Dewa Yadnya*), ancestors (*Pitra Yadnya*), human beings (*Manusa Yadnya*), priests (*Resi Yadnya*) and 'demons' (*Buta Yadnya*).

yayasan (S): foundation (corporate body).

zakat (A): Islamic religious alms.

zaman modern (A, D): modern times.

zelfbestuurder (D): 'self-ruler'; title conferred to the Balinese rajas by the Dutch colonial administration in 1938.

Bibliography

Abalahin, Andrew J. 2005. "A Sixth Religion? Confucianism and the Negotiation of Indonesian-Chinese Identity under the Pancasila State", in Andrew C. Willford and Kenneth M. George, eds, *Spirited Politics. Religion and Public Life in Contemporary Southeast Asia*. Ithaca: Southeast Asia Program Publications, Cornell University, pp. 119–42.

Abbasi, Rushain. 2021. "Islam and the Invention of Religion: A Study of Medieval Muslim Discourses on *Dīn*", *Studia Islamica* 116: 1–106.

Abdullah, Taufik. 1966. "*Adat* and Islam: An Examination of Conflict in Minangkabau", *Indonesia* 2: 1–24.

———. 1971. *Schools and Politics. The Kaum Muda Movement in West Sumatra*. Ithaca: Modern Indonesia Project, Cornell University.

Abeyasekere, Susan. 1972. "Partai Indonesia Raja, 1936–42: A Study in Cooperative Nationalism", *Journal of Southeast Asian Studies* 3, 2: 262–76.

Acciaioli, Gregory L. 1985. "Culture as Art. From Practice to Spectacle in Indonesia", *Canberra Anthropology* 8, 1–2: 148–74.

———. 1996. "Pavilions and Posters: Showcasing Diversity and Development in Contemporary Indonesia", *Eikon* 1: 27–42.

———. 2001. "'Archipelagic Culture' as an Exclusionary Government Discourse in Indonesia", *The Asia Pacific Journal of Anthropology* 2, 1: 1–23.

———. 2007. "From Customary Law to Indigenous Sovereignty: Reconceptualizing the Scope and Significance of *Masyarakat Adat* in Contemporary Indonesia", in Jamie S. Davidson and David Henley, eds, *The Revival of Tradition in Indonesian Politics: The Deployment of Adat from Colonialism to Indigenism*. London & New York: Routledge, pp. 295–318.

Acharya, Amitav. 2013. *Civilizations in Embrace: The Spread of Ideas and the Transformation of Power. India and Southeast Asia in the Classical Age*. Singapore: Institute of Southeast Asian Studies.

Acri, Andrea. 2006. "The Sanskrit-Old Javanese Tutur Literature from Bali: The Textual Basis of Śaivism in Ancient Indonesia", *Rivista di Studi Sudasiatici* 1: 105–35.

———. 2011. "A New Perspective for 'Balinese Hinduism' in the Light of the Premodern Religious Discourse: A Textual-Historical Approach", in Michel Picard and Rémy Madinier, eds, *The Politics of Religion in Indonesia. Syncretism, Orthodoxy, and Religious Contention in Java and Bali*. London & New York: Routledge, pp. 142–66.

———. 2013. "Modern Hindu Intellectuals and Ancient Texts: Reforming Śaiva Yoga in Bali", *Bijdragen tot de Taal-, Land- en Volkenkunde* 169, 1: 68–103.

———. 2015. "Revisiting the Cult of 'Śiva-Buddha' in Java and Bali", in D. Christian Lammerts, ed., *Buddhist Dynamics in Premodern and Early Modern Southeast Asia*. Singapore: Institute of Southeast Asian Studies, pp. 261–82.

———, ed. 2016. *Esoteric Buddhism in Mediaeval Maritime Asia: Networks of Masters, Texts, Icons*. Singapore: Institute of Southeast Asian Studies.

———. 2017a. "Tantrism Seen from the East", in Andrea Acri, Roger Blench and Alexandra Landmann, eds, *Spirits and Ships: Cultural Transfers in Early Monsoon Asia*. Singapore: Institute of Southeast Asian Studies, pp. 71–144.

———. 2017b. "'Local' vs. 'Cosmopolitan' in the Study of Premodern Southeast Asia", *Suvannabhumi* 9, 1: 7–52.

Acri, Andrea, and Michele Stephen. 2018. "Mantras to Make Demons into Gods. Old Javanese Texts and the Balinese *Bhūtayajñas*", *Bulletin de l'École française d'Extrême-Orient* 104: 141–203.

Adam, Ahmat B. 1995. *The Vernacular Press and the Emergence of Modern Indonesian Consciousness (1855–1913)*. Ithaca: Southeast Asia Program, Cornell University.

Adams, Kathleen M. 1995. "Making-up the Toraja? The Appropriation of Tourism, Anthropology, and Museums for Politics in Upland Sulawesi, Indonesia", *Ethnology* 34, 2: 143–53.

Aditjondro, George Junus. 1995. *Bali, Jakarta's Colony: Social and Ecological Impacts of Jakarta-Based Conglomerates in Bali's Tourism Industry*. Perth: Asia Research Centre Working Paper, Murdoch University.

Agastia, Ida Bagus Gede. 1996. *Eka Dasa Rudra, Eka Bhuwana* [Eleven Rudras, One World]. Denpasar: Parisada Hindu Dharma Pusat.

Agung, Ide Anak Agung Gde. 1985. *Dari Negara Indonesia Timur ke Republik Indonesia Serikat* [From the State of East Indonesia to the United States of Indonesia].Yogyakarta: UGM Press.

———. 1991. *Bali in the 19th Century*. Jakarta: Yayasan Obor Indonesia.

Alexander, Paul, ed. 1989. *Creating Indonesian Cultures*. Sydney: Oceania Publications.

Ali, Muhamad. 2007. "Categorizing Muslims in Postcolonial Indonesia", *Moussons* 11: 33–62.

Aljunied, Syed Muhd Khairudin. 2004. *Raffles and Religion: A Study of Sir Thomas Stamford Raffles' Discourse on Religions amongst Malays*. Kuala Lumpur: The Other Press.

Allen, Pamela. 2007. "Challenging Diversity?: Indonesia's Anti-pornography Bill", *Asian Studies Review* 31: 101–15.

Allen, Pamela, and Carmencita Palermo. 2005. "*Ajeg Bali*: Multiple Meanings, Diverse Agendas", *Indonesia and the Malay World* 33, 97: 239–55.

AMHI. 1968. *Seminar Tampaksiring, Tgl. 30 Djuni s/d 5 Djuli 1968* [Tampaksiring Seminar, June 30 – July 5, 1968] Djakarta & Denpasar, DPP. Angkatan Muda Hindu Indonesia.

Anandakusuma, Sri Reshi. 1954. *Dharma Shastra Agama Hindu Bali* [Dharma Literature of the Balinese Hindu Religion]. Denpasar: Balimas.

———. 1966. *Pergolakan Hindu Dharma II* [The Upheaval of Hindu Dharma II]. Klungkung.

———. 1972. "Perspektif Hari Depan Pulau Bali", Prasaran Musjawarah Tjendikiawan/Sardjana Hindu-Dharma (Indonesia) Seluruh Indonesia ["Perspectives on Bali's Future", Conference of Hindu-Dharma Intellectuals/Scholars (Indonesia) All over Indonesia]. Klungkung.

———. 1985. *Manifes Satya Hindu Dharma* [Satya Hindu Dharma Manifesto]. Klungkung.

———. 1986. *Kamus Bahasa Bali* [Balinese Dictionary]. Denpasar: C.V. Kayumas.

Anderson, Benedict R.O'G. 1990. "Language, Fantasy, Revolution: Java 1900–1945", *Prisma* 50: 25–39.

———. 1991 [1983]. *Imagined Communities: Reflections on the Origin and Spread of Nationalism*. London: Verso.

Anggaran Dasar Madjelis Hinduisme [Statutes of Madjelis Hinduisme]. 1950. Klungkung.

Anggaran Dasar Panti Agama Hindu Bali [Statutes of Panti Agama Hindu Bali]. 1951. Singaradja.

Anggaran Dasar Satya Hindu Dharma Indonesia [Statutes of Satya Hindu Dharma Indonesia]. 1956. Klungkung.

Anggraeni, Dewi. 2003. *Who Did This to Our Bali?* Briar Hill: Indra Publishing.

Aragon, Lorraine V. 2000. *Fields of the Lord: Animism, Christian Minorities, and State Development in Indonesia*. Honolulu: University of Hawai'i Press.

———. 2003. "Missions and Omissions of the Supernatural: Indigenous Cosmologies and the Legitimisation of 'Religion' in Indonesia", *Anthropological Forum* 13, 2: 131–40.

———. 2021. "Regulating Religion and Recognizing 'Animist Beliefs' in Indonesian Law and Life", in Chiara Formichi, ed., *Religious Pluralism in Indonesia. Threats and Opportunities for Democracy*. Ithaca & London: Cornell University Press, pp. 135–62.

Ardika, I Wayan. 2018. "Early Contacts between Bali and India", in Shyam Saran, ed., *Cultural and Civilisational Links Between India and Southeast Asia: Historical and Contemporary Dimensions*. Singapore: Palgrave Macmillan, pp. 19–29.

Ardika, I Wayan, and I Nyoman Darma Putra, eds. 2004. *Politik Kebudayaan dan Identitas Etnik* [Cultural Politics and Ethnic Identity]. Denpasar: Fakultas Sastra Universitas Udayana and Balimangsi Press.

Ari Dwipayana, AA. GN. 2001. *Kelas dan Kasta. Pergulatan Kelas Menengah Bali* [Class and Caste. Bali's Middle Class Struggle]. Yogyakarta: Lapera Pustaka Utama.

———. 2005. *GloBALIsm: Pergulatan Politik Representasi atas Bali* [GloBALIsm: The Political Struggle of Representation over Bali]. Denpasar: Uluangkep.

———. 2021. "Keluar dari Pusaran: Aktivisme Hindu dalam Menghadapi Tantangan dan Masa Depan", Orasi Ilmiah Dies Natalis Pertama Universitas Hindu Negeri I Gusti Bagus Sugriwa ["Out of the Vortex: Hindu Activism in the Face of Challenges and the Future", Scientific Oration for the First Anniversary of the National Hindu University I Gusti Bagus Sugriwa]. Denpasar.

Aritonang, Jan Sihar, and Karel Steenbrink, eds. 2008. *A History of Christianity in Indonesia*. Leiden: Brill.

Arnal, William. 2000. "Definition [of Religion]", in Willi Braun and Russell T. McCutcheon, eds, *Guide to the Study of Religion*. London & New York: Cassell Academic, pp. 21–34.

Asad, Talal. 1986. "The Concept of Cultural Translation in British Social Anthropology", in James Clifford and George E. Marcus, eds, *Writing Culture: The Poetics and Politics of Ethnography*. Berkeley: University of California Press, pp. 141–64.

———. 1993. "The Construction of Religion as an Anthropological Category", in Talal Asad, *Genealogies of Religion. Discipline and Reasons of Power in Christianity and Islam*. Baltimore: The Johns Hopkins University Press, pp. 27–54.

———. 2001. "Reading a Modern Classic: W.C. Smith's *The Meaning and End of Religion*", in Hent de Vries and Samuel Weber, eds, *Religion and Media*. Stanford: Stanford University Press, pp. 131–47.

———. 2003. *Formations of the Secular: Christianity, Islam, Modernity*. Stanford: Stanford University Press.

Assmann, Jan. 2009 [2003]. *The Price of Monotheism*. Stanford: Stanford University Press.

Atkinson, Jane Monnig. 1987. "Religions in Dialogue: The Construction of an Indonesian Minority Religion", in Rita Smith Kipp and Susan Rodgers, eds, *Indonesian Religions in Transition*. Tucson: The University of Arizona Press, pp. 171–86.

Atmadja, Nengah Bawa. 2001. *Reformasi ke Arah Kemajuan yang Sempurna dan Holistik. Gagasan Perkumpulan Surya Kanta Tentang Bali di Masa Depan* [Reform towards Perfect and Holistic Progress. Surya Kanta Association's Idea of Bali in the Future]. Surabaya: Paramita.

———. 2010. *Ajeg Bali. Gerakan, Identitas Kultural, dan Globalisasi* [Ajeg Bali. Movement, Cultural Identity and Globalization]. Yogyakarta: LkiS.

Augé, Marc. 1982. *Génie du paganism* [The Genius of Paganism]. Paris: Gallimard.

Babadzan, Alain. 2009. *Le spectacle de la culture: Globalisation et traditionalismes en Océanie* [The Spectacle of Culture. Globalization and Traditionalisms in Oceania]. Paris: L'Harmattan.

Bachtiar, Harsja W. 1973. "The Religion of Java: A Commentary", *Madjalah Ilmu-Ilmu Sastra Indonesia* 5, 1: 85–118.

Bagus, I Gusti Ngurah. [n.d.]. "Hubungan Agama, Adat-istiadat, dan Kemasyarakatan", ["The Relationship between Religion, Customs, and Society", in *Anthropologi dan*

Segi2 Pembangunan di Bali [Anthropology and Aspects of Development in Bali]. Denpasar: Fakultas Sastra Udayana.

———. 1969. *Pertentangan kasta dalam bentuk baru pada masjarakat Bali* [Caste Conflict in a New Form in Balinese Society]. Denpasar: Universitas Udayana.

———. 1972. *A Short Note on the Modern Hindu Movements in Balinese Society*. Denpasar: Universitas Udayana.

———. 1974. "'Karya Taur Agung Ekadasa Rudra': rite centenaire de purification au temple de Besakih (Bali)" ["'Karya Taur Agung Ekadasa Rudra': Centenary Rite of Purification at the Temple of Besakih (Bali)"], *Archipel* 8: 59–66.

———. 1975. "Surya Kanta: A *kewangsaan* Movement of the *jaba* Caste in Bali", *Masyarakat Indonesia* 2, 2: 153–62.

———. 1991. "Bali in the 1950s: The Role of the *Pemuda Pejuang* in Balinese Political Processes", in Hildred Geertz, ed., *State and Society in Bali; Historical, Textual and Anthropological Approaches*. Leiden: KITLV Press, pp. 199–212.

———. 1996. "The Play 'Woman's Fidelity': Literature and Caste Conflict in Bali", in Adrian Vickers, ed., *Being Modern in Bali: Image and Change*. New Haven: Monograph 43, Yale University Southeast Asia Studies, pp. 92–114.

———. 2004. "The Parisada Hindu Dharma Indonesia in a Society in Transformation", in Martin Ramstedt, ed., *Hinduism in Modern Indonesia. A Minority Religion between Local, National, and Global Interests*. London & New York: RoutledgeCurzon. IIAS Asian Studies Series, pp. 84–92.

Baier, Martin. 2007. "The Development of the Hindu Kaharingan Religion: A New Dayak Religion in Central Kalimantan", *Anthropos* 102, 2: 566–70.

Bakhtin, Mikhail Mikhailovich. 1981. *The Dialogic Imagination: Four Essays by M.M. Bakhtin*, edited by Michael Holquist. Austin & London: University of Texas Press.

Bakker, Frederik Lambertus. 1993. *The Struggle of the Hindu Balinese Intellectuals. Developments in Modern Hindu Thinking in Independent Indonesia*. Amsterdam: VU University Press.

———. 1995. "The Renaissance of Balinese Hinduism in the Context of Independent Indonesia: Its Relationship with Politics", Paper presented at the 1st Conference of the European Association for Southeast Asian Studies (EUROSEAS), Leiden, 29 June – 1 July, 1995.

———. 1997. "Balinese Hinduism and the Indonesian State. Recent Developments", *Bijdragen tot de Taal- Land- en Volkenkunde* 153, 1: 15–41.

Bakker. Wim. 2018. *Visual Arts in Bali. A Century of Change 1900–2000*. Eindhoven: Lecturis.

Balagangadhara, S.N. 2005 [1994]. *'The Heathen in His Blindness...'. Asia, the West and the Dynamic of Religion*. Leiden: Brill.

Bandem, I Made. 1983. "The Evolution of *Legong* from Sacred to Secular Dance of Bali", *Dance Research Annual* 14: 113–19.

Bandem, I Made, and Fredrik Eugene deBoer. 1978. "Gambuh: A Classical Balinese Dance-Drama", *Asian Music* 10, 1: 115–27.

———. 1995 [1981]. *Balinese Dance in Transition: Kaja and Kelod*. Kuala Lumpur: Oxford University Press.

Barbu, Daniel. 2016. "Idolatry and the History of Religions", *Studi e Materiali di Storia delle Religioni* 82, 2: 537–70.

Barton, Carlin A., and Daniel Boyarin. 2016. *Imagine No Religion: How Modern Abstractions Hide Ancient Realities*. New York: Fordham University Press.

Basu, Shamita. 2002. *Religious Revivalism as Nationalist Discourse: Swami Vivekananda and New Hinduism in Nineteenth Century Bengal*. New Delhi: Oxford University Press.

Bateson, Gregory, and Margaret Mead. 1942. *Balinese Character. A Photographic Analysis*. New York: New York Academy of Sciences.

Baum, Vicki. 2011 [1937]. *Love and Death in Bali*. Singapore: Tuttle Publishing.

Bawa, I Wayan. 2004. "Apa yang dimaksud dengan Ajeg Bali?" ["What Is Meant by Ajeg Bali?"], in I Wayan Cika et al., eds, *Garitan Budaya Nusantara Dalam Perspektif Kebinekaan* [Archipelago Culture in the Perspective of Diversity]. Kuta: Larasan, pp. 251–8.

Bayly, Susan. 2004. "Imagining 'Greater India': French and Indian Visions of Colonialism in the Indic Mode", *Modern Asian Studies* 38, 3: 703–44.

———. 2007. "India's 'Empire of Culture'. Sylvain Lévi and the Greater India Society", in Lyne Bansat-Boudon and Roland Lardinois, eds, *Sylvain Lévi (1863–1933). Études indiennes, histoire sociale*. Turnhout: Brepols, pp. 193–212.

Beatty, Andrew. 1999. *Varieties of Javanese Religion. An Anthropological Account*. Cambridge: Cambridge University Press.

Becker, Judith. 2004 [1993]. *Gamelan Stories. Tantrism, Islam, and Aesthetics in Central Java*. Tempe: Arizona State University.

Bell, Catherine. 2006. "Paradigms behind (and before) the Modern Concept of Religion", *History and Theory* 45: 27–46.

Belo, Jane. 1949. *Bali: Rangda and Barong*. Seattle: University of Washington Press.

———. 1953. *Bali: Temple Festival*. Seattle: University of Washington Press.

Belo, Jane. 1960. *Trance in Bali*. New York: Columbia University Press.

———, ed. 1970. *Traditional Balinese Culture*. New York: Columbia University Press.

Benda, Harry J. 1966. "The Pattern of Administrative Reforms in the Closing Years of Dutch Rule in Indonesia", *The Journal of Asian Studies* 25, 4: 589–605.

———. 1983 [1958]. *The Crescent and the Rising Sun. Indonesian Islam under the Japanese Occupation 1942–1945*. Dordrecht: Foris Publications.

Bendesa, I Komang Gde, and Ni Made Asti Aksari. 2015. "From Agricultural to Tourism Hegemony: A Deep Socio-Economic Structural Transformation", in Sylvine Pickel-Chevalier, ed., *Tourism in Bali and the Challenge of Sustainable Development*. Newcastle upon Tyne: Cambridge Scholars Publishing, pp. 76–102.

Benedict, Ruth. 1934. *Patterns of Culture*. Boston & New York: Houghton Mifflin.

Benson, Stella. 1935. "Tourists in Bali", *London Mercury* 31: 261–8.

Berger, Peter L., and Thomas Luckmann. 1966. *The Social Construction of Reality. A Treatise in the Sociology of Knowledge.* Garden City: Doubleday.

Bernand, Carmen, and Serge Gruzinski. 1988. *De l'idolâtrie. Une archéologie des sciences religieuses* [On Idolatry. An Archaeology of Religious Sciences]. Paris: Éditions du Seuil.

Bernet Kempers, August Johan. 1990 [1977]. *Monumental Bali. Introduction to Balinese Archeology & Guide to the Monuments.* Berkeley: Periplus Editions.

Besant, Annie. 1902. *Sanâtana Dharma Catechism. A Catechism for Boys and Girls in Hindu Religion and Morals.* Benares:The Board of Trustees, Central Hindu College.

Bettini, Maurizio. 2016. *Éloge du polythéisme. Ce que peuvent nous apprendre les religions antiques* [In Praise of Polytheism. What Ancient Religions Can Teach Us]. Paris: Les Belles Lettres.

Beyer, Peter. 2003. "Conceptions of Religion: On Distinguishing Scientific, Theological, and 'Official' Meanings", *Social Compass* 50, 2: 141–60.

Bhadra, Wajan. 1953a. *Treaty tentang Agama Hindu Bali* [Treatise on Balinese Hindu Religion]. Singaradja: Kantor Penerangan Agama Propinsi Sunda-Ketjil.

———. 1953b. "Kaste Aspek Sosial dari Hinduisme" ["Caste, a Social Aspect of Hinduism"], *Suara Indonesia* 17 December 1953.

———. 1956. "A Balinese Looks at Bali", *Perspective of Indonesia*, supplement to *The Atlantic Monthly*, June 1956: 70–1.

BKUP. 1950. *Keputusan-keputusan Konperensi Peladjar Seberang 14–17 Djuli 1950 di Denpasar* [Decisions of the Conference of Overseas Students 14–17 July 1950 in Denpasar]. Malang: Badan Koordinator Usaha Peladjar.

Bloch, Esther, Marianne Keppens and Rajaram Hegde, eds. 2010. *Rethinking Religion in India. The Colonial Construction of Hinduism.* London & New York: Routledge.

Bloch, Maurice. 2008. "Why Religion Is Nothing Special but Is Central", *Philosophical Transactions of the Royal Society B* 363: 2055–61.

Bloembergen, Marieke. 2006. *Colonial Spectacles. The Netherlands and the Dutch East Indies at the World Exhibitions, 1880–1931.* Singapore: Singapore University Press.

Boland, Bernard Johan. 1982 [1971]. *The Struggle of Islam in Modern Indonesia.* The Hague: Martinus Nijhoff.

Bonneff, Marcel, et al. 1980. *Pantjasila. Trente années de débats politiques en Indonésie* [Pantjasila. Thirty Years of Political Debate in Indonesia]. Paris: Éditions de la Maison des Sciences de l'Homme.

Bonnet, Rudolf. 1936. "Beeldende Kunst in Gianjar" ["Fine Arts in Gianjar"], *Djawa* 16: 60–73.

Boon, James A. 1977. *The Anthropological Romance of Bali 1597–1972: Dynamic Perspectives in Marriage and Caste, Politics and Religion.* Cambridge: Cambridge University Press.

———. 1986. "Between-The-Wars Bali. Rereading the Relics", in G.W. Stocking Jr. ed., *History of Anthropology, Volume 4. Malinowski, Rivers, Benedict and Others.*

Essays on Culture and Personality. Madison: The University of Wisconsin Press, pp. 218–47.

Borgeaud, Philippe. 1994. "Le couple sacré/profane. Genèse et fortune d'un concept 'opératoire' en histoire des religions" ["The Sacred/Profane Couple. Genesis and Fortune of an 'Operative' Concept in the History of Religions"]. *Revue de l'Histoire des Religions* 211, 4: 387–418.

Borsboom, Ad, and Ton Otto. 1997. "Introduction: Transformation and Tradition in Oceanic religions", in Ton Otto and Ad Borsboom, eds, *Cultural Dynamics of Religious Change in Oceania*. Leiden: KITLV Press, pp. 1–9.

Bosch, Frederik David Kan. 1932a. "Een ontoelaatbaar experiment" ["An Inadmissable Experiment], *De Stuw* 3, 17: 205–7.

———. 1932b. "Bali en de zending: voorloopig antwoord aan Dr. H. Kraemer" ["Bali and Mission: Preliminary Response to Dr. H. Kraemer"], *De Stuw* 3, 19: 240–2.

———. 1933. "Bali en de zending" ["Bali and Mission"], *Djawa* 13: 1–39.

———. 1961. "The Problem of the Hindu Colonization of Indonesia", in Frederik David Kan Bosch, *Selected Studies in Indonesian Archeology*. The Hague: Martinus Nijhoff, pp. 1–22.

Bossy, John. 1985. *Christianity in the West, 1400–1700*. Oxford & New York: Oxford University Press.

Bouillier, Véronique. 1997. "Émergence d'un fondamentalisme hindou au Népal?" ["Emergence of a Hindu Fundamentalism in Nepal?"], *Archives de sciences sociales des religions* 99: 87–168.

Bourdieu, Pierre. 1971. "Genèse et structure du champ religieux" ["Genesis and Structure of the Religious Field"], *Revue Française de Sociologie* 12, 3: 295–334.

———. 1980. "L'identité et la représentation" ["Identity and Representation"], *Actes de la recherche en sciences sociales* 35: 63–72.

Boxer, Charles R. 1973 [1969]. *The Portuguese Seaborne Empire, 1415–1825*. Harmondsworth: Penguin.

———. 1990 [1965]. *The Dutch Seaborne Empire, 1600–1800*. Harmondsworth: Penguin.

Bräuchler, Birgit. 2018. "Diverging Ecologies on Bali", *Sojourn. Journal of Social Issues in Southeast Asia* 33, 2: 362–96.

———. 2020. "Bali Tolak Reklamasi: The Local Adoption of Global Protest", *Convergence. The International Journal of Research into New Media Technologies* 26, 3: 620–38.

Brekke, Torkel. 2002. *Makers of Modern Indian Religion in the Late Nineteenth Century*. Oxford: Oxford University Press.

Bronkhorst, Johannes. 2011. "The Spread of Sanskrit in Southeast Asia", in Pierre-Yves Manguin, A. Mani and Geoff Wade, eds, *Early Interactions between South and Southeast Asia: Reflections on Cross-cultural Exchange*. Singapore: Institute of Southeast Asian Studies, pp. 263–75.

———. 2016. *How the Brahmins Won. From Alexander to the Guptas*. Leiden & Boston: Brill.

Brown, Iem. 1987. "Contemporary Indonesian Buddhism and Monotheism", *Journal of Southeast Asian Studies* 17, 1: 108–17.

———. 2004. "The Revival of Buddhism in Modern Indonesia", in Martin Ramstedt, ed., *Hinduism in Modern Indonesia. A Minority Religion between Local, National, and Global Interests*. London & New York: RoutledgeCurzon—IIAS Asian Studies Series, pp. 45–55.

Brubaker, Rogers, and Frederick Cooper. 2000. "Beyond 'Identity'", *Theory and Society* 29, 1: 1-47.

Bruner, Edward M. 1987–88. "Introduction: Experiments in Ethnographic Writing", in Paul J. Benson, ed., *Conversations in Anthropology: Anthropology and Literature, Journal of the Steward Anthropological Society* 17, 1–2: 1–19.

———. 1995. "The Ethnographer/Tourist in Indonesia", in Marie-Françoise Lanfant, John B. Allcock and Edward M. Bruner, eds, *International Tourism: Identity and Change*. London: Sage Publications, pp. 224–41.

Brunner, Hélène. 1967. "À propos d'un rituel balinais" ["About a Balinese Ritual"], *Journal Asiatique* 255, 3–4: 409–22.

———. [n.d.]. *Agama*, Encyclopaedia Universalis.

Budharta, Ida Bagus Gde et al. 1986. *Pertumbuhan Ide Nasionalisme Dalam Masyarakat Bali* [The Growth of Nationalism in Balinese Society]. Denpasar: Fakultas Sastra Universitas Udayana.

Budiarna, I Nyoman, ed. 2009. *PHDI Setengah Abad. Menuju Paradigma Millenium Budaya* [PHDI Half a Century. Toward the Millennium Cultural Paradigm]. Jakarta: Parisada Hindu Dharma Indonesia.

Budiastra, Putu et al. 1998. *Museum Bali. Sejarah dan Masa Depannya* [Museum Bali. Its History and Future]. Denpasar: Museum Bali.

Budja, I Gusti Made. 1971. "Prasaran Conferentie International Angkatan Muda Hindu Indonesia" ["Indonesian Hindu Youth International Conference Address"], Jogjakarta.

Buehler, Michael. 2016. *The Politics of Shari'a Law: Islamist Activists and the State in Democratizing Indonesia*. Cambridge: Cambridge University Press.

Burhanuddin, Yudhis M. 2008. *Bali Yang Hilang: Pendatang Islam dan Etnisitas di Bali* [The Lost Bali: Islamic Migrants and Ethnicity in Bali]. Yogyakarta: Kanisius.

Burns, Peter. 1989. "The Myth of Adat", *The Journal of Legal Pluralism and Unofficial Law* 28: 1–127.

———. 2004. *The Leiden Legacy: Concepts of Law in Indonesia*. Leiden: KITLV Press.

Butt, Simon. 2020. "Constitutional Recognition of 'Beliefs' in Indonesia", *Journal of Law and Religion* 35, 3: 450–73.

Byrne, Peter. 1989. *Natural Religion and the Nature of Religion. The Legacy of Deism*. London: Routledge.

Cabasset, Christine, Jean Couteau and Michel Picard. 2017. "La poldérisation de la baie de Benoa à Bali: vers un nouveau *puputan*?" ["The Reclamation of Benoa Bay in Bali: Toward a New *Puputan*?"], *Archipel* 93: 151–97.

Caldwell, Ian. 1985. "Anak Agung Panji Tisna, Balinese raja and Indonesian novelist, 1908–78", *Indonesia Circle* 36: 55–79.

Carpenter, Bruce W. 1997. *W.O.J. Nieuwenkamp. First European Artist in Bali*. Singapore: Éditions Didier Millet.

———, ed. 2014. *Lempad of Bali: The Illuminating Line*. Ubud: Museum Puri Lukisan and Singapore: Éditions Didier Millet.

Carpenter, Bruce W., and Maria Hofker-Rueter. 1993. *Willem Hofker, Schilder van / Painter of Bali*. Wijk en Aalburg: Pictures Publishers.

Carter, John Ross, 1993, "The Origin and Development of 'Buddhism' and 'Religion' in the Study of the Theravada Buddhist Tradition", in John Ross Carter, *On Understanding Buddhists: Essays on the Theravada Tradition in Sri Lanka*. Albany: State University of New York Press, pp. 9–25.

Cederroth, Sven. 1996. "From Ancestor Worship to Monotheism: Politics of Religion in Lombok", *Temenos* 32: 7–36.

Cerita, I Nyoman, and Kathy Foley. 2022. "Balinese *Calonarang* in Performance", *Ecumenica. Performance and Religion* 15, 1: 42–65.

Chambert-Loir, Henri. 2015. "Confucius Crosses the South Seas", *Indonesia* 99: 1–41.

Chatterjee, Partha. 1986. *Nationalist Thought and the Colonial World. A Derivative Discourse*. London: Zed Books.

Chatterji, Suniti Kumar. 1931. "Historical and Cultural Research in Bali", *The Modern Review* 49, 2: 134–41.

Chidester, David. 2014. *Empire of Religion: Imperialism and Comparative Religion*. Chicago & London: The University of Chicago Press.

Clémentin-Ojha, Catherine. 1994. "La Śuddhi de l'Ārya Samāj ou l'invention d'un rituel de (re)conversion à l'hindouisme" ["The Śuddhi of the Ārya Samāj or the Invention of a Ritual for (Re)conversion to Hinduism"], *Archives de sciences sociales des religions* 87: 99–114.

———. 2014. "'India, that is Bharat'...: One Country, Two Names", *South Asia Multidisciplinary Academic Journal* 10: 1–21.

———. 2019. "La question de la définition de l'identité hindoue. La contribution de B.R. Ambedkar à son règlement politique (1951)" ["The Question of Defining Hindu Identity. The Contribution of B.R. Ambedkar to its Political Settlement (1951)"], *Archives de sciences sociales des religions* 186: 163–82.

Clifford, James. 1988. *The Predicament of Culture. Twentieth-Century Ethnography, Literature, and Art*. Cambridge, MA & London: Harvard University Press.

Clifton, Violet. 1927. *Islands of Indonesia*. London: Constable.

Coast, John. 1951. "The Clash of Cultures in Bali", *Pacific Affairs* 24, 4: 398–406.

———. 1954. *Dancing out of Bali*. London: Faber and Faber Limited.

Coedès, George. 1968 [1964]. *The Indianized States of Southeast Asia*. Honolulu: East-West Center Press.
Cohen, Matthew Isaac. 2006. *The Komedie Stamboel. Popular Theater in Colonial Indonesia (1891–1903)*. Athens, OH: Ohio University Press.
Cohn, Bernard S. 1987 *An Anthropologist among the Historians and Other Essays*. Delhi: Oxford University Press.
Cohn, Werner. 1969. "On the Problem of Religion in Non-Western Cultures", *International Yearbook for the Study of Religion* 5: 7–19.
Colchester, Marcus. 1986. "Unity and Diversity. Indonesian Policy towards Tribal Peoples", *The Ecologist* 16, 2–3: 89–98.
Connor, Linda H. 1982. "In Darkness and Light: A Study of Peasant Intellectuals in Bali", PhD Dissertation, Department of Anthropology, University of Sydney, Sydney.

———. 1996. "Contestation and Transformation of Balinese Ritual: The Case of Ngaben Ngirit", in Adrian Vickers, ed., *Being Modern in Bali. Image and Change*. New Haven: Yale University Southeast Asia Studies, pp. 179–211.

Connor, Linda, and Adrian Vickers. 2003. "Crisis, Citizenship, and Cosmopolitanism: Living in a Local and Global Risk Society in Bali", *Indonesia* 75: 153–80.
Couteau, Jean. 1986. "Milieu et peinture. Le cas de Bali" ["Environment and Painting: The Case of Bali"]. Thèse de doctorat, École des Hautes Études en Sciences Sociales, Paris.

———. 1999a. *Museum Puri Lukisan*. Ubud: Ratna Wartha Foundation.

———. 1999b. "Bali et l'islam: 1. Rencontre historique" ["Bali and Islam: 1. Historical Encounter"], *Archipel* 58: 159–88.

———. 2000. "Bali et l'islam: 2. Coexistence et perspectives contemporaines" ["Bali and Islam: 2. Coexistence and Contemporary Perspectives"], *Archipel* 60: 45–64.

———. 2002, "Bali: crise en paradis" ["Bali: Crisis in Paradise"], *Archipel* 64: 231–54.

———. 2003, "After the Kuta Bombing. In Search of the Balinese 'Soul'", *Antropologi Indonesia* 27, 70: 41–59.

Covarrubias, Miguel. 1937. *Island of Bali*. New York: Alfred A. Knopf.
Crawfurd, John. 1820a. "On the Existence of the Hindu Religion in the Island of Bali", *Asiatick Researches* 13: 128–70.

———. 1820b. *History of the Indian Archipelago*. Edinburgh: Archibald Constable.

Creese, Helen. 2000. "In Search of Majapahit. The Transformation of Balinese Identities", in Adrian Vickers and I Nyoman Darma Putra with Michele Ford, eds, *To Change Bali. Essays in Honour of I Gusti Ngurah Bagus*. Denpasar: Bali Post and University of Wollongong, Institute of Social Change and Critical Inquiry, pp. 15–46.

———. 2001. "Old Javanese Studies. A Review of the Field", *Bijdragen tot de Taal-, Land- en Volkenkunde* 157, 1: 3–33.

———. 2007. "Curious Modernities: Early Twentieth-Century Balinese Textual Explorations", *The Journal of Asian Studies* 66, 3: 723–58.

———. 2009a. "Old Javanese Legal Traditions in Pre-colonial Bali", *Bijdragen tot de Taal-, Land- en Volkenkunde* 165, 2–3: 241–90.

———. 2009b. "Judicial Processes and Legal Authority in Pre-colonial Bali", *Bijdragen tot de Taal-, Land- en Volkenkunde* 165, 4: 515–50.

———. 2016. *Bali in the Early Nineteenth Century: The Ethnographic Accounts of Pierre Dubois*. Leiden: Brill.

———. 2018. "*Bhuwanawinasa*: 'The Destruction of the World'. A Balinese Tale of Internal Conflict and Colonial Conquest", 22nd Biennial Conference of the Asia Studies Association of Australia, University of Sydney, July 3–5, 2018.

Creese, Helen, I Nyoman Darma Putra, and Henk Schulte Nordholt, eds. 2006. *Seabad Puputan Badung. Perspektif Belanda dan Bali* [A Century of Puputan Badung. Dutch and Balinese Perspectives]. Denpasar: Pustaka Lasaran, KITLV-Fakultas Sastra Universitas Udayana.

Cribb, Robert, Soe Hok Gie et al. 1990. "The Mass Killings in Bali", in Robert Cribb, ed., *The Indonesian Killings of 1965–1966*. Clayton: Monash University, Centre of Southeast Asian Studies, pp. 241–60.

Crouch, Melissa A. 2012. "Law and Religion in Indonesia: The Constitutional Court and the Blasphemy Law", *Asian Journal of Comparative Law* 7, 1: Article 3.

Dalmia, Vasudha. 1997. *The Nationalization of Hindu Traditions: Bhāratendu Hariśchandra and Nineteenth-Century Banaras*. Delhi: Oxford University Press.

Dalmia, Vasudha, and Heinrich Von Stietencron, eds. 1995. *Representing Hinduism. The Construction of Religious Traditions and National Identity*. New Delhi & London: Sage Publications.

Dalton, Bill. 1990. *Bali Handbook*. Chico: Moon Publications.

Dana, I N., ed., 2005, *Kompilasi Dokumen Literer 45 Tahun Parisada* [Compilation of 45 Years of Parisada Literary Documents]. Jakarta: Parisada Hindu Dharma Indonesia Pusat.

Darling, Diana. 2003. "Unity in Uniformity. Tendencies toward Militarism in Balinese Ritual Life", in Thomas A. Reuter, ed., *Inequality, Crisis and Social Change in Indonesia. The Muted Worlds of Bali*. London & New York: RoutledgeCurzon, pp. 196–202.

Darmaputera, Eka. 1988. *Pancasila and the Search for Identity and Modernity in Indonesian Society*. Leiden: E.J. Brill.

Darta, I Gusti Nyoman, Jean Couteau and Georges Breguet. 2013. *Time, Rites and Festivals in Bali*. Jakarta: BabBooks.

Das Gupta, Arun. 2002. "Rabindranath Tagore in Indonesia. An Experiment in Bridge-Building", *Bijdragen tot de Taal-, Land- en Volkenkunde* 158, 3: 451–77.

Davidson, Jamie S., and David Henley, eds. 2007. *The Revival of Tradition in Indonesian Politics: The Deployment of Adat from Colonialism to Indigenism*. London & New York: Routledge.

Davidson, Ronald M. 2002. *Indian Esoteric Buddhism: A Social History of the Tantric Movement*. New York: Columbia University Press.

Davies, Stephen. 2008. "The Origins of Balinese Legong", *Bijdragen tot de Taal-, Land- en Volkenkunde* 164, 2–3: 194–211.

Davis, Richard H. 1991. *Ritual in an Oscillating Universe: Worshipping Śiva in Medieval India*. Princeton: Princeton University Press.

De Casparis, Johannes Gijsbertus, and Ian W. Mabbett. 1992. "Religion and Popular Beliefs of Southeast Asia before c. 1500", in Nicholas Tarling, ed., *The Cambridge History of Southeast Asia, Volume One: From Early Times to c. 1800*. Cambridge: Cambridge University Press, pp. 276–339.

De Keyser, Édouard. 1933. *L'Ile des Seins Nus* [The Island of Bare Breasts]. Paris: Les Éditions de France.

De Kleen, Tyra. 1921. "Bali. Its Dances and Customs", *Sluyters' Monthly* 2: 127–32.

De Roever-Bonnet, H. 1993. *Rudolf Bonnet. Een zondagskind. Zijn leven en zijn werk* [Rudolf Bonnet. A Sunday Child. His Life and Work]. Wijk en Aalburg: Pictures Publishers.

De Zoete, Beryl, and Walter Spies. 1938. *Dance and Drama in Bali*. London: Faber & Faber.

Despland, Michel. 1980. *La Religion en Occident. Évolution des idées et du vécu* [Religion in the West. Evolution of Ideas and Experience]. Paris: Les Éditions du Cerf.

Dewantara, Ki Hadjar. 1950. "Kebudajaan dan Pendidikan" ["Culture and Education"], *Indonesia*, Edisi chusus: 87–91.

Dhana, I Nyoman. 2014. "United in Culture – Separate Ways in Religion? The Relationship between Hindu and Christian Balinese", in Brigitta Hauser-Schäublin and David D. Harnish, eds, *Between Harmony and Discrimination: Negotiating Religious Identities within Majority–Minority Relationships in Bali and Lombok*. Leiden & Boston: Brill, pp. 244–57.

Dherana, Tjokorda Raka. 1982. *Garis-garis Besar Pedoman Penulisan Awig-awig Desa Adat* [Outlines of Guidelines for Writing Regulations of Customary Villages]. Denpasar: Mabhakti.

Diantari, Putu. 1990. *Gerakan Pembaruan Hindu: Studi Tentang Perkembangan Pemikiran Intelektual Hindu di Bali Tahun 1925–1958* [Hindu Renewal Movement: A Study of the Development of Hindu Intellectual Thought in Bali, 1925-1958]. Denpasar: Fakultas Sastra Universitas Udayana.

Dibia, I Wayan, and Rucina Ballinger. 2004. *Balinese Dance, Drama and Music. A Guide to the Performing Arts of Bali*. Singapore: Periplus Editions.

Dimyati, Muhammad. 1952a. "Bahaja anarsisme dilapangan keagamaan" ["The Danger of Anarchism in the Religious Field"], *Siasat* 6, 275: 4–5.

———. 1952b. "Demokrasi dan Anarsi" ["Democracy and Anarchy"], *Siasat* 6, 281: 11, 16.

Dirgahayu, Ida Bagus. 1952. "Agama Hindu Bali Terantjam" ["Balinese Hindu Religion under Threat"], *Bhakti* 1, 10: 13–14.

Dirks, Nicholas B., ed. 1992, *Colonialism and Culture*. Ann Arbor: The University of Michigan Press.

Djelantik, Dr. Anak Agung Madé. 1997. *The Birthmark. Memoirs of a Balinese Prince*. Singapore: Periplus Editions.

Djlantik, Anak Agoeng Bagoes. [n.d.]. *Darmasoesila* [Religious Ethics]. Soerabaia: Van Dorp.

Djlantik, I Goesti Poetoe. 1924. *Penoentoen menghémat mengabén. Tanda peringatan dari I Goesti Poetoe Djlantik atas pembitjaraannja dalam vergadering Perkoempoelan Santy Singaradja pada 2 November 1924* [Guidebook to Economize on Cremations. A Memorial from I Goesti Poetoe Djlantik for his Talk at the Meeting of the Santy Association in Singaradja November 2, 1924]. Singaradja: I Goesti Bagoes Tjakra Tanaja.

Djuana, I Nyoman. 1987. *Peranan Organisasi Taman Siswa Dalam Pergerakan Nasional Di Bali 1933–1943* [The Role of Taman Siswa Organization in the National Movement in Bali 1933–1943]. Denpasar: Fakultas Sastra Universitas Udayana.

Dosther, Ida Bagus Gde. 2007. *Ida Bagus Gde Dosther 80 th. Air mengalir sampai akhir* [Ida Bagus Gde Dosther 80 Years Old. Water Flows to the End]. Denpasar: Manawa Bali.

Dove, Michael R., ed. 1988. *The Real and Imagined Role of Culture in Development: Case Studies from Indonesia*. Honolulu: University of Hawaii Press.

Dressler, Markus, and Arvind-Pal S Mandair, eds. 2011. *Secularism and Religion-Making*. Oxford & New York: Oxford University Press.

Dubuisson, Daniel. 2003 [1998]. *The Western Construction of Religion. Myths, Knowledge, and Ideology*. Baltimore: The Johns Hopkins University Press.

———. 2007. "Exporting the Local: Recent Perspectives on 'Religion' as a Cultural Category", *Religion Compass* 1, 6: 787–800.

———. 2016. *Religion and Magic in Western Culture*. Leiden & Boston: Brill.

———. 2019. *The Invention of Religions*. Sheffield: Equinox Publishing.

Durkheim, Émile. 1965 [1912]. *The Elementary Forms of the Religious Life*. New York: Free Press.

Dwikora, Putu Wirata. 2002. *Menjadi Pelayan Umat* [Serving the People]. Denpasar: Parisada Hindu Dharma Indonesia Propinsi Bali.

Dwyer, Leslie, and Degung Santikarma. 2003. "'When the World Turned to Chaos'. 1965 and Its Aftermath in Bali, Indonesia", in Robert Gellately and Ben Kierman, eds, *The Specter of Genocide. Mass Murder in Historical Perspective*. Cambridge: Cambridge University Press, pp. 289–305.

Eck, Diana L. 1982. "The Church in Bali: Mountainwards and Seawards", *The South East Asia Journal of Theology* 23, 2: 151–60.

Elegant, Robert. 1987. "Seeking the Spirits of Bali: Despite Fast Food and Discos, the Old Ways Live", *The New York Times*, March 8, 1987, pp. 9, 26.

El Hafidy, M. As'ad. 1997. *Aliran-Aliran Kepercayaan dan Kebatinan di Indonesia* [Currents of Belief and Spirituality in Indonesia]. Jakarta: Ghalia Indonesia.

Eliade, Mircea. 1958. *Patterns in Comparative Religion*. London & New York: Sheed and Ward.

Ellen, Roy F. 1983. "Social Theory, Ethnography and the Understanding of Practical Islam in South-East Asia", in M. Barry Hooker, ed., *Islam in South-East Asia*. Leiden: E.J. Brill, pp. 50–91.

Elmore, Mark. 2016. *Becoming Religious in a Secular Age*. Oakland: University of California Press.

Elson, Robert E. 2009. "Another Look at the Jakarta Charter Controversy of 1945", *Indonesia* 88: 105–30.

Emigh, John. 1984. "Dealing with the Demonic. Strategies for Containment in Hindu Iconography and Performance", *Asian Theatre Journal* 1, 1: 21–39.

Enklaar, I.H. 1989. "Leiden Orientalists and the Christian Mission", in Willem Otterspeer, ed., *Leiden Oriental Connections, 1850–1940*. Leiden: E.J. Brill and Universitaire Pers, pp. 168–86.

Ensink, Jacob. 1978. "Siva-Buddhism in Java and Bali", in Heinz Bechert, ed., *Buddhism in Ceylon and Studies on Religious Syncretism in Buddhist Countries*. Göttingen: Vandenhoech & Ruprecht, pp. 178–98.

Errington, Shelly. 1997. "The Cosmic Theme Park of the Javanese", *Review of Indonesian and Malaysian Affairs* 31, 1: 7–35.

Fabricius, Johan. 1941. *Eiland der Demonen: Een Bali-Roman* [Island of Demons: A Bali Novel]. Batavia: Unie Bibliotheek.

Fagertun, Anette. 2017. "Waves of Dispossession. The Conversion of Land and Labor in Bali's Recent History", *Social Analysis* 61, 3: 108–25.

Fasseur, Cees. 2007. "Colonial Dilemma: Van Vollenhoven and the Struggle between Adat Law and Western Law in Indonesia", in Jamie S. Davidson and David Henley, eds, *The Revival of Tradition in Indonesian Politics. The Deployment of Adat from Colonialism to Indigenism*. London & New York: Routledge, pp. 50–67.

Feillard, Andrée, and Rémy Madinier. 2011 [2006]. *The End of Innocence? Indonesian Islam and the Temptations of Radicalism*. Singapore: NUS Press.

Feith, Herbert. 1962. *The Decline of Constitutional Democracy in Indonesia*. Ithaca: Cornell University Press.

Fisher, Elaine M. 2018. "Hindu Pluralism: A Prehistory", *Religion Compass* 12, 3–4: 1–9.

Fitzgerald, Timothy. 1990. "Hinduism and the 'World Religion' Fallacy", *Religion* 20, 2: 101–18.

———. 1997. "A Critique of 'Religion' as a Cross-cultural Category", *Method and Theory in the Study of Religion* 9, 2: 35–47.

———. 2000. *The Ideology of Religious Studies*. Oxford & New York: Oxford University Press.

———. 2007. *Discourse on Civility and Barbarity. A Critical History of Religion and Related Categories*. Oxford & New York: Oxford University Press.

Florida, Nancy. 1995. *Writing the Past, Inscribing the Future: History as Prophecy in Colonial Java*. Durham, NC: Duke University Press.

Flügel, Peter. 2005. "The Invention of Jainism. A Short History of Jaina Studies", *International Journal of Jaina Studies* 1, 1: 1–14.

Forge, Anthony. 1980. "Balinese Religion and Indonesian Identity", in James J. Fox et al., eds, *Indonesia: Australian Perspectives*. Canberra: The Australian National University, pp. 221–33.

Formoso. Bernard. 2006. "L'Indochine vue de l'Ouest" ["Indochina Seen from the West"], *Gradhiva* 4: 35–51.

Foucault, Michel. 1971. *L'ordre du discours* [The Order of Discourse]. Paris: Gallimard.

Foulcher, Keith. 1986. *Social Commitment in Literature and the Arts: The Indonesia 'Institute of Peoples Culture' 1950–1965*. Clayton: Centre of Southeast Asian Studies, Monash University.

———. 1990. "The Construction of an Indonesian National Culture: Patterns of Hegemony and Resistance", in Arief Budiman, ed., *State and Civil Society in Indonesia*. Clayton: Centre of Southeast Asian Studies, Monash University, pp. 301–20.

———. 2000. "*Sumpah Pemuda*: The Making and Meaning of a Symbol of Indonesian Nationhood", *Asian Studies Review* 24, 3: 377–410.

Fox, Richard. 2010. "Why Media Matter: Critical Reflections on Religion and the Recent History of 'the Balinese'", *History of Religions* 41, 4: 354–92.

———. 2018. *More Than Words. Transforming Script, Agency, and Collective Life in Bali*. Ithaca & London: Cornell University Press.

FPHDI. 1996. *Menyambut, Memaknai dan Menyukseskan Mahasabha Sebuah Obsesi: Umat Bersatu Di Bawah Parisada* [Welcoming, Interpreting and Making a Successful Congress an Obsession: People Unite Under Parisada]. Denpasar: Forum Pemerhati Hindu Dharma Indonesia.

Friederich, Rudolf H.Th. 1849–50. "Voorlopig verslag van het eiland Bali" ["Preliminary Report on the Island of Bali"], *Verhandelingen van het Bataviaasch Genootschap van Kunsten en Wetenschappen* 22: 1–63; 23: 1–57.

———. 1959. *The Civilization and Culture of Bali*. Calcutta: Susil Gupta.

Friedman, Jonathan. 1993. "Will the Real Hawaiian Please Stand: Anthropologists and Natives in the Global Struggle for Identity", *Bijdragen tot de Taal-, Land- en Volkenkunde* 149, 4: 737–67.

Frykenberg, Robert Eric. 1993. "Constructions of Hinduism at the Nexus of History and Religion", *Journal of Interdisciplinary History* 23, 3: 523–50.

———. 2005 [1989]. "The Emergence of Modern 'Hinduism' as a Concept and as an Institution: A Reappraisal with Special Reference to South India", in Günther-Dietz Sontheimer and Hermann Kulke, eds, *Hinduism Reconsidered*. New Delhi: Manohar, pp. 82–107.

Gangoly, O.C. 1936. "Review of *Indian Influences in Old-Balinese Art* by Dr. W.F. Stutterheim, The India Society, London", *Journal of the Greater India Society* 3, 1: 124–34.

Gardet, Louis. 1965. "Dīn", in Bernard Lewis, Charles Pellat, and Joseph Schacht, eds, *The Encyclopaedia of Islam*, Vol. 2. Leiden: Brill, pp. 293–96.

Gauchet, Marcel. 1997 [1985]. *The Disenchantment of the World: A Political History of Religion*. Princeton: Princeton University Press.

Geertz, Clifford. 1959. "Form and Variation in Balinese Village Structure", *American Anthropologist* 61, 6: 991–1012.

———. 1960. *The Religion of Java*. Glencoe: The Free Press.

———. 1973 [1964]. "'Internal Conversion' in Contemporary Bali", in Clifford Geertz, *The Interpretation of Cultures*. New York: Basic Books, pp. 170–89.

———. 1980. *Negara. The Theatre State in Nineteenth-Century Bali*. Princeton: Princeton University Press.

———. 1990. "'Popular Art' and the Javanese Tradition", *Indonesia* 50: 77–94.

Geertz, Hildred. 1994. *Images of Power. Balinese Paintings Made for Gregory Bateson and Margaret Mead*. Honolulu: University of Hawaii Press.

———. 1995. "Sorcery and Social Change in Bali. The Sakti Conjecture", Third International Bali Studies Workshop, University of Sydney.

———. 2000. "How Can we Speak about Balinese religion?", Seminar *Bali in Reformation: Religious Change and Socio-Political Transformation*. Denpasar.

———. 2004. *The Life of a Balinese Temple. Artistry, Imagination, and History in a Peasant Village*. Honolulu: University of Hawai'i Press.

Geertz, Hildred, and Clifford Geertz. 1975. *Kinship in Bali*. Chicago: The University of Chicago Press.

Gelders, Raf. 2009. "Genealogy of Colonial Discourse: Hindu Traditions and the Limits of European Representation", *Comparative Studies in Society and History* 51, 3: 563–89.

Gerbault, Alain. 1941. *Iles de Beauté* [Islands of Beauty]. Paris: Gallimard.

Girardot, N.J. 1999. "'Finding the Way': James Legge and the Victorian Invention of Taoism", *Religion* 29, 2: 107–21.

GKB. 1957. *Laporan Dewan Pimpinan Gerakan Kumara Bhavana pada Konperensi ke-V Angkatan Muda Hindu Bali tahun 1957 di Denpasar* [Report of the Leadership Council of the Kumara Bhavana Movement at the Vth Conference of the Angkatan Muda Hindu Bali in 1957 in Denpasar]. Denpasar.

Gleason, Philip. 1983. "Identifying Identity: A Semantic History", *Journal of American History* 69, 4: 910–31.

Gonda, Jan. 1973 [1952]. *Sanskrit in Indonesia*. New Delhi: International Academy of Indian Culture.

———. 1975. "The Indian Religions in Pre-Islamic Indonesia and their Survival in Bali", in Hans Kähler, ed., *Handbuch der Orientalistik, Part 3: Indonesien, Malaysia und die Philippinen*. Leiden & Köln: E.J. Brill, pp. 1–54.

Goody, Jack. 1961. "Religion and Ritual: The Definitional Problem", *The British Journal of Sociology* 12, 2: 142–64.

Goossaert, Vincent, and David A. Palmer. 2011. *The Religious Question in Modern China*. Chicago & London: The University of Chicago Press.

Gorer, Geoffrey. 1936. *Bali and Angkor. Or Looking at Life and Death*. Boston: Little, Brown.

Goris, Roelof. 1926. *Bijdrage tot de kennis der Oud-Javaansche en Balineesche theologie* [Contribution to the Knowledge of Old Javanese and Balinese Theology]. Leiden: Vros.

———.1930. *Bali. Godsdienst en ceremoniën* [Bali. Religion and Ceremonies]. Batavia: Koninklijke Paketvaart-Maatschappij.

———. [n.d.] [1931]. "Godsdienst en gebruiken in Bali – Observations on the Customs and Life of the Balinese", in *Bali*. Batavia: Officieele Vereeniging voor Toeristenverkeer in Nederlandsch-Indië – Batavia: Travellers' Official Information Bureau for Netherland India, pp. 10–67.

———. 1931a. "Secten op Bali" ["Sects in Bali"], *Mededelingen Kirtya Liefrinck – Van der Tuuk* 3: 37–54.

———. 1931b. "Bali als arbeidsveld voor wetenschappelijk werk" ["Bali as a Field for Scientific Work"], *Tijdschrift Koninklijk Bataviaasch Genootschap van Kunsten en Wetenschappen* 71: 695–712.

———. 1933a. "Tooneel, dans en muziek op Bali" ["Theater, Dance and Music in Bali"], *Djawa* 13: 329–33.

———. 1933b. *'De strijd over Bali en de Zending'. De waarde van Dr. Kraemer's boek* ['The Controversy about Bali and Mission'. The Value of Dr. Kraemer's Book] Batavia: Minerva.

———. 1937. "Overzicht over de belangrijkste litteratuur betreffende de cultuur van Bali over het tijdvak 1920–1935" ["Survey on the Main Literature Concerning the Culture of Bali over the Period 1920-1935"], *Medeelingen van de Kirtya Liefrinck – Van der Tuuk* 5: 15–43.

———. 1952. [no title]. Tuka: Widya Wahana Library.

———. 1953. "Apakah: Ibadat Hindu Bali itu Agama atau Aliran?" ["Is Hindu Bali Worship a Religion or a Sect?"], *Bhakti* 2, 20: 10–13.

———. 1954a. *Prasasti Bali: Inscripties voor Anak Wungsu* [Prasasti Bali: Inscriptions Before Anak Wungsu]. Bandung: Masa Baru.

———. 1954b. "Tjeramah oleh I Gusti Bagus Sugriwa" ["Lecture by I Gusti Bagus Sugriwa"]. Tuka: Widya Wahana Library.

———. 1967. *Ancient History of Bali*. Denpasar: Faculty of Letters, Udayana University.

Gouda, Frances. 1995. *Dutch Culture Overseas. Colonial Practice in the Netherlands Indies 1900–1942*. Amsterdam: Amsterdam University Press.

Goudriaan, Teun. 1970. "Sanskrit Texts and Indian Religion in Bali", in Lokesh Chandra, ed., *India's Contribution to World Thought and Culture: Vivekananda Commemoration Volume*. Madras: Vivekananda Rock Memorial Committee, pp. 555–64.

———.1976. "Some Recent Publications on Balinese Religion", *Review of Indonesian and Malaysian Affairs* 10, 1: 121–32.

Gramsci, Antonio. 1971. *Selections from the Prison Notebooks of Antonio Gramsci*. New York: International Publishers.

Griffiths, Arlo. 2014. "Early Indic Inscriptions of Southeast Asia", in John Guy, ed., *Lost Kingdoms. Hindu-Buddhist Sculpture of Early Southeast Asia*. New York: The Metropolitan Museum of Art, pp. 53–7.

Guermonprez, Jean-François. 1987. *Les Pandé de Bali. La Formation d'une 'Caste' et la Valeur d'un Titre* [The Pandé of Bali. The Formation of a 'Caste' and the Value of a Title]. Paris: École française d'Extrême-Orient.

———. 1990. "On the Elusive Balinese Village: Hierarchy and Values versus Political Models", *Review of Indonesian and Malaysian Affairs* 24: 55–89.

———. 2001. "La religion balinaise dans le miroir de l'hindouisme" ["Balinese Religion in the Mirror of Hinduism"], *Bulletin de l'École française d'Extrême-Orient* 88: 271–93.

Haan, Michael. 2005. "Numbers in Nirvana: How the 1872–1921 Indian Censuses Helped Operationalise 'Hinduism'", *Religion* 35: 13–30.

Hacker, Paul. 1995. "Aspects of Neo-Hinduism as Contrasted with Surviving Traditional Hinduism", in Wilhelm Halbfass, ed., *Philology and Confrontation. Paul Hacker on Traditional and Modern Vedanta*. Albany: State University of New York Press, pp. 229–55.

Halbfass, Wilhelm. 1988 [1981]. *India and Europe: An Essay in Understanding*. New York: State University of New York Press.

Hall, Kenneth R. 2005. "Traditions of Knowledge in Old Javanese Literature, c. 1000–1500", *Journal of Southeast Asian Studies* 36, 1: 1–27.

Hamzah, Amir. 1933–5. "*Bhagawad-Gita* diterdjemahkan oleh Amir Hamzah" ["The Bhagavad-Gita Translated by Amir Hamzah"], *Poedjangga Baroe* 1, 1 (July 1933) and 2, 8 (February 1935).

Handler, Richard. 1994. "Is 'Identity' a Useful Cross-cultural Concept?", in John Gillis, ed., *Commemorations: The Politics of National Identity*. Princeton: Princeton University Press, pp. 27–40.

Handler, Richard, and Jocelyn Linnekin. 1984. "Tradition, Genuine or Spurious", *The Journal of American Folklore* 97, 385: 273–90.

Hanegraaff, Wouter J. 2016. "Reconstructing 'Religion' from the Bottom Up", *Numen* 63, 5–6: 577-606.

Hanna, Willard A. 2016 [1976]. *A Brief History of Bali. Piracy, Slavery, Opium and Guns: The Story of an Island Paradise*. Singapore: Tuttle Publishing.

Hannigan, Tim. 2012. *Raffles and the British Invasion of Java*. Burrough on the Hill: Monsoon Books.

Harrison, Peter. 1990. *'Religion' and the Religions in the English Enlightenment*. Cambridge: Cambridge University Press.

Hasan, Noorhaidi. 2008. "*Reformasi*, Religious Diversity, and Islamic Radicalism after Suharto", *Journal of Indonesian Social Sciences and Humanities* 1: 23–51.
Hauser-Schäublin, Brigitta. 2004. "'Bali Aga' and Islam: Ethnicity, Ritual Practice, and 'Old-Balinese' as an Anthropological Construct", *Indonesia* 77: 1–28.
———. 2011. "Spiritualized Politics and the Trademark of Culture: Political Actors and their use of *adat* and *agama* in post-Suharto Bali", in Michel Picard and Rémy Madinier, eds, *The Politics of Religion in Indonesia. Syncretism, Orthodoxy, and Religious Contention in Java and Bali*. London & New York: Routledge, pp. 192–213.
———. 2013. "How Indigenous are the Balinese? From National Marginalisation to Provincial Domination", in Brigitta Hauser-Schäublin, ed., *Adat and Indigeneity in Indonesia. Culture and Entitlements between Heteronomy and Self-Ascription*. Göttingen: Universitätsverlag Göttingen, pp. 133–48.
Hauser-Schäublin, Brigitta, and David D. Harnish, eds. 2014. *Between Harmony and Discrimination: Negotiating Religious Identities within Majority-Minority Relationships in Bali and Lombok*. Leiden & Boston: Brill.
Hawley, John Stratton. 1991. "Naming Hinduism", *Wilson Quarterly* 15, 3: 20–34.
Heesterman, Johannes Cornelius. 1989. "The 'Hindu Frontier'", *Itinerario* 13, 1: 1–15.
Hefner, Robert W. 1985. *Hindu Javanese. Tengger Tradition and Islam*. Princeton: Princeton University Press.
———. 1993a. "World Building and the Rationality of Conversion", in Robert W. Hefner, ed., *Conversion to Christianity. Historical and Anthropological Perspectives on a Great Transformation*. Berkeley: University of California Press, pp. 3–44.
———. 1993b. "Islam, State, and Civil Society: ICMI and the Struggle for the Indonesian Middle Class", *Indonesia* 56: 1–35.
———. 1998. "Secularization and Citizenship in Muslim Indonesia", in David Martin, Paul Heelas and Paul Morris, eds, *Religion, Modernity, and Postmodernity*. Oxford: Blackwell Publishers, pp. 147–68.
———. 1999. "Religion: Evolving Pluralism", in Donald K. Emmerson, ed., *Indonesia Beyond Suharto. Polity, Economy, Society, Transition*. Armonk & London: M.E. Sharpe, pp. 205–36.
———. 2004. "Hindu Reform in an Islamizing Java: Pluralism and Peril", in Martin Ramstedt, ed., *Hinduism in Modern Indonesia. A Minority Religion between Local, National, and Global Interests*. London & New York: RoutledgeCurzon—IIAS Asian Studies Series, pp. 93–108.
———. 2011. "Where Have all the *abangan* Gone? Religionization and the Decline of Non-Standard Islam in Contemporary Indonesia", in Michel Picard and Rémy Madinier, eds, *The Politics of Religion in Indonesia. Syncretism, Orthodoxy, and Religious Contention in Java and Bali*. London & New York: Routledge, pp. 71–91.

———. 2012. "Shari'a Politics and Indonesian Democracy", *The Review of Faith & International Affairs* 10, 4: 61–9.

———. 2018. "The Religious Field: Plural Legacies and Contemporary Contestations", in Robert W. Hefner, ed., *Routledge Handbook of Contemporary Indonesia*. New York: Routledge, pp. 211–25.

———. 2019. "Whatever Happened to Civil Islam? Islam and Democratisation in Indonesia, 20 Years On", *Asian Studies Review* 43, 3: 375–96.

———. 2021. "Islam and Institutional Religious Freedom in Indonesia", *Religions* 12, 6: Article 415.

Hellman, Eva. 1993. "Political Hinduism. The Challenge of the Vishva Hindu Parishad", PhD Dissertation, Department of the History of Religions, Uppsala University, Uppsala.

Heriyanto, Yang. 2005. "The History and Legal Position of Confucianism in Post-independence Indonesia", *Marburg Journal of Religion* 10, 1: 1–8.

Heryanto, Ariel. 1988. "The Development of 'Development'", *Indonesia* 46: 1–24.

Hidayah, Sita. 2012. "The Politics of Religion. The Invention of 'agama' in Indonesia", *Kawistara* 2, 2: 121–39.

Hinzler, H.I.R. 1976. "The Balinese Babad", in Sartono Kartodirdjo, ed., *Profiles of Malay Culture: Historiography, Religion and Politics*. Jakarta: Ministry of Education and Culture, Directorate General of Culture, pp. 39–52.

———. 1986a. "The *Usana Bali* as a Source of History", in Taufik Abdullah, ed., *Papers of the Fourth Indonesian-Dutch History Conference, Yogyakarta 24–29 July 1983, Volume Two: Literature and History*. Yogyakarta: Gadjah Mada University Press, pp. 124–62.

———. 1986b. "Facts, Myths, Legitimation and Time in Balinese Historiography", International Workshop on Indonesian Studies N°1, *Balinese State and Society*, Leiden, Royal Institute of Linguistics and Anthropology.

Hiss, Philip Hanson. 1941. *Bali*. New York: Duell, Sloan and Pearce.

Hitchcock, Michael. 1998. "Tourism, Taman Mini and National Identity", *Indonesia and the Malay World* 26, 74: 124–35.

Hitchcock, Michael, and Lucy Norris. 1995. *Bali: The Imaginary Museum. The Photographs of Walter Spies and Beryl de Zoete*. Kuala Lumpur: Oxford University Press.

Hitchcock, Michael, and I Nyoman Darma Putra. 2007. *Tourism, Development and Terrorism in Bali*. Aldershot: Ashgate.

Hitchcock, Michael, Victor T. King and Michael Parnwell, eds, 2009. *Tourism in Southeast Asia. Challenges and New Directions*. Copenhagen: NIAS Press.

Hoadley, Mason C., and M. Barry Hooker. 1981. *An Introduction to Javanese Law. A Translation of and Commentary on the Agama*. Tucson: The University of Arizona Press.

———. 1986. "The Law Texts of Java and Bali", in M. Barry Hooker, ed., *The Laws of South-East Asia. Volume 1: The Pre-modern Texts*. Singapore: Butterworths, pp. 241–346.

Hobart, Mark. 1985. "Is God Evil?", in David Parkin, ed., *The Anthropology of Evil*. Oxford: Blackwell, pp. 165–93.

———. 1989. "Western Knowledge and Bali: Towards the Emergence of Indonesian Social Theory", Lecture delivered at Udayana University, Denpasar.

———. 1990. "Who Do You Think You Are? The Authorized Balinese", in Richard Fardon, ed., *Regional Traditions of Ethnographic Writing*. Edinburgh: Scottish Academic Press & Washington, Smithsonian Institution Press, pp. 303–38.

———. 1997. "The Missing Subject: Balinese Time and the Elimination of History", *Review of Indonesian and Malaysian Affairs* 31, 1: 123–72.

———. 2000. "Introduction", in Mark Hobart, *After Culture. Anthropology as Radical Metaphysical Critique*. Yogyakarta: Duta Wacana University Press, pp. 1–53.

———. 2007. "Rethinking Balinese Dance", *Indonesia and the Malay World* 35, 101: 107–28.

———. 2015. "Bali is a Brand: A Critical Approach", in I Nyoman Darma Putra and Siobhan Campbell, eds, *Recent Developments in Bali Tourism. Culture, Heritage, and Landscape in an Open Fortress*. Denpasar: Buku Arti, pp. 11–38.

Hobsbawm, Eric J. 1983. "Introduction: Inventing Traditions", in Eric J. Hobsbawm and Terence Ranger, eds, *The Invention of Tradition*. Cambridge: Cambridge University Press, pp. 1–14.

Hoek, Anne-Lot. 2021. *De strijd om Bali. Imperialisme, verzet en onafhankelijkheid 1846–1950* [The Struggle for Bali. Imperialism, Resistance and Independence 1846–1950]. Amsterdam: De Bezige Bij.

Hoffman, John. 1979. "A Foreign Investment: Indies Malay to 1901", *Indonesia* 27: 65–92.

Holdrege, Barbara A. 2004. "Dharma", in Sushil Mittal and Gene Thursby, eds, *The Hindu World*. New York & London: Routledge, pp. 213–48.

Hollan, Douglas W. 1988. "Pockets Full of Mistakes: The Personal Consequences of Religious Change in a Toraja Village", *Oceania* 58, 4: 275–89.

Holleman, Johan F., ed. 1981. *Van Vollenhoven on Indonesian Adat Law*. The Hague: Martinus Nijhoff.

Holt, Claire. 1967. *Art in Indonesia. Continuities and Change*. Ithaca: Cornell University Press.

Hoogervorst, Tom G. 2013. *Southeast Asia in the Ancient Indian Ocean World*. Oxford: Archaeopress.

Hooker, Virginia Matheson, ed. 1993. *Culture and Society in New Order Indonesia*. Kuala Lumpur: Oxford University Press.

Hooykaas, Christiaan. 1959. "On Sylvain Lévi's Sanskrit Texts from Bali", *Oriens Extremus* 6, 1: 69–74.

———. 1962. "Śaiva Siddhānta in Java and Bali, Some Remarks on its Recent Study", *Bijdragen tot de Taal-, Land- en Volkenkunde* 118, 3: 309–27.

———. 1963. "Books Made in Bali", *Bijdragen tot de Taal-, Land- en Volkenkunde* 119, 4: 371–86.

———. 1964a. *Agama Tirtha. Five Studies in Hindu-Balinese Religion*. Amsterdam: N.V. Noord-Hollandsche Uitgevers Maatschappij.

———. 1964b. "Weda and Sisya, Rsi and Bhujangga in Present-Day Bali", *Bijdragen tot de Taal-, Land- en Volkenkunde* 120, 2: 231–44.

———. 1966. *Sūrya-Sevana: The Way to God of a Balinese Śiva Priest*. Amsterdam: N.V. Noord-Hollandsche Uitgevers Maatschappij.

———. 1973a. *Religion in Bali*. Leiden: E.J. Brill.

———. 1973b. "La conservation de la parole parlée et des manuscrits en Indonésie" ["Conservation of Spoken Word and Manuscripts in Indonesia"], *Archipel* 6: 33–41.

———. 1973c. *Balinese Bauddha Brahmans*. Amsterdam & London: N.V. Noord-Hollandsche Uitgevers Maatschappij.

———. 1975. "Pañca-yajña-s in India and Bali", *The Adyar Library Bulletin* 39: 240–59.

———. 1979a. "Preservation and Cataloguing of Manuscripts in Bali", *Bijdragen tot de Taal-, Land- en Volkenkunde* 135, 2–3: 347–53.

———. 1979b. *Introduction à la littérature balinaise* [Introduction to Balinese Literature]. Paris: Association Archipel.

Horii, Mitsutoshi. 2015. "Critical Reflections on the Category of 'Religion' in Contemporary Sociological Discourse", *Nordic Journal of Religion and Society* 28, 1: 21–36.

———. 2018. *The Category of 'Religion' in Contemporary Japan: Shūkyō and Temple Buddhism*. New York: Palgrave Macmillan.

Hornbacher, Annette, 2011, "The Withdrawal of the Gods: Remarks on Ritual Trance-Possession and its Decline in Bali", in Michel Picard and Rémy Madinier, eds, *The Politics of Religion in Indonesia. Syncretism, Orthodoxy, and Religious Contention in Java and Bali*. London & New York: Routledge, pp. 167–91.

———. 2014. "Contested Moksa in Balinese Agama Hindu. Balinese Death Rituals between Ancestor Worship and Modern Hinduism", in Volker Gottowik, ed., *Dynamics of Religion in Southeast Asia. Magic and Modernity*. Chicago: The University of Chicago Press and Amsterdam: Amsterdam University Press, pp. 237–60.

———. 2017. "Return to the Source: A Balinese Pilgrimage to India and the Re-enchantment of *agama Hindu* in Global Modernity", in Michel Picard, ed., *The Appropriation of Religion in Southeast Asia and Beyond*. New York: Palgrave Macmillan, pp. 153–83.

———. 2021. "Schizoid Balinese? Anthropology's Double Bind: Radical Alterity and Its Consequences for Schizophrenia", in William Sax and Claudia Lang, eds, *The

Movement for Global Mental Health: Critical Views from South and Southeast Asia. Amsterdam: Amsterdam University Press, pp. 65–99.

Hosen, Nadirsyah. 2005. "Religion and the Indonesian Constitution: A Recent Debate", *Journal of Southeast Asian Studies* 36, 3: 419–40.

Hough, Brett. 2000. "The College of Indonesian Arts, Denpasar: Nation, State and the Performing Arts in Bali", PhD Dissertation, Department of Asian Languages and Studies, Monash University, Melbourne.

Howe, Leo, E.A. 1985. "Caste in India and Bali: Levels of Comparison", in R.H. Barnes, Daniel de Coppet and R.J. Parkin, eds, *Contexts and Levels. Anthropological Essays on Hierarchy*. Oxford: JASO Occasional Papers n° 4, pp. 139–52.

———. 1996. "Kings and Priests in Bali", *Social Anthropology* 4, 3: 265–80.

———. 2001. *Hinduism & Hierarchy in Bali*. Oxford: James Currey and Santa Fe: School of American Research Press.

Howell, Julia Day. 1977. "Vehicles for the Kalki Avatar: The Experiments of a Javanese Guru in Rationalizing Ecstatic Religion", PhD Dissertation, Department of Anthropology, Stanford University, Palo Alto.

———. 1978. "Modernizing Religious Reform and the Far Eastern Religions in Twentieth Century Indonesia", in S. Udin, ed., *Spectrum. Essays Presented to Sutan Takdir Alisjahbana on his Seventieth Birthday*. Jakarta: Dian Rakyat, pp. 260–76.

———. 1982. "Indonesia: Searching for Consensus", in Carlo Caldarola, ed., *Religions and Societies: Asia and the Middle East*. Berlin: Mouton, pp. 497–548.

———. 2004. "'Spirituality' vs 'Religion' Indonesian Style: Framing and Re-framing Experiential Religiosity in Contemporary Indonesian Islam", Paper presented at the 15th Biennial Conference of the Asian Studies Association of Australia, Canberra, June 29–July 2, 2004.

———. 2005. "Muslims, the New Age and Marginal Religions in Indonesia: Changing Meanings of Religious Pluralism", *Social Compass* 52, 4: 473–43.

Hughes, Aaron W. 2012. *Abrahamic Religions: On the Uses and Abuses of History*. Oxford & New York: Oxford University Press.

Hunter, Thomas M. 2007. "The Body of the King: Reappraising Singhasari Period Syncretism", *Journal of Southeast Asian Studies* 38, 1: 27–53.

IBRD/IDA. 1974. *Bali Tourism Project. Appraisal Report*. Washington: Tourism Projects Department.

ICG. 2003. *The Perils of Private Security in Indonesia: Guards and Militias on Bali and Lombok*. ICG Asia Report N°67, Jakarta & Brussels: International Crisis Group.

Ichwan, Moch Nur. 2012. *The Making of a Pancasila State: Political Debates on Secularism, Islam and the State in Indonesia*. Tokyo: Sophia Organization for Islamic Area Studies, Institute of Asian Cultures, Sophia University.

———. 2013. "Towards a Puritanical Moderate Islam: The Majelis Ulama Indonesia and the Politics of Religious Orthodoxy", in Martin Van Bruinessen, ed., *Contemporary Developments in Indonesian Islam. Explaining the 'Conservative Turn'*. Singapore: Institute of Southeast Asian Studies.

Inden, Ronald B. 1986. "Orientalist Constructions of India", *Modern Asian Studies* 20, 3: 401–46.
Intan, Benyamin Fleming. 2006. *'Public Religion' and the Pancasila-Based State of Indonesia. An Ethical and Social Analysis.* New York: Peter Lang.
Jacknis, Ira. 1988. "Margaret Mead and Gregory Bateson in Bali: Their Use of Photography and Film", *Cultural Anthropology* 3, 2: 160–77.
Jansen, Frans, ed. 2007. *Bali in the 1930s: Photographs and Sculptures by Arthur Fleischmann.* Wijk en Aalburg: Pictures Publishers.
Jelantik, Ida Bagus. 2009. "Setengah Abad Kebangkitan Hindu Indonesia" ["Half a Century of Indonesian Hindu Revival"], in Agus S. Mantik et al., eds, *PHDI Setengah Abad. Sebuah Retrospeksi* [PHDI Half a Century. A Retrospective]. Jakarta: Parisada Hindu Dharma Indonesia, pp. 3–14.
Jendra, Wayan. 2007. *Sampradaya. Kelompok Belajar Weda, Aliran dalam Agama Hindu dan Budaya Bali* [Sampradaya. Study Group of Vedas, Currents of Hinduism and Balinese Culture]. Denpasar: Panakom.
Jensen, Gordon D., and Luh Ketut Suryani. 1992. *The Balinese People. A Reinvestigation of Character.* Singapore: Oxford University Press.
Jensen, Lionel. 1997. *Manufacturing Confucianism.* Durham, NC: Duke University Press.
Jha, Dwijendra Narayan. 2006. "Looking for a Hindu Identity", Presidential Address to the 66th Indian History Congress, Shantiniketan.
Johnsen, Scott A. 2007. "From Royal House to Nation: The Construction of Hinduism and Balinese Ethnicity in Indonesia", PhD Dissertation, Department of Anthropology, University of Virginia, Charlottesville.
Jolly, Margaret. 1992. "Specters of Inauthenticity", *The Contemporary Pacific* 4, 1: 49-72.
Jones, Tod. 2013. *Culture, Power, and Authoritarianism in the Indonesian State. Cultural Policy across the Twentieth Century to the Reform Era.* Leiden & Boston: Brill.
Jordaan, Roy E., and Robert Wessing. 1996. "Human Sacrifice at Prambanan", *Bijdragen tot de Taal-, Land- en Volkenkunde* 152, 1: 45–73.
Jordens, J.T.F. 1978. *Dayananda Sarasvati. His Life and Ideas.* Delhi: Oxford University Press.
———. 1991. "Reconversion to Hinduism: The Shuddhi of the Arya Samaj", in Geoffrey A. Oddie, ed., *Religion in South Asia. Religious Conversion and Revival Movements in South Asia in Medieval and Modern Times.* New Delhi: Manohar, pp. 215–30.
Josephson, Jason Ānanda. 2012. *The Invention of Religion in Japan.* Chicago & London: The University of Chicago Press.
Kadjeng, Njoman. 1929. "Voorloopig overzicht der op Bali aanwezige literatuurschat" ["Preliminary Overview of the Literature Treasure Present in Bali"], *Mededeelingen van de Kirtya Liefrinck – Van der Tuuk*, vol. 1, pp. 19–40.
Kahin, George McTurnan. 1952. *Nationalism and Revolution in Indonesia.* Ithaca: Cornell University Press.

Kahn, Joel S. 1993. *Constituting the Minangkabau. Peasants, Culture, and Modernity in Colonial Indonesia*. Oxford: Berg.

———. 1995. *Culture, Multiculture, Postculture*. London: Sage Publications.

Kaler, I Gusti Ketut. 1957. *Pendidikan Agama Untuk S.R.* [Religious Education for Elementary Schools]. Denpasar: Dinas Agama Otonoom Daerah Bali.

Kam, Garrett. 1993. *Perceptions of Paradise. Images of Bali in the Arts*. Ubud: Yayasan Dharma Seni Museum Neka.

Kamenuh, Ida Padanda Made. 1978. *Uraian singkat tentang Paruman Para Pendita Bali dan Lombok* [A Brief Description of the Paruman Para Pendita Bali dan Lombok]. Singaraja.

Kandia, I Ketut. 1954. "Sekedar Tentang Usaha Pembinaan Agama Hindu-Bali" ["On Hindu-Balinese Religious Development Efforts], *Bhakti* 3, 6: 1–3.

———. 1957. *Beberapa masalah Agama Hindu Bali* [Some Issues of the Balinese Hindu Religion]. Denpasar: Prasaran Konperensi-V Angkatan Muda Hindu Bali.

———. 1958. *Delegasi Tuntutan Bahagian Agama Hindu Bali di Kementerian Agama Republik Indonesia* [Delegation of Demands of the Balinese Hindu Religious Section at the Ministry of Religion of the Republic of Indonesia]. Tampaksiring, June 29, 1958.

Kane, Pandurang Vaman. 1968. *History of Dharmaśāstra (Ancient and Mediaeval Religious and Civil Law in India)*, vol. 1. Poona: Bhandarkar Oriental Research Institute.

Kapoor, Gopi Nath. 1958. *Indian Culture in Bali and Indonesia*. Calcutta: India Asia Cultural Society.

Karamustafa, Ahmet T. 2017. "Islamic *Dīn* as an Alternative to Western Models of 'Religion'", in Richard King, ed., *Religion, Theory, Critique. Classic and Contemporary Approaches and Methodologies*. New York: Columbia University Press, pp. 163–71.

Kasiri, J., and S. Nubaiti. 1992. "Hindu pun Bertuhan Satu" ["Hindus as well are Monotheists"], *Tempo*, February 15, 1992, p. 103.

Kats, Jacob. 1939. "Modern Art in Bali", *Indian Arts and Letters* 13, 1: 45–9.

Keesing, Roger M. 1989. "Creating the Past: Custom and Identity in the Contemporary Pacific", *The Contemporary Pacific* 1, 1–2: 19–42.

———. 1990. "Theories of Culture Revisited", *Canberra Anthropology* 13, 2: 46–60.

Keesing, Roger M., and Robert Tonkinson, eds, 1982. "Reinventing Traditional Culture: The Politics of *Kastom* in Island Melanesia", *Mankind*, 13/ 4.

Kejariwal, O.P. 1988. *The Asiatic Society of Bengal and the Discovery of India's Past*. New Delhi: Oxford University Press.

Kelabora, Lambert. 1976. "Religious Instruction Policy in Indonesia", *Asian Survey* 16, 3: 230–48.

Kementerian Penerangan. 1953. *Republik Indonesia: Propinsi Sunda Ketjil* [Republic of Indonesia: Province of Sunda Ketjil]. Djakarta.

Kemp, Peter. 1961. *Alms for Oblivion*. London: The Adventurers Club.

Kerepun, Made Kembar. 2007. *Mengurai Benang Kusut Kasta. Membedah Kiat Pengajegan Kasta di Bali* [Unraveling the Tangled Threads of Caste. Analyzing the Stratagems of Caste Cultivation in Bali]. Denpasar: Panakom.

Kersten, Johannes. 1940. *Bali. Hoe een missionaris het ziet* [Bali. How a Missionary Sees It]. Eindhoven: De Pelgrim.

Killingley, Dermot. 1993. *Rammohun Roy in Hindu and Christian Tradition*. Newcastle upon Tyne: Grevatt & Grevatt.

Kim, Hyung-Jun. 1998. "The Changing Interpretation of Religious Freedom in Indonesia", *Journal of Southeast Asian Studies*, 29, 2: 357–73.

King, Richard. 1999a. *Orientalism and Religion: Postcolonial Theory, India and the 'Mystic East'*. London & New York: Routledge.

———. 1999b. "Orientalism and the Modern Myth of 'Hinduism'", *Numen* 46, 2: 146–85.

———. 2011. "Imagining Religions in India: Colonialism and the Mapping of South Asian History and Culture", in Markus Dressler and Arvind-Pal S. Mandair, eds, *Secularism and Religion-Making*. Oxford & New York: Oxford University Press, pp. 37–61.

———. 2013. "The Copernican Turn in the Study of Religion", *Method and Theory in the Study of Religion* 25, 2: 137–59.

King, Ursula. 1989. "Some Reflections on Sociological Approaches to the Study of Modern Hinduism", *Numen* 36, 1: 72–97.

Kipp, Rita Smith. 1993. *Dissociated Identities. Ethnicity, Religion, and Class in an Indonesian Society*. Ann Arbor: The University of Michigan Press.

Kipp, Rita Smith, and Susan Rodgers. 1987. *Indonesian Religions in Transition*. Tucson: The University of Arizona Press.

Kobalen, AS. 2009. "World Hindu Parisada", in Agus S. Mantik et al., eds, *PHDI Setengah Abad. Sebuah Retrospeksi* [PHDI Half a Century. A Retrospective]. Jakarta: Parisada Hindu Dharma Indonesia, pp. 68–75.

Koentjaraningrat, R.M. 1985. *Javanese Culture*. Singapore: Oxford University Press.

Kopf, David. 1969. *British Orientalism and the Bengal Renaissance. The Dynamics of Indian Modernization 1773–1835*. Berkeley & Los Angeles: University of California Press.

———. 1979. *The Brahmo Samaj and the Shaping of the Modern Indian Mind*. Princeton: Princeton University Press.

Korn, Victor Emanuel. 1925. "Bali is apart... is fijner bezenuwd dan eenig ander deel van Indië" ["Bali is Distinct... Is More finely Wrought than Any Other Part of the Indies"], *Koloniaal Tijdschrift* 14: 44–53.

———. 1932 [1924]. *Het Adatrecht van Bali* [The Customary Law of Bali]. 's-Gravenhage: Naeff.

———. 1960 [1928]. "The Consecration of a Priest", in Jan Lodewijk Swellengrebel, ed., *Bali: Studies in Life, Thought, and Ritual*. The Hague: W. van Hoeve, pp. 131–53.

Kraemer, Hendrik. 1932a. "Het eenig-toelaatbaar experiment" ["The Only Admissible Experiment"], *De Stuw* 3, 18: 219–23.

———. 1932b. "Nog eens Bali en de zending" [Once again Bali and Mission"], *De Stuw* 3, 20: 248-9.

———. 1933a. "Repliek op 'Bali en de Zending'" ["Rejoinder to 'Bali and Mission'"], *Djawa* 13: 40–77.

———. 1933b. *De Strijd over Bali en de Zending. Een studie en een appèl* [The Struggle over Bali and Mission. A Study and Appeal]. Amsterdam: H.J. Paris.

———. 1958. "The Controversy around Bali and Mission", in *From Missionfield to Independent Church*. The Hague: Boekencentrum, pp. 159–86.

Krause, Gregor. 1920. *Bali. Volk-Land-Tänze-Feste-Tempel* [Bali. People-Country-Dances-Celebrations-Temples]. Hagen: Folkwang Verlag.

———. 1930. *Bali. La population, le pays, les danses, les fêtes, les temples, l'art* [Bali. The Population, the Country, the Dances, the Festivals, the Temples, the Art]. Paris: Éditions Duchartre et Van Buggenhoudt.

———. 1988. *Bali 1912*. Wellington: January Books.

Krause, Gregor, and Karl With. 2000. *Bali. People and Art*. Bangkok: White Lotus.

Krom, Nicolaas Johannes. 1926. *Hindoe-Javaansche Geschiedenis* [Hindu-Javanese History]. The Hague: Martinus Nijhoff.

Kulke, Hermann. 1990. "Indian Colonies, Indianization or Cultural Convergence? Reflections on the Changing Image of India's Role in South-East Asia", *Semaian* 3: 8–32.

Kumar, Ann. 1997. *Java and Modern Europe. Ambiguous Encounters*. Richmond: Curzon Press.

Kuper, Adam. 1999. *Culture. The Anthropologists' Account*. Cambridge, MA & London: Harvard University Press.

Kutoyo, S. et al. 1977–78. *Sejarah Kebangkitan Nasional (1900–1942) Daerah Bali* [History of National Awakening (1900–1942) Bali Region]. Jakarta: Proyek Penelitian dan Pencatatan Kebudayaan Daerah, Pusat Penelitian Sejarah dan Budaya, Departemen Pendidikan dan Kebudayaan.

Kwa, Chong-Guan, ed. 2013. *Early Southeast Asia Viewed from India. An Anthology of Articles from the Journal of the Greater India Society*. New Delhi: Manohar.

Ladeira, Juliana Coelho de Souza. 2022. "'To the Extremes of Asian Sensibility'. Balinese Performances at the 1931 International Colonial Exhibition", *Anthropological Journal of European Cultures* 31, 2: 38–64.

Landmann, Alexandra. 2012. "Hindu Class and Hindu Education System in Bali: Emergence, Organization, and Conception in the Context of Indonesian Educational and Religious Policies", PhD Dissertation, Goethe-Universität Frankfurt am Main.

Lane, Max. 1972. "Wedastera Suyasa in Balinese Politics, 1962–72: From Charismatic Politics to Socio-educational Activities", BA Thesis, University of Sydney, Sydney.

Lansing, John Stephen. 1977. "Rama's Kingdoms: Social Supportive Mechanisms for the Arts in Bali", PhD Dissertation, Department of Anthropology, University of Michigan, Ann Arbor.

———. 1979. "The Formation of the Court–Village Axis in the Balinese Arts", in Edward M. Bruner and Judith O. Becker, eds, *Art, Ritual and Society in Indonesia*. Athens, OH: Ohio University Center for International Studies, pp. 10–29.

———. 1983. "The 'Indianization of Bali'", *Journal of Southeast Asian Studies* 14, 2: 409–21.

Lanus, Sugi. 2014. "*Puja Tri Sandhyā*: Indian Mantras Recomposed and Standardised in Bali", *The Journal of Hindu Studies* 7, 2: 243–72.

———. 2016. "Benarkah Teluk Benoa Sebuah Kawasan Suci?" ["Is Benoa Bay Really a Sacred Area?"], *Media Hindu* 146: 8-16.

Lardinois, Roland. 2007. *L'Invention de l'Inde. Entre ésotérisme et érudition* [The Invention of India. Between Esotericism and Erudition]. Paris: CNRS Éditions.

Last, Jef. 1955. *Bali in de kentering* [Bali at the Turning Point]. Amsterdam: De Bezige Bij.

Lekkerkerker, Cornelis. 1920. *Bali en Lombok. Overzicht der litteratuur omtrent deze eilanden tot einde 1919* [Bali and Lombok. Overview of the Literature on these Islands until the End of 1919]. Rijswick: Blankwaardt & Schoonhoven.

Lekkerkerker, T.C. 1918. *Hindoë-Recht in Indonesië* [Hindu Law in Indonesia]. Amsterdam: J.H. de Bussy.

Levenson, Jon D. 2012. *Inheriting Abraham: The Legacy of the Patriarch in Judaism, Christianity, and Islam*. Princeton: Princeton University Press.

Lévi, Sylvain. 1933. *Sanskrit Texts from Bali*. Baroda: Oriental Institute.

Lévi-Strauss, Claude. 1972 [1963]. "The Bear and the Barber", in William Armand Lessa and Evon Zartman Vogt, eds, *Reader in Comparative Religion: An Anthropological Approach*. New York: Harper & Row, pp. 181–9.

———, ed. 1977. *L'Identité* [Identity]. Paris: Grasset.

Lewis, Jeff, and Belinda Lewis. 2009. *Bali's Silent Crisis. Desire, Tragedy, and Transition*. Lanham: Lexington Books.

Lewis, Jeff, Belinda Lewis and I Nyoman Darma Putra. 2013. "The Bali Bombings Monument: Ceremonial Cosmopolis", *The Journal of Asian Studies* 72, 1: 21–43.

Liddle, R. William. 1989. "The National Political Culture and the New Order", *Prisma* 46: 4–20.

———. 1996. "The Islamic Turn in Indonesia: A Political Explanation", *The Journal of Asian Studies* 55, 3: 613–34.

Liefrinck, Frederik Albert. 1890. "Bijdrage tot de kennis van het eiland Bali" ["Contribution to the Knowledge of the Island of Bali"], *Tijdschrift voor Indische Taal-, Land- en Volkenkunde* 33: 233–427.

Liem, Maya H.T. 2003. "The Turning Wheel of Time. Roda Jaman Berputar. Modernity and Writing Identity in Bali 1900–1970", PhD Dissertation, Leiden University, Leiden.

Lindsay, Jennifer. 1995. "Cultural Policy and the Performing Arts in Southeast Asia", *Bijdragen tot de Taal-, Land- en Volkenkunde* 151, 4: 656–71.

Lindsey, Tim, and Simon Butt. 2016. "State Power to Restrict Religious Freedom: An Overview of the Legal Framework", in Tim Lindsey and Helen Pausacker, eds, *Religion, Law and Intolerance in Indonesia*. London & New York: Routledge, pp. 19–41.

Linnekin, Jocelyn. 1992. "On the Theory and Politics of Cultural Construction in the Pacific", *Oceania* 62, 4: 249–63.

Lipner, Julius J. 2006. "The Rise of 'Hinduism'; or, How to Invent a World Religion with Only Moderate Success", *International Journal of Hindu Studies* 10, 1: 91–104.

Listibiya. 1973. *Pola Dasar Kebijaksanaan Pembinaan Kebudayaan Daerah Bali* [Basic Pattern of Bali's Cultural Development Policy]. Denpasar: Majelis Pertimbangan dan Pembinaan Kebudayaan Daerah Propinsi Bali.

Llewellyn, J.E. 1993. *The Arya Samaj as a Fundamentalist Movement. A Study in Comparative Fundamentalism*. New Delhi: Manohar.

Lombard, Denys, 1990. *Le carrefour javanais. Essai d'histoire globale* [The Javanese Crossroads. Essay of Global History]. Paris: École des Hautes Études en Sciences Sociales.

Lopez, Donald S. Jr., ed. 1995. *Curators of the Buddha. The Study of Buddhism under Colonialism*. Chicago & London: The University of Chicago Press.

Lorenzen, David N. 1999. "Who Invented Hinduism?", *Comparative Studies in Society and History* 41, 4: 630–59.

Lovric, Barbara J.A. 1987. "Rhetoric and Reality: The Hidden Nightmare. Myth and Magic as Representations and Reverberations of Morbid Realities", PhD Dissertation, Department of Indonesian and Malayan Studies, University of Sydney, Sydney.

Lukas, Helmut. 2003. "Theories of Indianization, Exemplified by Selected Case Studies from Indonesia (Insular Southeast Asia)", in *Proceedings of Papers: 'Sanskrit in Southeast Asia: The Harmonizing Factor of Cultures'*. Bangkok: Sanskrit Studies Centre and Department of Oriental Languages, Silpakorn University, pp. 82–107.

Lyon, Margaret Louise. 1977. "Politics and Religious Identity: Genesis of a Javanese-Hindu Movement in Rural Central Java", PhD Dissertation, Department of Anthropology, University of California, Berkeley.

Mabbett, Ian W. 1977. "The 'Indianization' of Southeast Asia: Reflections on the Historical Sources", *Journal of Southeast Asian Studies*, 8, 2: 143–61.

MacDougall, John M. 2003. "From *Puik* (Silencing) to *Politik*: Transformations in Political Action and Cultural Exclusion from Late-1990's", *Antropologi Indonesia*, 27, 70: 60–76.

———. 2005. "Buddhist Buda or Buda Buddhists?: Conversion, Religious Modernism and Conflict in the Minority Buda Sasak Communities of New Order and Post-Suharto Lombok", PhD Dissertation, Department of Anthropology, University of Princeton, Princeton.

MacRae, Graeme S. 1992. "Tourism and Balinese Culture", MA Thesis, University of Auckland, Auckland.

———. 1997. "Economy, Ritual and History in a Balinese Tourist Town", PhD Dissertation, University of Auckland, Auckland.

———. 2003. "The Value of Land in Bali. Land Tenure, Landreform and Commodification", in Thomas A. Reuter, ed., *Inequality, Crisis and Social Change in Indonesia. The muted worlds of Bali*. London & New York: RoutledgeCurzon, pp. 143–65.

———. 2010. "If Indonesia is Too Hard to Understand, Let's Start with Bali", *Journal of Indonesian Social Sciences and Humanities* 3: 11–36.

MacRae, Graeme S. and I Nyoman Darma Putra. 2007. "A New Theatre-State in Bali? Aristocracies, the Media and Cultural Revival in the 2005 Local Elections", *Asian Studies Review* 31: 171-89.

Madinier, Rémy. 2015 [2011]. *Islam and Politics in Indonesia: The Masyumi Party between Democracy and Integralism*. Singapore: NUS Press.

Magenda, Burhan D. 1988. "Ethnicity and State-Building in Indonesia: The Cultural Base of the New Order", in Remo Guidieri, Francesco Pellizzi and Stanley Jeyaraja Tambiah, eds, *Ethnicity and Nations. Processes of Interethnic Relations in Latin America, Southeast Asia, and the Pacific*. Austin: Rothko Chapel, pp. 345–61.

Maier, Henk M.J. 1993. "From Heteroglossia to Polyglossia: The Creation of Malay and Dutch in the Indies", *Indonesia* 56: 37–65.

Majumdar, Ramesh Chandra. 1944. *Hindu Colonies in the Far East*. Calcutta: General Printers & Publishers.

Malalgoda, Kitsiri. 1997. "Concepts and Confrontations: A Case Study of *Agama*", in Michael Roberts, ed., *Sri Lanka: Collective Identities Revisited*. Vol. 1, Colombo: Marga, pp. 55–77.

Mandair, Arvind-Pal S. 2009. *Religion and the Specter of the West: Sikhism, India, Postcoloniality, and the Politics of Translation*. New York: Columbia University Press.

Mandair, Arvind-Pal S., and Markus Dressler. 2011. "Introduction: Modernity, Religion-Making, and the Postsecular", in Markus Dressler and Arvind-Pal S. Mandair, eds, *Secularism and Religion-Making*. Oxford & New York: Oxford University Press, pp. 3–36.

Manguin, Pierre-Yves. 2011. "Introduction", in Pierre-Yves Manguin, A. Mani and Geoff Wade, eds, *Early Interactions Between South and Southeast Asia: Reflections on Cross-cultural Exchange*. Singapore: Institute of Southeast Asian Studies, pp. xiii-xxxi.

———. 2022. "Early States of Insular Southeast Asia", in Charles F.W. Higham and Nam C. Kim, eds, *The Oxford Handbook of Early Southeast Asia*. New York: Oxford University Press, pp. 765–90.

Mantik, Agus S. et al., eds, 2009. *PHDI Setengah Abad. Sebuah Retrospeksi* [PHDI Half a Century. A Retrospective]. Jakarta: Parisada Hindu Dharma Indonesia.

Mantra, Ida Bagus. 1951. "Soal Agama di Bali" ["Regarding Religion in Bali"], *Suara Indonesia* February 2, 1951.

———. 1955. "Hindu Literature and Religion in Indonesia", PhD Dissertation, Visva-Bharati University, Santiniketan.

———, ed. 1967. *Bhagawad-Gita, naskah Sanskreta, alih bahasa dan pendjelasan* [Bhagavad-Gita, Sanskrit Text, Translation and Commentary]. Denpasar: Parisada Hindu Dharma Pusat.

Marcus, George E., and Michael M.J. Fischer. 1986. *Anthropology as Cultural Critique. An Experimental Moment in the Human Sciences*. Chicago & London: The University of Chicago Press.

Marshall, Peter J. 1970. *The British Discovery of Hinduism in the Eighteenth Century*. Cambridge: Cambridge University Press.

Masuzawa, Tomoko. 2005. *The Invention of World Religions. Or How European Universalism Was Preserved in the Language of Pluralism*. Chicago: The University of Chicago Press.

Mathews, Anna. 1965. *The Night of Purnama*. London: Cape.

McCutcheon, Russell T. 1997. *Manufacturing Religion. The Discourse on sui generis Religion and the Politics of Nostalgia*. Oxford & New York: Oxford University Press.

———. 2004. "Religion, Ire, and Dangerous Things", *Journal of the American Academy of Religion* 72, 1: 173–93.

McDaniel, June. 2010. "Agama Hindu Dharma Indonesia as a New Religious Movement: Hinduism Recreated in the Image of Islam", *Nova Religio: The Journal of Alternative and Emergent Religions* 14, 1: 93–111.

———. 2013. "A Modern Hindu Monotheism: Indonesian Hindus as 'People of the Book'", *Journal of Hindu Studies* 6, 3: 333–62.

McKean, Philip Frick. 1973. "Cultural Involution: Tourists, Balinese, and the Process of Modernization in an Anthropological Perspective", PhD Dissertation, Department of Anthropology, Brown University, Providence, Rhode Island.

———. 1989. "Towards a Theoretical Analysis of Tourism: Economic Dualism and Cultural Involution in Bali", in Valene L. Smith, ed., *Hosts and Guests. The Anthropology of Tourism*. Philadelphia: University of Pennsylvania Press, pp. 119–38.

McKinnon, Andrew M. 2002. "Sociological Definitions, Language Games, and the 'Essence' of Religion", *Method and Theory in the Study of Religion* 14, 1: 61–83.

McPhee, Colin. 1944. *A House in Bali*. New York: The Asia Press with The John Day Company.

———. 1966. *Music in Bali*. New Haven: Yale University Press.

McVey, Ruth T. 1965. *The Rise of Indonesian Communism*. Ithaca: Cornell University Press.

———. 1967. "Taman Siswa and the Indonesian National Awakening", *Indonesia* 4: 128–49.

———. 1999 [1993]. *Redesigning the Cosmos. Belief Systems and State Power in Indonesia*. Copenhagen: Nordic Institute of Asian Studies.
Mead, George Herbert. 1934. *Mind, Self, and Society*. Chicago: University of Chicago Press.
Mead, Margaret. 1939. "Researches in Bali, 1936–1939", *Transactions of the New York Academy of Sciences* 2, 2: 24–31.
———. 1970 [1940]. "The Arts in Bali", in Jane Belo, ed., *Traditional Balinese Culture*. New York: Columbia University Press, pp. 331–40.
———. 1972. *Blackberry Winter. My Earlier Years*. New York: William Morrow.
———. 1977. *Letters from the Field, 1925–1975*. New York: Harper & Row.
Medhurst, Walter Henry. 1830. "Short Account of the Island of Bali. Particularly of Bali Baliling", *Singapore Chronicle* June, pp. 85–96.
Meier, Théo. 1975. *Bali. Ile des dieux, des esprits et des demons* [Bali. Island of Gods, Spirits and Demons]. Zurich: Éditions Silva.
Menchik, Jeremy. 2014. "Productive Intolerance: Godly Nationalism in Indonesia", *Comparative Studies in Society and History* 56, 3: 591–621.
Mershon, Katharane Edson. 1971. *Seven plus Seven: Mysterious Life-Rituals in Bali*. New York: Vantage Press.
Mihardja, Achdiat K. ed. 1948. *Polemik Kebudajaan* [Polemic on Culture]. Jakarta: Pustaka Jaya.
Miller, D.B. 1984. "Hinduism in Perspective: Bali and India Compared", *Review of Indonesian and Malaysian Affairs* 18, 2: 36–63.
Mitter, Partha. 1987. "Rammohun Roy and the New Language of Monotheism", *History and Anthropology* 3, 1: 177–208.
Moerdowo, Raden Mas. 1983. *Reflections on Balinese Traditional and Modern Arts*. Jakarta: Balai Pustaka.
Monier-Williams, Monier. 1877. *Hinduism*. London: Society for Promoting Christian Knowledge.
Mozaffari, Mehdi. 2007. "What is Islamism? History and Definition of a Concept", *Totalitarian Movements and Political Religions* 8, 1: 17–33.
MPLA. 1990. *Mengenal dan Pembinaan Desa Adat di Bali* [Getting to Know and Nurturing Traditional Villages in Bali]. Denpasar: Majelis Pembina Lembaga Adat Daerah Tingkat I Bali.
Mulder, Niels. 1998. *Mysticism in Java. Ideology in Indonesia*. Amsterdam & Singapore: The Pepin Press.
Mursalin, Ayub. 2019. "Les restrictions à la liberté de religion et de conviction en Indonésie: genèse et enjeux contemporains de la loi anti-blasphème de 1965" ["Restrictions on Freedom of Religion and Belief in Indonesia: Genesis and Contemporary Issues of the 1965 Anti-blasphemy Law"], Thèse de doctorat, Université Paris-Saclay, Paris.
Mus, Paul. 1977. *L'angle de l'Asie* [The Angle of Asia]. Paris: Hermann.

Nagazumi, Akira. 1972. *The Dawn of Indonesian Nationalism. The Early Years of the Budi Utomo, 1908–1918*. Tokyo: Institute of Developing Economies.

Nala, Ngurah. 2004. "The Development of Hindu Education in Bali", in Martin Ramstedt, ed., *Hinduism in Modern Indonesia. A Minority Religion between Local, National, and Global Interests*. London & New York: RoutledgeCurzon—IIAS Asian Studies Series, pp. 76–83.

Nash, Dennison, ed. 2007. *The Study of Tourism. Anthropological and Sociological Beginnings*. Oxford & Amsterdam: Elsevier.

Ness, Sally Ann. 2008. "Bali, the Camera, and Dance: Performance Studies and The Lost Legacy of the Mead/Bateson Collaboration", *The Journal of Asian Studies* 67, 4: 1251–76.

Ngendjung, Ida Pedanda Gede. 1951. "Agama Hindu jg berlaku di Bali dan Lombok" ["The Hindu Religion as Practiced in Bali and Lombok"], *Suara Indonesia* October 10, 1951.

Nieuwenkamp, W.O.J. 1910. *Zwerftochten op Bali* [Wanderings in Bali]. Amsterdam: Elsevier.

Nihom, Max. 1994. *Studies in Indian and Indo-Indonesian Tantrism. The Kuñjarakarṇadharmakathana and the Yogatantra*. Vienna: Sammlung De Nobili Institut für Indologie der Universität Wien.

Nilon Batan, Jro Mangku Ir. W., and Dewa Made Mudita. 2001. *Lebih Jauh Tentang Agni Hotra* [More about Agni Hotra]. Pesraman Liang Galang.

Nongbri, Brent. 2014. *Before Religion. A History of a Modern Concept*. New Haven & London: Yale University Press.

Noronha, Raymond. 1979. "Paradise Reviewed: Tourism in Bali", in Emanuel de Kadt, ed., *Tourism. Passport to Development? Perspectives on the Social and Cultural Effects of Tourism in Developing Countries*. New York: Oxford University Press, pp. 177–204.

Noszlopy, Laura. 2002. "The Bali Arts Festival – Pesta Kesenian Bali: Culture, Politics and the Arts in Contemporary Indonesia", PhD Dissertation, University of East Anglia, Norwich.

Nugraha, Iskandar P. 2011. *Theosofi, Nasionalisme & Elite Modern* [Theosophy, Nationalism & the Modern Elite]. Jakarta: Komunitas Bambu.

Nye, Malory. 2000. "Religion, Post-religionism, and Religioning: Religious Studies and Contemporary Cultural Debates", *Method and Theory in the Study of Religion* 12, 4: 447–76.

Oberoi, Harjot. 1994. *The Construction of Religious Boundaries: Culture, Identity, and Diversity in the Sikh Tradition*. Chicago & London: The University of Chicago Press.

O'Connell, Joseph T. 1973. "The Word 'Hindu' in Gaudiya Vaishnava Texts", *Journal of the American Oriental Society* 93, 3: 340–44.

Oddie, Geoffrey A. 2006. *Imagined Hinduism. British Protestant Missionary Constructions of Hinduism, 1793–1900*. New Delhi & London: Sage Publications.

Official Tourist Bureau. 1914. *Illustrated Tourist Guide to East Java, Bali and Lombok*. Weltevreden: Official Tourist Bureau.

———. 1923. *Short Guide to Bali*. Batavia: Official Tourist Bureau.

Oka, G.G. 1988. *Proses Pembentukan Pemerintah Daerah Bali* [The Formation Process of Bali's Regional Government]. Denpasar: Fakultas Sastra Universitas Udayana.

Olcott, Henry Steel. 1881. *A Buddhist Catechism, According to the Canon of the Southern Church*. Colombo: The Theosophical Society, Buddhist Section.

Olle, John. 2006. "The Campaign against 'Heresy'. State and Society in Negotiation in Indonesia", Paper presented at the 16th Biennial Conference of the Asian Studies Association of Australia in Wollongong June 26–29, 2006.

Ottino, Arlette. 2000a. *The Universe Within. A Balinese Village through its Ritual Practices*. Paris: Karthala.

———. 2000b. "Conflict Avoidance and Cohabitation of Different Religious Groups in Bali", in Henny Warsilah and Rahdi Koestoer, eds, *International Symposium on Management of Social Transformation in Indonesian Society: In Search of Models for Conflict Prevention*. Jakarta: MOST-UNESCO & PMB-LIPI, pp. 69–84.

Otto, Rudolf. 1950 [1917]. *The Idea of the Holy. An Inquiry into the Non-rational Factor in the Idea of the Divine and its Relation to the Rational*. Oxford: Oxford University Press.

Padmawati, Ni Putu. 1982. *Pertumbuhan Perkoempoelan Shanti di Singaraja Antara Tahun 1921–1924* [The Growth of Shanti Association in Singaraja Between 1921–1924]. Denpasar: Fakultas Sastra Universitas Udayana.

Padoux, André. 2017 [2010]. *The Hindu Tantric World: An Overview*. Chicago & London: The University of Chicago Press.

PAHB. 1951. *Ichtisar Rapat Propaganda dan Anggota P.A.H.B. Singaradja pada tanggal 11 Maart 1951* [Outline of the Meeting on Propaganda and Members of P.A.H.B. Singaradja, March 11, 1951]. Singaradja.

Pain, Frédéric. 2017. "Local vs. trans-Regional Perspectives on Southeast Asian 'Indianness'", *Anthropological Forum* 27, 2: 135–54.

Pangdjaja, Ida Bagus, ed. 1991. *Bali Arts Festival. Pesta Kesenian Bali*. Denpasar: Cita Budaya.

Panitia Perantjang. 1958. *Panitia Perantjang 'Hindu-Bali Sabha' (Dewan Agama Hindu-Bali)* [Committee of the 'Hindu-Bali Sabha' (Hindu-Bali Religious Council)]. Denpasar, December 7, 1958.

Parker, Lynette. 2000. "The Introduction of Western-Style Education to Bali: Domination by Consent?", Adrian Vickers and I Nyoman Darma Putra with Michele Ford, eds, *To Change Bali. Essays in Honour of I Gusti Ngurah Bagus*. Denpasar: Bali Post and University of Wollongong, Institute of Social Change and Critical Inquiry, pp. 47–69.

Pausacker, Helen. 2008. "Hot Debates: A Law on Pornography Still Divides the Community", *Inside Indonesia* 94: October–December.

PDHB. 1960. *Dharma Prawrtti Çastra* [Dharma Prawrtti Literature]. Denpasar.

———. 2007. *Laporan Lokasabha V di Pura Samuhan Tiga, Bedulu-Gianyar* [Report on the 5th Meeting at Samuhan Tiga Temple, Bedulu-Gianyar]. Denpasar.
Pelras, Christian. 1977. "Culture, ethnie, espace social: quelques réflexions autour du cas Bugis" ["Culture, Ethnicity, Social Space: Some Reflections on the Bugis Case"], *Asie du Sud-Est et Monde Insulindien* 8, 2: 57–79.
Pemberton, John. 1994a. *On the Subject of 'Java'*. Ithaca & London: Cornell University Press.
———. 1994b. "Recollections from 'Beautiful Indonesia' (Somewhere Beyond the Postmodern)", *Public Culture* 6, 2: 241–62.
Pemecutan, I Gusti Ngurah Oka, ed. 2007. *Perjalanan Parisada Bali (Parisada Dharma Hindu Bali)* [The Journey of Parisada Bali (Parisada Dharma Hindu Bali)]. Denpasar: Yayasan Kerti Budaya.
Pendit, Njoman Suwandhi. 1952. "Dua masalah harus diselesaikan" ["Two Problems Must be Solved"], *Siasat* 6, 278: 7, 16.
———. 1979 [1954]. *Bali Berjuang* [Bali is Fighting]. Jakarta: Gunung Agung.
———. 2001. "Perjuangan Eksistensi Agama Hindu" ["The Struggle for the Existence of the Hindu Religion"], *Bali Post* July 4, 2001.
Pengumuman Resmi Dewan Pemerintah Daerah Bali n°15 & n°19 [Bali Local Government Council Official Announcement n°15 & n°19]. 1953. Singaradja.
Pennington, Brian K. 2005. *Was Hinduism Invented? Britons, Indians, and the Colonial Construction of Religion*. Oxford: Oxford University Press.
Pernau, Margrit. 2011. "Maulawi Muhammad Zaka Ullah. Reflections of a Muslim Moralist on the Compatibility of Islam, Hinduism and Christianity", in Catherine Clémentin-Ojha, ed., *Convictions religieuses et engagement en Asie du Sud depuis 1850*. Paris: École française d'Extrême-Orient, pp. 31–47.
Perreira, Todd LeRoy. 2012. "Whence Theravāda? The Modern Genealogy of an Ancient Term", in Peter Skilling, Jason A. Carbine, Claudio Cicuzza and Santi Pakdeekham, eds, *How Theravāda is Theravāda? Exploring Buddhist Identities*. Chiang Mai: Silkworm Books, pp. 443–571.
Perret, Daniel. 1995. *La formation d'un paysage ethnique. Batak & Malais de Sumatra nord-est* [The Formation of an Ethnic Landscape. Batak & Malays of Northeast Sumatra]. Paris: École française d'Extrême-Orient.
Pertemuan Kerdja Sama Organisasi Agama Hindu Bali tentang Kedudukan Agama Hindu Bali dalam Organisasi Kementerian Agama Republik Indonesia [Cooperation Meeting of Balinese Hindu Religious Organizations on the Position of the Balinese Hindu Religion in the Organization of the Ministry of Religion of the Republic of Indonesia], Denpasar, June 26, 1958.
Peterson, Derek, and Darren Walhof, eds, 2002. *The Invention of Religion. Rethinking Belief in Politics and History*. New Brunswick: Rutgers University Press.
Phalgunadi, I Gusti Putu. 1991. *Evolution of Hindu Culture in Bali*. Delhi: Sundeep Prakashan.

PHD. 1968. *Pedoman Dasar dan Rumah Tangga* [Constitution and Bylaws]. Denpasar: Parisada Hindu Dharma.

———. 1970. *Pokok-pokok Sejarah Perkembangan Parisada Hindu Dharma* [Outline of the Development History of the *Parisada Hindu Dharma*]. Denpasar: Parisada Hindu Dharma.

PHD Kabupaten Badung. 1970. *Sambutan dan Hasil Keputusan Sabha (Kongres) II Parisada Hindu Dharma Seluruh Indonesia Tanggal 2 s/d 5 Desember 1968 di Denpasar-Bali* [Remarks and Decisions of the Second Sabha (Congress) of the Parisada Hindu Dharma All Indonesia, December 2 to 5, 1968 in Denpasar-Bali]. Denpasar: Parisada Hindu Dharma Kabupaten Badung.

PHDI. 1988a. *Himpunan Keputusan Seminar Kesatuan Tafsir Terhadap Aspek-Aspek Agama Hindu I–XIV* [Decisions of the Seminar on Unity of Interpretation of Aspects of the Hindu Religion I-XIV]. Denpasar: Parisada Hindu Dharma Indonesia Pusat.

———. 1988b. *Pedoman Pembinaan Umat Hindu Dharma Indonesia* [Guidelines for the Development of the Hindu Dharma Indonesian Community]. Denpasar: PT. Upada Sastra.

———. 2006a. *Laporan Pertanggungjawaban Pengurus Parisada Hindu Dharma Indonesia Pusat Masa Bhakti 2001–2006* [Accountability Report of the Board of Parisada Hindu Dharma Indonesia Center for the 2001–2006 Bhakti Period]. Jakarta: Parisada Hindu Dharma Indonesia.

———. 2006b. *Hasil-Hasil Maha Sabha IX Parisada Hindu Dharma Indonesia* [Results of the 9th Congress of Parisada Hindu Dharma Indonesia]. Jakarta: Parisada Hindu Dharma Indonesia.

———. 2011. *Materi Mahasabha X Parisada Hindu Dharma Indonesia* [Materials for the 10th Congress of Parisada Hindu Dharma Indonesia]. Jakarta: Parisada Hindu Dharma Indonesia.

———. 2016. *Hasil-Hasil Mahasabha XI Parisada Hindu Dharma Indonesia* [Results of the 11th Congress of Parisada Hindu Dharma Indonesia]. Jakarta: Parisada Hindu Dharma Indonesia.

PHDI Propinsi Bali. 2001. *Sejarah Parisada dan Hasil Lokasabha IV Parisada Hindu Dharma Indonesia Propinsi Bali* [History of Parisada and Results of the 4th Congress of Parisada Hindu Dharma Indonesia Bali Province]. Denpasar: PHDI Propinsi Bali.

Picard, Michel. 1983. "En feuilletant le 'Bali Post': à propos de l'interdiction des combats de coqs à Bali" ["Flipping through the 'Bali Post': About the Ban on Cockfighting in Bali"], *Archipel* 25: 171–80.

———. 1990. "'Cultural Tourism' in Bali. Cultural Performances as Tourist Attraction", *Indonesia* 49: 37–74.

———. 1996a. *Bali. Cultural Tourism and Touristic Culture*. Singapore: Archipelago Press.

———. 1996b. "Dance and Drama in Bali: The Making of an Indonesian Art Form", in Adrian Vickers, ed., *Being Modern in Bali. Image and Change*. New Haven: Yale University Southeast Asia Studies, pp. 115–57.

———. 1998. "Le *gambuh*: grandeur, décadence et renaissance (?) du théâtre à Bali" ["The *gambuh*: Grandeur, Decadence and Rebirth (?) of the Theater in Bali"], *Archipel* 55: 141–90.

———. 2007. "From Turkey to Bali: Cultural Identity as Tourist Attraction", in Dennison Nash, ed., *The Study of Tourism. Anthropological and Sociological Beginnings*. Oxford & Amsterdam: Elsevier, pp. 167–83.

———. 2012. "Polyglossie et vernacularisation à Bali: 'l'indianisation' par le théâtre" ["Polyglossia and Vernacularization in Bali: 'Indianization' through Theater"], in Hélène Bouvier and Gérard Toffin, eds, *Théâtres d'Asie à l'oeuvre*. Paris: École française d'Extrême-Orient, pp. 159–79.

Pigeaud, Theodoor G. Th. 1960–63. *Java in the Fourteenth Century: A Study in Cultural History. The Nagara-Kertagama by Rakawi Prapañca of Majapahit, 1365 A.D.* The Hague: Martinus Nijhof.

Pitana, I Gde. 1997. "In Search of Difference. Origin Groups, Status and Identity in Contemporary Bali", PhD Dissertation, Department of Anthropology, The Australian National University, Canberra.

———. 1999. "Status Struggles and the Priesthood in Contemporary Bali", in Raechelle Rubinstein and Linda H. Connor, eds, *Staying Local in the Global Village. Bali in the Twentieth Century*. Honolulu: University of Hawai'i Press, pp. 181–201.

———. 2001. "Sociology of the Temple. Issues Related to Rivalry in Status and Power", in Urs Ramseyer and I Gusti Raka Panji Tisna, eds, *Bali. Living in Two Worlds. A Critical Self-portrait*. Basel: Museum der Kulturen, pp. 117–27.

Pollmann, Tessel. 1990. "Margaret Mead's Balinese: The Fitting Symbols of the American Dream", *Indonesia* 49: 1–35.

Pollock, Sheldon. 1996. "The Sanskrit Cosmopolis, A.D. 300–1300: Transculturation, Vernacularization, and the Question of Ideology. The Ideology and Status of Sanskrit in South and Southeast Asia", in Jan E.M. Houben, ed., *Ideology and Status of Sanskrit: Contributions to the History of the Sanskrit Language*. Leiden: Brill, pp. 197–247.

———. 1998. "The Cosmopolitan Vernacular", *The Journal of Asian Studies* 57, 1: 6–37.

———. 2006. *The Language of the Gods in the World of Men. Sanskrit, Culture, and Power in Premodern India*. Berkeley: The University of California Press.

Powell, Hickman. 1930. *The Last Paradise*. New York: Jonathan Cape.

PPP. 1949. *Notulen-verslag dari Congres P.P.P. di Singaradja pada tg. 16 s/d 19 November 1949* [Minutes-report of the P.P.P. Congress in Singaradja November 16 to 19, 1949]. Singaradja.

Projek. 1971a. *Seminar Seni Sakral dan Provan Bidang Tari* [Seminar on Sacred and Profane Arts in the Field of Dance]. Denpasar: Projek Pemeliharaan dan Pengembangan Kebudajaan Daerah.

Projek. 1971b. *Hasil Keputusan Seminar Pariwisata Budaja Daerah Bali* [Decisions of the Bali Regional Cultural Tourism Seminar]. Denpasar: Projek Pemeliharaan dan Pengembangan Kebudajaan Daerah.

Punyatmadja, Ida Bagus Oka. 1970. *Panca Çraddha* [Five Articles of Faith]. Denpasar: Parisada Hindu Dharma Pusat.

———. 1992. *The Hindu Ethics of Holy Veda as Found in Bali.* Jakarta: World Hindu Federation.

Putra, Anak Agung Putu Oka. 1989. *Perkumpulan Bali Darma Laksana: Sebuah Organisasi Sosial di Bali, 1936–1942* [The Bali Darma Laksana Association: A Social Organization in Bali, 1936–1942]. Denpasar: Fakultas Sastra Universitas Udayana.

Putra, I Gusti Agung Gede. 1971. "Tari-tarian sakral dan provan dari segi rituil" ["Sacred and Profane Dances in Terms of Rituals"], in *Seminar Seni Sakral dan Provan Bidang Tari*. Denpasar: Projek Pemeliharaan dan Pengembangan Kebudajaan Daerah.

Putra, I Gusti Bagus Andika. 1997. *Pasang Surut Perguruan Rakyat Saraswati di Bali, 1946–1992* [The Rise and Fall of the Saraswati Institute of Popular Education in Bali, 1946–1992]. Denpasar: Fakultas Sastra Universitas Udayana.

Putra, I Nyoman Darma. 2000. "Bali and Modern Indonesian Literature: The 1950s", in Adrian Vickers and I Nyoman Darma Putra, with Michele Ford, eds, *To Change Bali. Essays in Honour of I Gusti Ngurah Bagus*. Denpasar: Bali Post and University of Wollongong, Institute of Social Change and Critical Inquiry, pp. 135–53.

———. 2003. "Reflections on Literature and Politics in Bali. The Development of Lekra, 1950–1966", in Thomas A. Reuter, ed., *Inequality, Crisis and Social Change in Indonesia. The muted worlds of Bali*. London & New York: RoutledgeCurzon, pp. 54–85.

———. 2004a. "Bali Pasca-Bom: Konflik, kekerasan, dan rekonstruksi identitas budaya seputar 'Ajeg Bali'" ["Post-Bomb Bali: Conflict, Violence, and the Reconstruction of Cultural Identity around 'Ajeg Bali'"], in I Wayan Cika et al., eds, *Garitan Budaya Nusantara Dalam Perspektif Kebinekaan* [Archipelago Culture in the Perspective of Diversity]. Kuta: Larasan, pp. 206–32.

———, ed. 2004b. *Bali. Menuju Jagaditha: Aneka Perspektif* [Bali. Toward Jagaditha: Various Perspectives]. Denpasar: Pustaka Bali Post.

———. 2011. *A Literary Mirror. Balinese Reflections on Modernity and Identity in the Twentieth Century*. Leiden: KITLV Press.

Putra Agung, Anak Agung Gde. 1972. "Lahirnja idee-idee pembaharuan dalam organisasi sosial di Bali" ["The Birth of Reform Ideas in Social Organizations in Bali"], *Basis* 21, 6: 183–9.

———. 1983. "Dampak Pendidikan Terhadap Perubahan Sosial di Bali" ["The Impact of Education on Social Change in Bali"]. Tesis, Universitas Gadjah Mada, Yogyakarta.

———, 2001, *Perubahan Sosial dan Pertentangan Kasta di Bali Utara* [Social Change and Caste Conflict in North Bali]. Yogyakarta: Yayasan Untuk Indonesia.

Quaritch Wales, Horace G. 1951. *The Making of Greater India. A Study in South-East Asian Culture Change.* London: Bernard Quaritch.

Quinn, George. 2012. "The Muslim Saints of Bali", Paper presented at the Bali in Global Asia Conference, Udayana University, Denpasar, July 16–18, 2012.

Radice, William, ed. 1998. *Swami Vivekananda and the Modernisation of Hinduism.* New Delhi: Oxford University Press.

Raffles, Thomas Stamford. 1817. *The History of Java.* London: Black, Parbury & Allen.

Ramanujan, Attipate Krishnaswami. 1989. "Is There an Indian Way of Thinking? An Informal Essay", *Contributions to Indian Sociology* 23, 1: 41–58.

Ramseyer, Urs. 1977. *The Art and Culture of Bali.* Oxford: Oxford University Press.

———. 2001. "Prologue: Tears in Paradise", in Urs Ramseyer and I Gusti Raka Panji Tisna, eds, *Bali. Living in Two Worlds. A Critical Self-Portrait.* Basel: Museum der Kulturen, pp. 9–14.

Ramstedt, Martin. 1992. "Indonesian Cultural Policy in Relation to the Development of Balinese Performing Arts", in Danker Schaareman, ed., *Balinese Music in Context.* Winterthur: Amadeus, Forum Ethnomusicologicum 4, pp. 59–84.

———. 2002. "Hinduism in Modern Indonesia", in Satish Chandra and Baladas Ghoshal, eds, *Indonesia: A New Beginning?* New Delhi: Sterling Publishers, pp. 140–68.

———. 2004a. "Introduction: Negotiating Identities – Indonesian 'Hindus' between Local, National, and Global Interests", in Martin Ramstedt, ed., *Hinduism in Modern Indonesia. A Minority Religion between Local, National, and Global Interests.* London & New York: RoutledgeCurzon—IIAS Asian Studies Series, pp. 1–34.

———. 2004b. "The Hinduization of Local Traditions in South Sulawesi", in Martin Ramstedt, ed., *Hinduism in Modern Indonesia. A Minority Religion between Local, National, and Global Interests.* London & New York: RoutledgeCurzon—IIAS Asian Studies Series, pp. 184–225.

———. 2008. "Hindu Bonds at Work: Spiritual and Commercial Ties between India and Bali", *The Journal of Asian Studies*, 67, 4: 1227–50.

———. 2009. "Regional Autonomy and Its Discontents. The Case of Post-New Order Bali", in Coen J.G. Holtzappel and Martin Ramstedt, eds, *Decentralization and Regional Autonomy in Indonesia: Implementation and Challenges.* Singapore: Institute of Southeast Asian Studies, pp. 329–79.

———. 2011. "Colonial Encounters between India and Indonesia", *South Asian History and Culture* 2, 4: 522–39.

———. 2012. "Processes of Disembedding and Displacement: Anomie and the Juridification of Religio-Ethnic Identity in Post-New Order Bali", *Asian Ethnicity* 13, 4: 323–39.

———. 2013. "Religion and Disputes in Bali's New Village Jurisdictions", in Franz von Benda-Beckmann, Keebet von Benda-Beckmann, Martin Ramstedt and Bertrand Turner, eds, *Religion in Disputes. Pervasiveness of Religious Normativity in Disputing Processes*. New York: Palgrave Macmillan, pp. 111–28.

———. 2014. "Discordant Temporalities in Bali's new Village Jurisdictions", *The Journal of Legal Pluralism and Unofficial Law* 46, 1: 60–78.

———. 2018. "Hinduism and Buddhism", in Robert W. Hefner, ed., *Routledge Handbook of Contemporary Indonesia*. New York: Routledge, pp. 267–83.

———. 2019. "Politics of Taxonomy in Postcolonial Indonesia: Ethnic Traditions between Religionisation and Secularisation", *Historical Social Research* 44, 3: 264–89.

Rath, Amanda. 1997. "Cultural Sublimation: The Museumizing of Indonesia", *Explorations in Southeast Asian Studies* 1, 1: 13–35.

Rawski, Frederick & MacDougall. John, 2004. "Regional Autonomy and Indigenous Exclusivism in Bali", *International Journal on Minority and Group Rights* 11: 143-57.

Reisnour, Nicole Joanna. 2018. "Voicing Selves: Ethics, Mediation, and the Politics of Religion in Post-authoritarian Bali", PhD Dissertation, Graduate School of Cornell University, Ithaca.

Resink, Thomas A. 1938. "Het Bali-Museum" ["The Bali-Museum"], *Djawa* 18: 72–82.

Reuter, Thomas A. 2001. "Great Expectations: Hindu Revival Movements in Java", *The Australian Journal of Anthropology* 12, 3: 327–38.

———. 2002. *Custodians of the Sacred Mountains. Culture and Society in the Highlands of Bali*. Honolulu: University of Hawai'i Press.

———. 2008. *Global Trends in Religion and the Reaffirmation of Hindu Identity in Bali*. Melbourne: Monash University Press, Working Paper 130.

———. 2014. "Is Ancestor Veneration the most Universal of all World Religions? A Critique of Modernist Cosmological Bias", *Wacana* 15, 2: 223–53.

Reynolds, Craig J. 1995. "A New Look at Old Southeast Asia", *The Journal of Asian Studies* 54, 2: 419–46.

Rhodius, Hans, and John Darling. 1980. *Walter Spies and Balinese Art*. Zutphen: Terra.

Ricklefs, Merle C. 2006. *Mystic Synthesis in Java: A History of Islamisation from the Fourteenth to the Early Nineteenth Centuries*. Norwalk: Eastbridge.

———. 2007. *Polarising Javanese Society. Islamic and Other Visions (c. 1830–1930)*. Leiden: KITLV Press.

———. 2008 [1981]. *A History of Modern Indonesia Since C.1200*. New York: Macmillan International Higher Education.

———. 2012. *Islamisation and Its Opponents in Java. A Political, Social, Cultural and Religious History, c. 1930 to the Present*. Singapore: NUS Press.

Rickner, Robert. 1972. "Theatre as Ritual: Artaud's Theatre of Cruelty and the Balinese Barong", PhD Dissertation, University of Hawaii.

Robinson, Geoffrey. 1995. *The Dark Side of Paradise. Political Violence in Bali*. Ithaca & London: Cornell University Press.

———. 2018. *The Killing Season: A History of the Indonesian Massacres, 1965–1966*. Princeton: Princeton University Press.

Robinson, Kathryn May. 1997. "History, Houses and Regional Identities", *The Australian Journal of Anthropology* 8, 1: 71–88.

Robson, Stuart. 1995. *Deśawarnana (Nāgarakrtāgama) by Mpu Prapañca*. Leiden: KITLV Press.

Rocher, Ludo. 2003. "The Dharmaśāstras", in Gavin Flood, ed., *The Blackwell Companion to Hinduism*. Oxford: Blackwell Publishing, pp. 102–15.

Rocher, Rosane. 1993. "British Orientalism in the Eighteenth Century: The Dialectics of Knowledge and Government", in Carol A. Breckenridge and Peter Van der Veer, eds, *Orientalism and the Postcolonial Predicament. Perspectives on South Asia*. Philadelphia: University of Pennsylvania Press, pp. 215–49.

Rodgers, Susan. 1979. "Advice to the Newlyweds: Sipirok Batak Wedding Speeches. Adat or Art?", in Edward M. Bruner and Judith O. Becker, eds, *Art, Ritual and Society in Indonesia*. Athens, OH: Ohio University, pp. 30–61.

———. 1993. "Batak Heritage and the Indonesian State: Print Literacy and the Construction of Ethnic Cultures in Indonesia", in Judith D. Toland, ed., *Ethnicity and the State*. New Brunswick: Transaction Publishers, pp. 147–76.

Roff, William R. 1962. "Kaum Muda—Kaum Tua: Innovation and Reaction amongst the Malays, 1900–1941", in K.G. Tregonning, ed., *Papers on Malayan History*. Singapore: University of Singapore, pp.162–92.

Roosa, John. 2020. *Buried Histories: The Anticommunist Massacres of 1965–1966 in Indonesia*. Madison: University of Wisconsin Press.

Ropi, Ismatu. 2016. "*Ketuhanan Yang Maha Esa*, the State and the Politics of Religious (In)Tolerance", in Tim Lindsey and Helen Pausacker, eds, *Religion, Law and Intolerance in Indonesia*. London & New York: Routledge, pp. 132–57.

———. 2017. *Religion and Regulation in Indonesia*. Singapore: Palgrave Macmillan.

Rubinstein, Raechelle. 2000. *Beyond the Realm of the Senses. The Balinese Ritual of Kekawin Composition*. Leiden: KITLV Press.

Rudyansjah, Tony. 1986. "Modernization and Religion on Bali. A Cultural-Sociological Study of the Parisada Hindu Dharma". MA Thesis, University of Indonesia, Jakarta.

Ryan, Michael T., 1981, "Assimilating New Worlds in the Sixteenth and Seventeenth Centuries", *Comparative Studies in Society and History* 23, 4: 519–38.

Sachot, Maurice. 1991. "'Religio/superstitio'. Historique d'une subversion et d'un retournement" ["'Religio/superstitio'. History of a Subversion and a Reversal"], *Revue de l'Histoire des Religions* 208, 4: 355–94.

———. 2007. *Quand le christianisme a changé le monde. La subversion chrétienne du monde antique* [When Christianity Changed the World. The Christian Subversion of the Ancient World]. Paris: Odile Jacob.

Sahlins, Marshall. 1993. "Goodbye to *Tristes Tropes*: Ethnography in the Context of Modern World History", *Journal of Modern History* 65, 1: 1–25.

———. 1999. "Two or Three Things that I Know about Culture", *Journal of the Royal Anthropological Institute* 5: 399–422.

———. 2017. "The Original Political Society", *HAU: Journal of Ethnographic Theory* 7, 2: 91–128.

———. 2021. "Cosmic Economics", *Annals of the Fondazione Luigi Einaudi* 55, 1: 255–78.

Said, Edward. 1978. *Orientalism. Western Conceptions of the Orient*. New York: Random House.

Saler, Benson. 2000 [1993]. *Conceptualizing Religion. Immanent Anthropologists, Transcendent Natives, and Unbounded Categories*. New York & Oxford: Berghahn Books.

Sanderson, Alexis. 2003–04. "The Śaiva Religion among the Khmers. Part I", *Bulletin de l'École française d'Extrême-Orient* 90–91: 349–462.

———. 2009. "The Śaiva Age. The Rise and Dominance of Śaivism during the Early Medieval Period", in Shingo Einoo, ed., *Genesis and Development of Tantrism*. University of Tokyo: Institute of Oriental Culture, pp. 41–349.

———. 2015. "Tolerance, Exclusivity, Inclusivity, and Persecution in Indian Religion During the Early Mediaeval Period", in John Makinson, ed., *Honoris Causa: Essays in Honour of Aveek Sarkar*. London: Allen Lane, pp. 155–224.

Santikarma, Degung. 2001. "The Power of 'Balinese Culture'", in Urs Ramseyer and I Gusti Raka Panji Tisna, eds, *Bali. Living in Two Worlds. A Critical Self-Portrait*. Basel: Museum der Kulturen, pp. 27–35.

———. 2003a. "The Model Militia: A New Security Force in Bali is Cloaked in Tradition", *Inside Indonesia* 73: 14–16.

———. 2003b. "Bali Erect", *Latitudes* 34: 12–17.

———. 2003c. "*Ajeg* Bali: Dari gadis cilik ke Made Schwarzenegger" ["*Ajeg* Bali: From Little Girl to Made Schwarzenegger"], *Kompas* December 7, 2003.

Santoso, Soewito. 1975. *Sutasoma: A Study in Javanese Wajrayana*. New Delhi: International Academy of Indian Culture.

Saraswati, Swami Prakashanand. 2014. *Kebenaran Sejarah Agama Hindu. The True History and the Religion of India*. Surabaya: World Hindu Parisad & Paramita.

Sarkar, Himansu Bhusan. 1934. *Indian Influences on the Literature of Java and Bali*. Calcutta: Greater India Society.

Satria Naradha, ABG, ed. 2004. *Ajeg Bali. Sebuah Cita-cita* [Ajeg Bali. An Ideal]. Denpasar: Pustaka Bali Post.

Savarkar, Vinayak Damodar. 1928. *Hindutva: Who Is a Hindu?* Bombay: Savarkar Sadan.

Sayoga, I Wayan. 2019. *Rekomendasi Simposium Demografi: "Dampak Perubahan Struktur Penduduk Bali terhadap Tatanan Kehidupan Masyarakat Bali yang dilandasi Nilai-Nilai Luhur Hindu Dharma" kepada berbagai Instansi/Lembaga Pemerintahan* [Demographic Symposium Recommendations: "The Impact of

Changes in Bali's Population Structure on the Order of Balinese Life Based on the Noble Values of Hindu Dharma" to Various Government Agencies/Institutions]. Denpasar: Forum Advokasi Hindu Dharma.

SCETO. 1971. *Bali Tourism Study. Report to the Government of Indonesia.* Paris: UNDP/IBRD.

Schaareman, Danker. 1986. *Tatulingga: Tradition and Continuity. An Investigation in Ritual and Social Organization in Bali.* Basel: Ethnologisches Seminar der Universität und Museum für Völkerkunde.

Schärer, Hans. 1963. *Ngaju Religion. The Conception of God Among a South Borneo People.* The Hague: Martinus Nijhoff.

Schefold, Reimar. 1998. "The Domestication of Culture. Nation-Building and Ethnic Diversity in Indonesia", *Bijdragen tot de Taal-, Land- en Volkenkunde*, 154, 2: 259-80.

Scherer, Sawitri P. 1975. "Harmony and Dissonance: Early Nationalist Thought in Java", MA Thesis, Cornell University, Ithaca.

Schiller, Anne. 1997. *Small Sacrifices. Religious Change and Cultural Identity among the Ngaju of Indonesia.* New York: Oxford University Press.

Schoterman, Jan Anthony. 1979. "A Note on Balinese Sanskrit", *Bijdragen tot de Taal-, Land- en Volkenkunde* 135, 2–3: 323–46.

Schuh, Gotthard. 1954. *Iles des Dieux* [Islands of the Gods]. Lausanne: Éditions Clairefontaine.

Schulte Nordholt, Henk. 1986. *Bali: Colonial Conceptions and Political Change, 1700–1940. From Shifting Hierarchies to 'Fixed Order'.* Rotterdam: Comparative Asian Studies Programme, Erasmus University.

———. 1991. *State, Village, and Ritual in Bali.* Amsterdam: VU University Press.

———. 1992. "Origin, Descent, and Destruction: Text and Context in Balinese Representations of the Past", *Indonesia* 54: 27–58.

———. 1994. "The Making of Traditional Bali: Colonial Ethnography and Bureaucratic Reproduction", *History and Anthropology* 8, 1–4: 89–127.

———. 1996. *The Spell of Power. A History of Balinese politics 1650–1940.* Leiden: KITLV Press.

———. 2000. "From *Wangsa* to *Bangsa*: Subaltern Voices and Personal Ambivalences in 1930s Colonial Bali", in Adrian Vickers and I Nyoman Darma Putra with Michele Ford, eds, *To Change Bali. Essays In Honour of I Gusti Ngurah Bagus.* Denpasar: Bali Post and University of Wollongong, Institute of Social Change and Critical Inquiry, pp. 71–88.

———. 2007. *Bali. An Open Fortress. Regional Autonomy, Electoral Democracy and Entrenched Identities.* Leiden: KITLV Press.

Scott, David. 1996. "Religion in Colonial Civil Society. Buddhism and Modernity in 19th-century Sri Lanka", *Cultural Dynamics* 8, 1: 7–23.

Sears, Laurie J. 1996. *Shadows of Empire. Colonial Discourse and Javanese Tales.* Durham, NC: Duke University Press.

Segal, Robert A. 1983. "In Defense of Reductionism", *Journal of the American Academy of Religion* 51, 1: 97–124.

Sendra, I Made. 2013. "Pergolakan Elite dalam Panggung Politik di Bali 1945–1950" ["Elite Upheaval on the Political Stage in Bali 1945–1950"], *Jurnal Kajian Bali* 3, 1: 87–114.

Setia, Putu, ed. 1992. *Cendekiawan Hindu Bicara* [Hindu Scholars Speak Out]. Denpasar: Yayasan Dharma Naradha.

———. 1993. *Kebangkitan Hindu Menyongsong Abad ke-21* [Hindu Revival into the 21st Century]. Jakarta: Pustaka Manikgeni.

———, ed. 2001. *Eksistensi Sadhaka dalam Agama Hindu* [The Existence of Sadhaka in the Hindu Religion]. Denpasar: Pustaka Manikgeni.

———. 2002. *Mendebat Bali. Catatan Perjalanan Budaya Bali Hingga Bom Kuta* [Debating Bali. Notes on Bali's Cultural Journey Until the Kuta Bombing]. Denpasar: Pustaka Manikgeni.

Shadeg, Norbert. 1989. *Bali Notes: Religious Transformation and Development in Bali*. Tuka: Widya Wahana Library.

Shanty, Putu. 1951. "Panti Agama Hindu-Bali" ["Institution of the Hindu-Balinese Religion"], *Suara Indonesia* September 7 and 8, 1951.

———. 1952a. "Sebuah persoalan antara: Agama Tirtha dan Hindu-Bali" ["An Issue Between: Tirtha and Hindu-Bali Religion"], *Siasat* 6, 264: 7.

———. 1952b. "Agama + Demokrasi + Pantjasila" ["Religion + Democracy + Pantjasila"], *Siasat* 6, 268: 7.

———. 1953. "Negara Indonesia musti berdasarkan nasional. Aliran Islam akan mengakibatkan perpetjahan persatuan" ["The Indonesian State must be Nationally Based. The Sect of Islam will Lead to a Split in Unity"], *Bhakti* 2, 7: 2–4.

———, 1954. "Perhatian kepada Agama" ["Concern for Religion"] *Bhakti* 3, 1: 4–5.

Sharma, Arvind. 1994. "The Bearing of the Different Understandings of the Words *religion*, *dharma* and *dīn* on Religious Study and Research", in Ugo Bianchi, ed., *The Notion of 'Religion' in Comparative Research: Selected Proceedings of the XVI IAHR Congress*. Rome: Bretshneider, pp. 591–602.

———. 2002. "On Hindu, Hindustan, Hinduism and Hindutva", *Numen* 49, 1: 1–36.

Sharpe, Eric J. 1986. *Comparative Religion: A History*. La Salle: Open Court.

Shastri, Narendra Dev Pandit. 1951. *Dasa Sila Agama Bali* [The Ten Tenets of Balinese Religion]. Singaradja.

———. 1955a. *Intisari Hindu Dharma* [Essentials of Hindu Dharma]. Denpasar.

———. 1955b. *Dharmopadeça (Pengadjaran Çiwa-Buddha)* [Dharmopadeça (Teaching of Çiwa-Buddha)]. Denpasar: Bhuvana Saraswati Publications.

———. 195?, *Tri Sandhya*. Denpasar: Bhuvana Saraswati Publications.

Shavit, David. 2003. *Bali and the Tourist Industry. A History, 1906–1942*. Jefferson & London: McFarland.

Shiraishi, Takashi. 1981. "The Disputes Between Tjipto Mangoenkoesoemo and Soetatmo Soeriokoesoemo: Satria vs. Pandita", *Indonesia* 32: 93–108.

———. 1990. *An Age in Motion. Popular Radicalism in Java, 1912–1926*. Ithaca & London: Cornell University Press.

Slama, Martin. 2014. "From Wali Songo to Wali Pitu: The Travelling of Islamic Saint Veneration to Bali", in Brigitta Hauser-Schäublin and David D. Harnish, eds, *Between Harmony and Discrimination: Negotiating Religious Identities within Majority-Minority Relationships in Bali and Lombok*. Leiden & Boston: Brill, pp. 112–43.

Smith, Jonathan Z. 1982. *Imagining Religion: From Babylon to Jonestown*. Chicago & London: The University of Chicago Press.

———. 1998. "Religion, Religions, Religious", in Mark C. Taylor, ed., *Critical Terms for Religious Studies*, Chicago & London: The University of Chicago Press, pp. 275–80.

Smith, Wilfred Cantwell. 1959. "Comparative Religion: Whither—and Why?", in Mircea Eliade and Joseph M. Kitagawa, eds, *The History of Religions: Essays in Methodology*. Chicago: The University of Chicago Press, pp. 31–58.

———. 1962. *The Meaning and End of Religion. A New Approach to the Religious Traditions of Mankind*. New York: The Macmillan Company.

Snouck Hurgronje, Christiaan. 1893. *De Atjèhers* [The Acehnese]. Batavia: Landsdrukkerij and Leiden: E.J. Brill.

Soebadio, Haryati. 1971. *Jñānasiddhânta. Secret Lore of the Balinese Śaiva Priest*. The Hague: Martinus Nijhoff.

———. 1985. *Cultural Policy in Indonesia*. Paris: Unesco.

Soegeriwa, I.G.B. 1938. "Agama", *Djatajoe* 3, 2: 70–99.

Soe Lie Piet. [n.d.]. *Pengoendjoekan Poelo Bali Atawa Gids Bali* [Bali Island Presentation or Bali Guide]. Malang: Paragon Press.

Sökefeld, Martin. 2001. "Reconsidering Identity", *Anthropos* 96, 2: 527–44.

Somvir, Yadav. 2004. "Cultural and Religous Interaction between Modern India and Indonesia", in Martin Ramstedt, ed., *Hinduism in Modern Indonesia. A Minority Religion between Local, National, and Global Interests*. London & New York: RoutledgeCurzon—IIAS Asian Studies Series, pp. 255–63.

Sontheimer, Günther-Dietz, and Hermann Kulke, eds. 2005 [1989]. *Hinduism Reconsidered*. New Delhi: Manohar.

Southwold, Martin. 1978. "Buddhism and the Definition of Religion", *Man* 13, 3: 362–79.

Spies, Walter. 1936. "Bericht über den zustand von Tanz und Musik in der Negara Gianjar" ["Report on the State of Dance and Music in the Negara Gianjar"], *Djawa* 16: 51–56 [with a synopsis from the editor, "Music and Dancing in Present Bali and more Specially in Gianjar": 58–59].

Spies, Walter, and Roelof Goris. 1937. "Overzicht van dans en tooneel in Bali" ["Overview of Dance and Theater in Bali"], *Djawa* 17: 205–29.

Spiro, Melford E. 1966. "Religion: Problems of Definition and Explanation", in Michael Banton, ed., *Anthropological Approaches to the Study of Religion*. London: Tavistock Publications, pp. 85-126.

Spruit, Ruud. 1995. *Artists on Bali*. Amsterdam & Kuala Lumpur: The Pepin Press.

Srinivas, Mysore Narasimhachar. 1952. *Religion and Society Among the Coorgs of South India*. Oxford: Clarendon Press.

Staal, J. Frits. 1963. "Sanskrit and Sanskritization", *The Journal of Asian Studies* 22, 3: 261–75.

———. 1995. *Mantras between Fire and Water. Reflections on a Balinese Rite*. Amsterdam: Koningklijke Nederlandse Akademie van Wetenschappen.

———. 1996 [1990]. "Religions", in *Ritual and Mantras. Rules without Meaning*. Delhi: Motilal Banarsidass, pp. 387–420.

———. 2008. *Discovering the Vedas. Origins, Mantras, Rituals, Insights*. New Delhi: Penguin Books.

Stange, Paul. 1986."'Legitimate' Mysticism in Indonesia", *Review of Indonesian and Malayan Affairs* 20, 2: 76–117.

———. 1990. "Javanism as Text or Praxis", *Anthropological Forum* 6, 2: 237–55.

Steenbrink, Karel. 1993. *Dutch Colonialism and Indonesian Islam. Contacts and Conflicts 1596–1950*. Amsterdam: Rodopi.

———. 2013. "Buddhism in Muslim Indonesia", *Studia Islamika* 20, 1: 1–34.

Steenbrink, Karel, and Jan Sihar Aritonang. 2008. "A Small Christian Flock in Bali", in Jan Sihar Aritonang and Karel Steenbrink, eds, *A History of Christianity in Indonesia*. Leiden: Brill, pp. 731–45.

Stephen, Michele. 2001. "Barong and Rangda in the Context of Balinese Religion", *Review of Indonesian and Malaysian Affairs* 35, 1: 137–93.

———. 2002. "Returning to Original Form. A Central Dynamic in Balinese Ritual", *Bijdragen tot de Taal-, Land- en Volkenkunde*, 158, 1: 61–94.

———. 2005. *Desire. Divine and Demonic. Balinese Mysticism in the Paintings of I Ketut Budiana and I Gusti Nyoman Mirdiana*. Honolulu: University of Hawai'i Press.

———. 2010. "The Yogic Art of Dying, Kuṇḍalinī Yoga, and the Balinese *pitra yadnya*", *Bijdragen tot de Taal-, Land- en Volkenkunde* 166, 4: 426–74.

———. 2014. "The *Dasaksara* and Yoga in Bali", *The Journal of Hindu Studies* 7: 179–216.

———. 2015. "*Sūrya-Sevana*: A Balinese Tantric Practice", *Archipel* 89: 95–124.

Stowell, John. 2011. *Walter Spies: A Life in Art*. Jakarta: Afterhours Books.

Strathern, Alan. 2019. *Unearthly Powers. Religious and Political Change in World History*. Cambridge: Cambridge University Press.

Stroumsa, Guy. 2010. *A New Science: The Discovery of Religion in the Age of Reason*. Cambridge, MA & London: Harvard University Press.

Stuart-Fox, David J. 1982. *Once a Century: Pura Besakih and the Eka Dasa Rudra Festival*. Jakarta: Sinar Harapan & Citra Indonesia.

———. 2002. *Pura Besakih. Temple, Religion and Society in Bali*. Leiden: KITLV Press.

Stutterheim, Willem F. 1929. *Oudheden van Bali* [Antiquities of Bali]. Singaradja: Bali Kirtya Liefrinck-Van der Tuuk.

——. 1932a. "Old and New Art in Bali", *Indian Arts and Letters* 6, 1: 1–9.

——. 1932b, *Indische cultuurgeschiedenis I: De Hindu's* [Indian Cultural History I: The Hindus]. Groningen-Batavia: J.B. Wolters' Uitgeversmaatschappij.

Suartika, Gusti Ayu Made. 2010. *Morphing Bali. The State, Planning, and Culture*. Saarbrücken: Lambert Academic Publishing.

Suaryana, I Nyoman. 1982. "Perkembangan Agama Hindu di Bali (1950–1971)" [The Development of the Hindu Religion in Bali (1950–1971)"], MA Thesis, Fakultas Sastra Universitas Udayana, Denpasar.

Suasta, Putu, and Linda H. Connor. 1999. "Democratic Mobilization and Political Authoritarianism: Tourism Development in Bali", in Raechelle Rubinstein and Linda H. Connor, eds, *Staying Local in the Global Village. Bali in the Twentieth Century*. Honolulu: University of Hawai'i Press, pp. 91–122.

Subagiasta, I Ketut. 2009. *Reformasi Agama Hindu Dalam Perubahan Sosial Di Bali 1950–1959* [Hindu Reform in Social Change in Bali 1950-1959]. Surabaya: Paramita.

Subagya, Rahmat. 1976. *Kepercayaan Kebatinan Kejiwaan Kerohanian dan Agama* [Spirituality and Religious Beliefs]. Yogyakarta: Kanisius.

Sudharta, Tjokorda Rai, and Ida Bagus Oka Punia Atmadja. 1967. *Upadeśa Tentang Adjaran-Adjaran Agama Hindu* [Upadeśa on the Teachings of the Hindu Religion]. Denpasar: Parisada Hindu Dharma.

Sudharta, Tjokorda Rai, and I Wayan Surpha. 2006. *Parisada Hindu Dharma dengan konsolidasinya* [Parisada Hindu Dharma with its Consolidation]. Surabaya: Paramita.

Sugirtharajah, Sharada. 2003. *Imagining Hinduism. A Postcolonial Perspective*. London & New York: Routledge.

Sugriwa, I Gusti Bagus. 1953a. "Mungkinkah: Negara Indonesia Mendjadi Islam?" ["Could it Be: Indonesia Becomes Islamic?"], *Bhakti* 2, 5: 5–6; 2, 6: 4.

——. 1953b. "Pantja Sila dan Negara Islam" ["Pantja Sila and the Islamic State"], *Damai* 1, 2: 1–7.

——. 1953c. "Çiwa-Buddha, Bhinneka Tunggal Ika" ["Çiwa-Buddha, Unity in Diversity"], *Indonesia* 4, 12: 733–46.

——. 1954. "Tjeramah Agama terhadap rombongan mahasiswa pada tgl. 19 Oktober 1953 dibalai masjarakat Denpasar" [Religious lecture to a group of students, October 19, 1953 at the Denpasar community hall"], *Bahasa dan Budaja* 2, 6: 40–45.

——. 1955. "Konstituante" [The Constituent Assembly], *Damai* 3, 12: 3.

——. 1968. *Sedjarah dan Falsafah Agama Hindu Bali, Djilid 1* [History and Philosophy of the Balinese Hindu Religion, Volume 1]. Denpasar: Pustaka Balimas.

———. 1973. *Riwayat hidup I Gusti Bagus Sugriwa sebagaimana disampaikan kepada Ida Bagus Gede Agastia* [Life History of I Gusti Bagus Sugriwa as Told to Ida Bagus Gede Agastia]. Denpasar: Yayasan Dharma Sastra.

Sujana, Nyoman Naya. 1988. "Orang Bali Semakin Kehilangan Kebaliannya" ["The Balinese are Increasingly Losing their Balinese-ness"], *Bali Post* December 3, 1988, p. 7.

Sukahet, Ida Pangelingsir Agung Putra. 2016. *Hindu Bali. Menjawab Masalah Aktual* [Hindu Bali. Answering Current Problems]. Denpasar: Wisnu Press.

Sukarniti, Ni Luh Ketut. 1985. *Perkembangan Parindra di Bali 1938–1942* [The Development of Parindra in Bali 1938-1942]. Denpasar: Fakultas Sastra Universitas Udayana.

Sukarsa, K. Kebek. 1972. *Beberapa Titik-titik Pemikiran Untuk Dipersembahkan Kepada Musjawarah Tjendikiawan/Sardjana Hindu-Dharma (Indonesia) Seluruh Indonesia* [Some Points of Thought to be Presented to the Deliberation of Hindu-Dharma Intellectuals/Scholars (Indonesia) Throughout Indonesia]. Denpasar.

Sullivan, Gerald. 1999. *Margaret Mead, Gregory Bateson, and Highland Bali. Fieldwork Photographs of Bayung Gedé, 1936–1939*. Chicago: The University of Chicago Press.

Sumartana, Th. 1991. *Mission at the Crossroads. Indigenous Churches, European Missionaries, Islamic Association and Socio-Religious Change in Java 1812–1936*. Jakarta: BPK Gunung Mulia.

Sunjayadi, Achmad. 2019. *Pariwisata di Hindia Belanda (1891–1942)* [Tourism in the Dutch East Indies (1891–1942)]. Jakarta: Kepustakaan Populer Gramedia & École française d'Extrême-Orient.

Supartha, I Wayan, ed. 1994. *Memahami Aliran Kepercayaan* [Understanding Belief Currents]. Denpasar: Penerbit BP.

———, ed. 1998. *Baliku Tersayang. Baliku Malang* [My Dear Bali: My Unfortunate Bali]. Denpasar: Pustaka Bali Post.

Supartha, I Wayan, Ketut Nadha and Gde Sudibya, 1995. *Dharma Agama dan Dharma Negara* [State Dharma and Religious Dharma]. Denpasar: Penerbit BP.

Surpha, I Wayan. 1986. *Eksistensi Desa Adat di Bali dengan Diundangkannya Undang-undang N°5 Th. 1979 (Tentang Pemerintahan Desa)* [The Existence of Customary Villages in Bali with the Promulgation of Law N°5 1979 (on Village Government). Denpasar.

———. 2002. *Seputar Desa Pakraman dan Adat* [About Customary Villages and Customs]. Denpasar: Penerbit BP.

Surpi Aryadharma, Ni Kadek. 2011. *Membedah Kasus Konversi Agama di Bali* [Analyzing Religious Conversion Cases in Bali]. Surabaya: Paramita.

Suryani, Luh Ketut, and Gordon D. Jensen. 1993. *Trance and Possession in Bali. A Window on Western Multiple Personality, Possession Disorder, and Suicide*. Kuala Lumpur: Oxford University Press.

Suryawan, I Ngurah. 2004. "'Ajeg Bali' dan Lahirnya 'Jago-jago' Kebudayaan" ["'Ajeg Bali' and the Birth of Cultural 'Champions'"], *Kompas* January 7, 2004.

———. 2009. *Bali Pascakolonial. Jejak Kekerasan dan Sikap Kajian Budaya* [Postcolonial Bali. Traces of Violence and the Attitude of Cultural Studies].Yogyakarta: Kepel Press.

Sutherland, Heather. 1968. "Pudjangga Baru: Aspects of Indonesian Intellectual Life in the 1930s", *Indonesia* 6: 106–27.

Sutrisna, S. 1954. "Agama adalah soal kepertjajaan, bukan soal pengakuan" ["Religion is a Matter of Belief, not a Matter of Recognition"], *Bhakti* 3, 9: 6–7.

Suyasa, I Made Wedastera. 1952. "Agama Hindu Bali Terantjam" [The Balinese Hindu Religion is under Threat"], *Bhakti* 1, 6: 10–11, 19.

———. 1956. *Menjambut Konstituante Republik Indonesia* [Welcoming the Constituent Assembly of the Republic of Indonesia]. Djakarta: D.P. Gerakan Kumara Bhavana.

———. 1957a. *Surat kepada Presiden dan Perdana Menteri RI. Perihal: Wakil Umat Hindu-Bali dalam Dewan Nasional* [Letter to the President and Prime Minister of Indonesia. Subject: Representation of Balinese Hindus in the National Council]. Djakarta, April 27, 1957.

———. 1957b. *Konperensi-V Angkatan Muda Hindu-Bali* [Fifth Conference of the Angkatan Muda Hindu-Bali]. Denpasar.

———. 1957c. *Presidium Konperensi Angkatan Muda Hindu-Bali* [Presidium of the Angkatan Muda Hindu-Bali]. Denpasar.

———. 1958. *Gerakan Aksi-Bersama menuntut 'Bagian Hindu-Bali' dalam Kementerian Agama Republik Indonesia* [Joint Action Movement Demanding a 'Hindu-Bali Section' within the Ministry of Religion of the Republic of Indonesia]. Denpasar.

Sweeney, Amin. 1987. *A Full Hearing. Orality and Literacy in the Malay World*. Berkeley & Los Angeles: University of California Press.

Sweetman, Will. 2003. *Mapping Hinduism. 'Hinduism' and the Study of Indian Religions, 1600–1776*. Halle: Franckesche Stiftungen.

Swellengrebel, Jan Lodewijk. 1948. *Kerk en Tempel op Bali* [Church and Temple in Bali]. 'S-Gravenhage: W. van Hoeve.

———. 1960. "Introduction", in Jan Lodewijk Swellengrebel, ed., *Bali: Studies in Life, Thought, and Ritual*. The Hague: W. van Hoeve, pp. 1–76.

———. 1966. "In Memoriam Dr. Roelof Goris", *Bijdragen tot de Taal-, Land- en Volkenkunde* 122, 2: 205–28.

Tagore, Rabindranath. 1928. "Letters from Java", *The Visva-Bharati Quarterly* 5, 4: 323-38; 6, 1: 1–13.

Tarot, Camille. 2008. *Le symbolique et le sacré. Théories de la religion* [The Symbolic and the Sacred. Theories of Religion]. Paris: Éditions La Découverte.

Taylor, Paul Michael. 1994. "The *Nusantara* Concept of Culture: Local Traditions and National Identity as Expressed in Indonesia's Museums", in Paul Michael Taylor, ed., *Fragile Traditions. Indonesian Art in Jeopardy*. Honolulu: University of Hawaii Press, pp. 71–90.

Tedlock, Dennis. 1987. "Questions concerning Dialogical Anthropology", *Journal of Anthropological Research* 43, 4: 325–37.
Te Flierhaar, Hendrik. 1941. "De aanpassing van het inlandsch onderwijs op Bali aan de eigen sfeer" ["The Adaptation of Native Education in Bali to its own Atmosphere"], *Koloniale Studiën* 25: 135–59.
Tenzer, Michael. 2000. *Gamelan Gong Kebyar. The Art of Twentieth-Century Balinese Music*. Chicago: The University of Chicago Press.
Thangaraj, M. Thomas. 1999. "The Bible as *Veda*: Biblical Hermeneutics in Tamil Christianity", in R.S. Sugirtharajah, ed., *Vernacular Hermeneutics*. Sheffield: Sheffield Academic Press, pp. 133–43.
Thapar, Romila. 1989. "Imagined Religious Communities? Ancient History and the Modern Search for a Hindu Identity", *Modern Asian Studies* 23, 2: 209–31.
———. 2000 [1989]. "Syndicated Hinduism", in Günther-Dietz Sontheimer and Hermann Kulke, eds, *Hinduism Reconsidered*. New Delhi: Manohar, pp. 54–81.
Thomas, Nicholas. 1994. *Colonialism's Culture. Anthropology, Travel and Government*. Princeton: Princeton University Press.
Tiliander, Bror. 1974. *Christian and Hindu Terminology: A Study of Their Mutual Relations with Special Reference to the Tamil Area*. Uppsala: Almqvist & Wiksell Tryckeri.
Tillich, Paul. 1969. *What Is Religion?* New York: Harper & Row.
Tim Peneliti WHP/WHC. 2015. *Konsep dan Praktik Agama Hindu di Bali* [Concepts and Practices of Hindu Religion in Bali]. Surabaya: World Hindu Parisad & Paramita.
Titib, I Made. 1991. *Pedoman Upacara Śuddhi Wadāni* [Śuddhi Wadāni Ceremony Guidelines]. Denpasar: Upada Sastra.
———. 1997. *Pedoman Sembahyang dan Tirthayatra bagi Umat Hindu* [Guidelines for Worship and Tirthayatra for Hindus]. Denpasar: Upada Sastra.
———, ed. 2005. *Dialog Ajeg Bali* [Ajeg Bali Dialogue]. Paramita: Surabaya.
Tollenaere, Herman A.O. de. 1996. *The Politics of Divine Wisdom. Theosophy and Labour, National, and Women's Movements in Indonesia and South Asia, 1875–1947*. Nijmegen: Uitgeverij Katholieke Universiteit Nijmegen.
Tonkinson, Robert. 1993. "Understanding 'Tradition' – Ten Years On", *Anthropological Forum* 6, 4: 597–606.
Travellers Official Information Bureau. 1935. *Bali, The Eastern Paradise*. Batavia: The Travellers Official Information Bureau of the Netherlands Indies.
Tsuchiya, Kenji. 1987. *Democracy and Leadership. The Rise of the Taman Siswa Movement in Indonesia*. Honolulu: University of Hawaii Press.
Turner, Alicia. 2014. *Saving Buddhism: The Impermanence of Religion in Colonial Burma*. Honolulu: University of Hawai'i Press.
Tylor, Edward Burnett. 1871. *Primitive Culture: Researches into the Development of Mythology, Philosophy, Religion, Art, and Custom*. London: J. Murray.
Ubbens, Jop, and Cathinka Huizing. 1995. *Adrien Jean Le Mayeur de Merprès. Painter-Traveller / Schilder-Reiziger*. Wijk en Aalburg: Pictures Publishers.

Umeda, Hideharu. 2005. "Cultural Policy on Balinese Performing Arts: The First Decade of LISTIBIYA", *Senri Ethnological Reports* 65: 43–59.
UNDP/World Bank. 2003. *Bali, Beyond the Tragedy. Impact and Challenges for Tourism-led Development in Indonesia.* Jakarta: UNDP/USAID/The World Bank.
Urry, John. 1990. *The Tourist Gaze.* London: Sage Publications.
Van Bruinessen, Martin. 2002. "Genealogies of Islamic Radicalism in Post-Suharto Indonesia", *South East Asia Research* 10, 2: 117–54.
Vandenberg, Andrew, and Nazrina Zuryani, eds. 2021. *Security, Democracy, and Society in Bali. Trouble with Protection.* Singapore: Palgrave Macmillan.
Van den Boogert, Jochem. 2015. "Rethinking Javanese Islam. Towards new Descriptions of Javanese Traditions", PhD Dissertation, Leiden University, Leiden.
Vandenbosch, Amry. 1934. "Missions on the Island of Bali", *International Review of Missions* 23: 205–14.
Van der Kop, G.G. 1924. "Lights and Shadows on Bali and the Balinese", *Inter-Ocean* 5, 10: 645–9, 681.
Van der Kroef, Justus M. 1953. "Conflicts of Religious Policy in Indonesia", *Far Eastern Survey* 22, 10: 121–5.
Van der Meeberg, Mel. 1946. "Balinese Await Restoration of Dutch Authority", *Knickerbocker Weekly* 6, 4: 9.
Van der Meer, Arnout. 2020. *Performing Power. Cultural Hegemony, Identity, and Resistance in Colonial Indonesia.* Ithaca & London: Cornell University Press.
Van der Tuuk, Herman Neubronner. 1881. "Notes on the Kawi Language and Literature", *Journal of the Royal Asiatic Society. New Series* xiii: 42–58.
Van der Veer, Peter. 2014. *The Modern Spirit of Asia. The Spiritual and the Secular in China and India.* Princeton & Oxford: Princeton University Press.
Van Hoëvell, Wolter Robert Baron. 1846. *Nederland en Bali. Eene stem uit Indië tot het Nederlandsche volk* [The Netherlands and Bali. A Voice from the Indies to the Dutch People]. Groningen.
———. 1848. "Recent Scientific Researches on the Islands of Bali and Lombok", *The Journal of the Indian Archipelago and Eastern Asia* 2: 151–9.
Van Leur, Jacob Cornelis. 1955. *Indonesian Trade and Society. Essays in Asian Social and Economic History.* The Hague: W. van Hoeve.
Van Niel, Robert. 1984 [1960]. *The Emergence of the Modern Indonesian Elite.* Dordrecht: Foris Publications
Van Vollenhoven, Cornelis. 1928. *De Ontdekking van het Adatrecht* [The Discovery of Customary Law]. Leiden: Brill.
Vermeulen, Hans, and Cora Govers. 1997. "From Political Mobilization to the Politics of Consciousness", in Cora Govers and Hans Vermeulen, eds, *The Politics of Ethnic Consciousness.* London: MacMillan Press, pp. 1–30.
Vickers, Adrian, 1987. "Hinduism and Islam in Indonesia: Bali and the Pasisir World", *Indonesia* 44: 31–58.

———, ed. 1994. *Travelling to Bali. Four Hundred Years of Journeys*. Kuala Lumpur: Oxford University Press.

———. 1996. "Modernity and Being *Moderen*: An Introduction", in Adrian Vickers, ed., *Being Modern in Bali. Image and Change*, New Haven: Yale University Southeast Asia Studies, pp.1–36.

———. 1998. "Reopening Old Wounds: Bali and the Indonesian Killings. A Review Article", *The Journal of Asian Studies* 57, 3: 774–85.

———. 2000. "I Nengah Metra 1902–1946: Thoughts on the Biography of a Modern Balinese", in Adrian Vickers and I Nyoman Darma Putra with Michele Ford, eds, *To Change Bali. Essays In Honour of I Gusti Ngurah Bagus*. Denpasar: Bali Post and University of Wollongong, Institute of Social Change and Critical Inquiry, pp. 89–112.

———. 2002. "Bali Merdeka? Internal Migration, Tourism and Hindu Revivalism", in Minako Sakai, ed., *Beyond Jakarta. Regional Autonomy and Local Society in Indonesia*. Adelaide: Crawford House, pp. 80–101.

———. 2003. "Being Modern in Bali after Suharto", in Thomas A. Reuter, ed., *Inequality, Crisis and Social Change in Indonesia. The Muted Worlds of Bali*. London & New York: RoutledgeCurzon, pp. 17–29.

———. 2009. "When Did *legong* Start? A Reply to Stephen Davies", *Bijdragen tot de Taal-, Land- en Volkenkunde*, 165, 1: 1–7.

———. 2011. "Bali Rebuilds its Tourist Industry", *Bijdragen tot de Taal-, Land- en Volkenkunde*, 167, 4: 459–81.

———. 2012a [1989]. *Bali: A Paradise Created*. Singapore: Tuttle Publishing.

———. 2012b. *Balinese Art. Paintings and Drawings of Bali, 1800–2010*. Singapore: Tuttle Publishing.

Vignato, Silvia. 2000. *Au nom de l'hindouisme. Reconfigurations ethniques chez les Tamouls et les Karo en Indonésie* [In the Name of Hinduism. Ethnic Reconfigurations among Tamils and Karos in Indonesia]. Paris: L'Harmattan.

Vira, Raghu. 1978. *India and Asia. A Cultural Symphony: A Collection of Some Notes, Articles, Poems, and Letters of the Late Prof. Dr. Raghuvira Published Posthumously on his 75th Birth Anniversary*. New Delhi: International Academy of Indian Culture.

Volkman, Toby Alice. 1984. "Great Performances: Toraja Cultural Identity in the 1970s", *American Ethnologist* 11, 1: 152–69.

Voloshinov, Valentin Nicolaevich. 1973. *Marxism and the Philosophy of Language*. Cambridge, MA: Harvard University Press.

Von Benda-Beckmann, Franz, and Keebet Von Benda-Beckmann. 1988. "*Adat* and Religion in Minangkabau and Ambon", in Henri J.M. Claessen and David S. Moyer, eds, *Time Past, Time Present, Time Future. Perspectives on Indonesian Culture. Essays in Honour of Prof. P.E. De Josselin De Jong*. Dordrecht: Foris Publications, pp.195–212.

———. 2011. "Myths and Stereotypes about Adat Law. A Reassessment of Van Vollenhoven in the Light of Current Struggles over Adat Law in Indonesia", *Bijdragen tot de Taal-, Land- en Volkenkunde* 167, 2–3: 167–95.
Von Stietencron, Heinrich. 1997. *Hindu Religious Traditions and the Concept of 'Religion'*. 1996 Gonda Lecture. Amsterdam: Royal Nethelands Academy of Arts and Sciences.
———. 2005 [1989]. "Hinduism: On the Proper Use of a Deceptive Term", in Günther-Dietz Sontheimer and Hermann Kulke, eds, *Hinduism Reconsidered*. New Delhi: Manohar, pp. 32-53.
Wagner, Roy. 1981. *The Invention of Culture*. Chicago & London: The University of Chicago Press.
Walker, Edward W. 2003. "Islam, Islamism and Political Order in Central Asia", *Journal of International Affairs* 56, 2: 21–41.
Wardana, Agung. 2019. *Contemporary Bali. Contested Space and Governance*. Singapore: Palgrave Macmillan.
Warna, Wayan et al. 1990. *Kamus Bali-Indonesia* [Balinese–Indonesian Dictionary]. Denpasar: Dinas Pendidikan Dasar Propinsi Dati I Bali.
Warren, Carol. 1990. *The Bureaucratisation of Local Government in Indonesia: The Impact of the Village Government Law (UU N°5 1979) in Bali*. Clayton: Monash University, Working Paper 66.
———. 1993. Adat *and* Dinas. *Balinese Communities in the Indonesian State*. Kuala Lumpur: Oxford University Press.
———. 1998a. "Tanah Lot: The Cultural and Environmental Politics of Resort Development in Bali", in Philip Hirsch and Carol Warren, eds, *The Politics of Environment in Southeast Asia*. London & New York: Routledge, pp. 229–61.
———. 1998b. "Symbols and Displacement. The Emergence of Environmental Activism on Bali", in Arne Kalland and Gerard Persoon, eds, *Environmental Movements in Asia*. Richmond: Curzon, pp. 179–204.
———. 2000. "*Adat* and the Discourses of Modernity in Bali", in Adrian Vickers and I Nyoman Darma Putra with Michele Ford, eds, *To Change Bali. Essays In Honour of I Gusti Ngurah Bagus*. Denpasar: Bali Post and University of Wollongong, Institute of Social Change and Critical Inquiry, pp. 1–14.
———. 2007. "*Adat* in Balinese Discourse and Practice. Locating Citizenship and the Commonweal", in Jamie S. Davidson and David Henley, eds, *The Revival of Tradition in Indonesian Politics. The Deployment of Adat from Colonialism to Indigenism*. London & New York: Routledge, pp. 170–202.
Wedakarna, Anak Agung Ngurah Arya. 2002. "Mempertanyakan aksi 'Bali for The World'" ["Questioning the 'Bali for The World' Action"], *Bali Post* December 22, 2002.
Weinstock, Joseph A. 1987. "Kaharingan: Life and Death in Southern Borneo", in Rita Smith Kipp and Susan Rodgers, eds, *Indonesian Religions in Transition*. Tucson: The University of Arizona Press, pp. 71–97.

Weiss, Richard S. 2019. *The Emergence of Modern Hinduism. Religion on the Margins of Colonialism*. Oakland: University of California Press.

Wheatley, Paul. 1982. "Presidential Address: India Beyond the Ganges – Desultory Reflections on the Origins of Civilization in Southeast Asia", *The Journal of Asian Studies* 42, 1: 13–28.

Whittier, Herbert L. 1978. "Concepts of *adat* and Cosmology among the Kenyah Dayak of Borneo: Coping with the Changing Socio-cultural Milieu", *The Sarawak Museum Journal* 26, 47: 103–13.

Wiana, Ketut. 2006. *Memahami Perbedaan Catur Varna, Kasta dan Wangsa* [Understanding the Difference between Varna, Caste and Wangsa]. Surabaya: Paramita.

Wiana, Ketut, and Raka Santeri. 1993. *Kasta dalam Hindu. Kesalahpahaman Berabad-abad* [Caste in Hinduism. Centuries of Misunderstanding]. Denpasar: Yayasan Dharma Naradha.

Widia, I Ketut. 2010. *Pecalang Benteng Terakhir Bali* [Pecalang, Bali's Last Bastion] Surabaya: Paramita.

Wiebe, Dustin. 2014. "Performing Christian *Kebalian*: Balinese Music and Dance as Interreligious Drama", in Brigitta Hauser-Schäublin and David D. Harnish, eds, *Between Harmony and Discrimination: Negotiating Religious Identities within Majority-Minority Relationships in Bali and Lombok*. Leiden & Boston: Brill, pp. 221–43.

Wiener, Margaret J. [n.d.], [1990]. "Kings or Committees: Changing Ritual Hegemonies in Bali", unpublished paper.

———. 1994. "Object Lessons: Dutch Colonialism and the Looting of Bali", *History and Anthropology* 6, 4: 347–70.

———. 1995. *Visible and Invisible Realms. Power, Magic, and Colonial Conquest in Bali*. Chicago: The University of Chicago Press.

Wijaya, I Nyoman. 1990. *Dari Agama Bali Menuju Hindu Dharma: Studi Tentang Konflik Sosial di Bali 1913–1959* [From Balinese Religion to Hindu Dharma: A Study of Social Conflict in Bali 1913-1959]. Denpasar: Fakultas Sastra Universitas Udayana.

———. 2004. "Melawan Ajeg Bali: Antara Eksklusivitas dan Komersialisasi" ["Against Ajeg Bali: Between Exclusivity and Commercialization"], *Tantular. Jurnal Ilmu Sejarah* 2: 158–78.

———. 2007. "Mencintai Diri Sendiri: Memutar Gerakan Ajeg Bali Ke Masa Lampau 1910–2002" ["Loving Oneself: Turning the Ajeg Bali Movement Back in Time 1910-2002"], MA Thesis, Program Studi Sejarah, Universitas Gajah Mada, Yogyakarta.

———. 2009. "Mencintai Diri Sendiri: Gerakan Ajeg Bali dalam Sejarah Kebudayaan Bali 1910–2007" ["Loving Oneself: The Ajeg Bali Movement in Balinese Cultural History 1910-2007"], PhD Dissertation, Program Pascasarjana Fakultas Ilmu Budaya, Universitas Gajah Mada, Yogyakarta.

———. 2012. *Merayap di Akar Rumput. Sejarah Kelompok Minoritas Kreatif Membangun Gereja Kristen Protestan di Bali 1931–2011* [Creeping at the Grassroots. History of Creative Minority Groups Building Protestant Christian Churches in Bali 1931–2011]. Denpasar: Yayasan Samaritan and Yogyakarta: Pustaka Pelajar.

Wijaya, I Nyoman, Putra, I Nyoman Darma, and Adrian Vickers. 2021. "The Social Realist Stories of Putu Shanty as Historical Record. Balinese Culture and Indonesian National Politics in the 1950s", *Bijdragen tot de Taal-, Land- en Volkenkunde* 177, 2–3: 265–89.

Williams, Adriana, and Yu-Chee Chong. 2005. *Covarrubias in Bali*. Singapore: Éditions Didier Millet.

Wirawan, I Made Adi. 2011. *Tri Hita Karana: Kajian Teologi, Sosiologi dan Ekologi Menurut Veda* [The Three Sources of Well-Being: A Study of Theology, Sociology and Ecology According to the Vedas]. Surabaya: Paramita.

Wirjasutha, I Goesti Njoman Mas. [n.d.], [1939]. *Tjatoer Wangse di Bali* [The Four Peoples in Bali].

Wiryatnaya, Usadi. 1995. "Bali Dalam Pandangan Orang Kristen Bali" ["Bali in the View of Balinese Christians"], in Usadi Wiryatnaya and Jean Couteau, eds, *Bali di Persimpangan Jalan. Sebuah Bunga Rampai*, vol. 2. Denpasar: NusaData IndoBudaya, pp. 134–63.

Wolters, Oliver W. 1999 [1982]. *History, Culture, and Region in Southeast Asian Perspectives*. Ithaca: Southeast Asia Program Publications, Cornell University and Singapore: The Institute of Southeast Asian Studies.

Woodward, Mark R. 1989. *Islam in Java: Normative Piety and Mysticism in the Sultanate of Yogyakarta*. Tucson: University of Arizona Press.

Yamashita, Shinji. 1999. "Review of Michel Picard, *Bali. Cultural Tourism and Touristic Culture*, Singapore, Archipelago Press, 1996", *Indonesia* 67: 177–82.

———. 2003. *Bali and Beyond. Explorations in the Anthropology of Tourism*. New York & Oxford: Berghahn Books.

Yamashita, Shinji, J.S. Eades, and Kadir H. Din. 1997. "Introduction: Tourism and Cultural Development in Asia and Oceania", in Shinji Yamashita, Kadir H. Din and J.S. Eades, eds, *Tourism and Cultural Development in Asia and Oceania*. Bangi: Penerbit Universiti Kebangsaan Malaysia, pp. 13–31.

Yampolsky, Philip. 1995. "Forces for Change in the Regional Performing Arts of Indonesia", *Bijdragen tot de Taal-, Land- en Volkenkunde* 151, 4: 700–25.

Yates, Helen Eva. [n.d.], [1930]. *Bali. The Enchanted Isle*. Weltevreden: K.P.M.

———. 1933. *Bali: Enchanted Isle. A Travel Book*. London: George Allen & Unwin.

Young, Richard Fox. 1981. *Resistant Hinduism. Sanskrit Sources on Anti-Christian Apologetics in Early Nineteenth-Century India*. Vienna: De Nobili Research Foundation.

Zoetmulder, Petrus Josephus. 1974. *Kalangwan: A Survey of Old Javanese Literature*. The Hague: Martinus Nijhoff.

———. 1982. *Old Javanese—English Dictionary*. 's- Gravenhage: Martinus Nijhoff.
Zuhri, H. 2022. "Beyond Syncretism. Evidence of the Vernacularization of Islamic Theological Terms in Javanese Literature in the 19th Century", *Al-Jāmi'ah: Journal of Islamic Studies* 60, 2: 373–98.
Zuhri, Syaifudin. 2022. *Wali Pitu and Muslim Pilgrimage in Bali, Indonesia. Inventing a Sacred Tradition*. Leiden: Leiden University Press.
Zurbuchen, Mary Sabina. 1990. "Images of Culture and National Development in Indonesia: *The Cockroach Opera*", *Asian Theatre Journal* 7, 2: 127–50.

Balinese Periodicals
Aditya (1993–95)
Bali Adnjana (1924–30)
Bali Post (1971–)
Bhakti (1952–54)
Bhāwanāgara (1930–35)
Damai (1953–56)
Djatajoe (1936–41)
Media Hindu (2004–)
Raditya (1995–)
Sarad (2000–10)
Suara Indonesia (1948–66)
Surya Kanta (1925–27)
Warta Hindu Dharma (1967–)

Index

abangan, 17, 163, 167–8, 205, 218–9
acara, 11, 13, 83
adat, 1, 3–4, 6, 8–9, 27, 56, 58–9, 73, 79–94, 96, 98, 102, 137, 142, 149, 151, 155, 161–2, 166, 168, 171–2, 175, 189, 220, 222–4, 228, 230, 238, 240, 247–8, 253–5, 260, 264–72, 282–3, 287, 293, 302, 312, 326, 330–3, 337–40, 343
   adat istiadat, 85, 331
   adat keagamaan, 247
   adat kebiasaan, 83, 247
   adatrecht, 59, 84, 95, 104, 162
agama, 1, 3–4, 6, 8–9, 12, 23, 26–7, 33, 46, 73, 80–90, 93, 99, 103–5, 138, 149–52, 156, 162–3, 166–9, 172, 180–1, 187, 190, 194, 200, 204, 212, 214–5, 218–20, 222, 224–5, 229, 241–2, 246, 248–9, 255–6, 271, 283, 288, 291, 294, 312–3, 318, 331–4, 341, 344–5
   āgama, 80, 211
   Agama, 49, 58, 67, 73, 82, 86, 100
   agama adat, 247
   agama Bali, 10, 89, 137, 149, 151, 161, 183, 187, 206, 308, 333
   agama Bali Hindu, 87, 89–91, 151, 176
   agama Buda, 34–5, 46, 72, 89–90, 151, 220
   agama bumi, 231
   agama Hindu, 10, 15–6, 27, 89–90, 137, 142, 151, 161, 173, 175, 177, 181, 195, 198, 205–8, 210–3, 215–6, 219–21, 224–35, 238, 240–1, 283, 293, 296, 298, 300, 302, 304, 306–10, 313–4, 317–8, 320, 325–7, 335–9, 341–3
   agama Hindu Bali, 87, 89–91, 151, 169, 173–8, 180, 186–96, 198, 200, 202–6, 225, 227, 234, 305, 307–13, 326, 333–5, 339–40, 343
   agama Islam, 175
   agama Katolik Roma, 166
   agama Khonghucu, 213, 289
   agama Kristen Protestan, 166
   agama leluhur, 311
   agama Nasrani, 166
   agama samawi, 168
   agama Siwa, 45–6, 89–90, 151, 172–3
   agama Siwa–Buda, 89–90, 151, 172–3, 187
   agama suku, 166, 168, 214
   agama Tirta, 89–90, 142, 151, 173, 178
   agama Trimurti, 89, 151, 175
   agama wahyu, 232
Agastia, Ida Bagus Gede, 238, 309
Agni Hotra, 238, 302, 337
Agung, Ide Anak Agung Gde Agung, 171, 234
aja wera, 88, 152, 176, 201
Ajeg Bali, 277–83, 310, 340–1
Akademi Seni Tari Indonesia (ASTI), 257
Alangkahi Karang Hulu, 74, 175
Aliansi Masyarakat Adat Nusantara (AMAN), 266

Index

Anandakusuma, Sri Reshi, 85, 175, 195–6, 200, 205–6, 212, 223–4
Angkatan Muda Hindu–Bali (AMHB), 173, 194
Angkatan Muda Hindu Indonesia (AMHI), 221
art (*seni, kesenian*), 102, 104, 115, 186, 245–6, 248, 254–7, 332
Arya Samaj, 14, 182, 184–5, 207, 225, 238, 301, 322
Asu Pundung, 74, 175
autonomy
  regional autonomy (*otonomi daerah*), 266, 269, 271–3, 279, 292, 309, 339
  special autonomy (*otonomi khusus*), 272–3, 319

Badan Koordinator Usaha Pelajar (BKUP), 173, 194
Badan Penyelidik Usaha–usaha Persiapan Kemerdekaan Indonesia (BPUPKI), 164
Bagus, I Gusti Ngurah, 232, 234, 282, 296
Bali Adnjana, 64–5, 68–72, 75–80, 88–95, 100–3, 134–5, 138, 152, 157–8, 177, 282, 305, 312
Bali Arts Festival (*Pesta Kesenian Bali*), 258
Bali Darma Laksana (BDL), 129–37, 149, 151–2, 155–61, 171, 178, 188, 198, 311
Bali Museum, 99, 119, 205
Bali Nirwana Resort (BNR), 233, 261, 287, 303
Balinese–ness (*Kebalian*), 3, 5, 7, 9, 78, 81, 253, 272–4, 278–81, 283, 328, 331, 333, 341
Bali Post, 186, 253, 261, 264, 269, 272, 278–9, 284, 287
Balisch Studiefonds, 131
Baliseering, 62–3, 136–7, 171, 282
bangsa, 73, 80, 94, 102–3, 158, 163, 330

banjar, 66, 74, 208, 224
banten, 207, 309–10
Barong, 117–8, 121
batara, 34, 148, 179, 188, 209–10, 310–1
Bateson, Gregory, 120–1, 128
Baum, Vicki, 56, 112, 115
Belo, Jane, 115–6, 120–2, 128
Bendesa, 59
Benoa Bay reclamation project, 284–9
Beratha, I Dewa Made, 238, 269, 279, 299, 321
Bhadra, I Wayan, 98, 131, 133, 149, 176–8, 181–2, 184, 187–8, 193–4, 226
bhakti, 23, 42, 229, 240
Bhakti, 187, 189, 191, 193
Bhāwanāgara, 98–108, 116, 129–31, 134–5, 138, 145, 153, 255
bhisama, 233, 236, 287–8, 296, 298, 302–3
Bonnet, Rudolph, 62, 119
Bosch, Frederik David Kan, 31, 141–2, 145
Brahma, 91, 119, 155–6, 184, 212–3, 312
Brahmans, 46–7
Brahmanism, Brahmanization, 11, 13, 32–3, 37, 240
brahmana, 11, 31, 37, 40–1, 45, 49–51, 53, 57–8, 69, 74–7, 90, 94, 104, 134, 143–4, 173, 181–2, 198–9, 201, 223–4, 226, 234, 237–8, 242, 296–7, 300, 302, 306, 312–3, 328, 338–40
Brahmo Samaj, 14, 53
Buddhism, 12, 24, 33–6, 50–1, 90, 105, 120, 125, 151–2, 175, 188–9, 192, 194, 207, 214, 219, 222, 232, 293
Budi Utomo, 67, 71–2, 151, 158, 168

caste (*kasta*), 11, 32, 40, 47, 49, 58–9, 61, 63, 74–7, 88, 92, 102, 113, 134, 143, 174, 177, 184, 193, 226, 232, 237, 313
  caste conflict (*pertentangan kasta*), 69–70, 312

Christianity, 8–10, 12–7, 20–6, 44, 50, 56, 79, 81–2, 84–90, 123, 125, 133, 138–51, 153, 155–6, 162–9, 175, 178, 185–8, 190–3, 201–2, 204, 207, 211, 221–2, 225–6, 230–3, 248, 271, 283–4, 292, 297, 304–5, 313, 315–9, 324, 329–37, 341–2, 344–5
Colonial Exposition, 107, 109, 117
colonialism, 3, 5–10, 12, 14–7, 20, 22–5, 29–30, 37, 39, 45–6, 48–74, 80–1, 84–7, 92–8, 100, 102, 108–10, 112, 115, 122–3, 127, 129–45, 148–9, 153, 156–63, 167–8, 170–1, 173, 215–6, 232, 237, 243–4, 255, 267–9, 272, 328–30, 332–3, 339
Confucianism, 24, 214, 218, 290, 292
Covarrubias, Miguel, 39, 78, 111–5, 120, 126, 128, 138, 146–7, 209
Crawfurd, John, 39, 46–7, 49–51, 87, 189
cremation (*ngaben*), 49, 73, 94, 109, 112, 147–8, 184, 189, 193, 204–5, 208, 245, 261
culture (*budaya, kebudayaan*), 3–4, 6, 8–9, 103, 223, 227, 256, 278, 318, 333
   Balinese culture (*kebudayaan Bali*), 245, 252, 278–279, 283
   cultural arts (*seni budaya*), 255–6
   cultural capital (*modal budaya*), 252
   cultural diplomacy (*diplomasi kebudayaan*), 181, 257
   cultural heritage (*warisan budaya*), 252, 255
   cultural peaks (*puncak–puncak kebudayaan*), 256
   cultural pollution (*polusi kebudayaan*), 245, 251
   cultural preservation (*pelestarian budaya*), 280
   cultural renaissance (*renaissance budaya*), 251
   regional culture (*kebudayaan daerah*), 255–6
   polemic on culture (*polemik kebudayaan*), 71

dadia, 66, 205, 211
Damai, 193
dance, 107, 116–8, 121–3, 128, 144, 226, 228, 246–8, 255–8, 318, 321
Danghyang Astapaka, 37, 41
Danghyang Nirartha, 37, 41, 187, 205, 312, 321
Departemen Pendidikan dan Kebudayaan, 220
desa (village), 57, 86, 267–8
   desa adat (customary village), 57–8, 148, 205, 208, 213, 267–9, 327, 329, 339
   desa dinas (administrative village), 57, 267–70, 329
   desa kala patra, 16, 156, 224
   desa pakraman (customary village), 58, 269–71, 276, 288, 294, 303, 311, 339
   krama desa, 143, 269
dewa, 83, 155, 209–10, 212–3, 310–1, 317
Dewan Nasional, 195, 200
Dewan Pemerintah Daerah (DPD), 172, 175
Dewan Persatuan Pasraman Bali (DPPB), 314, 323
Dewan Perwakilan Daerah (DPD), 289, 317
Dewan Perwakilan Rakyat (DPR), 172, 194, 273, 291
Dewan Perwakilan Rakyat Daerah (DPRD), 273
Dewan Perwakilan Rakyat Daerah Sementara (DPRDS), 172
Dewan Raja–Raja, 133, 171–3
Dewantara, Ki Hadjar, 62, 130, 256
De Zoete, Beryl, 107, 118, 120
dharma, 11–4, 16, 23, 83–4, 86–7, 162, 180, 201, 203–4, 211, 226, 331–2

Hindu Dharma, 186, 196, 202, 206–7, 224–5, 240, 319, 323–5, 336, 343
Sanatana Dharma, 14, 207, 211–2, 324
dialogic, 1–3, 6, 29, 96
Dinas Agama Otonoom Daerah Bali, 192, 195–7, 203
Direktorat Jenderal Bimbingan Masyarakat Hindu, 306
Direktorat Jenderal Bimbingan Masyarakat Hindu Bali dan Buddha, 218, 223
Direktorat Jenderal Bimbingan Masyarakat Hindu dan Buddha, 223, 306
Direktorat Jenderal Kebudayaan, 220
Direktorat Pembinaan Penghayat Kepercayaan Terhadap Tuhan Yang Maha Esa, 220
discourse, 3–4, 6–8, 20, 32, 45, 63–5, 111, 128, 244, 252, 268, 279–81, 330, 341, 345
Djatajoe, 130–8, 149–56, 158–61, 184, 246, 296, 320
Djelantik, Anak Agung Made, 132, 158, 234
Djlantik, I Gusti Bagus, 67, 69
Djlantik, I Gusti Putu, 68, 71, 73, 98, 100, 133
Dosther, Ida Bagus Gde, 195, 197, 206, 211, 234, 301, 308–9, 314
Durga, 118
Dwikora, Putu Wirata, 289, 301, 305, 312

Eka Dasa Rudra, 226, 230, 238
Eka Laksana, 131
ethnicity, 217, 254, 257, 263, 336

Flierhaar, H. te, 62–3, 137
Forum Advokasi Hindu Dharma (FAHD), 318–9
Forum Bali Harmoni, 285
Forum Cendekiawan Hindu Indonesia (FCHI), 232, 235–7, 275
Forum Komunikasi Taksu Bali, 327
Forum Pemerhati Hindu Dharma Indonesia (FPHDI), 234–6, 301, 310
Forum Penyadaran Dharma, 234, 295
Forum Rakyat Bali Tolak Reklamasi Teluk Benoa (ForBALI), 285–8
Friederich, Rudolph, 49–51, 87, 106, 239

Geertz, Clifford, 17, 40, 66
Geertz, Hildred, 40, 43–4, 58, 66, 205
Gerakan Kumara Bhavana (GKB), 195
Golongan Karya (Golkar), 219, 222, 224, 227, 234–5, 299, 305, 312
Goris, Roelof, 37, 56, 62, 70, 100–1, 104–7, 110, 118, 128, 133, 141, 145, 153, 178, 182, 184, 186–9, 193, 212
Greater India Society, 30–1, 53, 83
gria, 202, 297
Guided Democracy (*Demokrasi Terpimpin*), 194
Gunung, Ida Padanda Gede Made, 299–301, 306–8, 314, 323

Habibie, Bacharuddin Jusuf, 231, 262, 266
Hatta, Mohammad, 165, 167
Hinduism, 9 10, 13–8, 22, 24, 27, 29–30, 33–4, 40–2, 44, 46–7, 49–54, 87–9, 92, 104–7, 138, 141–3, 145, 151–3, 155, 162, 173, 177–8, 181–9, 191–7, 199, 201–3, 206–9, 219, 222, 225–6, 232, 234, 273, 295, 299, 302, 304–5, 309–10, 313, 316, 320–6, 328–9, 332, 335, 342–5
Hindu Revival (*Kebangkitan Hindu*), 232, 241, 314–5, 337–8
Hinduization, 8, 10, 16–7, 29, 43, 142, 185, 221, 328, 335, 344
Neo–Hinduism, 15–6, 183, 203, 214, 217, 234, 237, 239, 242, 312, 323, 336, 338–9, 344–5

holy book (*kitab suci*), 24, 26, 84, 155–6, 160, 169, 174–5, 179–80, 184, 187, 190, 192, 194, 197, 310–1, 331, 334
Hooykaas, Christiaan, 30, 50, 52, 82, 101, 104, 213, 229

identity, 2–9, 25, 64, 97
    Balinese identity, 1, 3, 5–6, 53, 63, 65, 67, 70, 79–81, 87, 89, 96, 102–3, 128, 237, 243–4, 251–2, 265, 275, 278–81, 311, 317, 329–33, 340, 345–6
    cultural identity, 2, 51, 78, 102, 161, 178, 244–5, 248–9, 253, 256, 259, 281, 283, 294, 339, 342
    ethnic identity, 27–8, 86, 162, 169, 217, 242, 254–5, 270, 281, 283, 332, 336, 339, 342
    religious identity, 16, 27, 29–30, 131, 138, 149, 161–2, 173, 232, 239, 241–2, 264, 266, 284, 288, 299, 316, 319, 333, 337–9, 344–5
Ikatan Cendekiawan Muslim Indonesia (ICMI), 231
Ikatan Pemuda Hindu Indonesia (IPHI), 234–5
India, 10–7, 27, 30–6, 40–53, 56, 59, 67, 69, 75, 80, 82–4, 87–8, 90, 92, 101, 105–6, 117, 142–3, 152–3, 177–8, 181–6, 191, 194, 196, 199–201, 203, 206–7, 214, 226, 228, 230, 232, 235, 239–42, 283, 297, 302, 304–5, 308–9, 311–2, 319–26, 328–31, 335–6, 340, 342–4
    Indianization, 29–36, 42, 106, 217, 299, 303, 313, 328, 340–1
Indonesianization, 6, 217, 222, 228–9, 231, 254, 257–8, 313, 336–7, 340
Institut Hindu Dharma (IHD), 205, 306
Institut Hindu Dharma Negeri (IHDN), 306

intelligentsia, 8, 13, 65–7, 71, 79, 93, 96, 101, 131, 137, 150, 153, 161, 172, 187, 235, 294, 303, 330, 340
International Academy of Indian Culture, 182–3, 185, 239
International Society for Krishna Consciousness (ISKCON), 240, 298, 300, 322–3, 326–7, 338
Islam, 9–10, 13, 17, 24, 26, 29–30, 39, 45, 48, 56, 60–3, 66–7, 71, 73, 81–2, 84–9, 92–3, 105, 136, 139, 146, 151, 153, 155, 157, 162–9, 173, 175–6, 178–80, 185, 187–8, 190–5, 201–4, 207–8, 212, 214–5, 217–22, 225–33, 239, 265–6, 269, 273, 275, 277, 279–84, 290–5, 304, 310, 313, 315–25, 328–37, 339–45
    Islamization, 34–5, 41, 51, 168, 218, 222, 232, 290, 308, 316

jaba, 58, 68–78, 81, 88–94, 96, 102, 133–4, 158, 173–4, 177, 232, 237–8, 242, 298, 312–3, 332, 337, 339
Java, 5, 17, 30, 34–43, 45–52, 56–8, 61–2, 66–7, 71–9, 82–3, 90, 92–4, 104–5, 109, 117, 136, 140, 147, 157–9, 164, 166, 168–9, 171, 174, 179–80, 188, 190, 194, 206, 215, 220–3, 229–30, 254, 260, 276, 283, 299, 308–9, 316, 320, 328, 342
    Indo–Javanese, 17, 29–30, 38–9, 49–51, 57, 68–9, 104, 203, 329, 333
    Java–Instituut, 107, 141
    Javanism (*Kejawen*), 17, 164, 166, 168, 219
    Javanization, 37, 42, 67
    Old Javanese, 34–7, 39–40, 79, 82–3, 98, 101, 103–4, 131, 142, 155, 175, 180, 184, 189, 213–4
jero, 58, 77

Kadjeng, I Nyoman, 91, 98, 100–1, 131–2, 173, 176, 178, 187–8, 198, 200
Kaharingan, 221, 236, 307, 309
kahyangan, 204–5, 208, 213, 269
Kaler, I Gusti Ketut, 196, 216
Kamenuh, Ida Padanda Made, 173, 178–9, 183, 187–8, 197, 200
Kandia, I Ketut, 176, 197, 200
Kantor Urusan Agama Daerah Bali (KUAD), 176, 192, 203–4
Kantor Urusan Agama Propinsi Sunda Kecil (KUAP), 176, 178, 181, 192–4, 203
Karangasem, Anak Agung Agung Anglurah Ketut, 61, 67, 100, 156, 173
Kawi, 39–40, 47, 49, 51, 59, 67–8, 75, 79, 104, 179, 239
kawitan, 38, 311
kebatinan, 166, 168–9, 197, 215, 219–20
Keluarga Besar Bhujangga Waisnawa, 237–8
kepercayaan, 166–7, 169, 190–1, 215, 219–20, 241, 291, 297, 312, 314, 334
Kesatuan Mahasiswa Hindu Dharma Indonesia (KMHDI), 234–5
Ketuhanan Yang Maha Esa, 163, 165–6, 179, 197, 218–9, 334
Kirtya Liefrinck–Van der Tuuk, 87, 98–101, 104–5, 131, 154, 156, 182
Komite Nasional Indonesia Daerah (KNID), 170–1
Komite Nasional Indonesia Pusat (KNIP), 167
Koninklijk Bataviaasch Genootschap van Kunsten en Wetenschappen, 48, 101, 104, 107
Koninklijk Nederlands Indisch Leger (KNIL), 171
Koninklijke Paketvaart–Maatschappij (KPM), 109
Konservatori Karawitan (KOKAR), 257

Korn, Victor Emanuel, 54, 56, 60–2, 101–2, 105, 123–4, 138–9
Koster, I Wayan, 289
Kraemer, Hendrik, 140–5, 149
krama, 86, 269, 280
　krama banjar, 208
　krama desa, 143, 208, 269
　krama dura, 270
　krama tamiu, 270
　krama wed, 270
Krause, Gregor, 112–4, 128
Kuta bombing, 273–5, 279–80

law (*hukum*), 11–2, 25–6, 31, 50, 58–9, 68–9, 74, 83–7, 93, 104, 162, 165, 169, 180, 206, 214, 216, 218, 266–73, 279, 290–1, 302, 316, 331–2, 334, 339
　Blasphemy Law, 214–5, 218, 293
　customary law (*adatrecht, hukum adat*), 56–7, 60, 85, 105, 174–5, 265, 268–9, 283, 331
　Islamic law (*syariah*), 60, 164, 292–3, 317
　Pornography Law, 294, 316
Lekkerkerker, Cornelis, 105, 139
Lembaga Kebudayaan Rakyat (Lekra), 176
Lévi, Sylvain, 31, 39, 52, 83, 125
living museum, 29–30, 48, 96, 108, 127, 244, 282, 329, 333
lontar, 67, 75–7, 79–80, 89, 101, 154, 156, 179, 185, 187, 310–1

Maha Gotra Pasek Sanak Sapta Rsi, 237, 301
Maha Semaya Warga Pande, 237
Majapahit, 34–5, 37–42, 49, 51, 58, 75, 78, 80, 92, 105, 152, 182, 186, 190, 196, 203, 230, 232, 238, 269, 283, 298, 308, 310, 312, 316, 328–9, 335, 340, 344
Majelis Desa Adat Provinsi Bali (MDA), 327

Majelis Hinduisme, 176, 178, 197
Majelis Pembina Lembaga Adat (MPLA), 268
Majelis Permusyarawatan Rakyat (MPR), 194–5, 219–20, 228, 262, 266, 290, 292
Majelis Permusyarawatan Rakyat Sementara (MPRS), 206
Majelis Pertimbangan dan Pembinaan Kebudayaan Daerah Propinsi Bali (Listibiya), 258
Majelis Syuro Muslimin Indonesia (Masyumi), 164
Majelis Ulama Indonesia (MUI), 221, 293
Majelis Utama Desa Pakraman (MUDP), 269, 311
mantra, 13, 41, 50, 53, 101, 106, 184, 186, 204, 239, 281
Mantra, Ida Bagus, 181–3, 185–6, 199–201, 206–8, 211, 213, 226, 239, 251, 258–9, 268
Manuaba, Ida Bagus Putera, 160–1, 171, 190
McPhee, Colin, 115
Mead, Margaret, 97, 114, 120–2, 125, 128
Media Hindu, 305, 314, 316, 318, 325
Megawati Sukarnoputri, 262, 265–6, 276, 279
Mershon, Katharane, 120–1
Metra, I Nengah, 68, 74, 134–5
Ministry of Religion (Kementerian Agama Republik Indonesia, KAGRI; Departemen Agama, Depag), 166–70, 173, 175–6, 178–81, 187–8, 190–207, 212, 215, 218, 222–3, 231, 313, 321, 323, 334–5, 338, 341–2, 345
missions, missionaries, 8, 11–4, 22, 24–5, 45, 48, 51, 56, 63, 84, 87, 123, 127, 131, 138–46, 149, 151, 186–8, 201, 297, 317, 319, 329–32
Mpu Kuturan, 37, 213, 238, 308, 323
Muhammadiyah, 164, 292

Nahdlatul Ulama, 164, 215, 262, 292
Nasa, I Ktut, 68, 71–2, 76, 80, 91, 103
Nasakom, 215
nationalism, 16, 62, 67, 71, 93–4, 131, 139, 157–60, 164, 215, 239
negara, 37, 61–2, 98, 157, 164, 166, 170, 172, 174, 192, 194–5, 203, 219
negara–bestuurder, 61, 68, 95, 101, 132–3, 149, 157–8
Negara Indonesia Timur (NIT), 171
Netherlands East Indies (Nederlands Oost Indië), 5, 9, 17, 29, 39, 48, 51, 54, 64, 66–7, 73, 93, 98, 109, 114, 117, 159, 161, 171, 244, 328
Netherlands Indies Civil Administration (NICA), 171
New Order (*Orde Baru*), 9, 217–9, 221–2, 224, 228, 230, 234, 237, 240, 243, 251, 254–5, 257, 259–62, 265, 267, 279–80, 283, 290, 295, 314, 337, 339, 341
Ngendjung, Ida Padanda Gede, 174, 176, 184, 193
Nieuwenkamp, Vijnand Otto Jan, 112
niskala, 42, 80, 89, 209, 211, 216, 274, 288, 320, 336
Nyepi, 203, 225, 229–30

odalan, 42, 205, 210, 319
Oka, Gedong Bagoes, 232, 234, 240
Oka, Ida Bagus, 238, 259, 261
Oka Geg, Ida I Dewa Agung Gede, 101, 173, 196–7
Orientalism, orientalist, 5–6, 8–9, 13, 16–7, 24–5, 29–31, 38–9, 45–8, 50–1, 54, 56, 58–9, 62–3, 87, 90, 92, 96, 98, 100–1, 103–4, 106, 108, 110–1, 120, 128–9, 131, 138–9, 141, 143, 145, 149, 151, 153, 186, 239, 302, 329–30, 333

pacalang, 265, 270, 276
padanda, 40–1, 50, 52, 59, 65, 69, 74, 77, 89–91, 93–4, 98, 144, 149, 153–6,

173–8, 184–6, 188–9, 193, 201–3, 205, 223–4, 226, 234–9, 295–300, 303, 307–8, 312–3, 315, 321, 328, 338, 340
padanda Boda, 40–1, 90–1, 104, 174, 180, 238, 302
padanda Siwa, 40–1, 50, 90–1, 104, 173–4, 184, 238, 302
padiksan, 193, 204, 223, 302
padmasana, 205
pamangku, 41–2, 147, 175, 178, 223
Panca Çraddha, 186, 202, 208, 212, 214, 335
Pancasila, 164, 166, 175, 187, 191, 194–6, 208, 218, 228, 291, 334
Panca Wali Krama, 238, 302
Pande, 59, 91, 94, 237–8
pandita, 223, 225, 236, 288–9, 298, 300, 302–3, 308–9
Pandji Tisna, I Gusti Nyoman, 133
Panetje, I Gde, 100, 133, 136
Panitia Persiapan Kemerdekaan Indonesia (PPKI), 165, 167
Panti Agama Hindu–Bali (PAHB), 176–8, 187, 191, 193, 197–8, 200, 207
paradise, 110, 125, 243
　last paradise, 96, 108, 111, 125, 333
　lost paradise, 123, 125
Parisada, 199
　Parisada Besakih, 301–8, 340
　Parisada Campuan, 299–308, 311, 340
　Parisada Dharma Hindu Bali (PDHB), 184, 200–7, 308–11, 313, 335–6, 341
　Parisada Hindu Dharma (PHD), 184, 207–14, 221–7, 336
　Parisada Hindu Dharma Indonesia (PHDI), 227–36, 238, 240–2, 248, 287–8, 294–310, 313–5, 318–23, 325–7, 337–8, 340–3
　Parisada Hindu Dharma Indonesia Propinsi Bali (PHDI Bali), 227, 297–308, 312–3, 315, 326–7, 340

　Parisada Hindu Dunia, 322
Partai Demokrasi Indonesia (PDI), 218
Partai Demokrasi Indonesia–Perjuangan (PDI-P), 265
Partai Indonesia Raya (Parindra), 158–61, 171
Partai Komunis Indonesia (PKI), 94, 172, 176, 200, 215–7, 219
Partai Nasional Hindu Bali, 196–7
Partai Nasional Indonesia (PNI), 172, 174, 190, 200, 215–6, 222
Partai Persatuan Pembangunan (PPP), 218, 266
Paruman Agung, 62, 160, 170–2
Paruman Kerta Negara, 61, 156
Paruman Negara, 62, 170, 172
Paruman Pandita Dharma, 173
Paruman Para Pandita Bali Lombok (PPP), 173–4, 177–9, 197, 200
Pasek, 59, 237–8, 298, 301
Pastika, I Made Mangku, 274, 284–6, 322–3, 326
pawintenan, 223, 240
Pemuda Hindu Indonesia (PHI), 227, 234, 305
pendatang, 264–5, 312.
Pendit, I Nyoman Suwandhi, 179, 185–7, 232
peradaban, 99, 102–3, 254
Perhimpunan Pemuda Hindu Indonesia (Peradah), 227, 305
piagam,
　Piagam Bali (Bali Charter), 322–3, 326, 343
　Piagam Campuan (Campuan Charter), 203, 299–300, 306
　Piagam Jakarta (Jakarta Charter), 165–6, 218, 292
　Piagam Parisada (Parisada Charter), 200
　Piagam Samuan Tiga (Samuan Tiga Charter), 308, 310–1

pinandita, 223, 225
Pita Maha, 119
Prajaniti Hindu Indonesia, 222, 234, 319
priest, 35, 38, 41, 46, 49–51, 53, 55, 57–8, 69, 89–91, 94, 104, 143–4, 146–7, 154–5, 173–4, 185, 187, 201–4, 209, 213, 223–4, 228–9, 235–9, 246, 288, 295–9, 302–3, 308, 311, 318, 329, 335–6, 338
    priesthood, 21, 35, 40, 45, 75, 94, 173–4, 197, 202, 204, 231, 237–8, 288, 302, 309, 312–3, 328, 335, 338
progress, 54, 69–74, 77–80, 84, 88, 93, 97, 100–1, 130, 135, 174, 191, 239, 331–2
prophet (*nabi*), 26, 84, 155–6, 169, 175, 179–80, 187, 190, 192, 194, 197, 331, 334
Pudja, I Gusti Ketut, 100, 165, 170–1, 173
Punyatmadja, Ida Bagus Oka, 182–3, 206, 211, 234, 301, 322
puputan, 55, 109, 112, 171, 205, 215, 287
pura, 41–2, 99, 115, 187, 204, 210, 226, 233, 288, 303, 310, 318–9, 321
    Pura Agung Jagatnatha, 205, 230
    pura bale agung, 205
    pura dadia, 210
    pura dalem, 205, 213
    pura desa, 152, 205, 213
    Pura Gunung Lebah, 299
    pura kahyangan, 204
    pura kahyangan jagat, 230
    pura kawitan, 204, 210, 237
    Pura Luhur Uluwatu, 321
    Pura Mandara Giri Semeru Agung, 229
    Pura Panataran Agung, 175, 230, 301
    pura puseh, 205, 213
    Pura Samuan Tiga, 308, 323
puri, 37, 55, 98–9, 115, 202, 261, 297, 299
    Puri Lukisan, Museum Kesenian Bali Modern, 119
purohita, 40

Putra, I Gusti Agung Gede, 232, 248

Raad van Kerta, 58, 68, 74, 87
Raditya, 232, 235, 283, 295, 305, 311
Raffles, Thomas Stamford, 38–9, 47–50
raja, 37, 54–5, 57–8, 61–2, 68, 93, 95, 109, 115, 133, 170–6, 199–200, 202–3, 232, 272, 304
Rake, I Gusti Gde, 131–2, 135–6, 156, 160
Rangda, 117–8, 120–1
Reformasi, 9, 262, 265, 271, 278, 282, 290, 295, 339, 341–2, 344
religion, 3–4, 8–15, 17–27, 29, 31, 33, 35, 50, 59, 61, 63, 76, 81–2, 84–7, 97, 99–100, 102–5, 149, 164–70, 187, 201, 203, 215, 217–27, 239–42, 246, 248–9, 290–3, 310, 318, 321, 328, 331–4, 345
    Abrahamic religions, 17, 22, 24, 155, 169, 180, 194, 199, 208, 225, 320, 345
    Balinese religion, 16, 29–30, 39–40, 42–8, 51, 56, 68–9, 88–92, 106–7, 117, 123–4, 128–9, 134, 137–9, 141–5, 150–7, 160–3, 171–97, 199, 203–4, 206–7, 209, 214, 221, 229–34, 271, 283, 290, 298, 308–9, 312–3, 320, 327–9, 334–45
    religionization, 18, 25, 27, 291, 328, 345
Rencana Pembangunan Lima Tahun (Repelita), 222
Republik Indonesia Serikat (RIS), 168
resi, rsi, 213, 224, 227
    resi bhujangga, 35, 224, 237–8, 302
    Resi Dharmakirti, 211–4
    Rsi Markandeya, 37, 299
Roosevelt, André, 77, 115, 126
Roy, Rammohun, 13–4

sadhaka (*sarwa sadhaka, tri sadhaka*), 238, 302
sakala, 42, 80, 274, 288

sakti, kasaktian, 43–4, 89, 118, 144, 147, 212, 241
sampradaya, 11–2, 16, 23, 200, 237, 240–2, 271, 295–8, 300, 303–4, 308, 313–5, 321, 323, 326–7, 337–41
Sandi, I Ktut, 67–8
sanggah, 42, 143, 148, 175, 187, 210, 310
Sang Hyang Wid(h)i (Wasa), 155, 179–80, 186, 188, 204–5, 207–14, 309–11, 318, 336
Santi, 68–71, 75, 88, 90–1
Sarad, 242, 266, 282–3, 304, 314
Sarasvati, Dayananda, 14, 208, 232, 239, 302
Sarekat Islam, 67, 93
satria, 40, 58–59, 183, 328
Satria Naradha, Anak Bagus Gede, 278–81
Satya Hindu Dharma Indonesia, 196–7
Sebali Tianyar Arimbawa, Ida Padanda Gde Ketut, 232, 289, 298, 307, 314, 320–3, 325
Setia, Putu, 206, 232, 275, 283, 308, 311
Setiti Bali, 67
Setiti Gama Siwa Buda, 69
Shadeg, Norbert, 187–8
Shanty, Putu, 176–7, 187, 191
Shastri, Narendra Dev. Pandit, 183–6, 208, 211, 213
Shiva, 13, 34–5, 50, 69, 82–3, 184
    Shaiva Siddhanta, Siwa Siddhanta, 82, 311
    Shaivism, 12, 34–6, 50, 90, 180, 188, 207, 212–3, 311, 344
    Siwa, 118, 155–6, 173, 175, 179, 188, 204–5, 208, 212–3, 225–6, 238, 308, 310, 312
Somvir, Yadav, 321
soroh, 16, 237–8, 295, 302–3, 310
Spies, Walter, 62, 107, 114–5, 118–21, 124, 128
Sri Sathya Sai Baba, 240, 300, 323, 338

Stutterheim, Willem Frederik, 56, 62, 101, 105, 124, 153
Suara Indonesia, 181, 183, 278
Suardana, I Wayan Gendo, 285, 287
subak, 66, 208, 224
Sudarsana, Ida Bagus Putu, 309–10
Sudharta, Tjokorda Rai, 183, 186, 200, 204, 206–8, 211, 299, 301, 304
Sudhi Wadani, 226
Sudirta, I Wayan, 227, 232, 234, 301, 305, 307
sudra, 40, 58–9, 76–7, 237
Sugriwa, I Gusti Bagus, 134, 175–7, 179, 184, 188–90, 195, 200, 207, 212, 306, 309, 313
Suharto, 9, 217–9, 222, 228, 231, 242–3, 251, 254, 256, 258–9, 262–3, 265, 285, 290, 295, 337, 339
Suita Gama Tirta, 68
Sukarno, 66, 74, 159, 164–5, 167–8, 192–5, 197–8, 206, 214–8, 220, 222, 262, 293, 336
Sukawati, Tjokorda Gde Agung, 119
Sukawati, Tjokorda Gde Raka, 67, 69, 100, 107, 114, 119, 134, 139–40, 145, 171
sulinggih, 201, 203, 223–4, 236, 308–9, 311
Surpha, I Wayan, 84, 225, 305
Surya Kanta, *Surya Kanta,* 64–5, 68–80, 87–94, 100–3, 108, 124, 129–30, 134–5, 138, 152, 157–8, 177–8, 182, 223, 232, 237, 282, 305, 312–3, 320
Sutedja, Anak Agung Bagus, 172, 198–9, 216
Suyasa, I Made Wedastera, 174, 191, 195–6, 200, 222, 224, 317
Swastha, I Dewa Gede Ngurah, 233–4, 301, 310, 327

Tagore, Rabindranath, 30, 52–3, 90, 92, 104, 106, 143, 181, 186
Taman Mini Indonesia Indah, 256, 307

Taman Siswa, 130, 151, 168, 186
tantra, tantric, tantrism, 34–7, 41, 43–4, 82, 90, 117, 142, 212, 214, 311, 320, 331, 344–5
tattwa, 35–6, 43, 79, 101, 197, 204, 212–3, 310, 320
Theosophy, Theosophical Society, 34, 67, 151, 166, 168, 211
tirt(h)a, 40, 68, 91, 94, 144, 173, 201, 295
   tirt(h)a yatra, 52, 240, 321, 338
Titib, I Made, 239, 283, 298
Tjakra Tanaya, I Gusti Bagus, 67–70, 73, 75–9, 88, 91–5, 100, 134, 152, 182, 312–3
Tjatur Wangsa Deriya Gama Hindu Bali (Tjwadega Hindu Bali), 69, 75
tourism, 1–5, 98, 108–10, 125–8, 141, 145, 195, 216, 222, 225–6, 228, 233, 242–54, 258, 260–1, 263, 266, 271–2, 274, 276–8, 281–2, 284–9, 294, 317, 320, 333, 339, 345
   cultural tourism (*Pariwisata Budaya*), 2, 5, 8–9, 225, 244–5, 249, 251–2, 257–8, 281, 317
   touristic culture (*budaya pariwisata*), 246
   touristification, 2, 6, 249, 254, 257
Triguna, Ida Bagus Gde Yudha, 306, 309, 323
Tri Hita Karana, 216–7, 269, 324
Trimurti, 176, 312
Tri Sandhya, 184–5, 202, 214, 229, 335
tutur, 34–6, 43, 50, 79, 101, 187

Ubud Writers and Readers Festival, 287
Universitas Hindu Indonesia (UNHI), 206, 236, 296–7, 306, 313
Universitas Hindu Negeri I Gusti Bagus Sugriwa Denpasar (UHN), 306
Universitas Udayana (UNUD), 200, 286
upacara, 204, 212–3, 229, 247, 320
Upadesa, 202, 211–4, 235

Van Hoëvell, Wolter Robert Baron, 48–51
varna, 11, 40, 52, 240, 302
   varnashrama dharma, 11–2, 14, 84
Veda, 11–4, 47, 49–50, 101, 106, 154–5, 179–81, 184, 186, 191, 197, 213, 228–9, 239–40, 297, 302, 304–5, 310–1, 314, 324–5, 338
Vereenigde Oost–Indisch Compagnie (VOC), 38, 46, 54
Vereeniging Toeristenverkeer, 109
Vishnu, 13, 184
   Vaishnavism, 12, 33–4
Vishva Hindu Parishad, 183, 201, 297, 322–3
Vivekananda, 14, 80
Volksraad, 67, 100, 134, 139–40, 159

Wahid, Abdurrahman, 262, 290, 307
walaka, 201, 203, 223–4, 236, 288–9, 298, 300, 303, 305, 308, 311
Wali Pitu, 316
Wali Songo, 316
wangsa, 40, 75, 80, 158, 232, 299, 302
   catur wangsa, 69, 75, 91, 103, 184, 313
   triwangsa, 58–9, 68–71, 74–81, 88–94, 96, 102, 130, 133–4, 158, 173, 175, 177, 201, 227, 232, 234, 237–8, 242, 300–1, 303, 308, 312–3, 328, 332, 337–9, 341
warga, 224, 237–9, 242, 295–303, 313, 315, 337–41
warna, 40, 75, 232, 302
   catur warna, 40, 75, 302
Warta Hindu Dharma, 202, 305
weda, 50, 101, 153, 204, 212, 217, 310
Wedakarna, I Gusti Ngurah Arya, 317, 322
Werdhi Budaya, 258
wesia, 40, 58, 328
Wiana, I Ketut, 237, 283, 288, 297
Widodo, Joko, 262, 286–287, 289, 317

Wirjasutha, I Nyoman Mas, 100, 130, 134, 153
Wisnu, 90, 155, 212–3, 261, 312
Wiwada Sastra Sabha, 177–8
World Hindu Federation (Vishwa Hindu Mahasangh), 183, 322, 325, 343
World Hindu Parisad (Parisada Hindu Dunia), 322–7, 343–4

yadnya, yajna, 42, 116, 180, 193, 302–3
   Buta Yadnya, 184, 213, 238
   Dewa Yadnya, 184, 213
   Manusa Yadnya, 184, 213
   panca yadnya, 184, 213, 310
   Pitra Yadnya, 184, 213, 303, 311
   Resi Yadnya, 184, 213
Yudhoyono, Susilo Bambang, 262, 286, 322

zelfbestuurder, 61–2, 160, 170